Financial Accounting Theory

CRAIG DEEGAN

Financial Accounting Theory

CRAIG DEEGAN

The McGraw-Hill Companies, Inc.

Beijing Bogotá Boston Burr Ridge IL Caracas
Dubuque IA Lisbon London Madison WI
Madrid Mexico City Milan New Delhi New York
San Francisco Santiago Seoul Singapore
St Louis Sydney Taipei Toronto

McGraw·Hill Australia

A Division of The McGraw·Hill Companies

National Library of Australia Cataloguing-in-Publication data;

Deegan, Craig Michael, 1960–.
Financial accounting theory.

   Includes index.
   ISBN 0 074 70766 3

   1. Accounting. 2. Accounting – Study and teaching. I. Title.

657.48

Published in Australia by
McGraw-Hill Book Company Australia Pty Limited
4 Barcoo Street, Roseville NSW 2069, Australia
Acquisitions Editors: Karolina Kocalevski, Jae Chung
Production Supervisor: Jo Munnelly
Editor: Ken Tate
Designer: Green Words & Images
Permissions Editor: Leanne Peters
Typeset in Bembo 10.5 by Keyboard Wizards, Hazelbrook, NSW
Printed by Brown Prior Anderson

Contents

Preface

This book has been written to provide readers with a balanced discussion of different theories of financial accounting. Various theories for and against regulation of financial accounting are critically discussed and various theoretical perspectives, including those provided by Positive Accounting Theory, Political Economy Theory, Stakeholder Theory and Legitimacy Theory are introduced to explain different types of voluntary reporting decisions. The book also describes and evaluates the development of various normative theories of accounting, including various approaches developed to account for changing prices, different normative perspectives about the accountability of business entities, as well as various conceptual framework projects. It also emphasises the role of issues such as culture in explaining international differences in accounting.

Apart from providing explanations for why or how organisations should disclose particular items of financial information, the book investigates research that explores how or whether people at an aggregate and individual level demand or react to particular disclosures. Reflecting the growing relevance of social and environmental reporting issues to students, government, industry and the accounting profession, social and environmental reporting issues are discussed in depth. The book also provides an insight into the role of financial accounting from the perspective of a group of researchers who are often described as working from a critical perspective.

Being divided into twelve chapters sequenced in a logical order, this book provides the basis for subjects or units that investigate financial accounting theory. The entire book could realistically be used in the average 12 to 14 week university term, with chapters being studied in the sequence in which they are presented. Because it provides a balanced perspective of alternative and sometimes conflicting theories of financial accounting, it also provides a sound basis for readers contemplating further research in different areas of financial accounting. In writing this book a style has been adopted that enables students at both the undergraduate and post-graduate level to gain a sound understanding of financial accounting theory. Each chapter incorporates research from throughout the world, hence the book is of relevance to financial accounting theory students internationally. To assist in the learning process, each chapter provides learning objectives, chapter summaries and end-of-chapter discussion questions. Throughout the book readers are encouraged to critically evaluate and challenge the various views presented. To give the various perspectives a 'real world' feel, many chapters use recent articles from various newspapers, directly relating to the issues under consideration.

Many people must be thanked for helping me write this book. First I thank Michaela Rankin who helps me in so many of my endeavours. In this project she has acted as a great sounding-board for many of my ideas, as well as assisting in the review of draft chapters. Without her ongoing support, projects such as this would become a great deal more difficult. In the early stages of developing this book a number of individuals generously provided some very useful ideas. Professor Rob Gray from the University of Glasgow is to be thanked for some useful and insightful advice and, through his Centre for Social and Environmental Accounting Research, for generously providing a deal of useful research material. I must also thank Professor David Owen from the University of Sheffield for his advice and encouragement throughout the writing of this book. Dr Julie Cotter from the University of Southern Queenland is also to be thanked for her views about how the book should be structured and for her assistance in the writing of Chapter 10. I also thank Professor Reg Mathews (Massey University), Brian Millanta (Macquarie University); Colin Dolley (Edith Cowan University); Dean Adern (La Trobe University); Natalie Gallery (Griffith University); for providing critical comments in relation to a number of the chapters, and Tanya Ziebell (University of Queensland) for unearthing some difficult-to-find research papers. I must also thank my colleagues at the University of Southern Queenland for providing a supportive and friendly environment in which to undertake projects such as this book. Lastly, I thank the staff at McGraw-Hill Book Company for supporting this project. Particular thanks go to Jae Chung, Karolina Kocalevski, Jo Munnelly and Ken Tate.

I hope readers find this book to be interesting, informative and enjoyable to read and I would welcome constructive feedback.

Craig Deegan

About the Author

Craig Deegan, B.Com (University of NSW), M.Com (Hons) (University of NSW), PhD (University of Queensland), FCA is Professor of Accounting and Faculty Director of Research and Research Higher Degrees at the University of Southern Queensland. He has taught at Australian universities for sixteen years in both undergraduate and postgraduate courses and has presented lectures internationally within the United States, England, Wales, Scotland, Malaysia, Singapore, South Africa, New Zealand, South Korea, France and China.

Prior to his time within the university sector, Craig worked as a chartered accountant in practice. He is an active researcher, with publications in Australian and international professional and academic journals and he regularly provides consulting services to corporations, government, and industry bodies. His main research interests are in the area of social and environmental accountability and reporting and he is the author of the leading Australian financial accounting textbook, *Australian Financial Accounting*.

Craig has been the recipient of various teaching and research awards including teaching prizes sponsored by KPMG Peat Marwick, and the Institute of Chartered Accountants in Australia. In July 1998 he was the recipient of the *Peter Brownell Manuscript Award*, an annual research award presented by the Accounting Association of Australia and New Zealand. In 1998 he was also awarded the *University of Southern Queensland Award for Excellence in Research*.

Chapter 1

Introduction to financial accounting theory

Learning objectives

Upon completing this chapter readers should:

- understand that there are many theories of financial accounting;

- understand that the different theories of financial accounting are often developed to perform different functions, such as to *describe* accounting practice, or to *prescribe* particular accounting practices;

- understand that theories, including theories of accounting, are developed as a result of applying various value judgements and that acceptance of one theory, in preference to others, will in part be tied to one's own value judgements;

- be aware that we should critically evaluate theories (in terms of such things as the underlying logic, assumptions made, and evidence produced) before accepting them.

Opening issues to consider

At the beginning of each chapter a number of issues or problems are raised that relate to the material covered. On completion of the chapter you should be able to supply answers to the problems. In this introductory chapter, some of the issues that we can initially consider are as follows:

(a) Why do students of financial accounting need to bother with the study of 'theories'? Why not just study some more of the numerous Accounting Standards (and there are certainly plenty of them!) or other pronouncements of the accounting profession?

(b) Why would (or perhaps 'should') accounting practitioners and accounting regulators consider various theories of accounting?

(c) Do all 'theories of accounting' seek to fulfil the same role, and if there are alternative theories to explain or guide particular practice, how does somebody select one theory in preference to another?

No specific answers are provided for each chapter's opening issues. Rather, as a result of reading the respective chapters, readers should be able to provide their own answers to the particular issues. They might like to consider providing an answer to the opening issues before reading the material provided in the chapters, and then on completing the chapter, revisit the opening issue, and see whether they might change their opinions as a result of being exposed to particular points of view.

What is a theory?

We consider various theories of financial accounting. As such, we should first consider what we mean by a 'theory'. There are various perspectives of what constitutes a theory. The Macquarie Dictionary provides various definitions, including:

A coherent group of general propositions used as principles of explanation for a class of phenomena.

The accounting researcher Hendriksen (1970, p. 1) defines a theory as:

A coherent set of hypothetical, conceptual and pragmatic principles forming the general framework of reference for a field of inquiry.

The definition provided by Hendriksen is very similar to the US Financial Accounting Standards Board's definition of their Conceptual Framework Project (which in itself is deemed to be a *normative* theory of accounting), which is defined as 'a coherent system of interrelated objectives and fundamentals that is expected to lead to consistent standards'.

What the above definitions imply is that a theory should be based on logical (coherent) reasoning. As we will see, some accounting theories are developed on the basis of past observations (empirically based) of which some are further developed to make predictions about likely occurrences (and sometimes also to provide explanations of why the events occur). That is, particular theories may be generated and subsequently supported by undertaking numerous observations of the actual phenomena in question. Such empirically based theories are said to be based on inductive reasoning and are often labelled 'scientific', as, like many theories in the 'sciences', they are based on observation. Alternatively, other accounting theories that we also consider do not seek to provide explanations or predictions of particular phenomena, but rather, *prescribe* what *should* be done (as opposed to describing or predicting what *is* done) in particular circumstances. We stress that different theories of accounting often have different objectives.

Because accounting is a human activity (you cannot have 'accounting' without accountants), theories of financial accounting (and there are many) will consider such things as people's behaviour and/or people's needs as regards financial accounting information, or the reasons why people within organisations might elect to supply particular information to particular stakeholder groups. For example, we consider, among others, theories that:

- *prescribe* how, based upon a particular perspective of the role of accounting, assets *should* be valued for external reporting purposes (we consider such prescriptive or normative theories in Chapters 4 and 5);

- *predict* that managers paid bonuses on the basis of measures such as profits will seek to adopt those accounting methods that lead to an increase in reported profits (we consider such descriptive or positive theories in Chapter 7);

- seek to *explain* how an individual's cultural background will impact on the types of accounting information that the individual seeks to provide to people outside the organisation (we consider such a theory in Chapter 6);

- *prescribe* the accounting information that should be provided to particular classes of stakeholders on the basis of their perceived information needs (such theories are often referred to as decision usefulness theories, and we discuss them in Chapter 4);

- *predict* that the relative power of a particular stakeholder group (with 'power' often being defined in terms of the group's control over scarce resources) will determine whether that group receives the accounting information it desires (which derives from a branch of Stakeholder Theory, which is discussed in Chapter 8);

- *predict* that organisations seek to be perceived by the community as *legitimate* and that accounting information can be used as one means to bring legitimacy to the organisation (which derives from Legitimacy Theory, considered in Chapter 8).

A brief overview of theories of accounting

There are many theories of financial accounting. That is, there is no universally accepted theory of financial accounting, or indeed, any universally agreed perspective of how accounting theories should be developed. In part this is because different researchers have different perspectives of the role of accounting theory and/or what the central objective, role and scope of financial accounting should be. For example, some researchers believe that the principal role of accounting theory should be to *explain* and *predict* particular accounting-related phenomena (for example, to explain why some accountants adopt one particular accounting method, while others elect to adopt an alternative approach), while other researchers believe that the role of accounting theory is to *prescribe* (as opposed to *describe*) particular approaches to accounting (for example, based on a perspective of the role of accounting, there is a theory that prescribes that assets *should* be valued on the basis of market values rather than historical costs).

Early development of accounting theory relied on the process of induction, that is, the development of ideas or theories through observation. From approximately the 1920s to the 1960s, theories of accounting were predominantly developed on the basis of observation of what accountants actually did in practice. Common practices were then codified in the form of doctrines or conventions of accounting (for example, the doctrine of conservatism). Notable theorists at this time included Paton, 1922; Hatfield, 1927; Paton and Littleton, 1940; and Canning, 1929. Henderson, Peirson and Brown (1992, p. 61) describe the approaches adopted by these theorists as follows:

> *Careful observation of accounting practice revealed patterns of consistent behaviour. For example, it could be observed that accountants tended to be very prudent in measuring both revenues and expenses. Where judgement was necessary it was observed that accountants usually underestimated revenues and overstated expenses. The result was a conservative measure of profit. Similarly, it could be observed that accountants behaved as if the value of money, which was the unit of account, remained constant. These observations of accounting practice led to the formulation of a number of hypotheses such as 'that where judgement is needed, a conservative procedure is adopted' and 'that it is assumed that the value of money remains constant'. These hypotheses were confirmed by many observations of the behaviour of accountants.*

While there was a general shift towards prescriptive research in the 1960s, some research of an inductive nature still occurs. Research based on the inductive approach has been subject to many criticisms. For example, Gray, Owen and Maunders (1987, p. 66) state:

Studying extant practice is a study of 'what is' and, by definition does not study 'what is not' or 'what should be'. It therefore concentrates on the status quo, is reactionary in attitude, and cannot provide a basis upon which current practice may be evaluated or from which future improvements may be deduced.

In generating theories of accounting based upon what accountants actually do, it is assumed (often implicitly) that what is done by the majority of accountants is the most appropriate practice. In adopting such a perspective there is, in a sense, a perspective of *accounting Darwinism*—a view that accounting practice has evolved, and the fittest, or perhaps 'best', practices have survived. Prescriptions or advice are provided to others on the basis of what most accountants do—the 'logic' being that the majority of accountants must be doing the most appropriate thing. What do you think of the logic of such an argument?

As a specific example of this inductive approach to theory development we can consider the work of Grady (1965). His research was commissioned by the American Institute of Certified Public Accountants (AICPA) and was undertaken at a time when there was a great deal of prescriptive (as opposed to descriptive) research being undertaken. Interestingly, and as indicated in Deegan (1999, p. 38), in 1961 and 1962 the Accounting Research Division of the AICPA had already commissioned studies by Moonitz (1961), and by Sprouse and Moonitz (1962). In these studies the authors proposed that accounting measurement systems be changed from historical cost to a system based on current values. However, before the release of these research works, the AICPA released a statement saying that 'while these studies are a valuable contribution to accounting principles, they are too radically different from generally accepted principles for acceptance at this time' (Statement by the Accounting Principles Board, AICPA, April, 1962).

History shows that rarely have regulatory bodies accepted suggestions for significant changes to accounting practice. This is an interesting issue considered more fully in Chapter 5 when we discuss conceptual framework projects. However, it is useful to consider at this point a statement made in the US by Miller and Reading (1986, p. 64):

The mere discovery of a problem is not sufficient to assure that the FASB will undertake its solution . . . There must be a suitably high likelihood that the Board can resolve the issues in a manner that will be acceptable to the constituency—without some prior sense of the likelihood that the Board members will be able to reach a consensus, it is generally not advisable to undertake a formal project.

Grady's (1965) work formed the basis of APB Statement No. 4, 'Basic Concepts and Accounting Principles Underlying the Financial Statements of Business Enterprises'. In effect, APB Statement No. 4 simply reflected the generally accepted accounting principles of the time. It was therefore not controversial and had a high probability of being acceptable to the AICPA's constituency (Miller and Reading, 1986).

Following the 'inductive era' of accounting research, a great deal of work being undertaken by accounting researchers in the 1960s and 1970s sought to *prescribe* particular accounting procedures, and as such was not driven by existing practices. At this time there tended to be widespread inflation throughout various countries of the world and much of the research and the related theories sought to explain the limitations of historical cost accounting and to provide improved approaches (based upon particular value judgements held by the researchers) for asset valuation in times of rapidly rising prices.

In the mid- to late 1970s there were further changes in the focus of accounting research and theory development. At this time a great deal of accounting research had the major aim of *explaining* and *predicting* accounting practice, rather than *prescribing* particular approaches. As we indicate, there is a movement by many accounting researchers away from descriptive research and again towards prescriptive research. Nevertheless many researchers still undertake descriptive research.

In reading accounting research you will see that much research is labelled either *positive research* or *normative research*. Research that seeks to predict and explain particular phenomena (as opposed to prescribing particular activity) is classified as *positive research* and the associated theories are referred to as *positive theories*. Henderson, Peirson and Brown (1992, p. 326) provide a useful description of positive theories. They state:

> *A positive theory begins with some assumption(s) and, through logical deduction, enables some prediction(s) to be made about the way things will be. If the prediction is sufficiently accurate when tested against observations of reality, then the story is regarded as having provided an explanation of why things are as they are. For example, in climatology, a positive theory of rainfall may yield a prediction that, if certain conditions are met, then heavy rainfall will be observed. In economics, a positive theory of prices may yield a prediction that, if certain conditions are met, then rapidly rising prices will be observed. Similarly, a positive theory of accounting may yield a prediction that, if certain conditions are met, then particular accounting practices will be observed.*

As noted above, positive theories are typically based on observation. Empirically (observation) based theories can continue to be tested and perhaps refined through further observation, perhaps in different institutional or geographical settings and a great deal of published research is undertaken to see if particular results can be replicated in different settings, thereby increasing the generalisability of the theory in question. Apart from providing the basis for predicting future actions or effects, positive accounting research often goes to the next step of attempting to provide explanations for the phenomena in question.

In Chapter 7 we consider a positive theory of accounting principally developed by Watts and Zimmerman [relying upon the works of others, such as Jensen and Meckling (1976) and Gordon (1964)]. Their positive theory of accounting, which they called *Positive Accounting Theory*, seeks to predict and explain why accountants elect to adopt particular accounting methods in preference to others.[1]

Chapter 7 demonstrates that the development of Positive Accounting Theory relied in great part on work undertaken in the field of economics, and central to the development of Positive Accounting Theory was the acceptance of the economics based 'rational economic person assumption'. That is, an assumption was made that accountants (and, in fact, all individuals) are primarily motivated by self-interest (tied to wealth maximisation), and that the particular accounting method selected (where alternatives are available) will be dependent upon certain considerations:

- whether the accountant is rewarded in terms of accounting-based bonus systems (for example, whether they receive a bonus tied to reported profits);

- whether the organisation they work for is close to breaching negotiated accounting-based debt covenants (such as a debt-to-asset constraint);

- whether the organisation that employs them is subject to political scrutiny from various external groups, such as government, employee groups or environmental groups (with that scrutiny being focused on the organisation's reported profits).

The assumption of self-interest challenges the view that accountants will predominantly be objective when determining which accounting methods should be used to record particular transactions and events (objectivity is a qualitative characteristic promoted within various conceptual frameworks of accounting, as we see in Chapter 5).

Positive theories of accounting do not seek to tell us that what is being done in practice is the most efficient or equitable process. For example, while we have a (positive) theory of accounting, developed to predict which accounting methods most accountants will use in particular circumstances (Positive Accounting Theory), this theory will not tell us anything about the efficiency of what is being done. As Watts and Zimmerman (1986, p. 7) state:

> It [Positive Accounting Theory] is concerned with explaining [accounting] practice. It is designed to explain and predict which firms will and which firms will not use a particular [accounting method] . . . but it says nothing as to which method a firm should use.

---

1. It should be noted at this point that Positive Accounting Theory is one of several positive theories of accounting (other positive theories that relate to accounting would include legitimacy theory and certain branches of stakeholder theory). We will refer to the general class of theories that attempt to explain and predict accounting practice in lower case (that is, as positive theories of accounting) and we will refer to Watts and Zimmerman's positive theory of accounting as Positive Accounting Theory (that is, in upper case).

As we will see shortly, the practice of electing not to advise others as to what should be done in particular circumstances has been the subject of criticism of positive accounting research.

While positive theories tend to be based on empirical observation, there are other theories based not upon observation but rather on what the researcher believes *should* occur in particular circumstances. For example, in Chapter 4 we discuss a theory of accounting developed by the famous Australian academic, Raymond Chambers. His theory of accounting, called *Continuously Contemporary Accounting*, describes how financial accounting *should* be undertaken. That is, his theory is prescriptive. Central to his theory is a view that the most useful information about an organisation's assets for the purposes of economic decision making is information about their 'current cash equivalents'—a measure tied to their current net market values. As such, he prescribes that assets *should* be valued on the basis of their net market values. Theories that prescribe (as opposed to describe) particular actions are called normative theories (they are also often referred to as prescriptive theories). The dichotomy of positive and normative theories is one often used to categorise accounting theories and it is adopted in this book.

As noted above, normative theories of accounting are not necessarily based on observation and therefore cannot (or should not) be evaluated on whether they reflect actual accounting practice. In fact they may suggest radical changes to current practice. For example, for a number of decades, Chambers has been advocating the valuation of assets on a basis related to their net market values—a prescription that challenged the widespread use of historical cost accounting (it is interesting to note, however, that the use of market values for asset valuation has gained popularity in recent years). Other researchers concerned about the social and environmental implications of business (see Gray, Owen and Adams, 1996; Mathews, 1993) have developed theories that prescribe significant changes to traditional financial accounting practice (Chapter 9 of this book considers such theories). The Conceptual Framework of Accounting that we discuss in Chapter 5 is an example of a normative theory of accounting. Relying upon various assumptions about the types or attributes of information useful for decision making, it provides guidance on how assets, liabilities, expenses, revenues and equity should be defined, when they should be recognised, and ultimately how they should be measured. The Australian Conceptual Framework (particularly SAC 4) made a number of prescriptive suggestions that represented considerable changes to existing practice.[2]

As we see in later chapters, normative theories can be further subdivided. For example, we can classify some normative theories as 'true income

---

2. Some have argued that this is probably the main reason why the Statements of Accounting Concepts (issued as part of the Conceptual Framework Project) were never made mandatory, even though there was an original expectation that they would be. We discuss some theoretical perspectives about why the SACs were not made mandatory in Chapter 5.

theories' and other theories as 'decision usefulness theories'. The true income theories make certain assumptions about the role of accounting and then seek to provide a single 'best measure' of profits (for example, see Lee, 1974).[3]

Decision usefulness theories ascribe a particular type of information for particular classes of users on the basis of assumed decision making needs. According to Gray, Laughlin and Bebbington (1996, p. 491) the decision usefulness approach can be considered to have two branches, the *decision-makers emphasis*, and the *decision-models emphasis*. The decision-makers emphasis relies on undertaking research that seeks to ask them what information they want.[4] Once that is determined, this knowledge is used to prescribe what information should be supplied to the users of financial statements. Much of this research is questionnaire based. This branch of research tends to be fairly disjointed as different studies typically address different types of information, with limited linkage between them.

Another variant of the decision-makers emphasis, which we explore in Chapter 10, is security price research. Briefly, security price research works on the assumption that if the capital market responds to information (as evidenced through price changes that occur around the time of the release of particular information) the information must be useful.[5] This forms the basis for subsequent prescriptions about the types of information that should be provided to users of financial statements. It also has been used to determine whether particular mandatory reporting requirements (such as the introduction of new Accounting Standards) were necessary or effective, the rationale being that if a new Accounting Standard does not evoke a market reaction, then it is questionable whether the new requirement is useful or necessary. Research that evaluates information on the basis of whether it evokes a market reaction, or whether stakeholders indicate that it is useful to them, ignores the possibility that there could be information that is 'better' than that provided or sought. There is also a broader philosophical issue of whether what they 'want' is actually what they 'need'. These broader issues are explored throughout this book.

On the other hand, proponents of the *decision-models emphasis* develop models based upon the researchers' perceptions of what is necessary for efficient decision making. Information prescriptions follow (for example, that information should be provided about the market value of the reporting entity's assets). This branch of research typically assumes that classes of

---

3. Much of the work undertaken in developing 'true income theories' relies upon the work of Hicks (1946). Hicks defined 'income' as the maximum amount that can be consumed by a person or an organisation in a particular period without depleting the wealth that existed for that person or organisation at the start of the period.

4. For example, in recent years a number of research studies have asked a number of different stakeholder groups what types of environmental performance information the stakeholders considered to be useful to their various decision making processes.

5. Based on the Efficient Markets Hypothesis that the stock market instantaneously reacts, through price adjustments (changes), to all relevant publicly available information.

stakeholders have identical information needs. Unlike the decision-makers emphasis, the decision models emphasis does not ask the decision makers what information they want but, instead, concentrates on the types of information considered useful for decision making. As Wolk and Tearney (1997, p. 39) indicate, a premise underlying this research is that decision makers may need to be taught how to use this information if they are unfamiliar with it.

Evaluating theories of accounting

In the process of studying accounting, students will typically be exposed to numerous theories of accounting, and accompanying research and argument which attempts to either support or reject the particular theories in question. In undertaking this study students should consider the merit of the argument and the research methods employed. What many students find interesting is that many researchers seem to adopt one theory of accounting and thereafter adopt various strategies (including overt condemnation of alternative theories) in an endeavour to support their own research and theoretical perspective. In some respects, the attitudes of some researchers are akin to those of the disciples of particular religions. (In fact, Chambers (1993) refers to advocates of Positive Accounting Theory as belonging to the 'PA Cult'.) In Deegan (1997) a series of quotes are provided from the works of various high profile researchers which are opposed to Watts and Zimmerman's *Positive Theory of Accounting*. In providing arguments against the validity of Positive Accounting Theory, the opponents used such terms and descriptions as:

- it is a dead philosophical movement (Christenson, 1983, p. 7);

- it has provided no accomplishments (Sterling, 1990, p. 97);

- it is marred by oversights, inconsistencies and paradoxes (Chambers, 1993, p. 1);

- it is imperiously dictatorial (Sterling, 1990, p. 121);

- it is empty and commonplace (Sterling, 1990, p. 130);

- it is akin to a cottage industry (Sterling, 1990, p. 132);

- it is responsible for turning back the clock of research 1000 years (Chambers, 1993, p. 22);

- it suffers from logical incoherence (Williams, 1989, p. 459); and

- it is a wasted effort (Sterling, 1990, p. 132).

The quoted criticisms clearly indicate the degree of emotion that a particular theory (Positive Accounting Theory) has stimulated among its critics, particularly those who see the role of accounting theory as providing prescription, rather than description. Students of financial accounting theory will find it interesting to ponder why some people are so angered by such a theory—after all, it is just a theory (isn't it?). Many proponents of Positive Accounting Theory have also tended to be very critical of normative theorists.

In explaining or describing why a certain 'camp' of researchers might try to denigrate the credibility of alternative research paradigms (consistent with Kuhn (1962), a paradigm can be defined as an approach to knowledge advancement that adopts particular theoretical assumptions, research goals and research methods) it is relevant to consider one of the various views about how knowledge advances.[6] Kuhn (1962) explained how knowledge, or science, develops: scientific progress is not evolutionary, but rather, revolutionary. His view is that knowledge advances when one theory is replaced by another as particular researchers attack the credibility of an existing paradigm and advance an alternative, promoted as being superior, thereby potentially bringing the existing paradigm into 'crisis'. As knowledge develops, the new paradigm may be replaced by a further research perspective, or a prior paradigm may be resurrected. In discussing the process of how researchers switch from one research perspective to another, Kuhn likens it to one of 'religious conversion'.[7] While the perspective provided by Kuhn does appear to have some relevance to explaining developments in the advancement of accounting theory, so far no accounting theory has ever been successful in overthrowing all other alternatives. There have been, and apparently will continue to be, advocates of various alternative theories of accounting—many of which are discussed.

Returning to our brief review of financial accounting theories, we have stated previously that positive theories of accounting do not seek to prescribe. Critical of this perspective, it has been argued that the decision not to prescribe could alienate academic accountants from their counterparts within the profession. As Howieson (1996, p. 31) states:

> . . . an unwillingness to tackle policy issues is arguably an abrogation of academics' duty to serve the community which supports them. Among other activities, practitioners are concerned on a day-to-day basis with the question of which accounting policies they should choose. Traditionally, academics have acted as commentators and reformers on such normative issues. By concentrating on positive questions, they risk neglecting one of their important roles in the community.

---

6. A similar definition of a paradigm is provided by Wolk and Tearney (1997, p. 47). They define a paradigm as a shared problem-solving view among members of a science or discipline.

7. Kuhn's 'revolutionary' perspective about the development of knowledge is a theory, and as with financial accounting theories, there are alternative views of how knowledge develops and advances. Although a review of the various perspectives of the development of science is beyond the scope of this book, interested readers are referred to Popper (1959), Lakatos and Musgrove (1974), Feyerabend (1975), and Chalmers (1982).

Counter to this view, many proponents of Positive Accounting Theory have, at different times, tried to undermine normative research because it was not based on observation (observation-based research was deemed to be 'scientific', and 'scientific research' was considered to be akin to 'good research'), but rather, was based on personal opinion about what *should* happen. Positive Accounting theorists often argue that in undertaking research they do not want to impose their own views on others as this is 'unscientific', but rather, they prefer to provide information about the expected implications of particular actions (for example, the selection of a particular accounting method) and thereafter let people decide for themselves what they should do (for example, they may provide evidence to support a prediction that organisations that are close to breaching accounting-based debt covenants will adopt accounting methods that increase the firm's reported profits and assets).

However, as a number of accounting academics have quite rightly pointed out, and as we should remember when reading this book, selecting a theory to adopt for research (such as Public Interest Theory, Capture Theory, Legitimacy Theory, Stakeholder Theory or Positive Accounting Theory) is based on a value judgement; what to research is based on a value judgement; believing that all individual action is driven by self-interest as the Positive Accounting theorists do is a value judgement; and so on. Hence, no research, whether utilising Positive Accounting Theory or otherwise, is value free and asserting that it is is arguably quite wrong. As Gray, Owen and Maunders (1987, p. 66) state:

> *In common with all forms of empirical investigation we must recognise that all perception is theory-laden. That is, our preconceptions about the world significantly colour what we observe and which aspects of particular events we focus upon. Thus accountants are more likely to view the world through accounting frameworks and conventions.*

Watts and Zimmerman (1990, p. 146) did modify their original stance in relation to the objectivity of their research and conceded that value judgements do play a part in positive research as they do in normative research. As they stated:

> *Positive theories are value laden. Tinker et al. (1982, p. 167) argue that all research is value laden and not socially neutral. Specifically, 'Realism operating in the clothes of positive theory claims theoretical supremacy because it is born of fact, not values' (p. 172). We concede the importance of values in determining research: both the researcher's and user's preferences affect the process.*
>
> *Competition among theories to meet users' demand constrains the extent to which researcher values influence research design. Positive theories are 'If . . . then' propositions that are both predictive and explanatory. Researchers choose the topics to investigate, the methods to use, and the assumptions to make. Researchers' preferences and expected pay-offs (publications and citations) affect the choice of topics, methods and assumptions. In this sense, all research, including positive research, is 'value laden'.*

The position taken in this book is that theories of accounting, of necessity, are abstractions of reality, and the choice of one theory in preference to another is based on particular value judgements. Some of us may prefer particular theories to others because they more closely reflect how we believe people do, or should, act. We cannot really expect to provide perfect explanations or predictions of human behaviour, nor can we expect to assess perfectly what types of information the users of financial statements actually need—my perceptions of information needs will most probably be different to your views about information needs. There is a role for prescription if it is based on logical argument and there is a role for research that provides predictions if the research methods employed to provide the predictions are assessed as valid.

Evaluating theories—considerations of logic and evidence

Throughout this book we discuss various theories of financial accounting. Where appropriate, we also undertake an evaluation of the theories. We consider such issues as whether the argument supporting the theories is (or at least appears to be) logical and/or whether we agree with the central assumptions (if any) that are being made. If possible we should try to break the argument or theory into its main premises to see if the argument, in simplified form, appears logical. What we emphasise is that we/you must question the theories that we are exposed to—not simply accept them. Acceptance of a theory and its associated hypotheses (hypotheses can be described as predictions typically expressed in the form of a relationship between one or more variables) must be tied to whether we accept the logic of the argument, the underlying assumptions, and any supporting evidence provided.

As an example of logical deduction, consider the following simplistic non-accounting related argument (reflecting the author's own biases—it refers to surfing). It shows that although the argument may be logical (if we accept the premises), if it can be shown that one of the premises is untrue or in doubt, then the conclusions or predictions may be rejected. Where we have a number of premises and a conclusion we often refer to this as a syllogism.

- All surfers over the age of 35 ride longboards.

- Jack is a surfer over the age of 35.

- Jack therefore rides a longboard.

If we accept the above premises, we might accept the conclusion. It is logical. To determine the logic of the argument we do not need to understand what is a 'surfer' or what is a 'longboard'. That is, we do not need to refer to 'real world' observations. We could have deconstructed the argument to the form:

- All A's ride a B.
- C is an A.
- Therefore C rides a B.

An argument is logical to the extent that *if* the premises on which it is based are true, *then* the conclusion will be true. That is, the argument (even if logical) will only provide a true account of the real world if the premises on which it is based are true. Referring to the above syllogism, evidence gathered through observation will show that the first premise does not always hold. There are surfers over 35 who do not ride longboards. Hence we reject the conclusion on the basis of observation, not on the basis of logic. Therefore we had two considerations. If the argument seeks to provide an account of real world phenomena we must consider the logic of the premises and the correspondence between the premises and actual observation. However, it should be remembered that not all theories or arguments seek to correspond with real world phenomena—for example, some normative theories of accounting promote radical changes to existing practices. For many normative theories we might consider only the logic of the argument and whether we are prepared to accept the premises on which the argument is based.

Returning to the subject of the syllogism provided above, we could have argued alternatively that:

- A lot of surfers over 35 ride longboards.
- Jack is a surfer over 35.
- Therefore Jack rides a longboard.

The above is not a logical argument. The first premise has admitted alternatives and hence the conclusion, which does not admit alternatives, does not follow. We can dismiss the argument on the basis of a logical flaw without actually seeking any evidence to support the premises.

In Chapter 7 we review in greater depth Positive Accounting Theory as developed by such researchers as Jensen and Meckling (1976) and Watts and Zimmerman (1978). As noted earlier, their positive theory of accounting has a number of central assumptions, including an assumption that all people are *opportunistic* and will adopt particular strategies to the extent that such strategies lead to an increase in the personal wealth of those parties making the decisions. Wealth accumulation is assumed to be at the centre of all decisions. The theory does not incorporate considerations of morality, loyalty, social responsibility, and the like.

If we were to accept the economics-based assumption or premise of researchers such as Watts and Zimmerman that:

- self-interest tied to wealth maximisation motivates *all* decisions by individuals,

plus *if* we accept the following premises (which we might confirm through direct observation or through research undertaken by others) that:

- manager X is paid on the basis of reported profits (for example, he/she is given a bonus of five per cent of profits); and

- accounting method Y is an available method of accounting that will increase reported profits relative to other methods,

then we might accept a prediction that, all other things being equal:

- manager X will adopt accounting method Y.

The above argument appears logical. Whether Manager X is paid on the basis of reported profits and whether accounting method Y will increase reported profits are matters that can be confirmed though observation. But if the premises are both logical and true then the conclusion will be true.

The above argument may be logical but we might only accept it if we accept the critical assumption of *wealth maximisation*. If we do not accept the central assumption, then we may reject the prediction. What is being emphasised here is that you need to consider whether you are prepared to accept the logic and the assumptions upon which the arguments are based. If not, then we may reject the theory and the associated predictions. For example, in Gray, Owen and Adams (1996) the authors explicitly state that they reject the central assumptions of Positive Accounting Theory (although by their own admission it has 'some useful insights') and that they will not use it as a means of explaining or describing the practice of corporate social responsibility reporting. (Corporate social reporting is a topic covered in Chapter 9 of this book.) As they state (p. 75):

> There is little doubt that these theories have provided some useful insights into the way in which they model the world. There is equally little doubt that some company management and many gambling investors may act in line with these theories. It is also the case that some authors have found the form of analysis employed in these theories useful for explaining corporate social reporting; but apart from the limitations which must arise from a pristine liberal economic perspective on the world and the profound philosophical limitations of the approach, the approach cannot offer any justification why we might accept the description of the world as a desirable one. It is a morally bankrupt view of the world in general and accounting in particular. Its (usual) exclusion of corporate social reporting is therefore actually attractive as an argument for corporate social reporting.

In Chapter 5 we discuss the Conceptual Framework Project, which is considered to be a normative theory of accounting (applying a decision usefulness perspective). This framework provides a view about the objective of general purpose financial reporting (to provide information that is useful for economics-based decisions) and the qualitative characteristics that financial information should possess. It also provides definitions of the elements of accounting (assets, liabilities, revenues, expenses, equity) and prescribes recognition criteria for each of the elements. It is based on a central premise that the objective of financial accounting is to provide information that allows users of general purpose financial reports to make and evaluate decisions about the allocation of scarce resources. If we were not to accept this central premise then we could reject the guidance provided by the framework, even though it could be considered to be logically structured.

While the in-depth study of logic and a critique of argument are beyond the scope of this book, interested readers should consider studying books or articles that concentrate on the development of logical argument.[8] Thouless (1974) describes various approaches to identifying logical flaws in arguments and he also identifies 38 'dishonest tricks in argument' that some writers use to support their argument. Some of the 'tricks' he refers to are:

- the use of emotionally toned words;

- making a statement in which 'all' is implied but 'some' is true;

- evasion of a sound refutation of an argument by use of a sophisticated formula;

- diversion to another question, to a side issue, or by irrelevant objection;

- the use of an argument of logically unsound form;

- the use of speculative argument;

- change in the meaning of a term during the course of an argument;

- suggestion by repeated affirmation;

- prestige by false credentials;

- the appeal to mere authority; and

- argument by mere analogy.

When reading documents written to support particular ideas or theories, we must also be vigilant to ensure that our acceptance of a theory has not, in a sense, been coerced through the use of colourful or emotive language, or an incorrect appeal to authority. We referred to some earlier quotes from critics of Positive Accounting Theory—some of which were very emotive. Quite often (but not always) emotive or colourful language is introduced to support an otherwise weak argument. Where emotive or colourful language has been used, we should perhaps consider whether we would take the same position in terms of accepting the author's arguments if that author had used relatively neutral language. Thouless (1974, p. 24) provides some advice in this regard. He suggests:

---

8. A good book in this regard is entitled *Straight and Crooked Thinking*, written by Robert H. Thouless. Sterling (1970) is also useful.

The practical exercise which I recommend is one that I have already performed on some passages in which truth seemed to be obscured by emotional thinking. I suggest that readers should copy out controversial passages from newspapers, books, or speeches which contain emotionally coloured words. They should then underline all the emotional words, afterwards rewriting the passages with the emotional words replaced by neutral ones. Examine the passage then in its new form in which it merely states facts without indicating the writer's emotional attitude towards them, and see whether it is still good evidence for the proposition it is trying to prove. If it is, the passage is a piece of straight thinking in which emotionally coloured words have been introduced merely as an ornament. If not, it is crooked thinking, because the conclusion depends not on the factual meaning of the passage but on the emotions roused by the words.

While we must always consider the logic of an argument and the various assumptions that have been made, what we also must remember is that theories, particularly those in the social sciences, are by nature, abstractions of reality. We cannot really expect particular theories about human behaviour to apply all the time. People (thankfully) are different and to expect theories or models of human behaviour to have perfect predictive ability would be naive. If a number of theories are available to describe a particular phenomenon, then considering more than one theory may provide a more rounded perspective. Difficulties will arise if the theories provide diametrically opposite predictions or explanations—in such cases a choice of theory must generally be made.

For those theories that attempt to predict and explain accounting practice (positive theories of accounting) it is common practice to empirically test the theories in various settings and for various types of decisions—but what if the particular theories do not seem to hold in all settings? Should the theories be abandoned? Can we accept a theory that admits exceptions? Certainly, readings of various accounting research journals will show that many studies that adopt Positive Accounting Theory as the theoretical basis of the argument fail to generate findings consistent with the theory (however, many do). According to Christenson (1983, p. 18), an outspoken critic of Positive Accounting Theory:

We are told, for example, that 'we can only expect a positive theory to hold on average' [Watts and Zimmerman, 1978, p. 127, n. 37]. We are also advised 'to remember that as in all empirical theories we are concerned with general trends' [Watts and Zimmerman, 1978, pp. 288–289], where 'general' is used in the weak sense of 'true or applicable in most instances but not all' rather than in the strong sense of 'relating to, concerned with, or applicable to every member of a class' [American Heritage Dictionary, 1969, p. 548] . . . A law that admits exceptions has no significance, and knowledge of it is not of the slightest use. By arguing that their theories admit exceptions, Watts and Zimmerman condemn them as insignificant and useless.

Christenson uses the fact that Positive Accounting Theory is not always supported in practice to reject it.[9] However, as stressed previously, as a study of people (accountants, not 'accounting'), it is very hard to see how any model or theory could ever fully explain human action. In fact, ability to do so would constitute a very dehumanising view of people. Hence, I believe that the failure of a particular study to support a theory should not in itself provide a basis for rejecting a theory as 'useless and insignificant'. From another perspective, the failure to support the theory may have been due to the data being inappropriately collected or that the data did not provide a sound correspondence with the theoretical variables involved. However, if the theory in question continuously fails to be supported, then its acceptance will obviously be threatened. At this point we could speculate whether in fact there are any theories pertaining to human activities that always hold.

As we will see when reading accounting (and other) research, researchers often generalise the results they derive from particular samples of observations to the broader population of the phenomenon in question. While a comprehensive review of research methods is beyond the scope of this book, if researchers are attempting to generalise the findings of their studies (based on particular samples) to a larger population, we need to consider the data on which the generalisation is based.[10] For example, if we are going to generalise our findings from a sample (we typically cannot test the whole population), then we must consider how the sample was chosen. For example, if we have a prediction that all companies will adopt a particular accounting method in times of inflation and we test this prediction against the ten largest companies listed on the stock exchange in a period of inflation, then commonsense should dictate that the findings really should not be considered generalisable. Can we really be confident about what small companies will do? Hence, throughout your readings of various research studies you should consider not only how the argument is developed, but also how it is tested. If there are flaws in how the testing has been done, we may question or reject the significance of the findings. We must evaluate whether the data collected really represent valid measures of the theoretical variables in question.

As noted previously, for normative theories it is usually not appropriate to test them empirically. If researchers are arguing that accountants should provide particular types of accounting information, or if other researchers are providing a view that organisations have a social responsibility to consider the

---

9. Where a proposition is not supported in a particular instance, many of us have probably heard the phrase 'the exception proves the rule' being applied. Such a statement implies that we cannot accept a rule or proposition unless we find some evidence that appears to refute it. This clearly is illogical argument. As emphasised above, we must always guard against accepting arguments that are not logically sound.

10. Entire books are dedicated to research methods. Interested readers may refer to Cooper, D. R., Emory, C. W., *Business Research Methods*, Irwin, Chicago, 1995; Hussey, J., Hussey, R., *Business Research*, Macmillan Press, London, 1997; Dooley, D., *Social Research Methods*, Prentice-Hall, 2nd edition, 1990.

needs of all stakeholders, then this does not mean that what they are prescribing actually exists in practice. For example, if Chambers' model of accounting prescribes that all assets should be valued at their net market value, and we go out and find that accountants predominantly value their assets on the basis of historical cost, we should not reject Chambers' theory as he was *prescribing*, not *predicting* or *describing*. We should always keep in mind what the researchers are attempting to achieve. Our acceptance of Chambers' theory is dependent upon whether we accept the logic of the argument as well as the assumptions made by Chambers, including the assumption that the central role of accounting should be to provide information about an entity's ability to adapt to changing circumstances (which he argues is best reflected by measures of assets that are tied to their net market values), and the assumption that firms should exist primarily to increase the wealth of the owners.

Why would students of financial accounting need to study theories?

As students of financial accounting you will be required to learn how to construct and read financial statements prepared in conformity with various Accounting Standards and other professional and statutory requirements. When you receive your qualifications you could be involved in such activities as compiling financial statements for others to read, in analysing financial statements for the purposes of making particular decisions, or in generating accounting guidance or rules for others to follow. As a result of studying various theories of financial accounting you will be exposed to various issues, including:

- how the various elements of accounting should be measured;
- what motivates organisations to provide certain types of accounting information;
- what motivates individuals to support and perhaps lobby regulators for some accounting methods in preference to others;
- what the implications for particular types of organisations and their stakeholders are if one method of accounting is chosen or mandated in preference to other methods;
- how and why the capital markets react to particular accounting information;
- whether there is a 'true measure' of income.

Accounting plays a very important part in society. To simply learn the various rules of financial accounting (as embodied within Accounting Standards and the like) without considering the implications that accounting information will have would seem illogical. Many important decisions are made on the basis of information that accountants provide (or in some circumstances, elect not to provide). Accountants are indeed very powerful people. The information generated by accountants enables others to make important decisions, for example, should they support the organisation? Is the organisation earning sufficient 'profits'? Is it earning excessive 'profits'? Is the organisation fulfilling its social responsibilities by investing in community support programs and recycling initiatives and if so, how much? In considering profits, is profitability a valid measure of organisational success? Further, if the accountant/accounting profession emphasises particular attributes of organisational performance (for example, profitability) does this in turn impact on what society perceives as the legitimate goals of business?[11]

Such issues should arguably be considered by all financial accountants. As a result of considering various theories of financial accounting, we provide some answers to the above important issues.

Outline of this book

In a book of this size we cannot expect to cover all the theories of financial accounting. We nevertheless cover those theories that have tended to gain widespread acceptance by various sectors of the accounting community.

In Chapter 2 we provide an overview of various financial reporting decisions that entities typically face, emphasising that some reporting pertaining to particular transactions and events is regulated, while some is unregulated. We emphasise that financial accountants typically make many professional judgements throughout the accounting process and we discuss the qualitative attribute of objectivity, but emphasise that considerations (other than the pursuit of objectivity) may sometimes influence accounting method selection and disclosure practices.

Chapter 3 provides an overview of various arguments for and against the regulation of financial reporting, with an overview of various perspectives on the *costs* and *benefits* of regulating financial reporting. The chapter explores why some accounting approaches and/or methods are adopted by regulators and/or the profession, while others are not. The political process involved in the setting of accounting standards is highlighted.

Chapter 4 gives an overview of various normative (or prescriptive) theories of accounting that have been advanced to deal with various accounting issues associated with periods of rising prices (inflation). The

---

11. In Chapters 2 and 3 we consider some research (for example, Hines, 1988) which suggests that accountants and accounting do not necessarily provide an unbiased account of reality, but rather, create reality. If the accounting profession emphasises a measure (such as profitability) as being a measure of success and legitimacy, then in turn, profitable companies will be considered successful and legitimate. If something other than profitability had been supported as a valid measure, then this may not have been the case.

chapter considers such issues as whether there is a *true measure* of income. Conceptual Frameworks as normative theories of accounting are considered in Chapter 5. Applying material covered in Chapter 3, Chapters 4 and 5 also consider why various normative theories of accounting did not gain favour with the accounting profession or the accounting standard-setters.

Chapter 6 explores the international harmonisation of accounting requirements. Recently, moves have been made to internationally harmonise accounting requirements. Australia is at the forefront of such moves. This chapter considers some potential costs and benefits of this process. Particular consideration is given to issues of *culture* and how *cultural differences* have typically been proposed as a reason to explain international differences in accounting requirements. International harmonisation ignores this research and assumes that all countries (with different cultures) can simply adopt the same accounting practices.

Chapters 7 and 8 show that while much financial reporting is regulated, organisations still have some scope for voluntarily selecting between alternative accounting methods for particular types of transactions. The treatment of many transactions and the disclosure of many/most issues associated with various social and environmental events relating to an organisation is unregulated. Chapters 7 and 8 consider some theoretical perspectives (including Positive Accounting Theory, Legitimacy Theory, Stakeholder Theory, Political Economy Theory) about what drives the various unregulated/voluntary reporting decisions.

Chapter 9 considers the development and use of new systems of accounting that incorporate the economic, social and environmental performance of an organisation. The relationship between accounting and sustainable development is explored. This chapter includes a consideration of the limitations of traditional financial accounting, with particular focus on its inability to incorporate social and environmental issues.

Chapters 10 and 11 consider how individuals and capital markets react to various corporate disclosures. These chapters consider the various theories that have been used to test whether the market is actually using particular types of disclosures, as well as theories that indicate how individuals use accounting information. The chapters also consider who should be deemed to be the users of various types of disclosures. Issues associated with stakeholder *rights to know* are also explored.

The concluding chapter, Chapter 12, provides an overview of various critical perspectives of accounting—perspectives that tend to criticise the entire system of accounting as it stands (accounting practice is anthropocentric, masculine, etc.) arguing that accounting tends to support current social systems, which favour those with capital but undermine the power of parties without the control of necessary resources.

In summary, the balance of this book can be presented diagrammatically, as in Figure 1.1 on page 22.

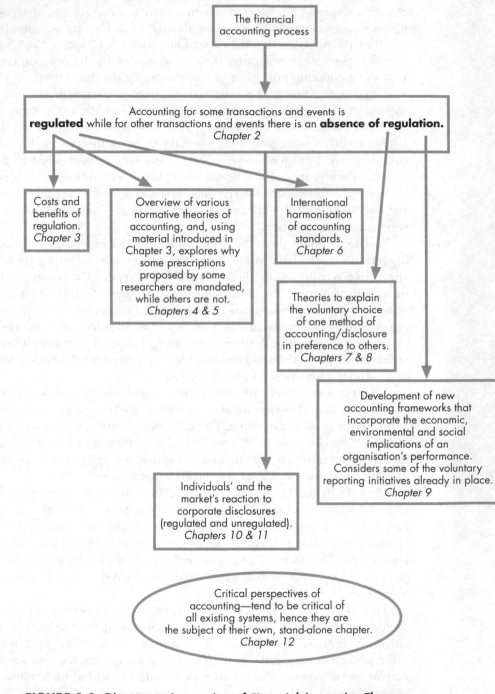

FIGURE 1.1 Diagrammatic overview of *Financial Accounting Theory*

The financial accounting process

Accounting for some transactions and events is **regulated** while for other transactions and events there is an **absence of regulation.**
Chapter 2

Costs and benefits of regulation.
Chapter 3

Overview of various normative theories of accounting, and, using material introduced in Chapter 3, explores why some prescriptions proposed by some researchers are mandated, while others are not.
Chapters 4 & 5

International harmonisation of accounting standards.
Chapter 6

Theories to explain the voluntary choice of one method of accounting/disclosure in preference to others.
Chapters 7 & 8

Development of new accounting frameworks that incorporate the economic, environmental and social implications of an organisation's performance. Considers some of the voluntary reporting initiatives already in place.
Chapter 9

Individuals' and the market's reaction to corporate disclosures (regulated and unregulated).
Chapters 10 & 11

Critical perspectives of accounting—tend to be critical of all existing systems, hence they are the subject of their own, stand-alone chapter.
Chapter 12

References

Canning, J.D., *The Economics of Accountancy*, Ronald Press, New York, 1929.

Chalmers, A.F., *What is this Thing Called Science?*, University of Queensland Press, 1982.

Chambers, R.J., '*Positive Accounting Theory and the PA Cult*', ABACUS, Vol. 29, No. 1, pp. 1–26, 1993.

Christensen, C., 'The Methodology of Positive Accounting', *The Accounting Review*, Vol. 58, pp. 1–22, January 1983.

Deegan, C., 'Varied Perceptions of Positive Accounting Theory: A Useful Tool for Explanation and Prediction, or a Body of Vacuous, Insidious and Discredited Thoughts?', *Accounting Forum*, Vol. 20, No. 5, pp. 63–73, 1997.

Deegan, C., *Australian Financial Accounting*, McGraw-Hill Book Company, 2nd edition, Sydney, 1999.

Feyerabend, P., *Against Method: Outline of an Anarchic Theory of Knowledge*, New Left Books, London, 1975.

Gordon, M.J., 'Postulates, Principles, and Research in Accounting', *The Accounting Review*, Vol. 39, pp. 251–63, April 1964.

Grady, P., *An Inventory of Generally Accepted Accounting Principles for Business Enterprises*, Accounting Research Study No. 7, AICPA, New York, 1965.

Gray, R, Owen, D., Adams, C., *Accounting and Accountability: Changes and Challenges in Corporate and Social Reporting*, Prentice-Hall, London, 1996.

Gray, R., Laughlin, R., Bebbington, J., *Financial Accounting: Method and Meaning*, International Thomson Business Press, London, 1996.

Gray, R., Owen, D., Maunders, K.T., *Corporate Social Reporting: Accounting and Accountability*, Prentice-Hall, Hemel Hempstead, 1987.

Hatfield, H.R., *Accounting, its Principles and Problems*, D. Appleton & Co, New York, 1927.

Henderson, S., Peirson, G., Brown, R., *Financial Accounting Theory: Its Nature and Development*, 2nd edition, Longman Cheshire, Melbourne, 1992.

Hendriksen, E., *Accounting Theory*, Richard D. Irwin, Illinois, 1970.

Hicks, J.R., *Value and Capital*, Oxford University Press, 1946.

Hines, R., 'Financial Accounting: In Communicating Reality, We Construct Reality', *Accounting Organizations and Society*, Vol. 13, No. 3, pp. 251–62, 1988.

Howieson, B., 'Whither Financial Accounting Research: A Modern-day Bo-Peep?', *Australian Accounting Review*, Vol. 6, No. 1, pp. 29–36, 1996.

Jensen, M.C., Meckling, W.H., 'Theory of the Firm: Managerial Behavior, Agency Costs and Ownership Structure', *Journal of Financial Economics*, Vol. 3, pp. 305–60, October 1976.

Kuhn, T.S., *The Structure of Scientific Revolutions*, University of Chicago Press, 1962.

Lakatos, I., Musgrove, A., *Criticism and the Growth of Knowledge*, Cambridge University Press, 1974.

Lee, T.A., 'Enterprise Income—Survival or Decline and Fall', *Accounting and Business Research*, No. 15, pp. 178–92, 1974.

Mathews, M.R., *Socially Responsible Accounting*, Chapman and Hall, London, 1993.

Miller, P.B.W., Reading, R., *The FASB: The People, the Process, and the Politics*, Irwin, Illinois, 1986.

Moonitz, M., *The Basic Postulates of Accounting*, Accounting Research Study No. 1, AICPA, New York, 1961.

Paton, W.A., *Accounting Theory*, Scholars Book Co, Kansas, 1922 (reprinted 1973).

Paton, W.A., Littleton, A.C., *An Introduction to Corporate Accounting Standards*, American Accounting Association, 1940.

Popper, K.R., *The Logic of Scientific Discovery*, Hutchinson, London, 1959.

Sprouse, R.T., Moonitz, M., *A Tentative Set of Broad Accounting Principles for Business Enterprises*, Accounting Research Study No. 3, AICPA, New York, 1962.

Sterling, R.R., 'On Theory Construction and Verification', *Accounting Review*, July 1970.

Sterling, R.R, 'Positive Accounting: An Assessment', *ABACUS*, Vol. 26, No. 2, pp. 97–135, 1990.

Thouless, R.H., *Straight and Crooked Thinking*, Pan Books, London, 1974.

Tinker, A.M., Merino, B.D., Neimark, M.D., 'The Normative Origins of Positive Theories: Ideology and Accounting Thought', *Accounting Organizations and Society*, Vol. 7, No. 2, pp. 167–200, 1982.

Watts, R.L., Zimmerman, J.L., 'Positive Accounting Theory: A Ten Year Perspective', *The Accounting Review*, Vol. 65, No. 1, pp. 259–85, 1990.

Watts, R.L., Zimmerman, J.L., 'Towards a Positive Theory of the Determinants of Accounting Standards,' *The Accounting Review*, Vol. 53, pp. 112–34, January 1978.

Watts, R.L., Zimmerman, J.L., *Positive Accounting Theory*, Prentice-Hall, Englewood Cliffs, New Jersey, 1986.

Williams, P.F., 'The Logic of Positive Accounting Research', *Accounting Organizations and Society*, Vol. 14, No. 5/6, pp. 455–68, 1989.

Wolk, H.I., Tearney, M.G., *Accounting Theory: A Conceptual and Institutional Approach*, International Thomson Publishing, 1997.

Questions

1.1 What is the difference between a positive theory of accounting and a normative theory of accounting?

1.2 Why would it not be appropriate to reject a normative theory of accounting because its prescriptions could not be confirmed through empirical observation?

1.3 Is the study of financial accounting theory a waste of time for accounting students? Explain your answer.

1.4 In the 1960s a number of accounting researchers concentrated on developing theories of accounting based on observing and documenting the behaviour of practising accountants. Do you think that such research is useful in improving the practice of financial accounting? Explain your answer.

1.5 Explain the meaning of the following paragraph and evaluate the logic of the perspective described:

In generating theories of accounting that are based upon what accountants actually do, it is assumed (often implicitly) that what is done by the majority of accountants is the most appropriate practice. In adopting such a perspective there is, in a sense, a perspective of accounting Darwinism—a view that accounting practice has evolved, and the fittest, or perhaps 'best', practices have survived. Prescriptions or advice are provided to others on the basis of what most accountants do—the logic being that the majority of accountants must be doing the most appropriate thing.

1.6 This chapter explains that in 1961 and 1962 the Accounting Research Division of the American Institute of Certified Public Accountants commissioned studies by Moonitz, and by Sprouse and Moonitz, respectively. These studies proposed that accounting measurement systems be changed from historical cost to a system based on current values. However, before the release of these studies, the AICPA released a statement saying that 'while these studies are a valuable contribution to accounting principles, they are too radically different from generally accepted principles for acceptance at this time' (Statement by the Accounting Principles Board, AICPA, April 1962). Explain why if something is 'radically different' (though it might be logically sound) this difference in itself might be enough to stop regulators embracing a particular approach to accounting.

1.7 Read the following quotation from Miller and Reading (1986). If constituency support is necessary before particular accounting approaches become embodied in accounting standards, does this have implications for the 'neutrality' and 'representational faithfulness' (qualitative characteristics that exist in various Conceptual Framework Projects around the world) of reports generated in accordance with accounting standards?

The mere discovery of a problem is not sufficient to assure that the FASB will undertake its solution . . . There must be a suitably high likelihood that the Board can resolve the issues in a manner that will be acceptable to the constituency—without some prior sense of the likelihood that the Board members will be able to reach a consensus, it is generally not advisable to undertake a formal project (Miller and Reading, 1986, p. 64).

1.8 As Watts and Zimmerman (1986, p. 7) state, Positive Accounting Theory is concerned with explaining accounting practice. It is designed to explain and predict which firms will, and which firms will not, use a particular accounting method, but says nothing as to which method a firm should use. Do you think that this represents an 'abrogation of the academics' duty to serve the community that supports them'?

1.9 This chapter describes two branches of 'decision usefulness' theories. Briefly identify and explain what they are.

1.10 Briefly explain the *revolutionary perspective* of knowledge advancement proposed by Kuhn (1962).

1.11 In your opinion, can accounting research be 'value free'? Explain your answer.

1.12 Assume that you have been asked to evaluate a particular theory of accounting. What factors would you consider before making a judgement that the theory appears 'sound'?

1.13 If you were trying to convince another party to support your theory about a particular facet of financial accounting, would you be inclined to use emotive or colourful language? Why, or why not?

1.14 What do we mean when we say that 'theories are abstractions of reality'? Do you agree that theories of accounting are necessarily abstractions of reality?

1.15 Would you reject as 'insignificant and useless' a positive theory of accounting on the basis that in a particular research study the results derived failed to support the hypotheses and the related theory? Explain your answer.

1.16 If a researcher tested a theory on a particular sample of companies, what considerations would you examine before you would agree with the researcher that the results can be generalised to the larger population of companies?

Chapter 2

The financial reporting environment

Learning objectives

Upon completing this chapter readers should:

- have a broad understanding of the history of the accounting profession and of accounting regulation;

- be aware of some of the arguments for and against the existence of accounting regulation;

- be aware of some of the theoretical perspectives used to explain the existence of regulation;

- be aware of how and why various groups within society try to influence the accounting standard–setting process;

- acknowledge that many accounting decisions are based on professional opinions and have an awareness of some of the theories used to explain what influences the accountant to choose one accounting method in preference to another;

- be aware of some of the arguments advanced to support a view that the accountant can be considered to be a powerful member of society.

Opening issues

Through such mechanisms as Conceptual Framework Programs, accounting professions throughout the world promote a view that accounting reports, when prepared properly, will be objective and will faithfully represent the underlying transactions and events of the reporting entity. Is it in the interests of the accounting profession to promote this view of objectivity and neutrality, and if so, why? Further, because of the economic and social impacts of many accounting decisions (for example, decisions that involve choosing one method of accounting in preference to another), and because accounting standard-setters take such economic and social impacts into account when developing new accounting standards, standard-setters themselves are not developing accounting standards that can subsequently enable a reliable account of organisational performance to be provided. Do you agree or disagree with this view, and why?

Introduction

Financial accounting is a process involving the collection and processing of financial information to assist in the making of various decisions by many parties external to the organisation. These parties are diverse and include present and potential investors, lenders, suppliers, employees, customers, governments, parties performing a review or oversight function, and the media. Financial accounting deals with the provision of information to parties not involved in the day-to-day running of the organisation. As there are many parties external to the firm, with potentially vastly different information demands and needs, it is not possible to generate reports that will satisfy each party's specific needs (reports that meet specific information needs are often referred to as special-purpose reports). As such, the process of financial accounting leads to the generation of reports deemed to be general purpose financial reports.[1]

Financial accounting tends to be heavily regulated in most countries, with many accounting standards governing how particular transactions and events shall be recognised, measured and disclosed. The reports generated, such as the statement of financial position (or balance sheet), statement of financial performance (or profit and loss account), statement of cash flows, and supporting notes, are directly impacted by the various accounting standards in place. When existing accounting standards change, or new accounting standards are released, this will typically have an impact on the various

---

1. Within Australia, general purpose financial reports are defined (in Statement of Accounting Concept No. 1) as reports intended to meet the information needs common to users who are unable to command the preparation of reports tailored so as to satisfy, specifically, all of their information needs.

numbers (such as particular revenues, expenses, assets and liabilities) included in the reports provided to the public.

Ideally, users of financial reports should have a sound working knowledge of the various accounting standards because, arguably, without such a knowledge it can be difficult (or perhaps near impossible) to interpret what the reports are actually reflecting. For example, 'profit' is the outcome of applying particular accounting rules and conventions, many of which are contained within accounting standards. As these rules change (as they frequently do), the same series of transactions will lead to different measures of 'profits' and net assets. Such a situation leads to an obvious question: should readers of financial reports be expected to understand financial accounting? The answer is yes, even though many users of financial statements (including many company directors and financial analysts) have a very poor working knowledge of accounting.

Throughout the world, various professional accounting bodies have stated specifically that users of financial reports do need to have some level of knowledge of financial accounting if they are to properly understand financial reports. For example, within Australia, Statement of Accounting Concepts No. 3 (paragraph 36) states:

> *General purpose financial reports ought to be constructed having regard to the interests of users who are prepared to exercise diligence in reviewing those reports and who possess the proficiency necessary to comprehend the significance of contemporary accounting practices.*[2]

If we are to review an annual report of a company listed on a stock exchange, we will soon realise just how confusing such a document would be to readers with a limited knowledge of accounting (and if we are to be honest, many of us with formal qualifications in accounting will also have trouble interpreting many of the numbers). Unfortunately, many readers of financial statements consider figures such as 'profits' or 'assets' as being 'hard' objective numbers which are not subject to various professional judgements. Hence, although such users may not understand some of the descriptions of accounting methods used, they believe that they understand what 'profits' and 'net assets' mean. As we know, however, the accounting results will be heavily dependent upon the particular accounting methods chosen, as well as upon various professional judgements made. Depending upon who compiles the accounting reports, measures of profits and net assets can vary greatly.[3]

---

2. Within the United States Conceptual Framework Project, reference is made to the 'informed reader' who should have sufficient knowledge of accounting to be able to appropriately interpret financial statements compiled in accordance with generally accepted accounting principles.

3. Yet all the various financial statements may be deemed to be *true and fair*—which implies that accountants are able to provide different versions of the 'truth'.

A review of annual reports will indicate that many companies are providing highlight statements at the beginning of the reports. Often, multi-year summaries are given of such figures as profits, return on assets, earnings per share, dividend yield, and net asset backing per share. By highlighting particular information, management could be deemed to be helping the less accounting-literate readers to focus on the important results. However, a down-side of this is that management is selecting the information to be highlighted (that is, such disclosures are voluntary) and as a result, a deal of otherwise important information may be overlooked.

Financial accounting can be contrasted with management accounting. Management accounting focuses on providing information for decision making by parties that work within an organisation (that is, for internal as opposed to external users) and it is largely unregulated. While we will find that most countries have a multitude of financial accounting standards that are often given the force of law, the same cannot be said for management accounting. Because management accounting relates to the provision of information for parties within the organisation, the view taken is that there is no need to protect their information needs or rights. It is the information rights of outsiders who are not involved in the day-to-day management of an entity that must be protected. Management accounting generates such information as cash flow projections, sales budgets, production requirements, inventory requirements, and so on. While management accounting tends to be forward focused (for example, on projections of future results, given particular strategies) financial accounting tends to be historical. Because financial reports are often used as a source of information for parties contemplating transferring resources to an organisation, it is arguably important that certain rules be put in place to govern how the information should be compiled. That is (adopting a pro-regulation perspective), to protect the interests of parties external to a firm, some regulation relating to accounting information is required. We now briefly consider the history of accounting practice and its associated regulation.

An overview of the development and regulation of accounting practice

While the practice of financial accounting can be traced back many hundreds of years, the regulation of financial accounting generally commenced in the twentieth century. In part this lack of regulation in the early days may have been due to the fact that until recent centuries there was a limited separation between the ownership and management of business entities, and as such, most systems of accounting were designed to provide information to the owner/manager. In the last century there has been an increase in the degree of separation between ownership and management, and with this increased separation has come an increased tendency to regulate accounting disclosures.

Early systems of double entry accounting, similar to the system we use today, have been traced back to thirteenth and fourteenth century Northern Italy. One of the first to document the practice of double entry accounting was a Franciscan monk by the name of Pacioli. His most famous work, entitled *Summa de Arithmetica, Geometrica, Proportioni et Proportionalita*, was published in Venice in 1494. A review of this work (there are translated versions) indicates that our current system of double entry accounting is very similar to that developed many hundreds of years ago. Even in the days of Pacioli there were debits and credits, with debits going on the left, credits on the right. There were also journals and ledgers.[4] Reflecting on the origins of double entry accounting, Hendriksen and Van Breda (1992, p. 36) state:

> *Debits, credits, journal entries, ledgers, accounts, trial balances, balance sheets and income statements all date back to the Renaissance. Accounting, therefore, can claim as noble a lineage as many of the liberal arts. Accounting students can take pride in their heritage. Part of this heritage is a rich vocabulary, almost all of which dates back to this period and much of which is fascinating in its origin.*

Debits and credits, which as we now know originated a number of centuries ago, have, over the ages, proved to be the bane of many an accounting student. So, did we really need them? Why couldn't we have simply used positive and negative numbers? For example, if we were to pay wages, why couldn't we have simply put a positive number under the wages column and a negative number under the cash column? The simple answer to this appears to be that negative numbers were not really used in mathematics until the seventeenth century. Hence, the t-account was devised to solve this problem with increases being on one side, and decreases on the other. But why keep the t-account, now that we accept the existence of negative numbers? Pondering this issue, Hendriksen and Van Breda (1992, p. 51) comment:

> *Textbook writers still explain how debits are found on the left and credits on the right and teach students the subtraction-by-opposition technique that was made obsolete in arithmetic three centuries ago. Programmers then faithfully seek to reflect these medieval ideas on the modern computer screen.*

As we will see in subsequent chapters, there are many criticisms of our financial accounting systems. There is an increasing trend towards the view that financial accounting should reflect the various social and environmental consequences of a reporting entity's existence. Unfortunately, however, our 'dated' double entry system has a general inability to take such consequences into account—but we will cover more of this in later chapters, particularly in Chapter 9.

---

4. According to Hendriksen and Van Breda (1992, p. 36), our use of the word debit can be traced back to the word *debere* (which is shortened to dr) which means to owe. The word credit is derived from the word *creed*, which abbreviates to cr.

While accounting and accountants have existed for hundreds of years, it was not until the nineteenth century that accountants within the United Kingdom and the United States banded together to form professional associations. According to Goldberg (1949), a Society of Accountants was formed in Edinburgh in 1854, later to be followed by a number of other bodies, including the Institute of Chartered Accountants in England and Wales (ICAEW), which was established in 1880. According to Mathews and Perera (1996, p. 16), from the early years, the ICAEW was very concerned about the reputation of its members and as a result set conditions for admission, including general education examinations, five years of articles served with a member of the institute, and intermediate and final examinations in a range of subjects.

Within the United States the American Association of Public Accountants was formed in 1887 (Goldberg, 1949). This association went on to form the basis of the American Institute of Certified Public Accountants (AICPA). While members of these bodies were often called upon to perform audits in particular circumstances, and while companies were generally required to prepare accounting reports subject to various company laws and stock exchange requirements,[5] there was a general absence of regulation about what the reports should disclose or how the accounting numbers should be compiled.[6]

In the early part of the twentieth century there was limited work undertaken to codify particular accounting principles or rules. Basically, accountants used those rules that they were aware of and which they (hopefully) believed were most appropriate to the particular circumstances. There was very limited uniformity between the accounting methods adopted by different organisations, thereby creating obvious comparability problems. Around the 1920s a number of people undertook research that sought to observe practice and to identify commonly accepted accounting conventions. That is, they sought to describe 'what was', rather than assuming a normative position with regards to 'what should be'. By simply describing current practice, the researchers gave themselves limited possibility for actually improving accounting procedures. As Mathews and Perera (1996, p. 20) state:

---

5. For example, within the United Kingdom the Joint Stock Companies Registration Act 1844 required that companies produce a balance sheet and an auditor's report thereon for distribution to shareholders before its annual meeting. This requirement was removed in a 1862 Act, but reinstated in a 1900 Act. In 1929 a requirement to produce a profit and loss account was introduced.

6. In 1900 the New York Stock Exchange required companies applying for listing to prepare financial statements showing the results of their operations as well as details about their financial position. In 1926 the exchange further required that all listed companies provide their shareholders with an annual financial report in advance of the companies' annual general meetings. The report did not have to be audited.

This led to a practice-theory-practice cycle and tended to retard the progress of accounting, because there was no value judgement exercised in respect of the practices which were observed. In other words, there was no opportunity to examine critically what was being practised before the next generation of accountants were prepared in the same manner.

Early researchers who provided detailed descriptions of existing conventions of accounting included Paton (1922), Paton and Littleton (1940), Sanders, Hatfield and Moore (1938) and Gilman (1939). These studies described such things as the doctrines of conservatism, concepts of materiality, consistency, the entity assumption, and the matching principle.

A great deal of the early work undertaken to establish particular accounting rules and doctrines was undertaken in the United States. In 1930 the accounting profession within the United States cooperated with the New York Stock Exchange (NYSE) to develop a list of broadly used accounting principles. According to Zeff (1972), this publication is one of the most important documents in the history of accounting regulation and set the foundation for the codification and acceptance of generally accepted accounting principles. The NYSE requested the accounting profession to compile the document as it was concerned that many companies were using a variety of (typically undisclosed) accounting methods.[7]

Within the United States it was not until 1934 that specific disclosures of financial information were required by organisations seeking to trade their securities. The Securities Exchange Act of 1934, as administered by the Securities Exchange Commission (SEC), stipulated the disclosure of specific financial information. The SEC was given authority to stipulate accounting principles and reporting practices. However, it allowed the accounting profession to take charge of this activity as long as it could clearly indicate that it would perform such duties diligently. In an effort to convince the SEC that it could identify acceptable accounting practices, the American Institute of Accountants (one of the predecessors of the AICPA) released, in 1937, a study by Sanders, Hatfield and Moore entitled *A Statement of Accounting Principles*.

In 1938 the SEC stated (within Accounting Series Release No. 4) that it would only accept financial statements prepared in accordance with the generally accepted accounting principles of the accounting profession— thereby giving a great deal of power to the profession. In part, ASR No. 4 stated:

---

7. Five of the identified principles subsequently formed the basis of Chapter 1 of Accounting Research Bulletin No. 43, as issued by the Committee on Accounting Procedure.

In cases where financial statements filed with the Commission . . . are prepared in accordance with accounting principles for which there is no substantial authoritative support, such financial statements will be presumed to be misleading or inaccurate despite disclosures contained in the certificate of the accountant or in footnotes to the statements provided the matters are material. In cases where there is a difference of opinion between the Commission and the registrant as to proper principles of accounting to be followed, disclosure will be accepted in lieu of correction of the financial statements themselves, only if the points involved are such that there is substantial authoritative support for the practices followed by the registrant and the position of the Commission has not previously been expressed in rules, regulations, or other releases of the Commission, including the published opinion of its chief accountant.

While the above statement does indicate that the SEC was to allow the accounting profession to determine acceptable practice, many considered that the SEC was also warning the accounting profession that it must take an authoritative lead in developing accounting standards, otherwise the SEC would take over the role (Zeff, 1972). From 1939 the Committee on Accounting Procedure, a committee of the accounting profession, began issuing statements on accounting principles, and between 1938 and 1939 it released 12 *Accounting Research Bulletins* (Zeff, 1972).

The development of mandatory accounting standards is a relatively recent phenomenon. In the United Kingdom it was not until 1970, when the Accounting Standards Steering Committee was established (later to become the Accounting Standards Committee), that UK accountants had to conform with professionally developed mandatory accounting standards. Prior to this time the ICAEW had released a series of 'recommendations' to members. In the United States, although there had been Accounting Research Bulletins (released by the Committee on Accounting Procedure, formed in 1938), and Opinions (released by the Accounting Principles Board, formed in 1959), these Bulletins and Opinions were not mandatory. Rather they indicated perceived best practice. There tended to be many corporate departures from these Bulletins and Opinions and as a result, in 1965 a rule (Rule 203 of the AICPA) was introduced that required departures from principles published in APB Opinions to be disclosed in footnotes to financial statements. From 1 July 1973 the APB was replaced by the Financial Accounting Standards Board (FASB), which has subsequently released many accounting standards that are mandatory.

As might be expected, given overseas experience, the history of accounting regulation within Australia is quite recent. In 1946 the Institute of Chartered Accountants in Australia (ICAA) released five *Recommendations on Accounting Principles*, which were largely based on documents released by the ICAEW. In 1956 a number of recommendations were released by the Australian Society of Accountants (now the Australian Society of CPAs). In later years the two bodies agreed to issue statements and recommendations jointly through the Australian Accounting Research Foundation (AARF), a body jointly funded by the ICAA and the Australian Society of CPAs (ASCPA). More recently the AARF has collaborated with the Australian Accounting Standards Board (a government funded body) in developing accounting standards that have the force of law.

The rationale for regulating financial accounting practice

As indicated above, even though financial reports have been in existence for hundreds of years, the regulation of accounting is a fairly recent phenomenon. Early moves for regulation of accounting were introduced in the United States around the 1930s and followed events such as the Great Depression. Rightly or wrongly it was argued that problems inherent to accounting led to many poor and uninformed investment decisions (Ray, 1960; Boer, 1994). Obviously, it would probably be quite unfair to blame events such as the Great Depression on accounting (and therefore on accountants) but such events did fuel the public desire for information generated by companies to be subject to greater regulation.

In most developed countries there is a multitude of accounting standards covering a broad cross-section of issues—but do we really need all this regulation? As we will see in the next chapter, there are two broad schools of thought on this issue. There are parties who argue that regulation is necessary, with reasons including:

- markets for information are not efficient and without regulation a sub-optimal amount of information will be produced;
- while proponents of the 'free-market' approach may argue that the market *on average* is efficient, such *on average* arguments ignore the rights of individual investors, some of whom can lose their savings as a result of relying upon unregulated disclosures;
- those who demand information can often do so due to power over scarce resources. Parties with limited power (limited resources) will generally be unable to secure information about an organisation, even though that organisation may impact on their existence;
- investors need protection from fraudulent organisations that may produce misleading information, which due to information asymmetries, cannot be known to be fraudulent when used;
- regulation leads to uniform methods being adopted by different entities, thus enhancing comparability.

Others argue that regulation is not necessary, particularly to the extent that it currently exists. Some of the reasons cited include:

- accounting information is like any other good, and people (financial statement users) will be prepared to pay for it to the extent that it has use. This will lead to an optimal supply of information by entities;[8,9]

- capital markets require information, and any organisation that fails to provide information will be punished by the market—an absence of information will be deemed to imply bad news;[10]

- because users of financial information typically do not bear its cost of production, regulation will lead to over-supply of information (at cost to the producing firms) as users will tend to overstate the need for the information;

- regulation typically restricts the accounting methods that may be used. This means that some organisations will be prohibited from using accounting methods that they believe best reflect their particular performance and position. This is considered to impact on the efficiency with which the firm can inform the markets about its operations.

When regulation is introduced, there are various theories available to describe who benefits from such regulation. There is the *public interest theory* of regulation which proposes that regulation be introduced to protect the public. This protection may be required as a result of inefficient markets. Public interest theory assumes that the regulatory body (usually government) is a neutral arbiter of the 'public interest' and does not let its own self-interest impact on its rule-making processes. According to Scott (1997, p. 357), following public interest theory, the regulator does its best to regulate so as to maximise overall social welfare. Consequently, regulation is thought of as a trade-off between the costs of regulation and its social benefits in the form of improved operation of markets.

A contrary perspective of regulation is provided by *capture theory* which argues that although regulation is often introduced to protect the public, the regulatory mechanisms are often subsequently controlled (captured) so as to protect the interests of particular self-interested groups within society, typically those whose activities are most affected by the regulation. That is, the 'regulated' tend to capture the 'regulator'. Posner (1974, p. 342) argues that 'the original purposes of the regulatory program are later thwarted through the efforts of the interest group'.

---

8. Advocates of a regulated approach would argue, however, that accounting information is a public good and as a result, many individuals will obtain the information for free (this is often referred to as the 'free-rider' problem). Once this occurs, reliance on market-mechanism arguments tends to be flawed and the usual pricing mechanisms of a market cannot be expected to operate (Cooper and Keim, 1983).

9. This 'free-market' perspective is adopted by researchers who work within the agency theory paradigm. This paradigm is discussed in Chapter 7.

10. Accepting this perspective, and consistent with Akerlof (1970), companies that fail to produce necessary information, particularly if the information is being produced by other entities, will be viewed as 'lemons', and these 'lemons' will find it more costly to attract funds than other ('non-lemon') entities.

As an example of capture theory, Walker (1987) argues that in less than two years following the establishment of the Accounting Standards Review Board (subsequently replaced by the Australian Accounting Standards Board) the Australian accounting profession (the 'industry' subject to the regulation) was able to control, or capture, the ASRB's regulatory process. Walker provides evidence to support this claim including the subsequent merger of the Australian Accounting Research Foundation (the professionally funded body) with the AASB (the government body), and that the great majority of issues to be addressed in accounting standards were raised by the accounting profession itself.[11]

Both public interest theories and capture theories of regulation assert that initially regulation is put in place to protect the public (capture theory simply asserts that the regulated will then subsequently attempt to control the regulatory process). Another view, which is often referred to as *private interest theory* (or *economic interest group theory*), is proposed by researchers such as Stigler (1971) and Peltzman (1976). This theory relaxes the assumption that regulations are initially put in place to protect the public interest, as well as the assumption that government regulators are neutral arbiters not driven by self-interest. Stigler (1971) proposes that governments are made up of individuals who are self-interested and will introduce regulations more likely to lead to their re-election. In deciding upon particular regulation they will consider the impacts upon key voters, as well as on election campaign finances. Individuals with an interest in particular legislation are deemed more likely to get their preferred legislation if they can form themselves into large organised groups with strong cohesive voting power. These theories of regulation (public interest theory, capture theory, and private interest theory), as well as others, are further considered in Chapter 3.

If we are to accept the need for accounting regulation, a further issue to consider is who should be responsible for the regulation—should it be in the hands of the private sector (such as the accounting profession), or in the hands of government?[12] Can private sector regulators be expected to put in

---

11. The establishment of the ASRB in the first place, however, can be explained by a public interest theory perspective. Prior to the establishment of the ASRB, accounting standards in Australia were released by the private sector body, the Australian Accounting Research Foundation. The AARF had limited ability to impose sanctions against entities that did not follow the AARF standards. This was believed to be a major cause of the numerous corporate non-compliances, and the associated social and economic costs that such non-compliances might cause. The ASRB, a government body, was established to give legal backing to accounting standards through the operation of the Corporations Law. With renewed confidence in the information being produced, there was also a view that the capital markets would function more efficiently—which would be considered to be in the public interest.

12. In some countries, accounting regulation is in the hands of both private sector and public sector entities. As an example, within Australia, Accounting Standards have been jointly developed by a public sector entity (the Australian Accounting Standards Board) and a private sector entity (the Australian Accounting Research Foundation). In the United States, both the Financial Accounting Standards Board (private sector) and the SEC (public sector) have released accounting standards.

place regulations that are always in the public interest, or will they seek to put in place rules that favour their own constituency? Advocates of private sector accounting standard-setting of rules would argue that the accounting profession is best able to develop accounting standards because of its superior knowledge of accounting, and because of the greater likelihood that its rules and regulations would be accepted by the business community. Proponents of public sector accounting standard-setting argue that government has greater enforcement powers, hence the rules of government are more likely to be followed. It might also be less responsive to pressures exerted by business, and more likely to consider overall public interest.

What we demonstrate in subsequent chapters is that the regulation of accounting (or indeed an absence of regulation) can have many economic and social consequences. As such, the accounting standard-setting process is typically considered to be a very political process, with various interested parties lobbying the standard-setters.

The role of professional judgement in financial accounting

As we would know from studying accounting, the process involved in generating accounts depends upon many professional judgements. While the accounting treatment of many transactions and events is regulated, a great deal of accounting treatment pertaining to other transactions and events is unregulated. Even when particular regulations are in place, for example, that buildings must be depreciated, there is still scope to select the useful life of the building and the residual value. Many such judgements must be made— should an item be capitalised or expensed? This in turn will depend upon crucial assessments as to whether the expenditure is likely to generate future economic benefits.

At the core of the accounting process is an expectation that accountants should be objective and free from bias when performing their duties. The information being generated should *faithfully represent* the underlying transactions and events and it should be *neutral* and *verifiable* (FASB Statement No. 2, 1980).[13] However, can we really accept that accounting can be 'neutral' or objective? Throughout the world, many accounting standard-setters explicitly consider the economic and social implications of possible accounting standards prior to their introduction (the consideration of economic and social consequences is referred to in a number of countries' conceptual framework projects). If the economic or social implications of a

---

13. According to Hines (1991, p. 330) it is in the accounting profession's interest to publicly promote a perspective of objectivity. As she states, 'the very talk, predicated on an assumption of an objective world to which accountants have privileged access via their "measurement expertise", serves to construct a perceived legitimacy for the profession's power and autonomy'.

particular accounting standard are deemed to be significant, then it is likely that the introduction of the standard will be abandoned—even though the particular standard may be deemed to more accurately reflect particular transactions or events. While it is difficult to criticise a process that considers potential impacts on others, it is nevertheless difficult to accept that accounting standards are neutral or unbiased. In a sense the acceptance of the need to consider economic and social consequences as part of the standard-setting process has created a dilemma for standard-setters. According to Zeff (1978, p. 62):

> The board (FASB) is thus faced with a dilemma which requires a delicate balancing of accounting and non-accounting variables. Although its decisions should rest—and be seen to rest—chiefly on accounting considerations, it must also study—and be seen to study—the possible adverse economic and social consequences of its proposed actions . . . What is abundantly clear is that we have entered an era in which economic and social consequences may no longer be ignored as a substantive issue in the setting of accounting standards. The profession must respond to the changing tenor of the times while continuing to perform its essential role in the areas in which it possesses undoubted expertise.

In Chapters 7 and 8 we consider various theoretical perspectives proposed as explanations for why particular accounting methods may be implemented by a reporting entity (remember, the accounting treatment of many transactions and events is not subject to accounting standards). Consistent with a perspective of objectivity is a view that organisations are best served by selecting accounting methods that best reflect their underlying performance. This is referred to as an 'efficiency perspective' (derived from Positive Accounting Theory). The efficiency perspective asserts that different organisational characteristics explain why different firms adopt different accounting methods (Jensen and Meckling, 1976). For example, firms that have different patterns of use in relation to a particular type of asset will be predicted to adopt different amortisation policies. Advocates of the efficiency perspective argue that firms should be allowed to choose those accounting methods that best reflect their performance, and that accounting regulations that restrict the set of available accounting techniques will be costly. For example, if a new accounting standard is released that bans a particular accounting method being used by a reporting entity, then this will lead to inefficiencies as the resulting financial statements may no longer provide the best reflection of the performance of the organisation. It would be argued that management is best able to select which accounting methods are appropriate in given circumstances, and government or other bodies should not intervene in the standard-setting process. This perspective, however, does not consider that some financial statement preparers may be less than objective (that is, they may be *creative*) when preparing the financial reports. The efficiency perspective also dismisses the comparability benefits that may arise if standard-setters reduce the available set of accounting methods.

An alternative perspective to explain why particular accounting methods are selected (and which is also derived from Positive Accounting Theory) is the 'opportunistic perspective'. This perspective does not assume that those responsible for selecting accounting methods will be objective. Rather, it assumes that they will be driven by self-interest (Watts and Zimmerman, 1978). This perspective provides an explanation of the practice of *creative accounting*, which is defined as an approach to accounting wherein objectivity is not employed, but rather, refers to a situation where those responsible for the preparation of accounts select accounting methods that provide the result desired by the preparers. As an example, an organisation might opportunistically elect to capitalise particular expenditure, not because they believe it will generate future economic benefits, but perhaps because they are close to breaching particular accounting-based agreements negotiated with external parties, such as loan agreements which have a stipulated minimum allowable debt to asset ratio, below which particular assets of the reporting entity may be seized.

Apart from the efficiency and opportunistic perspectives, there are a number of other theoretical perspectives proposed to explain why an entity may select particular accounting and disclosure policies (other perspectives include legitimacy theory, political economy theory, and stakeholder theory). Chapter 8 further explores the alternative perspectives. However, what is being emphasised at this point is that although there is much accounting regulation in place (and there are various theories to explain the existence of regulation), there are also many accounting decisions that are unregulated (giving rise to various theories to explain the choice of particular accounting methods from the set of available alternatives).

How powerful is the accountant?

Accountants are often the butt of many a cruel joke. They are often portrayed as small, weak individuals with poor social skills. For example, consider the depictions of accountants in various movies and television programs. In the (in)famous Monty Python Lion Tamer sketch, in which Cleese is cast as a recruitment consultant who interviews Michael Palin (who plays Mr Anchovy the accountant and aspiring lion tamer), Cleese describes the accountant as:

> *An extremely dull fellow, unimaginative, timid, lacking in initiative, spineless, easily dominated . . . Whereas in most professions these would be considerable drawbacks, in accountancy they are a positive boon.*[14]

Most of us would also probably remember such characters as Louis Tully, the 'nerd' accountant in Ghostbusters and Leo Getz the bumbling accountant in Lethal Weapon 2 and 3. These are only two of many poor depictions that

14. Smith and Briggs (1999) provide a more thorough overview of how accountants have been portrayed in movies and on television.

movies make of accountants. While accountants may be the subject of such (poorly informed and unpleasant) depictions and taunts, we can rest in the knowledge that we accountants are indeed very powerful individuals. The assertion that accountants are *powerful* (which is obviously flattering to students of accounting) is based on a number of perspectives, as follows:

- The output of the accounting process (for example, *profits* or *net asset backing per share*) impacts on many decisions such as whether to invest in or lend funds to an entity, whether to lobby for increased wages based on profitability, whether to place an entity into technical default for failure to comply with previously agreed accounting-based restrictions, whether to lobby government for intervention because of excessive *profits*, and so on. That is, many transfers of funds (and therefore wealth) arise as a result of reports generated by accountants through the accounting process. Because accounting is heavily reliant on professional judgement, the judgement of the accountant can directly impact on various parties' wealth.

- There is also a perspective that accountants, in providing objective information to interested parties can, in a sense, provide or transfer to them a source of 'power' to drive changes to corporations' behaviour. As Gray (1992, p. 404) states:

  . . . power can be exercised in some degree by all . . . external parties. For that power to be exercised there is a basic need for information (as an essential element of the participatory democratic process . . .) and this information will be an extension of that currently available. That is, the widest possible range of participants must be emancipated and enabled through the manifestation of existing but unfulfilled rights to information.

- By emphasising particular performance attributes (such as profits), accountants can tend to give legitimacy to organisations that otherwise may not be deemed to be legitimate.

Further reflecting on the above points, we can consider the work of Hines (1988, 1991). Hines (1991, p. 313) stresses a perspective that 'financial accounting practices are implicated in the construction and reproduction of the social world'. What she is arguing is that by emphasising measures such as profits (which ignores many social and environmental impacts) accounting can cause people to support organisations that may not otherwise be supported. By holding profitability out as some ideal in terms of performance, profitable companies are considered to be *good* companies.

Consider Exhibit 2.1. The newspaper report emphasises the profits of Rothmans. If profits increase, this is typically portrayed as a sign of sound management. The earning of profits tends to be seen as consistent with a notion of legitimacy—profits are reported and emphasised as some form of objective measure of performance. But as we know, and what the media typically neglects to note, is that the measure of profits really depends on the assumptions and judgements made by the particular team of accountants

EXHIBIT 2.1 Profits as an indicator of organisational performance

Rothmans lift payout after 20pc profit climb

Andrew White

Cigarette maker Rothmans Holdings has lifted its final dividend 10c to 45c after hoisting earnings 20 per cent on the back of continued market share gains in Australia.

Rothmans posted net earnings of $119.1 million, up 20 per cent after excluding the effect of last year's $74.5 million abnormal gain on changes in the collection of franchise fees. Including the abnormal item in comparisons, net profit was down 20 per cent on last year's $145 million.

The performance included a 25.9 per cent jump in second half earnings to $59.8 million, reflecting higher earnings in Australia and New Zealand and reduced losses in Indonesia.

Rothmans managing director Gary Krelle said the company had continued to take market share from its merger partner WD&HO Wills, adding nearly 1.5 per cent to 34.7 per cent over the past two years.

Mr Krelle said sales were up 22 per cent to $3 billion, and appeared to be benefiting from the buoyant economic conditions as smokers traded back up from discount to premium and middle-market brands.

'What I think is happening is a continued strengthening of brands that people have been comfortable with for a long time,' he said.

He warned that the company's earnings would be affected by tax changes in the pipeline, including the goods and services tax and a shift in tobacco excise from a per-gram to a per-stick regime.

The Federal Government has estimated the per-stick regime will add $420 million to federal tobacco revenues, but Mr Krelle estimates it could be as high as $550 million.

The increase in the final dividend takes Rothmans' total payout to 85c a share, compared to $1.65 last year, which included a $1 special dividend.

The Australian, **20 May 1999, p. 24.**

involved. As can be seen from Exhibit 2.1, no mention is made of the accounting methods employed by Rothmans. This is typical of media coverage given to corporate performance, with accounting results (for example, profits) being apparently promoted as hard, objective calculations. Financial accounting can engender such views because it is promoted (through such media as conceptual frameworks) as being objective and reliable and having the capacity to accurately reflect underlying facts.[15] As Hines (1991, p. 315) states in relation to conceptual framework projects:

> *It appears that the ontological assumption underpinning the CF is that the relationship between financial accounting and economic reality is a unidirectional, reflecting or faithfully reproducing relationship: economic reality exists objectively, inter-subjectively, concretely and independently of financial accounting practices; financial accounting reflects, mirrors, represents or measures this pre-existent reality.*

---

15. Authors such as Molotch and Boden (1985) provide a view that a form of social power is attributed to those people and professions able to 'trade on the objectivity assumption' (p. 281).

What also should be appreciated is that the measures of profit calculated for Rothmans (and also other organisations) ignore many social and environmental externalities caused by the reporting entity. In the case of a cigarette manufacturer such as Rothmans there is scientific evidence that their product causes major adverse social (and related economic) consequences. Accounting, however, ignores these externalities.

A counter view to the above perspective that accounting is *objective* and provides an accurate reflection of a pre-existent reality, and the view adopted by Hines, is that accountants can, in a sense, create different realities, depending upon the particular judgements taken, the accounting standards available, and so on. That is, accounting does not objectively reflect a particular reality—it creates it. This view is also provided by Handel (1982, p. 36) who states:

Things may exist independently of our accounts, but they have no human existence until they become accountable. Things may not exist, but they may take on human significance by becoming accountable . . . Accounts define reality and at the same time they are that reality . . . The processes by which accounts are offered and accepted are the fundamental social process . . . Accounts do not more or less accurately describe things. Instead they establish what is accountable in the setting in which they occur. Whether they are accurate or inaccurate by some other standards, accounts define reality for a situation in the sense that people act on the basis of what is accountable in the situation of their action. The account provides a basis for action, a definition of what is real, and it is acted on so long as it remains accountable.

While one team of accountants may make various accounting assumptions and judgements that lead to a profit being reported, it is possible that another team of accountants may make different assumptions and judgements that lead to the same organisation (with the same transactions and events) reporting a loss. Recording a loss may generate many negative reactions from various stakeholder groups (for example, from shareholders, media, and analysts) and may create real negative cash-flow consequences for the reporting entity. Hines (1991, p. 20) further reflects on the power of the accounting profession. She states:

If, say, auditors qualify their report with respect to the going-concern assumption, and/or insist that a corporation's financial statements be prepared on the basis of liquidation values, this in itself may precipitate the failure of a company which may otherwise have traded out of its difficulties.

Another point to be made (which is related to the above point), and one which we consider further in Chapter 3, is that few, if any, accounting standards are introduced without some form of economic and social impact (which as we know from previous discussion in this chapter is considered by many accounting standard-setters). As an example, we can consider the various arguments that have been raised internationally with regard to the requirement to amortise purchased goodwill. As Deegan (1999, p. 230) indicates, many Australian companies have claimed that the accounting requirement to amortise goodwill impacts negatively on their international competitiveness, particularly against those countries that have less rigid amortisation requirements.[16] Solomons (1978, p. 67) also states that similar arguments have been made in the United States. He states that the accounting requirement that United States companies must write off purchased goodwill is said to give an advantage to foreign companies in bidding for American businesses because, not being subject to the same accounting requirement, they can afford to offer a higher price. Further, Solomon, (1978, p. 63) states:

> FASB Statement No. 2, Accounting for Research and Development Costs, which requires that R & D be expensed as incurred, has been said to constitute a threat to technological progress, especially by smaller companies that may be contemplating seeking access to the capital market and will therefore want to show good profits.

As such, perspectives of accounting as being neutral in its effects are now widely dismissed (Zeff, 1978). Most standard-setting bodies throughout the world explicitly state in their various documents (which often form part of their respective conceptual frameworks) that economic and social implications of particular pronouncements must be considered prior to the introduction of new accounting rules.[17] As Zeff (1978, p. 60) states:

> The issue of economic consequences has, therefore, changed from one having only procedural implications for the standard-setting process to one which is now firmly a part of the standard-setters' substantive policy framework.

Hence we are left with a view that while the notion of objectivity and neutrality is promoted within various conceptual frameworks (perhaps, as Hines suggests, as a means of constructing a perceived legitimacy for the accounting profession), various factors such as the possible economic and social implications, and the potential influences of management self-interest (culminating in some form of *creative accounting*) can lead us to question such claims of objectivity. This chapter has also promoted a view that accountants do have quite a degree of *power*—many decisions with real economic and social implications are made on the basis of accounting information. Whether accounting information is like any other good that can be freely traded in the marketplace, or whether it should be subject to regulation is an issue that we further investigate in the next chapter.

---

16. Such claims have been made by a number of Australian companies, including Pacific Dunlop Ltd, Mayne Nickless Ltd and Amcor Ltd. However, Miller (1995) rejects such 'competitiveness arguments'. He proposes that 'sophisticated investors' should be able to distinguish between a real cash-flow effect, and a bookkeeping effect.

17. For example, within Australia, Statement of Accounting Concept No. 3, paragraph 45, states that 'in the process of setting standards, standard-setters seek to consider all costs and benefits in relation to financial reporting generally, and not just as they pertain to individual reporting entities'.

Chapter summary

In this chapter we explored how the output of the financial accounting process is used in many different decisions by parties both within, and outside, an organisation. Because the financial accounting process provides information to parties external to the organisation who otherwise would not have information, and because this information is often used as the basis for many decisions, it is generally accepted that it is necessary to regulate the practice of financial accounting.

Financial accounting practices are heavily regulated. However, the history of financial accounting regulation is relatively recent and there was a general absence of such regulation prior to the twentieth century. In the early parts of the twentieth century, accounting research often involved documenting commonly used accounting practices. This research led to the development and acceptance of broad principles of accounting that all accountants were expected to follow. Over time, broad principles gave way to the development of specific accounting standards. Accounting standards began to be released by various accounting professional bodies throughout the world around the 1970s and standard-setting activity has tended to increase since then. Financial accounting practices throughout the world today are generally regulated by a large number of accounting standards.

The act of regulating accounting practices through the continual release of new and revised accounting standards has led to various arguments for and against regulation. The arguments range from the belief that there is no need to regulate accounting practices (the 'free-market' approach) to a view that regulation is necessary to protect the interests of those parties with a stake in a reporting entity. Arguments against regulation often rely upon the view that the output of the financial accounting system should be treated like any other good, and if the market is left to operate freely, optimal amounts of accounting information will be produced. Introducing regulation leads to an oversupply of accounting information and can cause organisations to use accounting methods that do not efficiently reflect their actual operations, financial position, and financial performance. As we see in subsequent chapters, such 'free-market' arguments are challenged by many people.

This chapter has also briefly considered various theories about who is likely to benefit from regulation once it is introduced (Chapter 3 extends much of this discussion). We considered Public Interest Theory which proposes that regulation is introduced to protect the public and when putting regulation in place, regulators seek to maximise the overall welfare of the community (which obviously requires trade-offs of particular costs and benefits). Another theory that we considered was Capture Theory which proposes that while regulation might initially be introduced for the public's benefit, ultimately the group that is regulated will gain control of the regulation process. That is, they will eventually 'capture' the regulatory process. We also considered private interest theories of regulation, which propose that the regulators introduce regulation that best serves the regulators' own private interests. That is, regulators are motivated not by the public interest, but by their own self-interests. For example, politicians will introduce regulation likely to generate enough support to ensure their re-election.

We also considered issues associated with the 'power' of accountants. Arguments were advanced to support a view that accountants hold a very powerful role within society (which stands in contrast to how they are often portrayed in the media). Accountants provide information that is used in many decisions and they are able to highlight or downplay particular facets of an organisation's performance.

References

Akerlof, G.A., 'The Market for "Lemons": Quality Uncertainty and the Market Mechanism', *Quarterly Journal of Economics*, 84, pp. 488–500, August 1970.

Boer, G., 'Five Modern Management Accounting Myths', *Management Accounting*, pp. 22–27, January 1994.

Cooper, K., Keim, G., 'The Economic Rationale for the Nature and Extent of Corporate Financial Disclosure Regulation: A Critical Assessment', *Journal of Accounting and Public Policy*, Vol. 2, 1983.

Deegan, C., *Australian Financial Accounting*, Irwin/McGraw-Hill, 2nd edition, Sydney, 1999.

Gilman, S., *Accounting Concepts of Profits*, Ronald Press, New York, 1939.

Goldberg, L., The Development of Accounting, in C.T. Gibson, C.G. Meredith and R. Peterson (Eds), *Accounting Concepts Readings*, Cassell, Melbourne, 1949.

Gray, R., 'Accounting and Environmentalism: An Exploration of the Challenge of Gently Accounting for Accountability, Transparency and Sustainability', *Accounting Organizations and Society*, Vol. 17, No. 5, pp. 399–426, 1992.

Handel, W., *Ethnomethodology: How People Make Sense*, Prentice-Hall, 1982.

Hendriksen, E.S., Van Breda, M.F., *Accounting Theory*, Irwin, 5th edition, Boston, 1992.

Hines, R., 'Financial Accounting: In Communicating Reality, We Construct Reality', *Accounting Organizations and Society*, Vol. 13, No. 3, pp. 251–62, 1988.

Hines, R., 'The FASB's Conceptual Framework, Financial Accounting and the Maintenance of the Social World', *Accounting Organizations and Society*, Vol. 16, No. 4, pp. 313–51, 1991.

Jensen, M.C., Meckling, W.H., 'Theory of the Firm: Managerial Behavior, Agency Costs and Ownership Structure', *Journal of Financial Economics*, Vol. 3, pp. 305–60, October 1976.

Mathews, M.R., Perera, M.H.B., *Accounting Theory and Development*, 3rd edition, Thomas Nelson Australia, 1996.

Miller, M.C., 'Goodwill Discontent: The Meshing of Australian and International Accounting Policy', *Australian Accounting Review*, Issue 9, Vol. 5, No. 1, pp. 3–16, 1995.

Molotch, H.L., Boden, D., 'Talking Social Structure: Discourse, Domination and the Watergate Hearings', *American Sociological Review*, pp. 477–86, 1985.

Paton, W.A., *Accounting Theory*, Scholars Book Co, Kansas, 1922 (reprinted 1973).

Paton, W.A., Littleton, A.C., *An Introduction to Corporate Accounting Standards*, American Accounting Association, 1940.

Peltzman, S., 'Towards a More General Theory of Regulation', *Journal of Law and Economics*, pp. 211–40, August 1976.

Posner, R.A., 'Theories of Economic Regulation', *Bell Journal of Economics and Management Science*, Vol. 5, pp. 335–58, Autumn 1974.

Ray, D.D., *Accounting and Business Fluctuations*, University of Florida Press, 1960.

Sanders, T.H., Hatfield, H.R., Moore, U., *A Statement of Accounting Principles*, American Institute of Accountants, 1938 (reprinted AAA 1959).

Scott, W.R., *Financial Accounting Theory*, Prentice-Hall, New Jersey, 1997.

Smith, M., Briggs, S., 'From Beancounter to Action Hero', *Charter*, Vol. 70, No. 1, pp. 36–9, February 1999.

Solomons, D., 'The Politicisation of Accounting', *Journal of Accountancy*, Vol. 146. No. 5, pp. 65–72, November 1978.

Stigler, G., 'The Theory of Economic Regulation', *Bell Journal of Economics and Management Science*, pp. 2–21, 1971.

Walker, R.G., 'Australia's ASRB—A Case Study of Political Activity and Regulatory Capture', *Accounting and Business Research*, Vol. 17, No. 67, pp. 269–86, 1987.

Watts, R.L., Zimmerman, J.L., 'Towards a Positive Theory of the Determinants of Accounting Standards', *The Accounting Review*, Vol. 53, pp. 112–34, January 1978.

Zeff, S.A., *Forging Accounting Principles in Five Countries*, Stipes Publishing Co., 1972.

Zeff, S.A., 'The Rise of Economic Consequences', *Journal of Accountancy*, Vol. 146, No. 6, pp. 56–63, December 1978.

Questions

2.1 Do you consider that users of financial reports should have a sound working knowledge of the various accounting standards in use? Explain your answer.

2.2 Do you believe that the media portray accounting numbers, such as profits, as some sort of 'hard' and objective performance indicator? Why do you think they might do this, and if they do, what are some of the implications that might arise as a result of this approach?

2.3 Briefly outline some arguments in favour of regulating the practice of financial accounting.

2.4 Briefly outline some arguments in favour of eliminating the regulation pertaining to financial accounting.

2.5 As this chapter indicates, Stigler (1971) proposes a theory (*private interest theory*) in which it is proposed that regulatory bodies (including accounting standard-setters) are made up of individuals who are self-interested, and these individuals will introduce regulation that best serves their own self-interest. Under this perspective, the view that regulators act in the public interest is rejected. From your experience, do you think that this is an acceptable assumption? Assuming that you reject this central assumption, would this have implications for whether you would be prepared to accept any predictions generated by the private interest theory?

2.6 Because accounting standard-setters throughout the world typically consider the potential economic and social consequences of potential accounting standards when developing accounting standards, it has been argued that reports developed in accordance with the accounting standards cannot be considered neutral or unbiased. Do you agree with this perspective? Is this perspective consistent with the qualitative attributes typically promoted in accounting conceptual framework projects?

2.7 Hines (1991) promotes a view that it is in the interest of the accounting profession to publicly promote a view that the information they generate is 'objective'. Why do you think this is the case?

2.8 Solomons (1978, p. 69) quotes the American Accounting Association: 'Every policy choice represents a trade-off among differing individual preferences, and possibly among alternative consequences, regardless of whether the policy-makers see it that way or not. In this sense, accounting policy choices can never be neutral. There is someone who is granted his preference, and someone who is not.'

Required: Evaluate the above statement.

2.9 While it is difficult to criticise a process that considers potential impacts on others, at the same time it is difficult to accept that accounting standards are neutral or unbiased.

Required: Evaluate the above statement.

2.10 Hines (1991, p. 313) stresses a view that 'financial accounting practices are implicated in the construction and reproduction of the social world'.

Required: What does Hines mean in the above statement? Do you agree or disagree with her, and why?

2.11 Why might accountants be construed as being powerful individuals?

Chapter 3

The regulation of financial accounting

Learning objectives

Upon completing this chapter readers should:

- understand some of the various theoretical arguments that have been proposed in favour of reducing the extent of regulation of financial accounting;

- understand some of the various theoretical arguments for regulating the practice of financial accounting;

- understand various theoretical perspectives that describe who is likely to gain the greatest advantage from the implementation of accounting regulation;

- understand that the accounting standard-setting process is a very political process that seeks the views of a broad cross-section of account users;

- understand the relevance of potential economic and social impacts to the accounting standard-setting process.

Opening issues

(a) Throughout the world in recent years a number of industries have been deregulated, for example, the banking industry, the telecommunications industry, and the airline industry. There have been numerous similar calls for a reduction in accounting regulations (using such terminology as *accounting standard overload*)—but what could be some of the implications if financial accounting were to be deregulated?

(b) If financial accounting were to be deregulated, what incentives or mechanisms might operate to cause an organisation to produce publicly available financial statements? Would these mechanisms operate to ensure that an optimal amount of information is produced? What is the 'optimal' amount of information?

Introduction

In Chapter 2 we briefly considered a number of theories to explain the existence of accounting regulation. This chapter extends that discussion. While financial accounting is quite heavily regulated in many countries, and would be expected to remain so, it is nevertheless interesting to consider arguments for and against the continued existence of regulation. It is also interesting to consider various theories that explain what drives the imposition of regulation. By considering such theories we will be better placed to understand why some of the various accounting prescriptions become part of legislation, while others do not. Perhaps some proposed accounting regulations did not have the support of parties that have influence (or power) over the regulatory process. At issue here is whether issues of 'power' should be allowed to impact on the implementation of legislation, including accounting legislation. Is it realistic to expect that the interests of various affected parties will not impact on the final legislation? We will see that the accounting standard-setting process is a very political process. While some proposed requirements might appear technically sound and logical, we will see that this is not sufficient for them to be mandated. What often seems to be important is whether various parts of the constituency affected by the regulations are in favour of them.

In considering accounting regulations, we examine arguments for reducing or eliminating regulation, many of which propose that accounting information should be treated like any other good and that forces of *demand* and *supply* should be allowed to determine the optimal amount of information to be produced. Proponents of this 'free-market' approach (that is, proponents of the view that the provision of accounting information should be based on the laws of supply and demand rather than on regulation) have at times relied on the work of the famous 18th century economist, Adam Smith, and his much cited notion of the 'invisible hand'. However, we will see that he actually proposed the need for regulation to support the interests of those individuals who would otherwise be disadvantaged by the functioning of unregulated market systems.

We also consider a number of perspectives that explain why regulation might be necessary. We review the *public interest theory of regulation*. While the public interest theory provides an explanation of why regulation is necessary to protect the rights of the public, there are other theories (for example, *capture theory* and *private interest theory*) that we consider, that provide explanations of why regulations might be put in place that actually serve the interests of some groups at the expense of others (rather than serving the 'public interest'). This chapter also considers how perceptions about the economic and social consequences of potential accounting requirements affect the decisions of standard-setters and whether, in the light of regulators considering economic and social consequences, we can really say that financial accounting can ever be expected to have qualitative characteristics such as *neutrality* and *representational faithfulness*.

The 'free market' perspective

As indicated in Chapter 2, the proponents of a 'free-market' perspective to accounting regulation often provide a perspective that accounting information should be treated like other goods, and demand and supply forces should be allowed to operate so as to generate an optimal supply of information about an entity. In support of their claims a number of arguments are provided. One argument, based on the work of authors such as Jensen and Meckling (1976), Watts and Zimmerman (1978), Smith and Warner (1979), and Smith and Watts (1982) is that, even in the absence of regulation, there are private economics based incentives for the organisation to provide credible information about its operations and performance to certain parties outside the organisation, otherwise the costs of the organisation's operations will rise. The basis of this view is that in the absence of information about the organisation's operations, other parties, including the owners of the firm (shareholders) who are not involved in the management of the organisation, will assume that the managers might be operating the business for their own benefit.[1] That is, the managers will operate the business for their own personal

---

1. The costs that arise from the perspective of the owner when the owner (or principal) appoints a manager (the agent) would include costs associated with the agent shirking (being idle) or consuming excessive perquisites (using the organisation's funds for the manager's private purposes). These are called agency costs. Agency costs can be defined as costs that arise as a result of the delegation of decision making from one party to another party (the agency relationship). They are more fully considered in Chapter 7 when we consider Agency Theory. Another agency cost that might arise when decision making is delegated to the agent could include the costs associated with the manager using information that is not available to the owners, for the manager's personal gain. Smith and Watts (1982) provide an overview of the conflicts of interest that arise between managers and owners.

gain, rather than with the aim of maximising the value of the organisation (there is assumed to be a lack of alignment of goals between the owners and the managers).[2] It is further assumed that potential shareholders will expect the managers to be opportunistic, and in the absence of safeguards will reduce the amount they will pay for the shares. Likewise, under this economics based perspective of 'rationality' (self-interest), potential debtholders are assumed to expect managers to undertake opportunistic actions with the funds the debtholders might advance, and therefore in the absence of safeguards the debtholders will charge the organisation a higher price for their funds.[3] That is, the debtholders will 'price-protect'—such that the higher the perceived risk, the higher is the demanded return.

The expectations noted above (which are based on the rather pessimistic assumption that all parties will assume that others will work in their own interests unless constrained to do otherwise) will have the effect of increasing the operating costs of the organisation—the cost of attracting capital will increase and this will have negative implications for the value of the organisation.[4] Given this expectation, it will be in the interests of maximising the value of the organisation that managers should enter contracts with shareholders and debtholders so as to make a clear commitment that management strategies, that might be against the interests of the shareholders and debtholders, will not be undertaken. For example, management might make an agreement with debtholders that they will keep future debt levels below a certain percentage of total assets (the view being that, all things being equal, the lower the ratio of debt to assets, the lower is the risk that the organisation will default on paying the debtholders). To further safeguard the debtholders' assets, the organisation might agree to ensure that profits will cover interest expense by a specified number of times (referred to as an interest coverage clause). In relation to concerns that the manager might 'shirk' (which might be of particular concern to shareholders, given that shareholders will share in any profits generated by the actions of the managers) the organisation might require managers to be rewarded on the

---

2. What should be appreciated at this point is that these arguments are based on a central assumption that individuals will act in their own self-interest, which, in itself, is a cornerstone of many economic theories. If an individual acts with self-interest with the intention of maximising personal wealth, this is typically referred to as being 'economically rational'. 'Economic rationality' is a theoretical assumption, and as might be expected, it is an assumption that is challenged by advocates of alternative views about what drives or motivates human behaviour.

3. In considering the relationship between the managers and the debtholders, the actions that would be detrimental to the interests of the debtholders would include managers paying excessive dividends; taking on additional and possibly excessive levels of debt; and using the advanced funds for risky ventures, thereby reducing the probability of repayment. Smith and Warner (1979) provide an overview of some of the conflicts of interest that arise between managers and debtholders.

4. This is based on the assumption that the value of the organisation is based on the present value of future net cash flows. A higher cost of capital will result in decreased net cash flows.

basis of a bonus tied to profits, so the higher the profit (which is in the interests of shareholders and debtholders), the higher will be the rewards paid to managers. Most private corporations will give their managers (particularly the more senior managers) some form of profit share (Deegan, 1997) as well as being involved in negotiated agreements with debtholders (such as debt to asset constraints and interest coverage requirements).

What should be obvious from the brief discussion above is that such contractual arrangements are tied to accounting numbers. Hence the argument by some advocates of the 'free-market' perspective is that in the absence of regulation there will be private incentives to produce accounting information. That is, proponents of this view (based on Agency Theory which is more fully discussed in Chapter 7) assert that there will (naturally) be conflicts between owners and managers, and the costs of these potential conflicts will be mitigated through the process of private contracting and associated financial reporting.[5] Organisations that do not produce information will be penalised by higher costs of capital. Further, depending upon the parties involved and the types of assets in place, the organisation will be best placed to determine what information should be produced to increase the confidence of external stakeholders (thereby decreasing the organisation's cost of attracting capital). Imposing regulation that restricts the available set of accounting methods (for example, banning a particular method of amortisation that was previously used by some organisations) will decrease the efficiency with which negotiated contracts will reduce agency costs.[6] Given the theoretical economics-based assumption that managers will act in their own self-interest there will also be a contractual demand to have the accounting reports audited by an external party. Such an activity will increase the perceived reliability of the data, and this in turn is expected to reduce the perceived risk of the external stakeholders, thus further decreasing the organisation's cost of capital (Watts, 1977; Watts and Zimmerman, 1983; Francis and Wilson, 1988). That is, financial statement audits can also be expected to be undertaken, even in the absence of regulation, and evidence indicates that many organisations did have their financial statements audited prior to any legislative requirements to do so (Morris, 1984).[7]

Hence, if we accept the above arguments, we can propose that in the presence of a limited number of contracting parties then, perhaps, reducing regulation might seem reasonable given the view that various items of

---

5. This is consistent with the usual notion of 'stewardship' wherein management is expected to provide an account of how it has utilised the funds that have been provided.

6. It has also been argued that certain mandated disclosures will be costly to the organisation if they enable competitors to take advantage of certain proprietary information. Hakansson (1977) used this argument to explain costs that would be imposed as a result of mandating segment disclosures.

7. As Cooper and Keim (1983, p. 199) indicate, to be an effective strategy, 'the auditor must be perceived to be truly independent and the accounting methods employed and the statements' prescribed content must be sufficiently well-defined'.

financial information (as negotiated between the various parties) will be provided. Further, such information will be expected to be subject, where deemed necessary by the contracting parties, to an audit by an independent third party. However, in the presence of a multitude of different parties the argument seems to break down. As Scott (1997, p. 332) states:

> *Unfortunately, while direct contracting for information production may be fine in principle, it will not always work in practice. In many cases there are simply too many parties for contracts to be feasible. If the firm manager were to attempt to negotiate a contract for information production with every potential investor, the negotiation costs alone would be prohibitive. In addition, to the extent that different investors want different information, the firm's cost of information production would also be prohibitive. If, as an alternative, the manager attempted to negotiate a single contract with all investors, these investors would have to agree on what information they wanted. Again, given the disparate information needs of different investors, this process would be extremely time-consuming and costly, if indeed, it was possible at all. Hence, the contracting approach seems feasible only when there are few parties involved.*

While the above arguments are based on a private contracting perspective, there are further arguments for reducing or eliminating accounting regulation which are based on various market-related incentives, principally tied to the 'market for managers' and the 'market for corporate takeovers'. The 'market for managers' argument (see Fama, 1980) relies upon an assumption of an efficient market for managers and that managers' previous performance will impact on how much remuneration they command in future periods, either from their current employer, or elsewhere. Adopting this perspective, it is assumed that, even in the absence of contractual requirements, managers will be encouraged to adopt strategies to maximise the value of their organisation (which provides a favourable view of their own performance) and these strategies would include providing an optimal amount of financial accounting information. However, arguments such as this are based on assumptions that the managerial labour market operates efficiently, and that information about past managerial performance will not only be known by other prospective employers, but will also be fully impounded in future salaries. It also assumes that the capital market is efficient when determining the value of the organisation and that effective managerial strategies will be reflected in positive share price movements. In reality, these assumptions will clearly not always be met. Markets will not always be efficient. The arguments can also break down if the managers involved are approaching retirement, in which case future market prices for their services in the 'market for managers' may be irrelevant.

The 'market for corporate takeovers' argument works on the assumption that an under-performing organisation will be taken over by another entity that will subsequently replace the existing management team. With such a perceived threat, managers would be motivated to maximise firm value to minimise the likelihood that outsiders could seize control of the organisation at low cost. The 'market for corporate takeovers' and the 'market for managers' arguments assume that information will be produced to minimise the organisation's cost of capital and thereby increase the value of the organisation. Therefore, the arguments assume that management will know the *marginal costs* and *marginal benefits* involved in providing information, and in accord with economic theories about the production of other goods, management will provide information to the point where the marginal cost equals the marginal benefit. Clearly, working out the marginal costs and marginal benefits of information production would be difficult, and to assume that the majority of corporate managers have the expertise to determine such costs and benefits is again, perhaps, somewhat unrealistic.

There is also a perspective that even in the absence of regulation, organisations would still be motivated to disclose both good and bad news about their financial position and performance. Such a perspective is often referred to as the 'market for lemons' perspective (Akerlof, 1970), the view being that in the absence of disclosure the capital market will assume that the organisation is a 'lemon'.[8] That is, *no information* is viewed in the same light as *bad information*. Hence, even though the firm may be worried about disclosing bad news, the market may make an assessment that silence implies that the organisation has very bad news to disclose (otherwise, they would disclose it). This 'market for lemons' perspective provides an incentive for managers to release information in the absence of regulation, as failure to do so will have implications for the manager's wealth (perhaps in the form of current lower remuneration and a decreased value in the market for managers). That is, 'non-lemon owners have an incentive to communicate' (Spence, 1974, p. 93).

Drawing upon arguments such as those adopted in the 'lemons' argument above and applying them to preliminary profit announcements, Skinner (1994, p. 39) states:

> *Managers may incur reputational costs if they fail to disclose bad news in a timely manner. Money managers, stockholders, security analysts, and other investors dislike adverse earnings surprises, and may impose costs on firms whose managers are less than candid about potential earnings problems. For example, money managers may choose not to hold the stocks of firms whose managers have a reputation for withholding bad news and analysts may choose not to follow these firms' stocks . . . Articles in the financial press suggest that professional money managers, security analysts, and other investors impose costs on firms when their managers appear to delay bad news disclosures. These articles claim that firms whose managers acquire a reputation for failing to disclose bad news are less likely to be followed by analysts and money managers, thus reducing the price and/or liquidity of their firms' stocks.*

---

8. Something is a 'lemon' if it initially appears or is assumed (due to insufficient information) to be of a quality comparable to other products, but later turns out to be inferior. Acquiring the 'lemon' will be the result of information asymmetry in favour of the seller.

Reviewing previous studies, Skinner (p. 44) notes that there is evidence that managers disclose both good and bad news forecasts voluntarily. These findings are supported by his own empirical research which shows that when firms are performing well, managers make 'good news disclosures' to distinguish their firms from those doing less well, and when firms are not doing so well, managers make pre-emptive bad news disclosures consistent with 'reputational-effects' arguments (p. 58).

Arguments that the market will penalise organisations for failure to disclose information (which may or may not be bad) of course assumes that the market knows that the manager has particular information to disclose. This expectation might not always be so realistic, as the market will not always know that there is information available to disclose. That is, in the presence of information asymmetry the manager might know of some bad news, but the market might not expect any information disclosures at that time. However, if it does subsequently come to light that news was available that was not disclosed, then we could perhaps expect the market to react (and in the presence of regulation, we could expect regulators to react as failure to disclose information in a timely manner may be in contravention of particular laws in that jurisdiction). Also, at certain times, withholding information (particularly of a proprietary nature) could be in the interests of the organisation. For example, the organisation may not want to disclose information about certain market opportunities for fear of competitors utilising such information.

So, in summary to this point, there are various arguments or mechanisms in favour of reducing accounting regulation (including private contracting, markets for managers, and markets for corporate takeovers), as even in the absence of regulation, firms will have incentives to make disclosures. We now consider some alternative arguments in favour of regulating the practice of financial accounting.

The 'pro-regulation' perspective

In the above discussion we have considered a number of reasons proffered in favour of reducing or eliminating regulation. One of the most simple of arguments is that if somebody really desired information about an organisation, they would be prepared to pay for it (perhaps in the form of reducing their required rate of return) and the forces of supply and demand should operate to ensure an optimal amount of information is produced. Another perspective was that if information is not produced, there will be greater uncertainty about the performance of the entity and this will translate to increased costs for the organisation. With this in mind, organisations would, it is argued, elect to produce information to reduce costs. However, arguments in favour of a 'free-market' rely upon users paying for the goods or services that are being produced and consumed. Such arguments can break down when we consider the consumption of 'free' or 'public' goods.

Accounting information is a public good—once available, people can use it without paying and can pass it on to others. Parties that use goods or services without incurring some of the associated production costs are referred to as 'free-riders'. In the presence of free-riders, true demand is understated because people know they can get the goods or services without paying for them. Few people will have an incentive to pay for the goods or services, as they know that they themselves might be able to act as free-riders. This dilemma in turn is argued to provide a lack of incentive for producers of the particular good or service, which in turn leads to an underproduction of information. As Cooper and Keim (1983, p. 190) state:

Market failure occurs in the case of a public good because, since other individuals (without paying) can receive the good, the price system cannot function. Public goods lack the exclusion *attribute, i.e., the price system cannot function properly if it is not possible to exclude nonpurchasers (those who will not pay the asked price) from consuming the good in question.*

To alleviate this underproduction, regulation is argued to be necessary to reduce the impacts of market failure.[9] In specific relation to the production of information, Demski and Feltham (1976, p. 209) state:

Unlike pretzels and automobiles, [information] is not necessarily destroyed or even altered through private consumption by one individual....This characteristic may induce market failure. In particular, if those who do not pay for information cannot be excluded from using it and if the information is valuable to these 'free riders', then information is a public good. That is, under these circumstances, production of information by any single individuals or firm will costlessly make that information available to all . . . Hence, a more collective approach to production may be desirable.

However, as we often come to expect, there are counter-arguments to the perspective that the supply of 'free-goods' should be regulated. Some economists argue that free goods are often over-produced as a result of regulation. The argument is that segments of the public (the users of the good or service), knowing that they do not have to pay for the free good, will overstate their need for the good or service. This argument could perhaps be applied to investment analysts. They will typically be a main user of accounting information. If they lobby for additional regulation that requires further disclosure they will tend to receive a disproportionate amount of the benefits relative to the costs of producing the information. When considering the consumption of free goods it is argued by some that non-users effectively subsidise the consumers of the public good as, like other parties, the non-users pay for the production of the good without benefiting from its consumption. The result of concerted lobbying by particular parties, such as analysts, could

---

9. Scott (1997, p. 329) defines market failure as 'an inability of market forces to produce a socially "right" amount of information, that is, to produce information to the point where its marginal cost to society equals its marginal benefit'.

in turn lead to the existence of what has been termed an *accounting standards overload* which creates a cost for companies in terms of compliance. However, if we do not regulate, then in the presence of the 'free-riders' we could arguably have an underproduction of accounting information. Clearly, this is not an easy thing to balance and we can start to understand the difficult position in which legislators find themselves.

Regulators often use the 'level playing-field' argument to justify putting legislation in place. From a financial accounting perspective, everybody should (on the basis of fairness) have access to the same information. This is the basis of laws that prohibit insider trading, which rely upon an acceptance of the view that there will not be, or perhaps should not be, transfers of wealth between those parties that have access to information and those that do not.[10] Putting in place greater disclosure regulations will increase the confidence of external stakeholders that they are playing on a 'level playing-field'. If the community has confidence in the capital markets, then this is often deemed to be in 'the public interest'. However, we will always be left with the issue as to what is the socially right level of information. Arguably, such a question cannot be answered with any level of certainty.

It is interesting to see that when one reads various material relating to the benefits of free-market trading it becomes apparent that some of this material uses the work of the famous 18th century economist, Adam Smith, as a basis for supporting the free market approach. Adam Smith has become famous for his notion of the 'invisible hand'. The 'invisible hand', which was mentioned only once in his five-book treatise, appears in Book Four of the *Wealth of Nations*, referring to the distribution of capital in society: 'the annual revenue . . . is always equal to the whole product of its industry . . . as every individual attempts to employ his [her] capital . . . every individual necessarily endeavors the capital as great as he can . . . he intends only his own industry . . . his own gain . . . led by an invisible hand by it.'[11]

Subsequent free market exponents have drawn on the notion of the 'invisible hand' to promote a belief 'in market omnipotence', arguing against state involvement because it 'disturbs the spontaneous order and the spontaneous society' (Lehman, 1991, p. xi). That is, without regulatory involvement there is a view than somehow, as if by an 'invisible hand', productive resources will, as a result of individuals pursuing their self-interest, find their way to their most productive uses. Some writers actually went to the next step by arguing that leaving activities to be controlled by market mechanisms will actually protect market participants. For example, Milton Friedman (1962, p. 82) states:

---

10. There is also a view (Ronen, 1977) that extensive insider trading will erode investor confidence such that market efficiency will be impaired.

11. This quote is reproduced from Lehman (1991).

The central feature of the market organisation of economic activity is that it prevents one person from interfering with another in respect of most of its activities. The consumer is protected from coercion by the seller because of the presence of other sellers with whom he can deal. The seller is protected from coercion by the consumer because of other consumers to whom he can sell.

Such views ignore market failures and uneven distributions of power. Particular problems might occur when a monopolistic situation arises where prices for needed goods might be driven up by suppliers. Smith was particularly concerned where monopolistic powers were created as a result of government intervention. In these cases, he believed that it might have been better to 'let the market alone'. According to Collison (1998, p. 11):

Smith's advice to 'let the market alone' was partly prompted by the centuries old practice of conferring monopoly powers on certain favoured subjects: 'It is to prevent this reduction of price, and consequently of wages and profit, by restraining that free competition which would most certainly occasion it, that all corporations, and the greater part of corporations laws, have been established.'

However, Smith did not advocate no regulatory intervention. He was aware of the problems that might arise in an unregulated free-market, and while it is rarely mentioned by the advocates of the 'free-market', Smith actually wrote of the need for the government to be involved in the 'public interest' to protect the more vulnerable. As Lehman (1991, p. x) states:

Among the passages revealing Smith's concern for harmful unintended consequences [of the free-market approach] are those appearing in Book V, Chapter 1, where Smith writes that in the progress of the division of labour, the progress of the great body of people will be the man [or woman] who spends much time doing a few simple operations, with no invention, with no tender sentiment, incapable of judging, incapable of defending the country in war. In every society, the great body of people will fall this way, 'unless the government takes some pains to prevent it'.

This view is also supported by Collison (1998, p. 9) who states:

Adam Smith himself was well aware that conditions in the world he inhabited did not conform to the competitive ideal: he was not opposed to government action in pursuit of general welfare; indeed he favoured it, and was acutely conscious of the danger of undue power in the hands of the capitalist class.

So if we accept that Smith's work has been misrepresented as a treatise in favour of the 'free-market' (as a number of authors suggest), why has it been misrepresented? Collison (1998) argues that it is in the interests of many businesses that regulatory interference (such as minimum wage controls) be reduced. As such, he provides a view that many businesses used the work of acclaimed economists (such as Smith) as a form of 'propaganda' to support their position for reduced regulation.[12] This perspective is consistent with the economic interest theory of regulation, which we consider later in this chapter.

While we have provided only a fairly brief overview of the free-market versus regulation arguments, it should be stressed that this is an argument that is ongoing in respect of many activities and industries, with various vested interests putting forward many different and often conflicting arguments for or against regulation. It is an argument that is often the subject of heated debate within many economics and accounting departments throughout the world. What do you think? Should financial accounting be regulated, and if so, how much regulation should be put in place?

As an example of the 'regulate or not to regulate' debate, consider Exhibit 3.1, which details arguments for and against regulating *insider trading*. The researchers in question argue that regulating against insider trading can introduce inefficiencies into the market. They question the need for 'fairness at the expense of efficiency'.

Public interest theory

According to Posner (1974, p. 335) public interest theory 'holds that regulation is supplied in response to the demand of the public for the correction of inefficient or inequitable market practices'. That is, regulation is initially put in place to benefit society as a whole, rather than particular vested interests, and the regulatory body is considered to represent the interests of the society in which it operates, rather that the private interests of the regulators.[13] The enactment of legislation is considered a balancing act between the social benefits and the social costs of the regulation. Applying this argument to financial accounting, and accepting the existence of a capitalist economy, the society needs confidence in the capital markets to help ensure that resources are directed to productive assets. Regulation is deemed to be an instrument to create such confidence.

Many people are critical of this fairly simplistic perspective of why regulation is introduced (for example, Stigler, 1971; Posner, 1974; Peltzman, 1976). Posner (1974) questions the 'assumptions that economic markets are extremely fragile and apt to operate very inefficiently (or inequitably) if left alone; the other that government regulation is virtually costless' (p. 336). Posner also criticises arguments that legislation is typically initially put in place

---

12. Other authors (such as Carey, 1997) have argued that many larger business were able to influence academics (through the provision of funding) to support particular views. The results of the academic research studies were then provided to government to substantiate or support particular positions.

13. This perspective would not be accepted by advocates of the 'rational economic person' assumption as they would argue that all activities, including the activities of regulators and politicians, are primarily motivated by a desire to maximise personal wealth rather than any notion of *public interest*.

EXHIBIT 3.1 Perspectives about the costs and benefits of regulation

Study finds a case for insider trading

Nicholas Reece

Insider trading may be a 'necessary evil' and play a vital function in market efficiency without harming market integrity, according to a new academic study.

The study from the University of Technology Sydney says Australia's insider-trading regulations have been fuelled by excessive reaction by politicians and regulators to the notion of fairness at the expense of efficiency.

The academics say insider trading can enhance market efficiency by quickly providing accurate signals to the market about the true value of a company's shares.

Insider trading can be seen as a way to compensate and motivate management for entrepreneurial skills, although the UTS study acknowledges that this ignores the possible 'moral hazard' that not all insiders will deserve the reward.

The academics argue that empirical studies suggest that insider-trading regulations are ineffective and difficult to enforce. Private contracts, it is argued, provide a private and cheaper way of limiting insider trading.

The controversial claims are part of a broader argument that Australia's insider-trading regulations are too broad compared with regulations in other prominent securities markets and that there is a 'compelling need' for their revision.

The arguments are made in a paper by finance and legal academics Ms Lori Semaan, Associate Professor Mark Freeman and Associate Professor Michael Adams in the latest edition of the *Companies and Securities Law Journal*.

The article compares Australia's insider-trading regulations with six other competing regimes including the US (Nasdaq), Japan, Hong Kong, Indonesia, India and the UK.

In all regimes, it is found that regulation of insider trading has been excessively fuelled by equity objectives at the expense of an efficiency objective.

However, the academics say regulations in Australia are less soundly based in policy compared with overseas regimes and this may lead to even greater inefficiencies in Australian securities markets.

Australia is the only regime where the public policy behind insider-trading regulations gives primacy to the principle of equal access to information.

Under this policy objective, market fairness requires that all investors have equal access to information and insider trading is seen as unfair because it means people with better access to information can gain benefits.

Regulatory regimes in other countries are based on alternative policy arguments that centre on the fiduciary duty of 'insiders' to the company whose stock is traded or at the misappropriation of proprietary information.

Australia, it is argued, has failed to build on regulatory experience in the US and other securities regimes, whose regulations are not based on the policy of equal access to information and accordingly are narrower.

In particular, Australia's wide insider-trading regulations may have a dangerous effect on the efficiency role played by broker-analysts and insiders.

In other regimes, broker-analysts and insiders do not face the same disincentives as in Australia, meaning that new information is more quickly reflected in a company's share price.

Australia enacted insider trading regulations after the mining company scandals of the early 1970s. The lack of convictions combined with survey results showing that 5 per cent of all trades are possibly insider trades caused the regulations to be reviewed by the Griffiths committee in 1989.

On the back of the Griffiths report, new laws were introduced that removed a single section and replaced it with a whole division in the Corporations Law.

The new, widened insider-trading regulations apply to anyone who possesses information that is ultimately from company sources and not publicly available.

It is illegal to buy or sell shares on the basis of this information.

The Australian Financial Review, **Wednesday 21 July 1999, p. 4.**

for 'the public good' but only fails to achieve its aims due to government ineptitude, mismanagement, or lack of funds. As he states (p. 337):

> [There is] a good deal of evidence that the socially undesirable results of regulation are frequently desired by groups influential in the enactment of the legislation setting up the regulatory scheme . . . Sometimes the regulatory statute itself reveals an unmistakable purpose of altering the operation of markets in directions inexplicable on public interest grounds . . . The evidence that has been offered to show mismanagement by the regulatory body is surprisingly weak. Much of it is consistent with the rival theory that the typical regulatory agency operates with reasonable efficiency to attain deliberately inefficient or inequitable goals set by the legislature that created it.

Proponents of the economics based assumption of 'self-interest' would argue against accepting that any legislation was put in place by particular parties because they genuinely believed that it was in the public interest. Rather, they consider that legislators will only put in place legislation because it might increase their own wealth (perhaps through increasing their likelihood of being re-elected), and people will only lobby for particular legislation if it is in their own self-interest. Obviously, as with most theoretical assumptions, this self-interest assumption is one that (hopefully!) will not always hold. We consider the private interest group theory of regulation later in this chapter. In the following discussion we consider the regulatory capture theory of regulation. Unlike the private interest group theory of regulation, capture theory admits the possibility that regulation might initially be put in place for the public interest. However, it argues that the regulation will ultimately become controlled by those parties that it was supposed to control.

Capture theory

Under this perspective the regulated party seeks to take charge of (capture) the regulator with the intention that the rules subsequently released (post-capture) will be advantageous to those parties subject to the requirements. Mitnick (1980, p. 95 as reproduced in Walker, 1987, p. 281) provides a useful description:

> Capture is said to occur if the regulated interest controls the regulation and the regulated agency; or if the regulated parties succeed in coordinating the regulatory body's activities with their activities so that their private interest is satisfied; or if the regulated party somehow manages to neutralise or ensure non-performance (or mediocre performance) by the regulating body; or if in a subtle process of interaction with the regulators the regulated party succeeds (perhaps not even deliberately) in co-opting the regulators into seeing things from their own perspective and thus giving them the regulation they want; or if, quite independently of the formal or conscious desires of either the regulators or the regulated parties, the basic structure of the reward system leads neither venal nor incompetent regulators inevitably to a community of interests with the regulated party.

While the introduction of regulation can, in many cases, be explained in terms of protecting the 'public interest', it is argued that it is difficult for a regulator to remain independent of those being regulated, as continuity over a period of time often depends on satisfying the expectations of the regulated.

At various times and in various jurisdictions it has been argued that the large accounting firms have captured the accounting standard-setting process. This was of such concern in the United States that in 1977 the United States Congress investigated whether the Big Eight accounting firms had 'captured' the standard-setting process (Metcalf Inquiry). In Australia, Walker (1987) provides an interesting analysis of the early existence of the Accounting Standards Review Board (subsequently replaced by the Australian Accounting Standards Board). His analysis is consistent with a perspective that the ASRB, a government body, was 'captured' by the accounting profession (using the definition of 'capture' provided above by Mitnick, 1980).[14]

Proponents of capture theory typically argue that regulation is usually introduced, or regulatory bodies are established, to protect the public interest. This would seem to be the case in Australia with regard to the establishment of the ASRB. Prior to the establishment of the ASRB, accounting standards were issued by the accounting profession and sanctions for non-compliance (which were very rarely imposed) could only be made against members of the profession. Walker (1987, p. 270) notes that throughout the 1970s (which was prior to the establishment of the ASRB in 1984) monitoring activities by government agencies revealed a high incidence of non-compliance with profession-sponsored accounting rules.[15] This non-compliance was argued to reduce the confidence of the public in the capital market, which was not, in itself, deemed to be in the public interest. Government sponsored standards, with associated legal sanctions, should, it was thought, increase the level of compliance, and hence the confidence of the public in company reporting practices. Interestingly, in the 1970s the profession acknowledged the high level of non-compliance, but argued that the best alternative was to give automatic statutory backing to professionally developed standards (thereby increasing the 'force' of the standards, but leaving the standard-setting process in the hands of the profession).

While discussions proceeded relating to the establishment of the ASRB, suggestions were received by government from various sources that the

---

14. Walker was a member of the ASRB from 1984 to 1985. In commenting on his motivation for documenting the case study of the ASRB, Walker states (p. 285) that: 'The main concern was to highlight the way that a set of standard setting arrangements designed to permit widespread consultation and participation were subverted by some likeable, well-meaning individuals who were trying only to promote the interests of their fellow accountants.'

15. According to Walker, the New South Wales Corporate Affairs Commission reviewed the financial statements of 8699 companies over the period 1978–82 with the finding that 3528 (41%) had failed to comply with one or more professionally sanctioned accounting standards.

possibility of statutory accounting standards being developed other than by the accounting profession should be considered. It was also suggested that the ASRB be given the power to determine the priorities of various standard-setting issues, as well being able to appoint a 'research director'. The accounting profession was quite vocal in its opposition to such moves, as it was against the possibility of government itself (through the ASRB) being involved in the actual development of accounting standards. According to Walker (1987, p. 271):

> The accounting profession strongly opposed the 'costly and possibly bureaucratic step' of involving government in the preparation of accounting rules. It publicised counter-proposals that existing rules contained in Schedule 7 of the Companies Act and Codes should be scrapped and that legislative backing be extended to the profession's own standards. The files of the Commonwealth Attorney-General's Department relating to the establishment of the ASRB (copies of which were obtained in terms of Commonwealth Freedom of Information legislation) record that National Companies and Securities Commission Chairman Leigh Masel referred to a 'concerted lobby by the accounting profession' on these matters.

According to Walker (1987), Masel telexed members of the Commonwealth Government's Ministerial Council advising that the National Companies and Securities Commission (NCSC) had received submissions opposing the profession's proposals. Part of the message stated:

> A particular concern expressed in discussions with some respondents was that, if the accounting profession's proposals are accepted, the status and income of the profession would, effectively, be accorded statutory protection without any corresponding requirement for public reporting and accountability by that profession. For reasons readily apparent, there are many in the profession who would welcome the safe harbour which legislative recognition would provide.

After reviewing the available evidence, Walker argues that 'the ASRB's early history can be considered a case study in regulatory capture'. He provides the following evidence (p. 282):

(i)   Before the board was established, the accountancy bodies lobbied to ensure that the ASRB was not to have an independent research capability, was not to have an academic as chairman and was to be provided with an administrative officer rather than a research director; all of these objectives were achieved.

(ii) In 1984 the Board established its priorities on the basis of public submissions; by November 1985 its agenda represented the standards that the Australian Accounting Research Foundation (a professionally sponsored body) intimated it was prepared to submit; in December 1985 new ASRB procedures ensured that 'priorities would only be set after consultation with AARF' (the profession's own research body).

(iii)   *In 1984 the Board published a set of procedures (Release 200) which treated AARF and other interest groups on a similar footing. Accordingly the Board refused to place a standard submitted earlier by the Australian Shareholders' Association on its agenda, on the ground that the Association had not provided all the supporting documentation and an assignment of copyright as required by Release 200. Yet in November 1985 an ASRB advertisement announced that the Board would be reviewing a series of standards yet to be submitted by AARF; the Board, while abandoning the requirement of Release 200 for AARF, continued to impose them on the Australian Shareholders' Association. In December 1985 the ASRB reported that it had adopted 'fast-track' procedures for handling standards—but after six months had only applied these to submissions from AARF while it imposed more stringent requirements to submissions from other sources.*

(iv)   *Prior to its establishment, it was suggested that the ASRB would be independent of the accounting profession, and representative of a wide range of community interests. In 1984 the Board membership included nominees of the Australian Council of Trade Unions, and the Australian Shareholders Association and (it is understood) the Australian Merchant Bankers Association. The 1986 membership consisted of two former national presidents of the Australian Society of Accountants (including one who was a current member of AARF's Accounting Standards Board); a former national president of the Institute of Chartered Accountants in Australia; a former state president of the Australian Society of Accountants; a state councillor of the Australian Society of Accountants (and former chairman of AARF), an academic active in committee work for the Australian Society of Accountants—and only one other (the executive director of the Australian Associated Stock Exchanges).*

In providing a concluding comment on the ASRB's 'capture', Walker (1987, p. 282) states:

During 1984–5 the profession had ensured the non-performance of the ASRB and by the beginning of 1986 the profession had managed to influence the procedures, the priorities and the output of the Board. It was controlling both the regulations and the regulatory agency; it had managed to achieve coordination of the ASRB's activities; and it appears to have influenced new appointments so that virtually all members of the Board might reasonably be expected to have some community of interests with the professional associations. The ASRB had been 'captured' by the profession within only 24 months.

As we appreciate from reading previous chapters in this book, while a particular theory, such as Capture Theory, may be embraced by some researchers, there will be others who oppose such theories. Posner (1974), an advocate of the economic (private-interests) theory of regulation (which we will look at next), argues against a regular sequence wherein the original purposes of a regulatory program are subsequently thwarted though the efforts of the regulated group.

> *No reason is suggested as to why the regulated industry should be the only interest group to influence an agency. Customers of the regulated firm have an obvious interest in the outcome of the regulatory process—why may they not be able to 'capture' the agency as effectively as the regulated firms, or more so? No reason is suggested as to why industries are able to capture only existing agencies—never to procure the creation of an agency that will promote their interests—or why an industry strong enough to capture an agency set up to tame it could not prevent the creation of the agency in the first place (p. 340).*

Economic interest group theory of regulation

The economic interest group theory of regulation (or as it is sometimes called, the private interest theory of regulation) assumes that groups will form to protect particular economic interests. Different groups are viewed as often being in conflict with each other and the different groups will lobby government to put in place legislation that economically benefits them (at the expense of others). As an example, consumers might lobby government for price protection, or producers lobby for tariff protection. This theoretical perspective adopts no notion of *public interest*—rather, private interests are considered to dominate the legislative process.[16]

In relation to financial accounting, particular industry groups may lobby the regulator (the accounting standard-setter) to accept or reject a particular accounting standard. For example, in Australia an Accounting Standard relating to the activities of general insurers was released in 1990 (AASB 1023: Financial Reporting of General Insurance Activities). One requirement of this standard that was particularly unpopular with some insurance firms was that their investments be valued at net market value, and any changes therein be taken directly to the profit and loss account. To a number of firms, this introduced unwanted volatility in earnings, which they considered would negatively impact on their operations. They lobbied the Australian Accounting Standards Board to amend the requirement (Deegan, 1999, p. 617). As another example, many corporations have lobbied the AASB to remove the requirement that purchased goodwill must be amortised to the profit and loss account over a maximum period of twenty years (required in Australia by AASB 1013), the argument being that it was impacting on their international competitiveness (Deegan, 1999, p. 229). The accounting standards relating to

---

16. As Posner (1974) states, 'the economic theory of regulation is committed to the strong assumptions of economic theory generally, notably that people seek to advance their self-interest and do so rationally.'

goodwill and general insurers have not been amended to take account of these concerns. If we accept the economic interest group theory of regulation, the lack of success must be due to the fact that a more powerful interest group favoured the alternative situation.[17]

Watts and Zimmerman (1978) reviewed the lobbying behaviour of United States corporations in relation to a proposal for the introduction of general price level accounting—a method of accounting that, in periods of inflation, would lead to a reduction in reported profits. They demonstrated that large politically sensitive firms favoured the proposed method of accounting, which led to reduced profits. This was counter to normal expectations that companies generally would prefer to show higher rather than lower earnings. It was explained on the (self-interest) basis that it was the larger firms that would be seen more favourably if they reported lower profits. Hence, by reporting lower profits, there was less likely to be negative wealth implications for the organisations (perhaps in the forms of government intervention, consumer boycotts, claims for higher wages).

Accounting firms also make submissions as part of the accounting standard-setting process. If we are to embrace the interest group theory of regulation, we would argue that these submissions can be explained by efforts to protect the interests of professional accountants. Perhaps auditors favour rules that reduce the risk involved in an audit, as more standardisation and less judgement reduces the risk of an audit, and therefore the potential for costly law suits. Evidence in Deegan, Morris and Stokes (1990) also supports the view that audit firms are relatively more likely to lobby in favour of particular accounting methods if those methods are already in use by a number of their clients. Analysts also frequently lobby regulators for increased disclosure, perhaps because they can use the information in their job, but pay only a very small amount for it (other non-users will effectively subsidise the costs of the information).

Under the economic interest group theory of regulation, the regulator itself is an interest group—a group that is motivated to embrace strategies to ensure re-election, or to ensure the maintenance of its position of power or privilege within the community. While not strictly embracing the economic interest theory of regulation, Walker and Robinson (1994) document an interesting case in which the Australian accounting profession effectively tried to impede the development of a particular accounting standard until another body threatened its position of dominance in relation to setting accounting

---

17. In recent years, environmental groups have also lobbied government to introduce a requirement for companies to report various items of social and environmental information. Such submissions could perhaps prove a problem for advocates of the view that lobbying behaviour will be dictated by private concerns about wealth maximisation (the rational economic person assumption). Perhaps (and I am clutching at straws here!) to maintain support for their 'self-interest' view of the world, proponents of the economic interest theory of regulation might argue that the submissions are made by officers of the environmental lobby group in an endeavour to increase their probability of reappointment.

standards. The Australian Accounting Research Foundation (sponsored by the accounting profession) had supported the disclosure of *funds statements* in preference to the alternative *statement of cash flows*. The AARF allegedly put in place strategies to slow the Accounting Standards Review Board (the government body that subsequently became the Australian Accounting Standards Board) developing standards pertaining to statements of cash flows. However, in 1990 the Australian Stock Exchange indicated that by 1992 it would be requiring listed companies, as part of their listing requirements, to provide a statement of cash flows in conformity with a disclosure format to be determined by the Stock Exchange. The Stock Exchange further provided that it would only introduce its own requirements if either the Accounting Standards Review Board, or the accounting profession, did not release an accounting standard pertaining to statements of cash flows. The accounting profession thereafter worked towards developing a standard, which was ultimately released in December 1991. According to Walker and Robinson, it was the threat of intervention by the Australian Stock Exchange into the domain of the accountants that motivated the accounting profession to effectively abandon their public position in support of the funds statements, and to release a standard relating to Statements of Cash Flow (AASB 1026).

We should remember that regulatory bodies can be very powerful. The regulatory body, typically government controlled, has a resource (potential legislation) that can increase or decrease the wealth of various sectors of the constituency. As Stigler (1971, p. 3) states:

> The state—the machinery and power of the state—is a potential resource or threat to every industry in society . . . Regulation may be actively sought by an industry, or it may be thrust upon it. A central thesis of this paper is that, as a rule, regulation is acquired by the industry and is designed and operated primarily for its benefit . . . We propose the general hypothesis: every industry or occupation that has enough political power to utilise the state will seek to control entry.

Under this 'economic interest' perspective of regulation, rather than regulation initially being put in place for the *public interest* (as is initially assumed within capture theory and also in public interest theory), it is proposed that regulation is put in place to serve the *private interests* of particular parties, including politicians who seek re-election. According to Posner (1974, p. 343), economic interest theories of regulation insist that economic regulation serves the private interests of politically effective groups. Further, Stigler (1971, p. 12) states:

> The industry which seeks regulation must be prepared to pay with the two things a party needs: votes and resources. The resources may be provided by campaign contributions, contributed services (the businessman heads a fund-raising committee), and more indirect methods such as the employment of party workers. The votes in support of the measure are rallied, and the votes in opposition are dispersed, by expensive programs to educate (or uneducate)

members of the industry and other concerned industries . . . The smallest industries are therefore effectively precluded from the political process unless they have some special advantage such as geographical concentration in a sparsely settled political subdivision.[18]

Under the economic interest theory of regulation, the regulation itself is considered to be a *commodity* subject to the economic principles of supply and demand. According to Posner (1974, p. 344):

Since the coercive power of government can be used to give valuable benefits to particular individuals or groups, economic regulation—the expression of that power in the economic sphere—can be viewed as a product whose allocation is governed by laws of supply and demand . . . There are a fair number of case studies—of trucking, airlines, railroads, and many other industries—that support the view that economic regulation is better explained as a product supplied to interest groups than as an expression of the social interest in efficiency or justice.

The above position is consistent with that adopted by Peltzman (1976). He states (p. 212):

The essential commodity being transacted in the political market is a transfer of wealth, with constituents on the demand side and their political representatives on the supply side. Viewed in this way, the market here, as elsewhere, will distribute more of the good to those whose effective demand is the highest . . . I begin with the assumption that what is basically at stake in the regulatory process is a transfer of wealth.

The idea being promoted by the advocates of economic interest group theories of regulation is that if a particular group (perhaps a minority) does not have sufficient power (which might be proxied by number of controlled votes, or by the potential funds available to support an election campaign) then that group will not be able to effectively lobby for regulation that might protect its various interests. This is a view which, in a sense, has been accepted by a number of critical theorists who often argue that the legislation supporting our social system (including corporations law and accounting standards) acts to protect and maintain the position of those with power (capital) and suppresses the ability of others (those without financial wealth) to have an ability to have a great deal of influence within society. For example, in a review of the United States Securities Acts of 1933 and 1934, Merino and Neimark (1982, p. 49) conclude that:

---

18. As an example, Stigler (1971, p. 8) refers to the railroad industry. 'The railroad industry took early cognizance of this emerging competitor, and one of the methods by which trucking was combatted was state regulation. By the early 1930s all states regulated the dimensions and weight of trucks.'

The security acts were designed to maintain the ideological, social and economic status quo while restoring confidence in the existing system and its institutions.

They further state (p. 51) that the establishment of the Securities Acts:

. . . may have further contributed to the virtual absence of any serious attempts to ensure corporate accountability by broadening the set of transactions for which corporations are to be held accountable.

We consider the works of some critical theorists in greater depth in Chapter 12.

Accounting regulation as an output of a political process

If we accept that the accounting standard-setting process is a political process, then the view that financial accounting should be *objective*, *neutral* and *apolitical* (as espoused internationally within various conceptual framework projects) is something that can be easily challenged. Because financial accounting affects the distribution of wealth within society it consequently will be political.[19] While Conceptual Frameworks typically state that financial reports should be objective, neutral, and representationally faithful, they also typically state that the social and economic consequences of accounting standards must be considered by the standard-setters prior to their release.[20]

Standard-setting bodies typically encourage various affected parties to make submissions on draft versions of proposed accounting standards. This is deemed to be part of the normal 'due process'.[21] If the views of various parts of the constituency are not considered, the implication might be that the very existence of the regulatory body might be challenged. As Gerboth (1973, p. 497) states:

When a decision making process depends for its success on the public confidence, the critical issues are not technical; they are political . . . In the face of conflict between competing interests, rationality as well as prudence lies not in seeking final answers, but rather in compromise—essentially a political process.

---

19. For example, whether dividends are paid to shareholders will be dependent upon whether there are reported profits. Further, whether a company incurs the costs associated with defaulting on an accounting based debt agreement may be dependent upon the accounting methods it is permitted to apply.
20. For example, within Australia, Statement of Accounting Concepts No. 3, paragraph 45, states that 'in the process of setting standards, standard setters seek to consider all costs and benefits in relation to financial reporting generally, and not just as they pertain to individual reporting entities'.
21. Due process can be defined as a process wherein the regulator involves those parties likely to be affected by the proposed regulation in the discussions leading to the regulation—it provides an opportunity to 'be heard'.

If we accept that the standard-setters give due consideration to the views expressed in the various submissions they receive, then we must accept that accounting standards, and therefore financial accounting reports, are the result of various social and economic considerations.[22] Hence they are very much tied to the values, norms and expectations of the society in which the standards are developed. Therefore, it is arguably very questionable whether financial accounting should claim to be *neutral* or *objective* (Hines, 1988; 1991). While it is frequently argued within conceptual frameworks that proposed disclosures should be useful for decision making, this in itself is not enough. The proposed requirements must be acceptable to various parts of the constituency, and the benefits to be derived from the proposals must, it is argued, exceed the costs that might arise. Obviously determining these costs and benefits is very problematic and this is an area where academic advice and academic research is often used. According to Beaver (1973, p. 56):

> . . . *without a knowledge of consequences . . . it is inconceivable that a policy-making body . . . will be able to select optimal accounting standards.*

May and Sundem (1976) take the argument further. They argue that:

> *If the social welfare impact of accounting policy decisions were ignored, the basis for the existence of a regulatory body would disappear (p. 750).*

Any consideration of possible economic consequences necessarily involves a trade-off between the various consequences. For example, if neutrality/representational faithfulness is sacrificed to reduce potential negative impacts on some parties (for example, preparers who might have otherwise been required to disclose proprietary information, or to amend their accounting policies with the implication that they will default on existing debt contracts) this may have negative consequences for users seeking to make decisions on the basis of information provided.

While it is accepted that accounting standards are developed having regard to social and economic consequences, it is also a requirement in many jurisdictions that corporate financial statements be 'true and fair'. Australian research (Deegan, Kent and Lin, 1994) indicates that auditors generally consider that compliance with accounting standards is necessary and often sufficient for them to decide that the auditee's financial statements are true and fair. But can we really say they are *true* when the standards are determined depending upon various economic and social consequences? Perhaps it is easier to say they are *fair*. 'Truth' itself is obviously a difficult concept to define and this might explain why in some jurisdictions it was decided that financial reports should satisfy the requirement that they comply with relevant accounting regulations and generally accepted accounting

---

22. At this point we will not pursue the perspective adopted by the economic interest group theory of regulation. If we had persisted with this perspective, we would argue that the standard-setters would support those submissions which best served the standard-setters' self-interest.

practice, rather than being assessed in terms of whether they satisfy the qualitative test of being *true and fair*.

As another issue to consider, would it be reasonable to assume that users of financial reports generally know that accounting reports are the outcome of various political pressures, or would they expect that the reports are objective and accurate reflections of an organisation's performance and financial position? There could in fact be an accounting report *expectations gap* in this regard, although there is limited evidence of this.[23] According to Solomons (1978, p. 71), 'It is perfectly proper for measurements to be selected with particular political ends if it is made clear to users of the measurement what is being done.' However, is it realistic or practical to assume that users of financial statements would be able or prepared to accept that financial accounting necessarily needs to accommodate political considerations? Further, could or would users rely upon financial statements if they had such knowledge? Would there be a reduction of confidence in capital markets?

The argument that economic consequences need to be taken into account before new rules are introduced (or existing rules are changed) also assumes that in the first instance (before any amendments are to be made) there was some sort of equity that did not need addressing or rebalancing. As Collett (1995, p. 27) states:

> The claim that all affected parties such as the preparers of reports are entitled to have their interest taken into account in deciding on a standard, and not only dependent users, assumes that the position immediately prior to implementing the standard was equitable. If, however, users were being misled prior to the standard—for example, because certain liabilities were being kept off the balance sheet—then the argument that the interests of preparers of reports were being neglected in the standard-setting process would lose its force.

As a further related issue for readers to consider, is it appropriate for regulators to consider the views of financial statement preparers when developing accounting standards, given that accounting standards are put in place to limit what preparers are allowed to do, that is, to regulate their behaviour in the *public interest*? As we can hopefully see, regulating accounting practice requires many difficult assessments.

Chapter summary

In this chapter we considered various arguments that either supported or opposed the regulation of financial accounting. We saw that advocates of the 'free-market' (anti-regulation) approach argue that there are private economic

---

23. Liggio (1974) and Deegan and Rankin (1999) provide definitions of the expectations gap. An expectations gap is considered to exist when there is a difference between the expectations users have with regard to particular attributes of information, and the expectations preparers believe users have in regard to that information.

incentives for organisations to produce accounting information voluntarily, and imposing accounting regulation leads to costly inefficiencies. To support their argument for a reduction in financial accounting regulation, the 'free-market' advocates rely upon such mechanisms as private contracting (to reduce agency costs), the market for managers, and the market for takeovers.

Advocates of the 'pro-regulation' perspective argue that accounting information should not be treated like other goods, as being a 'public good' it is unrealistic to rely upon the forces of supply and demand. Because users of financial information can obtain the information at zero cost (they can be 'free-riders') producers will tend to produce a lower amount of information than might be socially optimal (which in itself is obviously difficult to determine). Further, there is a view that the stakeholders of an organisation have a right to various information about an entity, and regulation is typically needed to ensure that this obligation is adhered to by all reporting entities. Regulation itself is often introduced on the basis that it is in the 'public interest' to do so—the view being that regulators balance the costs of the regulation against the economic and social benefits that the legislation will bring. Clearly, assessments of costs and benefits are difficult to undertake and will almost always be subject to critical comment.

There are alternative views as to why regulation is put in place in the first place. There is one perspective (referred to above) that legislation is put in place for the *public interest* by regulators who are working for the interests of the constituency (public interest theory). Public interest theory does not assume that individuals are primarily driven by their own self-interest. However, an assumption of self-interest is made by other researchers who argue in favour of an economic interest theory of regulation. They argue that *all* action by *all* individuals can be traced back to self-interest in which all people will be seeking to increase their own economic wealth.[24] Under this perspective, regulators will be seeking votes and election funding/support, and will tend to provide the legislation to groups who can pay for it.

Capture theory provides another perspective of the development of regulation. It argues that while regulation might initially be put in place for well-intentioned reasons (for example, in the 'public interest'), the regulated party will, over time, tend to gain control of (or capture) the regulator so that the regulation will ultimately favour those parties that the regulation was initially intended to control.

In this chapter we have also considered how perceptions about potential economic and social consequences impact on the development of accounting standards. In the light of this we have questioned whether financial accounting reports can really be considered as neutral, objective, and representationally faithful.

---

24. There are, of course, many researchers who opposed this (rather cynical) view of human behaviour (authors such as Gray, Owen and Adams (1996) refer to this perspective as being 'morally bankrupt'). We consider some of these alternative perspectives in Chapters 8 and 9.

References

Akerlof, G.A., 'The Market for "Lemons": Quality Uncertainty and the Market Mechanism', *Quarterly Journal of Economics*, Vol. 84, pp. 488–500, August 1970.

Beaver, W.H., 'What Should be the FASB's Objectives?', *The Journal of Accountancy*, Vol. 136, pp. 49–56, 1973.

Carey, A., *Taking the Risk out of Democracy: Corporate Propaganda versus Freedom and Liberty*, University of Illinois Press, 1997.

Collett, P., 'Standard Setting and Economic Consequences: An Ethical Issue', *ABACUS*, Vol. 31, No 1. pp. 18–30, 1995.

Collison, D., 'Propaganda, Accounting and Finance: An Exploration', Dundee Discussion Papers, Department of Accountancy and Business Finance, University of Dundee, 1998.

Cooper, K., Keim, G., 'The Economic Rationale for the Nature and Extent of Corporate Financial Disclosure Regulation: A Critical Assessment', *Journal of Accounting and Public Policy*, Vol. 2, 1983.

Deegan, C., 'The Design of Efficient Management Remuneration Contracts: A Consideration of Specific Human Capital Investments', *Accounting and Finance*, Vol. 37, No 1, pp. 1–40, May 1997.

Deegan, C., *Australian Financial Accounting*, McGraw-Hill/Irwin, 2nd edition, Sydney, 1999.

Deegan, C., Kent, P., Lin, C., 'The True and Fair View: A Study of Australian Auditors' Application of the Concept', *Australian Accounting Review*, Issue 7, Vol. 4, No. 1, pp. 2–12, 1994.

Deegan, C., Morris, R., Stokes, D., 'Audit Firm Lobbying on Proposed Accounting Disclosure Requirements', *Australian Journal of Management*, Vol. 15, No. 2, pp. 261–80, December 1990.

Deegan, C., Rankin, M., 'The Environmental Reporting Expectations Gap: Australian Evidence', *British Accounting Review*, Vol. 31, No. 3, September 1999.

Demski, J., Feltham, G., *Cost Determination: A Conceptual Approach*, The Iowa State University Press, 1976.

Fama, E.F., 'Agency Problems and the Theory of the Firm', *Journal of Political Economy*, pp. 288–307, April 1980.

Francis, J.R., Wilson, E.R., 'Auditor Changes: A Joint Test of Theories Relating to Agency Costs and Auditor Differentiation', *The Accounting Review*, Vol. 63, No. 4, pp. 663–82, October 1988.

Friedman, M., *Capitalism and Freedom*, University of Chicago Press, Chicago, 1962.

Gerboth, D.L., 'Research, Intuition, and Politics in Accounting Inquiry', *The Accounting Review*, July 1973.

Gray, R., Owen, D., Adams, C., *Accounting and Accountability: Changes and Challenges in Corporate and Social Reporting*, Prentice-Hall, London, 1996.

Hakansson, N.H., 'Interim Disclosure and Public Forecasts: An Economic Analysis and Framework for Choice', *The Accounting Review*, pp. 396–416, April 1977.

Hines, R., 'Financial Accounting: In Communicating Reality, We Construct Reality', *Accounting Organizations and Society*, Vol. 13, No. 3, pp. 251–62, 1988.

Hines, R., 'The FASB's Conceptual Framework, Financial Accounting and the Maintenance of the Social World', *Accounting Organizations and Society*, Vol. 16, No. 4, pp. 313–51, 1991.

Jensen, M.C., Meckling, W.H., 'Theory of the Firm: Managerial Behavior, Agency Costs and Ownership Structure', *Journal of Financial Economics*, Vol. 3, pp. 305–60, October 1976.

Lehman, C., 'Editorial: The Invisible Adam Smith', *Advances in Public Interest Accounting*, Vol. 4, pp. ix–xiv, 1991.

Liggio, C.D., 'The Expectations Gap: The Accountant's Waterloo', *Journal of Contemporary Business*, Vol. 3, No 3, pp. 27–44, 1974.

May, R.G., Sundem, G.L., 'Research for Accounting Policy: An Overview', *The Accounting Review*, Vol. 51, No. 4, pp. 747–63, October, 1976.

Merino, B., Neimark, M., 'Disclosure Regulation and Public Policy: A Socio-Historical Appraisal', *Journal of Accounting and Public Policy*, Vol. 1, pp. 33–57, 1982.

Mitnick, B.M., *The Political Economy of Regulation*, Columbia University Press, 1980.

Morris, R., 'Corporate Disclosure in a Substantially Unregulated Environment', *ABACUS*, pp. 52–86, June 1984.

Peltzman, S., 'Towards a More General Theory of Regulation', *Journal of Law and Economics*, August 1976.

Posner, R.A., 'Theories of Economic Regulation', *Bell Journal of Economics and Management Science*, pp. 335–58, Autumn, 1974.

Ronen, J., 'The Effect of Insider Trading Rules on Information Generation and Disclosure by Corporations', *The Accounting Review*, Vol. 52, pp. 438–49, 1977.

Scott, W.R., *Financial Accounting Theory*, Prentice-Hall, New Jersey, 1997.

Skinner, D.J., 'Why Firms Voluntarily Disclose Bad News', *Journal of Accounting Research*, Vol. 32, No 1, pp. 38–60, 1994.

Smith, A., *The Wealth of Nations*, Modern Library, New York, 1937 (originally published in 1776).

Smith, C.W., Warner, J.B., 'On Financial Contracting: An Analysis of Bond Covenants', *Journal of Financial Economics*, pp. 117–61, June 1979.

Smith, C.W., Watts, R., 'Incentive and Tax Effects of Executive Compensation Plans', *Australian Journal of Management*, pp. 139–57, December 1982.

Solomons, D., 'The Politicisation of Accounting', *Journal of Accountancy*, Vol. 146, No. 5, pp. 65–72, November 1978.

Spence, A., *Market Signalling: Information Transfer in Hiring and Related Screening Processes*, Harvard University Press, 1974.

Stigler, G.J., 'The Theory of Economic Regulation', *Bell Journal of Economics and Management Science*, pp. 2–21, Spring 1971.

Walker, R.G., 'Australia's ASRB: A Case Study of Political Activity and Regulatory Capture', *Accounting and Business Research*, Vol. 17, No. 67, pp. 269–86, 1987.

Walker, R.G., Robinson, P., 'Competing Regulatory Agencies with Conflicting Agendas: Setting Standards for Cash Flow Reporting in Australia', *ABACUS*, Vol. 30, No. 2, pp. 119–37, 1994.

Watts, R.L., Zimmerman, J.L., 'Agency Problems: Auditing and the Theory of the Firm: Some Evidence', *Journal of Law and Economics*, Vol. 26, pp. 613–34, October 1983.

Watts, R.L., 'Corporate Financial Statements: A Product of the Market and Political Processes', *Australian Journal of Management*, pp. 53–75, April 1977.

Watts, R.L., Zimmerman, J.L., 'Towards a Positive Theory of the Determinants of Accounting Standards', *The Accounting Review*, Vol. 53, pp. 112–34, January 1978.

Questions

3.1 As this chapter indicates, some people argue that the extent of regulation relating to financial accounting is excessive and should be reduced.

(a) What arguments do these people use to support this view?

(b) How would you rate the arguments in terms of their logic?

3.2 What is the basis of the 'lemons' argument?

3.3 What is meant by saying that financial accounting information is a 'public good'?

3.4 Is regulation more likely to be required in respect of *public goods* than other goods? Why?

3.5 Why would an 'accounting standards overload' occur?

3.6 Can regulatory intervention be explained on fairness or equity grounds? If so, what is the basis of this argument?

3.7 Read and evaluate the following paragraph extracted from Cooper and Keim (1983, p. 202):

It should also be noted that the nature and degree of the effect of disclosure requirements (and other aspects of security regulation) on public confidence in the financial markets is unknown. Investors who have never read a prospectus or even thumbed through a 10-K report may have a great deal more confidence in the capital markets because the SEC and its regulations are an integral aspect of the financial system. The salutary effect of such enhancement of the perceived integrity and credibility of the investment process is to reduce the cost of capital for all firms, and the magnitude of this effect may be quite significant.

3.8 Private contractual incentives will assist in ensuring that even in the absence of regulation, organisations will provide such information as is demanded by its respective stakeholders. Evaluate this argument.

3.9 Why would the managerial labour market motivate the manager to voluntarily provide information to outside parties?

3.10 A newspaper article entitled 'Hannes "knew of TNT valuation"' (*The Australian*, 18 June 1999, p. 24) reported a case involving a person who was before the courts on a charge of insider trading. In part, the article stated:

Macquarie Bank executive director Simon Hannes learnt of the value the bank had placed on TNT shares three months before the transport giant was subject to a takeover bid by Dutch company KPN, a jury heard yesterday.

The Crown has alleged that Mr Hannes, using the alias Mark Booth, used that confidential information to make a $2 million profit trading in TNT options at the time of the October 1996 takeover offer. Macquarie was advising TNT on the bid and the Downing Centre District Court jury has previously heard Mr Hannes claimed to have had only a general knowledge of a possible transaction involving TNT. Mr Hannes, 39, has pleaded not guilty to one charge of insider trading and two of structuring bank withdrawals to avoid reporting requirements.

Required:

(a) Which of the theoretical perspectives of regulation reviewed in this chapter might best explain the existence of laws that prohibit insider trading?

(b) How would advocates of a 'free market' approach justify the removal of legislation pertaining to insider trading?

3.11 What assumptions are made about the motivations of the regulators in:

(a) the public interest theory of regulation?

(b) the capture theory of regulation?

(c) the economic interest theory of regulation?

3.12 Is it realistic to assume, in accordance with 'public interest theory', that regulators will not be driven by their own self-interest when designing regulations?

3.13 Is it in the 'public interest' for regulators to be driven by their own self-interest?

3.14 Under the economic interest theory of regulation, what factors will determine whether a particular interest group is able to secure legislation that directly favours that group above all others?

3.15 What do we mean when we say that financial accounting standards are the outcome of a political process? Why is the process political?

3.16 Is the fact that accounting standard-setters consider the economic and social consequences of accounting standards consistent with a view that accounting reports, if compiled in accordance with accounting standards and other generally accepted accounting principles, will be neutral and objective?

3.17 If an accounting standard-setter deems that a particular accounting standard is likely to adversely impact some preparers of financial statements, what do you think it should do?

3.18 Read Exhibit 3.2 which relates to the opposition of some companies within the Australian insurance industry to a particular accounting standard, and answer the following questions:

(a) What do you think is the underlying motivation of those insurance companies lobbying against the accounting standard?

(b) Should the economic consequences of the standard on the financial statement preparers be used as an argument to amend the accounting standard?

(c) If the accounting standard-setter does not amend the accounting standard even under the pressure of the insurance companies, does this imply that the accounting standard-setters are driven by the 'public interest'? How would the advocates of the economic interest theory of regulation explain the fact that the insurance companies' wishes were not met?

EXHIBIT 3.2 Lobbying efforts against an accounting standard

Fierce debate raging on new accounting standard

Christopher Jay

The recent turmoil in Australia's bond markets, with some issues showing capital losses of 25 to 30 per cent, has thrown into sharp relief one of the burning issues in general insurance—the treatment of unrealised gains and losses.

The controversy has shown no signs of abating since a new accounting standard for the insurance industry, AASB 1023 was issued in December 1990, with mandatory effect from the financial year ending June 30 1992.

AASB 1023 requires general insurance groups to include in their profit and loss accounts changes in the market value of their investment assets, even if they have no intention of actually selling them.

Its supporters, including the chairman of the Australian Accounting Standards Board, Mr Peter Day, believe the effects of market price changes, even if un-realised, should be included in profit and loss to give an accurate financial picture.

After all, even if a general insurer holds aloof from the hurly burly of day-to-day trading, one reason for holding these investments is to provide liquidity if required. If something like pay-outs on an earthquake in Newcastle, a cyclone in Darwin or unexpected flooding in Sydney requires these assets to be cashed in, what matters is their market price at the time, and not their potential yield on maturity.

Opponents of the provisions, which include most general insurance companies, the Insurance Council of Australia, most investment bankers, analysts and actuarial firms, contend that they distort the underlying performance of general insurers. Their essential concern is the volatility of investment markets, particularly equities and bonds. They consider an insurance group holding equities for their long-term yield can ride out short-term volatility.

If it intends holding bonds to maturity, cashing them in eventually at face value, then notional market losses in the meantime are beside the point.

The Insurance Council of Australia has made various submissions seeking amendments to AASB 1023, the most recent written one in December, 1993.

There was a presentation to the Accounting Standards Boards in March, 1994, resulting in a joint committee to review the operations of the standard.

The joint committee includes representatives of the Insurance Council of Australia, the Institute of Chartered Accountants, the Big Six chartered accounting firms and the Accounting

(continued)

EXHIBIT 3.2 (continued)

Standards Board themselves. Industry representatives hope this may produce some results by the end of this year.

With the exception of the GIO, the opposition to inclusion of unrealised gains and losses in the profit and loss account has been strongly pursued among the handful of companies either listed or hoping to list on the Australian share markets.

Mr Douglas Pearce, general manager, finance and administration for NRMA, pointed out that including market fluctuations in the bottom line particularly affected groups with high asset backing in relation to premium income.

General insurers must have asset backing equivalent to at least 20 per cent of the value of annual premium income, but most are well above that.

NRMA, for instance, has a group solvency of around 150–160 per cent.

The paradox is that the groups which are in the most secure positions, with high asset backing to cover their liabilities, become the ones most exposed to the fluctuations that occur in the share and bond markets, precisely because they have a large volume of assets to fluctuate. Mr Pearce said: 'It's an interesting anomaly that the better your prudential position, the more volatility there is in your profit and loss.'

Mr Bill Bartlett, chairman of Ernst & Young's international insurance practice, notes that government bonds are bought by insurance companies in maturity patterns to release funds to match anticipated future liabilities.

If the companies trade in the bonds it is reasonable to require them to be revalued at current prices ('mark to market'), but not if they are to be held to maturity.

'There's a new accounting standard in the US called FAS 115,' Mr Bartlett said. 'It says if you trade in bonds you mark to market, but if you intend to hold the bonds to maturity, you don't. It's a purpose-led approach.'

A submission for amendment of AASB 1023 put forward by the insurance industry recommends adoption of the principles of US Standard FAS 115.

The chief executive officer of the Insurance Council of Australia, Mr Peter Daly, said: 'Developments in the US and Europe in general insurance accounting since AASB 1023 was promulgated indicate that Australian insurance company accounts will be unique until beyond the year 2000.

'Adoption of the principles of FAS 115 would go some way towards rectifying this situation.'

The Australian Financial Review,
31 August 1994, p. 35

Chapter 4

Normative theories of accounting—the case of accounting for changing prices

Learning objectives

Upon completing this chapter readers should:

- be aware of some particular limitations of historical cost accounting in terms of its ability to cope with various issues associated with changing prices;

- be aware of a number of alternative methods of accounting that have been developed to address problems associated with changing prices;

- be able to identify some of the strengths and weaknesses of the various alternative accounting methods;

- understand that the calculation of income under a particular method of accounting will depend on the perspective of capital maintenance that has been adopted.

Opening issues

If we look at the financial statements of large corporations we find that various asset valuation approaches are often adopted. We also find that non-current assets acquired or perhaps valued in different years will simply be added together to give a total dollar value, even though the various costs or valuations might provide little reflection of the current values of the respective assets. For example, if we look at the notes to BHP Ltd's 1999 balance sheet, we find the following note related to land and buildings (all numbers are in $millions):

TABLE 4.1 A note to the 1999 Balance Sheet of BHP Ltd

Note 19:

	Gross value of assets $m	Accumulated depreciation $m	Net value of assets $m
Land and buildings			
At directors' valuation			
1974	94	79	15
1976	36	12	24
1979	1	1	—
1981	52	32	20
1984	18	12	6
1997	5	1	4
1998	22	2	20
1999	90	—	90
At cost	2661	847	1814
	2979	986	1993

Issues to consider:

(a) What are some of the criticisms that can be made in relation to the practice of accounting, wherein we add together, without adjustment, assets that have been acquired or valued in different years, when the purchasing power of the dollar was conceivably quite different?

(b) What are some of the alternative methods of accounting (alternatives to historical cost accounting) that have been advanced to cope with the issue of changing prices, and what acceptance have these alternatives received from the accounting profession?

(c) What are some of the strengths and weaknesses of the various alternatives to historical cost?

Introduction

In Chapter 3 we considered various theoretical explanations about why regulation might be put in place. Perspectives derived from *public interest theory*, *capture theory* and the *economic interest theory of regulation* did not attempt to explain what form of regulation was most optimal or efficient. Rather, by adopting certain theoretical assumptions about individual behaviour and motivations, these theories attempted to explain which parties were most likely to attempt to, and perhaps succeed in, impacting on the regulatory process.

In this chapter we consider a number of *normative theories* of accounting. Based upon particular judgements about the types of information people *need* (which could be different to what they *want*) the various normative theories provide prescriptions about how the process of financial accounting *should* be undertaken.[1]

Across time, numerous normative theories of accounting have been developed by a number of well respected academics. However, they have typically failed to be embraced by the accounting profession, or to be mandated within financial accounting regulations. Relying in part on material introduced in Chapter 3, we consider why some proposed methods of accounting are ultimately accepted by the profession and/or accounting standard-setters, while many are rejected. We question whether the rejection is related to the *merit* of their arguments (or lack thereof), or due to the *political nature* of the standard-setting process wherein various vested interests and economic implications are considered. In this chapter we specifically consider various prescriptive theories of accounting that were advanced by various people on the basis that historical cost accounting has too many shortcomings, particularly in times of rising prices.

Limitations of historical cost accounting in times of rising prices

Over time, criticisms of historical cost accounting have been raised by a number of notable scholars, particularly in relation to its ability to provide useful information in times of rising prices. For example, criticisms have been raised by Sweeney, MacNeal, Canning and Paton in the 1920s and 1930s. From the 1950s the levels of criticism increased, with notable academics (such as Chambers, Sterling, Edwards and Bell) prescribing different models of accounting that they considered provided more useful information than was available under conventional historical cost accounting. Such work continued through to the early 1980s, but declined thereafter as levels of inflation throughout the world began to drop. Nevertheless, the debate continues.

Historical cost accounting assumes that money holds a constant purchasing power. As Elliot (1986, p. 33) states:

---

1. Positive theories, by contrast, attempt to explain and predict accounting practice without seeking to prescribe particular actions. Positive accounting theories are the subject of analysis in Chapter 7.

An implicit and troublesome assumption in the historical cost model is that the monetary unit is fixed and constant over time. However, there are three components of the modern economy that make this assumption less valid than it was at the time the model was developed.[2]

One component is specific price-level changes, occasioned by such things as technological advances and shifts in consumer preferences; the second component is general price-level changes (inflation); and the third component is the fluctuation in exchange rates for currencies. Thus, the book value of a company, as reported in its financial statements, only coincidentally reflects the current value of assets.

While there was much criticism of historical cost accounting during the high inflation periods of the 1970s and 1980s, there were also many who supported historical cost accounting. As we would appreciate, the method of accounting predominantly used today is based on historical cost accounting. Hence the accounting profession and reporting entities have tended to maintain the support for this approach.[3] The very fact that historical cost accounting has continued to be applied by business entities has been used by a number of academics to support its continued use (which in a sense is a form of *accounting-Darwinism* perspective—the view that those things that are most efficient and effective will survive over time). For example, Mautz (1973) states:

Accounting is what it is today not so much because of the desire of accountants as because of the influence of businessmen. If those who make management and investment decisions had not found financial reports based on historical cost useful over the years, changes in accounting would long since have been made.[4,5]

---

2. As indicated in Chapter 2, the historical cost method of accounting can be traced to the work of a Franciscan monk by the name of Pacioli. His most famous work, entitled *Summa de Arithmetica, Geometrica, Proportioni et Proportionalita*, was published in Venice in 1494.

3. In many countries we do have the capacity to revalue non-current assets (which in itself means that a modified version of historical cost accounting is in use), which is one way to take account of changing values. Basing revised depreciation on the revalued amounts, which is generally the requirement in those countries in which revaluations are permitted, is one limited way of accounting for the effects of changing prices.

4. However, because something continues to be used does not mean that there is nothing else that might not be better. This is a common error made by proponents of decision usefulness studies. Such studies attempt to provide either support for, or rejection of, something on the basis that particular respondents or users indicated that it would, or would not, be useful for their particular purposes. Often there are things that might be more 'useful'—but they are unknown by the respondents. As Gray, Owen and Adams (1996, p. 75) state: 'Decision usefulness purports to describe the central characteristics of accounting in general and financial statements in particular. To describe accounting as useful for decisions is no more illuminating than describing a screwdriver as being useful for digging a hole—it is better than nothing (and therefore "useful") but hardly what one might ideally like for such a task.'

5. Reflective of the lack of agreement in the area, Elliot (1986) adopts a contrary view. Still relying upon metaphors associated with evolution, Elliot (1986, p. 35) states: 'There is growing evidence in the market place . . . that historical cost-basis information is of ever declining usefulness to the modern business world. The issue for the financial accounting profession is to move the accounting model toward greater relevance or face the fate of the dinosaur and the passenger pigeon.'

It has been argued (for example, Chambers, 1966) that historical cost accounting information suffers from problems of relevance in times of rising prices. That is, it is questioned whether it is useful to be informed that something cost a particular amount many years ago when its current value (as perhaps reflected by its replacement cost, or current market value) might be considerably different. It has also been argued that there is a real problem of additivity. At issue is whether it is really logical to add together assets acquired in different periods when those assets were acquired with dollars of different purchasing power.

In a number of countries, organisations are permitted to revalue their non-current assets. What often happens, however, is that different assets are revalued in different periods (with the dollar having different purchasing power), yet the revalued assets might all be added together, along with assets that have continued to be valued at cost, for the purposes of balance sheet disclosure. For example, if we consider the 1999 financial statements of the Australian company CSR Ltd, we find the following information (Table 4.2)

TABLE 4.2 Valuations of plant and equipment using valuations from different time periods

Note 17:	1999 $A million	1998 $A million
Plant and equipment		
At directors' valuation		
1985	15.1	15.1
1992	24.8	32.5
1993	3.3	3.6
1995	1.4	1.4
1996	0.2	0.3
1997	3.9	6.5
1998	175.1	175.1
1999	8.3	
Assessed value of leased assets	1.6	17.4
Accumulated depreciation and amortisation	(40.7)	(52.3)
	193	199.6
At cost	4720.7	4647.0
Accumulated depreciation	(2156.7)	(2089.3)
	2564.0	2557.7
Total plant and equipment	**2757.0**	**2757.3**

relating to the plant and equipment held by the CSR Group as at 31 March 1999. Different valuations undertaken in different years (the different valuations would relate to different assets) are simply added together, along with those assets that are valued at cost (and the assets valued at cost were probably acquired in different years) to give a total dollar value for property plant and equipment.[6]

There is also an argument that methods of accounting that do not take account of changing prices, such as historical cost accounting, can tend to overstate profits in times of rising prices, and that distribution of historical cost profits can actually lead to an erosion of operating capacity. For example, assume that a company commenced operations at the beginning of the year 2000 with $100,000 in inventory made up of 20,000 units at $5.00 each. If at the end of the year all the inventory had been sold, there were assets (cash) of $120,000, and throughout the year there had been no contributions from owners, no borrowings, and no distributions to owners, then profit under an historical cost system would be $20,000. If the entire profit of $20,000 was distributed to owners in the form of dividends, then the financial capital would be the same as it was at the beginning of the year. Financial capital would remain intact.

However, if prices had increased throughout the period, then the actual operating capacity of the entity may not have remained intact. Let us assume that the company referred to above wishes to acquire another 20,000 units of inventory after it has paid $20,000 in dividends, but finds that the financial year end replacement cost has increased to $5.40 per unit. The company will only be able to acquire 18,518 units with the $100,000 it still has available. By distributing its total historical cost profit of $20,000, with no adjustments being made for rising prices, the company's ability to acquire goods and services has fallen from one period to the next. Some advocates of alternative approaches to accounting would prescribe that the profit of the period is more accurately recorded as $120,000 less 20,000 units at $5.40 per unit which then equals $12,000. That is, if $12,000 is distributed in dividends, the company can still buy the same amount of inventory (20,000 units) as it had at the beginning of the period—its purchasing power remains intact.[7]

It has also been argued that historical cost accounting distorts the current year's operating results by including in the current year's income holding gains

---

6. Within Australia a new accounting standard becomes effective from July 2001, requiring that if assets are recorded on the basis of valuation, then the entire class of assets must be revalued every three years.

7. In some countries, such as the United States, inventory can be valued on the basis of the Last-in-First-Out method (this method is not allowed in some countries, for example, in Australia). The effect of employing LIFO is that cost of goods sold will be determined on the basis of the latest cost, which in times of rising prices will be higher, thereby leading to a reduction in reported profits. This does provide some level of (although certainly not complete) protection against the possibility of eroding the real operating capacity of the organisation.

that actually accrued in previous periods.[8] For example, some assets may have been acquired at a very low cost in a previous period (and perhaps in anticipation of future price increases pertaining to the assets), yet under historical cost accounting, the gains attributable to such actions will only be recognised in the subsequent periods when the assets are ultimately sold.

There is a generally accepted view that dividends should only be paid from income (and this is enshrined within the corporations laws of many countries). However, one central issue relates to how we measure *income*. There are various definitions of income. One famous definition was provided by Hicks (1946), that is, that *income* is the maximum amount that can be consumed during a period while still expecting to be as *well off* at the end of the period as at the beginning of the period. Any consideration of '*well-offness*' relies upon a notion of capital maintenance—but which one? Different notions will provide different perspectives of *income*.

There are a number of perspectives of *capital maintenance*. One version of capital maintenance is based on maintaining financial capital intact, and this is the position taken in historical cost accounting. Under historical cost accounting, dividends should normally only be paid to the extent that the payment will not erode financial capital, as illustrated in the previous example where $20,000 is distributed to owners in the form of dividends and no adjustment is made to take account of changes in prices and the related impact on the purchasing power of the entity.

Another perspective of capital maintenance is one that aims at maintaining purchasing power intact.[9] Under this perspective, historical cost accounts are adjusted for changes in the purchasing power of the dollar (typically by use of the price index) which, in times of rising prices, will lead to a reduction in income relative to income calculations under historical cost accounting. As an example, under general price level adjustment accounting (which we will consider more fully later in this chapter) the historical cost of an item is adjusted by multiplying it by the chosen price index at the end of the current period, divided by the price index at the time the asset was acquired. For example, if some land, which was sold for $1,200,000, was initially acquired for $1,000,000 when the price index was 100, and the price index at the end of the current period is 118 (reflecting an increase in prices of 18 per cent), then the adjusted cost would be $1,180,000. The adjusted profit

---

8. Holding gains are those that arise while an asset is in the possession of the reporting entity.

9. Gray, Owen, and Adams (1996, p. 74) also provide yet another concept of capital maintenance—one that includes environmental capital. They state 'it is quite a simple matter to demonstrate that company "income" contains a significant element of capital distribution—in this case "environmental capital". An essential tenet of accounting is that income must allow for the maintenance of capital. Current organisational behaviour clearly does not maintain environmental capital and so overstates earnings. If diminution of environmental capital is factored into the income figure it seems likely that no company in the western world has actually made any kind of a profit for many years.' We will consider this issue further in Chapter 9.

would be $20,000 (compared to an historical cost profit of $200,000).[10] What should be realised is that under this approach to accounting where adjustments are made by way of an index, the value of $1,180,000 will not necessarily (except due to chance) reflect the current market value of the land. Various assets will be adjusted using the same general price index.

Use of actual current values (as opposed to adjustments to historical cost using price indices) is made under another approach to accounting which seeks to provide a measure of profits which, if distributed, maintains physical operating capital intact. This approach to accounting (which could be referred to as *current cost accounting*) relies upon the use of current values, which could be based on present values, entry prices (for example, replacement costs), or exit prices.

Reflective of the attention that the impact of inflation was having on financial statements, Exhibit 4.1 reproduces an article that appeared in *The Australian* in April 1975 (a period of high inflation—and a time when debate in this area of accounting was widespread).

In the discussion that follows we consider a number of different approaches to undertaking financial accounting in times of rising prices. This discussion is by no means exhaustive but does give some insight into some of the various models that have been prescribed by various parties.[11]

Current purchasing power accounting

Current purchasing power accounting (or as it is also called, general purchasing power accounting; general price level accounting; or constant dollar accounting) can be traced to the early works of such authors as Sweeny (1936) and has since been favoured by a number of other researchers. Current purchasing power accounting (CPPA) has also, at various times, been supported by professional accounting bodies throughout the world (but more in the form of supplementary disclosures to accompany financial statements prepared consistent with historical cost accounting principles). CPPA was developed on the basis of a view that in times of rising prices, if an entity

---

10. Hence, if $20,000 is distributed as dividends, the entity would still be in a position to acquire the same land that it had at the beginning of the period (assuming that actual prices increased by the same amount as the particular price index used).

11. For example, we will not be considering one approach to determining income based on present values which did not have wide support, but would be consistent with Hicks' income definition (and which might be considered as a *true income* approach). A present value approach would determine the discounted present value of the firm's assets and liabilities and use this as the basis for the financial statements. Under such an approach the calculated value of assets will depend upon various expectations, such as expectations about the cash flows the asset would return through its use in production (its value in use) or its current market value (value in exchange). Such an approach relies upon many assumptions and judgements, including the determination of the appropriate discount rate. Under a present value approach to accounting, profit would be determined as the amount that could be withdrawn, yet maintain the present value of the net assets intact from one period to the next.

EXHIBIT 4.1   An insight into some professional initiatives in the area of accounting for changing prices

Call for inflated books

Brian Mahoney

With their capitalist ship slowly sinking from the weight of inflation, company directors and accountants are at last doing something about the problem.

They are not exactly finding a way to overcome it, but they have decided on a way of recording the effects of inflation in company accounts.

Members of the Institute of Chartered Accountants in Australia at the annual Victorian congress last weekend and a panel of directors at the Institute of Directors in Australia in Sydney on Wednesday called for the introduction of some form of accounting for inflation.

At present there is a preliminary exposure draft of one such form of accounting—Changes in the Purchasing Power of Money—distributed by the Institute of Chartered Accountants and the Australian Society of Accountants.

Under CPP, figures are adjusted by an index to a constant purchasing power.

Another such draft of another form of inflation accounting—Replacement Cost—is expected within a few months and hopefully some decision will be made after that as to what form of accounting will be encouraged.

RC accounting aims at showing the replacement value of non-monetary assets expected to be replaced, with consequential adjustments to profits.

As the ICAA pointed out at its Victorian meeting, a company reporting a steady profit in times of 20 per cent inflation would show adjusted earnings actually 20 per cent lower under the new schemes.

The present historical cost accounting, where companies compared different value dollars without converting them by any 'inflation exchange rate', has led some companies effectively to pay dividends out of capital.

Over 200 directors at the institute's seminar at the Wentworth Hotel, Sydney, were told until companies start to show the real effect of inflation on their earnings they could not hope to see any government moves similar to that of Finland where an index of inflation is declared each quarter.

Mr R. N. H. Denton, an accountant with Irish, Young and Outhwaite, told them: 'I prophesize (sic) that more and more companies will be seeking capital issues merely to maintain their level of operations.

'This is in a capital market where confidence has been severely shaken and which is in doubt as to whether industry can now earn an adequate return to service capital in real terms.

'To add to the problem, no recognition is given to our taxation policy to the effect that inflation exerts. The rate of 45 per cent, after a hopelessly inadequate reduction of 2.5 per cent, is really significantly higher on real earnings,' he said.

The Australian, **11 April 1975, p. 12.**

were to distribute unadjusted profits based on historical costs, the result could be a reduction in the real value of an entity—that is, in real terms the entity could otherwise distribute part of its capital.

In considering the development of accounting for changing prices, the majority of research initially related to restating historical costs to account for changing prices by using historical cost accounts as the basis, but restating the accounts by use of particular price indices. This is the approach that we consider in this section of the chapter. The literature then tended to move towards current cost accounting (which we consider later in this chapter) which changed the basis of measurement to current values as opposed to restated historical values. Consistent with this trend, the accounting profession initially tended to favour price-level-adjusted accounts (using indices), but then tended to switch to current cost accounting which required the entity to find the *current values* of the individual assets held by the reporting entity.[12,13]

Current purchasing power accounting with its reliance on the use of indices is generally accepted as being easier and less costly to apply than methods that rely upon current valuations of particular assets.[14] It was initially considered by some people that it would be too costly and perhaps unnecessary to attempt to find current values for all the individual assets. Rather than considering the price changes of specific goods and services, it was suggested on practical grounds that price indices be used.

Calculating indices

When applying general price level accounting, a price index must be applied. A price index is a weighted average of the current prices of goods and services relative to a weighted average of prices in a prior period, often referred to as a base period. Price indices may be broad, or narrow—they may relate to changes in prices of particular assets within a particular industry (a specific price index), or they might be based on a broad cross-section of goods and services that are consumed (a general price index, such as the Australian Consumer Price Index).

But which price indices should be used? Should we use changes in a general price index (for example, as reflected in Australia by the Consumer Price Index) or should we use an index that is more closely tied to the acquisition of production-related resources? There is no clear answer. From the shareholders' perspective the CPI may more accurately reflect their buying pattern—but prices will not change by the same amount for shareholders in different locations. Further, not everybody will have the same consumption patterns as is assumed when constructing a particular index. The choice of an index can be very subjective. Where CPPA has been recommended by particular professional bodies, *CPI-type* indices have been suggested.

Because CPPA relies upon the use of price indices, it is useful to consider how such indices are constructed. To explain one common way that indices may be constructed we can consider the following example which is

---

12. Current values could be based on *entry* or *exit* prices. As we will see, there is much debate as to which 'current' value is most appropriate.

13. The professional support for the use of replacement costs appeared to heighten around the time of the 1976 release of ASR 190 within the United States.

14. However, many questions can be raised with regard to what the restated value actually represents after being multiplied by an index such as the CPI. This confusion is reflected in studies that question the relevance of information restated for changes in purchasing power.

consistent with how the Australian Consumer Price Index is determined. Let us assume that there are three types of commodities (A, B, and C) that are consumed in the following base year quantities and at the following prices:

Year	Commodity A Price	Quantity	Commodity B Price	Quantity	Commodity C Price	Quantity
Base year (2000)	10.00	100	15.00	200	20.00	250
2001	12.00		15.50		21.20	

From the above data we can see that prices have increased. The price index in the base is frequently given a value of 100 and it is also frequently assumed that consumption quantities thereafter remain the same, such that the price index at the end of year 2001 would be calculated as:

$$100 \times \frac{(12.00 \times 100) + (15.50 \times 200) + (21.20 \times 250)}{(10.00 \times 100) + (15.00 \times 200) + (20.00 \times 250)}$$

$$= 106.67$$

From the above calculations we can see that the prices within this particular 'bundle' of goods have been calculated as rising on average by 6.67 per cent from the year 2000 to the year 2001. The reciprocal of the price index represents the change in general purchasing power across the period. For example, if the index increased from 100 to 106.67, as in the above example, the purchasing power of the dollar would be 93.75 per cent (100/106.67) of what it was previously. That is, the purchasing power of the dollar has decreased.

Performing current purchase power adjustments

When applying CPPA, all adjustments are done at the end of the period, with the adjustments being applied to accounts prepared under the historical cost convention. When considering changes in the value of assets as a result of changes in the purchasing power of money (due to inflation) it is necessary to consider monetary assets and non-monetary assets separately. Monetary assets are those assets that remain fixed in terms of their monetary value, for example, cash and claims to a specified amount of cash (such as accounts receivable and investments that are redeemable for a set amount of cash). These assets will not change their monetary value as a result of inflation. For example, if we are holding $10 in cash and there is rapid inflation, we will still be holding $10 in cash, but the asset's purchasing power will have decreased over time.

Non-monetary assets can be defined as those assets whose monetary equivalents will change over time as a result of inflation, and would include such things as plant and equipment and inventory. For example, inventory may cost $100 at the beginning of the year, but the same inventory could cost, say, $110 at the end of the year due to inflation. Relative to monetary assets, the purchasing power of non-monetary assets is assumed to remain relatively constant as a result of inflation.

Most liabilities are fixed in monetary terms (there is an obligation to pay a pre-specified amount of cash at a particular time in the future independent of the change in the purchasing power of the particular currency) and hence liabilities would typically be considered as monetary items (monetary liabilities). Non-monetary liabilities, on the other hand, although less common, would include obligations to transfer goods and services in the future, items which could change in terms of their monetary equivalents.

Net monetary assets would be defined as monetary assets less monetary liabilities. In times of inflation, holders of monetary assets will lose in real terms as a result of holding the monetary assets, as the assets will have less purchasing power at the end of the period relative to what they had at the beginning of the period. Conversely, holders of monetary liabilities will gain, given that the amount they have to repay at the end of the period will be worth less (in terms of purchasing power) than it was at the beginning of the period.

Let us consider an example to demonstrate how gains and losses might be calculated on monetary items (and under CPPA, gains and losses will relate to net monetary assets rather than net non-monetary assets). Let us assume that an organisation holds the following assets and liabilities at the beginning of the financial year:

	$
Current Assets	
Cash	6,000
Inventory	9,000
	15,000
Non-current Assets	
Land	10,000
Total Assets	25,000
Liabilities	
Bank loan	5,000
Owners' Equity	20,000

Let us also assume that the general level of prices has increased 5 per cent since the beginning of the year and let us make a further simplifying assumption (which will be relaxed later) that the company did not trade during the year and that the same assets and liabilities were in place at the end of the year as at the beginning. Assuming that general prices, perhaps as reflected by changes in the CPI, have increased by 5 per cent, then the CPI-adjusted values would be:

	Unadjusted $	Price adjustment factor	Adjusted $
Current Assets			
Cash	6,000		6,000
Inventory	9,000	0.05	9,450
	15,000		15,450
Non-current Assets			
Land	10,000	0.05	10,500
Total Assets	25,000		25,950
Liabilities			
Bank loan	5,000		5,000
Owners' Equity	20,000		20,950

Again, monetary items are not adjusted by the change in the particular price index because they will retain the same monetary value regardless of inflation. Under CPPA there is an assumption that the organisation has not gained or lost in terms of the purchasing power attributed to the non-monetary assets, but rather, it will gain or lose in terms of purchasing power changes attributable to its holdings of the net monetary assets. In the above example, to be as 'well off' at the end of the period the entity would need $21,000 in net assets (which equals $20,000 × 1.05) to have the same purchasing power as it had one year earlier (given the general increase in prices of five per cent). In terms of end-of-year dollars, in the above illustration the entity is $50 worse off in adjusted terms (it only has net assets with an adjusted value of $20,950, which does not have the same purchasing power as $20,000 did at the beginning of the period). As indicated, above, this $50 loss relates to the holdings on net monetary assets and not to the holding of non-monetary assets, and is calculated as the balance of cash, less the balance of the bank loan, multiplied by the general price level increase. That is, ($6,000 – $5,000) × 0.05. If the monetary liabilities had exceeded the monetary assets throughout the period, a purchasing power gain would have been recorded.

Again, it is stressed that under current purchasing power accounting, no change in the purchasing power of the entity is assumed to arise as a result of holding non-monetary assets. Under general price level accounting, non-monetary assets are restated to current purchasing power and no gain or loss is recognised. Purchasing power losses arise only as a result of holding net monetary assets. As noted at paragraph 7 of Provisional Statement of Standard Accounting Practice 7 (PSSAP 7), issued in the UK in 1974:

> *Holders of non-monetary assets are assumed neither to gain nor to lose purchasing power by reason only of inflation as changes in the prices of these assets will tend to compensate for any changes in the purchasing power of the pound.*

An important issue to consider is how the purchasing power gains and losses should be treated for income purposes. Should they be treated as part of the period's profit or loss, or should they be transferred directly to a reserve? Generally, where this method of accounting has been recommended it has been advised that the gain or loss should be included in income. Such recommendations are found in Accounting Research Bulletin No. 6, and APB statement No. 3 (issued in 1969 by AICPA); in FASB Exposure Draft entitled 'Financial Reporting in Units of General Purchasing Power'; and within Provisional Statement of Accounting Practice No. 7 issued by the Accounting Standards Steering Committee (UK) in 1974.

As a further example of calculating gains or losses in purchasing power pertaining to monetary items, let us assume four quarters with the following CPI index figures:

At the beginning of the year	120
At the end of the first quarter	125
At the end of the second quarter	130
At the end of the third quarter	132
At the end of the fourth quarter	135

Let us also assume the following movements in net monetary assets (total monetary assets less total monetary liabilities):

Opening net monetary assets		$100,000
Inflows:		
First quarter net inflow	20,000	
Second quarter net inflow	24,000	44,000
Outflows:		
Third quarter net outflow	(17,000)	
Fourth quarter net outflow	(13,000)	(30,000)
Closing net monetary assets		$114,000

In terms of year-end purchasing power dollars, the purchasing power gain or loss can be calculated as:

	Unadjusted dollars	Price index		Adjusted dollars
Opening net monetary assets	$100,000	× 135/120	=	$112,500
Inflows:				
First quarter net inflow	$20,000	× 135/125	=	$21,600
Second quarter net inflow	$24,000	× 135/130	=	$24,923
Outflows:				
Third quarter net outflow	$(17,000)	× 135/132	=	$(17,386)
Fourth quarter net outflow	$(13,000)	× 135/135	=	$(13,000)
Net monetary assets adjusted for changes in purchasing power				$128,637

What the above calculation reflects is that to have the same purchasing power as when the particular transactions took place, then in terms of end-of-period dollars, $128,637 in net monetary assets would need to be on hand at year end.[15] The actual balance on hand however is $114,000. Hence, there is a purchasing power loss of $14,637 which under CPPA would be treated as an expense in the profit and loss account.

Let us now consider a more realistic example of CPPA adjustments. We will restate the financial statements to reflect purchasing power as at the end of the current financial year. Let us assume that the entity commenced operation on 1 January 2000 and the unadjusted statement of financial position is as follows:

CPP Limited
Statement of Financial Position as at 1 January 2000

Current Assets

Cash	10,000	
Inventory	25,000	35,000

Non-current Assets

Plant and equipment	90,000	
Land	75,000	165,000
Total Assets		200,000

Current Liabilities

Bank overdraft	10,000

Non-current Liabilities

Bank loan	10,000
Total Liabilities	20,000
Net Assets	180,000

Represented by:

Shareholders' Funds

Paid up capital	180,000

---

15. For example, we can consider the initial net monetary asset balance of $100,000 at the beginning of the period. For illustration, we can assume that this was represented by cash of $100,000. Given the inflation which has caused general prices to rise from a base of 120 to 135, to have the same general purchasing power at the end of the period an amount of cash equal to $112,500 would need to be on hand. The difference between the required amount of $112,500 and the actual balance of $100,000 is treated as a purchasing power loss relating to holding the cash. Conversely, if the net monetary balance had been ($100,000), meaning that monetary liabilities exceeded monetary assets, then we would have gained, as the purchasing power of what we must pay has decreased over time.

As a result of its operations for the year, CPP Limited had the historical cost statement of financial performance (profit and loss statement) and statement of financial position (balance sheet) at year end as shown below:

CPP Ltd
Statement of Financial Performance for year ended
31 December 2000

Sales Revenue		200,000
Less:		
Cost of goods sold		
Opening inventory	25,000	
Purchases	110,000	
	135,000	
Closing inventory	35,000	100,000
Gross profit		100,000
Other expenses		
Administrative expenses	9,000	
Interest expense	1,000	
Depreciation	9,000	19,000
Operating profit before tax		81,000
Tax		26,000
Operating profit after tax		55,000
Opening retained earnings		0
Dividends proposed		15,000
Closing retained earnings		40,000

CPP Limited
Statement of Financial Position as at 31 December 2000

Current Assets

Cash	100,000	
Accounts receivable	20,000	
Inventory	35,000	155,000

(continued)

Non-current Assets

Plant and equipment	90,000	
Accumulated depreciation	(9,000)	
Land	75,000	156,000
Total Assets		311,000

Current Liabilities

Bank overdraft	10,000	
Accounts payable	30,000	
Tax payable	26,000	
Provision for dividends	15,000	81,000

Non-current Liabilities

Bank loan	10,000
Total Liabilities	91,000
Net Assets	220,000

Represented by:

Shareholders' Funds

Paid up capital	180,000
Retained earnings	40,000
	220,000

As we have already stated, under CPPA, gains or losses only occur as a result of holding net monetary assets. To determine the gain or loss, we must consider the movements in the net monetary assets. For example, if the organisation sold inventory during the year, this will ultimately impact on cash. However, over time, the cash will be worth less in terms of its ability to acquire goods and services, hence there will be a purchasing power loss on the cash that was received during the year. Conversely, expenses will decrease cash during the year. In times of rising prices, more cash would be required to pay for the expense, hence in a sense we gain in relation to those expenses that were incurred earlier in the year (the logic being that if the expenses were incurred later in the year, more cash would have been required).

We must identify changes in net monetary assets from the beginning of the period until the end of the period.

Movement in net-monetary assets
from 1 January 2000 to 31 December 2000

	1 January 2000	31 December 2000
Monetary assets		
Cash	10,000	100,000
Accounts receivable		20,000
	10,000	120,000
Less:		
Monetary liabilities		
Bank overdraft	10,000	10,000
Accounts payable		30,000
Tax payable		26,000
Provision for dividends		15,000
Bank loan	10,000	10,000
Net monetary assets	(10,000)	29,000

To determine any adjustments in CPP we must identify the reasons for the change in net monetary assets.

Reconciliation of opening and closing net monetary assets

Opening net monetary assets	(10,000)
Sales	200,000
Purchases of inventory	(110,000)
Payment of interest	(1,000)
Payment of administrative expenses	(9,000)
Tax expense	(26,000)
Dividends	(15,000)
Closing net monetary assets	29,000

What we need to determine is whether, had all the transactions taken place at year end, the company would have had to transfer the same amount, measured in monetary terms, as it actually did. Any payments to outside parties throughout the period would have required a greater payment at the end of the period if the same items were to be transferred. Any receipts during the year will, however, be worth less in purchasing power.

To adjust for changes in purchasing power we need to have details about how prices have changed during the period, and we also need to know when the actual changes took place. We make the following assumptions:

- The interest expense and administrative expenses were incurred uniformly throughout the year.

- The tax liability did not arise until year end.

- The dividends were declared at the end of the year.

- The inventory on hand at year end was acquired in the last quarter of the year.

- Inventory purchases occurred uniformly throughout the year.

- Sales occurred uniformly throughout the year.

We also assume that the price level index at the beginning of the year was 130. Subsequent indices were as follows:

31 December 2000	140
Average for the year	135
Average for first quarter	132
Average for second quarter	135
Average for third quarter	137
Average for fourth quarter	139

Rather than using price indices as at the particular dates of transactions (which would generally not be available) it is common to use averages for a particular period.

	Unadjusted	Index	Adjusted
Opening net monetary assets	(10,000)	140/130	(10,769)
Sales	200,000	140/135	207,407
Purchases of inventory	(110,000)	140/135	(114,074)
Payment of interest	(1,000)	140/135	(1,037)
Payment of administrative expenses	(9,000)	140/135	(9,333)
Tax expense	(26,000)	140/140	(26,000)
Dividends	(15,000)	140/140	(15,000)
Closing net monetary assets	29,000		31,194

The difference between $29,000 and the amount of $31,194 represents a loss of $2,194. It is considered to be a loss, because to have the same purchasing power at year end as when the entity held the particular net monetary assets, the entity would need the adjusted amount of $31,194, rather than the actual amount of $29,000.

Price Level Adjusted Statement of Financial Performance
for year ended 31 December 2000

Sales revenue	200,000	140/135	207,407
Less Cost of goods sold			
Opening inventory	25,000	140/130	26,923
Purchases	110,000	140/135	114,074
	135,000		140,997
Closing inventory	35,000	140/139	35,252
	100,000		105,745
Gross profit	100,000		101,662
Other expenses			
Administrative expenses	9,000	140/135	9,333
Interest expense	1,000	140/135	1,037
Depreciation	9,000	140/130	9,692
	19,000		20,062
Operating profit before tax	81,000		81,600
Tax	26,000	140/140	26,000
Operating profit after tax	55,000		55,600
Loss on purchasing power			2,194
			53,406
Opening retained earnings	0		0
Dividends proposed	15,000	140/140	15,000
Closing retained earnings	40,000		38,406

Price Level Adjusted Statement of Financial Position
As at 31 December 2000

Current Assets			
Cash	100,000		100,000
Accounts receivable	20,000		20,000
Inventory	35,000	140/139	35,252
	155,000		155,252
Non-current Assets			
Plant and equipment	90,000	140/130	96,923
Accumulated depreciation	(9,000)	140/130	(9,692)
Land	75,000	140/130	80,769
	156,000		168,000
Total Assets	311,000		323,252

Current Liabilities

Bank overdraft	10,000		10,000
Accounts payable	30,000		30,000
Tax payable	26,000		26,000
Provision for dividends	15,000		15,000

Non-Current Liabilities

Bank loan	10,000		10,000
Total liabilities	91,000		91,000
Net Assets	220,000		232,252

Represented by:

Shareholders' Funds

Paid up capital	180,000	140/130	193,846
Retained earnings	40,000		38,406
	220,000		232,252

From the above statement of financial position (balance sheet) we can again emphasise that the non-monetary items are translated into dollars of year-end purchasing power, whereas the monetary items are already stated in current purchasing power dollars, and hence no changes are made to the reported balances of monetary assets.

One main strength of CPPA is its ease of application. The method relies on data that would already be available under historical cost accounting and does not require the reporting entity to incur the cost or effort involved in collecting data about the current values of the various non-monetary assets. CPI data would also be readily available. However, and as indicated previously, movements in the prices of goods and services included in a general price index might not be reflective of price movements involved in the goods and services involved in different industries. That is, different industries may be impacted differently by inflation.

Another possible limitation is that the information generated under CPPA might actually be confusing to users. They might consider that the adjusted amounts reflect the specific value of specific assets (and this is a criticism that can also be made of historical cost information). However, as the same index is used for all assets, this will rarely be the case. Another potential limitation that we consider at the end of the chapter is that various studies (which have looked at such things as movements in share prices around the time of disclosure of CPPA information) have failed to find much support for the view that the data generated under CPPA are relevant for decision making (the information when released caused little if any share price reaction).

Following the initial acceptance of CPPA in the 1970s there was a move towards methods of accounting that used actual current values. We will now consider such approaches.

Current cost accounting

Current cost accounting (CCA) is one of the various alternatives to historical cost accounting that has tended to gain the most acceptance. Notable advocates of this approach have included Paton, and Edwards and Bell. Such authors decided to reject historical cost accounting and current purchasing power accounting in favour of a method that considered actual valuations. As we will see, unlike historical cost accounting, CCA differentiates between profits from trading, and those gains that result from holding an asset.

Holding gains can be considered as *realised* or *unrealised*. If a financial capital maintenance perspective is adopted with respect to the recognition of income, then holding gains or losses can be treated as income. Alternatively they can be treated as capital adjustments if a physical capital maintenance approach is adopted.[16] Some versions of CCA, such as that proposed by Edwards and Bell, adopt a physical capital maintenance approach to income recognition. In this approach, which determines valuations on the basis of replacement costs,[17] operating income represents realised revenues, less the replacement cost of the assets in question. It is considered that this generates a measure of income that represents the maximum amount that can be distributed, while maintaining operating capacity intact. For example, assume that an entity acquired 150 items of inventory at a cost of $10.00 each and sold 100 of the items for $15 each when the replacement cost to the entity was $12 each. We will also assume that the replacement cost of the 50 remaining items of inventory at year end was $14. Under the Edwards and Bell approach the operating profit that would be available for dividends would be $300 which is $100 \times (\$15 - \$12)$. There would be a realised holding gain on the inventory that was sold, which would amount to $100 \times (\$12 - \$10)$, or $200, and there would be an unrealised holding gain in relation to closing inventory of $50 \times (\$14 - \$10)$, or $200. Neither the realised nor the unrealised holding gain would be considered to be available for dividend distribution.[18]

In undertaking current cost accounting, adjustments are usually made at year end using the historical cost accounts as the basis of adjustments. If we adopt the Edwards and Bell approach to profit calculation, operating profit

---

16. In some countries non-current assets can be revalued upward by way of an increase in the asset account and an increase in a reserve, such as an asset revaluation reserve. This increment is typically not treated as income and therefore the treatment is consistent with a physical capital maintenance approach to income recognition.

17. We will also see later in this chapter that there are approaches to current cost accounting that rely upon exit (sales) prices.

18. Comparing this approach to income calculations under historical cost accounting we see that if we add the current cost accounting operating profit of $300 and the realised holding gain of $200, then this will give the same total as we would have calculated for income under historical cost accounting.

is derived after ensuring that the operating capacity of the organisation is maintained intact. Edwards and Bell believe operating profit is best calculated by using replacement costs.[19,20] As noted above, in calculating operating profit, gains that accrue from holding an asset (holding gains) are excluded and are not made available for dividends—although they are included when calculating what is referred to as *business profit*. For example, if an entity acquired inventory for $20 and sold it for $30, then business profit would be $10, meaning that $10 could be distributed and still leave financial capital intact. But if at the time the inventory was sold its replacement cost to the entity was $23, then $3 would be considered a holding gain, and to maintain physical operating capacity, only $7 could be distributed— current cost operating profit would be $7. No adjustment is made to sales revenue.

In relation to non–current assets, for the purposes of determining current cost operating profit, depreciation is based on the replacement cost of the asset. For example, if an item of machinery was acquired in 1999 for $100,000 and had a projected life of 10 years and no salvage value, then assuming the straight-line method of depreciation is used, its depreciation expense under historical cost accounting would be $10,000 per year. If at the end of 2000 its replacement cost had increased to $120,000, then under current cost accounting a further $2,000 would be deducted to determine current cost operating profit. However, this $2,000 would be treated as a realised cost saving (because historical cost profits would have been lower if the entity had not already acquired the asset) and would be recognised in *business profit* (it would be added back below operating profit) and the other $18,000 would be treated as an unrealised cost saving and would also be included in business profit. As with CPPA, no restatement of monetary assets is required as they are already recorded in current dollars and hence in terms of end-of-period purchasing power dollars.

As an example of one version of CCA (consistent with the Edwards and Bell proposals) let us consider the following example. CCA Ltd's statement of financial position at the commencement of the year is provided below. This is assumed to be the first year of CCA Ltd's operations.

---

19. In a sense, the Edwards and Bell approach represents a 'true income' approach to profit calculation. They believe that profit can only be correctly measured after considering the various asset replacement costs.

20. Those who favour a method of income calculation that requires a maintenance of financial capital (advocates of historical cost accounting) treat holding gains as income, while those who favour a maintenance of physical capital approach to income determination (such as Edwards and Bell) tend to exclude holding gains from income. A physical capital perspective was adopted by most countries in their professional releases pertaining to CCA.

CCA Limited
Statement of Financial Position as at 1 January 2000

Current Assets

Cash	10,000	
Inventory	25,000	35,000

Non-current Assets

Plant and equipment	90,000	
Land	75,000	165,000
Total Assets		200,000

Current Liabilities

Bank overdraft		10,000

Non-current Liabilities

Bank loan		10,000
Total liabilities		20,000
Net Assets		180,000

Represented by:

Shareholders' Funds

Paid up capital		180,000

The unadjusted statement of financial performance and statement of financial position for CCA Ltd after one year's operations are provided below.

CCA Ltd
Statement of Financial Performance for year ended 31 December 2000

Sales revenue		200,000
Less:		
Cost of goods sold		
Opening inventory	25,000	
Purchases	110,000	
	135,000	
Closing inventory	35,000	100,000
Gross profit		100,000

Other expenses		
Administrative expenses	9,000	
Interest expense	1,000	
Depreciation	9,000	19,000
Operating profit before tax		81,000
Tax		26,000
Operating profit after tax		55,000
Opening retained earnings		0
Dividends proposed		15,000
Closing retained earnings		40,000

CCA Limited
Statement of Financial Position as at 31 December 2000

Current Assets

Cash	100,000	
Accounts receivable	20,000	
Inventory	35,000	155,000

Non-current Assets

Plant and equipment	90,000	
Accumulated depreciation	(9,000)	
Land	75,000	156,000
Total Assets		311,000

Current Liabilities

Bank overdraft	10,000	
Accounts payable	30,000	
Tax payable	26,000	
Provision for dividends	15,000	81,000

Non-current Liabilities

Bank loan		10,000
Total liabilities		91,000
Net Assets		220,000

Represented by:

Shareholders' Funds

Paid up capital		180,000
Retained earnings		40,000
		220,000

We will assume that the inventory on hand at year end comprised 3,500 units that cost $10 per unit. The replacement cost at year end was $11.00 per unit. We will also assume that the replacement cost of the units actually sold during the year was $105,000 (as opposed to the historical cost of $100,000) and that the year-end replacement cost of the plant and equipment increased to $115,000.

CCA Ltd
Statement of Financial Performance for year ended 31 December 2000
Adjusted by application of current cost accounting

Sales revenue		200,000
Less:		
Cost of goods sold		105,000
		95,000
Other Expenses		
Administrative expenses	9,000	
Interest expense	1,000	
Tax	26,000	
Depreciation ($115,000 × 1/10)	11,500	47,500
Current cost operating profit		47,500
Realised Savings		
Savings related to inventory actually sold		5,000
Savings related to depreciation actually		
incurred [(115,000 − 90,000) × 1/10]		2,500
Historical cost profit		55,000
Unrealised savings		
Gains on holding inventory—yet to be realised		3,500
Gains on holding plant and machinery—not		
yet realised through the process of		
depreciation [(115,000 − 90,000) × 9/10)]		22,500
Business profit		81,000
Opening retained earnings		0
Dividends proposed		15,000
Closing retained earnings		66,000

CCA Limited
Statement of Financial Position as at 31 December 2000
Adjusted by application of current cost accounting

Current Assets

Cash	100,000	
Accounts receivable	20,000	
Inventory (3,500 × $11.00)	38,500	158,500

Non-current Assets

Plant and equipment	115,000	
Accumulated depreciation	(11,500)	
Land	75,000	178,500
Total Assets		337,000

Current Liabilities

Bank overdraft	10,000	
Accounts payable	30,000	
Tax payable	26,000	
Provision for dividends	15,000	81,000

Non-current Liabilities

Bank loan	10,000
Total liabilities	91,000
Net Assets	246,000

Represented by:

Shareholders' Funds

Paid up capital	180,000
Retained earnings	66,000
	246,000

Consistent with the CCA model prescribed by Edwards and Bell, all non-monetary assets have to be adjusted to their respective replacement costs. Unlike historical cost accounting, there is no need for inventory cost flow assumptions (such as last-in-first-out; first-in-first-out; weighted average). *Business profit* shows how the entity has gained in financial terms from the increase in cost of its resources—something typically ignored by historical cost accounting. In the above illustration, and consistent with a number of versions of CCA, no adjustments have been made for changes in the purchasing power of net monetary assets (in contrast with CPPA).[21]

The current cost operating profit before holding gains and losses, and the realised holding gains, are both tied to the notion of realisation, and hence the sum of the two equates to historical cost profit.

Differentiating operating profit from holding gains and losses (both realised and unrealised) has been claimed to enhance the usefulness of the information being provided. Holding gains are deemed to be different to trading income as they are due to market-wide movements, most of which are beyond the control of management. Edwards and Bell (1961, p. 73) state:

> *These two kinds of gains are often the result of quite different decisions. The business firm usually has considerable freedom in deciding what quantities of assets to hold over time at any or all stages of the production process and what quantity of assets to commit to the production process itself . . . The difference between the forces motivating the business firm to make profit by one means rather than by another and the difference between the events on which the two methods of making profit depend require that the two kinds of gain be separated if the two types of decisions involved are to be meaningfully evaluated.*

As with CPPA, the CCA model described above has been identified as having a number of strengths and weaknesses. Some of the criticisms relate to its reliance on replacement values. The CCA model we have just described uses replacement values, but what is the rationale for replacement cost? Perhaps it is a reflection of the 'real' value of the particular asset. If the market is prepared to pay the replacement cost, and if we assume economic rationality, then the amount paid must be a reflection of the returns it is expected to generate. However, it might not be worth that amount (the replacement cost) to all firms—some firms might not elect to replace a given asset if they have an option. Further, past costs are *sunk costs* and if the entity were required to acquire new plant, it might find it more efficient and less costly to acquire different types of assets. If they do buy it, then this might

---

21. Some variants of current cost accounting do include some purchasing power changes as part of the profit calculations. For example, if an entity issued $1 million of debt when the market required a rate of return of 6%, but that required rate subsequently rises to 8%, then the unrealised savings would include the difference between what the entity received for the debt and what they would receive at the new rate. This unrealised saving would benefit the organisation throughout the loan as a result of the lower interest charges.

reflect that it is actually worth much more. Further, replacement cost does not reflect what it would be worth if the firm decided to sell it.

As was indicated previously, it has been argued that separating holding gains and losses from other results provides a better insight into management performance, as such gains and losses are due to impacts generated outside the organisation—however, this can be criticised on the basis that acquiring assets in advance of price movements might also be part of efficient operations.

Another potential limitation of CCA is that it is often difficult to determine replacement costs. The approach also suffers from the criticism that allocating replacement cost via depreciation is still arbitrary, just as it is with historical cost accounting.

An advantage of CCA is better comparability of various entities' performance, as one entity's profits are not higher simply because they bought assets years earlier and therefore would have generated lower depreciation under historical cost accounting.

Chambers, an advocate of current cost accounting based on *exit values* was particularly critical of the Edwards and Bell model of accounting. He states (1995, p. 82) that:

> *In the context of judgement of the past and decision making for the future, the products of current value accounting of the Edwards and Bell variety are irrelevant and misleading.*

We now consider the alternative accounting model prescribed by Chambers and a number of others—a model that relies upon the use of *exit values*.

Exit price accounting: the case of Chambers' Continuously Contemporary Accounting

Exit price accounting has been proposed by researchers such as MacNeal, Sterling and Chambers. It is a form of current cost accounting which is based on valuing assets at their net selling prices (exit prices) at balance date and on the basis of orderly sales. Chambers coined the term *current cash equivalent* to refer to the cash that an entity would expect to receive through the orderly sale of an asset, and he had the view that information about current cash equivalents was fundamental to effective decision making. He labelled his method of accounting *Continuously Contemporary Accounting*, or *CoCoA*.

Although he generated some much cited research throughout the 1950s (such as Chambers, 1955) a great deal of his work culminated in 1966 in the publication of *Accounting, Evaluation and Economic Behavior*. This document stressed that the key information for economic decision making relates to *capacity to adapt*—a function of current cash equivalents. The statement of financial position (balance sheet) is considered to be the prime financial statement and should show the net selling prices of the entity's assets. Profit would directly relate to changes in *adaptive capital*, with adaptive capital reflected by the total exit values of the entity's assets.

As indicated previously in this chapter, how one calculates income is based, in part, on how one defines wealth. According to Sterling, an advocate of exit price accounting, (1970, p. 189).

> *The present [selling] price is the proper and correct valuation coefficient for the measurement of wealth at a point in time and income is the difference between dated wealths so calculated.*

Consistent with the views of Sterling, Chambers (1966, p. 91) states:

> *At any present time, all past prices are simply a matter of history. Only present prices have any bearing on the choice of an action. The price of a good ten years ago has no more relation to this question than the hypothetical price 20 years hence. As individual prices may change even over an interval when the purchasing power of money does not, and as the general purchasing power of money may change even though some individual prices do not, no useful inference may be drawn from past prices which has a necessary bearing on present capacity to operate in a market. Every measurement of a financial property for the purpose of choosing a course of action—to buy, to hold, to sell—is a measurement at a point in time, in the circumstances of the time, and in the units of currency at that time, even if the measurement process itself takes some time.*
>
> *Excluding all past prices, there are two prices which could be used to measure the monetary equivalent of any non-monetary good in possession: the buying price and the selling price. But the buying price, or replace price, does not indicate capacity, on the basis of present holdings, to go into a market with cash for the purpose of adapting oneself to contemporary conditions, whereas the selling price does. We propose, therefore, that the single financial property which is uniformly relevant at a point of time for all possible future actions in markets is the market selling price or realizable price of any goods held. Realizable price may be described as current cash equivalent. What men wish to know, for the purpose of adaptation, is the numerosity of the money tokens which could be substituted for particular objects and for collections of objects if money is required beyond the amount which one already holds.*[22]

We can see that Chambers has made a judgement about what people need in terms of information. Like authors such as Edwards and Bell, and unlike some of the earlier work which documented existing accounting practices to identify particular principles and postulates (descriptive research),[23] Chambers set out to develop what he considered was a superior model of

---

22. As quoted in Belkaoui, 1992, p. 286.

23. As a specific example of the inductive (descriptive) approach to theory development we can consider the work of Grady (1965). This research was commissioned by the American Institute of Certified Public Accountants and documented the generally accepted conventions of accounting of the time.

accounting—a model that represented quite a dramatic change from existing practice. We call this prescriptive or normative research. The research typically highlighted the limitations of historical cost accounting and then proposed an alternative on the basis that it would enable better decision making. Chambers adopts a *decision usefulness* approach and within this approach he adopts a *decision models perspective*.[24]

The Chambers' approach is focused on new opportunities—the ability or capacity of the entity to adapt to changing circumstances and the most important item of information to evaluate future decisions is, according to Chambers, current cash equivalents. Chambers makes an assumption about the objective of accounting—to guide future actions. *Capacity to adapt* is the key and the capacity to adapt to changing circumstances is dependent upon the current cash equivalents of the assets on hand. The higher the current market value of the entity's assets the greater is the ability of the organisation to adapt to changing circumstances.

As stated previously, in the Chambers' model, profit is directly tied to the increase (or decrease) in the current net selling prices of the entity's assets. No distinction is drawn between *realised* and *unrealised* gains. Unlike some other models of accounting, all gains are treated as part of profit. Profit is that amount that can be distributed, while maintaining the entity's adaptive ability (adaptive capital). CoCoA abandons notions of realisation in terms of recognising revenue, and hence, revenue recognition points change relative to historical cost accounting. Rather than relying on sales, revenues are recognised at such points as production or purchase.

Unlike the Edwards and Bell approach to current cost accounting, within CoCoA there is an adjustment to take account of changes in general purchasing power, which is referred to as a *capital maintenance adjustment*. The capital maintenance adjustment also forms part of the period's income, with a corresponding credit to a capital maintenance reserve (which forms part of owners' equity). In determining the capital maintenance adjustment, the opening residual equity of the entity (that is, the net assets) is multiplied by the proportionate change in the general price index from the beginning of the period to the end of the financial period. As an example, if opening residual equity was $5,000,000 and the price index increased from 140 to 148, then the capital maintenance adjustment (in the case of increasing prices,

---

24. As indicated in Chapter 1, decision usefulness research can be considered to have two branches, these being the *decision-makers' emphasis*, and the *decision-models emphasis*. The decision-makers' emphasis relies upon undertaking research that seeks to ask decision makers what information they want. Proponents of the *decision-models emphasis*, on the other hand, develop models based upon the researchers' perceptions about what is necessary for efficient decision making. Information prescriptions follow (for example, that information should be provided about the market value of the reporting entity's assets). This branch of research typically assumes that different classes of stakeholders have identical information needs. Unlike the decision-makers' emphasis, the decision-models emphasis does not ask the decision makers what information they want, but, instead, it concentrates on what types of information are considered to be useful for decision making.

an expense) would be calculated as $5,000,000 \times 8/140 = \$285,714$. According to Chambers (1995, p. 86):

Deduction of that amount, a capital maintenance or inflation adjustment, from the nominal difference between opening and closing capitals, would give the net increment in purchasing power, the real income, of a period. The inflation adjustment would automatically cover gains and losses in purchasing power from net holdings of money and money's worth. Net real income would then be the algebraic sum of (a) net realised revenues based on consummated transactions, or net cash flows, (b) the aggregate of price variation adjustments, the unrealised changes in value of assets on hand at balance date, and (c) the inflation adjustment. The amount of the inflation adjustment would be added proportionately to the opening balances of contributed capital and undivided surplus, giving closing amounts in units of up to date purchasing power.

We can now summarise some of the above points by referring to Exhibit 4.2 below which is a reproduction of an article that appeared in *The Australian Financial Review* (10 May 1973). It reported some of Chambers' concerns with regards to historical cost accounting.

EXHIBIT 4.2 Some views of Professor Raymond Chambers

Where company reports fail—Prof Chambers

Financial reports of companies generally failed to give a fair idea of their financial positions and profits, Professor R. J. Chambers, professor of accounting at the University of Sydney, said last night.

He called for amplification of the law on company reporting to ensure that balance sheets recognise changes in the prices of specific assets and profit and loss accounts reflect changes in the general purchasing power of money.

The accounting rules used were so different in effect that comparisons between companies were often quite misleading.

These rules had been debated for years among accountants but never yet had accountants settled on rules which gave consistent and up-to-date information year by year.

Addressing the university's Pacioli Society, Professor Chambers outlined specific amendments to the Companies

Acts which are contained in his new book, 'Securities and Obscurities'.

Professor Chambers' amendment to the laws governing balance sheet reporting was that no balance sheet should be deemed to give a true and fair view of the state of affairs of a company unless the amounts shown for the several assets were the best possible approximations of the net selling prices in the ordinary course of business.

Debts receivable should be the best possible approximations to the amounts expected at the date of the balance sheet to be receivable or recoverable.

On the profit and loss account, Professor Chambers urged that it be deemed to give a true and fair view only if the profit or loss was calculated so as to include changes during the year in the net selling prices of assets and the effects during the year of changes in the purchasing power of the unit of

(continued)

EXHIBIT 4.2 (continued)

account as specified in the Schedule of the Act.

Professor Chambers said thousands of shareholders had lost millions of dollars on security investments made on the basis of out-of-date information or on fictions which were reported as facts.

The Australian Financial Review, **10 May 1973, p. 30.**

As a simple illustration of CoCoA, consider the following information. Assume that Cocoa Ltd had the following balance sheets (statements of financial position) as at 30 June 2000, one compiled using historical cost accounting and the other using CoCoA.

Cocoa Ltd Historical cost Balance Sheet as at 30 June 2000		Cocoa Ltd CoCoA Balance Sheet as at 30 June 2000	
Assets		**Assets**	
Cash	6,000	Cash	6,000
Inventory	10,000	Inventory	16,000
Plant and equipment	24,000	Plant and equipment	28,000
Total Assets	40,000	**Total Assets**	50,000
Liabilities		**Liabilities**	
Bank loan	10,000	Bank loan	10,000
Net Assets	30,000	**Net Assets**	40,000
Represented by		Represented by	
Shareholders' Funds		**Shareholders' Funds**	
Paid up capital	10,000	Paid up capital	10,000
Retained earnings	20,000	Retained earnings	22,000
		Capital maintenance reserve	8,000
	30,000		40,000

We assume that in the financial year ending on 30 June 2001, all the opening inventory was sold for $16,000 and the same quantity of inventory was reacquired at a cost of $11,000 (and which had a retail price of $18,000). There were salaries of $2,000 and historical cost depreciation was based on 5 per cent of book value of plant and equipment. Prices rose generally throughout the period by 10 per cent and the net market value of the plant and equipment was assessed as $29,000.

The income determined for the year ended 30 June 2001 under both historical cost accounting and CoCoA can be calculated as follows:

Cocoa Ltd Historical Cost Profit and Loss Statement for year ended 30 June 2001	
Sales	16,000
Cost of goods sold	(10,000)
Gross margin	6,000
Salaries expense	(2,000)
Depreciation	(1,200)
Net profit	2,800
Opening retained earnings	20,000
Closing retained earnings	22,800

Cocoa Ltd CoCoA Profit and Loss Statement for year ended 30 June 2001	
Sale price of inventory	18,000
Cost of inventory	11,000
Trading income	7,000
Salaries expense	(2,000)
Increase in exit value of plant	1,000
Capital maintenance Adjustment (40,000 × 0.10)	(4,000)
Net profit	2,000
Opening retained earnings	22,000
Closing retained earnings	24,000

Cocoa Ltd Historical Cost Balance Sheet as at 30 June 2001	
Assets	
Cash	9,000
Inventory	11,000
Plant and equipment (net)	22,800
Total Assets	42,800
Liabilities	
Bank loan	10,000
Net assets	32,800
Represented by	
Shareholders' Funds	
Paid up capital	10,000
Retained earnings	22,800
	32,800

Cocoa Ltd CoCoA Balance Sheet as at 30 June 2001	
Assets	
Cash	9,000
Inventory	18,000
Plant and equipment	29,000
Total Assets	56,000
Liabilities	
Bank loan	10,000
Net assets	46,000
Represented by	
Shareholders' Funds	
Paid up capital	10,000
Retained earnings	24,000
Capital maintenance reserve	12,000
	46,000

What must be remembered is that under CoCoA, when the inventory recorded above is sold for $18,000, no profit or loss will be recognised. Such gain was recognised when the inventory was purchased, with the gain being the difference between the expected retail price (net of related expenses) and the cost to Cocoa Ltd. Hence, it is again emphasised, CoCoA involves a fundamental shift in revenue recognition principles compared to historical cost accounting.

As with other methods of accounting, a number of strengths and weaknesses have been associated with CoCoA. Considering the strengths, advocates of CoCoA have argued that by using one method of valuation for all assets (exit value) the resulting numbers can logically be added together (this is often referred to as 'additivity').[25] When CoCoA is adopted there is also no need for arbitrary cost allocations for depreciation as depreciation will be based on movements in exit price.

Considering possible limitations, CoCoA has never gained widespread acceptance, despite being supported by a small number of widely respected academics (there was more support for replacement costs). Also, if CoCoA was implemented it would involve a fundamental and major shift in financial accounting (for example, including major shifts in revenue recognition points and major adjustments to asset valuations) and this in itself could lead to many unacceptable social and environmental consequences.

The relevance of exit prices has also been questioned, particularly if we do not expect to sell assets (just as we questioned the relevance of replacement costs if we do not expect to replace the asset). Further, under CoCoA, assets of a specialised nature (such as a blast furnace) are considered to have no value because they cannot be separately disposed of. This is an assertion that is often challenged because it ignores the 'value in use' of an asset.[26] Further, is it appropriate to value all assets on the basis of their exit values if the entity is considered to be a going concern? Determination of exit values can also be expected to introduce a degree of subjectivity into the accounts (relative to historical cost), particularly if the assets are unique.

CoCoA also requires assets to be valued separately with regard to their current cash equivalents, rather than as a bundle of assets. Hence, CoCoA would not recognise goodwill as an asset because it cannot be sold separately. Evidence shows that the value of assets sold together can be very different to what would be received if they were sold individually (Larson and Schattke, 1966).

Just as Chambers was critical of the Edwards and Bell model, Edwards and Bell were also critical of the Chambers approach. For example, Edwards (1975, p. 238) states:

> I am not convinced of the merit of adopting, as a normal basis for asset valuation in the going concern, exit prices in buyer markets. These are unusual values suitable for unusual situations. I would not object in principle to keeping track of such exit prices at all times and, as Solomons (1966) has suggested, substituting them for entry values when they are the lesser of the two and

---

25. This can be contrasted with the current situation where it is common to find that various classes of assets are valued using a different approach (for example, for inventories—lower of cost and net realisable value; for marketable securities—at market value; for buildings— at cost or revalued amount; for debtors—at face value, less a provision for doubtful debts), yet they are simply added together to give a *total asset* amount.

26. In considering 'value in use', logically, if an asset's 'value in use' exceeds its market value, then it will be retained, else it will be sold. Hence the point might be that there has actually been a choice not to sell the assets that the entity has on hand (Solomons, 1966). Further, specialised assets might be of particular value to one entity, but not to any others.

> the firm has taken a definite decision not to replace the asset, or even the function it performs.

The demand for price adjusted accounting information

One research method often used to assess the usefulness of particular disclosures is to look for a share market reaction around the time of the release of the information, the rationale being that if share prices react to the disclosures, then such disclosures must have information content. That is, the information impacts on the decisions made by individuals participating in the capital market. A number of studies have looked at the stock market reaction to current cost and CPPA information. Results are inconclusive, with studies such as Ro (1980, 1981), Beaver, Christie and Griffin (1980), Gheyara and Boatsman (1980), Beaver and Landsman (1987), Murdoch (1986), Schaefer (1984), Dyckman (1969), Morris (1975), and Peterson (1975) finding limited evidence of any price changes around the time of disclosure of current cost information. (However Lobo and Song (1989) and Bublitz, Freka and McKeown (1985) provide limited evidence that there is information content in current cost disclosures.)

While the majority of share price studies show little or no reaction to price adjusted accounting information, it is possible that the failure to find a significant share price reaction might have been due to limitations in the research methods used. For example, there could have been other information released around the time of the release of the CCA/CPPA information. However, with the weight of research that indicates little or no reaction by the share market, we are probably on safe ground to believe that the market does not value such information when disclosed within the annual report. Of course there are a number of issues in why the capital market might not react to such information. Perhaps individuals or organisations are able to obtain this information from sources other than corporate annual reports, and hence, as the market is already aware of the information, no reaction would then be expected when the annual reports are released.

Apart from analysing share price reactions, another way to investigate the apparent usefulness of particular information is to undertake surveys. Surveys of managers (for example, within Australia, Ferguson and Wines, 1986) have indicated limited corporate support for current cost accounting, with managers citing such issues as the expense, limited benefits from disclosure, and lack of agreement as to the appropriate approach.

In the United States, and in relation to the relevance of FASB Statement No. 33 (which required a mixture of CCA and CPPA information), Elliot (1986, p. 33) states:

> FASB Statement No. 33 requires the disclosure of value information on one or two bases, either price level adjusted or current cost. Surveys taken since

this rule became effective suggest that users do not find the information helpful, don't use it, and they say it doesn't tell them anything they didn't already know. Preparers of the information complain that it is a nuisance to assemble.

Given the above results, we can perhaps say that, in general, there is limited evidence to support the view that the methods used to account for changing prices have been deemed to be successful in providing information of relevance to financial statement users. This is an interesting outcome, particularly given that many organisations over time have elected to provide CCA/CPPA information in their annual reports even when there was no requirement to do so, and also given that many organisations have actively lobbied for or against the particular methods of accounting. Adopting the method for disclosure purposes, or lobbying for it, implies that corporate management, at least, considered that the information was relevant and likely to impact on behaviour—a view at odds with some of the surveys and share price studies reported earlier.

In relation to research that has attempted to analyse the motivations underlying the corporate adoption of alternative accounting methods, an influential paper was Watts and Zimmerman (1978). That paper is generally considered to be one of the most important papers in the development of Positive Accounting Theory (which we consider in Chapter 7). The authors investigated the lobbying positions taken by corporate managers with respect to the FASB's 1974 Discussion Memorandum on general price level accounting (current purchasing power accounting). As we know from material presented in this chapter, if general price level accounting were introduced, then in times of rising prices, reported profits would be reduced relative to profits reported under historical cost conventions. The reduction in profits would be due to such effects as higher depreciation, and purchasing power losses due to holding net monetary assets.

Watts and Zimmerman proposed that the political process was a major factor in explaining which corporate managers were more likely to favour or oppose the introduction of general price level accounting. The political process itself is seen as a competition for wealth transfers. For example, some groups may lobby government to transfer wealth away from particular companies or industries (for example, through increased taxes, decreased tariff support, decreased subsidies, increases in award wages, more stringent licensing arrangements), and towards other organisations or groups otherwise considered to be poorly treated. Apart from government, groups such as consumer groups (perhaps through product boycotts), employee groups (through wage demands or strikes), community interest groups (through impeding operations or lobbying government), can act to transfer wealth away from organisations through political processes.

The perspective of Watts and Zimmerman was that entities deemed to be politically visible are more likely to favour methods of accounting that allow them to reduce their reported profits. High profitability itself was considered to be one attribute that could lead to the unwanted (and perhaps, costly) attention and scrutiny of particular corporations.

The corporate lobbying positions in the submissions made to the FASB are explained by Watts and Zimmerman on the basis of *self-interest* considerations (rather than any consideration of such issues as the 'public interest').[27] The study suggests that large firms (and large firms are considered to be more politically sensitive) favour general price level accounting because it enables them to report lower profits.[28,29]

Other research has also shown that companies might support CCA for the political benefits it provides. In times of rising prices, the adoption of current cost accounting (as with general price level accounting) can lead to reduced profits. In a New Zealand study, Wong (1988) investigated the accounting practices of New Zealand companies between 1977 and 1981 and found that corporations that adopted CCA had higher effective tax rates and larger market concentration ratios than entities that did not adopt CCA, both variables being suggestive of political visibility. In a UK study, Sutton (1988) found that politically sensitive companies were more likely to lobby in favour of current cost accounting. Sutton investigated lobbying submissions made in the UK in relation to an exposure draft that recommended the disclosure of CCA information. Applying a Positive Accounting Theory perspective he found support for a view that organisations that considered they would benefit from the requirement tended to lobby in support of it. Those expected to benefit were:

- Capital intensive firms because it was expected that the adoption of CCA would lead to decreased profits (due to higher depreciation) and this would be particularly beneficial if the method was accepted for the purposes of taxation; and

- Politically sensitive firms, as it would allow them to show reduced profits.

Professional support for various approaches to accounting for changing prices

Over time, varying levels of support have been given to different approaches to accounting in times of rising prices. Current purchasing power accounting was generally favoured by accounting standard-setters from the 1960s to the mid-1970s, with a number of countries, including United States, United

---

27. As we discuss in Chapter 7, and as we already discussed in earlier chapters, one of the central assumptions of Positive Accounting Theory is that all individual action is motivated by self-interest considerations, with that interest being directly tied to the goal of maximising an individual's wealth.

28. Ball and Foster (1982) however, indicate that size can be a proxy for many things other than political sensitivity (such as industry membership).

29. Within the Watts and Zimmerman study many of the respondents were members of the oil industry and such industry members were also inclined to favour the introduction of general price level accounting. Consistent with the political cost hypothesis, 1974 (the time of the submissions) was a time of intense scrutiny of oil companies.

Kingdom, Canada, Australia, New Zealand, Ireland, Argentina, Chile and Mexico, issuing documents that supported the approach. For example, the AICPA supported general price-level restatement in Accounting Research Study No. 6 released in 1961. The Accounting Principles Board also supported the practice in Statement No. 3. Early in its existence, the FASB also issued an exposure draft supporting the use of general purchasing power—'Financial Reporting in Units of General Purchasing Power'—which required CPPA to be disclosed as supplementary information.

From about 1975, preference tended to shift to current cost accounting. In 1976 the SEC released ASR 190 which required certain large organisations to provide supplementary information about 'the estimated current replacement cost of inventories and productive capacity at the end of the fiscal year for which a balance sheet is required and the approximate amount of cost of sales and depreciation based on replacement cost for the two most recent full fiscal years'. In Australia, a Statement of Accounting Practice (SAP 1) entitled Current Cost Accounting was issued in 1983. Although not mandatory, SAP 1 recommended that reporting entities provide supplementary current cost accounting information. In the United Kingdom, support for current cost accounting was demonstrated by the Sandilands Committee (a government committee) in 1975. In 1980 the Accounting Standards Committee (UK) issued SSAP 16 which required supplementary disclosure of current cost data (SSAP was withdrawn in 1985).

In the late 1970s and early 1980s many accounting standard-setters issued recommendations that favoured disclosure based upon a mixture of current purchasing power accounting and current cost accounting. Such 'mixed' reporting recommendations were released in United States, United Kingdom, Canada, Australia, New Zealand, Ireland, West Germany, and Mexico. For example, In 1979 the FASB released SFAS 33 which required a mixture of information, including:

- Purchasing power gains and losses on net monetary assets;

- Income determined on a current cost basis; and

- Current costs of year-end inventory and property plant and equipment.

Around the mid-1980s, generally a time of falling inflation, accounting professions worldwide tended to move away from issues associated with accounting in times of changing prices. For example, in 1984 a member of the Accounting Standards Review Board (subsequently to become the Australian Accounting Standards Board), Mr Ron Cotton, was reported (*Australian Financial Review*, 19 January 1984) as saying 'there are far more important things for the board to look at when current cost accounting does not have the support of the public or the government'. He also said he would be 'surprised and disappointed' if the board put current cost accounting high on the list of priorities when it met for the first time in January 1984.

It is an interesting exercise to consider why particular methods of accounting did not gain and maintain professional support. Perhaps it was because the profession, like a number of researchers, questioned the relevance of the information, particularly in times of lower inflation. If they did question the relevance of the information to various parties (such as the capital market) it would be difficult for them to support regulation from a 'public interest' perspective, given the costs that would be involved in implementing a new system of accounting.

Even in the absence of concerns about the relevance of the information, standard-setters might have been concerned that a drastic change in our accounting conventions could cause widespread disruption and confusion in the capital markets and therefore might not be in the public interest. Although there have been numerous accounting controversies and disputes over time (for example, how to account for goodwill or research and development, or how to account for investments in associates), such controversies typically impact on only a small subset of accounts. Adopting a new model of accounting would have much more widespread effects, which again might not have been in the public interest.

It has also been speculated that the adoption of a new method of accounting could have consequences for the amount of taxation that the government ultimately collects from businesses. As Zeff and Dharan (1996, p. 632) state:

> Some governments fear that an accounting regimen of generally lower reported profits under current cost accounting (with physical capital maintenance) would lead to intensified pressure for a concomitant reform of corporate income tax law.

Throughout the 1970s and 1980s, many organisations opposed introduction of alternative methods of accounting (alternative to historical cost). Corporate opposition to various alternative methods of accounting could also be explained by the notion of *self-interest* as embraced within the economic interest theory of regulation. Under historical cost accounting, management has a mechanism available to manage its reported profitability. Holding gains might not be recognised for income purposes until such time as the assets are sold. For example, an organisation might have acquired shares in another organisation some years earlier. In periods in which reported profits are expected to be lower than management wants, management could elect to sell some of the shares to offset other losses. If alternative methods of accounting were introduced, this ability to manipulate reported results could be lost. Hence such corporations might have lobbied government, the basis of the submissions being rooted in self-interest. Because there are typically corporate or business representatives on most standard-setting bodies, there is also the possibility that corporations/business interests were able to effectively *capture* the standard-setting process (Walker, 1987).

As we have already seen in this chapter, there is some evidence that accounting information adjusted to take account of changing prices might not be relevant to the decision making processes of those parties involved in the capital market (as reflected by various share price studies) and hence the alternative models of accounting might not be favoured by analysts (accepting the private economic interest theory of regulation, analysts might have little to gain personally if the alternative methods of accounting were introduced).

Of course we will never know for sure why particular parties did not favour particular accounting models, but what we can see is that alternative explanations can be provided from public interest theory, capture theory, or the economic interest theory of regulation—theories that were discussed at greater length in earlier chapters.

Throughout the CCA/CPPA debates a number of key academics continued to promote their favoured methods of accounting (and some continued to do so through the 1990s), even going so far as to release their own exposure drafts (see Exhibit 4.3). We can obviously speculate what drove them—was it the public interest, or was it self-interest? What do you think?

In concluding this chapter, we can see that the debate is far from settled as to which method of accounting is most appropriate in accounting for changing prices. While debate in this area has generally abated since the mid-1980s it is very possible that, if levels of inflation increase to prior levels, such debates will again be ignited. Various authors have developed accounting models that differ in many respects. Some of these differences are due to

EXHIBIT 4.3 The case of a researcher being creative in gaining support for a particular approach to accounting

Chambers drafts a final method

Professor R. J. Chambers of the University of Sydney has dropped a bombshell on the accounting profession by issuing his own 'exposure draft' on accounting for inflation.

Professor Chambers' pet method—dubbed Continuously Contemporary Accounting (CoCoA)—rivals the two exposure drafts already issued by the Institute of Chartered Accountants and the Australian Society of Accountants.

These cover current purchasing power (CPP) and current value accounting (CVA). The drafts are open for comment and suggestions from the profession until December 31.

Professor Chambers' stand is certain to fragment even further the profession's very lively debate on the most acceptable method. Up until now CVA has been acknowledged to have a slight lead over CPP.

He includes an evaluation of the three methods in his exposure draft. Answering a series of rhetorical questions, his own method comes out clearly on top.

He also says CPP and CVA lead to odd consequences in accounts because they are only partial treatments of changes in prices and price levels.

'The prices of the particular assets of a firm cannot be expected to move at the same rate (or even in the same direction) as a general price index.

'CoCoA realises this fact, which is ignored by CPP—and also takes into account the fall in purchasing power of actual net assets which is ignored by CVA,' he says.

© *The Australian*, 3 November 1975, p. 9.

fundamental differences of opinion about the role of accounting and the sort of information necessary for effective decision making. Because information generated by systems of accounting based on the historical cost convention are used in many decisions, major change in accounting conventions would conceivably have widespread social and economic impacts. This in itself will restrict any major modifications/changes to our (somewhat outdated) accounting system. This perspective was reflected in the 1960s, and arguably the perspective is just as relevant now.

As an example of how the profession has typically been reluctant to implement major reforms, we can consider activities undertaken in 1961 and 1962 where the Accounting Research Division of the American Institute of Certified Public Accountants (AICPA) commissioned studies by Moonitz, and by Sprouse and Moonitz respectively. In these documents the authors proposed that accounting measurement systems be changed from historical cost to a system based on current values. However, prior to the release of the Sprouse and Moonitz study the Accounting Principles Board of the AICPA stated in relation to the Moonitz, and Sprouse and Moonitz studies that 'while these studies are a valuable contribution to accounting principles, they are too radically different from generally accepted principles for acceptance at this time' (Statement by the Accounting Principles Board, AICPA, April 1962).

While this chapter has emphasised various issues and debates associated with how best to measure the financial performance of an entity in times when prices are changing, we must remember that financial performance is only one facet of the total performance of an entity. As we see in Chapter 9, there is much debate about how to measure and report information on the social and environmental performance of reporting entities. As with the debate we have considered in this chapter, the debates about the appropriate methodology and relevance of social and environmental information are far from settled. As has been emphasised, the practice of accounting generates a multitude of interesting debates.

Chapter summary

This chapter has explored different models of accounting that have been developed to provide financial information in periods of rising prices. These models have been developed because of the perceived limitations of historical cost accounting, particularly in times of rising prices. Critics of historical cost accounting suggest that because historical cost adopts a capital maintenance perspective which is tied to maintaining financial capital intact, it tends to overstate profits in periods of rising prices. Historical cost accounting adopts an assumption that the purchasing power of the entity's currency remains constant over time. Debate about the best model of accounting to use in periods of rising prices was vigorous in the 1960s through to the mid-1980s. During this time, inflation levels tended to be relatively high. Since this time, inflation levels internationally have tended to be low and the debate about which model to adopt to adjust for rising prices has tended to wane.

A number of alternative models have been suggested. For example, Current Purchasing Power Accounting (CPPA) was one of the earlier models to be developed. CPPA was supported by a number of professional accounting bodies during the 1960s and 1970s, although support then tended to shift to Current Cost Accounting. CPPA uses numbers generated by the historical cost accounting as the basis of the financial statements and at the end of each period, CPPA applies a price index, typically a general price index, to adjust the historical cost numbers. For balance sheet purposes, adjustments are made to non-monetary assets. Monetary items are not adjusted by the price index. However, although monetary items are not adjusted for disclosure purposes, holding monetary items will lead to gains or losses in purchasing power which are recognised in the period's profit or loss. No gains or losses are recorded in relation to holding non-monetary items. One of the advantages of using CPPA is that it is easy to apply. It simply uses the historical cost accounting numbers that are already available and applies a price index to these numbers. A disadvantage is that the adjusted prices may provide a poor reflection of the actual value of the items in question.

Another model of accounting that we considered was Current Cost Accounting (CCA). It uses actual valuations of assets, typically based on replacement costs, and operating income is calculated after consideration of the replacement costs of the assets used in the production and sale cycle. Non-monetary assets are adjusted to take account of changes in replacement costs, and depreciation expenses are also adjusted on the basis of changes in replacement costs. While not in use today, CCA attracted support from professional accounting bodies in the early 1980s. Opponents of CCA argued that replacement costs have little relevance if an entity is not considering replacing an asset, and further, that replacement costs might not accurately reflect the current market values of the assets in question.

The final model of accounting considered was Continuously Contemporary Accounting (CoCoA). One key objective of CoCoA was to provide information about an entity's capacity to adapt to changing circumstances, with profit being directly related to changes in adaptive capacity. Profit is calculated as the amount that can be distributed while maintaining the adaptive capital intact. CoCoA does not differentiate between realised and unrealised gains. In support of CoCoA, it requires only one type of valuation for all assets (based on exit-prices). There is no need for arbitrary cost allocations, such as depreciation. Criticisms of CoCoA include the relevance of values based on exit (selling) prices if there is no intention of selling an item. Also, many people have challenged the perspective that if an asset cannot be sold separately, it has no value, for example, goodwill. It has also been argued that valuing items on the basis of sales prices can introduce an unacceptable degree of subjectivity into accounting, particularly if the items in question are quite specialised and rarely traded.

References

Ball, R.J., Foster, G., 'Corporate Financial Reporting: A Methodological Review of Empirical Research', *Studies on Current Research Methodologies in Accounting: A Critical Evaluation*, supplement to Vol. 20 of *Journal of Accounting Research*, pp. 161–234, 1982.

Beaver W., Christie, A., and Griffin, P., 'The Information Content of SEC ASR 190', *Journal of Accounting and Economics*, Vol. 2, 1980.

Beaver, W., Landsman, W., 'The Incremental Information Content of FAS 33 Disclosures', *Research Report*, FASB, Stamford, 1987.

Belkaoui, A.R., *Accounting Theory*, Third Edition, The Dryden Press, London, 1992.

Bublitz, B., Freka, T., McKeown, J., 'Market Association Tests and FASB Statement No. 33 Disclosures: A Re-examination', *Journal of Accounting Research*, Supplement, pp. 1–23, 1985.

Canning, J.B., *The Economics of Accountancy: A Critical Analysis of Accounting Theory*, Ronald Press, New York, 1929.

Chambers, R.J., 'An Introduction to Price Variation and Inflation Accounting Research', in *Accounting Theory: A Contemporary Review*, by S. Jones, C. Romana, J. Ratnatunga, Harcourt Brace, Sydney, 1995.

Chambers, R.J., 'Blueprint for a Theory of Accounting', *Accounting Research*, pp. 17–55, January 1955.

Chambers, R.J., *Accounting, Evaluation and Economic Behavior*, Prentice-Hall, Englewood Cliffs, N.J., 1966.

Dyckman, T.R., *Studies in Accounting Research No. 1: Investment Analysis and General Price Level Adjustments*, American Accounting Association, 1969.

Edwards, E., 'The State of Current Value Accounting', *Accounting Review*, Vol. 50, No. 2, pp. 235–45, April 1975.

Edwards, E.O., Bell, P.W., *The Theory and Measurement of Business Income*, University of California Press, Berkeley, 1961.

Elliot, R.K., 'Dinosaurs, Passenger Pigeons, and Financial Accountants', *World*, pp. 32–35, 1986, as reproduced in Zeff, S.A., Dharan, B.G., *Readings and Notes on Financial Accounting*, McGraw-Hill, 5th edition, New York, 1996.

Ferguson, C., Wines, G., 'Incidence of the Use of Current Cost Accounting in Published Annual Financial Statements', *Accounting Forum*, March 1986.

Gheyara, K., Boatsman, J., 'Market Reaction to the 1976 Replacement Cost Disclosures', *Journal of Accounting and Economics*, Vol. 2, 1980.

Grady, P., *An Inventory of Generally Accepted Accounting Principles for Business Enterprises*, Accounting Research Study No. 7, AICPA, New York, 1965.

Gray, R., Owen, D., Adams, C., *Accounting and Accountability: Changes and Challenges in Corporate and Social Reporting*, Prentice-Hall, London, 1996.

Hicks, J.R., *Value and Capital*, Oxford University Press, 1946.

Larson, K., Schattke, R., 'Current Cash Equivalent, Additivity and Financial Action', *Accounting Review*, October, 1966.

Lobo, G., Song, I., 'The Incremental Information in SFAS No. 33 Income Disclosures over Historical Cost Income and its Cash and Accrual Components', *Accounting Review*, Vol. 64, No. 2, pp. 329–43, April 1989.

MacNeal, K., *Truth in Accounting*, Scholars Book Company, Kansas, 1970 (originally published in 1939).

Mautz, R.K., 'A Few Words for Historical Cost', *Financial Executive*, pp. 23–7 & 93–8, January 1973.

Moonitz, M., *The Basic Postulates of Accounting*, Accounting Research Study No. 1, American Institute of Certified Public Accountants, New York, 1961.

Morris, R.C., 'Evidence of the Impact of Inflation on Share Prices', *Accounting and Business Research*, pp. 87–95, Spring 1975.

Murdoch, B., 'The Information Content of FAS 33 Returns on Equity', *The Accounting Review*, Vol. 61, No. 2, pp. 273–87, April 1986.

Paton, W.A., *Accounting Theory*, Scholars Book Co, Kansas, 1922 (reprinted 1973).

Peterson, R.J., 'A Portfolio Analysis of General Price-Level Restatement', *The Accounting Review*, Vol. 50, No. 3, pp. 525–32, July 1975.

Ro, B.T., 'The Adjustment of Security Returns to the Disclosure of Replacement Cost Accounting Information', *Journal of Accounting and Economics*, Vol. 2, 1980.

Ro, B.T., 'The Disclosure of Replacement Cost Accounting Data and its Effect on Transaction Volumes', *Accounting Review*, Vol. 56, No. 1, January 1981.

Schaefer, T., 'The Information Content of Current Cost Income Relative to Dividends and Historical Cost Income', *Journal of Accounting Research*, Vol. 22, pp. 647–56, Autumn 1984.

Solomons, D., 'An Overview of Exit Price Accounting', *ABACUS*, December 1966.

Sprouse, R., Moonitz, M., *A Tentative Set of Broad Accounting Principles for Business Enterprises*, Accounting Research Study No. 3, American Institute of Certified Public Accountants, New York, 1962.

Sterling, R.R., *Theory of the Measurement of Enterprise Income*, University of Kansas Press, 1970.

Sterling, R.R., 'On Theory Construction and Verification', *Accounting Review*, July 1970.

Sutton, T.G., 'The Proposed Introduction of Current Cost Accounting in the UK', *Journal of Accounting and Economics*, Vol. 10, pp. 127–49, 1988.

Sweeney, H.W., *Stabilised Accounting*, Holt Rinehart and Winston, 1964 (originally published in 1936).

Walker, R.G., 'Australia's ASRB—A Case Study of Political Activity and Regulatory Capture', *Accounting and Business Research*, Vol. 17, No. 67, pp. 269–86, 1987.

Watts, R., Zimmerman, J., 'Towards a Positive Theory of the Determination of Accounting Standards', *Accounting Review*, Vol. 53, pp. 112–34, January 1978.

Wong, J., 'Economic Incentives for the Voluntary Disclosure of Current Cost Financial Statements', *Journal of Accounting and Economics*, pp. 151–67, April 1988.

Zeff, S.A., Dharan, B.G., *Readings and Notes on Financial Accounting*, McGraw-Hill, 5th edition, New York, 1996.

Questions

4.1 What assumptions, if any, does historical cost accounting make about the purchasing power of the currency?

4.2 List some of the criticisms that can be made of historical cost accounting when it is applied in times of rising prices.

4.3 As shown in this chapter, Mautz (1973) made the following statement:

Accounting is what it is today not so much because of the desire of accountants as because of the influence of businessmen. If those who make management and investment decisions had not found financial reports based on historical cost useful over the years, changes in accounting would long since have been made.

Required: Evaluate the above statement.

4.4 What is the 'additivity' problem that Chambers refers to?

4.5 Explain the difference between income derived from the viewpoint of maintaining financial capital (as in historical cost accounting) and income derived from a system of ensuring that physical capital remains intact.

4.6 In Current Purchasing Power Accounting:

(a) Why is it necessary to consider monetary assets separately from non-monetary assets?

(b) Why will holding monetary assets lead to a purchasing power loss, but holding non-monetary assets does not lead to a purchasing power loss?

4.7 What is the basis of Chambers' argument against valuing assets on the basis of replacement costs?

4.8 If Continuously Contemporary Accounting is adopted and an organisation is involved with selling inventory, when would the profit from the sale of inventory be recognised? How does this compare with historical cost accounting?

4.9 What are holding gains, and how are holding gains treated if current cost accounting is applied? Do we need to differentiate between realised and unrealised holding gains?

4.10 What are some of the major strengths and weaknesses of historical cost accounting?

4.11 What are some of the major strengths and weaknesses of current purchasing power accounting?

4.12 What are some of the major strengths and weaknesses of current cost accounting (applying replacement costs)?

4.13 What are some of the major strengths and weaknesses of Continuously Contemporary Accounting?

4.14 Evaluate the statement of Chambers (1995, p. 82) that 'in the context of judgement of the past and decision making for the future, the products of Current Value Accounting of the Edwards and Bell variety are irrelevant and misleading. No budget can properly proceed except from an up-to-date statement of the amount of money's worth available to enter the budget period'.

4.15 Evaluate the statement of Edwards (1975, p. 238) that 'I am not convinced of the merit of adopting, as a normal basis for asset valuation in the going concern, exit prices in buyer markets. These are *unusual* values suitable for *unusual* situations. I would not object in principle to keeping track of such exit prices at all times and, as Solomons (1966) has suggested, substituting them for entry values when they are the lesser of the two *and* the firm has taken a definite decision not to replace the asset or even the function it performs'.

4.16 Despite the efforts of authors such as Chambers, Edwards and Bell, and Sterling, historical cost accounting has maintained its position of dominance in how we do financial accounting. Why do you think that historical cost accounting has remained the principal method of accounting?

4.17 As indicated in this chapter, various studies have provided support for a view that CCA/CPPA is of little relevance to users of financial statements. Nevertheless numerous organisations lobbied in support of the methods, as well as voluntarily providing such information in their annual reports. Why do you think this is so?

Chapter 5

Normative theories of accounting—the case of conceptual framework projects

Learning objectives

Upon completing this chapter readers should:

- understand the role that conceptual frameworks can play in the practice of financial reporting;
- be aware of the history of the development of the various existing conceptual framework projects;
- be able to identify, explain and critically evaluate the various building blocks that have been developed within various conceptual framework projects;
- be able to identify some of the perceived advantages and disadvantages that arise from the establishment and development of conceptual frameworks;

- be able to identify some factors, including political factors, that might help or hinder the development of conceptual framework projects;

- be able to explain which groups within society are likely to benefit from the establishment and development of conceptual framework projects.

Opening issues

For many years the practice of financial accounting lacked a generally accepted theory that clearly enunciated the objectives of financial reporting, the required qualitative characteristics of financial information, or provided clear guidance as to when and how to recognise and measure the various elements of accounting. In the absence of an accepted theory, accounting standards tended to be developed in a rather *ad hoc* manner with various inconsistencies between the various standards. For example, various accounting standards relating to different classes of assets use different recognition and measurement criteria. It has been argued that the development of a conceptual framework will lead to improved financial reporting, and this improved reporting will provide benefits to the various financial statement readers as it will enable them to make more informed resource allocation decisions. Do you agree with this argument, and what is the basis of your view?

Introduction

In Chapter 4 we considered a number of normative theories developed by some notable accounting academics to address various accounting issues associated with how financial accounting *should* be undertaken in the presence of changing prices (typically increasing prices associated with inflation). These theories included current purchasing power accounting, current cost accounting and continuously contemporary accounting (or exit price accounting). As revealed in Chapter 4, the various normative theories, which represented quite significant departures from existing accounting practice, failed to be embraced by professional accounting bodies and regulators throughout the world, and with the decline in levels of inflation within most countries, debate about the relative benefits of alternative approaches of accounting for changing prices has subsided in recent years.

While the various normative theories advanced to deal with changing prices did not ultimately gain the support of accounting professions, professional accounting bodies within countries such as the United States, United Kingdom, Canada, Australia and New Zealand (as well as the International Accounting Standards Committee) have undertaken work to develop conceptual frameworks for accounting, which in themselves can be considered to constitute *normative theories of accounting*. In this chapter we consider what is meant by the term 'conceptual framework' and we consider why particular professional bodies thought there was a need to develop them.

We see that there are numerous perceived advantages and disadvantages associated with conceptual frameworks and we consider certain arguments that have been advanced to suggest that conceptual frameworks play a part in *legitimising* the existence of the accounting profession.

What is a conceptual framework of accounting?

There is no definitive view of what constitutes a 'conceptual framework'. The Financial Accounting Standards Board (FASB) in the USA, which developed one of the first conceptual frameworks in accounting, defined its Conceptual Framework as 'a coherent system of interrelated objectives and fundamentals that is expected to lead to consistent standards' (Statement of Financial Accounting Concept No. 1: *Objectives of Financial Reporting by Business Enterprises, 1978*).

In Chapter 1 we provided a definition of 'theory' (from the Macquarie Dictionary) as 'a coherent group of general propositions used as principles of explanation for a class of phenomena'. This definition was very similar to that provided by the accounting researcher Hendriksen (1970, p. 1). He defined a theory as 'a coherent set of hypothetical, conceptual and pragmatic principles forming the general framework of reference for a field of inquiry'. Looking at these definitions of 'theory' and looking at the FASB's definition of its conceptual framework, it is reasonable to argue that the Conceptual Framework attempts to provide a theory of accounting, and one that appears quite structured. Because conceptual frameworks provide a great deal of *prescription* (that is, they prescribe certain actions, such as when to recognise an asset for financial statement purposes) they are considered to have *normative* characteristics. According to FASB, the Conceptual Framework 'prescribes the nature, function and limits of financial accounting and reporting' (as stated in Statement of Financial Accounting Concepts No. 1: *Objectives of Financial Reporting by Business Enterprises*, 1978).

The above view of a conceptual framework is also consistent with the definitions provided within other countries. For example, in Australia the conceptual framework being jointly developed by the Australian Accounting Standards Board and the Australian Accounting Research Foundation (through its Public Sector Accounting Standards Board) consists of a series of Statements of Accounting Concepts (SACs), with the various statements defining the nature, subject, purpose and broad content of general-purpose financial reporting in the private and public sectors (as stated in Policy Statement 5: *The Nature and Purpose of Statements of Accounting Concepts*, issued in 1990).

The view being taken by people involved in developing conceptual frameworks is that if the practice of financial reporting is to be developed logically and consistently (which might be important for creating public confidence in the practice of accounting) we first need to develop some consensus on important issues such as what we actually mean by *financial reporting* and what should be its scope; what organisational characteristics or attributes indicate that an entity should produce financial reports; what the *objective* of financial reporting is; what *qualitative characteristics* financial information should possess; what the elements of financial reporting are; what measurement rules should be employed in relation to the various elements of accounting; and so forth. It has been proposed that unless we have some agreement on fundamental issues, such as those mentioned above, accounting standards will be developed in a rather *ad hoc* or piecemeal manner with limited consistency between the various accounting standards developed over time. It is perhaps somewhat illogical to consider how to account for a particular item of expenditure if we have not agreed in the first place on what the *objective* of financial accounting actually is, or indeed on issues such as what an *asset* is or what a *liability* is. Nevertheless, for many years accounting standards were developed in many countries in the absence of conceptual frameworks.[1] This in itself led to a great deal of criticism. As Horngren (1981, p. 94) states:

> *All regulatory bodies have been flayed because they have used piecemeal approaches, solving one accounting issue at a time. Observers have alleged that not enough tidy rationality has been used in the process of accounting policymaking. Again and again, critics have cited a need for a conceptual framework.*

In developing a conceptual framework for accounting it is considered that there are a number of 'building blocks' that must be developed. The framework must be developed in a particular order, with some issues necessarily requiring agreement before work can move on to subsequent 'building blocks'. Figure 5.1 provides an overview of the framework adopted by Australian accounting standard-setters.

As we can see, the first issue to be addressed is the definition of *financial reporting*. Unless there is some agreement on this it would be difficult to construct a framework for financial reporting. Having determined what financial reporting means, attention is then turned to the *subject* of financial reporting, specifically which entities are required to produce general purpose financial reports.[2] Attention is then turned to the *objective* of

---

1. For example, in Australia the first Statement of Accounting Concept (SAC 1: Definition of the Reporting Entity) was released in 1990. However, recommendations related to the practice of accounting first started being released in the 1940s, followed some years later by accounting standards. By the time the first Statement of Accounting Concepts was issued there were already many accounting standards in place. Reflective of the lack of agreement in many key areas of financial reporting, there was a degree of inconsistency between the various accounting standards.

2. Conceptual frameworks of accounting relate to general purpose financial reporting (which meets the needs of a multitude of user groups, many of which have information needs in common) as opposed to special purpose financial reports (special purpose financial reports are specifically designed to meet the information needs of a specific user or group). We consider definitions of general purpose financial reporting in more depth later in this chapter.

Building blocks of a Conceptual Framework for general-purpose financial reporting

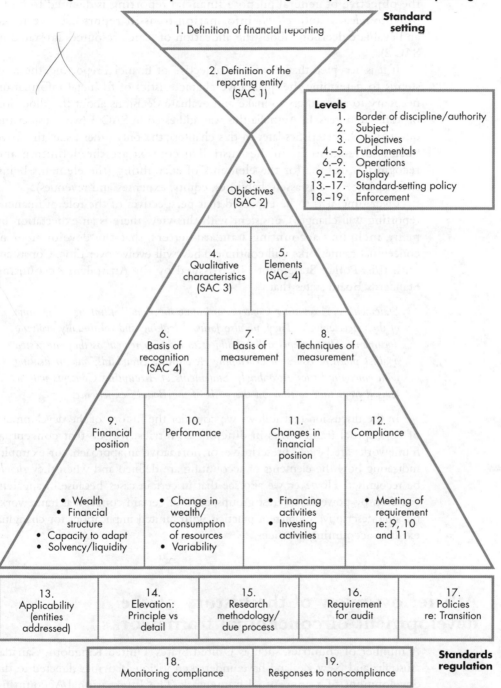

Source: Policy Statement 5—The Nature and Purpose of Statements of Accounting Concepts, issued in 1995.

FIGURE 5.1 **The conceptual framework**

financial reporting. As we will see shortly, in Australia, and elsewhere, the objective of general purpose financial reporting is deemed to be to provide *relevant* and *reliable* information to assist report users to make and evaluate decisions about the allocation of scarce resources (as stated in SAC 2).

If it is accepted that this is the objective of financial reporting, the next step is to determine the qualitative characteristics of financial information necessary to allow users to make and evaluate decisions about the allocation of scarce resources. In Australia this was addressed in SAC 3 (we consider the qualitative characteristics later in this chapter); the only other issues that have been addressed so far in the Australian context are the definition and recognition criteria for the elements of accounting (the elements being defined in SAC 4 as assets, liabilities, equity, expenses and revenues).

Over time, it is to be expected that perspectives of the role of financial reporting will change. Consistent with this view there is an expectation by many, including accounting standard-setters, that the development of conceptual frameworks will continue. They will evolve over time. Consistent with this, Policy Statement No. 5 issued by the Australian Accounting Standards Board states that:

> *Statements of Accounting Concepts articulate the Board's thinking at the time of their development. They are also forward looking and continually evolving documents. The concepts will be subject to ongoing review as they are tested against practical issues in developing Accounting Standards, and in dealing with emerging issues. Accordingly, Statements of Accounting Concepts will be revised from time to time on the basis of the Board's experience.*

In the discussion that follows we consider the history of the development of conceptual frameworks in different countries. We see that conceptual frameworks are largely prescriptive, or normative in approach, for example, indicating how the elements of accounting are defined and when they *should* be recognised. However, we also see that in certain cases, because of apparent coercion by powerful interest groups, parts of certain conceptual frameworks became descriptive of current practice, with limited implications for changing existing accounting practices.

A brief overview of the history of the development of conceptual frameworks

A number of countries, such as United States, United Kingdom, Canada, Australia and New Zealand have undertaken various activities directed to the development of a conceptual framework. The International Accounting Standards Committee has also done work to develop a conceptual framework. There are many similarities (and some differences) between the various conceptual frameworks being developed in the different jurisdictions.[3] No standard-setter anywhere in the world has developed what could be construed as a complete conceptual framework, and indeed most activities can be considered to be quite partial. Evidence also tends to show that in recent years, work on conceptual frameworks in various countries has tended to be put on hold, with limited progress being achieved recently. There is no clear reason for this, but some possible reasons are provided (including that conceptual frameworks tended to get to a stage where they became too controversial and not acceptable to broader business constituencies).

One country particularly active in developing frameworks in relation to financial reporting was the United States. Initially, some of the work involved developing *prescriptive* theories of how accounting *should* be undertaken, while other research related to the development of *descriptive* theories of how accounting was generally performed. For example, in 1961 and 1962 the Accounting Research Division of the American Institute of Certified Public Accountants (AICPA) commissioned studies by Moonitz (1961) and Sprouse and Moonitz (1962). These theorists prescribed that accounting practice should move towards a system based on current values, rather than historical cost. This work was considered 'too radically different from generally accepted principles' (AICPA, 1962) and was abandoned by the profession. The AICPA then commissioned Grady to develop a theory of accounting. Grady (1965) was basically descriptive of existing practice, thereby being quite uncontroversial. His work led to the release of APB Statement No. 4, *Basic Concepts and Accounting Principles Underlying the Financial Statements of Business Enterprises* in 1970. As it was not controversial and simply reflected generally accepted accounting principles of the time, APB Statement No. 4 had a high probability of being acceptable to the AICPA's constituency (Miller and Reading, 1986).

Although APB Statement No. 4 did not cause great controversy, the accounting profession was under some criticism for the apparent lack of any real framework.[4] The generally accepted accounting principles of the time allowed for much diversity in accounting treatments and this was seen by many to be a problem. There was an absence of agreement on key issues

---

3. This raises issues associated with the possible duplication of effort and whether it might be more cost-efficient for the various countries to pool their resources and develop one unified conceptual framework. However as Kenneth Most states in Staunton (1984, p. 87) when comparing the Australian and United States conceptual frameworks, 'a conceptual framework differs from a straight-jacket; one size does not fit all. The kind of doctrinaire thinkers who have dominated the standard-setting process in this country (United States) are not subject to the same economic, sociological, and professional influences that would affect Australians faced with a similar task'. Chapter 6 considers how issues such as *culture* are used to explain differences between the rules released by standard-setters in different countries.

4. In relation to APB Statement No. 4, Peasnell (1982, p. 245) notes that 'at best it was a defensive, descriptive document'.

about the role and objectives of financial reporting, appropriate definition, recognition and measurement rules for the elements of accounting, and so on. Responding to the criticism, the AICPA formed the Trueblood Committee (named after the committee chairman, Robert Trueblood) in 1971. It provided a report, The Trueblood Report (released in 1973 by the AICPA), which listed 12 objectives of accounting and seven qualitative characteristics that financial information should possess (relevance and materiality; form and substance; reliability; freedom from bias; comparability; consistency; understandability).

Objective 1 of the report was that financial statements are to provide information useful for making economic decisions. That is, there was a focus on the information needs of financial statement users. This objective, which was carried forward to subsequent documents, indicated that decision usefulness (as opposed to concepts such as *stewardship*) was a primary objective of financial statements.[5] This can be contrasted with previous perspectives of the role of accounting. For example, Accounting Terminology Bulletin No. 1 issued in 1953 by the AICPA made no reference to the information needs of users. It stated:

> *Accounting is the art of recording, classifying and summarizing in a significant manner and in terms of money, transactions and events which are in part at least of a financial character, and interpreting the results thereof.*

Objective 2 provided by the Trueblood Committee stated that financial statements are to primarily serve those users who have limited authority, ability, or resources to obtain information and who rely on financial statements as the principal source of information about an organisation's activities. This objective, which was also carried forward in subsequent work, was interesting in that it tended to be a departure from much research that was being carried on at the time. A great deal of research being undertaken in the late 1960s and thereafter had embraced the *efficient markets hypothesis* (discussed more fully in Chapter 10) that markets react quickly to impound the information content of publicly available information, whenever that information first becomes publicly available. Researchers working with the efficient markets hypothesis considered that as long as the information is publicly available to somebody, then given an assumption of market efficiency, this information would quickly be dispersed among all interested users. The Trueblood Committee and subsequent committees responsible for development of conceptual frameworks within the United States and elsewhere did not appear to embrace this view of market efficiency.

The Trueblood Committee acknowledged that a variety of different valuation methods were used for different classes of assets and liabilities. This

---

5. This focus on decision users' needs was also embraced in the earlier document, A Statement of Basic Accounting Theory, issued by the American Accounting Association in 1966. It was also embraced in APB Statement No. 4 released in 1970.

had been an issue that had concerned a number of researchers, such as Raymond Chambers (as indicated in Chapter 4). However, the Trueblood Committee noted that they considered that different valuation rules are relevant for different classes of assets, thereby ignoring the 'additivity problem' raised by individuals such as Chambers. As we will see shortly, prescribing a particular valuation or measurement approach is an activity that those responsible for developing conceptual frameworks have been reluctant to undertake.

In 1974 the Accounting Principles Board within the United States was replaced by the Financial Accounting Standards Board (FASB). The FASB embarked on its conceptual framework project early in its existence and the first release, Statement of Financial Accounting Concepts No. 1: *Objectives of Financial Reporting by Business Enterprises*, occurred in 1978. This was followed by the release of five more SFACs, with the latest one, SFAC No. 6, being issued in 1985. The initial SFACs were quite normative. However, when SFAC No. 5: *Recognition and Measurement in Financial Statements of Business Enterprises,* was released in 1984 the FASB appeared to opt for an approach largely descriptive of current practice. Rather than prescribe a particular valuation approach the FASB described some of the various valuation approaches commonly used: historical cost, current cost (replacement cost), current market value (exit value), net realisable value (amount gained from sale, less costs associated with the sale) and the present (discounted) value of future cash flows. The failure to take the lead and prescribe a particular valuation approach was referred to as a 'cop-out' by Solomons (1986). This view was also embraced by a number of others. For example, Nussbaumer (1992, p. 238) states:

> . . . the issuance of SFAC 5 (December 1984) marked the greatest disappointment of the FASB's project for the conceptual framework. It did nothing more than describe present practice; it was not prescriptive at all. The recognition and measurement issues, which the FASB promised to deal with in SFAC 5, were not settled, and the measurement issue was sidestepped. . . . If the FASB cannot reach an agreement when there are only seven members, it is unlikely that the profession as a whole will come to agreement on these issues either. The FASB should provide leadership to the profession on these issues and not compromise them for the sake of expediency.

In a similar vein, Miller (1990) argued that the FASB conceptual framework in accounting initially provided much needed reform to accounting. For example, SFAC No. 1 explicitly put financial report users' needs at the forefront of consideration. However, when SFAC No. 5 was released, 'momentum was lost when FASB did not have sufficient political will to face down the counter-reformation and endorse expanded use of current values in the recognition and measurement phase of the project' (Miller, 1990, p. 32). Interestingly, since SFAC 5 was released there has been very limited activity in the FASB conceptual framework project. SFAC 6 was released in 1985, but this was primarily a replacement of an early statement (SFAC 3). No further SFACs have been released. It would appear that measurement issues represented a real stumbling block for the project. Had the FASB supported one valuation method over and above others, this would have been a dramatic departure from current accounting practice and may not have been palatable to its constituents. Although this is conjecture, perhaps the FASB went as far as it could politically. We consider this issue in more depth later in this chapter.

If we turn our attention to other conceptual framework projects we see that their degree of progression has also been slow. In Australia, work on the conceptual framework started in the 1980s with the first Statement of Accounting Concept being issued in 1990. To date only four SACs have been released: Definitions of the Reporting Entity (SAC 1); Objectives of General Purpose Financial Reporting (SAC 2); Qualitative Characteristics of Financial Information (SAC 3); and Definition and Recognition of the Elements of Financial Statements (SAC 4). While a fifth SAC related to measurement issues has been expected for many years it has yet to be released.[6] As we see later in this chapter, the Australian conceptual framework had a number of similarities to the FASB project and as with the FASB, prescribing a particular measurement principle has appeared to be a major stumbling block.

In the United Kingdom an early move towards developing guidance in relation to the objectives and the identification of the users of financial statements, as well as the methods to be used in financial reporting, was provided by *The Corporate Report*—a discussion paper released in 1976 by the Accounting Standards Steering Committee of the Institute of Chartered Accountants in England and Wales. As we see in subsequent discussion in this chapter, *The Corporate Report* was particularly concerned with addressing the *rights* of the community in terms of their access to financial information about the entities operating in their community. The view taken was that if the community gives an organisation permission to operate, then that organisation has an *accountability* to the community and this accountability includes an obligation to provide information about its financial performance. This perspective of financial statement users was broader than that adopted in frameworks being developed in other countries and involved groups that did not have a direct financial interest in the organisation, but were nevertheless impacted by its ongoing operations.

The Corporate Report was also part of a UK Government Green Paper on Law Reform. The report ultimately did not become enshrined in law and its contents were generally not accepted by the accounting profession. In 1991 the Accounting Standards Board adopted the International Accounting Standards Committee's (IASC's) *Framework for the Preparation and Presentation of Financial Statements* and abandoned the broader notions of *users' rights* raised in *The Corporate Report*. The IASC framework is generally consistent with the United States and Australian frameworks.

Other countries such as Canada and New Zealand have devoted resources to the development of a conceptual framework. In Canada, initial efforts were

---

6. However, in December 1998 an Accounting Theory Monograph entitled *Measurement in Financial Accounting* was released by the Australian Accounting Research Foundation.

incorporated in a document entitled *Corporate Reporting: Its Future Evolution*, which was released in 1980. This report was written by Edward Stamp and became known as *The Stamp Report*. This report appeared to rely heavily on *The Corporate Report* and like *The Corporate Report*, was not embraced by the accounting profession. Subsequently, further work has been undertaken towards developing a conceptual framework with a number of similarities to the FASB project. In 1990 the Accounting Research and Standards Board in New Zealand also commenced some work related to a conceptual framework. It has many similarities to other frameworks developed in other countries.

What the above information demonstrates is that a number of countries have devoted resources to the development of a conceptual framework. What also is apparent is that those responsible for the frameworks have either been reluctant to promote significant changes from accounting practice (which obviously limits their ability to generate significant changes in financial reporting), or where frameworks have suggested significant changes, such changes have not been embraced by the accounting professions and many of their constituents. The reasons for this are provided in the discussion that follows.

Building blocks of a conceptual framework

In this section we consider some of the guidance that has already been produced in existing conceptual framework projects. We consider issues such as definition of a reporting entity; the objectives of general purpose financial reporting; the perceived users of general purpose financial reports; the qualitative characteristics that general purpose financial reports should possess; the elements of financial statements; and discussions of possible approaches to measuring the elements of financial statements.

Definition of the reporting entity

One key issue in any discussion about financial reporting is what characteristics of an entity provide an indication of an apparent need for it to produce general purpose financial reports. The term *general purpose financial reports* refers to financial reports that comply with accounting standards and other generally accepted accounting principles and are released by reporting entities to satisfy the information demands of a varied cross-section of users. They can be contrasted with special purpose financial reports, which are provided to meet the information demands of a particular user, or group of users. As stated earlier, the guidance that we consider in this chapter relates to general purpose financial reports.

Clearly, not all entities should be expected to produce general purpose financial reports. For example, there would be limited benefits in requiring a small owner/manager to prepare general purpose financial reports (which comply with the numerous accounting standards) for his or her small corner shop. There would be few external users with a significant stake or interest in the organisation. While limited guidance is provided by some conceptual frameworks in relation to this issue (for example, limited guidance is provided by the FASB framework), the Australian conceptual framework does provide some guidance in SAC 1: *Definition of the Reporting Entity*. According to SAC 1, general-purpose financial reports should be prepared by all *reporting entities*. Consistent with the discussion above, general-purpose financial reports are considered to be reports that comply with Statements of Accounting Concepts and Accounting Standards. Paragraph 6 of SAC 1 further defines them as reports:

> . . . intended to meet the information needs common to users who are unable to command the preparation of reports tailored so as to satisfy, specifically, all of their information needs.

Further, paragraph 8 of SAC 1 states that general-purpose financial reports should be prepared when there are users:

> . . . whose information needs have common elements, and those users cannot command the preparation of information to satisfy their individual information needs.

If an entity is not deemed to be a *reporting entity* (that is, there are no users dependent upon general purpose financial reports), it will not be required to produce general purpose financial reports—that is, it will not necessarily be required to comply with accounting standards.

Hence, whether an entity is classified as a *reporting entity* is determined by the information needs of the users, and relies upon professional judgement. When information relevant to decision making is not otherwise accessible to users who are judged to be dependent upon general-purpose financial reports to make and evaluate resource-allocation decisions, the entity is deemed to be a *reporting entity*. Where dependence is not readily apparent, SAC 1 suggests factors that may indicate a reporting entity (and hence a need to produce general purpose financial reports) including:

- the separation of management from those with an economic interest in the entity (paragraph 20)—as the spread of ownership increases and/or the separation of management and ownership increases, the greater the likelihood becomes that an entity will be considered to be a reporting entity;

- the economic or political importance/influence of the entity to/on other parties (paragraph 21)—as the entity's dominance in the market increases and/or its potential influence over the welfare of external parties increases, the greater is the likelihood that an entity will be considered to be a reporting entity;

- the financial characteristics of the entity (paragraph 22)—as the amount of sales, value of assets, extent of indebtedness, number of customers and number of employees increases, the greater is the likelihood that an entity will be considered to be a reporting entity.

Clearly, the approach adopted within Australia towards defining a reporting entity is highly subjective and could lead to conflicting opinions about whether an entity is a reporting entity or not. Interestingly, Australian law has developed more objective criteria for determining when a company is required to provide financial statements that comply with accounting standards, and these criteria, which are written into *The Corporations Law*, are related to measures such as gross revenue, dollar value of assets, and number of employees.[7]

Objectives of general purpose financial reporting

Over time, a number of objectives have been attributed to information provided with financial statements.[8] A traditionally cited objective was to enable outsiders to assess the *stewardship* of management. That is, whether the resources entrusted to management have been used for their intended or appropriate purposes. It is generally accepted that historical cost accounting enables management to effectively report on the stewardship of the resources provided to the reporting entity.

Another objective of financial reporting, and one that has become a commonly accepted goal of financial reporting, is to assist in report users' economic decision making. That is, in recent times, less emphasis is placed on the stewardship function of financial reports. For example, the FASB notes in SFAC 1 that a major objective of financial reporting is that it:

> . . . *should provide information that is useful to present and potential investors and creditors and other users in making rational investment, credit and similar decisions.*

This objective refers to 'rational' decisions. It is commonly accepted in the economics and accounting literature that a 'rational decision' is one that maximises expected utility, with this utility typically considered to be related to the maximisation of wealth. The FASB framework emphasises the information needs of those who have a financial stake in the reporting entity. For example, the above objective refers to the needs of present and potential investors and creditors. It also refers to the needs of 'others', but the 'others' are also explained in terms of having financial interests in the reporting entity.

This focus on the information needs of financial report users has also been embraced in other conceptual frameworks. For example, in SAC 2

---

7. Within Australia the SACs are not mandatory. Hence while SAC 1 provides guidance in determining whether an entity is a reporting entity, this guidance is not enforced.

8. In a FASB Discussion Memorandum released in 1974, the FASB defines an objective as 'something toward which effort is directed, an aim, or end of action, a goal'. It is perhaps questionable whether information itself can have objectives. Certainly, users of information can have objectives which can be achieved (or not) as a result of using information. Nevertheless, it is common for accounting standard-setters to talk about the objectives of financial information, and as such, we maintain this convention.

issued within Australia the objective of general-purpose financial reporting is deemed to be 'to provide information to users that is useful for making and evaluating decisions about the allocation of scarce resources'.[9]

Once we move towards *decision usefulness*, an objective recently embraced within conceptual framework projects, we might question whether historical cost information (which arguably is useful for assessing stewardship) is useful for financial report users' decisions, such as whether to invest in, or lend funds to, an organisation. Arguably, such decisions could be more effectively made if information on current market values was made available.[10]

Apart from *stewardship* and *decision usefulness*, another commonly cited objective of financial reporting is to enable reporting entities to demonstrate *accountability* between the entity and those parties to which the entity is deemed to be accountable. Gray, Owen and Adams (1996, p. 38) provide a definition of accountability: 'the duty to provide an account or reckoning of those actions for which one is held responsible'. Issues that arise here are *to whom* is a reporting entity accountable, and *for what*? There is a multitude of opinions on this. Within the FASB project it would appear that those responsible for developing a framework considered that there is a duty to provide an account of the entity's financial performance to those parties who have a direct financial stake in the reporting entity. Emphasis seems to be placed on economic efficiencies. This can be contrasted with the guidance provided by *The Corporate Report* (UK) which argues that society effectively allows organisations to exist as long as they accept certain responsibilities, one being that they are accountable for their actions to society generally, rather than solely to those that have a financial stake in the entity. *The Corporate Report* makes the following statement at paragraph 25:

> *The public's right to information arises not from a direct financial or human relationship with the reporting entity but from the general role played in our society by economic entities. Such organisations, which exist with the general consent of the community, are afforded special legal and operational privileges; they compete for resources of manpower, materials and energy and they make use of community owned assets such as roads and harbours.*

Although *The Corporate Report* emphasised an accountability perspective of financial reporting, it was generally not accepted, and the UK position, through its subsequent adoption of the IASC Framework, is basically one of

---

9. These objectives are also consistent with the IASC framework. It states that the objective of financial reporting is 'to provide information about the financial position, performance, and changes in financial position of an enterprise that is useful to a wide range of users in making economic decisions'.

10. Within Chambers' model of accounting, Continuously Contemporary Accounting, which is covered in Chapter 4, one objective of financial accounting is to provide information about the *adaptive capacity* of an entity. Historical cost information does not help meet this objective.

acceptance of the *decision makers' emphasis* with prime consideration being given to the needs of those with a financial interest or stake in the organisation.

Users of financial reports

In the above discussion we briefly considered perspectives of who the users of financial reports are. We now extend this discussion. We also consider the level of expertise such users are perceived to require. In Australia, SAC 2: *Objective of General-purpose Financial Reporting* identifies three primary user groups of general-purpose financial reports: resource providers, recipients of goods and services, and parties performing a review or oversight function. Resource providers are defined as including employees, lenders, creditors, suppliers, investors and contributors, while the recipients of goods and services are deemed to include customers and beneficiaries. Parties performing a review or oversight function include parliaments, governments, regulatory agencies, analysts, labour unions, employer groups, media, and special interest groups.

Hence, the definition of users provided by SAC 2 is quite broad, and through reference to such parties as 'special interest groups' could be construed as embracing the 'public'. While perhaps not as broad as the definition provided by *The Corporate Report* (UK) which considered 'rights' to information which are not necessarily linked to resource allocation decisions, the definition of users provided in the Australian document is broader than that provided by the FASB. In SFAC 1 the main focus of financial reports is present and potential investors and other users (with either a direct financial interest, or somehow related to those with a financial interest, for example, stockbrokers, analysts, lawyers, or regulatory bodies). Within SFAC 1 there appears to be limited consideration of the public being a legitimate user of financial reports.

The issue as to which groups should be considered to be legitimate users of financial information about an organisation is an argument that has attracted a great deal of debate. There are many, such as the authors of *The Corporate Report*, who hold that all groups impacted by an organisation's operations have *rights* to information about the reporting entity, including financial information, regardless of whether they are contemplating resource allocation decisions. In the Australian Conceptual Framework, however, whether an entity is deemed to be a *reporting entity* and therefore required to produce *general purpose financial reports* is related to future resource allocation decisions. SAC 1, paragraph 12, provides that:

> . . . *individual reporting entities be identified by reference to the existence of users who are dependent on general-purpose financial reports for information for making and evaluating resource allocation decisions.*

Many would question whether the need for information to enable 'resource allocation decisions' is the only or dominant issue to consider in determining whether an organisation has a public obligation to provide information about its performance.

In considering the issue of the level of expertise expected of financial report readers it has generally been accepted that readers are expected to have some proficiency in financial accounting, and as a result, accounting standards are developed on this basis. The FASB conceptual framework refers to the 'informed reader'. In Australia, Paragraph 36 of SAC 3 provides:

> General-purpose financial reports ought to be constructed having regard to the interests of users who are prepared to exercise diligence in reviewing those reports and who possess the proficiency necessary to comprehend the significance of contemporary accounting practices.

In considering the required qualitative characteristics financial information should possess (for example, relevance, understandability), some assumptions about the ability of report users are required. It would appear that those responsible for developing conceptual frameworks have accepted that individuals without any expertise in accounting are not the intended audience of reporting entities' reports (even though such people may have a considerable amount of their own wealth invested). We now consider some of the suggested *qualitative characteristics* of financial information.

Qualitative characteristics of financial reports

If it is accepted that financial information should be useful for economic decision making, as conceptual frameworks indicate, then a subsequent issue to consider (or in terms of the terminology used earlier, a subsequent 'building block' to consider) is the *qualitative characteristics* (attributes or qualities) that financial information should have if it is to be *useful* for such decisions (implying that an absence of such qualities would mean that the central objectives of general purpose financial reports would not be met).

Conceptual frameworks have dedicated a great deal of their material to discussing qualitative characteristics of financial information. The primary qualitative characteristics have been identified as *relevance* and *reliability*.[11] In the Australian Conceptual framework project, information is considered to be *reliable* if it 'faithfully represents' the entity's transactions and events (SAC 3, paragraph 16). For information to be reliable, it should be free from *bias* (paragraph 21) and be free from *undue error* (paragraph 22). Within the United States, SFAC 2 defines reliability as 'the quality of information that assures that information is reasonably free from error and bias and faithfully represents what it purports to represent'. SFAC 2 notes that reliability is a function of *representational faithfulness, verifiability,* and *neutrality.* According to SFAC 2,

---

11. For example, these have been identified as primary qualitative characteristics in SAC 3 and SFAC 2 as well as in earlier documents such as *A Statement of Basic Accounting Theory*, 1966; APB Statement No. 4, 1970; and *The Trueblood Report*, 1973. They are also identified in the IASC's *Framework for the Preparation and Presentation of Financial Statements*.

representational faithfulness refers to the 'correspondence or agreement between a measure or description and the phenomenon that it purports to represent'. *Verifiability* is defined in SFAC 2 as 'the ability through consensus among measurers to ensure that information represents what it purports to represent, or that the chosen method of measurement has been used without error or bias'. *Neutrality* implies that the information was not constructed or compiled to generate a predetermined result.

Introducing notions of reliability with the associated notions of *neutrality* and *representational faithfulness* have implications for how financial accounting has traditionally been practised. Traditionally, accountants have adopted the doctrine of conservatism. In practice, this means that asset values should never be shown at amounts in excess of their realisable values (but they can be understated), and liabilities should never be understated (although it is generally acceptable for liabilities to be overstated). That is, there has traditionally been a bias towards undervaluing the *net assets* of an entity. It would appear that such a doctrine is not consistent with the qualitative characteristic of 'freedom from bias', as financial statements should, arguably, not be biased in one direction or another.

Turning to the other primary qualitative characteristic, something is deemed to be *relevant* if it 'influences' decisions on the allocation of scarce resources (SAC 3). According to SFAC 2, something is relevant if it is 'capable of making a difference in a decision by helping users to form predictions about the outcomes of past, present and future events, or to confirm or correct expectations'. According to SFAC 2 there are two main aspects to relevance—for information to be relevant it should have both *predictive value* and *feedback value*, the latter referring to the information's utility in confirming or correcting earlier expectations.

Closely tied to the notion of *relevance* is the notion of *materiality*. This is embodied in various conceptual framework projects. For example, paragraph 48 of SAC 3 states that general-purpose financial reports shall include all financial information that satisfies the concepts of relevance and reliability to the extent that such information is *material*. According to the statement (paragraph 28), an item is material if:

> . . . *omission, misstatement or non-disclosure of an item of relevant and reliable information could affect decision-making about the allocation of scarce resources by the users of a general-purpose financial report of an entity.*

Within SFAC 2, something is deemed to be material if 'it is probable that the judgement of a reasonable person relying upon the report would have been changed or influenced by the inclusion or correction of the item'. Considerations of materiality provide the basis for restricting the amount of information provided to levels that are comprehensible to financial statement users. It would arguably be poor practice to provide hundreds of pages of potentially relevant and reliable information to report readers—this would only result in an overload of information. Nevertheless, materiality is a heavily judgemental issue and at times we could expect that it might actually be used as a justification for failing to disclose some information that might be deemed to be potentially harmful to the reporting entity.

Although *relevance* and *reliability* are identified as the primary qualitative characteristics that financial information should have, secondary characteristics have been identified to include comparability, uniformity, consistency and timeliness. Desirable characteristics such as uniformity and consistency imply that there are advantages in restricting the number of accounting methods that can be used by reporting entities. However, any actions that lead to a reduction in the accounting methods that can be used by reporting entities has been argued to lead potentially to reductions in the efficiency with which organisations operate (Watts and Zimmerman, 1986). For example, management might elect to use a particular accounting method because it believes that for their particular and perhaps unique circumstances the specific method of accounting best reflects their underlying performance. Restricting the use of the specific method can result in a reduction in how efficiently external parties can monitor the performance of the entity, and this in itself has been assumed to lead to increased costs for the reporting entity (this 'efficiency perspective', which has been applied in Positive Accounting Theory, is explored in Chapter 7).

If it is assumed, consistent with the *efficiency perspective* briefly mentioned above, that firms adopt particular accounting methods because the methods best reflect the underlying economic performance of the entity, then it is argued by some theorists that the regulation of financial accounting imposes unwarranted costs on reporting entities. For example, if a new accounting standard is released that bans an accounting method being used by particular organisations, this will lead to inefficiencies, as the resulting financial statements will no longer provide the best reflection of the performance of the organisation. Many theorists would argue that management is best able to select appropriate accounting methods in given circumstances, and government and/or others should not intervene.

Another consideration that needs to be addressed when deciding whether to disclose particular information is the *cost* of making the disclosures, versus the *benefits* such disclosures will generate. For example, in Australia, SAC 3 states (paragraphs 42 to 45):

> *A major difficulty facing preparers, auditors, standard-setters and others is whether the cost of providing certain financial information exceeds the benefits to be derived from its provision. The costs could include those of collection, storage, retrieval, presentation, analysis and interpretation of the information, possible loss or diminution of competitive position and, if the information is not reliable, misdirection of resources and other related undesirable consequences. The benefits of financial information will come from sound economic decision making by the various user groups . . . There is no universally acceptable methodology for measuring costs and benefits of financial information. It is a matter of professional judgement by those who have to prepare, or influence the preparation of, financial information. Standard-setters*

and regulators of financial information need to employ processes for gathering information about the merits of requirements they are proposing . . . In the process of setting accounting standards, standard-setters seek to consider all costs and benefits in relation to financial reporting generally, and not just as they pertain to individual reporting entities.

Obviously, consideration of costs and benefits of disclosure is a highly subjective activity and requires decisions about many issues (and we might question the statement made above that standard-setters seek to consider *all* costs and benefits—is this possible?). From whose perspective are we to consider costs and benefits? Are costs and benefits attributable to some users' groups more or less important than others, and so on. Any analysis of costs and benefits is highly judgemental and open to critical comment.

Can financial statements provide neutral and unbiased accounts of an entity's performance and position?

A review of existing conceptual frameworks, as reflected by some of the material provided above, indicates that they provide a perspective that accounting can, if performed properly, provide an *objective (neutral* and *representationally faithful)* view of the performance and position of a reporting entity. Reflecting on this apparent perspective, Hines (1991, p. 314) states:

. . . it appears that the ontological assumption underpinning the Conceptual Framework is that the relationship between financial accounting and economic reality is a unidirectional, reflecting or faithfully reproducing relationship: economic reality exists objectively, intersubjectively, concretely and independently of financial accounting practices; financial accounting reflects, mirrors, represents or measures the pre-existent reality.

In fact, the role of a well functioning system of accounting has been compared with that of cartography. That is, just as an area can be objectively 'mapped', some have argued that so can the financial position and performance of an organisation (Solomons, 1978). But as we would appreciate, the practice of accounting is heavily based on professional judgement. As we see in the next section, definitions of the elements of financial accounting are, in some jurisdictions, explicitly tied to assessments of probabilities. Clearly there is a degree of subjectivity associated with such assessments.

Although conceptual frameworks argue for attributes such as neutrality and representational faithfulness, we should perhaps take time to question whether it is valid or realistic to believe that financial accounting provides an objective perspective of an entity's performance. In Chapter 3 we considered research that investigated the economic consequences of accounting regulations. It was argued that before an accounting standard-setting body releases new or amended reporting requirements, it attempts to consider the economic consequences that would follow from the decision. Even if a proposed accounting rule was considered the *best* way to account (however this is determined—which of course would be an issue provoking much debate), if this would lead to significant costs being imposed on particular parties (for example, preparers) then plans to require the approach could be abandoned by the standard-setters. Once a profession starts considering the *economic consequences* of particular accounting standards, it is difficult to perceive that the accounting standards, and therefore accounting, can really be considered objective or neutral.

Tied to issues associated with economic implications, there is a body of literature (Positive Accounting Theory, which we have already briefly discussed and which we consider in Chapter 7) that suggests that those responsible for preparing financial statements will be driven by self-interest to select accounting methods that lead to outcomes that provide favourable outcomes for their own personal wealth. That is, this literature predicts that managers and others involved in the accounting function will always put their self-interests ahead of those of others.[12] *If* we accept this body of literature, we would perhaps dismiss notions of objectivity or neutrality as being unrealistic. Self-interest perspectives are often used to explain the phenomenon of 'creative accounting'—a situation where those responsible for the preparation of financial reports select accounting methods that provide the most desired outcomes from their own perspective.

Accounting Standards and Statements of Accounting Concepts form the foundation of general-purpose financial reporting. As we have noted in earlier chapters, Accounting Standards and Statements of Accounting Concepts are developed through public consultation, which involves the release of exposure drafts and, subsequently, a review of the written submissions made by various interested parties, including both the preparers and users of the financial information. Consequently, the process leading to finalised Accounting Standards and Statements of Accounting Concepts can be considered to be political. The political solutions and compromises impact on the financial information being presented and that information is, therefore, an outcome of a political process—a process where parties with particular attributes (power) may be able to have a relatively greater impact on final reporting requirements than other parties. This can be considered to have implications for the objectivity or neutrality of the financial information being disclosed.[13]

---

12. One example that is often provided by proponents of Positive Accounting Theory is managers being provided with a bonus tied to the output of the accounting system, for example, to profits. It would be argued in such a case that managers will have incentives to increase reported profits, rather than be objective.

13. Hines (1989, p. 80) argues that many individuals not involved in the standard-setting process would be very surprised to find out just how political the development of accounting standards actually is. She states 'an accounting outsider might find it remarkable that accounting knowledge should be articulated not only by professional accountants, but also by accounting information users—much like doctors and patients collaborating on the development of medical knowledge'.

Hines is one author who has written quite a deal of material on what she sees as the apparent 'myth' of accounting neutrality. Hines (1988) argues that parties involved in the practice and regulation of accounting impose their own judgements about what attributes of an entity's performance should be emphasised (for example, *profits* or *return on assets*), and also, what attributes of an entity's operations (for example, expenditure on employee health and safety initiatives) are not important enough to emphasise or highlight separately. The accountant can determine, under the 'guise' of objectivity, which attributes of an entity's operations are important and which can be used as a means of comparing the performance of different organisations. For example, we are informed in SFAC No. 1 that reported earnings measures an *enterprise's performance* during a period (paragraph 45)—but clearly there are other perspectives of organisational performance (clearly some that would take a more social, as opposed to financial, form)[14]. Hines emphasises that in *communicating reality*, accountants simultaneously *construct reality*.

> *If people take a definition or description of reality, for example, an organisational chart, or a budget, or a set of financial statements, to be reality, then they will act on the basis of it, and thereby perpetuate, and in so doing validate, that account of reality. Having acted on the basis of that definition of reality, and having thereby caused consequences to flow from that conception of reality, those same consequences will appear to social actors, in retrospect, to be proof that the definition of reality on which based their actions was real . . . Decisions and actions based on that account predicate consequences, which, in retrospect, generally confirm the validity of the subsequent account. For example, say an investigator, or a newspaper report, suggested that a 'healthy' set of financial statements is not faithfully representational, and that a firm 'really' is in trouble. If this new definition of reality is accepted by, say, creditors, they may panic and precipitate the failure of the firm, or through the court, they may petition for a liquidation. A new definition of reality, if accepted, will be 'real in its consequences', because people will act on the basis of it.* (Hines, 1991, p. 322)

Until accountants determine something is worthy of being the subject of the accounting system, then, in a sense, the issue or item does not exist. There is no transparency, and as such there is no perceived accountability in relation to the item. This perspective is adopted by Handel (1962, p. 36), who states:

> *Things may exist independently of our accounts, but they have no human existence until they become accountable. Things may not exist, but they may take on human significance by becoming accountable . . . Accounts define reality and at the same time they are that reality . . . The processes by which accounts*

---

14. And of course financial 'performance' is very much tied to the judgements about which particular accounting methods should be employed, over how many years an asset should be amortised, and so forth. Further, because accounting rules can change over time, this in itself can lead to a change in reported profits and hence a change in apparent 'performance'.

are offered and accepted are the fundamental social process . . . Accounts do not more or less accurately describe things. Instead they establish what is accountable in the setting in which they occur. Whether they are accurate or inaccurate by some other standards, accounts define reality for a situation in the sense that people act on the basis of what is accountable in the situation of their action. The account provides a basis for action, a definition of what is real, and it is acted on so long as it remains accountable.[15]

Hence, in concluding this section of the chapter we can see that there are a number of arguments that suggest that characteristics such as neutrality, while playing a part in the development of conceptual frameworks, do not, and perhaps may never be expected to, reflect the underlying characteristics of financial reports. As with much of the material presented in this book, whether we accept these arguments is a matter of personal opinion. As a concluding comment to challenge the belief in the objectivity or neutrality of accounting practice, we can reflect on the following statement of Baker and Bettner (1997, p. 293):

Accounting's capacity to create and control social reality translates into empowerment for those who use it. Such power resides in organizations and institutions, where it is used to instill values, sustain legitimizing myths, mask conflict and promote self-perpetuating social orders. Throughout society, the influence of accounting permeates fundamental issues concerning wealth distribution, social justice, political ideology and environmental degradation. Contrary to public opinion, accounting is not a static reflection of economic reality, but rather is a highly partisan activity.[16]

Definition and recognition of the elements of financial reporting

Having considered perspectives of the required qualitative characteristics of financial information, the next building block we can consider is the definition and recognition criteria of the elements of financial reporting. The definitions provided within conceptual frameworks indicate the characteristics or attributes that are required before an item can be considered as belonging to a particular class of element (for example, before it can be considered to be an *asset*). Recognition criteria, on the other hand, are employed to determine whether the item can actually be included within the financial reports.

Alternative approaches have been adopted in defining the elements of financial reporting. In Australia, SAC 4 identifies five elements of accounting: assets, liabilities, equity, expenses and revenues. This can be contrasted with the position in the United States where 10 elements of financial reporting are

---

15. As quoted in Hines (1991).

16. The view that the practice of accounting provides the means of maintaining existing positions of power and wealth by a favoured 'elite' is further investigated in Chapter 12 which considers the works of a body of theorists who are labelled *critical theorists*.

identified in SFAC 3, and subsequently in SFAC 6.[17] These elements are assets, liabilities, equity, investments, distributions, comprehensive income, revenues, expenses, gains, and losses. The IASC, in its Framework for the Preparation and Presentation of Financial Statements, adopts a position similar to that of the Australian framework. It identifies the five elements that have been identified by the Australian project, plus an additional one called *Income*.

Hence in the FASB conceptual framework, rather than simply having an element entitled revenue, two elements are provided, *revenues* and *gains*, where revenues relate to the 'ongoing major or central operations' of the entity, while gains relate to 'peripheral or incidental transactions'. Clearly the FASB classification system requires some judgement to be made about whether an item does or does not relate to the central operations of the entity. Such differentiation admits the possibility that managers might opportunistically manipulate whether items are treated as part of the ongoing operations of the entity, or whether they are treated as peripheral or incidental.

Definition and recognition of assets

In Australia, paragraph 14 of SAC 4 defines assets as:

> . . . *future economic benefits controlled by the entity as a result of past transactions, or other past events.*

This definition, which is similar to that adopted by FASB and IASC, identifies three key characteristics:

- There must be an expected future economic benefit.

- The reporting entity must control the future economic benefits.

- The transaction or other event giving rise to the reporting entity's control over the future economic benefits must have occurred.

SAC 4 provides that the future economic benefits can be distinguished from the source of the benefit—a particular object or right. The definition refers to the benefit and not the source. Thus whether an object or right is disclosed as an asset will be dependent upon the likely economic benefits flowing from it. In the absence of the benefits, the object should not be disclosed as an asset. As paragraph 23 of SAC 4 states:

> *The definition refers to the benefits and not to the source since, in the absence of future economic benefits, the object or right will not be of benefit to the entity and will not therefore qualify as an asset. This means that the assumption that a particular type of object or right will always be an asset is not justified. For example, while a machine would normally be associated with a future economic benefit, there may be circumstances where it would*

---

17. SFAC 3 was superseded by SFAC 6. SFAC 3 related to business enterprises. SFAC 6 includes non-business entities.

not qualify as an asset because it has become obsolete or unusable and has no scrap value.

Conceptual frameworks do not require that an item must have a value in exchange before it can be recognised as an *asset*. The economic benefits may result from its ongoing use within the organisation. This approach can be contrasted with the model of accounting proposed by Raymond Chambers: *Continuously Contemporary Accounting* (which we considered in Chapter 4). Under Chambers' approach to accounting, if an asset does not have a current market value (value in exchange) then it is to be excluded from the financial statements.

Considering the characteristic of *control*, paragraph 24 of SAC 4 provides that control relates to the capacity of a reporting entity to benefit from the asset and to deny or regulate the access of others to the benefit. Paragraph 25 provides that the capacity to control would normally stem from legal rights. However, legal enforceability is not a prerequisite for establishing the existence of control. Hence, it is important to realise that control, and not legal ownership, is required before an asset can be shown within the body of an entity's balance sheet. Frequently, controlled assets are owned but this is not always the case. Organisations frequently disclose leased assets as part of their total assets. Paragraph 30 provides that by requiring that the relevant transaction has already occurred, future economic benefits that are not currently controlled will be excluded from balance sheet recognition.

There are many resources that generate benefits for an entity, but fail to be recorded, owing to the absence of control. For example, paragraph 27 of SAC 4 states:

Some future economic benefits will not be controlled by the entity, because the entity cannot deny or regulate the access of other entities to the objects or rights in which the future economic benefits are embodied. For example, public highways represent future economic benefits to the entities that use them, but cannot qualify as assets of entities other than the entity or entities responsible for their operation. This is because the entities that use the highways are unable to control access to them by other entities. Similarly, general access to air or water does not qualify as assets of the entities that use them, even if the entities have incurred costs to help clean the environment.

In relation to the recognition criteria, paragraph 38 of SAC 4 provides that an asset shall be recognised in the financial statements when, and only when:

(a) *it is probable that the future economic benefits embodied in the asset will eventuate; and*

(b) *the asset possesses a cost or other value that can be measured reliably.*

Paragraph 40 of SAC 4 defines probable as 'more likely rather than less likely'. Obviously, considerations of *probability* can be very subjective, such that different people in different organisations might make different probability assessments for similar items. This will have implications for issues such as comparability—a qualitative characteristic of financial reporting.

Definition and recognition of liabilities

Paragraph 48 of SAC 4 defines liabilities as 'future sacrifices of economic benefits that the entity is presently obliged to make to other entities as a result of past transactions or other past events'. This definition is also very similar to the definition provided in other conceptual frameworks and as with the definition of assets, there are three key characteristics:

- *there must be an expected future disposition of economic benefits to other entities;*

- *it must be a present obligation; and*

- *a past transaction or other event must have created the obligation.*

In considering the requirement that it be a present obligation, SAC 4 requires the inclusion not only of legally enforceable obligations but also those imposed by notions of equity and fairness, or by custom or other business practices. The recognition criteria are consistent with those for assets. SAC 4 provides:

> *A liability shall be recognised in the statement of financial position when, and only when:*
>
> *(a) it is probable that the sacrifice of economic benefits will be required; and*
>
> *(b) the amount of the liability can be measured reliably.*

As with the other elements of accounting, the determination of probability, and hence the decision as to whether to disclose a liability, is very judgemental and therefore provides possible conflicts with desired qualitative characteristics such as comparability.

Requiring liability recognition to be dependent upon there being a present obligation to other entities has implications for the disclosure of various provision accounts, such as a provision for maintenance. Generally accepted accounting practice has required such amounts to be disclosed as a liability, even though it does not involve an obligation to an external party. This issue is addressed in paragraph 60 of SAC 4. It states:

> *Some entities that carry out overhauls, repairs and renewals relating to major items of property, plant and equipment regularly 'provide' in their financial reports for such work to be undertaken in the future, with concomitant recognition of an expense. These provisions do not satisfy the definition of liabilities, because the entity does not have a present obligation to an external party . . . Also, some entities create 'provisions' for uninsured future losses (sometimes known as 'self-insurance provisions') for the purpose of retaining funds in the entity to meet losses which may arise in the future. In these situations, the entity does not have an obligation to an external party.*

Although such accounts as provisions for repairs, or provisions for plant overhauls and the like, do not meet the definition of liabilities provided within existing conceptual frameworks, they are still typically disclosed as liabilities, providing evidence that the contents of the conceptual framework have not been fully embraced by reporting entities.

Definition and recognition of expenses

There are different approaches that can be applied to determining profits (revenues less expenses). Two such approaches are commonly referred to as the *asset/liability approach*, and the *revenue/expense approach*. The asset/liability approach links profit to changes that have occurred in the assets and liabilities of the reporting entity, whereas the revenue/expense approach tends to rely on concepts such as the matching principle, which is very much focused on actual transactions and which gives limited consideration to changes in the values of assets and liabilities.

The definition of expenses (and revenues) provided in SAC 4 is based on the asset/liability perspective of profit measurement, and hence is dependent upon the definitions given to assets and liabilities. Paragraph 117 of SAC 4 defines expenses as:

> . . . *consumptions or losses of future economic benefits in the form of reductions in assets or increases in liabilities of the entity, other than those relating to distributions to owners, that result in a decrease in equity during the reporting period.*

This definition is consistent with the definition provided by the IASC. There is no reference to traditional notions of 'matching' expenses with related revenues. The definition provided by the FASB in SFAC 3 and 6 is also similar, but restricts expenses to transactions or events relating to 'ongoing major or central operations'.[18] Expenses may therefore be considered as transactions or events that cause reductions in the net assets or equity of the reporting entity, other than those caused by distributions to the owners. An expense shall be recognised, according to paragraph 132, when:

> (a) *it is probable that the consumption or loss of future economic benefits resulting in a reduction in assets and/or an increase in liabilities has occurred; and*

> (b) *the consumption or loss of economic benefits can be measured reliably.*

---

18. The definition of expenses provided in SFAC 3 and 6 is 'outflows or other using up of the assets of the entity or incurrences of liabilities of an entity (or a combination of both) during a period that result from delivering or producing goods, rendering services, or carrying out other activities that constitute the entity's ongoing major or central operations'.

Reviewing the above definition we can see that if a resource is used up or damaged by an entity, but that entity does not *control* the resource—that is, it is not an *asset* of the entity—then to the extent that no liabilities or fines are imposed, no expenses will be recorded by the entity. For example, if an entity pollutes the environment but incurs no related fines, then no expense will be acknowledged, and reported profits will not be impacted, no matter how much pollution was emitted or how much damage was done to resources that are shared with others (and hence, not controlled by the reporting entity). This has been seen as a limitation of financial accounting and a number of experimental approaches have been adopted by a number of entities to recognise the externalities their operations can generate, but which would normally be ignored by traditional systems of accounting, including those proposed by the various conceptual framework projects. (Approaches used to incorporate externalities into financial accounting, often referred to as *full-cost accounting*, are explored in Chapter 9.)

Definition and recognition of revenues

As with expenses, the definition of revenues is dependent upon the definitions of assets and liabilities. Paragraph 111 of SAC 4 defines revenues as:

> . . . *inflows or other enhancements or savings in outflows of future economic benefits in the form of increases in assets or reductions in liabilities of the entity, other than those relating to contributions by owners, that result in an increase in equity during the reporting period.*

Again, this definition is consistent with that provided by the IASC and the FASB (except that the FASB definition in SFAC 3 and 6 restricts revenues to the transaction or events that relate to the 'ongoing major or central operations' of the entity). Revenues can therefore be considered as transactions or events that cause an increase in the net assets of the reporting entity, other than owner contributions. Strictly speaking, applying the definition of revenue, increases in the market values of assets could be treated as income. However, this is not always the case.

Within the Australian and IASC approaches, revenues can be recognised from normal trading relations, as well as from non-reciprocal transfers such as grants, donations, bequests, or where liabilities are forgiven. Consistent with expenses, paragraph 125 of SAC 4 requires that revenue be recognised when, and only when:

(a) *it is probable that the inflow or other enhancement or saving in outflows of future economic benefits has occurred; and*

(b) *the inflow or other enhancement or saving in outflows of future economic benefits can be measured reliably.*

Definition of equity

Paragraph 78 of SAC 4 defines equity as 'the residual interest in the assets of the entity after deduction of its liabilities'. This definition is essentially the same as that provided by the IASC and the FASB. The residual interest is a claim or right to the net assets of the reporting entity. As a residual interest, it ranks after liabilities in terms of a claim against the assets of a reporting entity. Consistent with revenues and expenses, the definition of equity is directly a function of the definitions of assets and liabilities. In considering the recognition of equity, paragraph 92 of SAC 4 provides that:

> *Since equity is the residual interest in the assets and the amount assigned to equity will always correspond to the excess of the amounts assigned to its assets over the amounts assigned to its liabilities, the criteria for the recognition of assets and liabilities provide the criteria for the recognition of equity.*

The Australian conceptual framework does not have a separate definition of profits or income, but rather, only defines expenses and revenues. Profit is a presentation issue and is represented as the difference between the two elements, revenues and expenses. This can be contrasted with the IASC and the FASB approaches in which they separately define *income* and *comprehensive income* respectively.

In concluding our discussion of the definition and recognition of the elements of financial accounting it is interesting to reflect upon the reaction that occurred when SAC 4 was released within Australia. On its initial release in 1992 it was stated that the statement would become mandatory for Australian reporting entities after an initial transitional period. This was met with a great deal of hostility from many parties in the business community. Had SAC 4 become mandatory, it would have created significant changes in reporting practices. For example, a number of liabilities that had previously not been recognised would need to be recognised, and a number of items that had previously been treated as equity items would have to be treated as liabilities[19]. As a result of the opposition to the statement, the mandatory status was removed in 1995 and the document subsequently was to provide guidance only. This was yet another clear illustration of how politically

---

19. For example, numerous Australian companies had issued preference shares, many of which were redeemable on a specific date. Common practice was to disclose these as equity when, in substance, they were debt. SAC 4 stated that such items should be disclosed as debt. This would have had some major implications for the debt/equity ratios, and other accounting ratios of reporting entities.

difficult it is for a standard-setter to make radical changes to generally accepted accounting practice.[20]

Measurement principles

Conceptual frameworks have provided very limited prescription in relation to measurement issues (Blocks 7 and 8 of Figure 5.1). At the present time, assets and liabilities are measured in a variety of ways depending upon the particular class of assets or liabilities being considered (and given the way assets and liabilities are defined this has direct implications for reported profits). For example, liabilities are frequently recorded at present value, face value or on some other basis. In relation to assets, there are various ways these are measured—on the basis of historical costs, current replacement costs, current selling prices and so forth.

Within Australia a Statement of Accounting Concept relating to measurement issues has been expected for many years—but it still has not appeared.[21] Clearly, if such a statement was released that prescribed particular measurement approaches and called for the abandonment of other approaches commonly used, then it would be reasonable to expect widespread opposition to the requirement. Perhaps this possibility has contributed somewhat to the delay (permanent or otherwise) in releasing a statement pertaining to measurement issues. As we saw in the last section of this chapter, when SAC 4 was released it represented significant departures from current practice, and as a result of much opposition to it, the mandatory status was revoked. While the Australian standard-setters have not released a statement on measurement issues, it is worth noting that they appear to have taken a position in favour of market values with a number of recently released accounting standards requiring the use of market values for particular classes of assets. Such an approach, however, does not resolve what some people (for example,

---

20. What should be appreciated is that standard-setting bodies are typically private sector bodies, rather than government bodies backed by the power of the law. As such, many standard-setting bodies are dependent upon support from their constituency for their survival. Throughout the world a number of standard-setting bodies have been disbanded, apparently because of widespread dissatisfaction with, or opposition to, their various releases. Government agencies are deemed to be somewhat more protected from such threats (but, not totally). As Dopuch and Sunder (1980, p. 18) state: 'Indeed, the demand to develop a conceptual framework may be inversely related to the power of enforcement which the standard-setting agency can command. For example, the Securities and Exchange Commission, which has the legal power to enforce its Accounting Series Releases, has not been hampered by the fact that it has not yet enunciated a conceptual framework of accounting.'

21. As noted previously, in December 1998 an Accounting Theory Monograph entitled *Measurement in Financial Accounting* was released by the Australian Accounting Research Foundation. Whether this actually leads to a concept statement being released is far from certain.

Chambers) have referred to as the additivity problem. Within Australia, various assets are required to be valued on different bases (for example, historical cost, lower of cost and net realisable value, market value) meaning that the aggregate sum called 'total assets' represents an amount calculated using many different approaches to valuation.

As we saw earlier in this chapter, issues associated with measurement appeared to represent a stumbling block in the development of the FASB conceptual framework. While the FASB framework was initially promoted as being prescriptive, when SFAC 5 was issued in 1984 the FASB appeared to side-step the difficult measurement issues, and rather, the statement provided a description of various approaches to measuring the elements of accounting. SFAC 5 simply notes that there are generally accepted to be five alternative measurement bases applied in practice: historical cost, current replacement cost, current market value, net realisable value, and present value. As noted previously in this chapter, such a descriptive approach was generally considered to represent a 'cop-out' on behalf of the FASB (Solomons, 1986). Australia perhaps attempted to delay this problem by separately considering recognition criteria (which are included in SAC 4) and measurement issues (which are yet to be addressed)—but does this make sense? Sterling (1985) argues that it is illogical to discuss how or when to recognise an element of accounting if we are not sure what measurement characteristics are to be recognised in relation to assets. What do you think of Sterling's argument that considering recognition issues in advance of measurement issues is akin to 'putting the cart before the horse'? Arguably, recognition and measurement go hand in hand and a central part of the measurement process is to decide on the subject to be measured, and when it should be measured (or recognised).

Benefits associated with having a conceptual framework

Conceptual frameworks are costly to develop and open to many forms of political interference. In some respects their degree of progress, while initially promising, has in recent years been rather slow and disappointing. Is it worth continuing with these frameworks? In this section we consider some perceived advantages that have been advanced by standard-setting bodies as being likely to follow from the development of a conceptual framework (we will also consider some criticisms).[22] These include:

---

22. A number of these perceived benefits are identified at Paragraph 7 of Policy Statement 5: *The Nature and Purpose of Statements of Accounting Concepts*, issued jointly in 1995 by the Australian Accounting Standards Board and the Public Sector Accounting Standards Board.

(a) Accounting Standards should be more consistent and logical because they are developed from an orderly set of concepts. The view is that in the absence of a coherent theory, the development of accounting standards could be somewhat *ad hoc*.

(b) Increased international compatibility of accounting standards should occur because they are based on a conceptual framework that is similar to the explicit conceptual frameworks used by the International Accounting Standards Committee and other overseas standard-setters.

(c) The standard-setters should be more accountable for their decisions because the thinking behind specific requirements should be more explicit, as should any departures from the concepts that may be included in particular accounting standards.

(d) The process of communication between the standard-setters and their constituents should be enhanced because the conceptual underpinnings of proposed accounting standards should be more apparent when the standard-setters seek public comment on them. Preparers and auditors will have a better understanding of why they are reporting/auditing. There is also a perspective that having a conceptual framework should alleviate some of the political pressure that might otherwise be exerted when accounting standards are developed—the conceptual framework could, in a sense, provide a defence against political attack.

(e) The development of accounting standards should be more economical because the concepts developed will guide the standard-setters in their decision making.

(f) Where statements of accounting concepts cover a particular issue, there might be a reduced need for developing additional accounting standards.

(g) Conceptual frameworks have had the effect of emphasising the 'decision usefulness' role of financial reports, rather than simply just restricting concern to issues associated with stewardship.

In terms of some possible disadvantages of conceptual frameworks, as with all activities based, at least in part, on lobbying processes and political actions, there will always be some parties potentially disadvantaged relative to others. Perhaps some smaller organisations feel that they are overburdened by reporting requirements because analysts have been able to convince regulators that particular information was necessary for an efficiently functioning economy.

Another criticism raised in terms of conceptual framework projects relates to their focus. Being principally economic in focus, general purpose financial reports (GPFRs) typically ignore transactions or events that have not involved market transactions or an exchange of property rights. That is, transactions or events that cannot be linked to a 'market price' are not recognised. For example, a great deal of recent literature has been critical of traditional financial accounting for its failure to recognise the environmental externalities caused by business entities (see Rubenstein, 1992; Gray, Owen and Adams, 1996; Deegan and Rankin, 1997).

Following on from the above point, it has been argued that by focusing on economic performance, this, in itself, further reinforces the importance of economic performance relative to various levels of social performance. Several writers such as Hines (1988) and Gray and Bebbington (1992) have argued that the accounting profession can play a large part in influencing the forms of social conduct acceptable to the broader community. As has been indicated previously, accounting can both reflect and construct social expectations. For example, if profits and associated financial data are promoted as the best measure of organisational success, it could be argued that dominant consideration—by both the organisation and the community—will only be given to activities that impact on this measure. If accountants were encouraged to embrace other types of performance indicators, including those that relate to environmental and other social performance, this may conceivably filter through to broadening people's expectations about organisational performance. Nevertheless, at the present time, profitability, as indicated by the output of the accounting system, is typically used as a guide to the success of the organisation.

Another criticism of conceptual frameworks is that they simply represent a codification of existing practice (Hines, 1989), putting in place a series of documents that describe existing practice, rather than prescribing an 'ideal' or logically derived approach to accounting. Hines (1989) also argues that accounting regulations, as generated by the accounting regulators, are no more than the residual of a political process and as such do not represent any form of *ideal* model.

It has also been argued that conceptual frameworks have a more important objective from the perspective of the accounting standard-setters and one that does not provide benefits to financial statement users. Hines (1989) provides evidence that conceptual framework projects were actually initiated at times when professions were under threat—that they are 'a strategic manoeuvre for providing legitimacy to standard-setting boards during periods of competition or threatened government intervention' (1989, p. 89).

In supporting her case, Hines refers to the relatively recent work being undertaken within Canada. The Canadian Institute of Chartered Accountants (CICA) had done very little throughout the 1980s in relation to its conceptual framework project. It had commenced the development of a framework in about 1980, a time Hines claims was 'a time of pressures for reform and criticisms of accounting standard-setting in Canada' (1989, p. 88). However, interest 'waned' until another Canadian professional accounting body, the Certified General Accountants Association, through its Accounting Standards Authority of Canada, commenced developing a conceptual framework in 1986. This was deemed to represent a threat to CICA 'who were motivated into action'. Solomons (1983) also provides an argument that conceptual frameworks are a defence against political interference by other interest groups.

Conceptual frameworks as a means of legitimising standard-setting bodies

While accounting standard-setters have promoted the benefits of conceptual frameworks, some of which have been discussed above, a number of writers (including Hines and Solomons, as identified above) have suggested that conceptual frameworks are created primarily to provide benefits to the parties that actually develop or commission the frameworks. It has been argued that they have been used as devices to help ensure the ongoing existence of the accounting profession by 'boosting' their public standing (Dopuch and Sunder, 1980, p. 17). As Hines (1989, p. 74) suggests:

> One of the main obstacles against which accountants have continually had to struggle in the professionalism quest has been the threat of an apparent absence of a formal body of accounting knowledge, and that creating the perception of possessing such knowledge has been an important part of creating and reproducing their social identity as a profession . . . Viewing these attempts (at establishing conceptual frameworks) as claims to accounting knowledge, which are used as a political resource in reducing the threat of government intervention and competing with other groups, in order to maintain and increase professionalism and social mobility seems to explain these projects better than viewing them from a technical/functional perspective.

It is argued that conceptual frameworks provide a means of increasing the ability of a profession to self-regulate, thereby counteracting the possibility that government intervention will occur. Hines (1991, p. 328) states:

> CFs presume, legitimise and reproduce the assumption of an objective world and as such they play a part in constituting the social world . . . CFs provide social legitimacy to the accounting profession.
>
> Since the objectivity assumption is the central premise of our society . . . . a fundamental form of social power accrues to those who are able to trade on the objectivity assumption. Legitimacy is achieved by tapping into this central proposition because accounts generated around this proposition are perceived as 'normal'. It is perhaps not surprising or anomalous then that CF projects continue to be undertaken which rely on information qualities such as 'representational faithfulness', 'neutrality', 'reliability', etc., which presume a concrete, objective world, even though past CFs have not succeeded in generating Accounting Standards which achieve these qualities. The very talk, predicated on the assumption of an objective world to which accountants have privileged access via their 'measurement expertise', serves to construct a perceived legitimacy for the profession's power and autonomy.

If we accept the argument of Hines, we would perhaps reject notions that the accounting profession was attempting to uncover any *truths* or *ideals*, and rather, we would consider that the development of conceptual frameworks was a political action to ensure the survival of the profession. Reflecting on the role of conceptual frameworks in assisting a professional accounting body to survive, Horngren (1981, p. 87) notes:

> *The useful life of the FASB is not going to rest on issues of technical competence. The pivotal issue will be the ability of the board to resolve conflicts among the various constituencies in a manner perceived to be acceptable to the ultimate constituent, the 800-pound gorilla in the form of the federal government, particularly the SEC (of course, the federal gorilla is also subject to pressure from its constituents). The ability will be manifested in the FASB's decisions, appointments and conceptual framework. So the conceptual framework is desirable if the survival of the FASB is considered to be desirable. That is, the framework is likely to help provide power to the board. After all, the board has no coercive power. Instead, the board must really rely on power by persuasion.*

Chapter summary

In this chapter we have considered the development of conceptual frameworks. We have seen that conceptual frameworks are made up of a number of building blocks that cover issues of central importance to the financial reporting process. From a technical or functional perspective it has been argued by accounting standard-setters that the development of a conceptual framework will lead to improvements in financial reporting practices, which will in turn lead to reports that are deemed more useful for the economic decisions made by the report users. With a well formulated conceptual framework there is an expectation that information will be generated that is of more relevance to report users, as well as being more reliable. The use of a logically derived conceptual framework will also lead to the development of accounting standards consistent within a country, and possibly with those released in other countries with similar frameworks. Further, there is a view that conceptual frameworks will allow constituents to understand more fully how and why particular accounting standards require specific approaches to be adopted, and will provide preparers with guidance when no specific accounting standards exist.

In considering the success of conceptual frameworks there are numerous authors who suggest that the frameworks have been a failure and have questioned whether such work should continue (Dopuch and Sunder, 1980). It has appeared that issues such as those relating to measurement have been very real stumbling blocks for the ongoing development of conceptual frameworks. The progress, or in some cases the lack of it, emphasises the political nature of the accounting standard-setting process and shows that where constituents do not support particular approaches, the standard-setters will quite often abandon particular endeavours.

While we can question the technical accomplishments of conceptual frameworks, some authors have suggested that technical advances were not the goal of the standard-setters. Rather, they have suggested that conceptual frameworks are actually established to bolster the ongoing existence and position of accountants in society. As Hines (1989, p. 79) states:

> *Since professional powers, professional prestige and financial rewards are legitimised in society by being assumed to be founded on a formal body of knowledge unique to the profession, the possibility of the loss of this mystique poses a threat to the successful advancement or social reproduction of the profession. The phenomenon of the proliferation of conceptual framework projects in the UK, USA, Canada and Australia is better understood as a response to such a threat than in the functional/technical terms in which the CFs have been articulated and discussed.*

Whether we accept that conceptual frameworks are developed to improve the practice of accounting, or that such frameworks are primarily created to assist those within the accounting profession, is obviously a matter of personal opinion. Having read this chapter you should be better informed to make a judgement.

References

American Institute of Certified Public Accountants, *Report of Study Group on Objectives of Financial Statements*, (The Trueblood Report), AICPA, New York, 1973.

Baker, C., Bettner, M., 'Interpretive and Critical Research in Accounting: A Commentary on its Absence from Mainstream Accounting Research', *Critical Perspectives on Accounting*, Vol. 8, pp. 293–310, 1997.

Chambers, R.J., *Accounting, Evaluation and Economic Behavior*, Prentice-Hall, Englewood Cliffs, 1966.

Deegan, C.M., Rankin, M., 'The Materiality of Environmental Information to Users of Accounting Reports', *Accounting, Auditing and Accountability Journal,* Vol. 10, No. 4, 1997.

Dopuch, N., Sunder, S., 'FASB's Statements on Objectives and Elements of Financial Accounting: A Review', *The Accounting Review,* Vol. LV, No. 1, January 1980.

Grady, P., *An Inventory of Generally Accepted Accounting Principles for Business Enterprises*, Accounting Research Study No. 7, AICPA, New York, 1965.

Gray, R., Bebbington, J., *Can the Grey Men Go Green?*, Discussion Paper, Centre for Social and Environmental Accounting Research, The University of Dundee, 1992.

Gray, R., Owen, D., Adams, C., *Accounting and Accountability: Changes and Challenges in Corporate Social and Environmental Reporting*, Prentice-Hall, London, 1996.

Handel, W., *Ethnomethodology: How People Make Sense*, Prentice-Hall, 1982.

Hendriksen, E., *Accounting Theory*, Richard D. Irwin, Illinois, 1970.

Hines, R., 'Financial Accounting: in Communicating Reality, We Construct Reality', *Accounting Organizations and Accountability,* Vol. 13, No. 3, pp. 251–61, 1988.

Hines, R.D., 'Financial Accounting Knowledge, Conceptual Framework Projects and the Social Construction of the Accounting Profession', *Accounting, Auditing and Accountability Journal,* Vol. 2, No. 2, pp. 72–92, 1989.

Hines, R., 'The FASB's Conceptual Framework, Financial Accounting and the Maintenance of the Social World', *Accounting, Organizations and Society,* Vol. 16, No. 4, pp. 313–32, 1991.

Horngren, C.T., 'Uses and Limitations of a Conceptual Framework', *Journal of Accountancy*, pp. 86–95, April 1981.

Miller, P.B.W., 'The Conceptual Framework as Reformation and Counterreformation', *Accounting Horizons*, pp. 23–32, June 1990.

Miller, P.B.W., Reading, R., *The FASB: The People, the Process, and the Politics*, Irwin, Illinois, 1986.

Moonitz, M., *The Basic Postulates of Accounting*, Accounting Research Study No. 1, American Institute of Certified Public Accountants, New York, 1961.

Nussbaumer, N., 'Does the FASB's Conceptual Framework Help Solve Real Accounting Issues?', *Journal of Accounting Education*, pp. 235–42, Spring 1992.

Peasnell, K.V., 'The Function of a Conceptual Framework for Corporate Financial Reporting', *Accounting and Business Research*, Vol. 12, No. 4, pp. 243–56, Autumn 1982.

Rubenstein, D.B., 'Bridging the Gap Between Green Accounting and Black Ink', *Accounting Organizations and Society*, Vol. 17, No. 5, pp. 501–8, 1992.

Solomons, D., 'The Politicization of Accounting', *Journal of Accounting*, pp. 65–72, November 1978.

Solomons, D., 'The Political Implications of Accounting and Accounting Standard Setting', *Accounting and Business Research*, Vol. 13, No. 56, pp. 107–18, Spring 1983.

Solomons, D., 'The FASB's Conceptual Framework: An Evaluation', *Journal of Accountancy*, pp. 114–24, June 1986.

Sprouse, R., Moonitz, M., *A Tentative Set of Broad Accounting Principles for Business Enterprises*, Accounting Research Study No. 3, American Institute of Certified Public Accountants, New York, 1962.

Stamp, E., *Corporate Reporting: Its Future Evolution*, Canadian Institute of Chartered Accountants, Toronto, 1980.

Staunton, J., 'Why a Conceptual Framework of Accounting?', *Accounting Forum*, Vol. 7, No. 2, pp. 85–90, 1984.

Sterling, R.R., *An Essay on Recognition*, The University of Sydney Accounting Research Centre, 1985.

The Accounting Standards Steering Committee, *The Corporate Report*, Institute of Chartered Accountants in England and Wales, London, 1975.

Watts, R.L., Zimmerman, J.L., *Positive Accounting Theory*, Prentice-Hall Inc., Englewood Cliffs, New Jersey, 1986.

Questions

5.1 What is a conceptual framework of accounting?

5.2 Do you consider that we need conceptual frameworks? Explain your answer.

5.3 What advantages or benefits have been advanced by standard-setters to support the development of conceptual framework projects? Do you agree that in practice such benefits will be achieved?

5.4 Conceptual framework projects identify a number of qualitative criteria that financial information should possess if it is to be useful for economic decision making. Two such attributes include neutrality and representational faithfulness. Do you believe that financial information can, in reality, be neutral and representationally faithful? Explain your answer.

5.5 The two main qualitative characteristics that financial information should possess have been identified as relevance and reliability. Is one more important than the other, or are they equally important?

5.6 What are some possible objectives of general purpose financial reporting? Which objective appears to have been embraced within existing conceptual framework projects?

5.7 Which groups within society are likely to benefit from the development of a conceptual framework of accounting?

5.8 Would you consider that conceptual frameworks have been successful in achieving their stated objectives? Why, or why not?

5.9 Conceptual frameworks have yet to provide prescription in relation to measurement issues. Why do you think this is the case?

5.10 Hines (1989, p. 89) argues that conceptual frameworks are 'a strategic manoeuvre for providing legitimacy to standard-setting boards during periods of competition or threatened government intervention'. Explain the basis of her argument and consider whether the history of the development of conceptual frameworks supports her position.

5.11 *The Corporate Report* (UK) referred to the 'public's right to information'. How does this differ from the perspectives adopted in other conceptual framework projects?

5.12 Hines (1991) states that 'in communicating reality, accountants simultaneously create reality'. What does she mean?

5.13 In this chapter we discussed how accounting standard-setters typically find it difficult to get support for newly developed requirements if those requirements represent major changes from existing practice. Why do you think this is the case and do you think the potential lack of support would influence the strategies adopted by accounting standard-setters?

5.14 As indicated in this chapter, when SAC 4: Definition and Recognition of the elements of Financial Statements was released in Australia, the initial intention was that its concepts were to become mandatory. Following a great deal of criticism of the statement, particularly from business representatives, the mandatory status was removed. Exhibit 5.1 below provides an article that describes the status change, as well as some of the criticisms made of SAC 4. Identify and critically evaluate the particular criticisms.

EXHIBIT 5.1   Criticisms raised in relation to SAC 4

Concept rumblings grow into a chorus of discontent

Tim Boreham

The intention of SAC 4 is to ensure a well-informed capital market, but the profession is worried about its direction, its jargon, and the conflict with existing standards.

Initial rumblings over the controversial Statement of Accounting Concepts number four (SAC 4) have grown into a chorus of discontent. This week, the Australian Accounting Standards Board bowed to pressure and removed the document's mandatory status. The extent of opposition to the standard setters was exemplified when KPMG Peat Marwick's new national chairman, John Harkness, condemned SAC 4 and called for it to be withdrawn. Bob Lamond, a senior Peat audit partner, went further, describing it as 'verbal diarrhoea strung together in incomprehensible jargon'.

Finance executives who have commented unfavourably on SAC 4 now include Chris Edwards, group accounting director of Qantas; QBE Insurance's chief executive, John Cloney; BHP's corporate general manager for accounting, Michael Gillian; and the Commonwealth Bank's senior manager for group accounting, Geoff Steel. The Institute of Chartered Accountants and Australian Society of CPAs, which have the power to veto AASB decisions, are also concerned about SAC 4's ramifications.

The future of SAC 4 is now in doubt. The statement was planned to be effective from January next year but implementation has now been put back 18 months to allow for more debate.

AASB chairman Peter Day and Australian Accounting Research Foundation executive director Warren McGregor are unfazed by the criticism. They concede, however, that the standard-setters have been remiss in communicating the basic purpose of concept statements, which they say is to improve the credibility of Australian Accounting Standards.

'This is not an agenda to push through various sacred cows,' Day says. 'There is a very healthy consensus component, but at the end of the day we have an accountability direct to Parliament to provide high-quality Accounting Standards that are going to improve Australia's international capital markets position.'

SAC 4, on the definition and recognition of the elements of financial statements, defines assets, liabilities, revenues, expenses and equity in a wider way than is traditional. It takes the view that the balance sheet is divided into these elements and, as a result, there is no room for deferred debits and credits. Assets, for instance, are described in terms of their service potential or future economic benefits, and liabilities are the 'future sacrifices of service potential or future economic benefits'.

Although criticised as esoteric and academic, the statement will have far-reaching effects on financial statements. For instance, items traditionally included as equity may have to be restated as liabilities. SAC 4 moves away from the idea of accounts being a parking place for items that should be spread over the years, doing away with the old concepts of contingencies and provisions. Instead, it takes the approach of providing for immediate recognition of future events affecting the entity. The old notion of ownership is replaced with a wider definition, 'control of economic benefit'.

The statement has been attacked on two fronts: its academic style and complex wording, and the specific changes to corporate reporting that would be made necessary. In an open letter, KPMG Peat Marwick's Lamond says SAC 4 epitomises the profession's abrogation of the old 'true and fair' concept of company

EXHIBIT 5.1 *(continued)*

reporting in favour of highly prescriptive measures. The trouble with this, he says, is that standards lack the flexibility to allow for the diversity of industries.

Lamond says the concept statement has the admirable objective of defining the elements of financial statements. 'However, it does not merely reiterate existing practice, but in some instances represents a major change, which will have a significant impact on reported financial positions and profits.'

Lamond wonders why the profession needed to produce a lengthy conceptual statement. 'Ten lines delivered to Moses was enough to outline the fundamentals of Christian life,' he says. He compares the current philosophy of the standard-setters to a statement on accounting principles produced by the institute in 1946. 'Businesses are so varied in their nature that there must be flexibility in the manner of presenting accounts,' the document says. 'A standard form to suit every industrial and commercial undertaking is neither practical nor desirable.'

Lamond says: 'Sadly, our current Corporations Law now prescribes a standard form in the fruitless pursuit of comparability between entities. Companies, like human beings, have many things in common while also having many substantial differences.' He says society and institute members' handbooks are bigger than corporations and income tax law combined. 'We have the temerity to call for the simplification and clarification of both these codes while we continue to generate similar incomprehensible material.'

Qantas's Edwards is among those who raised concerns about the statement's mandatory status. He says SAC 4 was far too wide-ranging, too uncertain and too pervasive of existing Accounting Standards to be made mandatory within the existing Australian financial reporting structure.

'SAC 4 purports to be a concept statement, yet covers a number of practical issues in some detail,' he says. 'As such, it is crossing through the provinces of several existing Accounting Standards. Qantas contends that such an accounting concept statement should be written at high level, with the Accounting Standards addressing the lower-level practical issues.'

Edwards says SAC 4 will create a balance-sheet emphasis, a fundamental change in accounting convention that is not necessarily supported. Specific concerns are that the resulting 'grossing-up' of the balance sheet will have an impact on ratios used in finance arrangements, and the profit and loss becomes a statement of movements in net worth and not an accurate reflection of performance.

The Commonwealth Bank's Geoff Steel says SAC 4 has the potential to create the biggest schism between the business community and standard-setters since the attempted introduction of current cost accounting in the 1970s. 'The question is, do we want a theoretically pure set of financial statements, or one that is understandable and meaningful?' he asks in the society's *Financial Forum* magazine.

Steel says some of the concepts contained in SAC 4 are meritorious, while others need refinement. 'The essence of the concepts is that they should apply equally to all business situations. This sounds good in theory, but in practice it has its drawbacks.' His main concerns are:

- SAC 4 adopts the 'probability' concept, which means that if a future event is likely to occur the related asset, liability expense or revenue item should be recognised immediately in the financial statements. In the case of mining companies, the effect is that capitalised exploration expenditure must be written off, reducing shareholders' equity and increasing gearing.
- Uncompleted contract obligations such as major capital work must be brought on to the balance sheet, rather than disclosed as a capital commitment in

(continued)

EXHIBIT 5.1 *(continued)*

notes to the accounts and treated as expenditure only when the expense is incurred. The gearing of a company would be affected as the item could be on the balance sheet long before any revenue is incurred.

- Provisioning must be based on fact, rather than anticipation of a future event. For instance, the bank's general provision for doubtful debts would show up on the profit and loss when the actual event has occurred.
- Certain items, such as convertible notes, can float between the two classifications, depending on the probability of their being converted into equity. Convertible notes subject to a conversion price above the current share market price, for instance, would be treated as a liability.

KPMG Peat Marwick's incoming national chairman John Harkness says the statement is not in harmony with good international practice and is not generally accepted by the business community. He says his firm has received numerous submissions from clients and other members of the business community that are highly critical of the Accounting Standards development process in general, and the content and thrust of SAC 4 in particular.

Harkness says the foundation knows and accepts that SAC 4 conflicts with a number of existing Accounting Standards. The boards have stated that, in cases of conflict, the Accounting Standards will prevail but eventually they will be amended to remove the conflict. 'However, we fail to see how in the meantime one can have two sets of existing rules side by side, both compulsory and yet fundamentally in conflict with each other. We believe it would be far better to develop a conceptual framework as a basis for future change and as a benchmark for evaluation of existing standards.'

However, the foundation's McGregor maintains that the document is robust. 'It is able to deal with the more specific issues, rather than trying to set everything in stone in terms of black-letter law,' he says.

McGregor believes that if accounts preparers subsequently have trouble interpreting the document on a specific issue, the Standards Board is quickly able to produce less formal guidelines.

He believes the debate is a healthy sign that accountants are thinking positively about both SAC 4's impact and the Accounting Standard-setting process in general. 'It is very healthy to see the level of input we are now getting,' he says. The disappointing aspect, he adds, is the lack of emphasis on the link between SAC 4 and improving financial reporting.

'There has not been any mention of what the Standards Board's objective is: to ensure we have a well informed capital market,' he says. 'I have been disappointed about the lack of comment from user groups, such as the Australian Stock Exchange, the Securities Institute of Australia and investment managers. I am concerned the focus of the debate has not been broad enough.'

Business Review Weekly, **28 May 1993**.

Chapter 6

International accounting and the effects of cultural differences and harmonisation efforts

Learning objectives

Upon completing this chapter readers should:

- appreciate that internationally there are many differences between some countries in the accounting policies and practices adopted;

- understand various explanations about why countries adopt particular accounting practices in preference to others;

- understand some of the arguments that suggest that it is appropriate that there are international differences in accounting practices;

- be able to explain what is meant by the term *harmonisation of accounting*;

- be able to identify and explain some of the perceived benefits of harmonising accounting practices on an international scale; and

- understand some of the obstacles to harmonisation, and the criticisms that efforts to harmonise accounting internationally have attracted.

Opening issue

A number of countries throughout the world have adopted, as their own, the accounting standards issued by the International Accounting Standards Committee (which are called International Accounting Standards). Many people argue that in the case of developing countries this is the most efficient policy to adopt because developing accounting standards and associated conceptual frameworks is an extremely costly and time consuming activity. Further, it has also been argued that the International Accounting Standards Committee, and its members who helped in the development of the International Accounting Standards, have a great deal of experience in determining the types of information likely to be *relevant* to financial statement readers.

Do you agree that this is the best avenue for developing countries to follow (rather than develop their own unique accounting standards), and can you identify any disadvantages in following this approach? Further, if the developing countries embarked on a process of developing their own accounting standards, do you think the standards would be more *relevant* to their particular country's environment compared to those developed by the International Accounting Standards Committee?

Introduction

In the previous chapters we considered how regulation can shape the practice of financial reporting. We learned that various factors can influence the actions of regulators (for example, their own perceptions about what is in the 'public interest', or about the economic implications of newly proposed accounting standards), and that various theoretical perspectives can be applied when making a judgement about the factors that will be more likely to impact on a regulator's ultimate decision to support or oppose particular financial accounting requirements. (For example, some perspectives may promote a view that regulators will adopt a public interest perspective, while other theoretical perspectives might provide a view that regulators are ultimately driven by self-interest.)

In Chapters 4 and 5 we considered various normative (prescriptive) theories of accounting that have provided guidance on how accounting *should* be undertaken. We learned that such normative theories did not have the force of law. While conceptual frameworks of accounting (Chapter 5) can arguably not be considered to be overwhelming successes in terms of improving the practice of financial reporting, it is nevertheless reasonable to believe that they are a factor that has had some influence on financial reporting.

In this chapter we consider other factors that might influence financial reporting. Specifically we consider the impacts that factors such as national *culture* might have on the practice of financial reporting and we see that there is some evidence that differences in the financial reporting practices between countries can, at least in part, be explained by underlying differences in various cultural attributes of the people of that country. That is, we consider arguments that the culture and beliefs of the community directly impact on how they elect to account.

We also consider other influences on financial reporting. We consider the role of the International Accounting Standards Committee (IASC) in influencing the practice of accounting within particular countries. We see that some countries, including some of those less developed economically, have elected to adopt accounting standards issued by the IASC. We consider the appropriateness of this action, particularly given that International Accounting Standards (IASs) are developed generally on the basis of accounting rules that exist in countries such as the United States, United Kingdom, Australia, Canada and New Zealand. We question whether such rules are appropriate in a different cultural setting, or conversely, whether similar accounting rules can be applied in countries with vastly different economic, political and cultural settings.

Having considered issues of culture and the efforts of the IASC, we conclude the chapter by considering recent attempts to harmonise accounting standards throughout the world. We consider the perceived benefits of such actions, as well as whether efforts towards harmonisation, and ultimately standardisation, are likely to succeed.

International accounting defined

The term 'international accounting' is used in a variety of ways and this can cause some confusion. Weirich, Avery and Anderson (1971) provide an overview of three different ways in which international accounting can be explained.[1] It can encompass:

1. Universal or world accounting,

2. Comparative or international accounting,

3. Parent–foreign subsidiary accounting.

Universal or *world* accounting considers issues (such as costs, benefits, likely impediments) associated with the implementation of a uniform set of accounting rules that would be used throughout the world. As Weirich, Avery and Anderson (1971) state:

> World Accounting. *In the framework of this concept, international accounting is considered to be a universal system that could be adopted in all countries. A world-wide set of generally accepted accounting principles (GAAP), such as the set maintained in the United States, would be established. Practices and principles would be developed which would be applicable to all countries. This concept would be the ultimate goal of an international system.*

---

1. As referenced in Riahi-Belkaoui (2000, p. 480).

In this chapter we consider research that relates to this category of international accounting. In particular we consider the efforts currently under way in which the IASC is attempting to develop a set of internationally acceptable accounting standards. The IASC has a long-term goal of global uniformity in accounting standards—a single set of high-quality accounting standards for all listed and economically significant business enterprises around the world. We will consider arguments that challenge the wisdom or logic of this aim.

Comparative or international accounting relates to efforts to document and explain differences in the ways different countries undertake the practice of financial accounting. For example, if we look at the accounting rules from various countries that have their own accounting rules or standards in place (and some do not) we find differences in such things as how they recognise and value their fixed assets (some countries predominantly use historical costs, whereas other countries use a mix of market and other valuations); how they account for their inventory; if, when and how they recognise goodwill; how they consolidate their foreign subsidiaries, and so forth. This is probably the major focus of research in international accounting. As Weirich, Avery and Anderson (1971) state:

> Comparative *or* International Accounting. *A second major concept of the term 'international accounting' involves a descriptive and informative approach. Under this concept, international accounting includes all varieties of principles, methods and standards of accounting of all countries. This concept includes a set of generally accepted accounting principles established for each country, thereby requiring the accountant to be multiple principle conscious when studying international accounting . . . No universal or perfect set of principles would be expected to be established. A collection of all principles, methods and standards of all countries would be considered as the international accounting system. These variations result because of differing geographic, social, economic, political and legal influences.*

This type of research provides an enhanced awareness of the influence of environmental factors on accounting development (Gray, 1988). In this chapter we review some research using comparative analysis of accounting methods of different countries that attempts to provide explanations of the apparent differences. We therefore also consider Weirich, Avery and Anderson's (1971) second branch of 'international accounting'.

The third classification of international accounting identified by Weirich, Avery and Anderson (1971), *parent–foreign subsidiary accounting*, refers to the practices employed in consolidating the financial statements of parent entities and those of their overseas subsidiaries. As Weirich, Avery and Anderson (1971) state:

> Accounting for Foreign Subsidiaries. *The third major concept that may be applied to 'international accounting' refers to the accounting practices of a parent company and a foreign subsidiary. A reference to a particular country or domicile is needed under the concept for effective internal financial reporting.*

The accountant is concerned mainly with the translation and adjustment of the subsidiary's financial statement. Different accounting problems arise and different accounting principles are to be followed depending upon which country is used as a reference for translation and adjustment purposes.

When considering the practice of consolidating foreign subsidiaries, different countries often adopt different approaches. Generally speaking the method used to consolidate the accounts of a foreign subsidiary will depend on whether the subsidiary operates in a way that is integrated with the parent entity, or operates independently. We do not consider issues associated with the consolidation of foreign subsidiaries in this book.[2]

Explanations of differences in accounting practices employed in different countries

We first consider the second branch of international accounting identified by Weirich, Avery and Anderson (1971), the branch that examines international differences in accounting practices. If we look at the accounting rules in place in different countries we see that there are typically numerous differences between them. Authors such as Perera (1989) have argued that accounting practices within particular countries evolve to suit the circumstances of a particular society, at a particular time. While there is a large variation in accounting systems adopted in different countries, it has been commonly accepted that there are two main models of financial accounting that have evolved within economically developed countries: the *Anglo–American Model* and the *Continental European Model* (Mueller, 1967; Nobes, 1984).[3] The Anglo-American Model is characterised by a system of accounting that is strongly influenced by professional accounting bodies rather than government, emphasises the importance of capital markets (the entities within the countries that use this model of accounting are typically very reliant on public sources of equity and debt finance), and relies upon terms such as *true and fair* or *presents fairly*, which in turn are based upon considerations of economic substance over and above legal form (legal form being bound by legislation).

The Continental European Model of accounting, on the other hand, typically is characterised by relatively small input from the accounting profession, little reliance upon qualitative requirements such as *true and fair*, and stronger reliance upon government. The accounting methods tend to be heavily associated with the tax rules in place, and the information tends to

---

2. This is an issue that tends to be covered in textbooks of a more 'practical' than 'theoretical' nature. For an explanation of how to apply the Australian rules pertaining to the translation of the accounts of foreign operations, reference can be made to Deegan, C., *Australian Financial Accounting*, McGraw-Hill, 1999.

3. For example, France and Germany are often presented as examples of the Continental European group, while countries such as the US, UK, Canada, Australia and New Zealand are often presented as examples of the Anglo-American group.

be of a nature to protect the interest of creditors, rather than investors *per se* (the entities within countries that use the Continental European Model tend to obtain most of their funds from lenders, often banks).

Over time, numerous reasons have been given for differences in the accounting methods of different countries. Mueller (1968) suggests that such differences might be caused by differences in the underlying laws of the country, the political systems in place (for example a capitalistic/free market system versus a centralised/communistic system), or their level of development from an economic perspective. As Mueller (1968, p. 95) explains:

> *In society, accounting performs a service function. This function is put in jeopardy unless accounting remains, above all, practically useful. Thus, it must respond to the ever-changing needs of society and must reflect the social, political, legal and economic conditions within which it operates. Its meaningfulness depends on its ability to mirror these conditions.*

Other reasons such as tax systems, level of education, and level of economic development have also been suggested to explain differences in accounting practices (Doupnik and Salter, 1995). At present there is no clear theory that explains international differences in accounting practices. Many different causes have been suggested. Nobes (1998) reviewed the literature and confirmed that numerous reasons have been proposed to explain the differences. These are summarised in Table 6.1.

TABLE 6.1 Reasons proposed for international accounting differences

1. Nature of business ownership and financing system
2. Colonial inheritance
3. Invasions
4. Taxation
5. Inflation
6. Level of education
7. Age and size of accountancy profession
8. Stage of economic development
9. Legal systems
10. Culture
11. History
12. Geography
13. Language
14. Influence of theory
15. Political systems, social climate
16. Religion
17. Accidents

Source: Nobes (1998, p. 163)

According to Nobes, many of the factors provided in Table 6.1 are interrelated. For example, a number are deemed to be 'institutional', and a number relate to the broader notion of *culture*. We consider some of the factors identified in Table 6.1. Specifically we consider the possible influences of culture, religion, and the nature of the business ownership and financing system.

Culture

Culture is a broad concept that would be expected to impact on legal systems, tax systems, the way businesses are formed and financed, and so on. For many years culture has been used in the psychology, anthropology and sociology literatures as the basis for explaining differences in social systems (Hofstede, 1980). In recent decades it has also been used to try to explain international differences in accounting systems. One of the earlier papers to consider the impacts of culture on accounting was Violet (1983) who argued that accounting is a 'socio–technical activity' that involved interaction between both human and non-human resources. Because the two interact, Violet claims that accounting cannot be considered culture-free. Relating accounting to culture, Violet (1983, p. 8) claims:

> *Accounting is a social institution established by most cultures to report and explain certain social phenomena occurring in economic transactions. As a social institution, accounting has integrated certain cultural customs and elements within the constraints of cultural postulates. Accounting cannot be isolated and analyzed as an independent component of a culture. It is, like mankind and other social institutions, a product of culture and contributes to the evolution of the culture which employs it. Since accounting is culturally determined, other cultural customs, beliefs, and institutions influence it.*

Takatera and Yamamoto (1987) have defined culture as 'an expression of norms, values and customs which reflect typical behavioural characteristics'. Hofstede (1980, p. 25) has defined culture as 'the collective programming of the mind which distinguishes the members of one human group from another'. It describes a system of societal or collectively held values (Gray, 1988, p. 4) rather than values held at an individual level. 'Values' are deemed to determine behaviour. Gray (1988, p. 4) explains that the term 'culture' is typically reserved for societies as a whole, or nations, whereas 'subculture' is used for the level of an organisation, profession (such as the accounting profession) or family. It is expected that different subcultures within a particular society will share common characteristics. In the discussion that follows we consider the work of Professor Sid Gray in some depth. This work is generally acknowledged as constituting some of the most rigorous research into accounting's relationship to, and to some extent dependence on, national culture.

Gray (1988, p. 5) argues that 'a methodological framework incorporating culture may be used to explain and predict international differences in accounting systems and patterns of accounting development internationally'. Any consideration of culture necessarily requires difficult choices as to aspects of culture that are important to the issue under consideration, and in turn, how one goes about measuring the relevant cultural attributes. As Perera (1989, p. 43) states, 'the study of culture is characterized by a unique problem arising from the inexhaustible nature of its components'.[4] Gray used the work of Hofstede (1980, 1983). Gray (1988, p. 5) explains:

Hofstede's (1980, 1983) research was aimed at detecting the structural elements of culture and particularly those which most strongly affect known behaviour in work situations in organizations and institutions. In what is probably one of the most extensive cross-cultural studies ever conducted, psychologists collected data about 'values' from the employees of a multinational corporation located in more than fifty countries. Subsequent statistical analysis and reasoning revealed four underlying societal value dimensions along which countries could be positioned. These dimensions, with substantial support from prior work in the field, were labeled Individualism, Power Distance, Uncertainty Avoidance, and Masculinity. Such dimensions were perceived to represent a common structure in cultural systems. It was also shown how countries could be grouped into culture areas, on the basis of their scores on the four dimensions, using cluster analysis and taking into account geographical and historical factors. The point of reviewing Hofstede's research is that if societal value orientations are related to the development of accounting systems at the subcultural level, given that such values permeate a nation's social system, then it may be hypothesised that there should be a close match between culture areas and patterns of accounting systems internationally. In order to explore further the relationship between culture and accounting systems in an international context it is necessary to identify the mechanism by which values at the societal level are linked to values at the accounting subcultural level as it is these latter values which are likely to influence directly the development of accounting systems in practice.

Gray argues that the value systems of accountants will be derived and related to societal values (which are reflected by Hofstede's cultural dimensions of Individualism, Power Distance, Uncertainty Avoidance and Masculinity).[5] The values of the accounting subculture will in turn, it is believed, impact on the development of the respective accounting systems at the national level. Therefore, at this point we can perhaps start to question whether accounting systems can be developed in a 'one-size-fits-all' perspective—an approach which, in some respects, the IASC appears to have

---

4. Perera (1989, p. 43) further states that 'it is essential, therefore, that in analyzing the impact of culture upon the behaviour of the members of any particular subculture, a researcher must select the cultural components or dimensions most pertinent to the particular facet of cultural behaviour being studied'. This is clearly not a straightforward task.

5. Hofstede's theory, while being applied to accounting issues, is from the cross-cultural psychology literature and was of itself not directly concerned with accounting.

adopted (we return to this point later in the chapter). However, while it is argued that there should be some association between various value systems and accounting systems, over time, many events would typically have occurred that confound this possible relationship. For example, in relation to developing countries, Baydoun and Willett (1995, p. 72) state:

> It is quite possible that had accounting systems evolved independently in developing countries they would have a rather different form from any we now witness in present day Europe. However, most accounting systems used in developing countries have been directly imported from the West through a variety of channels: by colonialism in the past; and through Western multinational companies, the influence of local professional associations (usually founded originally by Western counterpart organizations) and aid and loan agencies from the industrialised countries.

Returning to the work of Hofstede, the four societal value dimensions identified by Hofstede can be summarised as follows (from Hofstede, 1984):

Individualism versus Collectivism

> Individualism stands for a preference for a loosely knit social framework in society wherein individuals are supposed to take care of themselves and their immediate families only. Its opposite, Collectivism, stands for a preference for a tightly knit social framework in which individuals can expect their relatives, clan, or other in-group to look after them in exchange for unquestioning loyalty (it will be clear that the word 'collectivism' is not used here to describe any particular social system). The fundamental issue addressed by this dimension is the degree of interdependence a society maintains among individuals. It relates to people's self concept: 'I' or 'we'.

With regard to the cultural dimension of *Individualism versus Collectivism* it is interesting to note that a great deal of economic theory is based on the notion of *self-interest* and the *rational economic person* (one who undertakes action to maximise personal wealth at the expense of others). This is very much based in the *Individualism dimension*. In a culture that exhibited *Collectivism* it is expected that members of the society would look after each other and issues of loyalty would exist.[6]

---

6. Positive Accounting Theory, a theory developed by Watts and Zimmerman (and which we discuss in depth in Chapter 7), attempts to explain and predict managers' selection of accounting methods. In developing their theory, Watts and Zimmerman assume that individuals will *always* act in their own self-interest. Such an assumption would be invalid in a community which embraces a Collectivist perspective. In a similar vein, Hamid, Craig and Clarke (1993) suggest that finance theories developed in Western cultures will not apply in Islamic cultures. According to Hamid, Craig and Clarke (1993), the Islamic principles do not allow the payment of interest. They argue (p. 146) therefore that 'much of Western finance theory, in particular the capital asset pricing model, which draws upon interest-dependent explanations of risk, cannot be part of the (Islamic) accounting and finance package'.

Large versus Small Power Distance

Power Distance is the extent to which the members of a society accept that power in institutions and organisations is distributed unequally. This affects the behaviour of the less powerful as well as of the more powerful members of society. People in Large Power Distance societies accept a hierarchical order in which everybody has a place, which needs no further justification. People in Small Power Distance societies strive for power equalisation and demand justification for power inequities. The fundamental issue addressed by this dimension is how a society handles inequalities among people when they occur. This has obvious consequences for the way people build their institutions and organisations.

Strong versus Weak Uncertainty Avoidance

Uncertainty Avoidance is the degree to which the members of a society feel uncomfortable with uncertainty and ambiguity. This feeling leads them to beliefs promising certainty and to sustaining institutions protecting conformity. Strong Uncertainly Avoidance societies maintain rigid codes of belief and behaviour and are intolerant towards deviant persons and ideas. Weak Uncertainty Avoidance societies maintain a more relaxed atmosphere in which practice counts more than principles and deviance is more easily tolerated. The fundamental issue addressed by this dimension is how a society reacts to the fact that time only runs one way and that the future is unknown: whether it tries to control the future or to let it happen. Like Power Distance, Uncertainty Avoidance has consequences for the way people build their institutions and organisations.

Masculinity versus Femininity

Masculinity stands for a preference in society for achievement, heroism, assertiveness, and material success. Its opposite, Femininity, stands for a preference for relationships, modesty, caring for the weak, and the quality of life. The fundamental issue addressed by this dimension is the way in which a society allocates social (as opposed to biological) roles to the sexes.

Again, as stated earlier, when countries are given scores on the four value dimensions, a number of countries can be clustered together, reflecting that they have similar cultural values.[7] Having considered Hofstede's value dimensions, the next step for Gray was to relate them to the values that he perceived to be in place within the accounting subculture. Gray developed

---

7. For example, of the many groups, one group with similar scores on each of the four societal values comprises Australia, Canada, Ireland, New Zealand, UK, and USA. Another group is Denmark, Finland, Netherlands, Norway and Sweden, while another group comprises Indonesia, Pakistan, Taiwan and Thailand. The view is that people within these various groupings of countries share a similar culture and therefore share similar *norms* and *value systems*.

four accounting values that were deemed to relate to the accounting subculture with the intention that the accounting values would then be directly linked to Hofstede's four societal values (which we discussed above). Gray's four accounting values were defined as follows (1988, p. 8):

Professionalism versus Statutory Control

A preference for the existence of individual professional judgement and the maintenance of professional self-regulation, as opposed to compliance with prescriptive legal requirements and statutory control.

Uniformity versus Flexibility

A preference for the enforcement of uniform accounting practices between companies and the consistent use of such practices over time, as opposed to flexibility in accordance with the perceived circumstances of individual companies.

Conservatism versus Optimism

A preference for a cautious approach to measurement so as to cope with the uncertainty of future events, as opposed to a more optimistic, laissez-faire, risk-taking approach.

Secrecy versus Transparency

A preference for confidentiality and the restriction of disclosure of information about the business only to those who are closely involved with its management and financing, as opposed to a more transparent, open and publicly accountable approach.

Gray (1988) then developed a number of hypotheses relating Hofstede's four societal cultural dimensions to each one of his own four accounting values.[8] The hypotheses were as follows:

H1: The higher a country ranks in terms of *Individualism* and the lower it ranks in terms of *Uncertainty Avoidance* and *Power Distance*, then the more likely it is to rank highly in terms of *Professionalism*.

The basis for the above hypothesis was that a preference for applying judgement (for example, determining whether something is *true and fair*) rather than strict rules is more likely where people tend to be individualistic; where people are relatively more comfortable with people using their own judgement, rather than conforming to rigid codes of rules; and, where different people are allowed to make judgements rather than relying on strict rules 'from above' (lower Power Distance).

---

8. Although Gray (1988) developed four hypotheses, he did not test them empirically. To test them, as others have subsequently done, one must determine whether an accounting system scores high or low in a particular country on the four dimensions developed by Gray.

Gray's second hypothesis was:

H2: The higher a country ranks in terms of *Uncertainty Avoidance* and *Power Distance* and the lower it ranks in terms of *Individualism*, then the more likely it is to rank highly in terms of *Uniformity*.

The basis for the second hypothesis is that communities that prefer to avoid uncertainty prefer more rigid codes of behaviour and greater conformity. A desire for uniformity is also deemed to be consistent with a preference for Collectivism (as opposed to Individualism) and an acceptance of a relatively more Power Distance society in which laws are more likely to be accepted.

Gray's third hypothesis was:

H3: The higher a country ranks in terms of *Uncertainty Avoidance* and the lower it ranks in terms of *Individualism* and *Masculinity*, then the more likely it is to rank highly in terms of *Conservatism*.

As noted previously, Conservatism implies that accountants favour notions such as prudence (which traditionally means that profits and assets are calculated in a conservative manner with a tendency towards understatement rather than overstatement). The basis for the third hypothesis is that communities that have strong Uncertainty Avoidance characteristics tend to prefer a more cautious approach to cope with existing uncertainties. On the other hand, Conservatism is expected to be associated with communities that care less about individual achievement. Communities that tend to demonstrate masculine tendencies emphasise achievement—hence the expectation that lower levels of Masculinity will lead to higher preferences for conservative accounting principles. A more highly masculine community would be deemed to prefer to use methods of accounting that lead to higher levels of performance being reported.

Gray's fourth hypothesis is:

H4: The higher a country ranks in terms of *Uncertainty Avoidance* and *Power Distance* and the lower it ranks in terms of *Individualism* and *Masculinity*, then the more likely it is to rank highly in terms of *Secrecy*.

The basis for the fourth hypothesis is that communities that have a higher preference for Uncertainty Avoidance prefer not to disclose too much information because this could lead to conflict, competition and security problems. Also, communities that accept higher Power Distance would accept restricted information, as this acts to preserve power inequalities. Also, a community that prefers a collective approach, as opposed to an individualistic approach, would prefer to keep information disclosures to a minimum to protect those close to the firm and to reflect limited concern for those external to the organisation. A more *Masculine* community would be expected to provide more information about its financial position and performance to enable comparisons of the level of performance of different entities. (Masculine communities would be deemed to be more concerned with issues such as ranking the performance of one entity against another.) However, as a caveat to the general position that more Masculine communities disclose more accounting information, Gray (1988, p. 11) argues that 'a significant but less important link with masculinity also seems likely to the extent that more caring societies, where more emphasis is given to the quality of life, people and the environment, will tend to be more open, especially as regards socially related information'.[9] Table 6.2 summarises the hypothesised relationships between Gray's accounting values and Hofstede's cultural values.

TABLE 6.2 Summary of the hypothesised relationships between Gray's accounting values and Hofstede's cultural values

Cultural values (from Hofstede)	Accounting values (from Gray)			
	Professionalism	Uniformity	Conservatism	Secrecy
Power Distance	–	+	?	+
Uncertainty Avoidance	–	+	+	+
Individualism	+	–	–	–
Masculinity	?	?	–	–

Note: '+' indicates a positive relationship; '–' indicates a negative relationship; and '?' indicates that the direction of the relationship is unclear.

Gray (1988) further hypothesised that relationships can be established between accounting values and the *authority* and *enforcement* of accounting systems (the extent to which they are determined and enforced by statutory control or professional means), and the *measurement* and *disclosure* characteristics of the accounting systems. According to Gray (1988, p. 12):

> *Accounting value systems most relevant to the professional or statutory authority for accounting systems and their enforcement would seem to be the professionalism and uniformity dimensions, in that they are concerned with regulation and the extent of enforcement and conformity . . . Accounting values most relevant to the measurement practices used and the extent of information disclosed are self-evidently the conservatism and the secrecy dimensions.*

Gray's linkage between societal values, accounting values, and accounting practice can be summarised, as in Figure 6.1 (as summarised in Fechner and Kilgore, 1994, p. 269).

Perera (1989, p. 47) provides additional discussion in respect of the relationships summarised in Figure 6.1. He states:

---

9. Socially related information would relate to such issues as health and safety issues, employee education and training, charitable donations, support of community projects and environmental performance. A more Feminine (less Masculine) society would tend to consider these issues more important. Hence while Femininity might be associated with less financial disclosure, it is assumed to be associated with greater social disclosure.

The higher the degree of professionalism the greater the degree of professional self-regulation and the lower the need for government intervention. The degree of uniformity preferred in an accounting sub-culture would have an effect on the manner in which the accounting system is applied. The higher the degree of uniformity the lower the extent of professional judgement and the stronger the force applying accounting rules and procedures. The amount of conservatism preferred in an accounting sub-culture would influence the measurement practices used. The higher the degree of conservatism the stronger the ties with traditional measurement practices. The degree of secrecy preferred in an accounting sub-culture would influence the extent of the information disclosed in accounting reports. The higher the degree of secrecy, the lower the extent of disclosure.

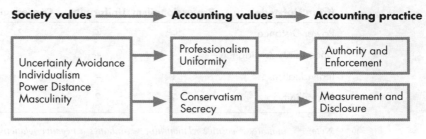

FIGURE 6.1 Gray's hypothesised relationships between society values, accounting values and accounting practice

One objective of Gray's research was to explain how differences between countries in respect of their culture may impede any moves towards international harmonisation of accounting standards. While some of the above material might appear a little confusing (perhaps not), it does represent quite an intellectual body of research, which is attempting to relate a fairly difficult to measure construct, *culture*, to differences in values of the accounting subculture, and ultimately to differences in the systems of accounting employed. While we might not be able to remember all the hypothesised relationships described above, what is important is that we appreciate how researchers have attempted to link cultural measures to accounting practice.

A number of other authors have also used Hofstede's cultural dimensions.[10] Zarzeski (1996) provides evidence that supports a view that entities located in countries classified as relatively more *Individualistic* and *Masculine* and relatively less in terms of *Uncertainty Avoidance* provide greater levels of disclosure. Zarzeski also considered issues associated with

---

10. Baydoun and Willett (1995, p. 72) identify a number of problems in testing the Hofstede–Gray theory. They emphasise that many accounting systems are imported from other countries with possibly different cultures. As they state: 'Due to the interference in what would otherwise have been the natural evolution of financial information requirements there are no uncontaminated examples of modern accounting practices in developing countries. Consequently great care has to be taken in using data from developing countries to draw inferences about relevance on the basis of the Hofstede–Gray framework.'

international profile and found that those entities with a relatively higher international profile tend to be less secretive than other entities. Further, entities from continental European countries, such as France and Germany, that tend to rely more heavily on debt financing than, say, Anglo–American companies, have lower levels of disclosure than Anglo–American companies. In relation to the issue of secrecy, Zarzeski shows that local enterprises are more likely to disclose information commensurate with the secrecy of their culture than are international enterprises. In explaining this she states (p. 20):

> The global market is just a different 'culture' than the one the firm faces at home. When a firm does business in the global market, it is operating in a different 'culture' and therefore may need to have different 'practices'. Higher levels of financial disclosures may be necessary for international survival because disclosure of quality operations should result in lower resource costs. When enterprises from more secretive countries perceive economic gain from increasing their financial disclosures, cultural borrowing may occur. The culture being borrowed will be a 'global market culture,' rather than a specific country culture.

Perera (1989) considered both Hofstede's cultural dimensions and Gray's accounting subcultural value dimensions and uses them to explain apparent differences in the accounting practices adopted in continental European countries and Anglo–American countries. According to Perera (p. 51):

> The Continental European countries, in particular France and West Germany, are high on the uncertainty avoidance scale, whereas Anglo-American countries are relatively low on the same scale. The characteristics of the uncertainty avoidance dimension reveals that in cultures which are high on the scale, behavior tends to be more rigidly prescribed, either by written rules or by unwritten social codes. The presence of these rules satisfied people's emotional needs for order and predictability in society, and people feel uncomfortable in situations where there are no rules. Therefore, in general, one can expect more formalization and institutionalization of procedures in strong uncertainty avoidance societies than in weak uncertainty avoidance countries.
>
> There is a preference for the existence of individual professional judgement, the maintenance of professional self-regulation, and flexibility in accordance with the perceived circumstances of individual companies in the accounting sub-culture of Anglo-American countries, whereas there is a preference for compliance with prescriptive legal requirements and statutory control, the maintenance of uniform accounting practices between companies, and the consistent application of such practices over time in the accounting sub-cultures of Continental Europe. Also, there is more support in the latter group for a prudent and cautious approach to income measurement to cope with the uncertainty of future events and the confidentiality of the information by restricting disclosures to only those involved with the management and financing of the organization.
>
> These characteristics, in turn, tend to influence the degree of disclosure expected in the respective accounting systems or practices. For example, in

France and West Germany, where the level of professionalism is relatively low and the preference for conservatism and secrecy is relatively high, the combined effect on the degree of disclosure will be negative. On the other hand, the collectivist or anti-individualist values of the society require business enterprises to be accountable to society by way of providing information. Therefore, it becomes necessary for the Government to intervene and prescribe certain disclosure requirements, including those in regard to social accounting. Furthermore, this situation is not likely to be rejected by the accounting profession, because here is a preference for compliance with prescriptive legal regulation and statutory control in the accounting sub-culture. By comparison, in the United States and U.K., although the relatively high level of professionalism and low level of preference for conservatism and secrecy tend to have a positive combined effect on the degree of disclosure in accounting practices, the individualistic values of the society are more concerned with the provision of information to shareholders or investors than those issues involving accountability to society at large.

Baydoun and Willett (1995) used the Hofstede–Gray theory to investigate the use of the French United Accounting System (which is ranked lowly in terms of Professionalism and highly in terms of Uniformity as well as being considered as quite conservative) in Lebanon. According to Baydoun and Willett, following World War I the Allied Supreme Council granted France a mandatory authority over Lebanon. Lebanon was a French colony until 1943 and French troops remained there until 1946. Strong trading relations between France and Lebanon still exist and in 1983 the French government sponsored the transfer of the French Uniform Accounting System (UAS) to Lebanon. What was of interest is whether the French system was actually suited to the Lebanon cultural environment. Baydoun and Willett provide evidence to suggest that Lebanon and France rank in a relatively similar manner in terms of Power Distance and Individualism. However, Lebanon is considered to rank lower in terms of Uncertainty Avoidance and higher in terms of Masculinity. On this basis (and we can refer back to Table 6.2), Baydoun and Willett (p. 81) conclude that 'it would appear that Lebanon's requirements are for less Uniformity, Conservatism and Secrecy in financial reporting practices'.[11] They further state (p. 87):

Assuming that cultural relevance is or should be a factor in determining the form of financial statements, we would expect Lebanese financial statements to be less uniform across time and between entities, to contain more market value information and provide more items of disaggregated information. Normal

---

11. In undertaking their work, Baydoun and Willett were, in a number of respects, critical of Gray's work. For example, they state (p. 82) that 'all of Gray's accounting values are defined in terms of preferences for particular courses of action, rather than in terms of apparent attributes of financial statements, such as the qualitative characteristics described in the FASB's conceptual framework project'. Also they state that Gray's theory does not clearly indicate what forms of financial statements might be preferred.

publication dates should be relatively flexible and there should be less call for conservative valuation rules such as lower of cost and market. It would appear that these and other similar prescriptions cannot be tested directly at present. Since 1983 all Lebanese firms have been required to follow UAS and this system has not yet been modified to accommodate any cultural differences between France and Lebanon . . . However, our analysis suggests that modifications along the lines described above either will or should take place in Lebanese accounting in the future.

Religion

A great deal of the culture-based research, particularly that based on the work of Hofstede and Gray, tends to lead to countries being grouped together in terms of both community and accounting subculture—this is perceived as providing guidance in the harmonisation process and, particularly, in identifying limits therein. That is, a feature of the work of Gray is that it relies on indigenous characteristics which are confined within the boundaries of the countries under review. In subsequent work, Hamid, Craig and Clarke (1993) consider the influence of one cultural input or factor, *religion*, on accounting practices. As they indicate, religion transcends national boundaries. They consider how Islamic cultures, which exist in numerous countries, have typically failed to embrace 'Western' accounting practices and they reflect upon how issues of religion had previously occupied minimal space in the accounting literature. They state (p. 134):

> *The existing literature dealing with the interaction of business activity and Islam needs extending to capture the particular effects which compliance with Islamic beliefs have on the structure of business and finance within an Islamic framework. In particular, the incompatibility of many Western accounting practices with Islamic principles requires explanation. For jurisprudential Islamic law influences the conduct of businesses in a manner not accommodated automatically by Anglo-American accounting practice. And many Western accounting practices draw upon assumptions which conflict with the tenets of Islam . . . There seems to be little understanding that, unlike the Western tradition, fundamental business ethics flow automatically from the practices of the religion, rather than from the codes (mainly of etiquette) devised and imposed upon members by professional associations.*

Hamid, Craig and Clarke (1993) point out that the Islamic tradition does have notions of stewardship—but to God rather than to suppliers of equity or debt capital. That is, Muslims believe that they hold assets not for themselves, but in trust for God. There are also other fundamental differences—for example, Islam precludes debt financing and prohibits the payment of interest. According to Hamid, Craig and Clarke (1993, p. 143):

> *The potential for the borrower to invest money and earn a profit introduces an unacceptable speculative element into the business undertaking. To exact*

a higher amount than the sum lent on that conjectural basis is regarded as being a kind of unjust exploitation. Injustice is presumed to arise wherever there is a guaranteed and fixed return to one party (in this case the lender), but an uncertain and variable return to the other (the borrower). As a consequence, all fixed income securities, such as preferred stock, are unlawful.

According to Hamid, Craig and Clarke (1993) the prohibition of interest on debt has significant implications for processes aimed at the international harmonisation of accounting standards, particularly:

. . . in-so-far as harmonisation is perceived necessary to entail implementation of many standard Western accounting procedures in which interest calculations are integral. Many past and present Western standards entail discounting procedures involving a time value of money concept, which is not admitted by Islam (p. 144).[12]

Hence, Hamid, Craig and Clarke (1993) appear to provide a logical argument that religion can have a major impact on the accounting system chosen. Religion can potentially affect how people do business and how they make decisions. As shown in Chapter 5, the conceptual framework projects being developed in countries such as the United States, Australia, Canada, United Kingdom and New Zealand (which, interestingly, have all been grouped together by Hofstede), and by the IASC, are based on the underlying objective that financial report users require financial information as the basis for making *rational economic decisions*. Such rational economic decisions also take into account the time value of money, which necessarily requires considerations of appropriate interest or discount rates. In some societies, such as Islamic states, this may not be a relevant objective. Further, any claims that particular frameworks of accounting are superior to others should only be made after considering the environments in which the frameworks are to be utilised.

Business ownership and financing system

In another paper, which attempted to provide an insight into explaining international differences in financial reporting, Nobes (1998) suggests that the major reason for international differences in financial reporting is different *purposes* for that reporting.

In particular, at a country level, it is suggested that the financing system is relevant in determining the purpose of financial reporting. Zysman (1983) distinguishes between three types of financing system: (a) capital market based, in which prices are established in competitive markets; (b) credit based system:

---

12. For example, notions of discounting are found in 'Western' accounting standards dealing with employee benefits, lease capitalisation, debt defeasance, and general insurers.

governmental, in which resources are administered by the government; and (c) credit-based system: financial institutions, in which banks and other financial institutions are dominant. Zysman suggested that the UK and the USA have a type (a) system, France and Japan a type (b) system, and Germany a type (c) system (p. 166).

Nobes suggests that for systems that rely on equity markets, which in turn typically creates large numbers of 'outsiders', there will be a demand for public disclosures, given that most investors are not involved in the day-to-day operation of the entity, and otherwise have no access to financial information.

The hypothesis predicting a correlation between the style of corporate financing and the type of accounting system is that the rule makers for, and the preparers of, financial reports in equity-outsider countries are largely concerned with the outside users. The conceptual frameworks used by the rule makers of the US, the UK, Australia and the IASC make it clear that this is so. In particular they state that they are concerned with financial reporting performance and enabling the prediction of future cash flows for relatively sophisticated outside users of financial statements of large companies. By contrast, credit based countries will be more concerned with the protection of creditors and therefore with prudent calculation of distributable profit. Their financiers (insiders) will not need externally audited, published accounts. The difference of purpose will lead to differences in accounting practice (p. 167).

In applying the above argument we can consider China. As Nobes states, China is not a country with a strong equity-outsider tradition, but it appears to be going this way. As such, systems of accounting such as those used in the US, UK, and Australia are following. Nobes suggests that apart from the finance system in place, other factors might also have implications for the system of financial accounting in place. He suggests that some underdeveloped countries sometimes have inappropriate accounting systems imposed upon them by more powerful countries. He also suggests that *colonial inheritance* is a major explanatory factor for the general system of financial accounting used in many countries outside Europe. Another influencing factor is *invasion*, but Nobes suggests that 'when the invader retires, any foreign accounting can be gradually removed if it does not suit the country' (p. 170). Nobes concludes his paper by suggesting that it is 'accounting practice systems, not countries, that should be classified. Some implications for the rule makers are suggested, warning against inappropriate transfers of technology' (p. 184).

In related research, Pratt and Behr (1987) compared the standard-setting processes adopted in the US and Switzerland. Differences in the standards and processes adopted were explained by differences in 'size, complexity, and diversity of capital transactions, the wide distribution of ownership, and the opportunistic nature of the capital market participants'.

Hence, in summarising this section of the chapter we can see that a number of reasons, including culture, religion (which is a subset of culture), and financing systems (which we could also imagine would be influenced by culture), have been advanced to explain the accounting systems in place. This discussion has by no means been exhaustive in identifying the many factors proposed to explain international differences in accounting systems, but nevertheless, the referenced research indicates that one general approach to accounting, such as that used in the US, UK, Australia, New Zealand or Canada, may suit a particular environment, but not others. Therefore, it is probably somewhat naive to claim that there is any one 'best' system of accounting. With this in mind we can reflect on the following claim. FASB Chairman Dennis Beresford recently claimed that the US accounting and reporting system is regarded by many as 'the most comprehensive and sophisticated system in the world' (as quoted in Wyatt and Yospe, 1993). Perhaps in some countries (perhaps the majority) the US system might be considered sophisticated—but in others it might be considered quite irrelevant.

International agencies and their impacts on accounting practice

We now turn to another branch of 'international accounting'. We consider efforts that have been undertaken to develop one system of accounting that is applicable to all countries. As we saw at the beginning of the chapter, this branch of international accounting was referred to as *universal* or *world accounting* by Weirich, Avery and Anderson (1971).

There are many institutions or bodies that can have an impact on the accounting policies used in particular countries. For example, multinational companies may export their accounting methods to various parts of the world. Large international accounting firms may have policies that prescribe that particular accounting methods be used by clients throughout the world. Large monetary organisations, such as the World Bank, may specify that a requirement of borrowing be that particular accounting methods be employed by borrowers. One institution that has had a major effect on accounting methods used throughout the world is the International Accounting Standards Committee (IASC).

The International Accounting Standards Committee

According to IASC (1998, p. 43), the IASC is an independent private sector body formed in 1973 through an agreement made by professional accounting bodies from Australia, Canada, France, Germany, Japan, Mexico, the Netherlands, The United Kingdom, Ireland and the United States of America. Since 1983, the IASC members have been all the professional accountancy bodies that are members of the International Federation of Accountants (IFAC). As of 1 November 1998, IASC and IFAC have 143 members in 103 countries.

The IASC is based in London. To date it has released over 30 International Accounting Standards (IASs) covering a wide cross-section of issues and has undertaken work on its conceptual framework which is entitled *Framework for the Preparation and Presentation of Financial Statements.* The IASC believes the framework helps it to achieve consistency within the International Accounting Standards that it develops. As we have indicated before, the conceptual framework adopted by the IASC is very similar to the conceptual framework projects developed in countries such as the US and Australia.

As in most standard-setting bodies, the development of IASs is a political process with members making submissions and voting on the acceptance, or otherwise, of particular accounting standards. The IASs themselves typically differ from the accounting standards used in the various countries that make up the membership of the IASC. Some individuals have referred to IASs as compromised outcomes. Although efforts have been made to harmonise accounting standards throughout the world, the IASC has no power to enforce the use of its standards in any jurisdiction. The objectives of IASC, as stated in its Constitution (as identified in IASC, 1998, p. 6) are:

(a) to formulate and publish in the public interest accounting standards to be observed in the presentation of financial statements and to promote their worldwide acceptance and observance; and

(b) to work generally for the improvement and harmonisation of regulations, accounting standards and procedures relating to the presentation of financial statements.

According to the IASC (1998), it has established some short-term and long-term aims (p. 8), these being:

(a) IASC's short-term aim should be for national accounting standards and International Accounting Standards to converge around high quality solutions; and

(b) IASC's aim in the longer term should be global uniformity—a single set of high-quality accounting standards for all listed and economically significant business enterprises around the world. It is not possible to forecast how long this will take, as different countries are likely to converge with uniform global standards at different rates.

In the previous section of this chapter we considered a number of factors that researchers claim will impede the convergence or standardisation of accounting standards on a worldwide scale, including differences of culture, religion, financing, and business structures.

The IASC believes that the development of International Accounting Standards has done a great deal both to *improve* and to *harmonise* financial reporting around the world. The IASC (1998, p. 3) states that they are used:

(a) as a basis for national accounting requirements in many countries;

(b) as an international benchmark by some countries that develop their own requirements (including certain major industrialised countries, regional organisations such as the European Union, and an increasing number of emerging markets such as China and many other countries in Asia, Central Europe and the countries of the former Soviet Union);

(c) by stock exchanges and regulatory authorities that allow foreign or domestic companies to present financial statements in accordance with International Accounting Standards;

(d) by supra-national bodies that rely on IASC to produce accounting standards that improve the quality of financial reporting and the comparability of financial statements, instead of developing their own requirements;

(e) by the World Bank Group and other development agencies that require borrowers and recipients of other forms of aid to follow high standards of financial reporting and accountability;

(f) by a growing number of individual companies.

In relation to the above points, stock exchanges such as the London and Hong Kong exchanges allow foreign companies to list on their exchange if they present financial statements prepared in accordance with IASs. Countries with quite significant differences in culture (relying upon measures provided by Hofstede (1980)), for example Singapore versus Jamaica, use IASs as the basis for developing their own standards, and other countries which also are deemed to be quite culturally different (for example, Botswana and Cyprus) have adopted the IASs as their own.

In recent years there seems to have been a sense of urgency in the efforts of the IASC and this is reflected in the following statement:

> The standards of many countries are already converging with International Accounting Standards. However, trends such as globalisation and the increasing pace of business and financial change have made this task more urgent. (IASC, 1998, p. 6).

Not all countries support IASs. However, one country that has been particularly supportive of IASs is Australia. Since about 1997 there has been considerable effort to harmonise Australian accounting standards with IASs. In Australia, according to APS 3: *Compatibility of Australian Accounting Standards and International Accounting Standards*, it is considered that an IASC standard should normally be considered to represent the minimum requirements for an Australian accounting standard that covers the same issue. APS 3 also requires that where an Australian standard is inconsistent with an existing IASC standard, this should be explicitly indicated within the body of the Australian standard.

Other international bodies

While the IASC clearly plays the dominant role in influencing accounting practices on an international basis, there are a number of other international organisations that have also provided input into accounting at an international level. For example, for a number of years the United Nations has called for moves towards 'uniform accounting'. Similar calls have also been made by the Organisation for Economic Cooperation and Development (OECD) and the European Economic Community (EEC).[13]

The European Union (EU) has also made calls for changes in accounting practice at an international level. In 1992 the EU released a document entitled *Towards Sustainability* as part of its *Fifth Action Programme*. In a document that suggested quite radical changes to the practice of accounting on a worldwide basis, one of the suggestions of the program was for the accounting profession to take a role in implementing costing systems that internalise many environmental costs which were previously ignored. Specifically, the EU called for a 'redefinition of accounting concepts, rules, conventions and methodology so as to ensure that the consumption and use of environmental resources are accounted for as part of the full cost of production and reflected in market prices' (European Commission, 1992, Vol. II, Section 7.4, p. 67).

The International Organization of Securities Commissions (IOSCO), a body that promotes the international harmonisation of the regulation and trading of securities, has also played a key role in influencing accounting practices on an international scale. In recent years IOSCO has been working with the IASC and has assisted IASs to achieve widespread acceptance by developing a plan that compliance with IASs will ultimately allow an organisation to have their securities listed in all global markets. The technical committee of IOSCO had claimed that 'a primary impediment to international offerings of securities is that different countries have different accounting standards' (as stated in IASC News, Vol. 18. No. 1, January 1998). In relation to its work with the IOSCO, IASC (1998, p. 47) states:

> *Many stock exchanges accept International Accounting Standards for cross-border listing purposes, but stock exchanges in Canada, Japan and the United States are currently exceptions. IASC has therefore adopted a work program to produce a comprehensive core set of high quality standards, aiming at more general acceptance of International Accounting Standards for cross-border listings. The Technical Committee of the International Organization of Securities Commissions (IOSCO) has agreed that when IASC completes the work programme to the Technical Committee's satisfaction, the Technical Committee will consider recommending that IOSCO should endorse International Accounting Standards for cross-border capital raising and listing purposes in all global markets. IASC aims to complete the core standards in 1998. If IOSCO endorses the International Accounting Standards (and International Standards on Auditing) there is likely to be a substantial increase in the credibility of financial statements prepared under International Accounting Standards and audited under International Standards on Auditing.*

---

13. For example, calls for the harmonisation of accounting were made in the EEC's *Treaty of Rome*, and the OECD issued a document in 1976 entitled *A Declaration on International Investment and Multinational Enterprises* which identified a number of suggested financial information disclosure items.

Another relevant body is the International Federation of Accounting Committee (IFAC) which in recent years has concentrated on international issues associated with the practice of auditing and accounting education, as well as issues associated with ethical conduct.

While the above bodies have attempted to implement strategies to harmonise or unify accounting practices on an international basis, we can appreciate, on the basis of the material covered earlier in this chapter, that there are many potential obstacles to restrict the achievement of such goals. It has also been argued that the efforts towards *assisting* countries, particularly developing countries, by providing them with mechanisms to use Western style accounting systems can actually cause harm (Briston, 1978). Reflecting on the efforts of the UK accounting profession in the 1970s with relation to developing countries, he states (p. 110):

> *Although it could be argued that some irrelevant accountancy training is better than none at all, the influence of the UK accountancy bodies upon developing countries is, on balance, highly detrimental . . . As an example, it was recommended that accountancy in the Seychelles should be encouraged by financing the training of a few students to become certified accountants (in the UK). Even if the students returned to the Seychelles after qualifying, they would probably hinder the development of a relevant accounting system in that country by many years. Instead of being encouraged in this way, accountants in developing countries should be positively discouraged from membership in the UK professional bodies, for these bodies make no concessions to overseas students and insist upon a set of knowledge which is largely peculiar to UK practice and almost certainly irrelevant and possibly harmful if applied in the wrong context.*

We now consider further the harmonisation efforts being undertaken by the IASC.

The harmonisation of accounting— a consideration of some perceived benefits and obstacles

As noted throughout this chapter, there are various efforts under way internationally to *harmonise* accounting standards, which refers to a process that attempts to make accounting standards released by different countries as similar as possible. Harmonisation does not imply absolute standardisation.

Australia was one of the first major accounting standard-setters to embark on a program that seeks to harmonise its Accounting Standards with those of the IASC. The harmonisation of Australian accounting standards with their international counterparts is typically justified on the basis that if Australia elects to retain accounting standards that are unique, then this will restrict the inflow of foreign investment into Australia. This view is promoted within the Australian Federal Government's Corporate Law Economic Reform Program

(CLERP). In its 1997 document *Accounting Standards: Building International Opportunities for Australian Business* it is stated (p. 15):

> There is no benefit in Australia having unique domestic accounting standards which, because of their unfamiliarity, would not be understood by the rest of the world. Even if those standards were considered to represent best practice, Australia would not necessarily be able to attract capital because foreign corporations and investors would not be able to make sensible assessments, especially on a comparative basis, of the value of the Australian enterprises.[14]
> The need for common accounting language to facilitate investor evaluation of domestic and foreign corporations and to avoid potentially costly accounting conventions by foreign listed companies are powerful arguments against the retention of purely domestic financial reporting regimes.

The above view is also consistent with the view provided in Policy Statement 6: *International Harmonisation Policy* (issued in April 1996 by the Australian Accounting Standards Board and the Public Sector Accounting Standards Board) which emphasises the need for international comparability of financial statements. As the Policy Statement notes in paragraph 1.2:

> The globalisation of capital markets has resulted in an increased demand for high quality, internationally comparable financial information. The Boards believe that they should facilitate the provision of this information by pursuing a policy of international harmonisation of Australian accounting standards. In this context, international harmonisation of Australian accounting standards refers to a process which leads to those standards being made compatible, in all significant respects, with the standards of other national and international standard-setters.

To support the standardisation effort, which is quite costly, in 1998 the Australian Stock Exchange announced the imposition of a 3% levy on annual listings. The purpose of this levy was to provide financial support to the Australian Accounting Standards Board in order to assist its harmonisation efforts.

Modifications to existing Australian accounting standards and the release of new standards related to the harmonisation process effectively began in 1997 with the release of a number of exposure drafts. Since 1998, over 20 new or revised accounting standards have been released (for some issues the revisions are fairly minor). No level of activity such as this has ever occurred before within the Australian accounting standard-setting arena. This has required much effort from local preparers of financial statements, users of

---

14. The view that harmonisation might lead to Australia abandoning particular standards that might represent 'best practice' is very interesting, implying that harmonisation might lead to systems of accounting that are less than ideal. Also, moving away from 'best practice' obviously has implications for qualitative characteristics such as *representational faithfulness* and *neutrality*.

financial statements, teachers of accounting, and so on. Such efforts required consideration prior to efforts to initiate the harmonisation project.

Paragraph 4.1 of Policy Statement 6 addresses some of the perceived barriers to harmonisation in 'the short to medium term'. According to the statement:

> *These barriers include the effects on standard-setting of different business environments, legal systems, cultures and political environments in different countries.*

If national culture has impacted on the approaches and decisions taken by accounting practitioners and accounting standard-setters within their own particular countries, is it appropriate to expect different countries, with varying cultural values, to adopt internationally compatible practices? Clearly a number of accounting standard-setting bodies believe it is appropriate, but as we have seen in previous discussion, many researchers adopt a contrary view. As an example of this, Perera (1989, p. 52) considers the potential success of transferring accounting skills from Anglo-American countries to developing countries. He notes:

> *The skill so transferred from Anglo-American countries may not work because they are culturally irrelevant or dysfunctional in the receiving countries' context.*

Perera (1989) also argues that the IASC standards themselves are strongly influenced by Anglo-American accounting models and, as such, the IASC standards tend to reflect the circumstances and patterns of thinking in a particular group of countries. He argues that IASC standards are likely to encounter problems of relevance in countries where different cultural environments from those found in Anglo-American countries exist. This is consistent with Gray (1988) who suggests that if policy makers consider cultural issues and the similarity between the cultural attributes of some countries, then 'policy-makers may be in a better position to predict problems that a country may be likely to face and identify solutions that may be feasible, given the experience of countries with similar development patterns' (p. 2).

In relation to Perera's point, which questions the relevance of IASs to some countries, the IASC (1998, p. 50) states:

> *Many developing and newly industrialised countries are using International Accounting Standards as their national requirements, or as the basis for their national requirements. These countries have a growing need for relevant and reliable financial information to meet the requirements both of domestic users and of international providers of the capital that they need.*

Again, whether the *imported* regulations provide *relevant* information is a point of some debate.

Perhaps it could be argued that with the increasing globalisation of business, international cultural differences will be reduced—but this is clearly speculative. Zarzeski (1996), however, provides evidence that business enterprises that operate on an international scale do appear to adopt a 'global market culture' (as discussed previously in this chapter) indicating that harmonisation efforts perhaps should be directed at larger international organisations, rather than organisations that operate domestically.

Apart from the attraction of foreign capital, other perceived benefits of the harmonisation process include:

- it is cheaper for developing countries to establish a national system of accounting (however, again we must consider issues of cultural relevance);

- it can lead to a reduction in costs for companies seeking listing on international stock exchanges—the costs necessary to restate financial statements to local generally accepted accounting standards would be lower;

- it would enable increased comparability between entities operating in different countries (which is important if we accept that *comparability* is an important qualitative characteristic, as is indicated in various conceptual framework projects);

- it would enable multinational corporations located in different countries to coordinate their efforts more efficiently and would allow the consolidation of foreign entities' financial statements to be done at less cost.

The whole area of harmonisation and the related issues of culture is an interesting area to study. Over time we can perhaps expect more refined measures of culture and more sophisticated analysis of the implications of cultural differences on accounting practice. It will be interesting to monitor the various current harmonisation efforts to see whether they lead to the benefits expected by the standard-setters, and whether cultural differences (however measured) do provide ongoing obstacles to the process.

Chapter summary

In this chapter we identified and considered international differences in accounting practices and we have seen that numerous reasons (generated from different theoretical perspectives) have been advanced to explain such differences (including differences in culture, religions as a subset of culture, financing systems, and capital structure). Much of the existing research into comparative international accounting questions whether it is appropriate to expect that we will ever have one system of accounting adopted uniformly throughout the world (which has been stated as a long-term objective of the IASC).

While many researchers question the relevance of 'Western style' accounting standards across all countries, efforts by a number of international organisations are nevertheless continuing to encourage quite culturally-disparate countries to adopt International Accounting Standards. This implies that the members of the international organisations (such as IASC, UN,

OECD, IOSCO) are either ignorant of the literature, or alternatively, choose to reject it as irrelevant. As efforts by a number of countries, such as Australia, continue in relation to harmonising domestic accounting standards with international standards, it is to be expected that this debate will continue.

References

Baydoun, N., Willett, R., 'Cultural Relevance of Western Accounting Systems to Developing Countries', *ABACUS*, Vol. 31, No. 1, pp. 67–92, 1995.

Briston, R.J., 'The Evolution of Accounting in Developing Countries', *The International Journal of Accounting Education and Research*, Vol. 14, No. 1, pp. 105–20, Fall 1978.

Commonwealth Government of Australia, *Accounting Standards: Building International Opportunities for Australian Business, Corporate Law Economic Reform Program Proposals for Reform: Paper No. 1*, Australian Government Printing Service, Canberra, 1997.

Deegan, C., *Australian Financial Accounting*, McGraw-Hill, Sydney, 1999.

Doupnik, T.S., Salter, S.B., 'External Environment, Culture, and Accounting Practice: A Preliminary Test of a General Model of International Accounting Development', *The International Journal of Accounting*, Vol. 30, No. 3, pp. 189–207, 1995.

European Union, *Fifth Action Programme*, Com (92) 23 final, Vols. I–III, Brussels, 1992.

Fechner, H.H.E., Kilgore, A., 'The Influence of Cultural Factors on Accounting Practice', *The International Journal of Accounting*, Vol. 29, pp. 265–77, 1994.

Gray, S.J., 'Towards a Theory of Cultural Influence on the Development of Accounting Systems Internationally', *ABACUS*, Vol. 24, No. 1, pp. 1–15, 1988.

Hamid, S., Craig, R., Clarke, F., 'Religion: A Confounding Cultural Element in the International Harmonization of Accounting?', *ABACUS*, Vol. 29, No. 2, pp. 131–48, 1993.

Hofstede, G., 'Cultural Dimensions in Management and Planning', *Asia Pacific Journal of Management*, January 1984.

Hofstede, G., 'Dimensions of National Cultures in Fifty Countries and Three Regions', in J.B. Derogowski, S. Dziuraweic, R. Annis (eds), *Expisations in Cross-Cultural Psychology*, Swets and Zeitlinger, 1983.

Hofstede, G., *Culture's Consequences: International Differences in Work-Related Values*, Sage Publications, 1980.

International Accounting Standards Committee, *Shaping IASC for the Future*, IASC, London, 1998.

Mueller, G.G., 'Accounting Principles Generally Accepted in the United States Versus Those Generally Accepted Elsewhere', *The International Journal of Accounting Education and Research*, Vol. 3, No. 2, pp. 91–103, Spring 1968.

Mueller, G.G., *International Accounting*, Macmillan, New York, 1967.

Nobes, C., 'Towards a General Model of the Reasons for International Differences in Financial Reporting', *ABACUS*, Vol. 34, No. 2, 1998.

Nobes, C., *International Classification of Financial Reporting*, Croom Helm, 1984.

Perera, H., 'Towards a Framework to Analyze the Impact of Culture on Accounting', *The International Journal of Accounting*, Vol. 24, No. 1, pp. 42–56, 1989.

Pratt, J., Behr, G., 'Environmental Factors, Transaction Costs, and External Reporting: A Cross National Comparison', *The International Journal of Accounting Education and Research*, Spring 1987.

Riahi-Belkaoui, A., *Accounting Theory*, 4th edn, Business Press–Thomson Learning, London, 2000.

Takatera, S., Yamamoto, M., 'The Cultural Significance of Accounting in Japan', paper presented at seminar on Accounting and Culture at the European Institute for Advanced Studies in Management, Brussels, 1987.

Violet, W.J., 'The Development of International Accounting Standards: An Anthropological Perspective', *The International Journal of Accounting Education and Research*, Vol. 18, No. 2, pp. 1–12, Spring 1983.

Watts, R.L., Zimmerman, J.L., *Positive Accounting Theory*, Prentice-Hall, Englewood Cliffs, New Jersey, 1986.

Weirich, T.R., Avery, C.G., Anderson, H.R., 'International Accounting: Varying Definitions', *The International Journal of Accounting Education and Research*, pp. 79–87, Fall 1971.

Wyatt, A.R., Yospe, J.F., 'Wake-Up Call to American Business: International Accounting Standards are on the Way', *Journal of Accountancy*, pp. 80–5, July 1993.

Zarzeski, M.T., 'Spontaneous Harmonization Effects of Culture and Market Forces on Accounting Disclosure Practices', *Accounting Horizons*, Vol. 10, No. 1, pp. 18–37, 1996.

Zysman, J., *Government, Markets and Growth: Financial Systems and the Politics of Change*, Cornell University Press, 1983.

Questions

6.1 In the context of financial accounting, what is harmonisation and how does it differ from standardisation?

6.2 Identify some factors that might be expected to explain why different countries use different systems of accounting.

6.3 After considering the Hofstede–Gray model, briefly explain the hypothesised link between society values, accounting values, and accounting practice.

6.4 Any efforts towards standardising accounting practices on an international basis implies a belief that a 'one-size-fits-all' approach is appropriate. Is this naive?

6.5 While it is often argued that within particular countries there should be some association between various value systems and accounting systems, it is also argued (for example, by Baydoun and Willett, 1995) that over time many events would typically have occurred that confound this expected relationship. What type of events might confound the expected relationship?

6.6 As noted in this chapter, Baydoun and Willett (1995, p. 72) identify a number of problems in testing the Hofstede–Gray theory. They emphasise that many accounting systems are imported from other countries with possibly different cultures. As they state: 'Due to the interference in what would otherwise have been the natural evolution of financial information requirements, there are no uncontaminated examples of modern accounting practices in developing countries. Consequently great care has to be taken in using data from developing countries to draw inferences about relevance on the basis of the Hofstede–Gray framework.' Explain the point of view being provided by Baydoun and Willett. Do you believe that they are correct?

6.7 As noted in this chapter, Hamid, Craig and Clarke (1993) provide an argument that religion can have a major impact on the accounting system chosen by particular countries and that before 'Western' methods of accounting are exported to particular countries, it must be determined whether particular religious beliefs will make the 'Western' accounting policies irrelevant. Provide an explanation of their argument.

6.8 Nobes (1998) suggests that for countries that have organisations that rely relatively heavily upon equity markets, as opposed to other sources of finance, there will be a greater propensity for such organisations to make public disclosures of information. What is the basis of this argument?

6.9 As noted in this chapter, in the early 1990s, FASB Chairman Dennis Beresford claimed that the U.S. accounting and reporting system is regarded by many as 'the most comprehensive and sophisticated system in the world'. Evaluate this statement. Do you think that the US system would be regarded as sophisticated in all cultural contexts?

6.10 In its 1998 document entitled *Shaping IASC for the Future* the IASC identified a long-term aim. It stated (p. 8). 'IASC's aim in the longer term should be global uniformity—a single set of high-quality accounting standards for all listed and economically significant business enterprises around the world. It is not possible to forecast how long this will take, as different countries are likely to converge with uniform global standards at different rates.' Do you think it is realistic to expect that one day there will be internationally uniform accounting standards? What factors would work for or against achieving this aim?

6.11 The harmonisation of Australian accounting standards with their international counterparts is typically justified on the basis that if Australia elects to retain accounting standards that are unique, then this will restrict the inflow of foreign investment into Australia. Evaluate this claim.

6.12 Paragraph 4.1 of Policy Statement 6 (issued in Australia) addresses some of the perceived barriers to harmonisation in 'the short to medium term'. According to the statement, these barriers include the effects on standard setting of different business environments, legal systems, cultures and political environments in different countries. Given these barriers, do you think that Australian standard setters have been naive in embracing the harmonisation process?

6.13 The IASC (1998, p. 50) states that 'many developing and newly industrialised countries are using International Accounting Standards as their national requirements, or as the basis for their national requirements. These countries have a growing need for relevant and reliable financial information to meet the requirements both of domestic users and of international providers of the capital that they need.' Do you think that International Accounting Standards will provide 'relevant and reliable information' that meets the needs of all financial statement users in all countries?

Chapter 7

Positive Accounting Theory

Learning objectives

Upon completing this chapter readers should understand:

- how a positive theory differs from a normative theory;

- the origins of Positive Accounting Theory;

- the perceived role of accounting in minimising the transaction costs of an organisation;

- how accounting can be used to reduce the costs associated with various political processes;

- how particular accounting based agreements with parties such as debtholders and managers can provide incentives for managers to manipulate accounting numbers;

- some of the criticisms of PAT.

Opening issues

Corporate management often expends considerable time and effort making submissions to accounting regulators on proposed introductions of, or amendments to, mandated accounting requirements. For example, in Australia a requirement was introduced in 1991 that all companies involved in the general insurance industry value their investment assets at net market value, with any changes in value to be included in the period's profit or loss. The introduction of this accounting method restricted the accounting methods available to an organisation, and introduced the possibility that companies would have to record gains or losses resulting from changes in the market value of the assets, even when such changes could be considered temporary. Many managers within general insurance companies lobbied against the proposed new requirement. What would have motivated such opposition?

Positive Accounting Theory defined

As indicated in Chapter 1, a *positive theory* is a theory that seeks to explain and predict particular phenomena. According to Watts (1995, p. 334), the use of the term *positive research* was popularised in economics by Friedman (1953) and was used to distinguish research which sought to *explain* and *predict*, from research which aimed to provide *prescription* (prescriptive research is often labelled *normative* research). Positive Accounting Theory, the topic discussed in this chapter and the theory popularised by Watts and Zimmerman, is one of several positive theories of accounting.[1] As indicated in Chapter 1, we can refer to the general class of theories that attempt to explain and predict accounting practice in lower case (that is, as positive theories of accounting), and we can refer to Watts and Zimmerman's particular positive theory of accounting as Positive Accounting Theory (that is, in upper case). Hence, while it might be confusing, we must remember that Watts and Zimmerman's Positive Accounting Theory is an example of *one* particular positive theory of accounting. This confusion might not have arisen had Watts and Zimmerman elected to adopt an alternative name (or 'trademark') for their particular theory. According to Watts and Zimmerman (1990, p. 148):

> *We adopted the label 'positive' from economics where it was used to distinguish research aimed at explanation and prediction from research whose objective was prescription. Given the connotation already attached to the term in economics we thought it would be useful in distinguishing accounting research*

---

1. Legitimacy Theory and Stakeholder Theory, both covered in Chapter 8, are other examples of positive theories. For example, Legitimacy Theory predicts that in certain circumstances organisations will use positive or favourable disclosures in an effort to restore the *legitimacy* of an organisation. These other positive theories are not grounded in classical economic theory, whereas Positive Accounting Theory is.

aimed at understanding accounting from research directed at generating prescriptions . . . The phrase 'positive' created a trademark and like all trademarks it conveys information. 'Coke', 'Kodak', 'Levi's' convey information.

As Watts and Zimmerman (1986, p. 7) state, Positive Accounting Theory (hereafter referred to as PAT):

. . . is concerned with explaining accounting practice. It is designed to explain and predict which firms will and which firms will not use a particular method . . . but it says nothing as to which method a firm should use.[2]

Positive theories can be contrasted with normative theories. In Chapters 4 and 5 we considered different normative theories of accounting. Normative theories prescribe how a particular practice *should* be undertaken and this prescription might be a significant departure from existing practice. A normative theory is generated as a result of the particular theorist applying some norm, standard, or objective against which actual practice should strive to achieve. For example, in Chapter 4 we considered Chambers' theory of accounting, which he labelled *Continuously Contemporary Accounting*. Under this theory Chambers prescribes that *all* assets should be measured at net market value and that such information is more useful for informed decision making than information based on historical costs, and which, according to Chambers, may actually be misleading. Chambers has made a judgement about the role of accounting (to provide information about an entity's *capacity to adapt* to changing circumstances) and as a result of this judgement he has prescribed particular accounting practice.

Returning our focus to PAT, we see in this chapter that PAT focuses on the relationships between the various individuals involved in providing resources to an organisation and how accounting is used to assist in the functioning of these relationships. Examples are the relationships between the owners (as suppliers of equity capital) and the managers (as suppliers of managerial labour), or between the managers and the firm's debt providers. Many relationships involve the delegation of decision making from one party (the principal) to another party (the agent)—this is referred to as an agency relationship. When decision-making authority is delegated, this can lead to some loss of efficiency and consequent costs. For example, if the owner (principal) delegates decision-making authority to a manager (agent) it is possible that the manager may not work as hard as would the owner, given that the manager might not share directly in the results of the organisation. Any potential loss of profits brought about by the manager under-performing is considered to be a cost that results from the decision-making delegation within this agency relationship—an agency cost. The agency costs that arise

---

2. Similarly, in Chapter 8 we see that two other positive theories, Stakeholder Theory (the managerial version) and Legitimacy Theory, provide alternative explanations (alternative to PAT) about what drives an organisation to make particular disclosures. These theoretical perspectives also do not prescribe particular actions, or methods of disclosure.

as a result of delegating decision-making authority from the owner to the manager are referred to in PAT as *agency costs of equity*.

PAT, as developed by Watts and Zimmerman and others, is based on the central economics-based assumption that all individuals' action is driven by *self-interest* and that individuals will act in an opportunistic manner to the extent that the actions will increase their wealth. Notions of loyalty, morality, and the like are not incorporated in the theory (as they typically are not incorporated in other accounting or economic theories). Given an assumption that self-interest drives all individual actions, PAT predicts that organisations will seek to put in place mechanisms that align the interests of the managers of the firm (the agents) with the interests of the owners of the firm (the principals). As we see later in this chapter, some of these methods of aligning interest will be based on the output of the accounting system (such as providing the manager with a share of the organisation's *profits*). Where such accounting-based 'alignment mechanisms' are in place, there will be a need for financial statements to be produced. Managers are predicted to 'bond' themselves to prepare these financial statements.[3] This is costly in itself, and in PAT would be referred to as a 'bonding cost'. If we assume that managers (agents) will be responsible for preparing the financial statements, then PAT also would predict that there would be a demand for those statements to be audited or monitored, otherwise agents would, assuming self-interest, try to overstate profits, thereby increasing their absolute share of profits. In PAT, the cost of undertaking an audit is referred to as a 'monitoring cost'.

To address the agency problems that arise within an organisation there may be various bonding and monitoring costs incurred. If it was assumed, contrary to the assumptions of PAT, that individuals always worked for the benefit of their employees, then there would not be such a demand for such activities—other than perhaps to review the efficiency with which the manager was operating the business. As PAT assumes that not all opportunistic actions of agents can be controlled by contractual arrangements or otherwise, there will always be some residual costs associated with appointing an agent.

Having provided this introductory overview of PAT we now turn to the origins and development of PAT. We return to the issue of how accounting can be used to reduce conflicts within the firm later in this chapter. The following discussion shows that PAT developed out of the economics literature and was heavily reliant on assumptions about the efficiency of markets (from the Efficient Markets Hypothesis); on research which considered the reactions of capital markets to accounting information (which was developed from models such as the Capital Assets Pricing Model); and, on the role of contractual arrangements in minimising conflicts within an organisation (from Agency Theory).

---

3. From the PAT perspective, *bonding* occurs when the agent gives a guarantee to undertake, or not to undertake, certain activities.

The origins and development of Positive Accounting Theory

Positive research in accounting started coming to prominence around the mid-1960s and appeared to become the dominant research paradigm in the 1970s and 1980s. Prior to this time the dominant type of accounting research was normative accounting research—research that sought to provide prescription based on the theorists' perspective of the underlying objective of accounting. High profile normative researchers of this time included Sterling, Edwards and Bell, and Chambers and the focus of much of the research at this time was how to undertake accounting in times of rising prices.[4] Such normative research did not rely on examining existing practice—that is, it did not tend to be empirical.

Watts (1995, p. 299) provides an insight into the trends in accounting research that occurred from the 1950s to 1970s. As evidence of the trends, and relying on the works of Dyckman and Zeff (1984), he documents the number of publications accepted by two dominant academic accounting journals—*The Accounting Review* and the *Journal of Accounting Research*.[5] He states:

> *The introduction of positive research into accounting in the mid-1960s represented a paradigm shift. Prior to that time, the most common type of paper published in the leading English language academic journal of the time (*The Accounting Review*) was normative (like the works of Edwards and Bell, Chambers and Sterling). In the period 1956–1963, 365 of* Accounting Review *articles were of this type. These papers use assumptions about phenomena and objectives to deduce their prescriptions. They do not use systematic evidence and/or advance hypotheses for formal testing. Only 3% of the articles published in* Accounting Review *in 1956–1963 were empirical and most were not designed to test hypotheses. Virtually none of the papers in this time period were attempts to explain current accounting using mathematical modelling or less formal techniques. Today, almost all papers in* Accounting Review *are in the positive tradition and the same is true of most other leading academic journals (all of which started in 1963 or later).*[6]

---

4. We considered the work of these theorists in Chapter 4. As indicated in Chapter 4 as well as in Chapter 1, researchers such as Sterling, Chambers and many others were particularly critical of positive research, and particularly of Positive Accounting Theory.

5. By relying on only two journals it could easily be argued, given that there are many other acounting journals, that the data may not be representative of all accounting research being undertaken. Further, evidence would indicate that the editors of these journals developed an extremely favourable disposition towards positive research, a disposition not necessarily shared by editors of other journals. Nevertheless, there was certainly a significant movement towards positive research in the 1960s and 1970s.

6. As we might imagine, there are many researchers who do not favour the positive research paradigm and hence would challenge Watts' view that journals that publish positive research are *leading* academic journals.

In reflecting on what caused the shift in paradigm from normative to positive research, Watts (1995, p. 299) argues that:

> The paradigm shift is associated with changes in US business schools in the late 1950s and early 1960s. Reports on business education commissioned by the Ford Foundation and the Carnegie Corporation of New York were catalysts for those changes . . . Hypothesis forming and testing were viewed as essential for good research.

It is also argued that around the mid-1960s and through the 1970s, computing facilities improved markedly, such that it became increasingly practical to undertake large-scale statistical analysis—an approach used within the positive research paradigm. As Watts and Zimmerman (1986, p. 339) state:

> Computers and large machine-readable data bases (CRSP and Compustat) became available in the 1960s. And, partially in response to the lowered cost of empirical work, finance and economic positive theories became available for accounting researchers' use. This led to the development of positive accounting research and to researchers trained in the methodology of positive theory.[7]

Watts considers that one paper that was crucial to the acceptance of the positive research paradigm was by two Australian researchers, Ray Ball and Phillip Brown. According to Watts (1995, p. 303), the Ball and Brown (1968) publication in *Journal of Accounting Research* caused widespread interest in accounting-related capital market research (research which seeks to explain and predict share price reaction to the public release of accounting information), and led to ever-increasing numbers of papers being published in the area (we will consider this paper shortly). Reflecting on the subsequent shift in publications towards positive research, Watts (1995, p. 303) states:

> Empirical papers as a proportion of papers published in Journal of Accounting Research *rose from 13 per cent in 1967 to 31 per cent in 1968 and to 60 per cent by 1972. Normative papers in* Journal of Accounting Research *fell from 24 per cent in 1967 to seven per cent in 1968 and by 1972 to zero.* Accounting Review *followed suit and stopped publishing normative papers. The empirical papers in the capital markets area*

---

7. Chapter 12 (which considers the views of the *critical theorists*) provides alternative views about why positive accounting flourished in the 1970s and 1980s. These theorists (for example, Mouck, 1992, Tinker, Lehman and Neimark, 1991) believe that many accounting researchers provide research results and perspectives that aim to legitimise and maintain particular political ideologies. As an example, in the late 1970s and in the 1980s there were moves by particular governments around the world towards deregulation. This was particularly the case in the United States and the United Kingdom. Around this time researchers working within the Positive Accounting Framework, and researchers who embraced the Efficient Market Hypothesis, came to prominence. The researchers typically took an anti-regulation stance, a stance that matched the views of the government of the time. Coincidentally, perhaps, the critical theorists show that such research, which supported calls for deregulation, tended to attract considerable government-sourced research funding, thereby providing further resources for the theory's development.

were in the positivist tradition. The normativists challenged the evidence and its interpretation, but did not supply their own counter-evidence. They did not have the training nor likely the desire to compete in this dimension.

One development from the 1960s that was crucial to the development of PAT was the work of theorists such as Fama, particularly work that related to the development of the Efficient Markets Hypothesis (EMH). The EMH is based on the assumption that capital markets react in an efficient and unbiased manner to publicly available information.[8] The perspective taken is that security prices reflect the information content of publicly available information and this information is not restricted to accounting disclosures. The capital market is considered to be highly competitive, and as a result, newly released public information is expected to be quickly impounded into share prices. As Watts and Zimmerman (1986, p. 6) state:

Underlying the EMH is competition for information. Competition drives investors and financial analysts to obtain information on the firm from many sources outside the firm's accounting reports and even outside the firm itself. For example, analysts obtain weekly production data on automobile firms and interview management. Analysts also interview competitors about a corporation's sales and creditors about the corporation's credit standing.

If accounting results are released by an organisation, and these results were already anticipated by the market (perhaps as a result of interim announcements), then the expectation is that the price of the security will not react to the release of the accounting results. Consistent with traditional finance theory, the price of a security is determined on the basis of beliefs about the present value of future cash flows pertaining to that security and when these beliefs change (as a result of particular information becoming available) the expectation is that the security's price will also change.[9]

Because share prices are expected to reflect information from various sources (as the information relates to predicting future cash flows), there was a view that management cannot manipulate share prices by changing accounting methods in an opportunistic manner. If the change in accounting method does not signal a change in cash flows, then early proponents of the

---

8. Research that subsequently tested the EMH predominantly adopted the assumption of *semi-strong form market efficiency*. Under the assumption of semi-strong form efficiency the market price of a firm's securities reflects all publicly available information. According to Watts and Zimmerman (1986, p. 19) the available evidence is generally consistent with the semi-strong form of the EMH. Two other forms of market efficiency (with less empirical support) have also been advanced. The *weak form* of market efficiency assumes that existing security prices simply reflect information about past prices and trading volumes. The *strong form* of market efficiency assumes that security prices reflect all information known to anyone at that point in time (including information which is not publicly available).

9. In studies that investigate the reaction of the capital market to earnings announcements, it is generally assumed that accounting earnings are highly correlated with cash flows, hence new information about accounting earnings is deemed to indicate new information about cash flows.

EMH would argue that the capital market will not react. Further, because there are many sources of data used by the capital market, if managers make less than truthful disclosures, which are not corroborated or contradict other available information, then, assuming that the market is efficient, the market will question the integrity of the managers. Consequently the market will tend to pay less attention to subsequent accounting disclosures made by such managers. Watts and Zimmerman (1986) rely upon this perspective to argue against the need for extensive accounting regulation. Because accounting information is only one source of information, because markets are assumed to be efficient in evaluating information, and because of the existence of other potentially non-corroboratory evidence, there is believed to be limited benefit in imposing accounting regulation.

Researchers such as Ball and Brown (1968) and Beaver (1968) sought to empirically investigate stock market reactions to accounting earnings announcements. Utilising monthly information about earnings announcements in the Wall Street Journal and information about share returns, Ball and Brown investigated whether unexpected changes in accounting earnings lead to abnormal returns on an organisation's securities. Relying upon the EMH, Ball and Brown proposed that if the earnings announcements were useful to the capital market (there was *new* or *unexpected* information in the announcement), then share prices would adjust to reflect the new information. As they stated (1968, p. 159):

> If security prices do in fact adjust rapidly to new information as it becomes available, then changes in security prices will reflect the flow of information to the market. An observed revision of stock prices associated with the release of the income report would thus provide evidence that the information reflected in income numbers is useful.

Hence Ball and Brown needed to determine whether the earnings announcement contained any information that was unexpected and therefore potentially 'useful'. Using statistical modelling they calculated an estimate of what was the *expected earnings* of the entity in the absence of the earnings announcement. They also needed a model to estimate what the market return from holding the entity's securities would have been in the absence of the information. That is, they needed to be able to determine what *normal* returns would have been on the securities so that they could then determine whether any *abnormal* returns arose (which would have been assumed to relate to the information disclosure).

In determining what normal returns would have been, had there been no unexpected information in the earnings announcement, reliance is placed on the Market Model which is derived from the Capital Assets Pricing Model (CAPM).[10] These models are more fully discussed in Chapter 10. Briefly, on

---

10. Share returns would generally be calculated by taking into account the change in the price of the security during the period, as well as any dividends received during the period.

the basis of past information, the CAPM provides an indication of the expected rate of return on securities by applying a linear model.[11] The expected return on a particular stock is calculated by considering the risk-free rate of return (for example, the return from holding government bonds), plus a risk/return component which is based on how the returns on the particular security have fluctuated historically relative to the movements in the overall (diversified) stock market. The difference between the expected return and the actual return constitutes the abnormal return. The results of the Ball and Brown study were generally supportive of the view that if earnings announcements provided unexpected information, the capital market reacted to the information, the reaction taking the form of abnormal returns on the entity's securities.

By indicating that earnings announcements (mainly based on historical cost accounting) were impacting share prices, Ball and Brown provided evidence that they considered was consistent with a view that historical cost information was useful to the market.[12] This was in direct conflict with various normative theorists (such as Chambers) who had argued that historical cost information is rather useless and misleading.[13] The capital market apparently thought otherwise (if we accept that the change in share price reflected the *usefulness* of the accounting information).[14] In this respect, Watts and Zimmerman (1986, p. 161) state:

---

11. The development of the CAPM is generally credited to the works of Sharpe (1964) and Lintner (1965).

12. Much research has followed Ball and Brown (1968). For example, subsequent research has shown that the relationship between the information content in earnings announcements and changes in share prices tends to be more significant for smaller firms. That is, in general, larger firms' earnings announcements have relatively less information content (for example, Freeman, 1987, Collins, Kothari, and Rayburn, 1987). This is consistent with the EMH and is explained by the fact that larger firms tend to have more information being circulated about them, as well as attracting more attention from such parties as security analysts. Hence, on average, earnings announcements for larger firms tend to be more anticipated, and hence already impounded in the share price prior to the earnings announcement.

13. Ball and Brown's results were also considered to be important because they emphasised that accounting numbers were not the sole (or predominant) source of information about an organisation. This was in contrast to the views held by many normative theorists who considered that accounting data were the sole, or at least the most important, source of information about an organisation, hence their concerns about getting the accounting numbers 'right'.

14. What should also be appreciated is that research such as that undertaken by Ball and Brown and subsequent researchers actually represents a joint test of the EMH, as well as the procedures used to estimate *expected earnings* and *normal returns*. That is, failure to generate significant results (or indeed, success in generating significant results) may be due to mis-specification problems in the calculation of expected earnings and normal returns, rather than problems with the hypothesis itself.

Some critics charge that, because earnings are calculated using several different methods of valuation (e.g. historical cost, current cost, and market value), the earnings numbers are meaningless and stock prices based on those numbers do not discriminate between efficient and less efficient firms. Given the EMH, evidence is inconsistent with this criticism. Positive stock price changes are associated with positive unexpected earnings and negative stock prices with negative unexpected earnings. Therefore, since the stock price is an unbiased estimate of value, earnings changes are measures of value changes.

Throughout the 1970s and subsequent years, many other studies were published that documented the relationship between accounting earnings and security returns (and a number of these are considered in Chapter 10). However, while supportive of the EMH, the literature was unable to explain *why* particular accounting methods might have been selected in the first place. That is, the research provided no hypotheses to *predict* and *explain* accounting choices—rather the existing research simply considered the market's reaction to the ultimate disclosures.

Much of the research based on EMH assumed that there were zero contracting and information costs, as well as assuming that the capital market could efficiently 'undo' the implications of management selecting different accounting methods.[15] For example, if an entity elected to switch its inventory cost flow assumptions and this led to an increase in reported income, then the market was assumed to be able to 'see through' this change, and to the extent that there were no apparent cash flow implications (for example, through changing taxes), there would be no share price reaction. Hence, if the particular accounting method had no direct taxation implications, there was an inability to explain why one method of accounting was selected in preference to another. As Watts and Zimmerman (1990, p. 132) state:

An important reason that the information perspective (e.g. Ball and Brown, 1968) failed to generate hypotheses explaining and predicting accounting choice is that in the finance theory underlying the empirical studies, accounting choice per se could not affect firm value. Information is costless and there are no transaction costs in the CAPM frameworks. Hence if accounting methods do not affect taxes they do not affect firm value. In that situation there is no basis for predicting and explaining accounting choice. Accounting is irrelevant.

---

15. As shown later in this chapter, however, subsequent arguments were developed to support a contrary view that a change in accounting method may have cash flow consequences (and therefore, consequences for share prices). For example, the new accounting method may be considered to provide information more efficiently about the performance of the firm, and hence may enable the firm to attract more funds at lower cost (perhaps because investors consider the available information to be more reliable). Further, and as shown shortly, many contractual arrangements with associated cash flows (for example, there might be an agreement that the manager gets paid a percentage of profits) are tied to accounting numbers and hence changing those numbers can ultimately change cash flows (and hence, firm value).

Yet, evidence indicated that corporate managers expended considerable resources lobbying regulators in regard to particular accounting methods. To such individuals, the choice of accounting method *did* matter. Further, there was evidence (for example, Kaplan and Roll, 1972) that firms within an entire industry often elected to switch accounting methods at a particular time.

A key to explaining managers' choice of particular accounting methods came from Agency Theory. Agency Theory provided a necessary explanation of why the selection of particular accounting methods might matter, and hence was an important facet in the development of PAT. Agency Theory focused on the relationships between principals and agents (for example, the relationship between shareholders and corporate managers), a relationship which, due to various information asymmetries, created much uncertainty. Agency theory accepted that transaction costs and information costs exist.

Jensen and Meckling (1976) was a key paper in the development of Agency Theory and was a paper that Watts and Zimmerman greatly relied upon when developing PAT. Jensen and Meckling defined the agency relationship (1976, p. 308) as:

> *A contract under which one or more (principals) engage another person (the agent) to perform some service on their behalf which involves delegating some decision-making authority to the agent.*[16]

Relying upon traditional economics literature (including accepting assumptions such as that all individuals are driven by desires to maximise their own wealth) Jensen and Meckling considered the relationships and conflicts between agents and principals and how efficient markets and various contractual mechanisms can assist in minimising the cost to the firm of these potential conflicts. A well-functioning firm was considered to be one that minimises its agency costs (those costs inherent in the principal/agent relationship). As indicated earlier in this chapter, if there is no mechanism to make an agent pay, then that agent (or manager) will, it is assumed, have an incentive to consume many perquisites, as well as to use confidential information for personal gain at the expense of the principals (the owners).

It is assumed within Agency Theory that principals will assume that the agent (like the principal) will be driven by self-interest, and therefore the principals will anticipate that the manager, unless restricted from doing otherwise, will undertake self-serving activities that could be detrimental to the economic welfare of the principals. In the absence of any contractual mechanisms to restrict the agents' potentially opportunistic behaviour, the principal will pay the agent a lower salary in anticipation of the opportunistic actions.[17] This lower salary will compensate the owners for the adverse actions

---

16. This *contract* does not have to be a written contract. That is, it may simply constitute implicit terms about how the principal expects the manager to behave.

17. Or if shares are being sold in a company, the shareholders will, in the absence of contractual restraints on the manager, pay a lower price for the shares in the organisation.

of the managers (this is referred to as *price protection*). Hence, the perspective is that it is the agents who, on average, pay for the principals' expectations of their opportunistic behaviour. The agents are therefore assumed to have an incentive to enter into contractual arrangements that appear to be able to reduce their ability to undertake actions detrimental to the interests of the principals. Consistent with this, Watts and Zimmerman (1986, p. 184) state:

> *This (perspective) provides the prime insight in the Jensen and Meckling analysis: the agent, not the principal, has the incentive to contract for monitoring. The outside shareholders do not care if monitoring (often involving accounting and auditing) is conducted. Competition in the capital markets leads to price protection and ensures that outside investors earn a normal return. Owner-managers (the agents) have the incentive to offer guarantees to limit their consumption of perks, for owner-managers receive all the gains . . . With competition and rational expectations, owner-managers who have incentives to take value reducing actions (opportunistic actions) such as over-consuming perks, shirking, or stealing when they sell outside shares, bear the costs of those dysfunctional actions. Hence they have incentives to contract to limit those actions and to have their actions monitored. The incentive is reduced (but not eliminated) by price protection in managerial labour markets.*[18]

That is, if it is assumed that managers would prefer higher salaries, then there will be an incentive for them to agree to enter into contractual arrangements that minimise their ability to undertake activities that might be detrimental to the interests of the owners (many of these contractual arrangements will be tied to accounting numbers). The managers (agents) will have incentives to provide information to demonstrate that they are not acting in a manner detrimental to the owners (principals).[19]

In the Agency Theory literature, the firm itself is considered to be a *nexus of contracts* and these contracts are put in place with the intention of ensuring that all parties, acting in their own self-interest, are at the same time motivated towards maximising the value of the organisation. The view of the firm as a nexus of contracts is consistent with Smith and Watts' (1983) definition of a corporation. They define the corporation as:

> . . . *a set of contracts among various parties who have a claim to a common output. These parties include stockholders, bondholders, managers, employees, suppliers and customers. The bounds of the corporation are defined by the*

---

18. In this context, reference is made to the owner/manager to imply that the manager might have some ownership in the organisation but does not own the entire organisation.

19. These arguments about managers' opportunistic behaviour are 'on average' arguments. Principals would not know with certainty whether specific agents will adopt particular opportunistic strategies which are detrimental to the principals' economic welfare. Rather, the principals will assume, on average, that the agent will adopt such strategies, and the principal will price protect accordingly. Hence the agent who does not commit to restrict the available set of actions will be penalised (in the form of lower salary) even though they individually may not ultimately elect to undertake actions detrimental to the principal.

set of rights under the contracts. The corporation has an indefinite life and the set of contracts which comprise the corporation evolves over time. (p. 3)

Agency Theory does not assume that individuals will ever act other than in self-interest, and the key to a well functioning organisation is to put in place mechanisms that ensure that actions that benefit the individual also benefit the organisation.[20]

Apart from the effects of various contractual arrangements, the literature of the 1970s also proposed that various markets, such as the *market for corporate control* and the *market for managers*, provided incentives for managers to work in the interests of the owners (Fama, 1980).[21] The view that agents have incentives to provide information to show they are working to the benefit of the owners (from Agency Theory), and the view that markets were efficient, was used as a basis for arguments against the regulation of accounting. Agents are deemed to have incentives to provide information that best reflects the underlying performance of the entity. Failure to do so will have negative implications for their reputation and hence will negatively impact on the total amount of income they can receive from within the organisation, or elsewhere. Referring to the work of Fama, Watts and Zimmerman (1986, p. 192) argue:

> *Fama (1980) suggests that information on managers' opportunistic value-reducing behavior eventually becomes known and affects their reputation. As a consequence, if managers consume a large quantity of perks (e.g., shirks), it eventually becomes known and they acquire a reputation. Such managers are expected to over-consume perks in the future, and their future compensation is reduced. Hence, even if managers' compensation is not adjusted in the period in which they over-consume, they still bear a cost for that over-consumption— the present value of the reductions in their future compensation. This effect is mitigated if the manager is close to retirement and does not have any deferred compensation (i.e., compensation paid after retirement).*

By the mid- to late 1970s, theory had therefore been developed that proposed that markets were efficient and that contractual arrangements were used as a basis for controlling the efforts of self-interested agents. This research provided the necessary basis for the development of PAT. PAT emphasised the role of accounting in reducing the agency costs of an organisation. It is also emphasised that efficiently written contracts, with many being tied to the

---

20. As shown later in this chapter, one way to align the interests of the manager with those of the owners of the firm might be for the manager to be given a share of profits in the organisation. Hence the manager would be motivated to increase profits (to increase his or her own wealth) and such self-interested activity will also provide benefits to the owners, who, all things being equal, will benefit from higher accounting earnings.

21. See Chapter 3 for an overview of the implications for managers of an efficiently functioning 'market for managers' and 'market for corporate takeovers'. In Chapter 3 we show that an assumption about efficiency in these markets provides a justification for some people to argue against regulating accounting disclosures.

output of the accounting system, were a crucial component of an efficient corporate governance structure.

One of the first papers to document how considerations of contracting costs,[22] as well as considerations of the political process, impacted on the choice of accounting methods was Watts (1977). This paper, published in the *Australian Journal of Management*, did not attract great attention. However, in the subsequent year, Watts and Zimmerman (1978) was published and this paper has become accepted as the key paper in the development and acceptance of PAT. It attempted to explain the lobbying positions taken by corporate managers in relation to the FASB's 1974 Discussion Memorandum on General Price Level Adjustments. According to Watts and Zimmerman (1978, p. 113):

> *In this paper, we assume that individuals act to maximise their own utility. In doing so they are resourceful and innovative. The obvious implication of this assumption is that management lobbies on accounting standards based on its own self-interest.*

As indicated in Chapter 4, General Price Level Accounting, through the use of a general price index, makes adjustments to historical cost profits to take into account the effects of changing prices. In times of inflation this typically has the effect of decreasing income, as well as increasing assets. Watts and Zimmerman considered how particular organisational attributes might affect whether the managers of an organisation supported, or opposed, a particular accounting requirement. Among the factors considered, two were the possibility that managers were paid bonuses tied to reported profits (the management compensation hypothesis), and the possibility that the organisation was subject to high levels of political scrutiny. In relation to the issue of political scrutiny and the associated costs, Watts and Zimmerman (1978, p. 115) state:

> *To counter potential government intrusions, corporations employ a number of devices, such as social responsibility campaigns in the media, government lobbying and selection of accounting procedures to minimise reported earnings. By avoiding the attention that 'high' profits draw because of the public's association of high reported profits and monopoly rents, management can reduce the likelihood of adverse political actions and, thereby, reduce its expected costs (including the legal costs the firm would incur opposing the political actions). Included in political costs are the costs labour unions impose through increased demands generated by large reported profits. The magnitude of the political costs is highly dependent on firm size.*

---

22. Contracting costs are costs that arise as a result of 'contracting' or formulating an agreement with another party (for example a manager) wherein one party provides a particular service for a particular payment. The contracting costs include: the costs of finding the other party to the contract; negotiating the agreement; costs associated with monitoring that the agreement has been carried out in the manner expected; possible renegotiation costs; and so on.

The results of Watts and Zimmerman (1978) did not provide support for the management compensation hypothesis. This was probably due to the fact that the discussion memorandum required GPLA disclosures to be provided as a supplement to the financial statements and did not require the financial statements themselves to be altered (and the bonus plans were expected to be tied to the numbers presented in the financial statements). However, significant findings were presented in relation to the political cost hypothesis.[23] More specifically, larger firms (who were deemed to be subject to higher political scrutiny) tended to support the Discussion Memorandum—an approach which would indicate (in times of rising prices) that the profits of the firm, adjusted for the effects of inflation, were lower than were otherwise reported. The view of Watts and Zimmerman was that, by presenting lower adjusted profits, these firms would attract less political attention and hence there would be less likelihood that parties would attempt to transfer wealth away from the firm (perhaps in the form of calls for increased taxes, for less tariff protection, for higher wages, etc.). In concluding their paper, Watts and Zimmerman (p. 131) state:

> *The single most important factor explaining managerial voting behavior on General Price Level Accounting is firm size (after controlling for the direction of change in earnings). The larger firms,* ceteris paribus, *are more likely to favour GPLA if earnings decline. This finding is consistent with our government intervention argument since the larger firms are more likely to be subjected to government interference and, hence, have more to lose than smaller organisations.*

Following the work of Watts and Zimmerman (1978), research in the area of PAT flourished. Much of this research sought to address some of the limitations inherent in Watts and Zimmerman's work. For example, subsequent research acknowledged that reported profits are impacted by many different accounting choices (rather than just the one choice, such as the choice to use GPLA), some of which may be income increasing, while others are income decreasing (thereby potentially offsetting each other). Zmijewski and Hagerman (1981) was an early paper that considered this issue and they undertook research in an endeavour to predict managements' choice in relation to four accounting methods choices, these relating to how to account for depreciation, inventory, investment tax credits and past pension costs.

In 1990 Watts and Zimmerman published an article in *The Accounting Review* that considered ten years of development of Positive Accounting Theory ('Positive Accounting Theory: A Ten Year Perspective'). They identified three key hypotheses that had become frequently used in the PAT literature to explain and predict whether an organisation would support or oppose a

---

23. Political costs are costs that particular groups external to the organisation may be able to impose on the organisation as a result of particular political actions. The costs could include increased taxes, increased wage claims or product boycotts.

particular accounting method. These hypotheses can be called the management compensation hypothesis (or bonus plan hypothesis), the debt hypothesis (or debt/equity hypothesis) and the political cost hypothesis. Watts and Zimmerman (1990) explain these hypotheses as follows:

> *The bonus plan hypothesis is that managers of firms with bonus plans are more likely to use accounting methods that increase current period reported income. Such selection will presumably increase the present value of bonuses if the compensation committee of the board of directors does not adjust for the method chosen. The choice studies to date find results generally consistent with the bonus plan hypothesis.* (1990, p. 138)

Hence, all things being equal, this hypothesis predicts that if a manager is rewarded in terms of a measure of performance such as accounting profits, that manager will attempt to increase profits to the extent that this leads to an increase in his or her bonus.

> *The debt/equity hypothesis predicts [that] the higher the firm's debt/equity ratio, the more likely managers use accounting methods that increase income. The higher the debt/equity ratio, the closer (i.e. tighter) the firm is to the constraints in the debt covenants. The tighter the covenant constraint, the greater [is] the probability of a covenant violation and of incurring costs from technical default. Managers exercising discretion by choosing income increasing accounting methods relax debt constraints and reduce the costs of technical default.* (1990, p. 139)

Hence, all things being equal, if a firm has entered into agreements with lenders, and these agreements involve accounting-based debt covenants (such as stipulating a maximum allowable debt/equity or debt/asset constraint) then managers have an incentive to adopt accounting methods that relax the potential impacts of the constraints (such as adopting accounting methods that increase reported income and assets).

> *The political cost hypothesis predicts [that] large firms rather than small firms are more likely to use accounting choices that reduce reported profits. Size is a proxy variable for political attention. Underlying this hypothesis is the assumption that it is costly for individuals to become informed about whether accounting profits really represent monopoly profits and to 'contract' with others in the political process to enact laws and regulations that enhance their welfare. Thus rational individuals are less than fully informed. The political process is no different from the market process in that respect. Given the cost of information and monitoring, managers have incentive to exercise discretion over accounting profits and the parties in the political process settle for a rational amount of ex post opportunism.* (1990, p. 139)

Hence, all things being equal, if managers consider that they are under a deal of political scrutiny, this could motivate them to adopt accounting methods that reduce reported income, and thereby reduce the possibility that people will argue that the organisation is exploiting other parties.

Researchers using the above three hypotheses (the management bonus hypothesis, the debt/equity hypothesis, and the political cost hypothesis), and there have been many such researchers, often adopted the perspective that managers (or agents) will act opportunistically when selecting particular accounting methods (for example, managers will select particular accounting methods because the choice will lead to an increase in profit and therefore to an increase in *their* bonus). Watts and Zimmerman (1978) was mainly grounded in the *opportunistic perspective*. However, a deal of the subsequent PAT research also adopted an *efficiency perspective*. This perspective proposes that managers will elect to use a particular accounting method because the method most efficiently provides a record of how the organisation performed. For example, the manager might have selected a particular depreciation method, not because it will lead to an increase in his or her bonus (the opportunistic perspective), but because the method most correctly reflects the use of the underlying asset. The following discussion considers the *opportunistic* and *efficiency* perspectives of PAT. In practice it is often difficult to determine whether opportunistic or efficiency considerations drove the managers' choice of a particular method—and this has been one limitation of much of this research.

Opportunistic and efficiency perspectives

As noted above, research that applies PAT typically adopts either an *efficiency perspective* or an *opportunistic perspective*. Within the efficiency perspective, researchers explain how various contracting mechanisms can be put in place to minimise the agency costs of the firm, that is, the costs associated with assigning decision making authority to the agent. The efficiency perspective is often referred to as an *ex ante* perspective—*ex ante* meaning before the fact—as it considers what mechanisms are put in place up front, with the objective of minimising future agency and contracting costs. For example, many organisations throughout the world voluntarily prepared publicly available financial statements before there was any regulatory requirement to do so. These financial statements were also frequently subjected to an audit, even when there also was no regulatory requirement to do so (Morris, 1984).[24] Researchers such as Jensen and Meckling (1976) argue that the practice of providing audited financial statements leads to real cost savings as it enables organisations to attract funds at lower cost. As a result of the audit, external parties have more reliable information about the resources and obligations of the organisation, which therefore enables the organisation to attract funds at a lower cost than would otherwise be possible, thereby increasing the value of the organisation.

---

24. Benston (1969) provides evidence that all of the firms listed on the New York Stock Exchange in 1926 published balance sheets when there was no direct requirement to do so. Further, 82 per cent were audited by a CPA when there was also no direct requirement to do so.

Within this efficiency (*ex ante*) perspective of PAT it is also argued that the accounting practices adopted by firms are often explained on the basis that such methods best reflect the underlying financial performance of the entity. Different organisational characteristics are used to explain why different firms adopt different accounting methods. For example, the selection of a particular goodwill amortisation rule from among alternative approaches is explained on the basis that it best reflects the underlying use of the asset. Firms that have different patterns of use in relation to an asset will be predicted to adopt different amortisation policies. By providing measures of performance that best reflect the underlying performance of the firm it is argued that investors and other parties will not need to gather additional information from other sources. This will consequently lead to cost savings.

As an illustration of research that adopts an efficiency perspective, Whittred (1987) sought to explain why firms voluntarily prepared publicly available consolidated financial statements in a period when there was no regulation that required them to do so. He found that when companies borrowed funds, security for debt often took the form of guarantees provided by other entities within the group of organisations. Consolidated financial statements were described as being a more efficient means of providing information about the group's ability to borrow and repay debts than providing lenders with separate financial statements for each entity in the group.[25]

If it is assumed, consistent with the efficiency perspective, that firms adopt particular accounting methods because the methods best reflect the underlying economic performance of the entity, then it is argued by PAT theorists that the regulation of financial accounting imposes unwarranted costs on reporting entities. For example, if a new accounting standard is released that bans an accounting method being used by particular organisations, this will lead to inefficiencies, as the resulting financial statements will no longer provide the best reflection of the performance of the organisation. Many PAT theorists would argue that management is best able to select appropriate accounting methods in given circumstances, and government should not intervene in the process.

The *opportunistic perspective* of PAT, on the other hand, takes as given the negotiated contractual arrangements of the firm (some of which are discussed later in this chapter) and seeks to explain and predict certain opportunistic behaviours that will subsequently occur. Initially, the particular contractual arrangements might have been negotiated because they were considered to

---

25. These results were also supported by Mian and Smith (1990). Using US data they found that the inclusion of financial subsidiaries in consolidated financial statements prior to Financial Accounting Standard 94 (which required the subsidiaries to be included within consolidated statements) was directly related to whether guarantees of debt were in existence between members of the group of companies. As Watts (1995, p. 332) indicates, the fact that two independent studies (Whittred, 1987; Mian and Smith, 1990) in different time periods and in different countries found the same results provides a stronger case that the efficiency perspective appears to explain this type of accounting choice.

be most efficient in aligning the interests of the various individuals within the firm. However, it is not possible or efficient to write complete contracts that provide guidance on all accounting methods to be used in all circumstances—hence there will always be some scope for managers to be opportunistic.

The opportunistic perspective is often referred to as an *ex post* perspective—*ex post* meaning after the fact—because it considers opportunistic actions that could be undertaken once various contractual arrangements have been put in place. For example, in an endeavour to minimise agency costs (an efficiency perspective), a contractual arrangement might be negotiated that provides the managers with a bonus based on the profits generated by the entity. Once it is in place, the manager could elect to adopt particular accounting methods that increase accounting profits, and therefore the size of the bonus (an opportunistic perspective). Managers might elect to adopt a particular goodwill amortisation method that increases income, even though it might not reflect the actual use of the asset. It is assumed within PAT that managers will opportunistically select particular accounting methods whenever they believe that this will lead to an increase in their personal wealth. PAT also assumes that principals would predict a manager to be opportunistic. With this in mind, principals often stipulate the accounting methods to be used for particular purposes. For example, a bonus plan agreement may stipulate that a particular amortisation method such as straight-line amortisation be adopted to calculate income for the determination of the bonus. However, as noted previously, it is assumed to be too costly to stipulate in advance all accounting rules to be used in all circumstances. Hence PAT proposes that there will always be scope for agents to opportunistically select particular accounting methods in preference to others.

The following discussion addresses the various contractual arrangements that may exist between owners and managers, and between debtholders and managers, particularly those contractual arrangements based on the output of the accounting system. Again, these contractual arrangements are initially assumed to be put in place to reduce the agency costs of the firm (the efficiency perspective). However, it is assumed by Positive Accounting theorists that once the arrangements are in place, parties will, if they can, adopt manipulative strategies to generate the greatest economic benefits to themselves (the opportunistic perspective). The following material also considers the political process and how firms might use accounting to minimise the costs of potential political scrutiny.

Owner/manager contracting

If the manager owned the firm, then that manager would bear the costs associated with their own perquisite consumption. Perquisite consumption could include consumption of the firm's resources for private purposes (for example, the manager may acquire an overly expensive company car, acquire overly luxurious offices, stay in overly expensive hotel accommodation) or the excessive generation and use of idle time. As the percentage ownership held by the manager decreases, that manager begins to bear less of the cost of his/her own perquisite consumption. The costs begin to be absorbed by the owners of the firm.

As noted previously, PAT adopts as a central assumption that all action by individuals is driven by self-interest, and that the major interest of individuals is to maximise their own wealth. Such an assumption is often referred to as the 'rational economic person' assumption. If all individuals are assumed to act in their own self-interest, then owners would expect the managers (their agents) to undertake activities that may not always be in the interest of the owners (the principals). Further, because of their position within the firm, the managers will have access to information not available to the principals (this problem is frequently referred to as 'information asymmetry') and this may further increase the manager's ability to undertake actions beneficial to themselves at the expense of the owners. The costs of the divergent behaviour that arises as a result of the agency relationship (that is, the relationship between the principal and the agent appointed to perform duties on behalf of the principal) are, as indicated previously, referred to as agency costs (Jensen and Meckling, 1976).

It is assumed in PAT that the principals hold expectations that their agents will undertake activities that may be disadvantageous to the value of the firm, and the principals will price this into the amounts they are prepared to pay the manager. That is, in the absence of controls to reduce the ability of the manager to act opportunistically, the principals expect such actions, and as a result, will pay the manager a lower salary. This lower salary compensates the principals for the expected opportunistic behaviour of the agents. The manager will therefore bear some of the costs of the potential opportunistic behaviours (the agency costs) that they may, or may not, undertake. If it is expected that managers would derive greater satisfaction from additional salary than from the perquisites that they will be predicted to consume, then managers may be better off if they are able to contractually commit themselves not to consume perquisites. That is, they contractually commit or bond themselves to reducing their set of available actions (some of which would not be beneficial to owners). Of course, the owners of the firm would need to ensure that any contractual commitments can be monitored for compliance before agreeing to increase the amounts paid to the managers. In a market where individuals are perfectly informed it could be assumed that managers would ultimately bear the costs associated with the bonding and monitoring mechanisms (Jensen and Meckling, 1976). However, markets are typically not perfectly informed.

Managers may be rewarded on a fixed basis (that is, a set salary independent of performance), on the basis of the results achieved, or on a combination of the two. If the manager was rewarded purely on a fixed basis, then assuming self-interest, that manager would not want to take great risks as he/she would not share in any potential gains. There would also be limited incentives for the manager to adopt strategies that increase the value of the firm (unlike equity owners whose share of the firm may increase in value). Like debtholders, managers with a fixed claim would want to protect their fixed income stream. Apart from rejecting risky projects, which may be beneficial to those with equity in the firm, the manager with a fixed income stream may also be reluctant to take on optimal levels of debt, as the claims of the debtholders would compete with the manager's own fixed income claim.

Assuming that self-interest drives the actions of the managers, it may be necessary to put in place remuneration schemes that reward the managers in a way that is, at least in part, tied to the performance of the firm. This will be in the interest of the manager as that manager will potentially receive greater rewards and will not have to bear the costs of the perceived opportunistic behaviours (which may not have been undertaken anyway). If the performance of the firm improves, the rewards paid to the manager correspondingly increase. Bonus schemes tied to the performance of the firm will be put in place to align the interests of the owners and the managers. If the firm performs well, both parties will benefit.

Bonus schemes generally

It is common practice for managers to be rewarded in line with the profits of the firm, sales of the firm, or return on assets. That is, for their remuneration to be based on the output of the accounting system. Table 7.1 describes some of the accounting-based remuneration plans found to have been used in Australia. It is also common for managers to be rewarded in line with the market price of the firm's shares. This may be through holding an equity interest in the firm, or perhaps by receiving a cash bonus explicitly tied to movements in the market value of the firm's securities.

Accounting-based bonus plans

Given that the amounts paid to the manager may be directly tied to accounting numbers (such as profits/sales/assets), any changes in the accounting methods being used by the organisation will affect the bonuses paid. Such a change may occur as a result of a new accounting standard being issued. For example, consider the consequences if a new rule was issued that required all research and development expenditure to be written off, as is the case in the US. With such a change, profits would decline, and the bonuses paid to managers may also change. If it is accepted, consistent with classical finance theory, that the value of the firm is a function of the future cash flows of the firm, then the value of the organisation may change. Hence, once we consider the contractual arrangements within a firm, Positive Accounting theorists would argue that we can start to appreciate that a change in accounting method can lead to a change in cash flows, and hence a change in the value of the organisation. This perspective is contrary to the views of early proponents of the EMH who argued that changes in accounting methods would not impact on share prices unless they had direct implications for expenses such as taxation.

TABLE 7.1 Accounting performance measures used within Australia as a basis for rewarding managers

- Percentage of after-tax profits of the last year
- Percentage of after-tax profits after adjustment for dividends paid
- Percentage of pre-tax profits of the last year
- Percentage of division's profit for the last year
- Percentage of division's sales for the last year
- Percentage of the last year's accounting rate of return on assets
- Percentage of previous year's division's sales, plus percentage of firm's after-tax profits
- Percentage of previous year's division's sales plus percentage of division's pre-tax profits
- Percentage of previous 2 years' division's sales, plus percentage of last 2 years' division's pre-tax profit
- Percentage of previous year's firm's sales, plus a percentage of firm's after-tax profit
- Average of pre-tax profit for the last 2 years
- Average of pre-tax profit for the last 3 years
- Percentage of the last six months' profit after tax

Source of data: Deegan (1997)

Of course it is possible that the bonus may be based on the 'old' accounting rules in place at the time the remuneration contract was negotiated (perhaps through a clause in the management compensation contract) such that a change in generally accepted accounting principles will not impact on the bonus, but this will not always be the case. Contracts that rely on accounting numbers may rely on 'floating' generally accepted accounting principles. This would suggest that should an accounting rule change, and should it affect an item used within a contract made by the firm, the value of the firm (through changes in related cash flows) might consequently change. PAT would suggest that if a change in accounting policy had no impact on the cash flows of the firm, then a firm would be indifferent to the change.

Incentives to manipulate accounting numbers

In considering the costs of implementing incentive schemes based on accounting output, there is a possibility that rewarding managers on the basis of accounting profits may induce them to manipulate the related accounting numbers to improve their apparent performance and, importantly, their related rewards (the opportunistic perspective). That is, accounting profits may not always provide an unbiased measure of firm performance or value. Healy (1985) provides an illustration of when managers may choose to manipulate accounting numbers opportunistically due to the presence of accounting-based bonus schemes. He found that when schemes existed that rewarded managers after a pre-specified level of earnings had been reached, the managers would adopt accounting methods consistent with maximising that bonus. In situations where the profits were not expected to reach the minimum level required by the plan, the managers appeared to adopt strategies that further reduced income in that period (frequently referred to as 'taking a bath'), but would lead to higher income in subsequent periods— periods when the profits may be above the required threshold. As an example, the manager may write off an asset in one period, when a bonus was not going to be earned anyway, such that there would be nothing further to depreciate in future periods when profit related bonuses may be paid.[26]

Investment strategies that maximise the present value of the firm's resources will not necessarily produce uniform periodic cash flows or accounting profits. It is possible that some strategies may generate minimal accounting returns in early years, yet still represent the best alternatives available to the firm. Rewarding management on the basis of accounting profits may discourage them from adopting such strategies. That is, it may encourage management to adopt a short-term, as opposed to long-term, focus.

In Lewellen, Loderer and Martin (1987) it was shown that US managers approaching retirement are less likely to undertake research and development expenditure if their rewards are based on accounting-based performance measures, such as profits. This is explained on the basis that all research and development has to be written off as incurred, in the US, and hence incurring research and development will lead directly to a reduction in profits. Although the research and development expenditure would be expected to lead to benefits in subsequent years, the retiring managers may not be there to share in the gains. Hence the *self-interested manager* that is rewarded on the basis of accounting profits is predicted not to undertake research and development in the periods close to the point of retirement. This may, of course, be detrimental to the ongoing operations of the business. In such a case it would be advisable from an *efficiency perspective* for an organisation that incurs research and development expenditure to take retiring managers off a profit-share bonus scheme, or alternatively, to calculate 'profits' for the purpose of the plan after adjusting for research and development expenditures.

---

26. Holthausen, Larcker and Sloan (1995) utilised private data on firms' compensation plans to also investigate managers' behaviour in the presence of management compensation plans. Their results confirmed those of Healy (1985), except that they did not find any evidence to support the view than management will 'take a bath' when earnings are below the lower pre-set bound.

Alternatively, managers approaching retirement could be rewarded in terms of market-based schemes. Such schemes are addressed below.

Market based bonus schemes

Firms involved in mining, or high technology research and development, may have accounting earnings that fluctuate greatly. Successful strategies may be put in place that will not provide accounting earnings for a number of periods. In such industries, Positive Accounting theorists may argue that it is more appropriate to reward the manager in terms of the market value of the firm's securities, which are assumed to be influenced by expectations about the net present value of expected future cash flows. This may be done either by basing a cash bonus on any increases in share prices, or by providing the manager with shares, or options to shares in the firm. If the value of the firm's shares increases, both the manager and the owners will benefit (their interests will be aligned). Importantly, the manager will be given an incentive to increase the value of the firm. In a survey of Australian managers, Deegan (1997) provides evidence that 21 per cent of the managers surveyed held shares in their employer.

As with accounting based bonus schemes, there are also problems associated with the manager being rewarded in terms of share price movements. First, the share price will be affected not only by factors controlled by the manager, but also by outside, market-wide factors. That is, share prices may provide a 'noisy' measure of management performance—'noisy' in the sense that they are not only affected by the actions of management but also are largely affected by general market movements over which the manager has no control. Further, only the senior managers would be likely to have a significant effect on the cash flows of the firm, and hence the value of the firm's securities. Therefore, market related incentives may only be appropriate for senior management. Offering shares to lower level management may be demotivational as their own individual actions would have little likelihood (relative to senior management) to impact on share prices, and therefore, their personal wealth. Consistent with this, within Australia it is more common for senior managers, relative to other employees, to hold shares in their employer. Within the Deegan (1997) sample, 35 per cent of the senior management, 16 per cent of the middle management, and 6 per cent of the lower management held shares in their employer.

Reflecting the way executives often share in the performance of an organisation, Exhibit 7.1 shows how Qantas rewards its executives by way of a scheme tied to the market value of the organisation's securities. It would be expected that rewarding the executives in the manner outlined should align the interests of the executives (agents) with those of the shareholders (principals)—a view consistent with Agency Theory and PAT. It would be expected that such schemes would be restricted to senior management as they have the greatest ability to have an impact on share prices.

EXHIBIT 7.1 An example of the use of market based incentives

Shares for Qantas high-flyers

Terry Plane
Steve Creedy

Aviation

Qantas shareholders were asked yesterday to approve the allocation of more than 1.5 million shares to the company's two top executives.

Chairman Gary Pemberton, backed by proxies already in, called on shareholders at the company's annual general meeting in Adelaide to vote for an allocation of 1.1 million shares to chief executive James Strong and 545,000 to chief financial officer Gary Toomey.

At yesterday's closing price of $4.99 (down 2c) the allocations would have been worth almost $5.5 million and just over $2.7 million.

'Both have made a substantial contribution to the success of Qantas,' Mr Pemberton said after outlining details of a new executive incentive plan.

He said there would be 'performance hurdles' all executives benefiting from the scheme would have to jump and that shares would be made available on a proportional formula from 2002.

In support of the scheme the chairman told the meeting the board was seeking to create 'competitive compensation' to help retain senior staff and to focus executives on shareholder wealth.

Mr Pemberton also asked the meeting to support an increase in maximum aggregate directors' fees from $750,000 to $1.1 million.

He revealed the board had this week discussed succession planning within the company.

'CEOs have a finite life,' he said. 'They should be well rewarded while they're performing, but they shouldn't be encouraged to stay too long.'

Mr Strong, at Qantas for six years, said after the meeting he was not planning to leave the company.

Mr Pemberton said the carrier would need continued productivity and efficiency improvements and higher revenue to meet increased costs.

He said the year-to-date profit was ahead of the same period last year.

Qantas reported a 38 percent jump to a record $420.9 million for the year ended June 30.

Passenger numbers on domestic operations had risen and international routes were showing some profit improvements, despite strong competitive pressures. Subsidiary operations were performing slightly ahead of expectations.

Mr Pemberton's comments were supported by Qantas figures which showed passenger numbers for September 8.4 percent higher than the same month last year and year-to-date figures up by 6.4 per cent.

The percentage of paying passengers on Qantas flights in September was up 4.9 points on September last year to 78.5 per cent for the month and four points to 77.1 per cent in the year-to-date figures, Mr Pemberton said.

'On the other hand, we are carrying increased costs associated with higher fuel prices, net of hedging, the cost of capacity increases and the start-up of new services,' Mr Pemberton said.

'As mentioned earlier, depreciation and funding costs will also increase this year and beyond, due to investments in new aircraft and significant investment over the last three years in aircraft refurbishments, customer service programs and lounge and terminal improvements.'

The Australian, **Thursday 18 November 1999, p. 25.**

In general it is argued that the likelihood of accounting-based or market-based performance measures or reward schemes being put in place will, in part, be driven by considerations of the relative 'noise' of market-based versus accounting-based performance measures. The relative reliance upon accounting or market-based measures may potentially be determined on the basis of the relative sensitivity of either measure to general market (largely uncontrollable) factors. Sloan (1993) indicates that CEO salary and bonus compensation appears to be relatively more aligned with accounting earnings in those firms where:

(a) share returns are relatively more sensitive to general market movements (relatively noisy);

(b) earnings have a high association with the firm-specific movement in the firm's share values;

(c) earnings have a less positive (more negative) association with market-wide movements in equity values.

Accounting-based rewards have the advantage that the accounting results may be based on subunit or divisional performance, but one would need to ensure that individuals do not focus on their division at the expense of the organisation as a whole.

PAT assumes that if a manager is rewarded on the basis of accounting numbers (for example, on the basis of a share of profits) then the manager will have an incentive to manipulate the accounting numbers. Given such an assumption, the value of audited financial statements becomes apparent. Rewarding managers in terms of accounting numbers (a strategy aimed at aligning the interests of owners and managers) may not be appropriate if management was solely responsible for compiling those numbers. The auditor will act to arbitrate on the reasonableness of the accounting methods adopted. However, it must be remembered that there will always be scope for opportunism.

The above arguments concentrate on how management's rewards will be directly impacted as particular accounting methods are chosen. Management might also be rewarded in other indirect ways as a result of electing to use particular accounting methods. For example, DeAngelo (1988) provided evidence that when individuals face a contest for their positions as managers of an organisation they will, prior to the contest, adopt accounting methods that lead to an increase in reported profits (and the increased reported earnings could not be associated with any apparent increase in cash flows) thereby bolstering their case for re-election. DeAngelo also showed that where the existing managers were nevertheless unsuccessful in retaining their positions within the organisation, the newly appointed managers were inclined to recognise many expenses as soon as they took office (that is, 'take a bath') in a bid to highlight the poor 'state of affairs' they had inherited.

Having considered the contractual relationship between managers and principals, and how accounting can be used as a means of reducing the costs associated with potential conflict, we can now consider the relationship between debtholders and managers. We will see that accounting can be used to restrict the implications of this conflict and thereby enable an organisation to attract funds at a lower cost than might otherwise be possible.

Debt contracting

When a party lends funds to another organisation the recipient of the funds may undertake activities that reduce or even eliminate the probability that the funds will be repaid. These costs that relate to the divergent behaviour of the borrower are referred to in PAT as the *agency costs of debt* and under PAT, lenders will anticipate divergent behaviour. For example, the recipient of the funds may pay excessive dividends, leaving few assets in the organisation to service the debt. Alternatively, the organisation may take on additional and perhaps excessive levels of debt. The new debtholders would then compete with the original debtholder for repayment.

Further, the firm may also invest in very high-risk projects. This strategy would not be beneficial to the debtholders. They have a fixed claim and hence if the project generates high profits they will receive no greater return, unlike the owners, who will share in the increased value of the firm. If the project fails, which is more likely with a risky project, the debtholders may receive nothing. The debtholders therefore do not share in any 'upside' (the profits), but suffer the consequences of any significant losses (the 'downside').

In the absence of safeguards that protect the interests of debtholders, the holders of debt will assume that management will take actions that might not always be in the debtholders' interest, and as a result, it is assumed that they will require the firm to pay higher costs of interest to compensate the debtholders for the high risk exposure (Smith and Warner, 1979).

If the firm agrees not to pay excessive dividends, not to take on high levels of debt, and not to invest in projects of an excessively risky nature, then it is assumed that the firm will be able to attract debt capital at a lower cost than would otherwise be possible. To the extent that the benefits of lower interest costs exceed the costs that may be associated with restricting how management can use the available funds, management will elect to sign agreements that restrict their subsequent actions. Australian evidence on debt contracts is provided by Whittred and Zimmer (1986) who find that:

> . . . *with few exceptions, trust deeds for public debt place restrictions on the amount of both total and secured liabilities that may exist. The constraints were most commonly defined relative to total tangible assets; less often relative to shareholders' funds. The most frequently observed constraints were those limiting total and secured liabilities to some fraction of total tangible assets.* (p. 22)

Cotter (1998) provides more recent Australian evidence about debt contracts. She finds that:

Leverage covenants are frequently used in bank loan contracts, with leverage most frequently measured as the ratio of total liabilities to total tangible assets. In addition, prior charges covenants that restrict the amount of secured debt owed to other lenders are typically included in the term loan agreements of larger firms, and are defined as a percentage of total tangible assets. (p. 187)[27]

Where covenants restrict the total level of debt that may be issued, this is assumed to lead to a reduction in the risk to existing debtholders. This is further assumed to translate to lower interest rates being charged by the 'protected' debtholders. It is worth noting that, in her unpublished PhD thesis, Cotter found that the definition of assets commonly used allowed for assets to be revalued. However, for the purposes of the debt restriction, some banks restricted the frequency of revaluations to once every two or three years, while others tended to exclude revaluations undertaken by directors of the firm. These restrictions lessen the ability of firms to loosen debt constraints by revaluing assets. Cotter (1998) found that apart from debt to assets constraints, interest coverage and current ratio clauses are frequently used in debt agreements. Interest coverage clauses typically require that the ratio of net profit, with interest and tax added back, to interest expense, be at least a minimum number of times. In the Cotter study, the number of times interest must be covered ranged from one-and-a-half to four times. The current ratio clauses reviewed by Cotter required that current assets be between one and two times the size of current liabilities, depending upon the size and industry of the borrowing firm.

As with management compensation contracts, PAT assumes that the existence of debt contracts (which are initially put in place as a mechanism to reduce the agency costs of debt and can be explained from an *efficiency perspective*) provides management with a subsequent (*ex post*) incentive to manipulate accounting numbers, with the incentive to manipulate the numbers increasing as the accounting-based constraint approaches violation. As Watts (1995, p. 323) states:

Early studies of debt contract-motivated choice test whether firms with higher leverage (gearing) are more likely to use earnings-increasing accounting methods to avoid default (leverage hypothesis). The underlying assumptions are that the higher the firm's leverage the less [is the] slack in debt covenants and the more likely the firm is to have changed accounting methods to have avoided default. This change is usually interpreted as opportunistic since technical default generates wealth transfers to creditors but it could also be efficient to the extent that it avoids real default and the deadweight loss associated with bankruptcy.

---

27. Cotter (1998) notes that in the 1990s banks became the major source of corporate debt in Australia. This can be contrasted with the earlier period reviewed by Whittred and Zimmer (1986). In the early 1980s Australian corporations placed relatively greater reliance on raising debt through public funding, rather than privately dealing with institutions such as banks.

For example, if the firm contractually agreed that the ratio, debt to total tangible assets, should be kept below a certain figure, then if that figure was likely to be exceeded (causing a technical default of the loan agreement), management may have an incentive to either inflate assets or deflate liabilities. This is consistent with the results reported in Christie (1990) and Watts and Zimmerman (1990). To the extent that such an action was not objective, management would obviously be acting opportunistically and not to the benefit of individuals holding debt claims against the firm. Debt agreements typically require financial statements to be audited.

Other research to consider how management might manipulate accounting numbers in the presence of debt agreements includes that undertaken by DeFond and Jiambalvo (1994) and Sweeney (1994). Both of these studies investigated the behaviour of managers of firms known to have defaulted on accounting-related debt covenants. DeFond and Jiambalvo (1994) provided evidence that the managers manipulated accounting accruals in the years before and the year after violation of the agreement. Similarly, Sweeney (1994) found that as a firm approaches violation of a debt agreement, managers have a greater propensity to adopt income–increasing strategies, relative to firms that are not approaching technical default of accounting-based debt covenants. The income-increasing accounting strategies included changing key assumptions when calculating pension liabilities and adopting LIFO cost flow assumptions for inventory.

Sweeney (1994) also showed that managers with an incentive to manipulate accounting earnings might also strategically determine when they will first adopt a new accounting requirement. When new accounting standards are issued there is typically a transition period (which could be a number of years) in which organisations can voluntarily opt to implement a new accounting requirement. After the transitional period the use of the new requirement becomes mandatory. Sweeney showed that organisations that defaulted on their debt agreements tended to adopt income–increasing requirements early, and deferred the adoption of accounting methods that would lead to a reduction in reported earnings.

Debt contracts occasionally restrict the accounting techniques that may be used by the firm, hence requiring adjustments to published accounting numbers. For example, and as stated above, Cotter (1998) shows that bank loan contracts sometimes do not allow the component related to asset revaluations to be included in the definition of 'assets' for the purpose of calculating ratios, such as 'debt to assets' restrictions. These evaluations are, however, allowed for external reporting purposes. Therefore, loan agreements sometimes require the revaluation component to be removed from the published accounting numbers prior to the calculation of any restrictive covenants included within the debt contract.

Within accounting, management usually has available a number of alternative ways to account for particular items. Hence management has at its disposal numerous ways to minimise the effects of existing accounting-based restrictions. Therefore, it may appear optimal for debtholders to stipulate in advance *all* accounting methods management must use. However, and as noted previously, it would be too costly, and for practical purposes impossible, to write 'complete' contracts up front. As a consequence, management will always have some discretionary ability, which may enable them to loosen the effects of debtholder-negotiated restrictions. The role of external auditors (if appointed) would be to arbitrate on the reasonableness of the accounting methods chosen.

In relation to auditors, and following discussion so far provided in this chapter, there would appear to be a particular demand for financial statement auditing (that is, monitoring by external parties) when:

(a) management is rewarded on the basis of numbers generated by the accounting system; and

(b) when the firm has borrowed funds, and accounting-based covenants are in place to protect the investments of the debtholders.

Consistent with the above, it could also be argued that as the managers' share of equity in the business decreases, and as the proportion of debt to total assets increases, there will be a corresponding increase in the demand for auditing. In this respect, Ettredge, Simon, Smith and Stone (1994) show that organisations that voluntarily elect to have interim financial statements audited tend to have greater leverage, and lower management shareholding in the firm.

In the discussion that follows we will consider how expectations about the *political process* can also impact on managers' choice of accounting methods.

Political costs

As indicated previously in this chapter, firms (particularly larger ones) are sometimes under scrutiny by various groups, for example, by government, employee groups, consumer groups, environmental lobby groups, and so on. For example, the size of a firm is often used as an indication of market power and this in itself can attract the attention of regulatory bodies such as the Trade Practices Commission (in Australia) or the Federal Trade Commission (in the US).

Government and interest groups may publicly promote the view that a particular organisation (typically large) is generating excessive profits and not paying its 'fair share' to other segments of the community (for example, the wages it is paying are too low, its product prices are too high, its financial commitment to environmental and community initiatives is too low, its tax payments are too low, and so on). Watts and Zimmerman (1978; 1986) highlight the highly publicised claims about US oil companies made by consumers, unions, and government within the US in the period of the late 1970s. The claims were that oil companies were making excessive reported profits and were in effect exploiting the nation. It is considered that such claims may have led to the imposition of additional taxes in the form of 'excess profits' taxes.

Consistent with the early work of Watts and Zimmerman (1978), it has been argued that to reduce the possibility of adverse political attention and the associated costs of this attention (for example, the costs associated with increased taxes, increased wage claims, or product boycotts), politically sensitive firms (typically large firms) should adopt accounting methods that lead to a reduction in reported profits.[28] However, the view that lower reported profits will lead to lower political scrutiny (and ultimately to lower wealth transfers away from the firm) assumes that parties involved in the political process are unable or not prepared to 'unravel' the implications of the managers' various accounting choices. That is, managers can somehow *fool* those involved in the political process by simply adopting one method of accounting (income decreasing) in preference to another. But, why would this be the case when elsewhere it has been assumed (consistent with the EMH) that individuals within other markets, such as the capital market, can efficiently unravel managements' choices of accounting methods?

From an economic perspective there is a view that in political markets there is limited expected 'pay-off' that can result from the actions of individuals (Downs, 1957). For example, if an individual seeks to know the real reasons why government elected to adopt a particular action from among many possible actions, then gathering such information would be costly. Yet that individual's vote would have very little likelihood of affecting the existence of the government. Hence, individuals will elect to remain *rationally uninformed*. However, should particular interest groups form, then such information costs can be shared and the ability to investigate government actions can increase. A similar perspective is taken with groups other than government, for example, representatives of labour unions, consumer bodies and so on. Officials of these bodies represent a diverse group of people, with the individual constituents again having limited incentive to be fully informed about the activities of the office-bearers.

Because PAT assumes that *all* actions by *all* individuals (including officials of interest groups, politicians, and so on) are driven by self-interest, representatives of interest groups are predicted to adopt strategies that maximise their own welfare in the knowledge that their constituents will have limited motivation to be fully informed about their activities.

With the above arguments in mind, we can consider the actions of politicians. Because politicians know that highly profitable companies could be unpopular with a large number of their constituency, the politicians could 'win' votes by taking actions against such companies. However, Watts and Zimmerman (1979) argue that politicians will claim that the actions they have

---

28. Difficulties with using firm size to proxy for political costs, including the likelihood that it can proxy for many other effects, such as industry membership, are discussed in Ball and Foster (1982).

taken were in the 'public interest' as obviously they need to disguise the fact that such actions best served the politicians' own interests. As Watts and Zimmerman (1979, p. 283) argue:

> In recent years economists have questioned whether the public interest assumption is consistent with observed phenomena. They have proposed an alternative assumption—that individuals involved in the political process act in their own self-interest (the self-interest assumption). This assumption yields implications which are more consistent with observed phenomena than those based on the public interest assumption.

To justify their own actions, politicians may simply rely on the reported profits of companies to provide an *excuse* for their actions, knowing that individual constituents are unlikely to face the cost of investigating the politicians' motives, or the cost of investigating how the corporation's profits were determined (that is, whether the profit resulted because a particular accounting method was used in a less than objective manner). To reduce the *excuses* of politicians, potentially politically sensitive firms are predicted to anticipate politicians' actions and therefore managements of politically vulnerable firms have an incentive to reduce their reported profits. As Watts and Zimmerman (1979, p. 281) state:

> Government commissions often use the contents of financial statements in the regulatory process (rate setting, anti-trust, etc.). Further, Congress often bases legislative actions on these statements. This, in turn, provides management with incentives to select accounting procedures which either reduce the costs they bear or increase the benefits they receive as a result of the actions of government regulators and legislators.

Interestingly, when the media reports a company's profitability it seldom gives any attention to the accounting methods used to calculate the profit. In a sense, profit is held out as some form of objective measure of organisational performance (much like governments might rely on profits to support a particular action). Media reports of high corporate profitability can potentially trigger political costs for a firm. In the discussion above we discussed how representatives of interest groups might use profits as a justification for particular actions. In this respect we can consider Exhibit 7.2 below. The author refers to comments made by a New Zealand 'union boss'. The 'union boss' identifies the high profits of particular organisations and notes that these profits have not been passed on in any real extent to the employees. In a sense, the reported accounting profits are used as an excuse to push for higher wages. Such a 'wage-push' could be costly for the particular organisations involved. Perhaps if reported profits were not so high, there would be less chance that demands for increased wages would be made. As Watts and Zimmerman (1978, p. 115) state:

> By avoiding the attention that high profits draw because of monopoly rents, management can reduce the likelihood of adverse political actions and, thereby, reduce its expected costs (including the legal costs the firm would incur opposing

EXHIBIT 7.2 Profits as a consideration in the political process

Union boss attacks profit surge, static pay

From Selwyn Parker, AFR Correspondent in Auckland

AVERAGE pay rates for shopfloor staff lag far behind the latest round of double-digit company profits, according to New Zealand's union boss, Mr Ken Douglas, in an attack on labour legislation.

Citing fast-rising profitability across most of the business spectrum, including claimed 56 per cent margins by US-owned Telecom New Zealand, Council of Trade Unions president Mr Douglas said yesterday it seemed that 'as the rate of economic expansion improves, real wages decline at an increasing rate'.

Mr Douglas, an arch opponent of New Zealand's Employment Contracts Act which abolished the unions' monopoly on wage negotiations, claims record GDP growth has bypassed workers.

According to CTU research released yesterday, profit increases of over 40 per cent were 'not uncommon' in the last half of 1994. Over that period, government agency Statistics New Zealand calculated that total pay increases averaged 1.2 per cent—or 1.6 per cent below the rate of inflation—over the whole of 1994.

At the same time, 'managerial pay has leapt ahead of the pay of workers'.

Among the companies Mr Douglas singled out for spectacular profits at workers' expense are Commonwealth Bank-owned ASB Bank which has just posted a 31 per cent after-tax profit increase, Fletcher Challenge (24 per cent), Air New Zealand (59 per cent), tourism-based Helicopter Line (47 per cent), and Steel and Tube (44 per cent).

Mr Douglas particularly criticised Telecom for the 'incredibly wide margins' that drove it to December quarter profits of NZ$158 million. He said Telecom's 56.4 per cent mark-up was unjustifiable.

Mr Douglas also noted a sharp increase in part-time employment since the ECA laws were introduced in late 1991.

However, Mr Douglas's comments follow consistently upbeat economic reports showing a general and sustained increase in GDP growth.

***Australian Financial Review*, 22 March 1995.**

the political actions). Included in political costs are the costs labour unions impose through increased demands generated by large reported profits.

Numerous studies have considered how particular accounting methods can be used in an endeavour to decrease political costs. We have already considered the work of Watts and Zimmerman. Other research has been undertaken by Jones (1991) who, in a US study, considered the behaviour of 23 domestic firms from five industries that were the subject of government import related investigations over the period from 1980 to 1985. These government investigations by the International Trade Commission sought to determine whether the domestic firms were under threat from foreign competition. Where this threat is deemed to be unfair, the government can grant relief by devices such as tariff protection. In making its d_____ the government relies upon a number of factors, including econom____ such as profits and sales. The results of the study show that in the ____ investigations the sample companies selected accounting strategie____ a decrease in reported profits. Such behaviour was not evidenced before or the year after the government investigation (perhaps indicating that the politicians are fairly 'short sighted' when undertaking investigations).

In a New Zealand study, Wong (1988) investigated the practice of NZ companies between 1977 and 1981 and found that those that adopted Current Cost Accounting (which had the effect of reducing reported profits) had higher effective tax rates and larger market concentration ratios than other firms. Effective tax rates and market concentration rates were both used as a measure of political sensitivity. In a UK study, Sutton (1988) found that politically sensitive companies were also more likely to lobby in favour of current cost accounting.[29]

Apart from adopting income reducing accounting techniques, authors such as Ness and Mirza (1991), and McComiskey (1995) have argued that particular voluntary social disclosures in an organisation's annual report can be explained as an effort to reduce the political costs of the disclosing entities. Ness and Mirza (1991) studied the environmental disclosure practices of a number of UK companies. They considered that companies in the oil industry had developed particularly poor reputations for their environmental practices and that such a reputation could be used by various interest groups to transfer wealth away from the firm (and presumably away from the managers). Such wealth transfers might be generated if certain groups lobbied government to impose particular taxes (perhaps related to their environmental performance), or perhaps if particular employee groups took actions to insist that the companies put in place strategies to improve their environmental performance and reputation. Ness and Mirza argued that if firms voluntarily provide environmental disclosures (typically of a positive or self-laudatory nature) then this may lead to a reduction in future wealth transfers away from the firm. They found, consistent with their expectations, that oil companies provided greater environmental disclosures within their annual reports than did companies operating in other industries. They argued that this was the case as oil companies had more potentially adverse wealth transfers at stake.

McComiskey (1995) adopted a political cost perspective to explain which companies would be more likely to voluntarily provide native title related disclosures within their annual report. It was argued that such disclosures occurred as an attempt to reduce wealth transfers from the mining industry to indigenous groups. A number of the disclosures called specifically for government action to reduce the uncertainties associated with native title claims. Specific illustrations of comments made within the directors' reports

---

29. While a number of studies considered in this chapter investigate the choice between alternative accounting methods, it should be noted that in recent years there has been an increased focus on studying the manipulation of accounting accruals. Relative to investigating the selection of particular accounting methods (for example, the use of straight line depreciation versus reducing balance depreciation), the study of accruals is more difficult and requires the use of modelling techniques to identify discretionary (those controlled by management) and non-discretionary accruals (Jones, 1991). The use of accruals can also be explained from either an *efficiency* or *opportunistic* perspective (Guay, Kothari and Watts, 1996).

incorporated within companies' annual reports (McComiskey, 1995, p. 45) include:

> *It is my opinion that the Federal Government should consider the industry's pleas for review of attitude in this matter and to restate the general principle of Crown ownership of minerals and that current mining titles are valid irrespective of the date on which they were issued (Mt Martin Gold Mines NL).*

> *The implications of Mabo have serious economic consequences for Australia . . . (Pasminco) . . . is working with State and Federal governments to achieve early resolution of the native title issues arising from Mabo (Pasminco Limited).*

> *In light of the recent developments in claims for native title it remains for Australian governments to make good their undertakings that previously granted title will be validated in the near term (QCT Limited).*

To this point, we have shown that PAT indicates that the selection of particular and alternative accounting methods may impact on the cash flows associated with debt contracts, the cash flows associated with management compensation plans, and the political costs of the firm. PAT indicates that these impacts can be used to explain why firms elect to use particular accounting methods in preference to others. PAT also indicates that the use of particular accounting methods may have opposing effects. For example, if a firm was to adopt a policy that increased income (for example, it may capitalise an item, rather than expensing it as incurred), then this may reduce the probability of violating a debt constraint. However, it may increase the political visibility of the firm due to the higher profits. Managers are assumed to select the accounting methods that best balance the conflicting effects (and also that maximise their own wealth).

We have demonstrated in this chapter that PAT became the dominant theory used by accounting researchers in the 1970s.[30] It represented a challenge to many normative theorists and conflicted with the views of many established researchers. Many individuals openly criticised PAT. In the concluding section of this chapter we now consider some of these criticisms.

Some criticisms of Positive Accounting Theory

One widespread criticism of PAT is that it does not provide *prescription* and therefore does not provide a means of improving accounting practice. It is argued that simply explaining and predicting accounting practice is not enough. Using a medical analogy, Sterling (1990, p. 130) states:

> *PAT cannot rise above giving the same answers because it restricts itself to the descriptive questions. If it ever asked how to solve a problem or correct*

---

30. While its popularity is still high, many accounting schools are now actively promoting alternative theories.

an error (both of which require going beyond a description to an evaluation of the situation), then it might go on to different questions and obtain different answers after the previous problem was solved. If we had restricted the medical question to the description of the smallpox virus, for example, precluding prescriptions to be vaccinated, we would need more and more descriptive studies as the virus population increased and mutations appeared. Luckily Edward Jenner was naughtily normative, which allowed him to discover how cowpox could be used as a vaccine so smallpox was eventually eliminated, which made room for different questions on the medical agenda.

Howieson (1996, p. 31) provides a view that by failing to provide prescription, Positive Accounting theorists may alienate themselves from practising accountants. As he states:

. . . an unwillingness to tackle policy issues is arguably an abrogation of academics' duty to serve the community which supports them. Among other activities, practitioners are concerned on a day-to-day basis with the question of which accounting policies they should choose. Traditionally, academics have acted as commentators and reformers on such normative issues. By concentrating on positive questions, they risk neglecting one of their important roles in the community.

A second criticism of PAT is that it is not *value free*, as it asserts. If we are to look at various research that has adopted PAT, we will see a general absence of prescription (that is, there is no guidance as to what people *should* do). This is normally justified by Positive Accounting theorists by saying that they do not want to impose their views on others, but rather would prefer to provide information about the expected implications of particular actions and let people decide for themselves what they should do (for example, they may provide evidence to support a prediction that organisations close to breaching accounting-based debt covenants will adopt accounting methods that increase the firm's reported profits and assets). However, as a number of accounting academics have pointed out, selecting a theory to adopt for research (such as PAT) is based on a value judgement; what to research is based on a value judgement; believing that all individual action is driven by self-interest is a value judgement; and, so on.[31] Also, Watts and Zimmerman appear to have taken a normative position when they identify the objective of accounting research. According to them, 'the objective of accounting theory is to explain and predict accounting practice' (1986, p. 2). Clearly, there are many other views about the role of accounting theory. Hence, no research, whether conducted under PAT or otherwise, is value free.

Following from the above points, a third criticism of PAT relates to the fundamental assumption that *all action* is driven by a desire to maximise one's wealth. To many researchers such an assumption represents a far too negative

---

31. In Chapter 12 we also see that some researchers argue that Positive Accounting theorists adopt a conservative right-wing ideology in promoting the virtues of markets, the rights of shareholders (the capitalist class), and so on.

and simplistic perspective of humankind. In this respect, Gray, Owen and Adams (1996, p. 75) state that PAT promotes 'a morally bankrupt view of the world'. Given that everybody is deemed to act in their own self-interest, the perspective of self-interest has also been applied to the research efforts of academics. For example, Watts and Zimmerman (1990, p. 146) argue that:

> *Researchers choose the topics to investigate, the methods to use, and the assumptions to make. Researchers' preferences and expected payoffs (publications and citations) affect their choice of topic, methods, and assumptions.*

Many academics would challenge this view and would argue that they undertake their research because of real personal interest in an issue. Another implication of the self-interest issue is that incorporation of this self-interest assumption into the teaching of undergraduate students (as has been done in many universities throughout the world) has the possible implication that students think that when they subsequently have to make decisions in the workplace, it is both acceptable and predictable for them to place their own interests above those of others. It is perhaps questionable whether such a philosophy is in the interests of the broader community. Nevertheless, while assuming that all action is driven by a desire to maximise one's own wealth is not an overly kind assumption about human nature, such an assumption has been the cornerstone of many past and existing theories used within the discipline of economics (and this is not a justification).

Another criticism of PAT is that since its general inception in the 1970s the issues being addressed have not shown great development. Since the early days of Watts and Zimmerman (1978) there have been three key hypotheses: the debt hypothesis (which proposes that organisations close to breaching accounting-based debt covenants will select accounting methods that lead to an increase in profits and assets); the bonus hypothesis (which proposes that managers on accounting-based bonus schemes will select accounting methods that lead to an increase in profits); and the political cost hypothesis (which proposes that firms subject to political scrutiny will adopt accounting methods that reduce reported income). A review of the recent PAT literature indicates that these hypotheses continue to be tested in different environments and in relation to different accounting policy issues—even after the passing of twenty years since Watts and Zimmerman (1978). In this respect, Sterling (1990, p. 130) poses the following question:

> *What are the potential accomplishments (of PAT)? I forecast more of the same: twenty years from now we will have been inundated with research reports that managers and others tend to manipulate accounting numerals when it is to their advantage to do so.*

A further criticism is that PAT is scientifically flawed. It has been argued that as the hypotheses generated pursuant to PAT (for example, the debt hypothesis, the bonus hypothesis, and the political cost hypothesis) are frequently not supported (they are falsified), then scientifically PAT should be rejected. Christenson (1983, p. 18) states:

> *We are told, for example, that 'we can only expect a positive theory to hold on average' [Watts and Zimmerman, 1978, p. 127, n. 37]. We are also advised 'to remember that as in all empirical theories we are concerned with general trends' [Watts and Zimmerman, 1978, pp. 288–9], where 'general' is used in the weak sense of 'true or applicable in most instances but not all' rather than in the strong sense of 'relating to, concerned with, or applicable to every member of a class' [American Heritage Dictionary, 1969, p. 548] . . . A law that admits exceptions has no significance, and knowledge of it is not of the slightest use. By arguing that their theories admit exceptions, Watts and Zimmerman condemn them as insignificant and useless.*

As a study of people, however, (accounting is a process undertaken by people and the accounting process itself cannot exist in the absence of accountants), it is hard to consider that any model or theory could ever fully explain human action. In fact, ability to do so would constitute a dehumanising action. Are there any theories of human activity or choice processes that always hold? In defence of the fact that PAT predictions do not always hold, Watts and Zimmerman (1990, p. 148) state:

> *But accounting research using this methodology has produced useful predictions of how the world works. A methodology that yields useful results should not be abandoned purely because it may not predict all human behaviour. Do we discard something that works in some situations because it may not work in every circumstance?*

Another criticism of PAT is that the positive researchers believe that they can generate laws and principles expected to operate in different situations, and that there is one underlying 'truth' that can be determined by an independent, impartial observer who is not influenced by individual perceptions, idiosyncrasies or biases (Tinker, Merino and Neimark (1982, p. 167)). That is, the apparent perspective is that reality exists objectively, and one observer's view of that reality will be the same as all other people's views. This is referred to as the 'realist philosophy'. A number of researchers have challenged this philosophy (for example, Hines, 1988). They have argued that in undertaking large-scale empirical research, positive researchers ignore many organisation-specific relationships and the information collected is only the information that the researchers consider relevant. A different person would possibly consider that other information is more relevant. Many researchers critical of the 'realist perspective' argue that more insights might be gained by undertaking in-depth case studies. Positive researchers would provide a counter-argument, however, that case study research is very specific to a particular time and place and therefore cannot be generalised to a broader population. Such arguments about research methodology abound in the literature with potentially very limited likelihood that researchers operating across different paradigms will ever agree on what constitutes valid research. As Watts and Zimmerman (1990, p. 149) concede when defending their research against numerous criticisms:

To most researchers, debating methodology is a 'no win' situation because each side argues from a different paradigm with different rules and no common ground. Our reason for replying here is that some have mistaken our lack of response as tacit acceptance of the criticisms.

While the above criticisms do, arguably, have some merit, PAT does continue to be used by many accounting researchers. Respected accounting research journals continue to publish PAT research (although the numbers appear to be declining). A number of the leading accounting research schools throughout the world continue to teach it. What must be remembered is that all theories of accounting will have limitations. They are, of necessity, abstractions of the 'real world'. Whether individually we prefer one theory of accounting in preference to another will be dependent upon our assumptions about many of the issues raised within this chapter.

Chapter summary

A positive theory seeks to explain and predict particular phenomena. In this chapter we considered Positive Accounting Theory (PAT), a theory that seeks to explain and predict managers' choices of accounting methods. PAT focuses on relationships between various individuals within and outside an organisation and explains how financial accounting can be used to minimise the costly implications associated with each contracting party operating in his or her own self-interest. The economic perspective that all individual behaviour is motivated by self-interest is central to PAT, and PAT predicts that contractual arrangements will be put in place to align the interests of the various self-interested parties. Many of these contractual arrangements will use the output of the accounting system.

PAT became a dominant research paradigm in the 1970s and 1980s and its development owed much to previous research work that had been undertaken, including work on the Efficient Markets Hypothesis (EMH) and Agency Theory. The EMH provided evidence that capital markets reacted to new information but it provided little explanation for why managers might elect to use particular accounting methods in preference to others. PAT was developed to fill this void.

Applying Agency Theory, PAT focused on relationships between principals and agents. PAT proposed that agents have incentives to enter various contracts. Firms themselves were considered as a nexus of contracts between many self-interested individuals. The contractual arrangements are initially put in place for efficiency reasons with well developed contracts reducing the overall agency costs that could arise within the firm. Further, agents are predicted to adopt those accounting methods that most efficiently reflect their own performance. Regulation is considered to introduce unnecessary costs and inefficiencies into the contractual arrangements, particularly as it often acts to reduce the methods of accounting that would otherwise be adopted.

Early work within PAT relied upon three central hypotheses: the bonus hypothesis, the debt hypothesis, and the political cost hypothesis. The bonus hypothesis predicts that from an efficiency perspective many organisations will elect to provide their managers with bonuses tied to the performance of the firm, with these bonuses often being directly related to accounting numbers (for example, management might be rewarded with a share of profits). Offering performance based rewards will motivate the self-interested manager to work also in the best interests of the owners. However, under the opportunistic perspective, PAT predicts that once bonus schemes are in place, managers will, to the extent that they can get away with it, manipulate performance indicators such as profits to generate higher individual rewards.

The debt hypothesis predicts that to reduce the cost of attracting debt capital, firms will enter into contractual arrangements with lenders which reduce the likelihood that the managers can expropriate the wealth of the debtholders. Arranging such agreements prior to obtaining debt finance is deemed to be an efficient way to attract lower cost funds. However, once a debt contract is in place, the opportunistic perspective of PAT predicts that firms, particularly those close to breaching debt covenants, will adopt accounting methods that act to minimise or loosen the effects of the debt constraint.

The political cost hypothesis explores the relationships between a firm and various outside parties who, although perhaps not having any direct contractual relationships, can nevertheless impose various types of wealth transfers away from the firm. It is argued that high profits can attract adverse and costly attention to the firm, and hence managers of politically vulnerable firms look for ways to reduce the level of political scrutiny. One way is to adopt accounting methods that lead to a reduction in reported profits. Most tests of the political cost hypothesis use size of the firm as a proxy for the existence of political scrutiny.

The chapter also provided a number of criticisms of PAT. Included among the various criticisms was a challenge to the central PAT assumption that *all* individual action is driven by self-interest.

References

Ball, R., Brown, P., 'An Empirical Evaluation of Accounting Numbers', *Journal of Accounting Research*, Vol. 7, pp. 159–78, Autumn 1968.

Ball, R., Foster, G., 'Corporate Financial Reporting: A Methodological Review of Empirical Research', *Journal of Accounting Research*, Vol. 20, Supplement, pp. 161–234, 1982.

Beaver, W., 'The Information Content of Annual Earnings Announcements', *Journal of Accounting Research*, Vol. 6, Supplement, pp. 67–92, 1968.

Benston, G.J., 'The Value of the SEC's Accounting Disclosure Requirements', *The Accounting Review*, pp. 515–32, July 1969.

Chambers, R.J., *Accounting, Evaluation and Economic Behavior*, Prentice-Hall, Englewood Cliffs, 1966.

Christenson, C., 'The Methodology of Positive Accounting', *The Accounting Review*, Vol. 58, pp. 1–22, January 1983.

Christie, A., 'Aggregation of Test Statistics: An Evaluation of the Evidence on Contracting and Size Hypotheses', *Journal of Accounting and Economics*, Vol. 12, pp. 15–36, 1990.

Collins, D., Kothari, S., Rayburn, J, 'Firm Size and Information Content of Prices with Respect to Earnings', *Journal of Accounting and Economics*, Vol. 9, pp. 111–38, 1987.

Cotter, J., 'Utilisation and Restrictiveness of Covenants in Australian Private Debt Contracts', *Accounting and Finance*, Vol. 38, No. 2, pp. 181-96, 1998.

Cotter, J., 'Asset Revaluations and Debt Contracting', unpublished PhD thesis, University of Queensland, 1998.

DeAngelo, L., 'Managerial Competition, Information Costs, and Corporate Governance: The Use of Accounting Performance Measures in Proxy Contests', *Journal of Accounting and Economics*, Vol. 10, pp. 3–36, January 1988.

Deegan, C., 'The Design of Efficient Management Remuneration Contracts: A Consideration of Specific Human Capital Investments', *Accounting and Finance*, Vol. 37, No. 1, pp. 1–40, May 1997.

DeFond, M., Jiambalvo, J., 'Debt Covenant Violation and Manipulation of Accruals', *Journal of Accounting and Economics*, Vol. 17, pp. 145–76, 1994.

Downs, A., An Economic Theory of Democracy, Harper and Row, New York, 1957.

Dyckman, A., Zeff, S., 'Two Decades of the Journal of Accounting Research', *Journal of Accounting Research*, Vol. 22, pp. 225–97, 1984.

Ettredge, M., Simon, D., Smith, D., Stone, M., 'Why Do Companies Purchase Timely Quarterly Reviews?' *Journal of Accounting and Economics*', Vol. 18, No. 2, pp. 131–56, September 1994.

Fama, E., 'The Behavior of Stock Market Prices', *Journal of Business,* Vol. 38, pp. 34–105, 1965.

Fama, E., 'Agency Problems and The Theory of the Firm', *Journal of Political Economy*, Vol. 88, pp. 288–307, April 1980.

Freeman, R., 'The Association Between Accounting Earnings and Security Returns for Large and Small Firms', *Journal of Accounting and Economics,* Vol. 9, pp. 195–228, 1987.

Friedman, M., *The Methodology of Positive Economics, Essays in Positive Economics*, University of Chicago Press, 1953 (reprinted in 1966 by Phoenix Books).

Gray, R., Owen, D., Adams, C., *Accounting and Accountability: Changes and Challenges in Corporate Social and Environmental Reporting*, Prentice-Hall, London, 1996.

Guay, W.R., Kothari, S.P., Watts, R.L., 'A Market-based Evaluation of Discretionary Accrual Models', *Journal of Accounting Research*, Vol. 34 Supplement, pp. 83–105, 1996.

Healy, P.M., 'The Effect of Bonus Schemes on Accounting Decisions', *Journal of Accounting and Economics*, Vol. 7, pp. 85–107, 1985.

Hines, R., 'Financial Accounting: In Communicating Reality, We Construct Reality', *Accounting Organizations and Society*, Vol. 13, No. 3, pp. 251–62, 1988.

Holthausen, R.W., Larcker, D.F., Sloan, R.G., 'Annual Bonus Schemes and the Manipulation of Earnings', *Journal of Accounting and Economics*, Vol. 19, 1995.

Howieson, B., 'Whither Financial Accounting Research: A Modern-day Bo-Peep?', *Australian Accounting Review*, Vol. 6, No. 1, pp. 29–36, 1996.

Jensen, M.C., Meckling, W.H., 'Theory of the Firm: Managerial Behavior, Agency Costs and Ownership Structure', *Journal of Financial Economics*, Vol. 3, pp. 305–60, October 1976.

Jones, J., 'Earnings Management During Import Relief Investigations', *Journal of Accounting Research*, Vol. 29, pp. 193–228, 1991.

Kaplan, R.S., Roll, R., 'Investor Evaluation of Accounting Information: Some Empirical Evidence', *Journal of Business*, Vol. 45, pp. 225–57, 1972.

Lewellen, R.A, Loderer, C., Martin, K., 'Executive Compensation and Executive Incentive Problems', *Journal of Accounting and Economics*, Vol. 9, pp. 287–310, 1987.

Lintner, J., 'The Valuation of Risk Assets and the Selection of Risky Investments in Stock Portfolios and Capital Budgets', *Review of Economics and Statistics*, Vol. 47, pp. 13–37, 1965.

McComiskey, T., *Native Title Related Disclosures: A Political Cost Perspective*, unpublished B.Com. Honours Degree Dissertation, Griffith University, 1995.

Mian, S.L., Smith, C.W., 'Incentives for Consolidated Financial Reporting', *Journal of Accounting and Economics*, Vol. 12, pp. 141–71, 1990.

Morris, R., 'Corporate Disclosure in a Substantially Unregulated Environment', *ABACUS*, Vol. 20, No. 1, pp. 52–86, June 1984.

Mouck, T., 'The Rhetoric of Science and the Rhetoric of Revolt in the Story of Positive Accounting Theory', *Accounting, Auditing and Accountability Journal*, pp. 35–56, 1992.

Ness, K., Mirza, A., 'Corporate Social Disclosure: A Note on the Test of Agency Theory', *British Accounting Review*, Vol. 23, pp. 211–17, 1991.

Sharpe, W.F., 'Capital Asset Prices: A Review of Market Equilibrium Under Conditions of Risk', *Journal of Finance*, Vol. 19, pp. 425–42, 1964.

Sloan, R.G., 'Accounting Earnings and Top Executive Compensation', *Journal of Accounting and Economics*, Vol. 16, pp. 55–100, 1993.

Smith, C.W., Warner, J.B., 'On Financial Contracting: An Analysis of Bond Covenants', *Journal of Financial Economics*, Vol. 7, pp. 117–61, June 1979.

Smith, C.W., Watts, R.L. 'The Structure of Executive Contracts and the Control of Management', unpublished manuscript, University of Rochester, 1983.

Sterling, R.R, 'Positive Accounting: An Assessment,' *ABACUS*, Vol. 26, No. 2, pp. 97–135, 1990.

Sutton, T.G., 'The Proposed Introduction of Current Cost Accounting in the UK: Determinants of Corporate Preference', *Journal of Accounting and Economics*, Vol. 10, pp. 127–49, April 1988.

Sweeney, A.P., 'Debt-Covenant Violations and Managers' Accounting Responses', *Journal of Accounting and Economics*, Vol. 17, pp. 281–308, 1994.

Tinker, A., Lehman, C., Neimark, M., 'Corporate Social Reporting: Falling Down the Hole in the Middle of the Road', *Accounting, Auditing and Accountability Journal*, Vol. 4, No. 1, pp. 28–54, 1991.

Tinker, A.M., Merino, B.D., Neimark, M.D., 'The Normative Origins of Positive Theories: Ideology and Accounting Thought', *Accounting Organizations and Society*, Vol. 7, No. 2, pp. 167–200, 1982.

Watts, R.L., 'Corporate Financial Statements: A Product of the Market and Political Process', *Australian Journal of Management*, Vol. 2, pp. 53–75, April 1977.

Watts, R.L., 'Nature and Origins of Positive Research in Accounting', in *Accounting Theory, a Contemporary Review*, (Eds Jones, S., Romano, C., Ratnatunga, J.) Harcourt Brace, Sydney, pp. 295–353, 1995.

Watts, R.L., Zimmerman, J.L., 'Towards a Positive Theory of the Determinants of Accounting Standards', *The Accounting Review*, Vol. LIII, No.1, pp. 112–34, January 1978.

Watts, R.L., Zimmerman, J.L., 'The Demand for and Supply of Accounting Theories: The Market for Excuses', *The Accounting Review*, Vol. LIV, No. 2, pp. 273–305, April 1979.

Watts, R.L., Zimmerman, J.L., *Positive Accounting Theory*, Prentice-Hall, Englewood Cliffs, New Jersey, 1986.

Watts, R.L., Zimmerman, J.L., 'Positive Accounting Theory: A Ten Year Perspective', *The Accounting Review*, Vol. 65, No. 1, pp. 259–85, 1990.

Whittred, G., 'The Derived Demand for Consolidated Financial Reporting', *Journal of Accounting and Economics*, Vol. 9, pp. 259–85, December 1987.

Whittred, G., Zimmer, I., 'Accounting Information in the Market for Debt', *Accounting and Finance*, Vol. 28, No. 1, pp. 1–12, November 1986.

Wong, J., 'Economic Incentives for the Voluntary Disclosure of Current Cost Financial Statements', *Journal of Accounting and Economics*, pp. 151–67, April 1988.

Zmijewski, M., Hagerman, R., 'An Income Strategy Approach to the Positive Theory of Accounting Standard Setting/Choice', *Journal of Accounting and Economics*, Vol. 3, pp. 129–49, 1981.

Questions

7.1 Early positive research investigated evidence of share price changes as a result of the disclosure of accounting information. However, such research did not explain why particular accounting methods were selected in the first place. How did Positive Accounting Theory fill this void?

7.2 Explain the *management bonus hypothesis* and the *debt hypothesis* of Positive Accounting Theory.

7.3 If a manager is paid a percentage of profits, does this generate a motive to manipulate profits? Would this be anticipated by principals, and if so, how would principals react to this expectation?

7.4 What is an *agency relationship* and what is an *agency cost*? How can agency costs be reduced?

7.5 Explain the *political cost hypothesis* of Positive Accounting Theory.

7.6 Explain the *efficiency perspective* and the *opportunistic perspective* of Positive Accounting Theory. Why is one considered to be *ex post* and the other *ex ante*?

7.7 Organisations typically have a number of contractual arrangements with debtholders, with many covenants written to incorporate accounting numbers.

(a) Why would an organisation agree to enter into such agreements with debtholders?

(b) On average, do debtholders gain from the existence of such agreements?

7.8 Positive Accounting theorists typically argue that managers can reduce political costs by simply adopting an accounting method that leads to a reduction in reported income. Does this imply anything about the perceived efficiency of those parties involved in the political process, and if so, what perception is held?

7.9 Positive Accounting Theory assumes that all individual action is driven by self-interest, with the self-interest being tied to wealth maximisation.

(a) Is this a useful and/or realistic assumption?

(b) Adopting this assumption, why would politicians introduce particular regulations?

(c) Why would researchers study particular issues?

7.10 What are some of the criticisms of PAT? Do you agree with them? Why or why not?

7.11 Read Exhibit 7.3, and, adopting a positive accounting perspective, consider the following issues:

(a) If a new accounting standard impacts on profits, should this impact on the value of the firm, and if so, why?

(b) Will the imposition of a particular accounting method have implications for the *efficiency* of the organisation?

EXHIBIT 7.3 The introduction of accounting regulation

Accountancy plan poses profit danger

Tim Boreham

Tax

AUSTRALIA'S leading companies face a $1.3 billion profit hit if a controversial offshore accounting standard is introduced here, according to a Deloitte Touche Tohmatsu analysis of brand-rich corporates.

The international accounting standard, IAS 38, would require companies to write down (amortise) intangibles, such as brands, mastheads and liquor licences, over a maximum 20-year period.

Australia does not have a specific standard for intangibles but requires acquired goodwill to be written off on a similar basis.

A general depreciation standard requires all assets to be depreciated in line with their 'useful lives'.

Under the proposed rule, companies would need to reverse previous upward revaluations of intangibles, unless they can prove there is an 'active market' for these assets.

This would result in at least $5.5 billion of assets vanishing from corporate balance sheets, according to Deloitte.

Deloitte's national technical partner, Bruce Porter, said the 'time was right' for Australia to come to grips with the issue.

'The market is keenly following this issue; we cannot operate in a policy vacuum,' Mr Porter said.

Deloitte has identified nine potentially affected companies from the Australian Stock Exchange 20 Leaders, media and telecommunications indices.

They are The News Corporation Ltd (publisher of *The Australian*), Publishing & Broadcasting Ltd, John Fairfax, Seven Network, Foster's, Cable & Wireless Optus, BHP, Pacific Dunlop and CST.

(continued)

EXHIBIT 7.3 *(continued)*

News alone would incur an extra amortisation charge of $1.008 billion and relinquish 4.7 billion of balance sheet value through revaluation reversals, according to the analysis.

A similar proposal was developed by local standard-setters in 1989 but was vetoed after a corporate outcry.

Since then, however, corporates and regulators alike have actively pushed for harmonised local and global accounting rules.

The chairman of the International Accounting Standards Committee, Stig Enevoldsen, said IAS 38 was approved by 12 of the 16 country representatives on the committee. 'IAS 38 has gone down quite well around the world,' Mr Enevoldsen said.

For its part, the Australian Securities and Investments Commission has launched a related crackdown on the treatment of intangibles under the current rules.

ASIC chief accountant Jan McCahey said regulators were scrutinising companies which claimed their assets had an indeterminate, or infinite, life.

'I don't think that is sufficient justification for not amortising,' she said.

While ASIC was not sure whether IAS 38 was the answer, Ms McCahey warned that the Australian intangibles treatment was out of step with other countries.

'We are perceived to be cowboys in the international arena.'

The Australian, **Wednesday 2 June 1999, p. 24.**

7.12 Applying Positive Accounting Theory, and after reading Exhibit 7.4, answer the following questions:

(a) From an efficiency perspective, why could the introduction of new rules on intangibles be costly for an organisation?

(b) Why could the introduction of the new rules on intangibles be costly for a manager?

(c) What would motivate the regulators to develop the new rules?

EXHIBIT 7.4 Introduction of accounting regulation for accounting for intangibles

ASIC in row with media players over intangible assets

Luke Collins

A legal showdown is looming between Australia's major media companies and the Australian Securities and Investments Commission over the contentious issue of valuing television licences and newspaper mastheads, collectively worth billions of dollars annually to the companies' balance sheets.

The commission wants media groups such as Publishing and Broadcasting, the Seven Network, News Corporation and John Fairfax Holdings to alter their accounting treatment of intangibles,

(continued)

EXHIBIT 7.4 *(continued)*

amortising the assets rather than simply ascribing a carrying value to them.

Adopting ASIC's approach would wipe hundreds of millions of dollars from the companies' bottom lines. The regulator is adamant the change should take place in accounts for the 1998–99 financial year to bring the companies back into line with Australian accounting standards.

'We have a wide range of enforcement mechanisms available,' the chief accountant of the ASIC, Ms Jan McCahey, said. 'I would think it's unlikely that we will have a problem with the companies that we've spoken to.'

However, *The Australian Financial Review* understands the situation is less clear-cut. The big five accounting firms which audit the companies' accounts are undecided about their approach to the issue, and the industry's two major professional accounting bodies are split on the subject.

That means ASIC seems likely to have to take action of some form against a company if it wishes to enforce the standard.

'We're trying to find out where it's all coming from because we don't quite understand the logic behind it,' a Seven spokeswoman said. 'There's no real benefit and no real market driver, except from ASIC. We're bemused, as is everyone else.'

TV licences and newspaper mastheads are not presently amortised as they are assumed to have an infinite useable life.

ASIC is determined to enforce the Australian Accounting Standards Board's AASB 1021, which requires intangible assets to be amortised.

While the Australian Society of CPAs backs the ASIC stance, its rival, the Institute of Chartered Accountants, believes the standard has not changed in the past financial year. The ICA's technical standards director, Mr Keith Reilly, said if the standard had not changed, 'nothing has changed'.

'What the institute has consistently said is we expect companies to comply [with AASB 1021],' Mr Reilly said. 'If you are effectively going to modify the standard, there's an appropriate mechanism to do that.'

The major issue appears to be an interpretation of the amortisation issue released by the AASB in June. That interpretation found 'identifiable intangible assets fall within the scope' of AASB 1021, but did not set a time period over which the mastheads and licences should be amortised.

ASCPA accounting and audit director Mr Colin Parker said the organisation expected 'those [assets] that haven't been depreciated in the past for whatever reason to now be depreciated'.

'The job of ASIC is to enforce the accounting standard,' Mr Parker said. 'We don't think the answer is with ASIC at the end of the day. It should be the standard setters that take the heat.'

The Australian Financial Review, **Monday 2 August 1999, p. 21.**

7.13 Read Exhibit 7.5 and explain why publicity such as this might be costly to an organisation. How would Positive Accounting theorists expect the banks to react to such publicity?

EXHIBIT 7.5 An illustration of an industry attracting negative political attention

Bank fee hike sparks anger from battlers

By David Luff

THE Commonwealth Bank yesterday unveiled a string of higher fees and transaction charges in the latest move to force customers to change their banking habits.

Consumer and retiree groups immediately criticised the move while the Federal Government said it was concerned with any moves affecting people on fixed incomes.

Under the schedule which starts on December 1, over-the-counter withdrawals will face a $2 fee, up from $1.50. Withdrawals from automatic teller machines will attract a 60c fee, up from 45c.

The Commonwealth Bank hopes to encourage more customers to use EFTPOS machines, clipping 5c off the withdrawal fee to bring it back to 40c.

An account-keeping option—enabling customers to avoid the fees—is available at a cost of $3 a month, a 50 percent increase.

The CBA move is the latest in a wave of new and higher bank fees announced by the major banks since the federal election, with National Australia Bank, ANZ, Westpac and St George increasing selected fees.

Prime Minister John Howard declined to attack the Commonwealth Bank's fee grab, ignoring Labor Party queries about the higher charges.

'It is unarguable that over the past two-and-a-half years there has not been a dramatic reduction in the cost of borrowing money,' he told Parliament.

Labor shadow treasurer Simon Crean said 'the Prime Minister's silence speaks volumes about his attitude to rising bank fees'.

The ALP pledged to introduce formal monitoring of bank fees as an election promise.

Family and Community Services Minister Jocelyn Newman acknowledged the impact of higher fees on elderly households.

'I am always concerned if people are taking money out of pensioners' pockets,' she said. The Australian Pensioners and Superannuants Federation said older people would be the obvious losers from the changes.

'Older people in particular don't like using ATMs and want to use over-the-counter withdrawals,' APSF spokeswoman Norah McGuire said.

The Australian Consumers' Association nominated the CBA as the bank leading the charge for extra fee revenue.

The Australian Bankers' Association estimates transaction account fees contribute about $1.5 billion a year to the annual income of the five major banks. The banks argue the moves are necessary to recover the costs accumulated in providing comprehensive banking services.

'The Commonwealth Bank remains firmly committed to offering more accessible and fairly priced banking services to more Australians than anyone else,' CBA products division head Neville Cox said.

Interest rate analysts said banks were forced to increasingly rely on fees and charges to overcome the dwindling margins on interest rate lending produced by heavy competition from non-banks.

Interest rate monitor MarketFaxts said fee income would continue to rise as banks looked for new avenues to recoup lost revenue from lending.

CBA managing director David Murray attracted criticism after the bank's $1.25 billion profit announcement by declaring Australian banks should be congratulated by its customers for closing branches and maintaining prudent financial management.

At the time, the CBA was facing a customer backlash for closing branches as

(continued)

EXHIBIT 7.5 *(continued)*

part of the move towards electronic banking.

Queensland credit unions said the fee hike would backfire on the Commonwealth and provide credit unions with more customers.

Industry group Credit Union Services said credit unions always experienced a membership increase following a major bank increasing its fees.

'A lot of our surveys show that people are moving across (to credit unions) because they have much fairer and lower fee structures,' public affairs general manager David Taylor said.

'Credit unions don't tend to charge fees just because people have low balances which is something that banks do.

'Most credit union fees are strictly related to usage and I don't know of many charging for over-the-counter transactions.

'Certainly customers have in the past moved across to credit unions because they have seen them as more favourable and that might occur again.'

Queensland credit unions said the fee hike would backfire on the Commonwealth and provide credit unions with more customers.

The Courier-Mail, **Tuesday 24 November 1998.**

Chapter 8

Unregulated financial reporting decisions: Considerations of systems oriented theories

Learning objectives

Upon completing this chapter readers should:

- understand how community or stakeholders' perceptions can influence the disclosure policies of an organisation;

- understand how Legitimacy Theory and Stakeholder Theory can be applied to help explain why an entity might elect to make particular voluntary disclosures;

- understand what we mean by *organisational legitimacy* and how corporate disclosures within such places as annual reports can be used as a strategy to maintain or restore the legitimacy of an organisation;

- understand how the respective *power* and information demands of particular stakeholder groups can influence corporate disclosure policies;

- understand the view that a successful organisation is one that is able to balance or manage the demands (sometimes conflicting), including information demands, of different stakeholder groups.

Opening issues

In *The Australian* newspaper on 18 October 1999 (p. 39) a headline read: *ANZ, Commonwealth share 'bastard bank' award*. The article was particularly critical of the ANZ Bank and the Commonwealth Bank for the number of jobs 'slashed' within both organisations.

Would you expect these banks to react to such negative media publicity, and if so, why? Further, would you expect them to make any disclosures within their respective annual reports in relation to the job cuts? What form would you expect these disclosures to take?

Introduction

In Chapter 7 we considered a number of theoretical arguments as to why corporate management might elect to voluntarily provide particular information to parties outside the organisation. These arguments were grounded within *Positive Accounting Theory*. In this chapter we consider some alternative theoretical perspectives that address this issue. Specifically we consider *Legitimacy Theory* and *Stakeholder Theory*.

As has been stressed throughout this book, and particularly in Chapter 1, theories are abstractions of reality and hence particular theories cannot be expected to provide a full account or description of particular behaviour. Hence, it is sometimes useful to consider the perspectives provided by alternative theories. Different researchers might study the same phenomenon but elect to adopt alternative theoretical perspectives.[1] The choice of one theoretical perspective in preference to others will, at least in part, be due to particular value judgements of the authors involved. As O'Leary (1985, p. 88) states:

> *Theorists' own values or ideological predispostions may be among the factors that determine which side of the argument they will adopt in respect of disputable connections of a theory with evidence.*

Legitimacy Theory and Stakeholder Theory are two theoretical perspectives that have been adopted by a number of researchers in recent years. These theories are sometimes referred to as 'systems-oriented theories'. In accordance with Gray, Owen and Adams (1996, p. 45):

> *. . . a systems-oriented view of the organisation and society . . . permits us to focus on the role of information and disclosure in the relationship(s) between organisations, the State, individuals and groups.*

---

1. For example, some researchers operating within the Positive Accounting Theory paradigm (e.g. Ness and Mirza, 1991) argue that the voluntary disclosure of social responsibility information can be explained as a strategy to reduce political costs. Social responsibility reporting has also been explained from a Legitimacy Theory perspective (e.g. Patten, 1991), and from a Stakeholder Theory perspective (e.g. Roberts, 1992).

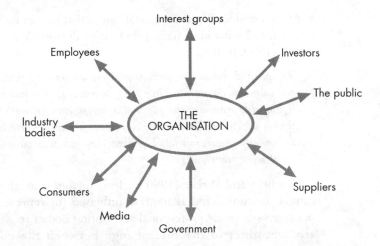

FIGURE 8.1 The organisation viewed as part of a wider social system

Within a *systems-based perspective*, the entity is assumed to be influenced by, and in turn to have influence upon, the society in which it operates. This is simplistically represented in Figure 8.1.

Within both Legitimacy Theory and Stakeholder Theory, accounting disclosure policies are considered to constitute a strategy to influence the organisation's relationships with the other parties with which it interacts. In recent times, Stakeholder Theory and Legitimacy Theory have been applied primarily to explain why organisations make certain social responsibility disclosures within their annual reports.[2] The theories could, however, also be applied to explain why companies adopt particular financial accounting techniques.

Political Economy Theory

According to Gray, Owen and Adams (1996), Legitimacy Theory and Stakeholder Theory are both derived from a broader theory which has been called *Political Economy Theory*. The 'political economy' itself has been defined by Gray, Owen and Adams (p. 47) as 'the social, political and economic framework within which human life takes place'. The perspective embraced is that *society*, *politics* and *economics* are inseparable, and economic issues cannot meaningfully be investigated in the absence of considerations about the political, social and institutional framework in which the economic activity takes place. It is argued that by considering the *political economy* a researcher

2. Social responsibility disclosures are considered more fully in Chapter 9. However, at this stage they can be defined as disclosures that provide information about the interaction of an organisation with its physical and social environment, inclusive of community involvement, the natural environment, human resources, energy and product safety (Mathews, 1993; Gray, Owen and Maunders, 1987).

is able to consider broader (societal) issues that impact on how an organisation operates, and what information it elects to disclose. According to Guthrie and Parker (1990, p. 166):

> The political economy perspective perceives accounting reports as social, political, and economic documents. They serve as a tool for constructing, sustaining, and legitimising economic and political arrangements, institutions, and ideological themes which contribute to the corporation's private interests. Disclosures have the capacity to transmit social, political, and economic meanings for a pluralistic set of report recipients.

Guthrie and Parker (1990, p. 166) further state that corporate reports cannot be considered as neutral, unbiased (or representationally faithful) documents as many professional accounting bodies might suggest, but rather are 'a product of the interchange between the corporation and its environment and attempt to mediate and accommodate a variety of sectional interests'.[3] This view is consistent with Burchell et al. (1980, p. 6) who suggest that accounting can 'not be seen as a mere assembly of calculative routines, it functions as a cohesive and influential mechanism for economic and social management'.

Political Economy Theory has been divided (perhaps somewhat simplistically, but nevertheless usefully) into two broad streams which Gray, Owen and Adams (1996, p. 47) have labelled 'classical' and 'bourgeois' political economy. Classical political economy is related to the works of philosophers such as Karl Marx, and explicitly places 'sectional (class) interests, structural conflict, inequity, and the role of the State at the heart of the analysis' (Gray, Owen and Adams, 1996, p. 47). This can be contrasted with 'bourgeois' political economy theory which, according to Gray, Kouhy and Lavers (1995, p. 53), largely ignores these elements and, as a result, is content to perceive the world as essentially pluralistic.

Classical political economy tends to perceive accounting reports and disclosures as a means of maintaining the favoured position of those who control scarce resources (capital), and as a means of undermining the position of those without scarce capital. It focuses on the structural conflicts within society.[4]

---

3. As we would appreciate, various professional accounting bodies throughout the world have released documents (normally as part of a conceptual framework project) indicating that financial reporting should embrace the attributes of *neutrality* and *representational faithfulness*. Proponents of political economy theories would argue that there are a multitude of political and social issues that make such a perspective unrealistic.

4. For example, in considering the practice of social responsibility reporting, classical political economists would typically argue that the growth of environmental disclosure by companies in the late 1980s and early 1990s can be seen as an attempt to act *as if* in response to environmental groups while, *actually*, attempting to wrest the initiative and control of the environment agenda from these groups in order to permit capital to carry on doing what it does best—making money from capital (Gray, Owen and Adams, 1996, p.47).

According to Cooper and Sherer (1984), the study of accounting should recognise *power* and *conflict* in society, and consequently should focus on the effects of accounting reports on the distribution of income, wealth and power in society. This is consistent with Lowe and Tinker (1977) who argue that the majority of accounting research is based on a *pluralist* conception of society.[5] According to Lowe and Tinker, this pluralistic view assumes (incorrectly, they argue) that power is widely diffused and that society is composed of individuals whose preferences are to predominate in social choices, and with no individual able to consistently influence that society (or the accounting function therein). Researchers such as Lowe and Tinker (1977) and Cooper and Sherer (1984) oppose such a view and provide a counter-perspective that the *pluralist* view ignores a deal of evidence that suggests that the majority of people in society are controlled by a small but 'well-defined elite'—an elite that uses accounting (as well as other mechanisms) as a means of maintaining their position of dominance. We further consider the works of authors who take this position when we consider *critical accounting perspectives* in Chapter 12. We show that such researchers tend to be extremely critical of current accounting and reporting techniques.

According to Gray, Owen and Adams (1996), and as briefly noted above, *bourgeois political economy*, on the other hand, does not explicitly consider structural conflicts and *class struggles* but rather 'tends to be concerned with interactions between groups in an essentially pluralistic world (for example, the negotiation between a company and an environmental pressure group, or between a local authority and the State)'. It is this branch of Political Economy Theory from which *Legitimacy Theory* and *Stakeholder Theory* derive. Neither theory questions or studies the various class structures (and possible struggles) within society.[6] We now turn our attention to these theories.

Legitimacy Theory

Legitimacy Theory asserts that organisations continually seek to ensure that they operate within the bounds and norms of their respective societies, that is, they attempt to ensure that their activities are perceived by outside parties as being 'legitimate'. These bounds and norms are not considered to be fixed, but rather, change over time, thereby requiring the organisation to be responsive to the environment in which they operate. Lindblom (1994) distinguishes between *legitimacy* which is considered to be a status or

---

5. A pluralistic perspective assumes (typically implicitly) that many classes of stakeholders have the power to influence various decisions by corporations, government and other entities. Accounting is not considered to be put in place to favour specific interests (sometimes referred to as 'elites'). By using 'society' as the topic of focus rather than *subgroups* within society, theories such as Legitimacy Theory ignore 'struggles and inequities within society' (Puxty, 1991).

6. Positive Accounting Theory, the focus of Chapter 7, also does not consider issues associated with inequities within society or the role of accounting in sustaining these inequities.

condition, and *legitimation* which she considers to be the process that leads to an organisation being adjudged *legitimate*. According to Lindblom (p. 2), legitimacy is:

> . . . *a condition or status which exists when an entity's value system is congruent with the value system of the larger social system of which the entity is a part. When a disparity, actual or potential, exists between the two value systems, there is a threat to the entity's legitimacy.*

Legitimacy Theory relies upon the notion that there is a 'social contract' between the organisation in question and the society in which in operates. The 'social contract' is not easy to define but the concept is used to represent the multitude of implicit and explicit expectations that society has about how the organisation should conduct its operations.[7] It can be argued that traditionally, profit maximisation *was* perceived to be the optimal measure of corporate performance (Ramanathan, 1976; Abbott and Monsen, 1979; Heard and Bolce, 1981; Patten, 1991, 1992). Under this notion a firm's profits were viewed as an all-inclusive measure of *organisational legitimacy* (Ramanathan, 1976). However, public expectations have undergone significant change in recent decades. Heard and Bolce (1981) note the expansion of the advocacy movement in the United States during the 1960s and 1970s, and the significant increase in legislation related to social issues, including the environment, and employees' health and safety, which was enacted in the United States within the same period. With heightened social expectations it is anticipated that successful business corporations will react and attend to the human, environmental and other social consequences of their activities (Heard and Bolce, 1981).

Society now expects business to '. . . make outlays to repair or prevent damage to the physical environment, to ensure the health and safety of consumers, employees, and those who reside in the communities where products are manufactured and wastes are dumped . . .' (Tinker and Niemark, 1987, p. 84). Consequently, companies with a poor social and environmental performance record may increasingly find it difficult to obtain the necessary resources and support to continue operations within a community that values a clean environment. Perhaps this was not the case a number of decades ago.

It is assumed that society allows the organisation to continue operations to the extent that it generally meets their expectations. Legitimacy Theory emphasises that the organisation must appear to consider the rights of the public at large, not merely those of its investors. Failure to comply with societal expectations (that is, comply with the terms of the 'social contract') may lead to sanctions being imposed by society, for example, in the form of legal restrictions imposed on its operations, limited resources (for example, financial capital and labour) being provided, and reduced demand for its products.

---

7. It can be argued that the requirements imposed by the law reflect the explicit terms of the social contract, while uncodified community expectations (and these will be perceived to be different by different people) constitute the implicit terms of the social contract.

In Exhibit 8.1, an executive of one of Australia's largest banks concedes that his organisation broke the 'social contract'. It is interesting to note that the notion of a social contract is something that is increasingly being referred to by managers (and we show further evidence of this later in this chapter).

Consistent with Legitimacy Theory, organisations are not considered to have any inherent right to resources. *Legitimacy* (from society's perspective) and the right to operate go hand in hand. As Mathews (1993, p. 26) states:

> *The social contract would exist between corporations (usually limited companies) and individual members of society. Society (as a collection of individuals) provides corporations with their legal standing and attributes and the authority to own and use natural resources and to hire employees. Organisations draw on community resources and output both goods and services and waste products to the general environment. The organisation has no inherent rights to these benefits, and in order to allow their existence, society would expect the benefits to exceed the costs to society.*

The idea of a 'social contract' is not new, having been discussed by philosophers such as Thomas Hobbes (1588–1679), John Locke (1632–1704), and Jean-Jacques Rousseau (1712–1778). Shocker and Sethi (1974, p. 67) provide a good overview of the concept of a social contract:

> *Any social institution—and business is no exception—operates in society via a social contract, expressed or implied, whereby its survival and growth are based on:*

EXHIBIT 8.1 The social contract between a bank and the community

Westpac chief admits banks failed in the bush

By Sid Marris

The rush by banks to shut branches in rural areas over the past decade was a 'mistake' and broke 'the social contract' with the community, a Westpac executive Michael Hawker said yesterday.

Mr Hawker, group executive for Business and Consumer Banking, said that in the face of intense competition following deregulation, banks had lost sight of the needs and fears of a number of their customers.

He told a National Farmers' Federation conference in Longreach that many of the rural closures should have been handled more sensitively. 'I think what we are saying is what we did was probably not the most appropriate thing to do,' he said.

'I think everyone in the community would say there's been a lot of dramatic change and I think we have made a number of mistakes. There is no doubt about that.'

Between 1990 and 1998, 1306 banks shut their doors across Australia—406 of them in country areas—while 1345 agencies also shut, 1071 outside major cities.

Mr Hawker said advances in technology meant 'in-store' banking—which provides basic teller transactions and a phone service at a sponsoring business—could spare rural communities from loss of services. Westpac initiated a $300 million review and refurbishment program last November for its 969 branches, which will see an estimated 150 convert to in-store operations.

The Australian, **20 May 1999, p. 1.**

(1) *the delivery of some socially desirable ends to society in general, and*

(2) *the distribution of economic, social, or political benefits to groups from which it derives its power.*

In a dynamic society, neither the sources of institutional power nor the needs for its services are permanent. Therefore, an institution must constantly meet the twin tests of legitimacy and relevance by demonstrating that society requires its services and that the groups benefiting from its rewards have society's approval.

As indicated above, and in Deegan and Rankin (1996, p. 54), in accord with Legitimacy Theory, if an organisation cannot justify its continued operation, then in a sense the community may revoke its 'contract' to continue its operations. Again, as indicated earlier, this may occur through consumers reducing or eliminating the demand for the products of the business, factor suppliers eliminating the supply of labour and financial capital to the business, or constituents lobbying government for increased taxes, fines or laws to prohibit actions that do not conform with the expectations of the community. Given the potential costs associated with conducting operations deemed to be outside the terms of the 'social contract', Dowling and Pfeffer (1975) state that organisations will take various actions to ensure that their operations are perceived to be legitimate. That is, they will attempt to establish congruence between 'the social values associated with or implied by their activities and the norms of acceptable behavior in the larger social system of which they are a part' (Dowling and Pfeffer, 1975, p. 122). As community expectations change, organisations must also adapt and change. The process of maintaining this congruence leads to what is known as organisational legitimacy (Dowling and Pfeffer, 1975). It is assumed that *effective* managers react swiftly to changes in community concerns and priorities.

Dowling and Pfeffer outline the means by which an organisation may legitimate its activities (p. 127):

- The organisation can adapt its output, goals and methods of operation to conform to prevailing definitions of legitimacy.

- The organisation can attempt, through communication, to alter the definition of social legitimacy so that it conforms to the organisation's present practices, output and values.

- The organisation can attempt through communication to become identified with symbols, values or institutions that have a strong base of legitimacy.

Consistent with Dowling and Pfeffer's strategy of 'communication', Lindblom (1994) proposes that if an organisation perceives that its legitimacy is in question it can adopt a number of strategies. Lindblom (1994) identifies four courses of action (there is some overlap with Dowling and Pfeffer) that an organisation can take to obtain, or maintain legitimacy. The organisation can:

1. seek to educate and inform its 'relevant publics' about (actual) changes in the organisation's performance and activities;

2. seek to change the perceptions of the 'relevant publics'—but not change its actual behaviour;

3. seek to manipulate perception by deflecting attention from the issue of concern to other related issues through an appeal to, for example, emotive symbols; or

4. seek to change external expectations of its performance.

According to Lindblom, and Dowling and Pfeffer, the public disclosure of information in such places as annual reports can be used by an organisation to implement each of the above strategies. Certainly this is a perspective that many researchers of social responsibility reporting have adopted, as we show shortly. For example, a firm may provide information to counter or offset negative news which may be publicly available, or it may simply provide information to inform the interested parties about attributes of the organisation that were previously unknown. In addition, organisations may draw attention to strengths, for instance environmental awards won, or safety initiatives that have been implemented, while sometimes neglecting, or down-playing information concerning negative implications of their activities, such as pollution or workplace accidents.[8]

Consistent with the positions taken by Dowling and Pfeffer, and Lindblom, Hurst (1970) suggests that one of the functions of accounting, and subsequently accounting reports, is to legitimate the existence of the corporation. Such views highlight the strategic nature of financial statements and other related disclosures.

The view within Legitimacy Theory that organisations will be penalised if they do not operate in a manner consistent with community expectations (that is, in accordance with the social contract) is a view being embraced publicly by many Australian (as well as overseas) corporate managers. This is reflected in some statements made by North Ltd (a large Australian mining company) in its stand-alone *Environment, Safety and Health '98 Annual Report*. In the report the directors of North Ltd state:

> One of the key features for North is whether the way we manage the environmental, social and economic implications of our business meets the expectations of the community. We recognise that our future commercial success depends on being accepted and valued by the communities in which we operate. Their acceptance depends upon our actions as a company, and the values which underpin them.

---

8. What is being stressed is that managing *legitimacy* is very much about managing the *perceptions* of others.

R.J. McNeilly, Chief Operating Officer of BHP Ltd, one of Australia's largest corporations, made the following statement in the 1998 Annual Report of BHP.

World class performance in the areas of safety, the environment and community relations is a business responsibility. Success in these areas is an investment in our global future and protects our licence to operate. Continual improvement is necessary to meet changing world standards and to meet the rising level of community expectations.

Consistent with Legitimacy Theory, the above statement reflects the view that organisations must adapt to community expectations if they are to be successful. This view is also reflected in WMC Ltd's 1997 annual report (WMC Ltd is also one of Australia's largest corporations). In the report the directors state:

WMC's environmental performance affects the Company's ability to attract skilled people, capital and community support. Good environmental management reduces costs, meets the expectations of the communities in which WMC operates, and enables the company to be more profitable.

Pearce Bowman, Executive General Manager (Copper and Uranium) of WMC Ltd also makes the following statement in WMC Ltd's third stand-alone environmental performance report, *WMC Limited Environmental Progress Report 1998*:

As a producer of uranium, as well as copper, Olympic Dam welcomes public scrutiny of its operations and provides extensive information about its environmental performance . . . It is good business to be responsible managers. Industry can no longer consider environmental and social issues as 'outside the fence'. Good environmental management requires more than written procedures and policies. We must continue translating our words into action. This has become more challenging as community expectations of business behaviour rise . . . A company that does not address public expectations cannot expect to maintain its 'license to operate' and will inevitably founder in increasing government regulation and public opposition.

At an industry level, The Mineral Council of Australia also makes public statements about the need to act in a manner consistent with community perceptions. The 1998 Annual Report of the Minerals Council of Australia states in relation to environmental performance (p. 12):

The environmental performance of the Australian minerals industry is an essential requirement for the industry's continued viability and success. It is only on the basis of high quality environmental performance and through striving for continual improvement in environmental management that the industry can credibly influence government environmental policies and seek the community's acceptance of the industry's licence to operate.

In three of the above quotes the term 'licence to operate' is used. It would appear that the term 'licence to operate', which in recent years seems to have become a quite common term for corporate management to use, is what many researchers might refer to as a 'social contract'.[9]

The above statements illustrate that the notions embodied within Legitimacy Theory are reflective of the public positions being taken by Australian corporate executives. Management appears to consider the expectations of the community in which it operates and realises that failure to do so will be detrimental to ongoing operations and survival.

Empirical tests of Legitimacy Theory

In recent years Legitimacy Theory has been used by numerous accounting researchers who have elected to study social and environmental reporting practices. A number of papers have identified specific types of social responsibility disclosures that have appeared within annual reports. The respective researchers have attempted to explain these disclosures on the basis that they form part of the portfolio of strategies undertaken by accountants and their managers to bring legitimacy to, or maintain the legitimacy of, their respective organisations. We now consider a number of such papers.

An early study that sought to link legitimacy theory to corporate social disclosure policies was conducted by Hogner (1982). This longitudinal study examined corporate social reporting in the annual reports of US Steel Corporation over a period of eighty years, commencing in 1901, the data being analysed for year to year variation. Hogner showed that the extent of social disclosures varied from year to year and he speculated that the variation could represent a response to society's changing expectations of corporate behaviour.

Patten (1992) focused on the change in the extent of environmental disclosures made by North American oil companies, other than just Exxon Oil Company, both before and after the *Exxon Valdez* incident in Alaska in 1989. He argued that if the Alaskan oil spill resulted in a threat to the legitimacy of the petroleum industry, and not just to Exxon, then Legitimacy Theory would suggest that companies operating within that industry would respond by increasing the amount of environmental disclosures in their annual reports. Patten's results indicate that there were increased environmental disclosures by the petroleum companies for the post-1989 period, consistent with a legitimation perspective. This disclosure reaction took place across the industry, even though the incident itself was directly related to one oil company. He argued (p. 475):

---

9. A number of organisations also refer to the *community* licence to operate.

. . . it appears that at least for environmental disclosures, threats to a firm's legitimacy do entice the firm to include more social responsibility information in its annual report.

In an Australian study, Deegan and Rankin (1996) utilised Legitimacy Theory to try to explain systematic changes in corporate annual report environmental disclosure policies around the time of proven environmental prosecutions. The authors examined the environmental disclosure practices of a sample of firms that were successfully prosecuted by the New South Wales and Victorian Environmental Protection Authorities (EPAs) for breaches of various environmental protection laws during the period 1990 to 1993 (any prosecutions by these agencies are reported in the EPAs' annual reports which are publicly available). The annual reports of a final sample of 20 firms, prosecuted a total of 78 times, were reviewed to ascertain the extent of the environmental disclosures. These annual reports were matched by industry and size to the annual reports of a control group of 20 firms that had not been prosecuted.

Of the 20 prosecuted firms, 18 provided environmental information in their annual report, but the disclosures were predominantly positive and qualitative. Only two organisations made any mention of the prosecutions. Deegan and Rankin found that prosecuted firms disclosed significantly more environmental information (of a favourable nature) in the year of prosecution than any other year in the sample period. Consistent with the view that companies increase disclosure to offset any effects of EPA prosecutions, the EPA-prosecuted firms also disclosed more environmental information, relative to non-prosecuted firms. The authors concluded that the public disclosure of proven environmental prosecutions has an impact on the disclosure policies of firms involved.

With the results of Patten (1992) and Deegan and Rankin (1996) in mind we can consider Exhibit 8.2, which documents the poor safety record of a number of companies in the mining industry. Read the exhibit and then consider how Legitimacy Theory could be used to predict how the organisations involved, as well as other companies in the industry, might react to such publicity. Do you think that the organisations would be deemed to have breached their 'social contract', and if so, do you think that they might use their annual reports in an attempt to reinstate their legitimacy?

In another study, Deegan and Gordon (1996) reviewed annual report environmental disclosures made by Australian companies from 1980 to 1991. They investigated the objectivity of corporate environmental disclosure practices and trends in environmental disclosures over time. They also sought to determine if environmental disclosures are related to concerns held by environmental groups about particular industries' environmental performance. The results derived by the Deegan and Gordon (1996) study confirm, among other findings, that: (1) increases in corporate environmental disclosures over time are positively associated with increases in the levels of environmental group membership; (2) Australian corporate environmental disclosures are

EXHIBIT 8.2 Negative media coverage of the mining industry's safety record

Deaths blamed on mine neglect

Penelope Green

SAFETY in Australia's coal mining industry came under another blistering attack yesterday after a former NSW judge recommended that mine owners be prosecuted for 'gross negligence' surrounding a mining disaster that claimed four lives in 1996.

He said more prosecutions and 'attitudinal change' were needed to secure mine safety in Australia.

'Mining companies and senior officials must be made aware, by timely prosecution, that they are accountable under the law for their actions,' Judge James Staunton said in his 749-page report on the disaster at the Gretley Colliery, near Newcastle.

He said 'disturbing and wrong assumptions' by mine surveyors and managers had jeopardised lives.

Judge Staunton recommended papers be referred to the NSW Crown Solicitor 'with a view to determining whether offences have been committed' by the mine's owner, Newcastle Wallsend Coal Co. Pty Ltd, under the Occupational Health and Safety Act 1983.

The judge said more than 33 miners had lost their lives in mining disasters in the State since 1990—many involving 'gross negligence and breaches of the law'—however no mining company or senior official had been prosecuted since April that year.

Two years ago, Australia's biggest mining company, BHP, was found to have been negligent in its operation of the Moura mine in Queensland where 11 miners died in an explosion but there were no prosecutions.

Edward Batterham, 49, Damon Murray, 19, Mark Kaiser, 30 and John Hunter, 36 were working to develop a roadway out of the Gretley colliery in the final hours of their 'dogwatch' night shift when they unwittingly drilled into the disused Young Wallsend Colliery.

The torrent of water that swept them to their deaths was so powerful it lifted a 50-tonne machine.

At the time of the incident, the miners were using inaccurate maps approved and provided to them by the Department which showed they were up to 100 metres away from the Young Wallsend Colliery, when their mechanical digger was about eight metres away.

Judge Staunton said a series of failures had led to the 1996 disaster, including the Department's creation of three false maps, one copied from a 19th century map of the area.

He said mining officials at the Newcastle Wallsend company had failed to research the true location of the Young Wallsend Colliery. The Department had failed to properly appraise and evaluate the mining application by Newcastle Wallsend and as a result 'a flawed system was approved'.

Recommending sweeping changes to regulation, Judge Staunton said the NSW government should establish an autonomous unit to investigate 'fatalities, serious bodily injuries and dangerous occurrences' in the industry.

NSW Mineral and Resources minister Bob Martin confirmed yesterday he would legislate to set up a 'high-powered' special investigative unit similar to air crash investigation units such as the Federal Bureau of Air Safety Investigation.

In a separate development, the Construction, Forestry, Mining and Energy Union said yesterday it would consider its own criminal prosecution. The company said it would 'take some time to read and interpret' the report.

The Australian, **Wednesday 18 July 1999, p. 1.**

overwhelmingly self-laudatory; and (3) there is a positive correlation between the environmental sensitivity of the industry to which the corporation belongs and the level of corporate environmental disclosure.[10] These results were deemed to be consistent with Legitimacy Theory.

Gray, Kouhy and Lavers (1995) performed a longitudinal review of UK corporate social and environmental disclosures for the period 1979 to 1991. In discussing the trends in corporate environmental disclosure policies, they made use of Legitimacy Theory, with specific reference to the strategies suggested by Lindblom (1994), which we considered earlier in this chapter. After considering the extent and types of corporate disclosures, they stated (p. 65):

> *The tone, orientation and focus of the environmental disclosures accord closely with Lindblom's first, second and third legitimation strategies. A significant minority of companies found it necessary to 'change their actual performance' with respect to environmental interactions (Lindblom's first strategy) and use corporate social reporting to inform their 'relevant publics' about this. Similarly, companies' environmental disclosure has also been an attempt, first, to change perceptions of environmental performance—to alter perceptions of whether certain industries were 'dirty' and 'irresponsible' (Lindblom's second strategy) and, second, as Lindblom notes, to distract attention from the central environmental issues (the third legitimation strategy). Increasingly, companies are being required to demonstrate a satisfactory performance within the environmental domain. Corporate social reporting would appear to be one on the mechanisms by which the organisations satisfy (and manipulate) that requirement.*

In relation to trends found in regard to health and safety disclosures Gray, Kouhy and Lavers (p. 65) state:

> *We are persuaded that companies were increasingly under pressure from various 'relevant publics' to improve their performance in the area of health and safety and employed corporate social reporting to manage this 'legitimacy gap'. That is, while the disclosure did not, as such, demonstrate improved health and safety records (lack of previous information makes such assessment impossible), it did paint a picture of increasing concern being given by companies to the matter of protecting and training their workforce. This disclosure then helped add to the image of a competent and concerned organisation which took its responsibilities in this field seriously. As such, health and safety disclosure appears to be a strong illustration of Lindblom's second legitimation strategy— 'changing perceptions'.*

---

10. Environmental sensitivity was determined by use of a questionnaire to Australian environmental lobby groups in which office bearers were required to rate industries (on a 0 to 5 scale) on the basis of whether the industry had been made the focus of action as a result of its environmental performance/implications.

Deegan, Rankin and Voght (2000) also utilised Legitimacy Theory to explain how the social disclosures included within the annual reports of companies in selected industries changed around the time of major social incidents or disasters that could be directly related to their particular industry. The results of the study are consistent with Legitimacy Theory and show that companies do appear to change their disclosure policies around the time of major company and industry related social events. The authors argue that 'the results highlight the strategic nature of voluntary social disclosures and are consistent with a view that management considers that annual report social disclosures are a useful device to reduce the effects upon a corporation of events that are perceived to be unfavourable to a corporation's image' (p. 127).

In a US study the choice of an accounting framework was deemed to be related to a desire to increase the legitimacy of an organisation. Carpenter and Feroz (1992) argue that the State of New York's (government) decision to adopt Generally Accepted Accounting Procedures (as opposed to a method of accounting based on cash flows rather than accruals) was 'an attempt to regain legitimacy for the State's financial management practices' (p. 613). According to Carpenter and Feroz, New York State was in a financial crisis in 1975, with the result that many parties began to question the adequacy of the financial reporting practices of all the associated government units. To regain legitimacy the State elected to implement GAAP (accruals–based accounting). As Carpenter and Feroz (pp. 635, 637) state:

> The state of New York needed a symbol of legitimacy to demonstrate to the public and the credit markets that the state's finances were well managed. GAAP, as an institutionalized legitimated practice, serves this purpose . . . We argue that New York's decision to adopt GAAP was an attempt to regain legitimacy for the state's financial management practices. Challenges to the state's financial management practices, led by the state comptroller, contributed to confusion and concern in the municipal securities market. The confusion resulted in a lowered credit rating. To restore the credit rating, a symbol of legitimacy in financial management practices was needed.
>
> It is debatable whether GAAP was the solution for the state's financial management problem. Indeed, there is strong evidence that GAAP did not solve the state's financial management problems.
>
> New York needed a symbol of legitimacy that could be easily recognised by the public. In the realm of financial reporting, 'GAAP' is the recognised symbol of legitimacy.

According to Carpenter and Feroz, few people would be likely to oppose a system that is 'generally accepted'—general acceptance provides an impression of legitimacy. As they state (p. 632):

> In discussing whether to use the term 'GAAP' instead of 'accrual' in promoting the accounting conversion efforts, panel members argued that no one could oppose a system that is generally accepted. The name implies that any other

accounting principles are not accepted in the accounting profession. GAAP is also seemingly apolitical.

As has been emphasised in this chapter, Legitimacy Theory proposes a relationship between corporate disclosures (and other corporate strategies) and community expectations, the view being that management reacts to community concerns and changes therein. But we are left with a question— how does management determine community expectations? There is evidence that management might rely on sources such as the media to determine community expectations. For example, O'Donovan (1999) provides the results of interviews with senior executives from three large Australian companies (Amcor Ltd, BHP Ltd, and ORICA Ltd). The executives confirmed that, from their perspective, the media does shape community expectations, and that corporate disclosure is one way to correct 'mis-perceptions held or presented by the media'. O'Donovan reproduced a number of statements made by the executives who were interviewed. These included:

If there was something that was given prominent press coverage, yes (news reports influence disclosure decisions). This year and last year we mentioned the ground water survey at Botany Bay as it attracted press coverage and was important to Sydney residents. (Company C—Interviewee No. 1)

The environmental issues that are covered in the annual report really try to address matters of current concern as depicted in the media. Shareholders then get an understanding on where our company stands on issues such as recycling, forestry, chlorine and greenhouse gases. (Company A—Interviewee No. 2)

Related to the results of O'Donovan (1999), Brown and Deegan (1999) investigated the relationship between the print media coverage given to various industries' environmental effects, and the levels of annual report environmental disclosures made by a sample of firms within those industries. The basis of the argument was that the media can be particularly effective in driving the community's concern about the environmental performance of particular organisations and where such concern is raised, organisations will respond by increasing the extent of disclosure of environmental information within the annual report.

Brown and Deegan use the extent of media coverage given to a particular issue as a measure (or proxy) of community concern. They make explicit reference to *Media Agenda Setting Theory*. Media Agenda Setting Theory proposes a relationship between the relative emphasis given by the media to various topics, and the degree of salience these topics have for the general public (Ader, 1995, p. 300).[11] In terms of causality, increased media attention

---

11. For an explanation of Media Agenda Setting Theory see McCombs and Shaw, 1972; Zucker, 1978; Eyal, Winter and DeGeorge, 1981; Blood, 1981; Mayer, 1980; McCombs, 1981; Ader, 1995.

is believed to lead to increased community concern for a particular issue. The media are not seen as mirroring public priorities; rather, they are seen as shaping them.[12] The arguments provided in Brown and Deegan (1999) can be summarised as:

(a) management uses the annual report as a tool to legitimise the ongoing operations of the organisation (from Legitimacy Theory);

(b) community concerns with the environmental performance of a specific firm in an industry will also impact on the disclosure strategies of firms across that industry (consistent with Patten, 1992, who adopted Legitimacy Theory); and

(c) the media are able to influence community perceptions about issues such as the environment (from Media Agenda Setting Theory).

The results in Brown and Deegan (1999) indicate that for the majority of the industries studied, higher levels of media attention (as determined by a review of a number of print media newspapers and journals) are significantly associated with higher levels of annual report environmental disclosures. This result was consistent with the interviews undertaken by O'Donovan, as mentioned previously.

In considering the proposed relationship between media attention, corporate legitimacy, and corporate disclosure policies (or strategies) it is interesting to consider Exhibit 8.3, which provides information about claims that have been made that John Laws, a leading radio personality within Australia with a daily national program, was paid by certain organisations to provide positive comments about the organisations' operations. Read the exhibit and consider whether you would think that what is said is consistent with some of the arguments already being presented in this chapter. Do you think that the organisations involved might use the broadcaster in an attempt to win community support for their organisations, and would you consider that such a strategy would complement, or be a substitute for, disclosures within an annual report? Further, do you think that the subsequent revelations and allegations about the 'multi-million dollar deal', as discussed in Exhibit 8.3, could damage the organisations' legitimacy?

Some writers have suggested that the propositions generated by Legitimacy Theory (that annual report disclosure practices can be used in a strategic manner to manage an organisation's relations with the community in which it operates) are very similar to the propositions generated by the Political Cost Hypothesis which is developed through Positive Accounting

---

12. An extreme, but somewhat interesting view of the media's power of influence is provided by White (1973, p. 23). In relation to the US he states that 'the power of the press in America is a primordial one. It sets the agenda of public discussion; and this sweeping political power is unrestrained by any law. It determines what people will talk and think about—an authority that in other nations is reserved for tyrants, priests, parties and mandarins'.

EXHIBIT 8.3 The role of the media in shaping community perceptions

Laws denies offering bank statements

Amanda Meade
Television writer

John Laws, claimed to be the nation's most influential broadcaster, yesterday denied asking the banks for a million-dollar deal to promote their image, despite evidence of the approach.

But Laws confirmed the deal was done.

Australian Bankers Association chief lobbyist Tony Aveling wrote in a confidential memo to member banks including Westpac, Colonial, ANZ and NAB that he had been approached about a sponsorship deal by an agency representing Laws, according to documents obtained by the ABC's Media Watch.

In the memo dated October 8, 1998, Mr Aveling recommended the approach by the Laws agency be taken up because the association needed 'Australia's most influential third party with the greatest audience reach on our side'.

A 12-month figure of $1.2 million was suggested for the arrangement.

Before Laws signed the deal with the ABA, he was, according to Media Watch, a vocal critic of the banks.

His morning radio program on 2UE is syndicated on 74 stations around the country, earning him $11.6 million last year, half in sponsorship deals.

Laws, who has an average of 2 million listeners a morning, also hosts an evening interview program on pay-television's Foxtel.

Laws' agent, John Fordham, said his client was flown by helicopter to record his television show in Newcastle yesterday and would be unavailable for comment.

A spokesman for Mr Aveling confirmed the banks' deal with Laws—but would not specify if the broadcaster or the ABA had made the first move.

The spokesman said the ABA stood by its arrangement with Laws, which includes a daily paid segment promoting the banks, and was not dismayed the arrangement had been made public.

When Media Watch raised the issue last month, Laws told listeners the banks had approached him, saying: 'Listen, if you're going to climb into us, what about you tell the whole story.'

But the ABA document which has been seen by *The Australian* contradicts Laws's version of events, a version he repeated on air yesterday.

'I at no time approached the banks, simple as that,' Laws said on air. 'I thought the suggestion was very good when it came my way, and of course I saw a commercial opportunity in it.

'You know you can call me all sorts of things, but don't call me a liar.'

The ABA memo outlines the strategy behind the deal: 'The objective is to reduce the negative comments about banks by John Laws from the present average of four a week to nil; concurrently to receive positive comments from Mr Laws (over and above the paid advertisements) and by doing so to shift Australians' perceptions of and attitudes towards banks.'

Mr Aveling's spokesman would not say whether Laws's contract includes refraining from negative comment as well as reading the promotional material.

Laws defended his right to promote products and institutions in return for money. 'If I have been given an ability that I can market successfully, then I have every intention of doing it. I don't believe that makes me a bad man.'

Change of tune
John Laws's anti-bank stance

• **November 24, 1997:** So here's how it works. The bank makes $2.2 billion profit, the bank closes branches, the bank loses 2500 staff. And then they do it all over again.

• **November 30, 1998:** When they go down to the bank, Uncle Scrooge down there behind the counter hits them with

(continued)

EXHIBIT 8.3 *(continued)*

a fee. How can you do that, you people? I mean, how can you really do it? *John Laws's pro-bank stance* **March 1, 1999:** So there you are. See, banks make very big profits, but are they	unreasonable about it? Maybe not when you know the whole story. **April 7, 1999:** You know we do forget sometimes when we criticise them that banks are made up of people too. ***The Australian*, 14 July 1999, p. 3.**

Theory (which we discussed in Chapter 7).[13] While there are some similarities, Legitimacy Theory relies upon the central notion of an organisation's 'social contract' with society and predicts that management will adopt particular strategies (including reporting strategies) in a bid to assure the society that the organisation is complying with the society's values and norms (which are predicted to change over time). Unlike Positive Accounting Theory, Legitimacy Theory does not rely upon the economics–based assumption that *all* action is driven by individual self-interest (tied to wealth maximisation) and it emphasises how the organisation is part of the social system in which it operates. Also, unlike Positive Accounting Theory, Legitimacy Theory makes no assumptions about the efficiency of markets, such as the capital market and the market for managers.

Stakeholder Theory

We now turn to Stakeholder Theory. It has both an ethical (moral) or normative branch (which is also considered as prescriptive), and a positive (managerial) branch.[14] We first consider the ethical branch. We then consider the positive (managerial) branch, which explicitly considers various groups (of stakeholders) that exist in society, and how the expectations of particular stakeholder groups may have more (or less) impact on corporate strategies.

---

13. As Chapter 7 indicates, Positive Accounting Theory proposes that managers are motivated to undertake actions that will maximise their own wealth. To the extent that mechanisms have been put in place to align the interests of the managers with the goals of maximising the value of the organisation, the manager will adopt those accounting and disclosure methods that minimise the wealth transfers away from the organisation—wealth transfers that might be due to various political processes.

14. Stakeholder Theory itself is a confusing term as many different researchers have stated that they have used Stakeholder Theory in their research. Yet when we look at the research we see that different theories with different aims and assumptions have been employed—yet they have all been labelled as *Stakeholder Theory*. As Hasnas (1998, p. 26) states, 'stakeholder theory is somewhat of a troublesome label because it is used to refer to both an empirical theory of management and a normative theory of business ethics, often without clearly distinguishing between the two'. More correctly, perhaps, we can think of the term Stakeholder Theory as an *umbrella term* that actually represents a number of alternative theories that address various issues associated with relationships with stakeholders, including considerations of the rights of stakeholders, the power of stakeholders, or the effective management of stakeholders.

This in turn has implications for how the stakeholders' expectations are considered or managed.

In the discussion that follows we see that there are many similarities between Legitimacy Theory and Stakeholder Theory, and as such, to treat them as two totally distinct theories would be incorrect. As Gray, Kouhy and Lavers (1995, p. 52) state:

> It seems to us that the essential problem in the literature arises from treating each as competing theories of reporting behaviour, when 'stakeholder theory' and 'legitimacy theory' are better seen as two (overlapping) perspectives of the issue which are set within a framework of assumptions about 'political economy'.

The ethical branch of Stakeholder Theory

The moral (and normative) perspective of Stakeholder Theory argues that all stakeholders have the right to be treated fairly by an organisation, and that issues of *stakeholder power* are not directly relevant. That is, regardless of whether *stakeholder management* leads to improved financial performance, managers *should* manage the organisation for the benefit of all stakeholders. As Hasnas (1998, p. 32) states:

> When viewed as a normative (ethical) theory, the stakeholder theory asserts that, regardless of whether stakeholder management leads to improved financial performance, managers should manage the business for the benefit of all stakeholders. It views the firm not as a mechanism for increasing the stockholders' financial returns, but as a vehicle for coordinating stakeholder interests, and sees management as having a fiduciary relationship not only to the stockholders, but to all stakeholders. According to the normative stakeholder theory, management must give equal consideration to the interests of all stakeholders and, when these interests conflict, manage the business so as to attain the optimal balance among them. This of course implies that there will be times when management is obliged to at least partially sacrifice the interests of the stockholders to those of the other stakeholders. Hence, in its normative form, the stakeholder theory does imply that business has true social responsibilities.

Within the ethical branch of Stakeholder Theory there is a view that stakeholders have intrinsic rights (for example, to safe working conditions, fair pay, etc.), and these rights should not be violated.[15] That is, each group of stakeholders merits consideration for its own sake and not merely because of its ability to further the interests of some other group, such as the shareholders (Donaldson and Preston, 1995, p. 66). Obviously, a normative discussion of

---

15. We can contrast this perspective with that provided in Friedman (1962). He states: 'few trends could so thoroughly undermine the very foundation of our free society as the acceptance by corporate officials of a social responsibility other than to make as much money for their stockholders as possible. This is a fundamentally subversive doctrine' (p. 133).

stakeholder rights requires some definition of *stakeholders*. One definition we can use is that provided by Freeman and Reed (1983, p. 91):

> *Any identifiable group or individual who can affect the achievement of an organisation's objectives, or is affected by the achievement of an organisation's objectives.*

Clearly, many people (or other subjects) can be classified as stakeholders if we apply the above definition (for example, shareholders, creditors, government, media, employees, employees' families, local communities, local charities, future generations, and so on). With this in mind, Clarkson (1995) sought to divide stakeholders into *primary* and *secondary* stakeholders. A primary stakeholder was defined as 'one without whose continuing participation the corporation cannot survive as a going concern' (p. 106). Secondary stakeholders were defined as 'those who influence or affect, or are influenced or affected by, the corporation, but they are not engaged in transactions with the corporation and are not essential for its survival' (p. 107). According to Clarkson, primary stakeholders are the ones that must primarily be considered by management, and for the organisation to succeed in the long run, the organisation must be run for the benefit of all primary stakeholders. This view would be challenged by proponents of the ethical branch of Stakeholder Theory who would argue that all stakeholders have a right to be considered by management. Clarkson's definition of primary stakeholders would be similar to the definition of stakeholders applied by many researchers working within a managerial perspective of stakeholder theory.

Returning to the broader ethical (and normative) perspective that all stakeholders (both *primary* and *secondary*) have certain minimum rights that must not be violated, we can acknowledge that this perspective can be extended to a notion that all stakeholders also have a right to be provided with information about how the organisation is impacting on them (perhaps through pollution, community sponsorship, provision of employment, safety initiatives, etc.), even if they choose not to use the information, and even if they cannot directly have an impact on the survival of the organisation.

In considering the notion of *rights to information* we can briefly consider Gray, Owen and Adams' (1996) perspective of accountability as used within their *accountability model*. They define accountability (1996, p. 38) as:

> *The duty to provide an account (by no means necessarily a financial account) or reckoning of those actions for which one is held responsible.*

According to Gray, Owen and Adams, accountability involves two responsibilities or duties:

(i) The responsibility to undertake certain actions (or to refrain from taking actions); and

(ii) The responsibility to provide an account of those actions.

Under their accountability model, reporting is assumed to be *responsibility* driven rather than *demand* driven. The view being projected is that people in society have a right to be informed about certain facets of the organisation's operations.[16] By considering *rights*, it is argued that the model avoids the problem of considering users' *needs* and how such needs are established (Gray, Owen and Maunders, 1991). Applying the accountability model to corporate social reporting, Gray, Owen and Maunders (1991, p. 15) argue that:

> . . . *the role of corporate social reporting is to provide society-at-large (the principal) with information (accountability?) about the extent to which the organisation (the agent) has met the responsibilities imposed upon it (has it played by the rules of the game?).*

That is, the role of a corporate report is to inform society about the extent to which actions for which an organisation is deemed to be responsible have been fulfilled. Under the accountability model, the argument is that the principal (society) can elect to be entirely passive with regard to their demand for information. Nevertheless the agent (the organisation) is still required to provide an account—the passive, non-demanding principal is merely electing not to use the information directly. Gray, Owen and Maunders state (p. 6) that 'if the principal chooses to ignore the account, this is his prerogative and matters not to the agent who, nevertheless, must account'.

Hurst (1970) also emphasises the importance of accountability. He states (p. 58) that 'an institution which wields practical power—which compels men's wills or behaviour—must be accountable for its purposes and its performance by criteria not in the control of the institution itself'. The need to demonstrate accountability has also been stressed by the Research and Policy Committee of the Committee for Economic Development (a US based organisation). The committee states (1974, p. 21) that 'the great growth of corporations in size, market power, and impact on society has naturally brought with it a commensurate growth in responsibility; in a democratic society, power sooner or later begets equivalent accountability'.

Gray, Owen and Adams (1996) make use of the concept of the social contract to theorise about the responsibilities of business (against which there is a perceived accountability). Under their perspective they also perceive the

---

16. Within the model they refer to society as the 'principal' and the organisation (that owes the accountability) as the 'agent'. However, according to Gray, Owen and Maunders (1991, p. 17), their 'principal–agent model must be distinguished from "agency theory" or "economic principal–agent theory" as employed in, for example, Jensen and Meckling (1976), Ronen (1979), Fellingham and Newman (1979), Jensen (1983, 1993), Watts and Zimmerman (1986). Economic agency theory is grounded in neo-classical economics and takes its assumptions from it. Most significant among these are the assumptions about the single-minded greed of the principal and agent who are actively seeking to gain at the other's expense. The principal–agent model we are using makes no such assumptions and adopts no assumptions from economics, but rather owes its genesis to jurisprudence (MacPherson, 1973)'.

law as providing the explicit terms of the social contract, while other non-legislated societal expectations embody the implicit terms of the contract.

In considering the above normative perspectives of how organisations *should* behave with respect to their stakeholders (relating to intrinsic rights including rights to information) it should be noted that these perspectives pertain to how the respective researchers believe organisations *should* act, which is not necessarily going to be the same as how they actually *do* act.[17] Hence, the various perspectives cannot be validated by empirical observation—as might be the case if the researchers were providing descriptive or predictive (positive) theories about organisational behaviour. As Donaldson and Preston (1995, p. 67) state:

> In normative uses, the correspondence between the theory and the observed facts of corporate life is not a significant issue, nor is the association between stakeholder management and conventional performance measures a critical test. Instead a normative theory attempts to interpret the function of, and offer guidance about, the investor-owned corporation on the basis of some underlying moral or philosophical principles.

The Managerial branch of Stakeholder Theory

We now turn to perspectives of Stakeholder Theory that attempt to explain when corporate management will be likely to attend to the expectations of particular (typically powerful) stakeholders. According to Gray, Owen and Adams (1996), this alternative perspective tends to be more 'organisation-centred'. Gray, Owen and Adams (1996, p. 45) state:

> Here (under this perspective), the stakeholders are identified by the organisation of concern, by reference to the extent to which the organisation believes the interplay with each group needs to be managed in order to further the interests of the organisation. (The interests of the organisation need not be restricted to conventional profit-seeking assumptions). The more important the stakeholder to the organisation, the more effort will be exerted in managing the relationship. Information is a major element that can be employed by the organisation to manage (or manipulate) the stakeholder in order to gain their support and approval, or to distract their opposition and disapproval.

Unlike the ethical branch of Stakeholder Theory, such (organisation centred) theories can and are often tested by way of empirical observation.

---

17. Nevertheless, Donaldson and Preston (1995) argue that observation suggests that corporate decisions are frequently made on the basis of ethical consideration, even when doing so could not enhance corporate profit or shareholder gain. According to Donaldson and Preston, such behaviour is deemed to be not only appropriate, but desirable. They argue that corporate officials are not less morally obliged than any other citizens to take ethical considerations into account, and it would be unwise social policy to preclude them from doing so.

As we learned earlier, within Legitimacy Theory the audience of interest is typically defined as *the society*. Within a descriptive managerial branch of Stakeholder Theory the organisation is also considered to be part of the wider social system, but this perspective of Stakeholder Theory specifically considers the different stakeholder groups within society and how they should best be managed if the organisation is to survive (hence we call it a 'managerial' perspective of Stakeholder Theory).[18] Like Legitimacy Theory, it is considered that the expectations of the various stakeholder groups will impact on the operating and disclosure policies of the organisation. The organisation will not respond to all stakeholders equally (from a practical perspective, they probably cannot), but rather, will respond to those that are deemed to be 'powerful'. Nasi et al. (1997) build on this perspective to suggest that the most powerful stakeholders will be attended to first. This is consistent with Wallace (1995, p. 87) who argues that 'the higher the group in the stakeholder hierarchy, the more clout they have and the more complex their requirements will be'.

A stakeholder's (for example, owner's, creditor's, or regulator's) power to influence corporate management is viewed as a function of the stakeholder's degree of control over resources required by the organisation (Ullmann, 1985). The more critical the stakeholder resources are to the continued viability and success of the organisation, the greater the expectation that stakeholder demands will be addressed. A successful organisation is considered to be one that satisfies the demands (sometimes conflicting) of the various powerful stakeholder groups.[19] In this respect Ullman (1985, p. 2) states:

> . . . our position is that organisations survive to the extent that they are effective. Their effectiveness derives from the management of demands, particularly the demands of interest groups upon which the organisation depends.

Power in itself will be stakeholder-organisation specific, but may be tied to such things as command of limited resources (finance, labour), access to influential media, ability to legislate against the company, or ability to influence the consumption of the organisation's goods and services. The behaviour of various stakeholder groups is considered a constraint on the strategy that is

---

18. By comparison, Donaldson and Preston (1995) refer to the *instrumental perspective* of Stakeholder Theory in which the principal focus of interest is the proposition that corporations practising stakeholder management will be relatively successful in conventional performance terms. This is obviously similar to our 'managerial' perspective of Stakeholder Theory.

19. In considering the managerial perspective of Stakeholder Theory, Hasnas (1998, p. 32) states: 'when viewed as an empirical theory of management designed to prescribe a method for improving a business's performance, the stakeholder theory does not imply that business has any social responsibilities'.

developed by management to best match corporate resources with its environment. Pursuit of profits for the benefit of investors is not sufficient.

Freeman (1984) discusses the dynamics of stakeholder influence on corporate decisions. A major role of corporate management is to assess the importance of meeting stakeholder demands in order to achieve the strategic objectives of the firm. Further, as the expectations and power relativities of the various stakeholder groups can change over time, organisations must continually adapt their operating and disclosure strategies. Roberts (1992, p. 598) states:

> *A major role of corporate management is to assess the importance of meeting stakeholder demands in order to achieve the strategic objectives of the firm. As the level of stakeholder power increases, the importance of meeting stakeholder demands increases also.*

If we accept the view that a 'good' management is one that can successfully attend to various and sometimes conflicting demands of various (important) stakeholder groups, then we might, consistent with Evan and Freeman (1988), actually redefine the purpose of the firm. According to Evan and Freeman (1988), 'the very purpose of the firm is, in our view, to serve as a vehicle for coordinating stakeholders. It is through the firm that each stakeholder group makes itself better off through voluntary exchanges' (p. 82).

As indicated above, as the level of *stakeholder power* increases, the importance of meeting stakeholder demands increases. Some of this demand may relate to the provision of information about the activities of the organisation. According to Ullman (1985), the greater the importance to the organisation of the respective stakeholder's resources/support, the greater the probability that the particular stakeholder's expectations will be incorporated within the organisation's operations. From this perspective, various activities undertaken by organisations, including public reporting, will be directly related to the expectations of particular stakeholder groups. Furthermore, organisations will have an incentive to disclose information about their various programs and initiatives to the respective stakeholder groups to clearly indicate that they are conforming with those stakeholders' expectations. Organisations must necessarily balance the expectations of the various stakeholder groups. As these expectations and power relativities can change over time, organisations must, it is argued, continually adapt their operating and reporting behaviours.

Within the managerial perspective of Stakeholder Theory, information (including financial accounting information and information about the organisation's social performance) 'is a major element that can be employed by the organisation to manage (or manipulate) the stakeholder in order to gain their support and approval, or to distract their opposition and disapproval' (Gray, Owen and Adams, 1996, p. 46). This is consistent with the strategies suggested by Lindblom (1994), as discussed earlier in this chapter. In relation to corporate social disclosures, Roberts (1992, p. 599) states:

> . . . *social responsibility activities are useful in developing and maintaining satisfactory relationships with stockholders, creditors, and political bodies. Developing a corporate reputation as being socially responsible through performing and disclosing social responsibility activities is part of a strategy for managing stakeholder relationships.*[20]

Empirical tests of Stakeholder Theory

Utilising Stakeholder Theory to test the ability of stakeholders to impact on corporate social responsibility disclosures, Roberts (1992) finds that measures of stakeholder power and their related information needs can provide some explanation about levels and types of corporate social disclosures.

Neu, Warsame and Pedwell (1998) also found support for the view that particular stakeholder groups can be more effective than others in demanding social responsibility disclosures. They reviewed the annual reports of a number of publicly traded Canadian companies operating in environmentally sensitive industries for the period from 1982 to 1991. A measure of correlation was sought between increases and decreases in environmental disclosure and the concerns held by particular stakeholder groups. The results indicated that the companies were more responsive to the demands or concerns of financial stakeholders and government regulators than to the concerns of environmentalists. They considered that these results supported a perspective that where corporations face situations where stakeholders have conflicting interests or expectations, the corporations will elect to provide information of a legitimising nature to those stakeholders deemed to be more important to the survival of the organisation, while down-playing the needs or expectations of less 'important' stakeholders.

Stakeholder Theory of the 'managerial' variety does not directly provide prescriptions about what information *should* be disclosed other than indicating that the provision of information, including information within an annual report, can, if thoughtfully considered, be useful to the continued operations of a business entity. Of course, if we accept this view of the world, we would still be left with the difficult problem of determining who are our most

---

20. Again, we find that most of the studies that use Stakeholder Theory (as with Legitimacy Theory) have researched issues associated with social and environmental disclosures. While these theories could be applied to financial disclosures, most researchers of financial accounting practices have, at least to date, tended to use other theories, such as Positive Accounting Theory. Issues associated with firms' capital structures have been studied from a Stakeholder Theory perspective by Barton, Hill and Sundaram (1989) and Cornell and Shapiro (1987).

important (powerful) stakeholders, and what their respective information demands are.[21]

As we have noted, organisations typically have a multitude of stakeholders with differing expectations about how the organisation should operate. Read Exhibits 8.4 and 8.5. Exhibit 8.4 is critical of banks in terms of their rising fees and the impact these rises have on the elderly. Would the elderly or the Council on the Ageing, in your view, be considered to be powerful stakeholders, such that their concerns would be met by the bank (adopting the managerial perspective of stakeholder theory)? How would this view be different if we were adopting a moral/ethical perspective of stakeholder theory?

Exhibit 8.5 relates to the large mining company Rio Tinto. In the article it is indicated that a particular union is very concerned about the company's record on human rights, labour relations, and environmental performance. After reading the Exhibit we can again consider whether the company would construe the union as being a powerful stakeholder, and if it is deemed to be so, we can also consider how or whether the company might make certain disclosures of information (perhaps what it is doing about ensuring that human rights are observed and that sound environmental management practices are put in place) to allay the concerns of the union.

As a concluding issue it should be realised that in the above discussion we have separately considered the normative moral/ethical perspective of Stakeholder Theory as well as the managerial (power based) perspective of Stakeholder Theory. By discussing them separately it could be construed that management might either be ethically/morally aware, or perhaps solely focused on the survival of the organisation. However, by separately considering the two perspectives we are only likely to get a partial view. Arguably, management will be driven by both ethical considerations and performance based decisions—not one or the other. As Wicks (1996) argues, many people have embraced a conceptual framework in which ethical considerations and market considerations are seen as constituting a categorically and independent realism. Wicks argues that this view is

---

21. Again it is emphasised that this will not always be an easy exercise. For example, and for the purpose of illustration (perhaps at an extreme) we may find that a company has elected to provide an elderly woman who lives in a modest house nearby with a report that details when coal dust can be expected to be released from the company's furnaces so that she can ensure that no washing is left out at this time. At face value such a person may not appear to be a powerful stakeholder and we as outsiders might question why the company provides such disclosures. However, we may find that the woman has a daughter who is a popular high profile radio personality who will readily complain on air, at some cost to the company in terms of community support, each time her mother's washing is put out and is subsequently covered with coal ash. Through her connections the elderly woman is a powerful stakeholder, and to alleviate her problems, coal-dust release information is provided so that she can schedule her washing. In relation to this illustration it should be noted that an ethical/moral view of stakeholder information rights would perhaps be that this person has a right to information, regardless of the fact that her daughter works in the media.

EXHIBIT 8.4 Stakeholders' concern about an attribute of an organisation's performance

Banking charges double in one year

David Luff and James Swanwich

A NATIONAL outcry over the rising bank fees heightened yesterday, with new figures showing some fees had more than doubled in the past year.

Almost all fees charged by major banks have increased, prompting aged groups to predict that hefty charges on over-the-counter transactions would add $100 a year to the cost of banking for elderly households.

A raft of new charges, including account-keeping fees, were introduced in the past year as the five major banks build their annual revenue from non-interest income to the $10 billion mark.

Transaction fees on deposits also were ushered in by some banks.

The Commonwealth Bank, under fire this week for raising fees, has increased its automatic teller machine withdrawal charge from 25c to 60c since last November.

ANZ has introduced a $1.25 fee for over-the-counter deposits in the past year, and over-the-counter withdrawals are up 50c to $2.50.

Westpac also has slugged some of its customers an extra $1 for over-the-counter withdrawals and National Australia Bank introduced a $4 monthly account-keeping fee.

Aged groups said the elderly were extremely concerned with fee increases, given the majority only used over-the-counter banking.

Council on the Ageing national executive director Dennis Correll said the fee hike had come at a time when the elderly could least afford it.

'They have a number of worries on their mind at the moment, including the GST,' Mr Correll said.

'They do not find ATMs easy to use, particularly the 75 to 80 age group, who are very unlikely to adapt to ATMs.'

Channel Nine's *A Current Affair* put $50 in 10 different bank and credit union accounts at the start of the year and did not touch the money.

Fees and account-keeping charges saw many of the accounts whittled away by more than half.

The St George Bank account was now only worth $8.98, the show reported last night.

Australia's biggest bank, National Australia Bank, yesterday said it had no plans to raise fees, but conceded the policy could be reviewed at any time— in line with the stance of other major banks.

And there are renewed fears of future transaction charges attracting the GST.

Treasurer Peter Costello said transaction charges would not be subject to the 10 percent GST, but the major banks declared they would push for the new tax not to apply to all financial services.

The Labor Party warned the impact of the GST would further tighten profit margins for banks, forcing them to raise fees to higher levels.

Assistant Treasurer Rod Kemp urged disgruntled bank customers to ditch loyalty and shop around for a better deal.

'Bank customers can maximise the benefits of competition by actively shopping around for the best products, services and prices to satisfy their needs,' he said.

The Courier Mail, **Wednesday 25 November 1998.**

EXHIBIT 8.5 A further example of stakeholders' concern about an attribute of an organisation's performance

UK protesters dig in on Rio Tinto

By Sean Smith and agencies

RIO Tinto's opponents have set the scene for another confrontation with the company in Australia later this month after a strong turnout at the London leg of its annual meeting yesterday.

In what is now commonplace for the Anglo-Australian mining giant, the meeting venue was picketed by protesters campaigning against its alleged anti-union stance and human rights abuses.

The protesters also kept the board busy inside, grilling directors on Rio Tinto's environmental policy and executive salaries. They will get a second shot at the miner on May 27 when it holds another meeting in Melbourne for its Australian shareholders.

Although the London meeting was peaceful, Rio Tinto chairman Robert Wilson angrily dismissed as 'systematic misrepresentation' a worldwide campaign against the group led by the Construction, Forestry, Mining and Energy Union.

'It is one of deceit in support of the indefensible and is propaganda at its most cynical,' Mr Wilson said. 'This company is not anti-union.'

He also lashed out at CFMEU president John Maitland, saying he made Britain's former coal miners' union boss Arthur Scargill 'look like a modern trade unionist'.

The union is part of the Brussels-based International Federation of Chemical, Energy, Mine and General Workers' Unions, which represent 20 million workers worldwide.

The federation, which has been critical of what it sees as Rio Tinto's poor record on human rights, labour relations and environmental performance, detailed its complaints in a document, *Rio Tinto Tainted Titan*, handed to shareholders.

'I have skimmed through it and I expect it is the usual catalogue of distortions, half-truths and probably even lies,' Mr Wilson said.

He said Rio Tinto's outlook had darkened since the February announcement of its profits, referring to 'a very fragile' Japanese economy and signs of weakness in China 'over the last couple of months'. But while Asia's economic woes were still making headlines, the commodities' outlook did 'not look too bad', he said.

'Indeed, despite the adverse effect of lower metal prices, our earnings for the first four months of 1998 are roughly in line with those in the same period of 1997.'

***Herald Sun*, Friday 15 May 1998.**

unrealistic since it implies that people cannot introduce 'moral imaginations when they act in the market world'. In terms of future research in Stakeholder Theory, Rowley (1998) provides some interesting advice. He states:

> *The blurring of normative and descriptive analysis is problematic for the field, however, dividing them into separate camps is equally hazardous. I believe that if our most challenging issues 10 years from now are to be different from today, we will need to collectively understand the complementary roles that normative and descriptive research play in our research questions. Like market and society we cannot think of one without the other (p. 2).*

Again, we are left with a view that particular theories (of accounting) can provide us with only a partial view, and hence it is sometimes useful to consider the insights provided by different theoretical perspectives.

Chapter summary

This chapter provides a number of perspectives about why management elects to make particular disclosures. Specifically, it reviews Legitimacy Theory and Stakeholder Theory—two theories that can be classified as systems-oriented theories. Systems-oriented theories see the organisation as being part of a broader social system.

Legitimacy Theory and Stakeholder Theory are both derived from Political Economy Theory wherein the political economy constitutes the social, political and economic framework within which human life takes place and social, political and economic issues are considered as inseparable. Political Economy Theory can be classified as either Classical or Bourgeois. Bourgeois Political Economy Theory ignores various tensions within society and accepts the world as essentially pluralistic with no particular class dominating another. Legitimacy Theory and Stakeholder Theory adopt the Bourgeois perspective.

Legitimacy Theory relies upon the notion of a social contract, which is an implied contract representing the norms and expectations of the community in which an organisation operates. An organisation is deemed to be legitimate to the extent that it complies with the terms of the social contract. Legitimacy and the right to operate are considered to go hand in hand. Accounting disclosures are considered to represent one way in which an organisation can legitimise its ongoing operations. Where legitimacy is threatened, disclosures are one strategy to restore legitimacy.

Two different categories of Stakeholder Theory have been reviewed, these being the ethical (or normative) branch, and the managerial branch. The ethical branch of Stakeholder Theory discusses issues associated with rights to information, rights that should be met regardless of the power of the stakeholders involved. Within the ethical branch, disclosures are considered to be responsibility driven. The managerial branch of Stakeholder Theory, on the other hand, predicts that organisations will tend to satisfy the information demands of those stakeholders who are important to the organisation's ongoing survival. Whether a particular stakeholder receives information will be dependent upon how powerful they are perceived to be, with power often considered in terms of the scarcity of the resources controlled by the respective stakeholders. The disclosure of information is considered to represent an important strategy in managing stakeholders.

References

Abbott, W. and Monsen, R., 'On the Measurement of Corporate Social Responsibility: Self-reported Disclosures as a Method of Measuring Corporate Social Involvement', *Academy of Management Journal*, Vol. 22, No. 3, pp. 501–15, 1979.

Ader, C., 'A Longitudinal Study of Agenda Setting for the Issue of Environmental Pollution', *Journalism & Mass Communication Quarterly*, Vol. 72, No. 3, (Summer), pp. 300–11, 1995.

Barton, S., Hill, N., Sundaram, S., 'An Empirical Test of Stakeholder Theory Predictions of Capital Structure', *Financial Management*, pp. 36–44, Spring 1989.

Blood, R.W., *Unobtrusive Issues and the Agenda-Setting Role of the Press*, Unpublished Doctoral Dissertation, Syracuse University, New York, 1981.

Brown, N. and Deegan, C., 'The Public Disclosure of Environmental Performance Information—A Dual Test of Media Agenda Setting Theory and Legitimacy Theory', *Accounting and Business Research*, Vol. 29, No. 1, pp. 21–41, 1999.

Burchell, S., Clubb, C., Hopwood, A., Hughes, J., Naphapiet, J., 'The Roles of Accounting in Organisations and Society', *Accounting, Organizations and Society*, pp. 5–28, 1980.

Carpenter, V., Feroz, E., 'GAAP as a Symbol of Legitimacy: New York State's Decision to Adopt Generally Accepted Accounting Principles', *Accounting, Organizations and Society*, Vol. 17, No. 7, pp. 613–43, 1992.

Clarkson, M., 'A Stakeholder Framework for Analyzing and Evaluating Corporate Social Performance', *Academy of Management Review*, Vol. 20, No. 1, pp. 92–118, 1995.

Committee for Economic Development, *Measuring Business Social Performance: The Corporate Social Audit*, Committee for Economic Development, New York, 1974.

Cornell, B., Shapiro, A., 'Corporate Stakeholders and Corporate Finance', *Financial Management*, pp. 5–14, Spring 1987.

Cooper, D.J., Sherer, M.J., 'The Value of Corporate Accounting Reports—Arguments for a Political Economy of Accounting', *Accounting, Organizations and Society*, Vol. 9, No. 3/4, pp. 207–32, 1984.

Deegan, C. and Gordon B., 'A Study of the Environmental Disclosure Practices of Australian Corporations', *Accounting and Business Research*, Vol. 26, No. 3, (Summer), pp. 187–99, 1996.

Deegan, C., Rankin, M., 'Do Australian companies report environmental news objectively? An analysis of environmental disclosures by firms prosecuted successfully by the Environmental Protection Authority', *Accounting, Auditing and Accountability Journal*, Vol. 9, No. 2, pp. 52–69, 1996.

Deegan, C., Rankin, M., Voght, P., 'Firms' Disclosure Reactions to Major Social Incidents: Australian Evidence', *Accounting Forum*, Special Issue on Social and Environmental Accounting, Vol. 24, No. 1, pp. 101–30, 2000.

Donaldson, T., Preston, L., 'The Stakeholder Theory of the Corporation—Concepts, Evidence, and Implications', *Academy of Management Review*, Vol. 20, No. 1, pp. 65–92, 1995.

Dowling, J., Pfeffer, J., 'Organisational Legitimacy: Social Values and Organisational Behavior', *Pacific Sociological Review*, Vol. 18, No. 1, pp. 122–36, January 1975.

Evan, W., Freeman, R., 'A Stakeholder Theory of the Modern Corporation: Kantian Capitalism', in T. Beauchamp and N. Bowie (Eds), *Ethical Theory and Business*, Englewood Cliffs, NJ, pp. 75–93, 1988.

Eyal, C.H., Winter, J.P. and DeGeorge, W.F., 'The Concept of Time Frame in Agenda Setting', *Mass Communication Yearbook*, Vol. 2 (Ed. G.C. Wilhoit, Beverly Hills), CA, Sage Publications Inc., 1981.

Fellingham, J., Newman, D., 'Monitoring Decisions in an Agency Setting', *Journal of Business Finance and Accounting*, Vol. 6, No. 2, pp. 203–22, 1979.

Freeman, R., *Strategic Management: A Stakeholder Approach*, Pitman, Marshall, MA, 1984.

Freeman, R., Reed, D., 'Stockholders and Stakeholders: A New Perspective on Corporate Governance', *Californian Management Review*, Vol. 25, No. 2, pp. 88–106, 1983.

Friedman, M., *Capitalism and Freedom*, University of Chicago Press, Chicago, 1962.

Gray, R., Kouhy, R., Lavers, S., 'Corporate Social and Environmental Reporting: A Review of the Literature and a Longitudinal Study of UK Disclosure', *Accounting, Auditing and Accountability Journal*, Vol. 8, No. 2, pp. 47–77, 1995.

Gray, R, Owen, D., Adams, C., *Accounting and Accountability: Changes and Challenges in Corporate Social and Environmental Reporting*, Prentice-Hall, London, 1996.

Gray, R., Owen, D., Maunders, K.T., *Corporate Social Reporting: Accounting and Accountability*, Prentice-Hall, Hemel Hempstead, 1987.

Gray, R., Owen, D., Maunders, K.T., 'Accountability, Corporate Social Reporting and the External Social Audits', *Advances in Public Interest Accounting*, Vol. 4, pp. 1–21, 1991.

Guthrie, J., Parker L., 'Corporate Social Disclosure Practice: A Comparative International Analysis', *Advances in Public Interest Accounting*, Vol. 3, pp. 159–75, 1990.

Hasnas, J., 'The Normative Theories of Business Ethics: A Guide for the Perplexed', *Business Ethics Quarterly*, Vol. 8, No. 1, pp. 19–42, January 1998.

Heard, J., Bolce, W., 'The Political Significance of Corporate Social Reporting in the United States of America', *Accounting Organizations and Society*, Vol. 6, No. 3, pp. 247–54, 1981.

Hogner, R.H., 'Corporate Social Reporting: Eight Decades of Development at US Steel', *Research in Corporate Performance and Policy*, Vol. 4, pp. 243–50, 1982.

Hurst, J.W., *The Legitimacy of the Business Corporation in the Law of the United States 1780–1970*, The University Press of Virginia, Charlottesville, 1970.

Jensen, M.C., 'Organisation Theory and Methodology', *The Accounting Review*, Vol. 58, pp. 319–39, April 1983.

Jensen, M.C., 'The Modern Industrial Revolution, Exit and Failure of Internal Control Systems', *Journal of Finance*, pp. 831–80, 1993.

Jensen, M.C., Meckling, W.H., 'Theory of the Firm: Managerial Behavior, Agency Costs and Ownership Structure', *Journal of Financial Economics*, pp. 305–60, October 1976.

Lindblom, C.K., 'The Implications of Organisational Legitimacy for Corporate Social Performance and Disclosure', Paper presented at the Critical Perspectives on Accounting Conference, New York, 1994.

Lowe, E.A., Tinker, A., 'Sighting the Accounting Problematic: Towards an Intellectual Emancipation of Accounting', *Journal of Business Finance and Accounting*, Vol. 4, No. 3, pp. 263–76, 1977.

Mathews, M.R., *Socially Responsible Accounting*, Chapman and Hall, London, 1993.

Mayer, H., 1980, 'Power and the Press', *Murdoch University News*, Vol. 7, No. 8, Murdoch University.

McCombs, M. and Shaw, D., 'The Agenda Setting Function of Mass Media', *Public Opinion Quarterly*, 36, pp. 176–87, 1972.

McCombs, M., 'The Agenda-Setting Approach', in *Handbook of Political Communication* (Eds. D. Nimmo and K. Sanders), Beverly Hills, California, Sage, 1981.

Macpherson, C.B., *Democratic Theory: Essays in Retrieval*, Oxford University Press, Oxford, 1973.

Nasi, J., Nasi, S., Phillips, N., Zyglidopoulos, S., 'The Evolution of Corporate Social Responsiveness—An Exploratory Study of Finnish and Canadian Forestry Companies', *Business & Society*, Vol. 38, No. 3, pp. 296–321, 1997.

Ness, K., Mirza, A., 'Corporate Social Disclosure: A Note on a Test of Agency Theory', *British Accounting Review*, Vol. 23, pp. 211–17, 1991.

Neu, D., Warsame, H., Pedwell, K., 'Managing Public Impressions: Environmental Disclosures in Annual Reports', *Accounting Organizations and Society*, Vol. 25, No. 3, pp. 265–82, 1998.

O'Donovan, G., 'Managing Legitimacy through Increased Corporate Environmental Reporting: An Exploratory Study', *Interdisciplinary Environmental Review*, Vol. 1, No. 1, pp. 63–99, 1999.

O'Leary, T., 'Observations on Corporate Financial Reporting in the Name of Politics', *Accounting, Organizations and Society*, Vol. 10, No. 1, pp. 87–102, 1985.

Patten, D.M., 'Exposure, Legitimacy and Social Disclosure', *Journal of Accounting and Public Policy*, Vol. 10, pp. 297–308, 1991.

Patten, D.M., 'Intra-industry Environmental Disclosures in Response to the Alaskan Oil Spill: A Note on Legitimacy Theory', *Accounting, Organizations and Society*, Vol. 15, No. 5, pp. 471–75, 1992.

Puxty, A., 'Social Accountability and Universal Pragmatics', *Advances in Public Interest Accounting*, Vol. 4, pp. 35–46, 1991.

Ramanathan, K.V., 'Toward a theory of corporate social accounting', *The Accounting Review*, Vol. 21, No. 3, pp. 516–28, 1976.

Roberts, R., 'Determinants of Corporate Social Responsibility Disclosure: An Application of Stakeholder Theory', *Accounting, Organizations and Society*, Vol. 17, No. 6, pp. 595–612, 1992.

Ronen, J., 'The Dual Role of Accounting: A Financial Economic Perspective', in J.L. Bicksler (Ed.), *Handbook of Financial Economics*, North Holland, 1979.

Rowley, T., 'A Normative Justification for Stakeholder Theory', *Business and Society*, Vol. 37, No. 1, pp. 105–7, 1998.

Shocker, A.D., Sethi, S.P., 'An Approach to Incorporating Social Preferences in Developing Corporate Action Strategies', in *The Unstable Ground: Corporate Social Policy in a Dynamic Society*. S.P. Sethi (Ed.), California: Melville, pp. 67–80, 1974.

Tinker, A., Neimark, M., 'The Role of Annual Reports in Gender and Class Contradictions at General Motors: 1917–1976', *Accounting, Organisations and Society*, Vol. 12, No. 1, pp. 71–88, 1987.

Ullman, A., 'Data in Search of a Theory: A Critical Examination of the Relationships Among Social Performance, Social Disclosure, and Economic Performance of US Firms, *Academy of Management Review*, Vol. 10, No. 3, pp. 540–57, 1985.

Wallace, G., 'Balancing Conflicting Stakeholder Requirements', *Journal for Quality and Participation*, Vol. 18, No. 2, pp. 84–98, 1995.

Watts, R.L., Zimmerman, J.L., *Positive Accounting Theory*, Prentice-Hall Inc., Englewood Cliffs, New Jersey, 1986.

White, T., *The Making of the President 1972*, Bantam Press, New York, 1973.

Wicks, A., 'Overcoming the Separation Thesis: The Need for a Reconsideration of Business and Business Research', *Business and Society*, Vol. 35, No. 1, pp. 89–118, 1996.

Zucker, H.G., 'The Variable Nature of News Media Influence', in *Communication Yearbook No. 2*, B.D. Rubin (Ed.), New Jersey, pp. 225–45, 1978.

Questions

8.1 Explain the notion of a *social contract* and what relevance the social contract has with respect to the *legitimacy* of an organisation.

8.2 What does the notion of legitimacy and social contract have to do with corporate disclosure policies?

8.3 How would corporate management determine the terms of the *social contract* (if this is indeed possible) and what would be the implications for a firm if it breached the terms of the contract?

8.4 If an organisation's management considered that the organisation might not have operated in accordance with community expectations (it broke the terms of the *social contract*), consistent with Legitimacy Theory, what actions would you expect management to undertake in the subsequent period?

8.5 If an organisation was involved in a major accident or incident, would you expect them to use vehicles such as an annual report to try to explain the incident? If so, explain *how* and *why* they would use the annual report in this way.

8.6 Consistent with the material provided in this chapter, would you expect management to make disclosures in relation to real-world events, or alternatively, in relation to how they believed the community perceived the real-world events? Why?

8.7 This chapter divided Stakeholder Theory into the *ethical branch* and the *managerial branch*. Explain the differences between the managerial and ethical branches of Stakeholder Theory in terms of the alternative perspectives about when information will, or should, be produced by an organisation.

8.8 Under the *managerial perspective* of Stakeholder Theory, when would we expect an organisation to meet the information demands of a particular stakeholder group?

8.9 Read Exhibit 8.4 on p. 276, an article that relates to increasing bank charges. After reading the exhibit:

(a) Apply the managerial perspective of Stakeholder Theory to explain whether management would care about the concerns of the *Council on the Ageing*.

(b) If we applied an ethical perspective of stakeholder theory, *should* they care?

(c) If society considered that the banks' policies were unreasonable, would you expect the banks to use their annual report to defend their position (legitimacy)?

8.10 Read Exhibit 8.6, and using Legitimacy Theory as a basis of your argument, explain why a company such as McDonald's would not want a radio station to make adverse comments about it. If the station does make adverse statements, how might McDonald's react from a corporate disclosure viewpoint?

EXHIBIT 8.6 The potential influence of the media on an organisation's perceived legitimacy

Lay off Big Macs, radio boss tells staff

Amanda Meade

Top management at radio 2UE ordered the station's broadcaster not to make derogatory comments about McDonald's on air or the station would lose its $170,000 advertising account with the fast-food chain, according to a leaked internal memo.

The memo from program director John Brennan in February reveals for the first time that the practice of tailoring editorial comment to suit 2UE's advertisers is an integral part of the top-rating radio station's culture.

'It's going to be a tough year for revenue and we need all the help we can get from everyone concerned,' the management memo says.

'It is obviously imperative that no derogatory comments about McDonald's are made by any broadcaster on the station. Any such comment would see an immediate cancellation of the contract.'

The memo will be investigated by the Australian Broadcasting Authority's inquiry into the radio station next month.

Mr Brennan's directive appears to contravene the Commercial Radio Code of Practice, under which a radio station must promote accuracy and fairness in news and current affairs programs. The code may be reviewed by the ABA in separate public hearings and may result in moves away from self-regulation.

The memo contradicts public statements by 2UE chief John Conde this week about the role of station management in the scandal involving John Laws and the now-defunct $1.2 million deal with the Australian Bankers Association.

The banks' deal with Laws also involved refraining from negative comments about the client on air.

McDonald's spokesman John Blyth said the company was unaware the 2UE directive had been issued and would never make its advertising contracts conditional on editorial comment.

The memo was addressed to Alan Jones, John Laws, John Stanley, Mike Carlton, Peter Bosly, Ray Hadley, Stan Zemanek and eight other on-air presenters.

Senior management was also party to the directive.

In a letter to *The Australian* yesterday, Mr Conde confirmed Mr Brennan wrote the memo, which had 'reflected (his) exuberance'. He said Mr Brennan had promptly clarified the memo, telling staff he only intended to avoid any announcer 'sending up' the McDonald's ads. 'It was made plain 2UE was not seeking to curtail editorial comment.'

In a separate statement, Mr Conde said 2UE and its affiliates were to receive $707,000 from the bank deal. Laws says his share was $300,000.

The Australian, **22 July 1999, p. 1.**

8.11 Read Exhibit 8.7, and with the material of this chapter in mind, explain *why* (or perhaps, *why not*) the community needs to be *protected* from the media.

EXHIBIT 8.7 The role of the media in influencing public opinion

A democratic duty not to abuse power

David Flint

The Australian Broadcasting Authority Inquiry, which began yesterday, goes to the integrity of commercial broadcasting.

The media play a central role in our democracy, which has a healthy suspicion of concentrations of power. And the media is one of the most important checks and balances against abuse of power. There is, in effect, a compact between society and the media. In return for its considerable freedom, the media has a duty to be responsible.

Being responsible means that news, as far as possible, is true. It means that news and opinion must be distinguished. And it means that opinion be bona fide. Any blurring between advertising, news and opinion—advertorials—should be identifiable.

It is a well-established principle that the press must not be subject to government regulation because it would be too dangerous to do this. This is another example of the checks and balances necessary to preserve freedom. This does not, of course, mean the press is immune from the law.

The electronic media is fundamentally different. It is (still) a scarce public resource. Without regulation there would be anarchy, so licensing is essential.

The question for any democratic society is how to regulate the electronic media so it, too, can fulfill its role of informing the people on matters of public interest, fairly and accurately. In this, Australia has been remarkably innovative. We devised a mixed system, an independent public broadcaster, along with commercial broadcasting. The virtues of this only began to dawn on the Europeans decades later. This mixed model, now expanded to include SBS and community broadcasting, is important. It ensures greater diversity than, say, in a free market. Under this it is far more likely that the people will be informed fairly and accurately on matters of public interest.

Until 1992, commercial broadcasting was subject to a high degree of regulation. But this was too often paralysed because of the complexities of the law. Who benefited? Certainly not the public. Under the 1992 legislation greater autonomy was given to commercial broadcasting. But this was not intended to be the degree of self-regulation the print media enjoys. Rather, it was to be a system of co-regulation. Codes of practice would be developed with public consultation. A breach of a code would not be a breach of the law or of any of the conditions in a licence. And only complaints the broadcaster could not resolve would come to the broadcasting authority. The strategy was to encourage good behaviour by example, transparency and persuasion. Hence the jibe the ABA is a 'toothless tiger'.

But if there is convincing evidence a code has failed to provide the community safeguards that society expects and the law requires, a more direct regulatory response can be designed to target a station, a network or even a whole broadcasting sector.

It would be premature to suggest this is going to happen. What the ABA has before it are allegations. Only through the discovery of documents and sworn evidence can the ABA determine the true state of affairs and take appropriate action.

Professor David Flint is Australian Broadcasting Authority chairman.

The Australian, **Thursday 22 July 1999, p. 2.**

8.12 Would you expect management to worry about attitudinal surveys, such as the one described in Exhibit 8.8? Explain your answer, as well as explaining how such surveys might impact on the disclosure policies of an organisation.

8.13 Read Exhibit 8.9 and explain whether you think the banks *would* or *should* respond to the concerns of the National Farmers' Federation. What theories did you rely upon (if any) to inform your judgement?

EXHIBIT 8.8 Determining community expectations—the role of attitudinal surveys

Health rates as top social issue

CANBERRA: Health has taken over from crime as the most important social issue seen to be facing Australia, figures showed yesterday.

The survey of people's views of environmental issues found the environment rated fifth in importance—even though three in four Australians had at least one environmental concern.

The Australian Bureau of Statistics (ABS) figures showed 29% of respondents believed health was the most important social issue.

This was followed by crime (24%), education and unemployment (both 16%), and environmental problems (16%).

In 1996, crime was seen as the most important social issue, followed by health, education, unemployment, then the environment.

In the latest survey, dated March 1998, health was the most important issue to older people and least important to people aged 35–44.

In general, younger people were more concerned about long-term environmental problems although 18–24 year olds, as well as 45–54 year olds, were most concerned about unemployment.

But the survey said 71% of Australians were concerned with at least one specific environmental problem.

The figure was up from 68% in 1996 but down from 75% in 1992.

People living in the ACT were most concerned while Tasmanians were the least concerned about environmental problems.

Air pollution continued to be the problem of greatest worry for Australians, with 32% reporting it as their major concern.

The Chronicle, **Friday 27 November 1998, p. 22.**

EXHIBIT 8.9 **Stakeholder concern with an attribute of an organisation's performance**

Union warns bank job losses may be as high as 40,000

Miranda McLachlan

ABOUT 40,000 banking industry jobs have gone in the past decade and the Finance Sector Union yesterday warned that another 40,000 would go if the Federal Government lifts its four pillars ban on big bank mergers.

That meant the Federal Government should establish a social charter for banks, the FSU said yesterday.

Westpac managing director David Morgan, who on Tuesday said his bank intended to shed 3000 jobs over the next two years, including at least 200 in Queensland, admitted then that his cost-squeezing would help ward off the threat of being taken over by another major bank if the ban was lifted.

'If a bank can't be competitive and give competitive returns . . . When the inevitable four pillars collapses, one will be taken over by the people with the strongest share price,' Dr Morgan said.

Since 1993, 1706 bank branches have been closed across the country—615 of them in the bush.

National Farmers' Federation executive director Wendy Craik said Westpac had assured the NFF that it would not reduce face to face services and would 'maintain a watching brief' to make sure that commitment was fulfilled.

Many of the job losses in the banks have come from converting customers to the ease of electronic forms of banking like automated telling machines, EFTPOS and the telephone.

The National Australia Bank yesterday was quick to distance itself from Westpac's suggestion that further significant staff-shedding was necessary.

The bank's chief executive of its Australian operations Gordon Wheaton said: 'We are totally opposed to a slash and burn approach to managing levels.'

Yet, NAB culled 4000 full-time equivalents in the past two years alone, while ANZ cut 1700 and the Commonwealth Bank 2000.

NAB's total job reductions have been masked by its acquisitions in Australia and overseas.

The FSU says it is braced for 1200 more job losses at AXA Australia (formerly National Mutual).

The FSU said the Federal Government should establish a social charter for banks to protect the community interest.

National FSU secretary Tony Beck said Westpac's 'callous and short-sighted' staff-slashing showed banks were incapable of managing the social responsibilities that came with their 'privileged position in the community'.

The Courier Mail, **Thursday 14 October 1999.**

BANK EMPLOYMENT

BANK	1990	1999
ANZ	48,182	29,644
CBA	34,772	28,964
Westpac	45,395	32,000
NAB	45,457	46,643

New systems of accounting—the incorporation of social and environmental factors within external reporting

Learning objectives

Upon completing this chapter readers should:

- be aware of various perspectives of the responsibilities of business;

- be able to provide an explanation of the relationship between organisational responsibility and organisational accountability;

- be aware of various theoretical perspectives that can explain why organisations might voluntarily elect to provide publicly available information about their social and environmental performance;

- be aware of some recent initiatives in social and environmental accounting;

- be able to explain the concept of *sustainable development* and be able to explain how organisations are reporting their progress towards the goal of sustainable development;

- be able to explain the relationship between sustainability and *eco-efficiency* and *eco-justice* issues;

- be able to identify some of the limitations of traditional financial accounting in enabling users of reports to assess a reporting entity's social and environmental performance.

Opening issues

1. Many companies throughout the world have recently released reports that discuss their economic, environmental and social performance. There are also numerous instances of companies publicly stating their commitment to sustainable development. In WMC Ltd's *Environmental Progress Report 1998* the following statements were made by the Chief Executive Officer, Mr Hugh Morgan:

   Looking beyond this report, we are considering public reporting in the wider context of sustainable development. Increasingly, this concept forms the basis for decision making by communities, governments and forward-thinking businesses. It involves integrating decision-making in developmental, environmental and social areas, and publicly reporting on performance. The roles of business, government and community groups in contributing to sustainable development are still evolving. Further debate is needed. It will only be productive if all participants accept the need for high levels of accountability, transparency and fairness. Future WMC reports will contribute to that debate.

   A further comment is made in WMC's report that 'our environmental policy commits us to operate in a way which is consistent with the principles of sustainable development'.

   Moves towards sustainable development require organisations to explicitly consider various facets of their economic, social and environmental performance. But why would companies embrace *sustainability* as a corporate goal rather than simply aiming for increased and continued profitability? Further, if an entity embraces triple bottom line reporting (reporting which provides information about economic, social and environmental performance) what does this imply about the perceived accountability of business? What sort of accounting system would enable an organisation to report its social and environmental performance?

2. Many professional accounting bodies throughout the world are actively sponsoring research that looks at various social and environmental

reporting issues (for example, in Australia the Institute of Chartered Accountants in Australia set up an Environmental Accounting Task Force in 1995 while in the UK the Association of Chartered Certified Accountants has sponsored an environmental reporting award since 1991 as well as funding various social and environmental reporting research projects).[1] Are social and environmental reporting issues really within the domain of professional accounting bodies? If not, who should be responsible for formulating social and environmental reporting guidelines?

Introduction

As we would appreciate from studying financial accounting, in most countries financial accounting, which provides information about the economic/financial performance of an entity, is heavily regulated according to corporations laws and accounting standards. On the other hand there is a relative absence of requirements relating to the public disclosure of information about the social and environmental performance of an entity. Nevertheless for a number of years many organisations throughout the world have been voluntarily providing public disclosures about their environmental, and to a lesser extent, their social performance.

During the last one to two years a number of corporations throughout the world have also commenced discussing various issues associated with what has become commonly termed *triple bottom line reporting*. This has been defined by Elkington (1997) as reporting that provides information about the economic, environmental, and social performance of an entity. It represents a departure from previous 'bottom line' perspectives, which have traditionally focused solely on an entity's financial or economic performance. The notion of reporting against the three components (or 'bottom lines') of economic, environmental, and social performance is directly tied to the concept and goal of *sustainable development*.[2]

Triple bottom line reporting, if properly implemented, will provide information to enable others to assess how sustainable an organisation's or a community's operations are. The perspective taken is that for an organisation (or a community) to be sustainable (a long-run perspective) it must be financially secure (as evidenced by such measures as profitability); it must minimise (or ideally eliminate) its negative environmental impacts; and it must act in conformity with societal expectations. These three factors are obviously highly interrelated.

---

1. Details of the award are available at: www.acca.org.uk.

2. As we see shortly, sustainable development has been defined as 'development that meets the needs of the present world without compromising the ability of future generations to meet their own needs' (Brundtland Report, 1987).

Reporting against the objective of sustainable development can be contrasted with the objective of general purpose financial reporting as prescribed in various existing Conceptual Framework projects. Within these frameworks the objective of general purpose financial reporting is usually described as providing information to enable users of financial statements to make informed resource allocation decisions. General purpose financial reporting (as the name would suggest) focuses on financial performance, and issues associated with environmental and social performance are usually excluded. Accounting standards are overwhelmingly concerned with providing guidance in relation to accounting for the financial performance and financial position of reporting entities.[3]

Where environment-related guidance has been released by accounting regulators (for example, in the UK, Canada and US) the guidance provided has tended to show how environmental issues can be considered within the context of conventional financial accounting systems. For example, guidance has been provided in relation to how to account for environment-related expenditure (that is, whether to expense or capitalise it) and how to account for environment-related liabilities that will not be settled for some time (for example, those that relate to cleaning up contaminated sites).[4]

What are the responsibilities of business?

The recent moves by many companies throughout the world to implement reporting mechanisms that provide information about the social and environmental performance of their entities implies that the management of these organisations consider that they have an accountability not only for their economic performance, but also for their social and environmental performance. While this is a view held by many individuals it is not necessarily a view that is accepted universally (however, as we see shortly, some quotes from corporate annual reports show that a number of organisations are publicly embracing sustainable development as a core business goal). Many people still consider that the major goal (and to some

---

3. Neither the Australian Accounting Standards Board nor the Australian Accounting Research Foundation have environmental or social reporting issues on their agendas. Nevertheless, the two major Australian professional accounting bodies (The Institute of Chartered Accountants in Australia and the Australian Society of CPAs) are funding research that considers various social and environmental reporting issues. Overseas, institutions such as the Institute of Chartered Accountants in England and Wales, the Institute of Chartered Accountants of Scotland, the Association of Chartered Certified Accountants, and the Canadian Institute of Chartered Accountants are actively pursuing various reporting issues of a social and environmental nature.

4. In the UK a new financial reporting standard, FRS12: Provisions, Contingent Liabilities and Contingent Assets, was released in 1999. While the standard applies to liabilities generally, it specifically requires full disclosure of liabilities relating to pollution risks and exposure. Consistent with generally accepted accounting principles, it requires full reporting and detailed explanation of present environmental liabilities arising from past events.

people, the *only* goal) of business entities is to generate profits for the benefit of shareholders, with higher profits being preferable to lower profits.

How does an entity determine its responsibilities, and perhaps more importantly, what its relevant stakeholders consider to be its responsibilities? Who in fact are the stakeholders of an organisation?[5] This is clearly based on the personal judgement of the management involved. Judgements about perceived responsibilities have implications for the information the entity elects to disclose (that is, how it elects to account). That is, the perceived *responsibility* of business and its *accountability* go hand in hand. Adopting a definition provided by Gray, Owen and Adams (1996, p. 38) we can define accountability as:

> *The duty to provide an account (by no means necessarily a financial account) or reckoning of those actions for which one is held responsible.*

As indicated in Chapter 8, according to Gray, Owen and Adams, accountability involves two responsibilities or duties, these being:

(i) the responsibility to undertake certain actions (or to refrain from taking actions); and

(ii) the responsibility to provide an account of those actions.

Any discussion of social responsibility reporting (which can be defined as the provision of information about the performance of an entity with regard to its interaction with its physical and social environment, inclusive of information about an entity's support of employees, local and overseas communities, safety record, and use of natural resources) necessarily needs to consider what the responsibilities of organisations are, or are perceived to be. Are businesses responsible to their direct owners (shareholders) alone, or do they owe a duty to the wider community in which they operate? Certainly, many organisations are making public statements to the effect that they consider that they do have responsibilities to parties other than just the shareholders. For example, in North Ltd's *1998 Environment, Safety and Health Report* the company states:

> *North recognises that as a company we have a responsibility to conduct our affairs in a way which benefits society as a whole. We also believe that our commercial objectives will best be achieved and enhanced by understanding community values and taking them into account in all of our activities.*

As another issue, is the responsibility of business restricted to current generations, or should the implications for future generations be factored into current management decisions? If sustainability is embraced then, as the Brundtland Report (1987) definition indicates, our current production patterns should not be such that they compromise the ability of future

---

5. Stakeholders have been defined in various ways. For our purposes we broadly define stakeholders as parties impacted by, or having an impact upon, the organisation in question. This is also consistent with definitions provided by Freeman (1984) and Gray, Owen and Adams (1996).

generations to satisfy their own needs. Such a view is also being publicly embraced throughout the world by many organisations. For example, consider the following statement by General Motors (US) in its *1997 Environmental, Health and Safety Report*:

> *Business opportunities and social responsibility go hand-in-hand. Corporations must act responsibly in regard to their business and to the natural environments in which they operate; successful companies do not separate the two. The balance of economic and environmental benefit is the cornerstone of sustainable development. It is for the subsequent generation that we must focus on sustainable development efforts.*

Such quotes reflect the public positions being promoted by many organisations. Whether these public positions actually dominate decision making within the firm is another issue—we clearly cannot be sure. Exhibit 9.1 provides a perspective of the responsibilities of business. Read the exhibit and consider whether you are inclined to agree with the perspective.

We have already considered various theories that can be applied to explain why organisations might elect to voluntarily provide information about their organisational strategies and their social and environmental performance.[6] For example:

(a) In Chapter 8 we considered Legitimacy Theory and the associated notion of a *social contract*. Adopting this perspective we could argue that an entity would undertake certain social activities (and provide an account thereof) if management perceived that the particular activities were expected by the communities in which it operates. Failure to undertake the expected activities may result in the entity no longer being considered legitimate (it is perceived as breaching its *social contract*) and this in turn will impact on the support it receives from the community, and hence, its survival.[7] Success is contingent upon complying with the social contract. Such a view is consistent with quotes provided in numerous corporate reports, including a quote by the Chief Executive of South African Breweries Ltd in its 1998 Corporate Citizenship Review. In it he states:

---

6. As we have stressed throughout this book, and in particular within Chapter 1, whether we elect to accept that a particular theory provides an explanation of a particular phenomenon will be dependent upon whether we are prepared to accept the underlying assumptions of the theory in question.

7. As indicated in Chapter 8, the *social contract* is a concept used to represent the multitude of implicit and explicit expectations that society has about how an organisation should conduct its business. It is assumed that society allows an organisation to continue operations to the extent that it generally meets society's expectations. These expectations will change over time and different individuals (including the organisation's managers) will have different perspectives about what these expectations actually encompass at a given point in time. Hence, to all intents and purposes it is not possible to provide any form of accurate depiction of what specifically are the terms of the social contract—nevertheless, it is arguably a useful construct to describe the relationship between an organisation and the society in which it operates.

EXHIBIT 9.1 A perspective of the social responsibility of business

Being socially responsible pays dividends

By Clive Mathieson

Companies that neglected their social responsibilities in favour of a narrow focus on shareholder returns risked limiting their long-term financial performance, Sydney Harbour Casino executive Anna Booth warned yesterday.

Ms Booth, a union leader before joining the casino this year as general manager of corporate and government communications, said directors should adopt a wider view of the 'stakeholders' in a company than merely those collecting a dividend and enjoying capital growth. Companies should place corporate conscience alongside shareholder returns when making strategic decisions that affected the performance of their business.

Although shareholders should be the 'ultimate beneficiaries' of corporate growth, other important stakeholders could include employees, customers, welfare groups, the local community and the government.

'I believe that by exercising good conscience you will ultimately generate more durable cash,' she told an Institute of Chartered Accountants lunch in Sydney.

'The socially responsible model, carefully implemented, can in fact deliver to the shareholders better than the shareholder model.'

Ms Booth said that as an SHC executive she was well placed to comment on companies' moral responsibilities, with the casino consistently forced to defend its operations against community groups concerned with the casino's contribution to gambling problems and crime in Sydney.

'We do truly welcome that debate because we recognise that unless we . . . acknowledge the harm that can fall to people by being patrons of our venue we're not going to be able to be in business for the long haul,' she said. 'If we don't think about those patrons in a social sense, then we are immoral but we also jeopardise our very existence.'

According to SHC chief executive Neil Gamble, the casino provides $8 million a year to fund counselling and other community programs to help with problem gambling. The casino also offers a hotline to provide emergency assistance to gamblers.

Ms Booth said SHC was undergoing a three-year licence review by regulators in NSW and considered its external relationships with employees, customers, community groups and the Government extremely important.

'Our behaviour as a corporate entity on social issues is critical to (the government's) willingness to entertain our commercial needs,' she said.

'Unless we adopt the stakeholder model as opposed to the shareholder model we can't succeed commercially.'

Ms Booth said SHC was reviewing its policy on ATMs at the casinos which provide customers with access to credit accounts, after concerns were raised at a meeting with church groups on Monday.

The Weekend Australian, **23–24 August 1997, p. 61.**

Our goal is to strengthen our license to trade, which is bestowed by the communities in which we function. As SAB prospers and grows, these communities will continue to benefit from both the value created by SAB and its behaviour as a corporate citizen.[8]

---

8. What SAB refers to as a 'license to trade' would appear to be equivalent to what many researchers refer to as a 'social contract'.

(b) In Chapter 8 we considered Stakeholder Theory. We learned that one version of Stakeholder Theory (the *positive* version and not the *normative* version) predicts that management is more likely to focus on the expectations of powerful stakeholders. Powerful stakeholders are those who control resources that are both scarce and essential to the organisation. Under this perspective, management would be expected to take on those activities expected by the powerful stakeholders, and to provide an account of those activities to these stakeholders.

(c) In Chapter 8 we considered the Accountability Model developed by Gray, Owen and Adams (1996). Under this model, organisations have many responsibilities (at a minimum, as required by law but expanded by society's expectations that have not also been codified within the law), and with every organisational responsibility comes a set of rights for stakeholders, including rights to information from the organisation to demonstrate its accountability in relation to the stakeholders' expectations. Obviously, determining responsibilities is not a straightforward exercise— different people will have different perspectives of the responsibilities of business, and hence the accountability of business.

(d) In Chapter 7 we considered Positive Accounting Theory. This theory predicts that all people are driven by self-interest.[9] As such, particular social and environmental activities, and their related disclosure, would only occur if it had positive wealth implications for the management involved.

As emphasised throughout, the acceptance of particular theories is, at least in part, tied to one's own value system. This is also clearly the case when we consider the responsibilities of business. Over time, many high profile people have provided their views about the responsibility of business. At one extreme are the views of the famous economist, Milton Friedman. In his widely cited book, *Capitalism and Freedom,* Friedman (1962) rejects the view that corporate managers have any *moral obligations*. In relation to the view that organisations have *moral responsibilities* he notes (p. 133) that such a view:

> . . . *shows a fundamental misconception of the character and nature of a free economy. In such an economy, there is one and only one social responsibility of business, to use its resources and engage in activities designed to increase*

9. As such, it is probably not a theory that provides a great deal of hope in terms of moves towards sustainable development—moves which, if we accept the Brundtland Report definition of sustainability, would require current generations to consider forgoing consumption to ensure that future generations' needs are met. Sacrificing current consumption for the benefit of future generations, and Positive Accounting Theory's central assumption of self-interest, could be deemed to be mutually inconsistent.

its profits as long as it stays within the rules of the game, which is to say, engages in open and free competition, without deception or fraud.[10]

Certainly we could be excused for thinking that many individuals working within the contemporary financial press hold the same view as Friedman. The financial press continues to praise companies for increased profitability and to criticise companies who are subject to falling profitability. They often do this with little or no regard to any social costs or social benefits being generated by the operations of the particular entities—costs and benefits not directly incorporated within reported profit. Another point, considered more fully in Chapter 12, is that 'profits' provide a measure of possible future returns (dividends) to one stakeholder group—shareholders. In commending organisations for high profits we are, perhaps, putting the interests of the investors (the owners) above the interests of other stakeholders. It is not uncommon to see a report in the financial press that a particular company generated a sound profit *despite* increased wage costs. In such a context there is an implication that returns to one stakeholder (employees) are somehow bad, but gains to other stakeholders (the owners of capital) are good. As Collison (1998, p. 7) states:

> *Financial description of the factors of production in the business media, and even in textbooks, makes clear that profit is an output to be maximised while recompense to labour is a cost to be minimised. Financial Times contributors are fond of words like 'ominous' to describe real wage rises: such words are not used to describe profit increases.*

As we see in Chapter 12, some accounting researchers whom we refer to as *critical theorists* would consider that our whole system of accounting acts to support the interests of those with power (often proxied by financial wealth), and to undermine others (such as employees). Promoting performance indicators, such as 'profits' will, it is argued, maintain the 'favoured' position of those in command of financial resources.

Consider Exhibit 9.2, which provides details of how an organisation 'axed' jobs in an endeavour to cut 'costs'. In the same way as our traditional systems of financial accounting ignore social costs, such media articles ignore the social costs that arise as a result of 'axing' employees and thereby making them unemployed.

---

10. According to Clarkson (1995, p. 103), 'Friedman chose to interpret social issues and social responsibilities to mean non-business issues and non-business responsibilities. He, like so many neo-classical economists, separated business from society, which enabled him to maintain that "the business of business is business". By placing the two abstractions of business and society into separate compartments, Friedman was able to deny the necessity, or even the validity, of the concept of corporate social responsibility, decrying it as a fundamentally subversive doctrine'.

Financial Accounting Theory

EXHIBIT 9.2 Example of media attention directed towards accounting profits to the exclusion of the consideration of 'other' costs

North axes 120 jobs to cut costs

Damon Frith

It's almost a local tradition for new chief executives to start their reign with sweeping management changes and staff shedding, and North's Malcolm Broomhead yesterday did both.

North is to axe 120 jobs from the Australian operations by June as part of a program to reduce costs by $130 million a year.

The positions will go as part of an improvement program to help North survive the weakened resources environment, as low commodity prices continue to take a big slice of the company's earnings.

The company has revealed it expects to save $US5 per tonne at its majority owned Iron Ore Co of Canada group by cutting 25 per cent of the workforce over the next five years through a recently ratified union agreement.

Managing director Mr Broomhead said: 'The loss to North of some dedicated and hard working people is a decision I regret a great deal but it is absolutely essential for the future of the company.'

North has overhauled senior management with Philip Shirvington, the chief executive of its wholly-owned Energy Resources of Australia, moving to a new 12 member executive decision making team at North.

Other members of the executive team will include senior management from corporate administration and operations and executive directors.

ERA deputy chief executive Robert Clearly will replace Mr Shirvington and additional members will join the team to enable the company's controversial Jabiluka uranium mine to be brought into production by 2001.

Mr Shirvington will resign from ERA on July 15 and said he was looking forward to his new role at North after spending five years on the development of Jabiluka.

Of the 120 jobs to go at North, 65 will be lost from head office (including exploration) with 55 people to leave the company and 10 others to be relocated to other positions in the group.

A company spokesman could not reveal the cost to the company of the redundancies but said they would be accounted for this financial year.

North announced last month it identified $130 million in cost savings after posting a dramatic fall in net profit during the March quarter to $9.8 million from $37.9 million on the back of weaker commodity prices.

Mr Broomhead, who took over as managing director on January 1, has also suggested possible non-core asset sales and an outsourcing of North's power, rail and forestry infra-structure.

The Australian, **Thursday 27 May 1999, p. 24.**

In applauding the results of 'profitable' organisations, the press also typically ignores the fact (perhaps through ignorance) that the calculated profit is directly tied to the particular accounting methods applied and that the selection of alternative accounting methods could have provided a significantly different accounting result (yet still be deemed to be *true and fair* by the external auditors). For example, consider Exhibit 9.3. The company is being praised for its increased profits—yet no details of how the profit has been impacted by the selection of particular accounting methods (this is the *normal* situation) is provided. In a sense, 'profit' is discussed as if it is a 'hard',

EXHIBIT 9.3 Example of how 'profit' is depicted as an all-encompassing measure of organisational performance

Rebel back on profit track

Australia's largest sporting goods retailer, Rebel Sport, is confident of a reversal this financial year of a profit fall suffered in 1998/99 with a decline in the sporting goods market having bottomed out.

Chairman Anthony Whatmore said yesterday sales in the first seven weeks of the new fiscal year were 12 percent ahead of last year with strong same-store sales.

'Our margins have also been strong. We are confident of a strong reversal of the profit decline experienced in 1999 in the 2000 fiscal year ahead,' he said.

Rebel earlier posted net profit of $3.72 million for the year ended April 3, 1999, down from $4.62 million in the previous year.

It cut its final dividend to a fully franked 3.15 cents from 4.25 cents. Profit before abnormals and tax decreased 14 per cent to $6.09 million and sales revenue grew 10 per cent to $179.2 million.

The company has also launched a new youth lifestyle format called Glue, in conjunction with Ernest Bloom, founder of the Cobra Athleisure stores in Sydney.

Rebel Sports plan to open at least another three new super stores in fiscal 2000. Shares in Rebel lost one cent to 90 cents.

The Weekend Australian, **29 May 1999,** *p. 38. © The Australian.*

objective number. As we know, however, profit as a residual is calculated as a result of making various judgements and assumptions about the expenses and revenues of the reporting entity.

Returning to the earlier view (Friedman, 1962) that the maximisation of profits is management's major priority, it should be noted that there is (as you might expect) a contrary view embraced by many researchers working in the area of corporate social reporting. This is that organisations, public or private, *earn* their right to operate within the community. This right, which we considered in Chapter 8, is provided by the society in which they exist, and not solely by those parties with a direct financial interest (such as the shareholders who directly benefit from increasing profits), or by government. That is, business organisations themselves are artificial entities that society chooses to create (Donaldson, 1982). Donaldson notes that if society chooses to create organisations, they can also choose either not to create them or to create different entities. The view held is that organisations do not have an inherent right to resources. As Mathews (1993, p. 26) states:

> Society (as a collection of individuals) provides corporations with their legal standing and attributes and the authority to own and use natural resources and to hire employees. Organisations draw on community resources and output both goods and services and waste products in the general environment. The organisation has no inherent rights to these benefits and, in order to allow their existence, society would expect the benefits to exceed the costs to society.

Consequently, the corporation receives its permission to operate from society,[11] and is ultimately accountable to society for how it operates and what it does (Benston, 1982).

If society considers that increasing profits is the overriding duty of organisations, then this factor alone may be sufficient (as Friedman argues) to ensure the business's survival. However, if society has greater expectations (such as that the organisation must provide goods or services that are safe; that it must not exploit its employees; that it must not exploit its physical environment; and so on) then it is arguable whether an organisation that is preoccupied with profitability could maintain an existence.

Many senior executives have recently released statements that indicate that they do not consider that pursuit of profits alone is an acceptable strategy. As the Chairman's Statement within Shell UK's *Report to Society 1998* says:

The days when individual companies were judged solely in terms of economic performance and wealth creation have long disappeared. Today, companies have far wider responsibilities to the community, to the environment and to improving the quality of life for all.

This sentiment is also echoed in the Chairman's Statement to BP UK's *1997 Health Safety and Environment Report*. It says:

Success in business is no longer measured by financial results alone. A company such as BP has to deliver not just outstanding competitive returns for its shareholders but also a standard of care in everything it does which matches society's expectations. Our success depends upon the fact that people choose to do business with us and our aspiration is to be the company of first choice. To achieve that we have to build and demonstrate an outstanding track record in terms of the way we do business as well as our financial performance.

In Chapter 8 we considered a study undertaken by Deegan and Rankin (1996) that explored how corporations altered their environmental disclosure policies around the time of environmental prosecutions. The results of the study supported a view that management considered that the prosecutions negatively impacted on the community's perception of the organisation, and as a result, management made other environmental disclosures (of a positive nature) in the annual report in order to limit the likely damage caused to the company's reputation as a result of the prosecutions.

In the light of the Deegan and Rankin (1996) study we can speculate about how some UK companies will react to a recent UK Government initiative. According to *Environmental Accounting and Auditing Reporter* (April 1999, p. 3), the UK Environment Agency has released what it refers to as the

---

11. Or as many organisations are now calling it (for example, WMC Ltd (Australia) in its Environmental Performance Report, 1997) their *public licence to operate*, or their *licence to trade* (for example, South African Breweries in its 1997 Corporate Citizen Report).

'Hall of Shame', a ranking of the ten worst corporate environmental offenders, ranked in order of size of total fines paid. Reflecting a view that 'shaming' an organisation might cause the organisation to reconsider its responsibilities, the Environment Agency's Director stated:

> Naturally we prefer to work with businesses to prevent pollution from occurring in the first place. However, if they do not take responsibility for their operations seriously, we will use all the powers at our disposal to make them change their minds. Businesses must understand that they have a responsibility to protect the environment. The companies included in our Hall of Shame have let the public down, the environment and their own industry.[12]

How do you think the 'shamed' organisations would react to being in the Hall of Shame? Do you think they are likely to respond by making disclosures within documents such as the annual report, and if so, why?

Sustainability—some further considerations

Since the 1970s there has been much discussion in various forums about the implications of continued development for the environment, and relatedly, for human-kind. Many companies worldwide have recently released documents that state that their organisation has a commitment to sustainable development and many companies are providing information to show how they are progressing and performing against the goal of sustainable development. Sustainable development is not something that will be easily achieved and many consider that, at least at this stage, it is nothing more than an ideal. Whatever the case, it is clearly not something that will be achieved easily. As Interface Incorporated (US) states in its 1998 *Sustainability Report:*[13]

> At Interface we are completely reimagining and redesigning everything we do, including the way we do business. While there is no one solution to the impact we now have on Earth and its ecosystems, the company shares one vision: to lead the way to the next industrial revolution by becoming the first sustainable corporation, and eventually a restorative enterprise. We know, broadly, what that means for us. It is daunting. It's a mountain to climb that is higher than Everest.

A significant step in placing *sustainability* on the agenda of governments and businesses worldwide was a report initiated by the General Assembly of

---

12. As quoted in *Environmental Accounting and Auditing Reporter* (April 1999, p. 3).

13. Interface Inc. is a resource intensive company whose largest divisions are petroleum dependent. Its main products are floor coverings. It produces at 26 sites, located in the United States, Canada, the United Kingdom, Holland, Australia and Thailand.

the United Nations. The report entitled *Our Common Future* was presented in 1987 by the World Commission of Environment and Development under the chairmanship of Gro Harlem Brundtland, the then Norwegian Prime Minister. This important document subsequently became known as *The Brundtland Report*. The brief of the report was to produce a global agenda for change in order to combat or alleviate the ongoing pressures on the global environment—pressures considered as being clearly unsustainable. It was generally accepted that business organisations must change the way they do business and they must learn to question traditionally held business goals and principles (perhaps with encouragement from government). As previously stated, *The Brundtland Report* defined sustainable development as:

> . . . development that meets the needs of the present world without compromising the ability of future generations to meet their own needs.

The Brundtland Report clearly identified that equity issues, and particularly issues associated with inter-generational equity are central to the sustainability agenda. That is, it is argued that globally we must ensure that our generation's consumption patterns do not negatively impact on future generations' quality of life. Specifically, we should be in a position to say that the planet that we leave our children is in as good a shape as the planet we inherited (and preferably, in better shape). The move towards sustainability implies that something other than short-term self-interest should drive decision making (a normative position). It implies that wealth creation for current generations should not be held as *the* all-consuming pursuit, and that consumption and personal wealth creation by us (now), while perhaps being considered as economically 'rational' (using the definition often applied in the economics literature) is not necessarily rational from a global and inter-generational perspective.

Implicit in the above definition of sustainability is also a requirement that intra-generational equity issues also be addressed—that is, the needs of all 'of the present world' inhabitants need to be met, which requires strategies to alleviate the poverty and starvation that currently besets the peoples of various countries. While from a moral perspective efforts should clearly be undertaken with a view to eradicating poverty and starvation (again, this is a normative assertion), from a broader perspective, communities cannot be expected to focus on local or global environmental issues (necessary for sustainability) if they are in desperate need of money (for example, if they are starving, can they really be expected to keep their forests intact when such forests provide a means of 'free' heating and income?). Decisions by particular impoverished nations, such as to remove significant tracts of rainforest, can have significant global implications. Any vision of sustainability clearly needs to address poverty.

A further significant event that followed *The Brundtland Report* was the 1992 *Earth Summit* in Rio de Janeiro which was attended by government representatives from around the world as well as numerous social and environmental experts and non-government organisations. The *Earth Summit* again placed the issue of sustainable development at the forefront of international politics and business. Globally, the Summit attracted considerable media attention. An important outcome of the *Earth Summit* was Agenda 21, which was deemed to be an action plan for the 21st century, which placed sustainability as the core consideration for ongoing national and global development.

In the same year as the *Earth Summit* (1992) the European Union (EU) released a document entitled *Towards Sustainability* as part of its *Fifth Action Programme*. One of the suggestions of the program was for the accounting profession to take a role in implementing costing systems that internalise many environmental costs. As we discuss shortly, traditional financial accounting typically ignores social and environmental costs and benefits. Specifically the EU called for a 'redefinition of accounting concepts, rules, conventions and methodology so as to ensure that the consumption and use of environmental resources are accounted for as part of the full cost of production and reflected in market prices' (European Commission, 1992, Vol. II, Section 7.4, p. 67). We return to this issue of 'full-cost' accounting later in this chapter, but the rationale for the EU's proposal was that if the prices reflected the 'full costs' of production, including environmental costs, then such costs would flow through the various production and consumption cycles, and as a result of the higher costs there would be an inclination towards more sustainable consumption patterns.[14]

Since these important early developments in the late 1980s/early 1990s, many governments, industry and professional associations (such as the Australian Business Council and the British Confederation of Industries), and non-government organisations have released various documents addressing the needs for shifts towards sustainable development.[15]

Sustainability appears to have become a central part of the language of government and business worldwide and the definition provided within *The Brundtland Report* has attracted widespread acceptance (for example, the definition has been directly adopted within reports released publicly by Australian companies such as North Ltd, Rio Tinto Ltd, WMC Ltd, and Body Shop Australia, and in numerous overseas companies). As an example, consider the following comments by the Chairman of Unilever in its *1998 Environment Report*:

---

14. There is an ethical issue here in that the higher priced goods will thereafter only be available to the more wealthy. That is, the supply of those goods with a high 'environmental price' will be restricted to the wealthier people.

15. The Business Council of Australia website (www.bca.com.au) provides an overview of the Council's view on sustainable development. In 1999 its website indicated that the Council had formed a partnership with the World Business Council on Sustainable Development.

At Unilever we want to create value for our consumers, employees and shareholders through profitable growth. We see this aim as entirely consistent with the idea of sustainable development: meeting the needs of the present without compromising the ability of future generations to meet their own needs. Our challenge is to improve continuously the competitiveness and appeal of our products. To do this we have to understand what our consumers value, because real value can only be delivered by aligning Unilever's values with those of the broader community. It is in this way that we will create the three pillars of sustainability: economic growth, environmental protection and social progress.[16]

Many organisations are now stating explicitly that their focus is on longer run sustainability considerations, which although having implications for near-term profitability, are essential for long-term survival (at both the corporate and global level).[17] As an example, in the report of the Royal Dutch/Shell Group of Companies, entitled *Profits or Principles—does there have to be a choice?* (Shell's current reports are available at www.shell.com), Shell states:

Shell companies have responsibilities to a wide range of interested parties, such as shareholders, employees, customers and others in society. And the responsibilities relate to our financial, environmental and social impacts on each of these groups. Living up to their expectations demands a long-term perspective, embraces many non-financial considerations, and calls for balance when requirements conflict.

Within Australia, numerous companies are also explicitly stating their commitment to sustainable development. For example, in Placer Pacific Ltd's 1998 document 'Taking on the Challenge Towards Sustainability', the Managing Director states (p. 3):

We need to adopt sustainability, not as added extra, but as a core aspect of our business strategy. We have decided to do so.

Other Australian companies, such as WMC Ltd, RGC Ltd, Rio Tinto Ltd, North Ltd, BHP Ltd, and Body Shop Australia have also recently publicly released documents that specifically refer to the necessity for business to focus on issues associated with sustainable development.

---

16. What should be noted is that there appears to be some differences in how organisations are interpreting the definition of sustainability. Many people would challenge whether Unilever's pursuit of economic growth is really part of a sustainability agenda.

17. Whether they are actually making any real progress towards sustainability is another issue.

Developments in the practice of social and environmental reporting

Moves towards sustainability, which will require fundamental changes to production and consumption patterns, are being promoted by many parties as being an immediate global necessity.[18] Adopting a perspective provided by Legitimacy Theory, we can further argue that if sustainability becomes part of the expectations held by society, then it must become a business goal. As the concept of sustainable development continues to become part of various communities' expectations, communities will expect to be provided with information about how organisations, governments and other entities have performed against the central requirements of sustainability.

Tied to the notion of organisational legitimacy, it has also been argued by some individuals that providing information about an organisation's social and environmental performance will increase the *trust* a community has in an organisation. For example, Greg Bourne, Chief Executive Officer of BP Australia Ltd, recently stated (1999) that:

> *At BP, detailed financial reporting began in 1948 with the inclusion of a consolidated balance sheet, ahead, I'm pleased to say, of legislation which tends to set the pace in these matters. In the 1980s we advanced into environmental reporting, again ahead of the legislators. In the last few years, we've moved into social reporting which accounts for our impact in the world, covering every aspect of our operations. The impetus for this was the need to operate in an atmosphere of trust, no matter where in the world we are.*

As noted above, the view that corporate survival and prosperity is tied to community perceptions (and trust) is certainly consistent with the central tenets of Legitimacy Theory (as discussed in Chapter 8) and it is a view that is being promoted, at least publicly, by many companies. This is reflected in some statements made by North Ltd in its first stand-alone Environment, Safety and Health Report issued late in 1997. In the report the directors of North Ltd state:

---

18. Numerous alarming statistics are available. For example, in *State of the World 1998: A Worldwatch Institute Report on Progress Towards a Sustainable Society* (released by Earthscan, London) statistics are provided that reveal such information as:

   a. sixteen million hectares of forest are being cleared each year, either by fire or chainsaw;
   b. twentieth century population has increased from 1 billion to 6 billion and expectations are that it will double within fifty years;
   c. with population increases the demand for food alone will require an additional 90 million hectares by 2010—equivalent to half the area of Indonesia;
   d. Australia has the world's worst modern record for mammalian extinction. Nineteen mammal species have become extinct since European settlement in the 18th century and at least one-quarter of the remaining native mammalian fauna remains threatened. This in itself has implications for ecological balance;
   e. fourteen species of rainforest-dwelling frogs have disappeared in Eastern Australia—also having consequences for ecological balance.

> *We recognise that the support we receive for our activities will depend largely on our ability to protect the health and well-being of the people and the environment around our operations. . . . The communities in which we operate have a right to understand the impact of our activities and a legitimate expectation that we will act responsibly to protect the quality of the environment. Similarly our workers and their families, who are part of those communities, have a right to be reassured that we are doing all we can to protect their safety and health . . . Performance in these areas is of critical importance to our employees and the community and is therefore essential to the future success of our Company.*

In another statement from a senior Australian corporate executive, the Chief Executive Officer of BHP Ltd, one of Australia's largest corporations, made the following statement at the front of the organisation's inaugural Environmental Report released in 1998:

> *We live in a time of great change: new environmental regulations, changing community expectations, and emerging scientific knowledge about the impacts of human activities. We will embrace these developments as part of our vision to be the world's best resources company.*

Consistent with Legitimacy Theory, the above statement reflects the view that organisations must adapt to community expectations if they are to be successful. This view is also reflected in WMC Ltd's 1997 annual report (WMC Ltd is also one of Australia's largest corporations). In the report, the directors state:

> *WMC's environmental performance affects the Company's ability to attract skilled people, capital and community support. Good environmental management reduces costs, meets the expectations of the communities in which WMC operates, and enables the company to be more profitable.*

The directors of WMC Ltd also make the following statement in their second stand-alone environmental performance report, issued in 1997:

> *WMC understands that its access to land and its public licence to operate depend to a considerable extent on informing and involving the communities in which it operates. The Company recognises the need for local communities to be more involved in decision making. Over time, community expectations change. WMC is looking to develop policies and processes to foster community consultation at all its operations.*

It would appear that the term 'public licence to operate' as used in the quote above is what many researchers might refer to as a 'social contract'. Increasingly, companies are using this term, which does provide some support for a view that companies do clearly see themselves as part of a broader social system in which the interests of not only the shareholders, but also the broader community must be considered.

While sustainability requires more than sound financial/economic performance, it is nevertheless a necessary component of sustainability. That is, moves towards sustainability do not require that profitability be dropped as an important organisational goal. Regardless of how good management's intentions are in relation to its environmental and social strategies, if it does not have any economic resources, then, given our current capitalistic structures, it will be unable to implement the strategies. It will not be able to survive. As Shell states in its 1998 report *Profits or Principles—does there have to be a choice?*:

> *Profits are essential to sustain a private business: without profits to reinvest, a business ceases to exist and contributes nothing. They also enable us to fulfil our social and environmental obligations . . . Business has a number of social and environmental responsibilities but without profits a company— no matter how big or small—ceases to exist and can make no contribution to any of its stakeholders.*[19]

But while 'profits' are important for survival, how profits are typically defined and measured is an issue of concern. In Chapter 2 we referred to *creative accounting* and in other chapters we considered various theoretical perspectives that could be used to explain why creative accounting might occur. But apart from the problems created by the possibility of people employing creative accounting, the conventions on which financial accounting is based are also a source of great concern. Even if generally accepted financial accounting principles are applied objectively, the resulting accounts fail to recognise many social and environmental costs (and benefits). We now consider such limitations.

Some possible limitations of traditional financial accounting

Financial accounting is often criticised on the basis that it ignores many of the *externalities* caused by the reporting entity.[20] Some of these effects relate to the social and environmental implications of the reporting entity's operations and would include such things as the effects that would be generated through pollution caused by the entity, or by injuries caused by the use of the entity's products. Briefly, some of the perceived limitations of traditional financial accounting could include:

---

19. In 1999, Shell continued its public commitment to triple bottom line reporting by issuing *The Shell Report 1999—People, Planets and Profits: An Act of Commitment*. Other related reports issued by Shell included *A Practical Guide to Human Rights*. Such reports are available at Shell's website which is www.shell.com.

20. Externalities can be defined as impacts that an entity has on parties (not necessarily restricted to humans) external to the organisation, parties that typically have no direct relationship with the organisation.

(a) Financial accounting focuses on the information needs of those parties involved in making resource allocation decisions. That is, the focus tends to be restricted to stakeholders with a financial interest in the entity, and the information that is provided consequently tends to be primarily of a financial or economic nature.[21] This has the effect of denying or restricting access to information by people who are impacted in a way that is not financial. But as we appreciate, companies can elect to voluntarily provide social and environmental information. Publications such as *The Corporate Report* (issued in 1975 by the Accounting Standards Steering Committee of the Institute of Chartered Accountants in England and Wales) have clearly indicated that information about corporate performance (including information of a non-financial nature) should be provided to a wider group than simply those with a financial interest. As paragraph 25 of *The Corporate Report* states:

> *The public's right to information arises not from a direct financial or human relationship with the reporting entity but from the general role played in our society by economic entities. Such organisations, which exist with the general consent of the community, are afforded special legal and operational privileges, they compete for resources of manpower, materials and energy and they make use of community owned assets such as roads and harbours.*

(b) Related to the above point, one of the cornerstones of financial accounting is the notion of 'materiality' which has tended to preclude the reporting of social and environmental information, given the difficulty associated with quantifying social and environmental costs. 'Materiality' in itself is an issue involving a great deal of professional judgement. Paragraph 4.1 of the Accounting Standard AASB 1031: Materiality, as issued by the Australian Accounting Standards Board, provides that information is material if its omission, misstatement or non-disclosure has the potential to adversely affect:

(i) decisions about the allocation of scarce resources made by users of the financial report; or

(ii) the discharge of accountability by the management or governing body of the entity.

Because materiality is heavily judgement based, numerous professional accounting bodies throughout the world have provided some guidelines. For example, within Australia, the guidelines provided in AASB 1031 indicate that if an amount is more than 10% of the total equity, or the appropriate total for the respective class of assets or liabilities, or is 10% of the operating profit or loss, then the item is material. If something is not considered to be material, it does not need to be disclosed in the

---

21. In Australia, Statement of Accounting Concept No. 2, paragraph 43, states that the objective of general purpose financial reporting is to provide information useful to users for making and evaluating decisions about the allocation of scarce resources.

financial reports. Unfortunately this has meant that if something cannot be quantified (as is the case for many social and environmental externalities) it is generally not considered to be material and therefore does not warrant separate disclosure. This obviously implies that materiality may not be a relevant criterion for the disclosure of social and environmental performance data. Social and environmental performance is quite different to financial performance. Yet many accountants have been conditioned through their education and training to adopt the *materiality* criterion to decide whether any information should be disclosed. In a review of British companies, Gray et al. (1998) indicate that companies frequently provide little or no information about environmental expenses (however defined) because individually the expenditure is not considered to be *material*.

(c) As highlighted in Gray, Owen and Adams (1996), another issue that arises is that reporting entities frequently discount liabilities, particularly those that will not be settled for many years, to their present value. This tends to make future expenditure less significant in the present period. For example, if our current activities are creating a need for future environmental expenditure of a remedial nature, but work will not be undertaken for many years, then as a result of discounting we will recognise little or no cost now (which does appear to be at odds with the sustainability agenda). For example, if we were anticipating that our activities would necessitate a clean-up bill of $100m in 30 years time to remove some contamination, and if we accept that our normal earnings rate is, say, 10 per cent, then the current expenses to be recognised in our financial statements under generally accepted accounting principles would be $5.73m. While discounting makes good *economic* sense, Gray, Owen and Adams (1996) argue that it does tend to make the clean-up somewhat trivial (and therefore, not that important) at the current time, perhaps thereby providing little current discouragement for an entity's contemplating undertaking activities that will damage the environment, but which will not be remediated for many years.

(d) Financial accounting adopts the 'entity assumption', which requires the organisation to be treated as an entity distinct from its owners, other organisations, and other stakeholders. If a transaction or event does not directly impact on the entity, the transaction or event is to be ignored for accounting purposes. This means that the externalities caused by reporting entities will typically be ignored, thereby meaning that performance measures (such as profitability) are incomplete from a broader societal (as opposed to a 'discrete entity') perspective. Consider Exhibit 9.4 which discusses the financial performance of Rothmans, a major cigarette manufacturer. It is generally accepted that cigarettes cause many health problems, yet externalities such as these that relate to the produce of a reporting entity are ignored for financial reporting purposes. Reported profits are not impacted by such externalities.

EXHIBIT 9.4 Recognition of profits in the absence of a consideration of possible externalities

Rothmans lifts payout after 20pc profit climb

Andrew White

Tobacco

CIGARETTE maker Rothmans Holdings has lifted its final dividend 10c to 45c after hoisting earnings 20 per cent on the back of continued market share gains in Australia.

Rothmans posted net earnings of $119.1 million, up 20 per cent after excluding the effect of last year's $74.5 million abnormal gain on changes in the collection of franchise fees. Including the abnormal item in comparisons, net profit was down 20 per cent on last year's $145 million.

The performance included a 25.9 per cent jump in second-half earnings to $59.8 million, reflecting higher earnings in Australia and New Zealand and reduced losses in Indonesia.

Rothmans managing director Gary Krelle said the company had continued to take market share from its merger partner WD&HO Wills, adding nearly 1.5 per cent to 34.7 per cent over the past two years.

Mr Krelle said sales were up 22 per cent to $3 billion, and appeared to be benefiting from the buoyant economic conditions as smokers traded back up from discount to premium and middle-market bands.

'What I think is happening is a continued strengthening of brands that people have been comfortable with for a long time,' he said.

He warned that the company's earnings would be affected by tax changes in the pipeline, including the goods and services tax and a shift in tobacco excise from a per-gram to a per-stick regime.

The Federal Government has estimated the per-stick regime will add $420 million to federal tobacco revenues, but Mr Krelle estimates it could be as high as $550 million.

The increase in the final dividend takes Rothmans total payout to 85c a share, compared to $1.65 last year, which included a $1 special dividend.

The Australian, **Thursday 20 May 1999, p. 24.**

Arguably, any moves towards accounting for sustainability would require a modification to, or a move away from, the entity assumption. A related area in which our traditional financial accounting system generates a rather strange outcome is the treatment of tradeable pollution permits. In a number of countries, certain organisations are provided with permits, often free of charge, which allow the holder to release a pre-specified amount of a particular pollutant. If the original recipient of the permit is not going to emit as much as the licence allows, then that party is allowed to sell the permit to another party. As such, what we are finding in some jurisdictions is that particular organisations are treating tradeable pollution permits as assets. This may make sense from an 'economic' perspective—but it is questionable whether something that will allow an organisation to pollute is an asset from a broader 'societal' perspective.[22]

(e) Expenses are defined in such a way as to exclude the recognition of any impacts on resources that are not controlled by the entity (such as the environment), unless fines or other cash flows result. For example, in Australia, *expenses* for financial reporting purposes are defined as:

> ... *consumptions of losses of future economic benefits in the form of reductions in assets or increases in liabilities of the entity, other than those relating to distributions to owners, that result in a decrease in equity during the reporting period.* (Paragraph 117 of Statement of Accounting Concept No. 4)

An understanding of *expenses* therefore requires an understanding of *assets*. Assets are defined as 'future economic benefits **controlled** by the entity as a result of past transactions or other past events' (SAC 4, paragraph 14, emphasis added). The recognition of assets therefore relies upon *control*. SAC 4, paragraph 27, explicitly states that environmental resources such as air and water are shared and not controlled by the organisation, and hence cannot be considered as assets. Therefore, their use, or abuse, are not considered as expenses. This is an important limitation of financial accounting and one that must be emphasised. As indicated in Deegan (1996), and using a rather extreme example, under traditional financial accounting if an entity were to destroy the quality of water in its local environs, thereby killing all local sea creatures and coastal vegetation, then to the extent that no fines or other related cash flows were incurred, reported profits would not be directly impacted. No externalities would be recognised, and the reported assets/profits of the organisation would not be affected. Adopting conventional financial reporting practices, the performance of such an organisation could, depending upon the financial transactions undertaken, be portrayed as being very successful. In this respect Gray and Bebbington (1992, p. 6) provide the following opinion of traditional financial accounting:

> ... *there is something profoundly wrong about a system of measurement, a system that makes things visible and which guides corporate and national decisions, that can signal success in the midst of desecration and destruction.*[23]

---

22. Related to this point, in 1999 the European Federation of Accountants released a Discussion Paper which addressed various environmental issues and their association with accounting. In the paper they suggested that with IAS 38 (Financial Instruments) the International Accounting Standards Committee should consider whether such items as pollution permits and emission rights qualify for recognition as intangible assets.

23. Motivated by their concern about the limitations of traditional financial accounting, Gray and Bebbington have sought to develop alternative methods of accounting—methods that embrace the sustainability agenda. We consider these prescriptions at a later point in this chapter.

(f) There is also the issue of 'measurability'. For an item to be recorded for financial accounting purposes it must be measurable with reasonable accuracy. For example, within Australia, *Statement of Accounting Concept No. 4* states that the recognition criteria for the elements of accounting (assets, liabilities, expenses, and revenues) are dependent upon the item having a cost or other value that can be measured reliably (issues associated with the probability of occurrence also need to be considered). Trying to place a value on the externalities caused by an entity often relies on various estimates and 'guesstimates', thereby typically precluding their recognition from the financial accounts on the basis of the potential inaccuracy of the measurement.

While criticisms abound (some provided above) as to how businesses calculate their financial performance in accordance with generally accepted accounting practice, criticisms can also be made of how countries calculate their economic success. For example, the performance of governments (and relatedly, of nations) is often related to the outputs of their systems of national accounts, a well-known output being gross domestic product (GDP). With such a system, the greater the levels of production, the better are the numbers. Obviously such a measure does not consider issues of resource efficiencies or the equities associated with how the resources are distributed. Current methods of calculating GDP provide some strange outcomes. For example, if we build more jails (perhaps reflective of a breakdown in society) this will have positive implications for GDP, as would the sale of harmful tobacco products to third world nations. Sustainability requires a reduced reliance upon indicators such as GDP. Criticisms of GDP abound internationally. For example, consider Exhibit 9.5, which provides a view from the UK that 'economic growth may disguise the fact that we are getting poorer'.

Various experiments worldwide have sought to 'Green GDP', which would monetarise various environmental effects for inclusion within traditionally calculated GDP. However, these experiments have been subject to various criticisms, many related to the lack of an accepted methodology. *The Economist* (18 April 1998, p. 77) highlighted the problems involved in placing a monetary valuation on certain environmental resources. It stated:

> *Some assets, such as timber, may have a market value, but that value does not encompass the trees' role in harbouring rare beetles, say, or their sheer beauty. Methods for valuing such benefits are controversial. To get round these problems, the UN guidelines suggest measuring the cost of repairing environmental damage. But some kinds of damage, such as extinction, are beyond costing, and others are hard to estimate.*

A US organisation named Redefining Progress is promoting various approaches to adjusting GDP to give 'truer' measures of national performance. According to their website:

EXHIBIT 9.5 Criticism of GDP as a measure of national performance

GDP Figures 'distorted' by pollution

The clean-up costs of pollution distort figures on national spending by almost 2 percent, according to a report published today. Economic growth may disguise the fact that we are getting poorer, writes David Nicholson-Lord.

The paper, from the New Economics Foundation, is timed to coincide with the release of the first quarter's figures on gross domestic product (GDP) which, it argues, is a highly inaccurate measure of national welfare, ignoring social and environmental factors.

UK spending on pollution abatement costs £8.8bn, equivalent to a 1.8 per cent addition to GDP, according to the foundation, which has circulated the report to MPs and peers along with a bottle of mineral water. 'The bottle makes the point that economic statistics can go up while the quality of our drinking water goes down,' Ed Mayo, the foundation's director, said.

The reports says that the Government should prepare a 'greener' GNP index measuring welfare and use resources, comparable to the system in the Netherlands. 'Our current way of calculating growth treats the Earth as if it were a business in liquidation,' Mr Mayo added.

***Independent*, Monday 26 April 1993.**

Redefining Progress created a more accurate measure of progress called the Genuine Progress Indicator (GPI). It starts with the same accounting framework as the GDP, but then makes some crucial distinctions. It adds in the economic contributions of households and volunteer work, but subtracts factors such as crime, pollution, and family breakdown. We continue to update the GPI on a yearly basis to document a more truthful picture of economic progress.

The Redefining Progress website can be found at www.rprogress.org.

Eco-justice and eco-efficiency reporting

If we return to our three components of sustainability, we recall that the components are economic, environmental and social performance[24]. When considering the environmental and social implications of a business, two separate components are often identified, *eco-efficiency* and *eco-justice* considerations. Where corporations have elected to produce stand-alone environmental reports (and numerous organisations throughout the world have done so) they have tended to focus on eco-efficiency issues alone. For true sustainability the two components must be addressed.

Eco-efficiency is concerned with maximising the use of a given quantity of resources and minimising the environmental implications of using the

---

24. At this point it might be interesting to consider how the concept of sustainable development as it applies to business entities compares to the accountant's notion of 'going concern'. Are they similar or are they quite different? What do you think?

resources—it relates to environmental protection. Considerations of eco-efficiency do not address the difficult issues of whether the goods being produced (which consume various resources) actually need to be produced. Eco-justice considerations, however, question what is produced, when it is produced, and for whom it is produced. According to Stone (1995, p. 97):

> It (eco-justice issues) may well point to the significant reduction or elimination of production of certain goods and services . . . Eco-justice will also demand a reduction in consumption and the material standard of living in affluent nations and a corresponding shift and a redistribution of (scarce) resources to more impoverished nations . . . and will at least challenge and probably reject the notion of economic growth as the dominant driving force and measure of economic health for nations, for organisations and for individuals.

As noted above, most environmental reports and supplementary disclosures in annual reports have, at least to date, considered eco-efficiency issues but not eco-justice issues. The concentration on eco-efficiency issues is probably due to such issues tending to be more technical or 'scientific', and less controversial than eco-justice issues. Eco-justice considerations are very value-laden and hence easily open to criticism. As Jonathon Porritt, Director of Forum for the Future (UK) states in relation to organisations embracing both eco-efficiency and eco-justice considerations:

> That's a huge challenge for both government and companies to take on, and more than once I've heard hard-pressed business people beg to be allowed to concentrate on dealing with their environmental impacts (which can at least be quantified, costed and conventionally managed) without cluttering the agenda 'with all this wishy-washy stuff about ethics and corporate social responsibility'. (Porritt, 1999, p. 21)

Eco-justice style reporting would indicate how the entity is using its limited resources to ensure that particularly disadvantaged groups are not being forgotten. Other issues to consider from an eco-justice perspective would include the creation of employment opportunities, education and health care; the observance of human rights and equal opportunities; impact on indigenous peoples; support for people in developing countries; and so forth. Consider Exhibit 9.6 which presents some eco-justice style disclosures made by Rio Tinto in its *1998 Social and environmental report: Minerals and metals of the world*. The extracts relate to employee programs related to language skills and health issues as well as to child safety issues.

As noted previously, in recent years there has been a move by numerous organisations to provide stand-alone environmental reports—reports that typically focus on eco-efficiency issues. These reports have typically provided information of a non-financial nature, such as emission levels of particular substances, details of environmental policies, environmental management systems, environmental incidents, environmental awards, stakeholder engagement, performance against best-practice guidelines, environmental risks and impacts, energy and water usage, life-cycle analysis, legislative non-

EXHIBIT 9.6 Voluntary eco-justice disclosure made by Rio Tinto in its *1998 Social and environmental report: Minerals and metals of the world*

Southern Africa

Educational assistance needs to go beyond upgrading physical facilities and ensuring quality tuition in those facilities. It also needs to focus on the development of life skills. These include entrepreneurship, environmental and conservation education and road safety. In KwaZulu Natal, Richards Bay Minerals (RBM) has introduced the 'child in traffic' programme to enable young children in the school playground to familiarise themselves with traffic signs, regulations and road usage.

Many children in rural areas have never been in town or experienced any form of traffic control. These play areas teach children to become safety conscious pedestrians. They also teach children to take responsibility for the surrounding plant life and to learn about various careers and entrepreneurial opportunities related to traffic and road usage. RBM has introduced two pilot projects, based on a concept designed by a local traffic authority, and hopes to introduce similar projects at other rural schools in the area.

Wales—Employee Language Skills

The preservation of cultural heritage is not confined to time or space. Within the UK, for example, there has been a heightened awareness in Wales, accompanied by resurgence in the Welsh language. At Anglesey in North Wales, 63 per cent of the people recorded themselves a few years ago as Welsh speaking. This is reflected in the employee composition of Anglesey Aluminium which includes several crews who routinely speak Welsh at work. The company has always treated the language with respect, but had no formal policy.

A Welsh language policy was developed by Anglesey Aluminium during 1998. It acknowledges that the principal language on their site will continue to be English but provides for Welsh to be given status appropriate to its significance in the community. Among the measures Anglesey Aluminium has introduced are bilingual telephone and face to face communication, sign posting and plant tours and consultative meetings with the local community. It is encouraging the development of language skills through training for staff.

Occupational Health

The Group incidence rate for all occupational health conditions in 1998 fell by 47 per cent to 100 per 10,000 employees from the 188 reported in 1997. Mild induced hearing impediment has become the most common condition at 31.

Although strains and sprains remain common, at a rate of 21, there was a significant fall from the 1997 rate of 78. This is the second year that Rio Tinto has collected and reported centrally on occupational health. The collection of data at Group operations has long been comprehensive, covering all forms of occupational disorders. The intention remains to record conditions at an early stage even if there may be some doubt as to a clear link with occupation.

In South Africa, changes to the law now require tuberculosis in workers exposed to dust containing crystalline silica to be recorded as occupational conditions if certain exposure criteria are met. Six cases of tuberculosis at one mine were reported to the authorities under this requirement. All the workers have been treated for tuberculosis. The major cause of increased levels of tuberculosis in South Africa is the rise in HIV/AIDS. The prevalence of HIV/AIDS is a concern in Rio Tinto's southern African operations. Death rates are increasing and are predicted not to peak until 2003 or later. The Group's southern African companies have active awareness programmes to help combat this. At two sites, monitoring of the rates of sexually transmitted diseases has shown reductions following community outreach activities directed at local schools.

compliances, and so on. Limited information of a financial nature has also been provided in stand-alone environmental reports, such as fines incurred for breaches of environmental laws, amounts spent on recycling initiatives, provisions for restoration, and decommissioning of facilities. Predominantly, such information has been produced voluntarily in the absence of any legislative requirements. Again, we can ponder why companies provide this information—and in doing so we can refer to some of the theoretical perspectives provided in earlier chapters. As an illustration of some contemporary environmental performance disclosures, consider Table 9.1 which provides a copy of a limited subset of the disclosures made by WMC Ltd in its *Environmental Progress Report 1998*.

In Australia, the mining industry has led the way in the production of such reports. In part this is probably due to the leadership taken by the Mineral Council of Australia (MCA). In 1996 it was instrumental in developing the Australian Minerals Industry Code for Environmental Management. Most large Australian companies involved in mineral exploration and development have become signatories to this code. The Code has a Statement of Principles to which signatories 'are committed to excellence in environmental management through: sustainable development, environmentally responsible culture, community partnership, risk management, integrated environmental management, performance targets, continual improvement, rehabilitation and decommissioning, and reporting'. In relation to reporting, organisations are to compile a publicly available environmental performance report within two years of registration with The Code. The

TABLE 9.1   Eco-efficiency disclosures made in the *WMC Ltd Environmental Progress Report 1998*

Eco-efficiency targets at 31 December 1998[1]	1994–95 base-year quantity	Target reduction	Target	Status	Improvements	Measure
Water	1.106 (1.100)[2]	15%	0.940	1.064	3.8%	Kilolitres per tonne of ore milled
Energy	747 (707)	15%	634	672	9.9%	Megajoules per tonne of ore milled
Carbon dioxide	102 (100)	15%	86	80	21.6%	Kilograms per tonne of ore milled
Sulphur dioxide	21.33 (19.33)	75%	5.33	1.67	92.2%	Kilograms per tonne of ore milled

1   Base-year targets have been recalculated to account for sites sold or closed since 1994–95. Figures in brackets present previously reported base years.
2   Figure changed from 1996–97 to account for Kambalda data.

Mineral Council has provided signatories with guidelines as to what could be disclosed in such a report. Hence, rather than leaving it to the government or the accounting profession to provide guidance on what to report publicly in relation to the environment, the MCA has taken the initiative in advising its members. However, the Code does not stipulate what *must* be disclosed. The Code only requires annual public environmental reporting.

We could speculate on why the MCA took this initiative of requiring public reporting. One perspective might be that the organisations considered that the act of requiring public reporting and developing (non-compulsory) guidelines for its members could mean that mandatory (and perhaps more onerous) reporting would not be thrust upon it by government regulation— in a sense the MCA may have sought to 'capture' the regulatory process. Another perspective (provided by Legitimacy Theory) could be that the industry considered that there was much concern in the community about the environmental performance of the minerals industry, and in an endeavour to maintain the perceived legitimacy of the industry it developed guidelines to allow the community to see that, on average, the mining industry was using the environment in a responsible manner. The MCA states (on its website, address www.minerals.org.au) that 'more than in any other way, the community judges the minerals industry by its environmental performance'. Another perspective (consistent with an accountability perspective) could be that the industry leaders considered that they had a responsibility to provide the public with disclosures that provided information about how the organisations had used the environmental resources entrusted to them.

Apart from the MCA guidelines, many other environmental reporting guidelines have been released. For example, within Australia the Environmental Protection Authority (NSW) released a report in 1997 entitled *Corporate Environmental Reporting: Why and How*. Some of the suggested disclosures included information about an organisation's:

- Activities, services and operations
- Environmental policies and systems
- Senior management's commitment to responsible environmental management
- Latest environmental policy with details of specific environmental goals
- Stakeholder consultation programs
- Environmental audit programs
- Complaint handling procedures
- Environmental training and awareness programs
- Water consumption
- Energy consumption
- Use of energy in transport
- Emissions to air

- Transport emissions
- Greenhouse gas production
- Emissions to water
- Waste generation and disposal
- Use of packaging
- Noise and odour production
- Legal compliance
- Life-cycle assessment procedures
- Environmental expenditure
- Environmental liabilities, and
- Donations and grants.

Internationally, environmental reporting guidelines have been released by various organisations, including:

- Confederation of British Industry (UK), *Introducing Environmental Reporting—Guidelines for Business* (1993).
- Deloitte and Touche (Denmark), *Assessor's Manual for the Analysis and Evaluation of Corporate Environmental Reporting* (1996).
- Environment Australia, *A Framework for Public Environmental Reporting: An Australian Approach (2000).*
- Environmental Task Force of the European Federation of Accountants, *FEE Discussion Paper Towards a Generally Accepted Framework for Environmental Reporting* (1999).
- European Chemical Industry Council, *Responsible Care: Health Safety and Environmental Reporting Guidelines* (1998).
- Global Environmental Management Initiative (USA), *Environment Reporting in a Total Quality Management Framework* (1994).
- Global Reporting Initiative (sponsored by Coalition for Environmentally Responsible Industries, US), *Sustainability Reporting Guidelines* (1999).
- Institute of Chartered Accountants in England and Wales, *Environmental Issues in Financial Reporting* (1996).
- Public Environmental Reporting Initiative (USA), *The PERI Guidelines* (1992).
- UK Government's Advisory Committee on Business and the Environment (UK), *Environmental Reporting and the Financial Sector—An Approach to Good Practice* (1997).
- United Nations Environment Programme (and SustainAbility), *Engaging Stakeholders—Second International Progress Report on Company Environmental Reporting* (1996).
- World Council for the Environment (now part of World Business Council for Sustainable Development), *Environmental Reporting—a Manager's Guide* (1994).

There is presently no conceptual framework for environmental reporting, and hence the inclusion of particular items for disclosure tends to be based on particular people's perceptions of the information needs of particular stakeholder groups. Much reliance also tends to be placed on what is acknowledged as best reporting practice (as perhaps evidenced by an entity winning a reporting award for its disclosures).

In March 1999 a new institution called the Global Reporting Initiative (GRI) released further guidelines which it referred to as *Sustainability Reporting Guidelines*.[25] This document was based heavily on the 1999 environmental reporting guidelines released by the European Federation of Accountants (FEE). However, unlike the FEE guidelines (which primarily relate to eco-efficiency issues), the GRI guidelines also included a number of social, or eco-justice issues.[26]

A problem that arises in relation to the current practice of environmental performance reporting is that many companies provide information about such things as emission levels, sometimes with trends over a number of years, but to the lay person the data do not mean a great deal. For example, consider Table 9.1 provided earlier. Would most of us really know the significance of '80 kilograms of carbon dioxide per tonne of ore milled'? Some considerations of the expected 'environmental-data-competence' of the report user is required in much the same way as conceptual frameworks for financial reporting state the expected accounting-competence levels of the financial report reader.[27]

From an accounting perspective it is generally accepted that information should be comparable over time and between entities (within Australia *SAC 3: Qualitative Characteristics of Financial Information* indicates that comparability is one of the qualitative attributes that financial accounting information should have). The attribute of comparability is also something promoted in the recently released *Sustainability Reporting Guidelines* issued by the Global Reporting Initiative. Within these guidelines it is stated that:

---

25. The Global Reporting Initiative was established in late 1997 with the mission of designing globally-applicable guidelines for preparing enterprise-level sustainability reports.

26. For example, in relation to employees, the guidelines suggested disclosure about workforce diversity (gender, race, age); child labour; turnover rate (recruitment and retention); compensation and benefits; flexibility in work arrangements; and assistance for displaced workers. In relation to community involvement, the guidelines suggested disclosures about such things as complaints, community reinvestment, activities in developing countries, philanthropy, and taxes.

27. For example, and as indicated in Chapter 2, in the Australian Conceptual Framework project it is stated (SAC 3, paragraph 36) that: 'General purpose financial reports ought to be constructed having regard to the interests of users who are prepared to exercise diligence in reviewing those reports and who have the proficiency necessary to comprehend the significance of contemporary accounting practices'. Within the United States Conceptual Framework Project, reference is made to the 'informed reader' who should have sufficient knowledge of accounting to be able to appropriately interpret financial statements that are compiled in accordance with generally accepted accounting principles.

Users of sustainability related information wish to monitor and compare performance over time, in order to identify significant trends. Users also wish to compare the results of different enterprises, particularly within industry sectors. Consistency in the recognition, measurement and presentation of sustainability related data is therefore essential.

Looking at figures such as those provided in Table 9.1 does not really provide much information in terms of real-world impacts and outcomes. Another problem is one of inter-firm comparisons (or benchmarking). Many organisations select their own unique measures and performance indicators, which means that benchmarking is difficult, if not possible. Given that the reports should provide a basis for assessing performance, this is an obvious limitation.

Interestingly, there appear to be international differences emerging in the practice of environmental reporting. For example, within the UK the most common approach to environmental performance reporting is one that reports progress against pre-specified targets. This is predominantly also the approach adopted within the US and Australia. In Germany, however, a commonly used approach is to adopt a mass-balance, or eco-balance (in Germany, referred to as Ökobilanz) approach, where a systems-based approach is implemented to describe the functioning of an organisation's operations, with all physical inputs to an organisation being traced through to their eventual end within the organisation, whether as product, packaging, emissions or waste. The flow is typically disclosed in diagrammatic form.

It is interesting to speculate why international differences in environmental reporting have emerged. Within Australia we have tended to follow the UK approach (as we have also done with our financial reporting requirements embodied within our corporate law, and accounting standards). If we were ever to attempt to harmonise environmental reporting (and there are many current efforts to harmonise financial reporting requirements) the various approaches would need to be evaluated. This is obviously some way off and perhaps may never happen.

Social accounting and social auditing

We now turn from eco-efficiency issues to eco-justice issues. As noted previously, eco-justice considerations relate to social-based issues such as the reporting entity's support of its employees, disadvantaged groups, community based projects, and so on. Consideration of social-based issues for external reporting purposes is often referred to as social accounting (which we can contrast with financial accounting and environmental accounting). According to Elkington (1997, p. 87):

Social accounting aims to assess the impact of an organisation or company on people both inside and outside. Issues often covered are community relations, product safety, training and education initiatives, sponsorship, charitable donations of money and time, and employment of disadvantaged groups.

Ramanathan (1976) also provides an interesting perspective of social accounting. He states (p. 519) that the purpose of social accounting is to help evaluate how well a firm is fulfilling its social contract. It would accomplish this purpose by providing visibility to the impact of a firm's activity upon society.

The practice of social reporting was widely promoted in the 1970s but lost prominence in the 1980s. In the early 1990s, attention was devoted to environmental reporting from an eco-efficiency perspective. Social reporting did not appear to re-emerge until the mid- to late 1990s. As Gray, Collison and Bebbington (1998, p. 303) state:

> In much the same way as environmental reporting has re-emerged, so social accounting and reporting has recently burst back to prominence with renewed vigour. Little illustrates this better than the public commitments in 1996 by Shell and BT to the development of their own social reporting processes. There are many reasons for this renewal of interest. The increasing concern with stakeholders, growing anxiety about business ethics and corporate social responsibilities, and the increasing importance of ethical investment, have all raised the need for new accounting and accounting methods through which organisations and their participants can address such matters. But probably the most important of all the influences has been the dawning realisation that environmental issues—especially when examined within the framework of sustainability—cannot be separated from social issues and the accompanying questions of justice, distribution, poverty, and so forth. Social accounting, in all its guises, is designed to deal exactly with these issues.

Social accounting necessarily acknowledges that the organisation has many stakeholders and for many of those organisations currently producing stand-alone social accounts, it is the stakeholders' expectations (learned through various consultation mechanisms) that are being used to drive the reporting process. For example, at the front of the *1996 Social Accounts* of APSO (an Irish aid agency) it is stated:

> A core principle of the Social Accounting methodology is the input from all stakeholder categories into the process of identifying the criteria against which the organisation's performance will be measured.

For many years, companies throughout the world, and within Australia, have been providing social information in annual reports. For example, if we review the annual reports of a number of large listed Australian companies we will often find information about their health and safety initiatives and performance, injury rates, training programs, relationships with indigenous peoples, and community support programs (and, as we have mentioned previously, information about environmental performance).[28] As another

---

28. A review of academic accounting journals reveals that there have been many studies over time that have sought to explain why these voluntary social disclosures were made by the disclosing entities. Commonly, these studies applied Positive Accounting Theory, Legitimacy Theory, or to a lesser extent, Stakeholder Theory in their endeavour to explain voluntary social reporting.

example of social disclosures, in the 1970s and 1980s many organisations throughout the world made specific reference to the fact that they did not invest in South African-based organisations. The reason typically cited was the existence of the apartheid doctrine, which was generally considered unacceptable to most stakeholders, and hence the company did not want to appear supportive of the country and, by association, its government.

The social disclosures being made in annual reports are typically rather *ad hoc* with minimal consistency in disclosures from year to year. Many companies have, at various times, also elected to disclose value-added statements within their annual reports. These statements typically reveal how the value added by the company has been distributed between the shareholders, employees, government (in the form of taxes) and providers of debt finance, as well as the amount of earnings that has been retained within the business.[29] Value-added statements can be considered to be a form of social accounting.

While a number of companies commenced producing stand-alone environmental reports in the early 1990s, in the late 1990s a number commenced producing stand-alone social reports. The practice is more common in Europe and the UK. Within Australia the practice is currently quite rare, with only a limited number of companies (such as Body Shop Australia) producing a social report. Organisations producing stand-alone social reports elsewhere include Body Shop (UK), Traidcraft (UK), NatWest (UK), Co-Operative Bank (UK), SbN Bank (Denmark), Ben and Jerry (USA), South African Brewing, APSO (Ireland), British Telecom, BP (UK), and Shell (UK). A review of the social accounts currently being produced indicates that a great many of the disclosures being made relate to whether the organisation is meeting stakeholder expectations, and if not, the remedial action that is being undertaken.[30] Stakeholder expectations are learned through direct consultation mechanisms which engage various stakeholder groups.

One of the first organisations to produce social accounts was the UK-based organisation, Traidcraft.[31] Within the *Traidcraft plc Social Accounts 1998* the company provides a summary of its approach to social accounting and reporting. This summary is reproduced below as Exhibit 9.7.

As an example of some social-performance-related disclosures we can consider Exhibit 9.8 which provides a reproduction of some performance-based disclosures made in the *Traidcraft plc Social Accounts 1998*.

While there have been many environmental reporting guidance documents released over recent years, this has not been the case in social reporting. In 1999, however, two documents were released that provide some guidance:

---

29. Value added is defined as turnover (typically sales) less the cost of purchased materials and services.

30. As an example of how some organisations are defining their stakeholders, in the social accounts of the Cooperative Bank (UK) the organisation defines its main stakeholders rather broadly as shareholders, customers, staff and their families, suppliers, local communities, national and international society, and past and future generations of cooperators.

31. Traidcraft is an organisation that sells products sourced from third world countries.

EXHIBIT 9.7 Extract from the *Traidcraft plc Social Accounts 1998*

The Social Accounting Method

Traidcraft plc has been a leader in Social Accounting since producing its first report in 1993. Social Accounting is a systematic approach for organisations to account for their social impacts and record the views of stakeholders. It recognises the right of all those who have a stake of interest in the organisation to information about its social impact and ethical performance.

Social Accounting:
- Identifies the social objectives and values of the organisation
- Defines the stakeholders
- Establishes indicators to measure performance against previous years and agreed targets
- Measures performance, keeps records and prepares accounts using principles such as relevance, understandability, objectivity and consistency
- Records the views of stakeholders to provide a baseline for future comparisons
- Submits the accounts to independent audit
- Publishes the accounts

EXHIBIT 9.8 Performance indicators included within *Traidcraft plc Social Accounts 1998*

Stakeholder: *Overseas Craft Suppliers*
Questions asked of stakeholder*:
Traidcraft pays fair prices
Traidcraft allows sufficient time for production
Fluctuations in orders do not cause problems
Traidcraft pays promptly
Traidcraft provides positive advice and inputs on quality
Traidcraft behaves openly and fairly in its business dealings
As producers we feel a sense of partnership with Traidcraft
As producers we feel we have sufficient information
As producers we feel adequately involved in decisions

Stakeholder: *Staff*
Questions asked of stakeholder*:
Traidcraft pays me a fair wage
Traidcraft recognises my worth and matches my skills and abilities to my job
Traidcraft gives me the opportunity for self-development within my job
Traidcraft provides adequate and safe facilities and equipment for me to do my work
Traidcraft provides me with opportunities and encouragement to participate in
  decisions
Traidcraft provides a caring and friendly atmosphere to work in
Traidcraft recognises my workload and offers flexibility to share work where
  necessary
Traidcraft offers opportunities in training and to develop my career

* All questions were on a 1 to 5 scale with one being *strongly disagree* and 5 being
  strongly agree. Comparative figures were provided for 1996/97 and 1997/98

- *Sustainability Reporting Guidelines*, issued by Global Reporting Initiative; and

- *Towards Standards in Social and Ethical Accounting, Auditing and Reporting* issued by The Institute of Social and Ethical AccountAbility (ISEA).

Closely linked to social accounting is the practice of social auditing. According to Elkington (1997, p. 88) the purpose of social auditing is for an organisation to assess its performance in relation to society's requirements and expectations. The results of a social audit often form the basis of an entity's publicly released social accounts (thereby increasing the apparent transparency of the organisation), and the outcomes of social audits can be considered as an important part of the ongoing dialogue with various stakeholder groups.

In a sense, the mechanisms employed by organisations such as Traidcraft plc (see Exhibits 9.7 and 9.8 above) where questionnaires are used to determine stakeholders' concerns and expectations, is a form of social audit. It provides details of where improvements are necessary from the perspective of the stakeholders. In undertaking a review of an organisation's actual social performance, and, importantly, the stakeholders' expectations about performance, there is a view that it is preferable to anticipate potential stakeholder backlash before a given activity is undertaken. This is a view endorsed by the management of the Royal Dutch/Shell Group as reflected in Exhibit 9.9.

Reflective of the recent interest in social accounting and social auditing, a social accounting standard was released in 1998 by the Council on Economic Priorities.[32] The standard entitled SA8000 (SA stands for Social Accountability) focuses on issues associated with human rights, health and safety, and equal opportunities.[33] According to Wright (1999), SA8000 requires an audit of site performance against the principles of the UN Declaration of Human Rights, the International Labour Organisation conventions, and the UN Convention on the Rights of the Child. There are strict procedures laid down to ensure that those carrying out the audit (who must receive special training to qualify) will get to learn of local opinion and operations. Auditors are to consult trade unions, workers, and local non-government organisations. People living close to a site have the right to appeal against an SA8000 award if they disagree with it. Arguably, the impetus for the development of SA8000 was controversies such as those (explained further below) that involved Nike (use of cheap labour in Indonesia—see Exhibit 9.13 below), Shell (human rights issues in Nigeria—as noted in Exhibit 9.9), and Disney (use of cheap labour in Haiti—see Exhibit 9.12 below). If an organisation can have its operations (particularly those undertaken in developing countries) certified to SA8000 standards (or other

---

32. The Council on Economic Priorities (CEP) is an organisation largely based in the USA. CEP describes its mission as providing accurate and impartial analysis of corporate social performance and promoting excellence in corporate citizenship. CEP also produces a *Corporate Report Card* in which various companies are rated on issues such as environmental stewardship and treatment of employees. For further details see www.cepnyc.org.

33. Given that the standard addresses a fairly small subset of corporate social responsibility it is arguable that the title is perhaps somewhat misleading.

EXHIBIT 9.9 Example of stakeholder consultation—the case of Shell

Human rights and environmental activists to participate in projects

Shell to consult pressure groups

By Robert Corzine

Royal Dutch/Shell, the largest international oil company, is to invite environmental and human rights groups to participate in some of its more sensitive projects in the developing world.

In a radical departure from past practice, the Anglo-Dutch oil group says the early involvement of the non-governmental organisations in sensitive projects, especially in Africa and Latin America, will become standard practice.

Managers at the company are believed to have reassessed the way it operates after international criticism of its record on human rights and environmental issues.

In 1995 Shell faced wide-spread condemnation of its activities in Nigeria following the execution of minority rights activist Ken Saro Wiwa and an outcry in Europe over its plan—later dropped—to dump the obsolete Brent Spar oil installation in the Atlantic Ocean.

'We learned from those two events that we have not been listening enough,' said Mr John Jennings, chairman of Shell Transport and Trading, the group's UK arm.

Shell hopes the new approach will identify environmental or social issues with the potential to flare up into serious problems.

Shell also plans to ask pressure groups to monitor and audit the implementation of sensitive projects. It says it will publish the results of the monitoring even if they are not flattering to the company.

'We should use the increased scrutiny of NGOs as a tool to strengthen our performance,' said Mr Jennings. Shell intends to use a wide range of pressure groups, 'including those who wish you were not there'.

Financial Times, **17 March 1997.**

similar standards) by an independent party, then it is very conceivable that its *legitimacy* from the perspective of its stakeholders will be enhanced relative to that of its competitors. This in itself should generate business benefits (and of course, more importantly, it should generate real benefits for the employees involved). Exhibit 9.10 provides further detail on the implementation of SA8000.

In late 1999 the Institute of Social and Ethical Accountability (ISEA) launched standard AA1000, which is concerned with processes relating to setting up and operating social and ethical accounting and auditing systems. The guidelines, which are voluntary, emphasise the need to clearly define social and ethical goals and targets, and to report levels of achievement in meeting targets. The importance of involving stakeholders in the process is heavily emphasised.[34] As *Environmental & Auditing Reporter* (January 2000, p. 2) states:

---

34. While documents such as AA1000 might change over time, or be replaced by other documents, the current efforts to develop such documents reflects the perspective that organisations are increasingly being expected to involve the broader community in decisions pertaining to corporate activities. Corporations are not considered as wholly autonomous units.

EXHIBIT 9.10 Detail about the development and implementation of SA8000

Profit bows to ethics

By Michael Prest

Some of the world's biggest companies are putting their weight behind a new, verifiable code of conduct intended to answer mounting consumer criticism of the exploitative conditions under which the goods they sell are produced in poor countries.

Among the well-known brand names are supermarket chain Sainsbury, cosmetic retailer Avon, athletic shoe maker Reebok, Toys 'R'Us, and the Body Shop.

The code, called SA8000, is the brainchild of the Council on Economic Priorities, an American public interest group, which tries to improve corporate responsibility. It has been drawn up by companies, non-governmental organisations, trade unions, and other interested groups, and is due to start operating next year.

The code covers the basic issues of child labour, forced labour, health and safety, trade union rights, discrimination, discipline, working hours, and pay.

Fitzroy Hilaire, Avon's director of supplier development said, 'There are real problems with child labour, low wages and so on.' The company was trying to find ways of dealing with these issues, he added.

Earlier initiatives by the International Labour Organisation and the United Nations, through the Universal Declaration on Human Rights and the UN Convention of the Rights of the Child, to tackle the problems substantially failed because they lacked teeth. Individual companies such as British supermarkets have also tried to improve standards, but supplier companies in developing countries often found that they were burdened with meeting different codes of conduct for different customers.

The new initiative seeks to get round these difficulties. As the name SA8000 suggests, it is the first to be modelled on existing and widely accepted commercial standards such as ISO9000, drawn up by the International Standards Organisation in Geneva, which is used to determine whether companies have the management systems to meet required product quality.

But the real strength of the new approach is commercial sanctions. A company which adopts the code also agrees to be independently inspected to see whether it is abiding by the conditions laid down. It will be able to attract customers and gain a competitive advantage by advertising the fact that its factories and suppliers meet the standard.

Verification will be conducted by independent commercial organisations, to whom companies will pay a fee for certification that they comply with the code. SGS-ICS, a Swiss company with more than a century's experience of independent monitoring of management processes, helped to draw up the code and will apply for accreditation as an inspector.

Tom DeLuca, vice president for imports at Toys'R'Us, which dominates a fifth of the huge American toy market, said that the company will ask all of its 5,000 suppliers to be certified. Avon intends to have its own 19 factories certified and to request that its suppliers do likewise.

Independent on Sunday, **26 October 1997.**

The process set out in AA1000 guides an organisation through the definition of goals and targets, the measurement of progress against these targets, the auditing and reporting on performance, and feedback mechanisms. The involvement of stakeholder groups is crucial to each stage of the process, building trust in the organisation and the ethical claims it makes. Whilst the process remains the same for each organisation, the goals and targets set will be specific to the needs of their stakeholders, covering a range of issues from employee rights through to conditions in supply chains.

AA1000 also provides guidance in developing programs to train social and ethical accountants and auditors, which possibly signals the genesis of a new subset of the accounting profession. In reflecting on the benefits to companies from complying with AA1000, Simon Zadek, a representative of ISEA, states (as quoted in *Environmental & Auditing Reporter,* January 2000, p. 2):

There is an increasing body of evidence that organisations which listen to their stakeholders are more likely to be successful in the long term. AA1000's continuous cycle of consultation with statkeholders is designed to encourage transparency, clear goal-setting and the building of trust in relationships with people. Organisations which adhere to its principles and processes will be able to draw strength from association with this quality standard and, ultimately, can expect to achieve competitive advantage. Companies like Railtrack and Monsanto must wish, in retrospect, they had invested in these kinds of processes to help avoid billions being wiped off their market values.[35]

Once activities such as social audits are undertaken they can act as a catalyst for organisations and, importantly, for senior management to embrace new values. A 'sustainable organisation' needs to ensure that it complies with community expectations. As such, activities such as social audits make good business sense. As noted in the above quotation from Simon Zadek, failure to comply with community expectations can have major implications for the survival of the organisation (regardless of how efficiently they are using the financial resources or the environment). As WMC Ltd states in its *Environmental Progress Report 1997,* 'the greater the community's confidence in a company, the more secure its longer-term viability'[36]. It also appears that some organisations are undertaking social audits as a means of gaining (or regaining) some legitimacy from the perspective of their stakeholders. Undertaking a social audit, particularly if the audit is undertaken by a credible, independent party, should act to increase the perceived transparency of the organisation. Exhibit 9.11 below supports this view in relation to the activities of Camelot—the organisation responsible for running lotteries within the UK. Camelot was seeking another term to run the lotteries, but had been the subject of much public criticism about how it was using the substantial funds it was attracting.

With the power of the media to beam information about an organisation's international operations into our lounge rooms, an organisation must arguably

---

35. ISEA's website is www.AccountAbility.org.uk.

36. Another mechanism that organisations could adopt in an endeavour to ensure that operations are consistent with stakeholders' expectations would be to open the membership of the board of directors (in the form of non-executive directors) to representatives from various stakeholder groups, for example, representatives from environmental groups, labour unions, consumer groups, and/or suppliers. However, there is no evidence of such a practice being adopted.

EXHIBIT 9.11 Implementing social audits as a possible means of establishing corporate legitimacy—the case of Camelot

Camelot puts itself on trial

Lottery firm's social audit aims to counter critics writes Roger Crowe

Camelot, the National Lottery Operator, has decided to conduct a social audit in an effort to rescue its reputation before bidding for a new licence in 2001.

The exercise will aim to give an independent seal of approval to the way the lottery has been run, countering accusations that Camelot has made too much money, failed customers and charities and abused its monopoly position.

It follows Camelot's appointment in July of the campaigner Sue Slipman to the new post of director of social responsibility. Ms Slipman will be responsible for the audit until next month. She has described it as 'a challenging project'.

The £250,000 audit will report the views of six groups including staff, retailers and the general public, on how the lottery company is carrying out its responsibilities.

The decision to follow companies such as Body Shop and Shell in seeking external scrutiny of its social role was taken by the board in June.

Companies such as BP and BT, as well as some of the international accountancy firms, have focused on social auditing as a means of justifying controversial actions and protecting reputations.

PriceWaterhouseCoopers (PWC), the international audit and consultancy firm, is preparing to launch a Reputation Assurance Service which aims to help multinationals assess their social and environmental impact. Glen Peters, the firm's director of futures, said that managing a company's reputation will be one of the greatest challenges of the next decade. He expects 1,000 companies in the US and Europe to embrace the notion

of wider accountability over the next five years.

Six large companies have been testing the PWC system, which will be launched in January. They are using the approach to examine their responsibilities to five groups—shareholders, employees, customers, society in general, and 'partners', including suppliers.

Mr Peters said big businesses were interested in such an exercise because of the need to back up promises such as 'the customer is number one' and 'employees are our most valuable asset'.

'Reputation is going to be a business's most important asset,' he said. 'Businesses will need to adopt a systematic approach to protecting their reputations.'

Camelot has adopted a social audit after facing a furore over bonuses for directors and accusations of misconduct against its technical supplier, GTech.

The lottery operator has commissioned the New Economics Foundation (NEF) to manage the audit. The NEF pioneered the concept in Britain, initially with Traidcraft, the Third World crafts importer, then the cosmetics chain, Body Shop.

Adrian Henriques, head of social audit at NEF, said: 'Social auditing is becoming part of the mainstream. It is about determining what impact a company has on society and how society affects the company.'

Richard Brown, director of government relations at Camelot, said it was crucial that an external agency such as the NEF was involved to counter accusations that this was merely a public relations exercise. 'NEF will ensure that all stakeholder groups are involved in ongoing dialogue which is externally verified.'

Mr Brown said the decision to undertake the audit was not driven solely

(continued)

EXHIBIT 9.11 *(continued)*

by the campaign to win a second licence term for the lottery. 'It is responding to changing values of the 1990s', he said. 'But it is also an important way of telling people there are plenty of things we can be proud of.'

He suggested the row over directors' bonuses might have been avoided if Camelot had been carrying out a social audit from the start, because the board would have understood how controversial the pay packages were.

Mr Brown dismissed worries about the link with GTech, which was originally a partner in the lottery consortium but is now merely a supplier.

'If people have concerns about GTech, we would like to know about it.'

One unusual feature of the Camelot audit will be the establishment of a permanent 'stakeholder council' which will oversee the process and continue to monitor action or issues arising from it.

The audit will take about 18 months to complete and is not expected to be published until 2000, when applications for the new lottery licence will be submitted. *Guardian*, **21 September 1998.**

not only consider the expectations of the local community in which it operates (whether gained through the process of a social audit, or otherwise), but its stakeholders worldwide—many of which will focus on eco-justice issues.[37]

Organisations must be able to indicate that they are not exploiting particular communities or sub-groups—even though they might be complying with local laws.[38] For example, consider the implications for Nike when it became apparent to others that the organisation was selling sportswear that was being produced in Indonesia by workers being paid less than $10 a week (at the same time it was paying Michael Jordan many millions of dollars to endorse the same products), or the implications for BHP Ltd when it became apparent to the world how much environmental damage was being caused in Papua New Guinea as a result of operations that BHP Ltd was associated with. Other examples would include Shell's operations in Nigeria in which it was deemed by many parties that Shell was appearing to be supportive of an oppressive regime, and Disney's use of cheap labour in Haiti. Exhibits 9.12 and 9.13 are reflective of the media coverage that was given to some of the above social performance issues.

---

37. In the 1997 *Health Safety and Environmental Report* of Shell International, the Chairman refers to the world in which we live as a 'CNN world'—a world in which global news networks will very quickly let us know about corporate misdemeanours, no matter where they occur.

38. As shown in Exhibits 9.12 and 9.13 some corporate managers have been known to defend their organisation's social performance in particular countries by saying that they are complying with local laws. Such a policy has been attacked by many groups, including many non-government organisations (NGOs). Essentially, an organisation can seek out countries that have limited regulation so they can produce goods in a manner that they could not do domestically (the restrictions may have been imposed domestically because of the potential harm to people and/or the environment). Many organisations try to distance themselves from such an approach by stating that they adopt world's best practice in all locations even though this may be beyond local requirements.

EXHIBIT 9.12 Media attention to poor corporate social performance— the case of Disney

No glamour for Disney's sweatshop toilers

Hercules, Disney's latest animated film, opened in London last night. Glenda Cooper, Social Affairs Correspondent, contrasts the glittering premiere with the wage of £2 a day paid to Haitian workers who make Disney products.

The charity World Development Movement (WDM) yesterday accused Disney—symbol of all American wholesomeness—for making huge profits in the United Kingdom and United States while buying from sweatshops in places such as Haiti.

Disney spent £22m marketing *Hercules* in the US, the charity says. Women sewing Disney T-shirts are being paid 17p an hour while Disney's chief executive, Michael Eisner, earns £6,250. To raise the daily wage rate from £1.35 to £2.81 as the workers wish would cost Disney 4 per cent of the money already taken from *Hercules*.

Disney, however, says there is another side to the story: the company complies with all the applicable laws. And in a country where 80 per cent of the population are unemployed, jobs are few and hard to come by. 'Companies moving out—that is definitely not what the workers want,' says Charles Arthur, of the Haiti Support Group. 'We wish they would send more orders. But they want to have their rights to a union respected.'

Haiti is one of the poorest countries in the world. The minimum daily wage has been set at 36 gourdes (£1.35) since 1995 but inflation is running at 117 per cent. Factory workers often share a bag of charcoal costing 20 gourdes (75p) because they cannot afford to buy it themselves. Food can take another half to one-third of the daily wage and even daily transport fares take out 1.5–2.5 gourdes for a single journey.

More than half the daily wage is spent on rent and women paid on Friday often do not have any money left to buy food for the children by Sunday, so they are forced to survive on loans.

In September, interviews were conducted on behalf of WDM with workers from three factories in Haiti: LV Myles; Buddy, Villard and Faubert (BVF) and Classic. All three are sub-contactors to Disney products.

More than 20,000 people work in assembly plants, one third of which produce clothes for Disney, mainly women's and children's wear, and 90 to 95 per cent of the employees are women, most of them young and single and many with several children to support.

The report concluded that factories are keeping wages down to the lowest level legally allowed; forcing workers to accept overtime with little additional pay; sacking workers who join unions; and refusing sickness and maternity leave.

The employees are paid according to work quotas, which they say are too high. Those who make the quota can have a bonus which raises their daily wage to 50 gourdes (almost £2) but workers reported that those who did not make their quotas were suspended for two or three days or even replaced by new workers. For sewing a £19 garment, a Haitian worker receives just under 5p.

One woman sewing sleeves said that there were 50 garments in a packet and to make the quota she has to produce 35 packets each day: 1,750 garments a day. Conditions were also criticised. One woman from BVF described that in their factory serving hundreds of people there were three lavatories for women, of which two were blocked.

The same woman said that as far as water facilities were concerned, the

(continued)

EXHIBIT 9.12 *(continued)*

workers were supposed to drink from a tank that had not been cleaned since the factory opened two years ago. Recently, a dead toad was found in the tank and a man who went to management to complain about this was fired. Workers now carry their own work-time drinking water from home.

People also complained that their workplace had inadequate ventilation. A woman working with LV Myles said the workers had asked for a cafeteria because at the moment they have to eat standing up in the road outside the factory.

'Improving conditions in these factories is not a *Herculean* task. Disney can well afford to give its workers a fair deal,' DM campaigner, Aditi Sharma said. 'Disney's Code of Conduct claims to recognise workers' rights but the Haitian workers have never even heard of it.'

But trying to get rid of such factories is not the answer, experts warn. Haiti is less dependent that it was in the mid-eighties when up to 120,000 people were employed in factories, James Ferguson, a researcher at the Latin American Bureau said. 'But in the capital, particularly for women from the poorer shanty towns with large families to support, it would be pretty disastrous if companies moved out. There's nowhere else to go to look for a job.'

A spokesman for the Disney Store said yesterday: 'Disney is extremely careful about the conditions under which its products are made and always operates within the particular employment, health and safety and environmental laws governing each country.

'In Haiti an inspection and review has demonstrated that we are adhering to all applicable laws and policies; workers who make Disney licensed goods do so in decent conditions and are paid above the local minimum wage.'

The Independent, **10 October 1997.**

Consistent with Media Agenda Setting Theory (see Chapter 8) it is reasonable to assume that such negative media coverage would have impacted on the public's perceptions of the legitimacy of the companies involved. Consistent with Lindblom (1994), an organisation that suffers a potential 'legitimacy crisis' may undertake certain actions in an attempt to improve its image in the eyes of its stakeholders, including educating and informing its stakeholders about changes in the organisation's performance and activities, or perhaps by attempting to change external expectations about an entity's performance (Lindblom's work is considered in Chapter 8). As noted earlier, social auditing and social reporting can be useful in this respect and it is interesting to find that many organisations challenged about their social conduct (with extensive negative media attention) have subsequently put in place social reporting and auditing mechanisms.

When reading Exhibits 9.12 and 9.13 we can consider whether the attitudes attributed to the management of Disney and Nike are consistent with the goal of sustainability publicly embraced by many corporations.

Undertaking social audits on a periodic basis is becoming accepted as a necessary part of a well functioning management system. For example, Nike now ensures that supply chains pay appropriate wage rates—had a social audit been undertaken previously Nike could have insisted on this earlier and its name would not have been so badly tarnished.

EXHIBIT 9.13 Media attention to poor corporate social performance—
the case of Nike

Nike work at 16p an hour? Just do it.

In the West trainers are equated with liberty but in Asia the shoe is on the other foot reports Rocasta Shakespeare

Sweating in the 90-degree heat, 22 year old Eni dabs paint on to the soles of freshly moulded Reebok, Nike and Adidas trainers as they pass along a production line in Jakarta's Eltri factory. Presses thump and hiss, glue stinks and rubber burns as machines drum 23,000 stitches into each leather upper. But the Nike advertisement posted to the wall above her head implores 'Just Do It'.

'If we make a mistake they call us dogs and prostitutes and sometimes they hit us', says Eni . . . Eni and her fellow workers on Line Four are paid 16 pence an hour. A pair of Reebok Instapump Fury Graphite costs £99.99.

Tomorrow Christian Aid will launch a campaign called 'The Globe-Trotting Sports Shoe' to highlight conditions in sport shoe factories in China, the Philippines and Thailand which, together with Indonesia, employ more than 75,000 workers. In an industry that spends millions of pounds on advertising campaigns and takes millions in profits, the labour costs are minute. For example, labour costs for a pair of Nike Air Pegasus shoes that retail for $70 are $1.66 (£1.07).

The Indonesian Government admits that its minimum wage of 4,600 rupiahs (£1.30) a day is fixed below the poverty line to encourage foreign investment. By that criterion, the policy has been a huge success. Nike started using subcontractors in Indonesia in the late 1980s when Korean wages increased. Top names such as Adidas, Puma, Converse, LA Gear and Fila followed and more than 25,000 workers—85 per cent of them women— are now employed in the shoe factories around Jakarta.

In Indonesia, free trade unions are illegal and attempts to organise one can end in violence or murder. Working conditions can be dangerous and hours long. Work begins at 7.30 am and can continue for up to 18 hours. While compulsory overtime is illegal, enforcement is lax. 'We are often forced to work until midnight or later if the factory has a high quota or deadline, like Christmas, to meet,' says 20 year old Lely, who works at the Pratama Abadi Indus factory outside Jakarta. 'If we refuse to do overtime we are fired.'

A complaint of any kind can result in sacking. Sadisah, 24, was fired in 1992 along with 23 fellow workers after striking to demand compliance with statutory labour laws at the Eltri factory. She now works at the Nikomas factory in Serang, a Jakarta suburb.

Dusty Kidd, Nike's head of communications, said: 'We can't dictate to governments how they run their labour laws.' He points out that in a country where the population is increasing at the rate of 2.5 million per year, with 40 per cent unemployment, it is better to work in a shoe factory than not to have a job at all.

Philip Knight, Nike's founder, says he wants Nike to be thought of as a company with 'a soul that recognises the value of human beings'.

Reebok intends to stay in Indonesia. Its founder, Paul Fireman, says: 'Rather than impose US culture on other countries, we work to make every country its own headquarters—sort of a "when in Rome do as the Romans" philosophy.'

Such a statement amazes Rahman, 20, a hot press operator at Jakarta's Nasa shoe factory. 'We need protection from our government. We don't need foreign companies to come to Indonesia to take advantage of Suharto's denial of human rights' . . .

(continued)

EXHIBIT 9.13 *(continued)*

The scene is about as far as you can get from the fit and aggressive image projected by the sports shoe companies in the West. Here, they spend millions signing up sports stars and then more millions on buying advertising space. In 1994, Reebok spent $70 million on US advertising alone; Nike spent £187 million. More than £6.5 m has been spent on advertising in Britain.

'To you in England these shoes have an image of freedom and individuality,' Sadisah says. 'To us they mean oppression' . . .

Nike's profits last year were $299 million while those of Reebok's were $254 million. It is not known how much of a shoe's price goes for profit or marketing, but neither can be insignificant in a market where image is everything. The endorsement deals are huge, with the likes of American star Michael Jordan being paid $20 million.

Peter Madden of Christian Aid says the irony is that companies which claim to be masters of the latest technology say they have no control of the factories. 'These companies are developing the most complex design specifications yet they are not able to regulate what goes on in the factories.'

***The Observer*, 3 December 1995.**

Reflective of the view that corporations will be increasingly likely to explicitly consider the social implications of their operations, many large accounting and consulting firms throughout the world (such as the 'Big 5' accounting firms) are acquiring or developing expertise to undertake such work. As an example of this, KPMG (one of the 'Big 5') elected to offer positions to key individuals who had been employed as part of the Body Shop (UK) social and ethical auditing team (Body Shop is widely recognised as a leader in this field). According to KPMG (UK) Senior Partner, Mike Rake:

> *In recent years it has become increasingly evident that a wide range of leading companies recognise that financial performance is not the only yardstick by which their sustainability should be measured . . . KPMG seek to be innovators in this field and by forming this strategic alliance with the recognised leader in sustainability reporting we shall be able to provide a unique service to our clients.*[39]

An organisation's operations can have many social impacts. A social audit (and related report) can obviously not cover all such impacts. Some prioritisation is necessary and this prioritisation will be dependent upon professional judgements. Considerations must be made of stakeholder needs, selection of appropriate performance indicators to satisfy information needs, and so on. Ideally, management should explain the reasons for selecting particular social areas for subsequent review.

Because sound social performance in the eyes of stakeholders is important for corporate survival, many organisations are implementing various

---

39. As quoted in *Environmental Accounting and Auditing Reporter* (February 1999, p. 1).

stakeholder consultation mechanisms to ensure that they are aware of various expectations within the community (becoming known as 'engaging the stakeholders'). Organisations must acknowledge that they have many different stakeholder groups with differing expectations. Definitions of stakeholders will differ. Previously in this chapter we have considered how Co-Operative Bank (UK) defines its stakeholders. As an Australian example, Placer Pacific reports in its 1998 document *Taking on the Challenge Towards Sustainability*:

> *We now define our stakeholders as a much broader group, including shareholders; employees; local community groups; existing and aspirant landowners; indigenous peoples; local, regional, national governments and policy makers; local, national and international non-government organisations (NGOs); academics and research institutions. Although we have found it difficult to engage all of our stakeholders in a meaningful and consistent manner, we believe there is scope for improvement. Hence we are developing a more coordinated approach to engagement.*

Apart from ensuring that stakeholders are consulted about particular operating and reporting decisions, many organisations are going further and actually entering into formal partnership arrangements with various stakeholder groups. The organisations are often finding that this provides beneficial outcomes for all parties involved. We will now consider such 'strategic alliances'.

Strategic alliances with stakeholder groups

Apart from consulting stakeholders in an endeavour to be aware of their expectations, many organisations are entering into strategic alliances or partnerships with other organisations, many of which at earlier points in time may have been considered as adversaries. For example, consider the timber industry. At a time when there was much consumer concern about the origin of timber supplies, the timber industry formed a partnership with World Wide Fund for Nature (WWF). As part of this partnership the Forest Stewardship Council was formed, which enabled timber to be certified if it was derived from an acceptable and sustainable source. Certification provided both environmental and business benefits. Subsequent to the Forest Stewardship Council, and following concerns about the sustainability of fishery operations, WWF was also instrumental in forming, in conjunction with the large multinational corporation Unilever, the Marine Stewardship Council. The products of participating fisheries will bear the MSC logo. Unilever made the following statements in its *1998 Environment Report*:

> *Worldwide demand for fish is rising, but the long-term supply is threatened by decades of over-fishing and indiscriminate fishing practices . . . In February 1996 Unilever formed a conservation partnership with the World Wide Fund for Nature (WWF). The aim was to create market incentives for sustainable fishing by establishing a certification scheme to use market forces and the power*

of consumer choice to encourage sustainable fishing . . . For WWF—one of the world's largest conservation organisations—this is an important step in conserving fish stocks and safeguarding the marine ecosystem. For Unilever sustainable fishing is essential to ensure long-term supply to sustain the business. The partnership is based on a common purpose: the long-term sustainability of global fish stocks and the integrity of the marine ecosystem.

Within Australia the representatives of the mining industry have held discussions with WWF Australia regarding the potential application of the 'Stewardship Council model' to the minerals industry. Interestingly also, WMC Ltd invited WWF to provide a one page commentary on its reporting policies for inclusion in its *Environmental Progress Report 1997.*[40]

With regard to the mining industry, it is interesting to note that in 1999, WWF developed a 'Scorecard' for evaluating the environmental reports released by signatories to the Minerals Industry Code for Environmental Management. They released their first 'scores' in May 1999.[41] In undertaking the process, WWF (1999) stated:

Consistent with WWF's strategic objectives, WWF is actively participating in constructive debate and projects with the mining sector and other organisations. Our goal is for the mineral exploration and extraction industries to improve their environmental and social performance and so contribute to ecological sustainable development . . . When linked to effective environmental management systems with responsible targets for environmental performance, corporate environmental reporting can be as critical to a company's success as its financial reporting . . . Environmental reporting is a way that mining companies can demonstrate their environmental credentials. It enables stakeholders and the community to differentiate one company's performance from another, and assists the process of continual improvement of environmental performance in the industry sector.

WWF was critical of the code because it did not stipulate what must be included in the reports, nor did it require any verification of the contents of the report. In regard to this latter point, WWF (1999, p. 6) states:

The significant shortcoming in all the reports was external verification. Only four (out of 11) had any external verification, with WMC and North being the only companies referring to an external panel or advisory committee for the reports. WWF believes external verification adds to the credibility and integrity of the report by providing stakeholders with an independent assessment of the report content. WWF believes that the companies should place as much importance on external verification of statements on environmental performance as they do for statements on financial performance.

---

40. A review of the WMC Ltd Environmental Progress Report 1998, however, did not provide evidence of any input from WWF, nor any reason for its omission in 1998.

41. The company that gained the highest score in the inaugural 'scorecard' was WMC Ltd, which received 77 out of a possible 100, followed by RGC with 66, and BHP with 54.

Within Australia we can also consider the partnership between Greenpeace and the Sydney Olympic Committee bid for the Olympic Games. In Northern NSW there has also been an interesting partnership struck up by a property developer, Rays Development Corporation, and the Australian Koala Foundation in which a 'koala friendly' residential development was established (called Koala Beach). Examples of other strategic alliances currently abound—yet if we go back only a few years there was a general absence of such alliances. Arguably, such initiatives are further evidence that corporations are coming to accept that to be viable they need to take on the views, and sometimes assistance, of stakeholder groups other than their shareholders.

Monetising environmental costs and benefits

Approaches such as *target-based reporting* and the *eco-balance approach*, as already briefly discussed, do not attempt to incorporate environmental factors into measures of financial performance. Rather, they stand apart from financial disclosures and calculations. This approach has been criticised as the success of an organisation is often gauged by its financial profit (even when other social and environmental information is provided) which, as we would appreciate, is considered by many people to be a very imperfect guide to the performance of an organisation.

Reflective of the fact that financial accounting typically ignores the environmental impacts of an entity's operations (part of the externalities of the business) there have been various experimental approaches throughout the world aiming to develop a 'full-cost' approach to profit calculation. The motivation for the push towards full-cost accounting is that market prices often do not reflect the scarcity of the resources involved, or the harm such resources can cause. There is a perceived requirement that all costs associated with a product or service should be reflected in the price of the good—that is, internalised by the organisation. Such an analysis, if done comprehensively, would require some form of life-cycle analysis of the product or service, thereby requiring consideration of the inputs and outputs from raw material acquisition to disposal. These costs would include those associated with pollution and health issues generated through production, use and subsequent disposal of the product. Such prices are often referred to as 'true prices'. A number of companies are experimenting with full-cost accounting, including Dow Europe, BSO/Origin (Netherlands), Volvo, Ontario Hydro, and IBM. Their approaches represent a dramatic departure from conventional accounting. In a recent report, Dow Europe has stated:

> When it comes to full-cost accounting, no one has all the answers. Certainly we don't, but we are beginning to take steps toward more realistic allocation of environmental costs. At Dow Europe we believe this is the first step in a long journey that may result in the more accurate 'environmental pricing' of our products. It will take years to accomplish, but when implemented correctly,

full-cost accounting has the potential to improve environmental performance more than any other program or regulation in place today. True pricing leads to informed consumer choices. By building costs into a product's price consumers no longer need to rely upon 'green' advertising, seals and guides. Provided all products reflect their true environmental price tag, consumers can be confident that they are making the best choice for both their wallet and the world.

In the remainder of this chapter we consider some initiatives implemented in an endeavour to recognise various social and environmental costs and to recognise these costs prior to calculating measures such as 'profit'. There is a range of approaches to quantifying environmental costs, ranging from fairly conservative approaches to 'full-cost accounting' to the more radical and experimental approaches that involve 'sustainable cost calculations' (Gray and Bebbington, 1992, 1997, 1998). The moves towards quantifying environmental costs and benefits is consistent with the call by the European Union Fifth Action Programme on the Environment (considered earlier in this chapter) which called for accounting to redefine its concepts, rules, conventions and methods so that products would reflect more fairly their full costs. Notable developments in the area of full-cost accounting include work undertaken at Baxter International Inc. (USA), Ontario Hydro (Canada), BSO/Origin (Netherlands), Landcare Research Ltd (New Zealand), and Earth Sanctuaries (Australia). We now briefly consider each of the approaches.

Baxter International

Baxter International is an organisation that produces, develops and distributes medical products and technologies. It has revenues in excess of US$5 billion. In the mid-1990s, Baxter decided to develop what it called its *Environment Financial Statement* (EFS). According to Bennett and James (1998, p. 295):

> . . . the purpose of the EFS was to collect together in a single report, annually, the total of the financial costs and benefits that could be attributed not only to the environmental programme itself but to the environmentally beneficial activities across the corporation. Its aim was to demonstrate that, contrary to the preconception of many, the environment need not be only a burden on business performance but could make a positive contribution.

Of the five entities' approaches to monetising environmental impacts that we consider, Baxter's approach is the most conservative. It ignores any externalities caused by the business, and considers only those costs and benefits that directly relate to actual cash flows. The Environmental Financial Statement from Baxter's *1998 Environmental, Health and Safety Performance Report* is reproduced in Table 9.2. In the statement, 'Income' refers to actual monies received in the report year; 'Savings' refers to reduction in costs between report year and prior year (an increase in actual costs is negative savings); and 'Cost Avoidance' refers to additional costs other than the report year's savings that were not incurred, but would have been incurred if the waste reduction activity had not taken place.

TABLE 9.2 Environmental Financial Statement as shown in the 1998 Environmental, Health and Safety Performance Report of Baxter International

Estimated Environmental Costs and Savings Worldwide ($ in millions)

ENVIRONMENTAL COSTS	1997	1996	1995[1]
Costs of Basic Program			
Corporate EHS—General and Shared Multidivisional Costs	1.5	1.4	1.4
Auditors' and Attorneys' Fees	0.5	0.5	0.3
Corporate EHS—Engineering/Facilities Engineering	0.6	0.6	0.7
Division/Regional/Facility EHS Professionals and Programs	5.8	6.3	6.8
Packaging Professionals and Programs for Packaging Reductions	0.8	1.0	2.3
Pollution Controls—Operations and Maintenance[2]	2.6	2.8	2.9
Pollution Controls—Depreciation	1.0	1.4	1.7
Total Costs of Basic Program	**12.8**	**14.0**	**16.1**
Remediation, Waste and Other Response Costs			
(Proactive environmental action will minimize costs)			
Attorneys' Fees for Cleanup Claims, NOVs	0.1	0.1	0.2
Settlements of Government Claims	0.0	0.1	0.0
Waste Disposal	3.1	3.0	2.6
Environmental Taxes for Packaging	0.3	0.3	0.3
Remediation/Cleanup—On-site[3]	0.3	0.3	0.3
Remediation/Cleanup—Off-site	0.0	0.1	0.6
Total Remediation and Waste, and Other Response Costs	**3.8**	**3.9**	**4.0**
TOTAL ENVIRONMENTAL COSTS	**16.6**	**17.9**	**20.1**
ENVIRONMENTAL SAVINGS			
Income, Savings and Costs Avoidance from 1997 Initiatives			
Ozone Depleting Substances Cost Reductions	1.7	0.6	0.5
Hazardous Waste Disposal Cost Reductions	0.0	(0.1)	0.1
Hazardous Waste Material Cost Reductions	(0.2)	(0.3)	0.2
Nonhazardous Waste Disposal Cost Reductions	0.2	(0.1)	0.1
Nonhazardous Waste Material Cost Reductions	2.9	1.3	(0.7)
Recycling Income	4.6	5.6	5.2
Energy Conservation Cost Savings	3.3	1.5	1.4
Packaging Cost Reductions	1.3	2.4	5.6
TOTAL 1997 ENVIRONMENTAL SAVINGS[4]	13.8	10.9	12.4
— As a Percentage of the Costs of Basic Program	108%	78%	77%

(*continued*)

TABLE 9.2 *(continued)*

SUMMARY OF SAVINGS

Total Report Year Savings[4]	13.8	10.9	12.4
Cost Avoidance in Report Year From Efforts **Initiated in Prior Years Back to 1990**	86.3	80.0	68.7
TOTAL INCOME, SAVINGS AND COST AVOIDANCE **IN REPORT YEAR**	100.1	90.9	81.1

1 These amounts have been adjusted from previous years to reflect the spin-off of Allegiance Healthcare Corporation operations.
2 Operational and maintenance costs for 1996 and 1995 were recalculated in the light of more accurate data received from this report.
3 An additional $0.4 million in on-site cleanup costs was incurred in 1997 from newly acquired operations.
4 Cost avoidance from initiatives completed in prior years is listed as a separate line item in this report.

In principle, all the figures presented in Baxter's EFS would be available from the organisation's main accounting system. No notional costs are calculated for externalities caused, such as the emission of ozone-depleting substances, releases to water, and so on. For example, where electricity costs have fallen as a result of decreasing use due to specific energy reduction initiatives, this reduction in cost is shown as a saving. No consideration is given to the fact that the electricity consumption is still resulting in the emission of harmful greenhouse gases. As such, the approach is rather uncontroversial from an accounting viewpoint. What it attempts to demonstrate is that by explicitly considering the environment, actual cost savings can be made. Without such an analysis these savings may be unknown and more emphasis may be placed on the cost of putting in place recycling initiatives, cleaner production techniques, and so on. By only considering the costs and savings incurred by the organisation, and by excluding recognition of externalities (impacts of greenhouse emissions, and so on), Baxter is still applying the usual 'entity assumption' when producing its EFS. This is reflected at page 30 of the Baxter Environmental, Health and Safety Report. It states:

> *Baxter's environmental initiatives saved the company almost $14 million in 1997. This was 108 per cent of the costs of the basic environmental program. Cost avoidance from efforts initiated in prior years back to 1990 was $86 million. This means that Baxter would have spent $100 million more in 1997 for raw material, production processes, disposal costs and packaging if no environmentally beneficial actions had been implemented by the company since 1990. Baxter's $16.6 million environmental expenditure was 0.3 per cent of its 1997 sales.*

Ontario Hydro

Ontario Hydro is an electricity distributor and its 1994 revenue was approximately $US8.7 billion. Its supply system includes nuclear, fossil-fuelled and hydro-electric energy stations. Its approach to full-cost accounting explicitly recognises the existence of externalities and therefore it represents a more 'radical' approach than that adopted by Baxter International. According to a case study undertaken by the US Environmental Protection Authority (USEPA, 1996), Ontario Hydro defines Full-Cost Accounting (FCA) as:

> A means by which environmental considerations can be integrated into business decisions. FCA incorporates environmental and other internal costs, with external impacts and costs/benefits of Ontario Hydro's activities on the environment and on human health. In cases where the external impacts cannot be monetised, qualitative evaluations are used.[42]

In quantifying and monetising externalities, Ontario Hydro adopt what they refer to as the 'damage function approach', an approach that uses site-specific data and modelling techniques combined with economic methods to estimate external impacts and costs. According to Bennett and James (1998, p. 315):

> The damage function approach attempts to place a dollar value on the actual impacts to human health and the environment by considering site-specific impacts. Ontario Hydro advocates using market prices to estimate monetary values for those impacts (e.g. crop losses) that are traded in the market. For impacts that are not explicitly traded in markets (e.g. human health and mortality), Ontario Hydro believes that a number of valuation techniques can be used to derive estimates of willingness to pay for (WTP) or willingness to accept (WTA) changes in environmental quality.

In relation to Ontario Hydro's approach to recognising externalities, USEPA (1996) further provides:

> Monetised external impacts are external impacts for which Ontario Hydro has developed monetary value. To date, Ontario Hydro has developed preliminary external cost estimates for the operation of its fossil stations and external cost estimates for fuel extraction through to decommissioning for its nuclear power stations. Ontario Hydro supports the Damage Function Approach, rather than the Cost of Control Approach, to identify, quantify, and where possible monetise, the external impacts of the full life cycle of its activities. This approach first considers site-specific environmental and health

---

42. According to Bennett and James (1998, p. 310), Ontario Hydro has undergone considerable change since the case study was prepared and now appears to place less emphasis on full-cost accounting. However, the details of the case remain of considerable interest.

data; then uses environmental modelling techniques which consider how emissions/effluents etc. are transported, dispersed or chemically transformed in the environment; and then considers what receptors (e.g., people, fish) are affected by these emissions. Finally economic valuation techniques are applied to translate physical impacts into monetary terms.

Table 9.3 provides the results of Ontario Hydro's FCA team's preliminary estimates of the system's average external costs due to the generation of electricity in Ontario using fossil fuels (USEPA, 1996, p. 31). Limited information is available about how Ontario Hydro put a value on mortality and morbidity, and clearly such a calculation would be highly subjective and based on various estimates (and 'guesstimates'). Nevertheless, the case does show how the organisation is trying to place a value on the impacts it causes to parties outside its organisation. This represents a departure from traditional accounting approaches, which tend to ignore social and environmental costs. It should be noted, however, that there have been many critics of approaches such as this that attempt to place a dollar value on human life and health. Do you think that life and health should be valued in dollar terms?

TABLE 9.3 Monetised external impacts of fossil generation in Ontario Hydro

Receptor	Pollutants of concern	Unit values	Monetised impacts $M 1992	¢/kW
Mortality (Statistical deaths)	SO_2, SO_4, O_3, NO_3	$4,725,600	21.40	0.088
Morbidity (Admissions)	SO_2, SO_4, O_3, NO_3, TSP	$44,700	50.83	0.210
Cancer cases	Trace metals	$408,397	9.53	0.039
Crops	O_3	N/A	8.32	0.034
Building materials	SO_2	N/A	5.71	0.024
TOTAL			95.79	0.395

Ontario Hydro advocates FCA as a necessary tool in an organisation's move towards sustainable development. According to USEPA (1996, p. 16), Ontario Hydro believes that FCA can support sustainable development by helping to ensure that internal and external environmental impacts and costs are factored into business decisions. By better understanding the internal and external environmental costs associated with its activities, including quantifying, and where possible monetising, externalities, and incorporating this information into planning and decision making, Ontario Hydro expects to be in a better position to fulfil its sustainable development mission and enhance its competitiveness. In 1993 Ontario Hydro listed the following expected benefits from introducing FCA:

- Provides a powerful incentive to search for the most economic ways of reducing environmental damage.

- Leads to choices that include explicit consideration of the present and future environmental impacts of alternative options.

- Should lead to a more efficient and effective use of resources.

- Should help in 'levelling the playing field' when evaluating demand and supply options (e.g., demand side management, alternative power generation technologies, conventional supply options).

BSO/Origin

BSO/Origin is a Dutch computer consultancy organisation. Over a number of years BSO/Origin provided some *environmental accounts* in which a notional value is placed on the environmental costs imposed upon society.[43] This value is then deducted from profits (with profits being determined using conventional financial accounting methods) to subsequently provide a measure of what is termed 'sustainable operating income'. As stated previously, quantifying environmental effects/impacts in financial terms requires many assumptions. The 1995 environmental accounts of BSO/Origin provide details of how it determines its environmental costs, and some of these details are provided in Exhibit 9.14.

BSO/Origin's *Environmental Result Statement* is reproduced in Table 9.4. The statement shows that 'extracted value' is deducted from operating income (with operating income determined in accord with generally accepted accounting principles) to give 'sustainable operating income'. According to BSO/Origin:

> *Extracted value is treated as a cost factor on top of existing costs categories. It means that environmental loss can be added to the bottom line, where it is subtracted from net income. The resulting figure could be termed sustainable net income. In this BSO/Origin annual report 1995, however, the calculated extracted value will be deducted from the operating income. The resulting management parameter BSO/Origin proposes to call: sustainable operating income.*

What should be appreciated, however, is that while a figure is provided for sustainable operating income, the calculations ignore many of the eco-justice considerations required in the pursuit of sustainability. However, the calculations do consider many externalities that are ignored by conventional financial accounting.

---

43. The year 1995 appears to be the last year that BSO/Origin produced environmental accounts, apparently due to particular changes in staffing. There is an expectation that the practice will be recommenced.

EXHIBIT 9.14 Extract from the 1995 Environmental Accounts of BSO/Origin

Calculation based on actual damage costs

Many methods are in use with just as many results. This report concentrates on two of these methods:

• Prevention costs, and
• Actual damage costs, consisting of damage repair and compensation costs.

For years direct valuation of damage has been striven for, but this has repeatedly proven to be extremely difficult. The prevention costs method was introduced as a short-cut method to establish total environmental damage by approximation. This method is based on hypothetical costs that would have been made to bridge the distance between the actual environmental situation and the desired quality level. Where at all possible BSO/Origin prefers actual damage costs over the prevention costs method.

Taking responsibility for the extracted value embodied in products

In the present environmental result statement, not only environmental loss incurred through BSO/Origin's use of energy is incorporated, but also loss incurred by the generation of energy (as well as by the disposal and treatment of waste). This means that BSO/Origin does not only include its own corporate activities in the valuation, but also those of some of its suppliers. The next step might be to include the disposal or recycling of used personal computers in the environmental result statement. Furthermore BSO/Origin may consider the valuation of environmental loss caused by the introduction and disposal of cars and buildings. Such developments would imply the extension of responsibilities for environmental loss from BSO/Origin's own activities to activities elsewhere in the production chain.

New Shadow Prices

BSO/Origin uses direct or indirect estimates of actual environmental damage for a first approximation of damage repair, and only uses prevention costs when no appropriate studies can be found. BSO/Origin opts for the use of zero environmental risk. Therefore, when literature shows divergent shadow prices for one and the same emission, BSO/Origin chooses the study in which sustainable shadow prices are best expressed.

Review of sustainable shadow prices for the year 1995

Object	NLG/kg	Source
CO_2	0.50	Prognos 1992
CO_2 air traffic	0.70	SNM 1995/Prognos 1992
NO_x	40.00	Ecoplan 1992
NO_x air traffic	70.00	SNM 1995/Ecoplan 1992
SO_2	7.00	T&E 1993
Noise road traffic	50.00/1,000 km	Infras 1992
CO	0.10	UPI 1993
VOC	18.00	Ecoplan 1992
Aerosols	7.00	UPI 1993

(continued)

EXHIBIT 9.14 *(continued)*

The basis for the shadow price of CO_2 emission reduction for air traffic is the Prognos 1992 report. As a preliminary estimation this value is doubled by BSO/Origin in view of the fact that noise disturbance by air-planes is not valued separately. A separate valuation will be included in next year's environmental result statement.

So far little is known about the environmental effects of NO_x emissions by aviation. BSO/Origin believes that the suspicion that emissions at cruising altitude are many times more damaging should be taken seriously. Starting from zero environmental risk, BSO/Origin expects an estimate of twice or three times the normal shadow price for NO_x (NLG 40.00 per kilogram), resulting in NLG 100.00 at cruising altitude to be reasonable. For this year's report an average of NLG 70.00 per kilogram is used for both cruising altitude and the landing and take-off cycles.

TABLE 9.4 BSO/Origin environmental result statement

ENVIRONMENTAL RESULT STATEMENT
(in thousands of Dutch guilders)

Atmospheric emissions	Emission (kg)	Shadow price (NLG/kg)	1995 Total cost (1,000 NLG)	1994* Total cost (1,000 NLG)
Fuel Consumption				
SO_2	932	7	7	
NO_x	1,132	40	45	41
CO_2	1,200 t	500 NLG/t	600	544
Total			652	585
Electricity consumption**				
SO_2	26,623	7	186	104
NO_x	9,692	40	388	344
CO_2	4,089 t	500 NLG/t	2,045	1,901
Total			2,619	2,349
Road traffic				
SO_2	4,046	7	28	20
NO_x	52,306	40	2,092	1,823
VOC	29,852	18	537	
CO	155,851	0.10	16	
CO_2	13,432 t	500 NLG/t	6,716	6,569
Aerosols	3,859	7	27	
Noise	68.8 min km	0.05 NLG/km	3,442	
Total			12,858	8,412

(continued)

TABLE 9.4 *(continued)*

Atmospheric emissions			1995	1994*
	Emission	Shadow price	Total cost	Total cost
	(kg)	(NLG/kg)	(1,000 NLG)	(1,000 NLG)
Air traffic				
SO_2	2,238	7	16	
NO_x***	12,736	70	891	220
VOC	1,910	18	34	
CO	5,749	0.10	1	
CO_2****	2,875 T	700 NLG/t	2,012	599
Total			2,954	819
Waste and waste water			300	257
(extrapolation of foregoing years)				
Extracted value			19,383	12,422
Operating income			18,949	13,557
Extracted value			−19,383	−12,422
Sustainable operating income			−434	1,135

* calculated with sustainable shadow-prices
** electricity now partly generated by wind-energy 'Windfonds'
*** average of cruising and 'landing and take-off' cycle
**** including noise overload

Landcare Ltd

Landcare is a New Zealand government-funded organisation with approximately 400 staff. It conducts research into sustainable management and land systems. The exploratory accounting work being undertaken at Landcare Ltd, and which is ongoing, commenced in 1996 and is being undertaken in conjunction with Rob Gray and Jan Bebbington from the Centre for Social and Environmental Accounting Research (CSEAR) at the University of Dundee.[44] The work builds on approaches to accounting for sustainability that have been in development at CSEAR since the early 1990s (see Gray, 1992; Gray and Bebbington, 1992).

Gray and Bebbington (1992, p. 15) discuss their approach to *full-cost accounting* which incorporates notions of *sustainability*. They state that:

---

44. In 2000, CSEAR moved its operations to the University of Glasgow.

. . . sustainable cost can be defined as the amount an organisation must spend to put the biosphere at the end of the accounting period back into the state (or its equivalent) it was in at the beginning of the accounting period. Such a figure would be a notional one, and disclosed as a charge to a company's profit and loss account. Thus we would be presented with a broad estimate of the extent to which the accounting profits had been generated from a sustainable source . . . our estimates suggest that the sustainable cost calculations would produce the sort of answer which would demonstrate that no Western company had made a profit of any kind in the last 50 years or so.

The project undertaken sought to work out the notional costs that would be incurred if the organisation was to have zero environmental impact.[45] According to Bebbington and Gray (1997, p. 10) the sustainable cost calculation involved two elements:

(i) a consideration of the costs required to ensure that inputs to the organisation have no adverse environmental impacts in their production. These are costs that arise in addition to those already internalised in the most environmentally sound products and services currently available; and

(ii) the costs required to remedy any environmental impacts that arise, even if the organisation's inputs had a zero environmental impact.

To understand the environmental impacts of the organisation it became apparent within the research project that initially an eco-balance must be constructed.[46] Without such a systematic approach to data gathering, many potentially significant environmental impacts may inadvertently be ignored. Other issues that arose were that, as in the case of the Ontario Hydro, many costs pertaining to particular externalities could not be determined. The research into the development of the sustainable cost calculation continues.

Earth Sanctuaries Ltd

An interesting approach adopted within Australia is that adopted by Earth Sanctuaries Ltd, a public company with reported assets (financial) as at 30 June 1999 of $20,916,020. Earth Sanctuaries Ltd aims to ensure the survival of the remaining Australian native flora and fauna within a commercial environment. Within the Earth Sanctuaries Ltd 1997 Annual Report the company provides a balance sheet, profit and loss account and statement of

---

45. While Bebbington and Gray refer to it as a sustainable cost calculation, it ignores eco-justice issues. As Bebbington and Gray (1997, p. 14) state, 'from the outset the sustainable cost calculation was recognised as not being a complete account of sustainability because the justice and equity elements of the concept were not addressed by the proposal'.

46. The concept of an eco-balance 'refers to a product's energy and material inputs and its impact in use and disposal. In other contexts the word is used to denote carrying capacity of an ecological system' (Gray et al., 1993, p. 170).

cash flows, constructed in accordance with traditional financial accounting principles (it must do this as a minimum to comply with the Corporations Law). As in 1996, it also does something different by providing a set of what it calls 'economic' accounts (a *consolidated economic profit and loss account*, and a *consolidated economic balance sheet*).

Within the Earth Sanctuaries Ltd economic reports there are some very interesting approaches to valuation, particularly in relation to wildlife. In relation to wildlife, Earth Sanctuaries uses the following approach to valuation (see page 37 of the 1997 Earth Sanctuaries Annual Report):

- For endangered species which probably will never be sold, we use, as an indicator, the amount spent by tourists coming to Australia as given by the Australian Tourist Commission Annual Report. The value placed on a whole species of mammal is 3% of this figure. The tourism for the year ending June 1996 is $13.1 billion. Therefore a species of endangered mammal is valued at $393 million (denoted by V). If Earth Sanctuaries controls C% of the species, then the value attributed to them (denoted by v) is $v = C$% of V.

- For common species which have bureaucratic restrictions on them that will probably be changed, such as platypus, we give the best conservative estimate of what we could reasonably be expected to recover over the next 5 years.

- For species we are presently able to sell, such as rare fish, we give 50% of the price we can sell them for.

Increases in the value of the vegetation and wildlife of the company are included in Earth Sanctuaries' periodic economic profit.

Obviously the approach adopted by Earth Sanctuaries in 1997 is open to criticism; for example, why 3%? Why is the life of an endangered mammal valued so much more than the life of another mammal? Also, many would argue that wildlife should not be valued in financial terms as this represents a commodification of nature and nature itself should be *above* financial quantification and in fact, above 'accounting' (conversely, this approach would be favoured by numerous environmental economists).[47] But, as with the other approaches we have considered, what Earth Sanctuaries is doing is very interesting and new, and can only help by adding to the debate in this new and exciting area of reporting. Further, as is noted in the Earth Sanctuaries Annual Report, adoption of such an approach enables stakeholders to see how conventional financial accounts grossly understate the environmental contribution of the company (conversely, it might be expected that if a similar approach were adopted by other organisations in other industries, those stakeholders might see how conventional financial accounts grossly overstate the real contribution of a company).

---

47. Chapter 12, pertaining to 'critical theorists', provides some views about how the practice of accounting, including 'full-cost' accounting, causes social and environmental problems.

In 1999, Earth Sanctuaries adopted an alternative method for valuing its native fauna—an approach which was quite different to that used previously. This in itself reflects the lack of an accepted method for valuing resources such as native fauna. Extracts from the 1999 annual report of Earth Sanctuaries are provided in Exhibit 9.15.

EXHIBIT 9.15 Extracts from the 1999 Annual Report of Earth Sanctuaries

Note 1(g) Native Fauna

The 'Earth Sanctuaries' represent protected compounds which are designed to facilitate the propagation of Australian fauna. This financial report recognises the net market value of threatened, rare and endangered Australian fauna controlled but not necessarily owned.

ESL believe there is no active and liquid market for vulnerable Australian fauna. Accordingly, the best indicator of net market value is to estimate the value by comparing similar translocation costs achieved in the market place.

Translocation costs represent a contribution to species conservation, being a recovery of sanctuary costs in re-establishing species population to cater for translocations.

The net market value of the native fauna is determined by species census of the individual species at balance date, multiplied by the current translocation cost.

For the 1998/99 financial year the following translocation costs have been applied:

Threatened:	$1,250 Per animal
Rare:	$2,500 Per animal
Endangered:	$5,000 Per animal

For the purpose of the valuation, the following definitions have been utilised:

Threatened: the species require some form of conservation action due to the species vulnerability.

Rare: the species numbers have declined and it is likely to move into the 'Endangered' category in the near future if causal factors continue.

Endangered: the species is in danger of extinction.

The species census of the native fauna as at 30 June 1999 has been determined from ESL's internal stock recording systems. A review, verifying the methodology applied by management in the species census, was conducted by Professor D. W. Cooper, Professor of Biology, Macquarie University.

Significant assumptions made in determining the net market value of the native fauna are:

(a) publications on Australia's mammals have been used to establish the threatened, rare and endangered classifications;

(b) translocation prices have been set at conservative levels by the Board, having taken into account documented relocation and translocation cost experienced by the group and general translocations documented in the media and other publications.

(continued)

EXHIBIT 9.15 (continued)

Note 14 Native Fauna outlines the various native species included in the sanctuary valuations and stock numbers as at balance date.

Note 1(h) Method chosen to determine the net increment in the net market values of native fauna recognised as revenue, and the determination of the net market value of the fauna translocated during the financial year recognised as revenue.
The net increment in net market value of the native fauna recognised as revenue, $844,750, is determined as the difference between the total net market values of the native fauna recognised as at the beginning of the financial year and the total net market values of the native fauna recognised as at the end of the financial year. Any costs incurred in properly managed translocations of native fauna are recognised as expenses when incurred and are reimbursed from the recipient of the native fauna. Therefore, those costs are not included in the determination of the net increment in the net market values.

14. NATIVE FAUNA (THREATENED/RARE/ENDANGERED)
The following reflects the species of Australian Natives kept at the sanctuaries, their current vulnerability classification and species census details. Net Market Values have been calculated in accordance with Note 1(g).

Species	Status	Number 1999	Number 1998	Net Market Value 1999	Net Market Value 1998
Southern Hairy Nosed Wombat	Threatened	100	100	125,000	125,000
Rufous Bettong	Threatened	97	86	121,250	107,500
Long-nosed Potoroo	Threatened	90	85	112,500	106,250
Southern Brown Bandicoot	Threatened	85	70	106,250	87,500
Tammar Wallaby	Threatened	42	36	52,500	45,000
Eastern Quoll	Threatened	36	18	45,000	22,500
Cream-striped Red-Necked Pademelon	Rare	45	35	112,500	87,500
Yellow-footed Rock-wallaby	Rare	120	120	300,000	300,000
Woylie	Endangered	341	297	1,705,000	1,485,000
Numbat	Endangered	130	61	650,000	305,000
Bilby	Endangered	38	18	190,000	90,000
Stick Nest Rat	Endangered	33	–	165,000	–
Bridled Nailtail Wallaby	Endangered	20	–	100,000	–
Boodie	Endangered	12	7	60,000	35,000
TOTAL		1,189	933	3,845,000	2,796,250

Other species, including the platypus, will not be included until acceptable methods are available for determining the number of these species.

As we would realise from reading the above material, there is still much work to be done in developing systems of accounting that can place a value on the social and environmental costs generated as a result of an entity's operations. Clearly, no one has the 'right' answer to the issue, and experimentation continues. Moves towards monetising the social and environmental costs and benefits of an entity will require detailed life-cycle analysis of an organisation's production and operations. But this in itself creates numerous issues. For example, should we adopt a discrete entity approach (as in conventional financial accounting) when considering an entity's social and environmental impacts? Arguably, individual corporate environmental management systems (and the related corporate reports) would probably not be very useful in assessing the sustainability of particular eco-systems. As such, governments need to assess changes at the eco-system level and continue to undertake necessary research in the area. As Owen (1996, p. 28) states:

> Broad eco-based methodologies require an understanding of cumulative environmental change, and particularly a recognition of the fact that changes may be non-linear, discontinuous, synergistic and, most importantly, beyond certain thresholds may well be irreversible. Therefore, measuring at the level of the individual company, as in our conventional accounting framework, may be insufficient. For many natural resources the key variable is not the cumulative impact of one firm but that of all firms using the resource. Recognition of this fact gives rise to a questioning of the validity of project- or firm-based assessments of environmental impact and suggests the need for research into integrating firm-based information with community or regionally developed ecological information systems.

Chapter summary

This chapter has reviewed various issues associated with corporate social and environmental reporting. Since around the early 1990s many organisations throughout the world have been providing information about their environmental performance. More recently, many organisations have commenced producing information about their social performance. These developments in reporting are probably a reflection of changing community expectations about the performance and responsibilities of business.

When a firm voluntarily discloses information publicly about its social and environmental performance this implies that the managers are acknowledging that they are accountable to a broad group of stakeholders in relation to not only their financial performance, but also their social and environmental performance. However, as the chapter indicates, not all people consider that managers have any social responsibilities to a broad group of stakeholders. Some researchers believe that the prime responsibility is to shareholders alone. However, this narrow perspective of corporate responsibility seems to be becoming less widely accepted.

This chapter explained how concerns associated with sustainability (which relates to economic, social and environmental performance issues) have increased since the early 1990s and the evolution of corporate social and environmental performance reporting appears to be related to these concerns. Reflecting the lack of an accepted methodology for providing social and environmental information, this chapter demonstrated that there are various approaches to providing social and environmental information. The chapter has also demonstrated that conventional financial accounting often ignores various social and environmental performance issues because of its focus on transactions and events that directly impact on the economic resources of the entity. Various experimental approaches to full-cost accounting were explored, a number of which attempt to put a cost on the social and environmental externalities created by business entities.

This chapter also reviewed the practice of social accounting and social auditing. Social accounting is explained as an approach to accounting that provides information about the organisation's impact on people both inside and outside it, while social auditing is defined as a process of assessing an organisation's performance in relation to society's requirements and expectations. Evidence shows that the practice of social accounting and social auditing, which was widely promoted in the 1970s, has re-emerged as a major issue in corporate accountability and reporting.

References

Bebbington, J., Gray, R., 'An Account of Sustainability: Failure, Success and Reconceptualisation', Working Paper, Centre for Social and Environmental Accounting Research, University of Dundee, 1997.

Bennett, M., James, P., 'Environment-related Management Accounting in North America and its implications for UK companies', *Environmental Accounting and Sustainable Development—The Final Report*, Limperg Institute, Amsterdam, pp. 41–67, 1996.

Bennett, M., James, P., *The Green Bottom Line: Environmental Accounting for Management—Current Practice and Future Trends*, Greenleaf Publishing, 1998.

Benston, G.J. 'Accounting and Corporate Accountability', *Accounting Organizations and Society*, Vol. 6, No. 2, pp. 87–105, 1982.

Clarkson, M., 'A Stakeholder Framework for Analyzing and Evaluating Corporate Social Performance', *Academy of Management Review*, Vol. 20, No. 1, pp. 92–118, 1995.

Collison, D., *Propaganda, Accounting and Finance: An Exploration*, Dundee Discussion Papers, Department of Accountancy and Business Finance, University of Dundee, 1998.

Deegan, C., 'A Review of Mandated Environmental Reporting Requirements for Australian Corporations together with an Analysis of Contemporary Australian and Overseas Environmental Reporting Practices', *Environmental and Planning Law Journal*, Vol. 13, No. 2, pp 120–32, April 1996.

Deegan, C., Rankin, M., 'Do Australian Companies Report Environmental News Objectively? An Analysis of Environmental Disclosures by Firms Prosecuted Successfully by the Environmental Protection Authority', *Accounting, Auditing and Accountability Journal*, Vol. 9, No. 2, pp. 52–69, 1996.

Deloitte and Touche (Denmark), *Assessor's Manual for the Analysis and Evaluation of Corporate Environmental Reporting*, 1996.

Donaldson, T., *Corporations and Morality*, Prentice-Hall, Englewood Cliffs, 1982.

Elkington, J., *Cannibals with Forks: The Triple Bottom Line of 21st Century Business*, Capstone, Oxford, 1997.

Environment Australia, *Public Environmental Reporting: An Australian Approach*, Environment Australia, Canberra, 2000.

Environmental Accounting and Auditing Reporter ('First standard for building corporate accountability and trust'), Vol. 5, No. 1, p. 2, January 2000.

Environmental Protection Authority (NSW), *Corporate Environmental Reporting: Why and How?*, EPA (NSW), Sydney, 1997.

European Commission, *Towards Sustainability: A Community Programme of Policy and Action in Relation to the Environment and Sustainable Development*, Brussels, 1992.

European Federation of Accountants (FEE), *FEE Discussion Paper Towards a Generally Accepted Framework for Environmental Reporting*, FEE, Brussels, 1999.

European Union, *Fifth Action Programme*, Com (92) 23 final—Vol. I–III, Brussels, 1992.

Freeman, R., *Strategic Management: A Stakeholder Approach*, Pitman, Marshall, MA, 1984.

Friedman, M., *Capitalism and Freedom*, University of Chicago Press, Chicago, 1962.

Global Environmental Management Initiative, *Environment Reporting in a Total Quality Management Framework*, GEMI, Washington, 1994.

Global Reporting Initiative, *Sustainability Reporting Guidelines: Exposure Draft for Public Comment and Testing*, GRI, London, March 1999.

Gray, R., 'Accounting and Environmentalism: An Exploration of the Challenge of Gently Accounting for Accountability, Transparency and Sustainability', *Accounting Organizations and Society*, Vol. 17, No. 5, pp. 399–425, 1992.

Gray, R, Owen, D., Adams, C., *Accounting and Accountability: Changes and Challenges in Corporate and Social Reporting*, Prentice-Hall, London, 1996.

Gray, R., Bebbington, J., 'Can the Grey Men Go Green?', Discussion Paper, Centre for Social and Environmental Accounting Research, University of Dundee, 1992.

Gray, R., Bebbington, J., Collison, D., Kouhy, R., Lyon, B., Reid, C., Russell, A., Stevenson, L., *The Valuation of Assets and Liabilities: Environmental Law and the Impact of the Environmental Agenda for Business*, Institute of Chartered Accountants in Scotland, Edinburgh, 1998.

Gray, R., Bebbington, J., Walters, D., *Accounting for the Environment*, Paul Chapman, London, 1993.

Gray, R., Collison, D., Bebbington, J., 'Environmental and Social Accounting and Reporting', in *Financial Reporting Today: Current and Emerging Issues*, ICAEW, London, 1998.

Institute of Chartered Accountants in England and Wales, *The Corporate Report*, ICAEW, London, 1975.

Institute of Social and Ethical AccountAbility, *Towards Standards in Social and Ethical Accounting, Auditing and Reporting—Consultation Draft*, ISEA, London, February 1999.

Lindblom, C.K., 'The Implications of Organisational Legitimacy for Corporate Social Performance and Disclosure', Paper presented at the Critical Perspectives on Accounting Conference, New York, 1994.

Mathews, M.R., *Socially Responsible Accounting*, Chapman and Hall, London, 1993.

Owen, D., 'A Critical Perspective on the Development of European Corporate Environmental Accounting and Reporting', *Environmental Accounting and Sustainable Development—The Final Report*, Limperg Institute, Amsterdam, pp. 21–31, 1996.

Porritt, J., 'Directions', *Green Futures*, p. 21, March/April 1999.

Public Environmental Reporting Initiative, *The PERI Guidelines*, PERI, USA, 1992.

Ramanathan, K.V., 'Towards a Theory of Corporate Social Accounting', *The Accounting Review*, Vol. 51, No. 3, pp. 516–28, 1976.

Stone, D., 'No Longer at the End of the Pipe, but Still a Long Way from Sustainability: A Look at Management Accounting for the Environment and Sustainable Development in the United States', *Accounting Forum*, Vol. 19, No. 2/3, pp. 95–110, 1995.

United Nations Environment Programme (and SustainAbility), *Engaging Stakeholders—Second International Progress Report on Company Environmental Reporting*, London, 1996.

United States Environmental Protection Authority, *Environmental Accounting Case Studies: Full Cost Accounting for Decision Making at Ontario Hydro*, USEPA, Washington, 1996.

World Commission on Environment and Development, *Our Common Future*, (The Brundtland Report), Oxford University Press, 1987.

World Council for the Environment (now part of WBCSD), *Environmental Reporting—a Manager's Guide*, 1994.

World Wide Fund For Nature (WWF), *Mining Environmental Report Scorecard*, WWF Melbourne, May 1999.

Wright, M., 'Do the Right Thing', *Green Futures*, pp. 24–8, March/April 1999.

Questions

9.1 What has the environment to do with accounting?

9.2 What is accountability and what is its relationship to:

(a) accounting?

(b) an organisation's responsibilities?

9.3 What do the terms eco-efficiency and eco-justice refer to?

9.4 What is sustainable development?

9.5 What is the relationship between eco-efficiency, eco-justice and sustainable development?

9.6 Are 'economic rationality' (as defined by economists) and 'sustainability' mutually inconsistent?

9.7 What is an externality, and why do financial accounting practices typically ignore externalities?

9.8 What is a social audit and why would a profit-seeking entity bother with one?

9.9 Why do you think the European Union called for a 'redefinition of accounting concepts, rules, conventions and methodology so as to ensure that the consumption and use of environmental resources are accounted for as part of the full cost of production and reflected in market prices' (European Commission, 1992, Vol. II, Section 7.4, p. 67)?

9.10 What is triple bottom line reporting, and what has it to do with sustainable development?

9.11 Of what relevance to the accounting profession is sustainable development?

9.12 Why do you think that the accounting profession has generally not released any accounting standards pertaining to the disclosure of environmental information?

9.13 Consider Exhibit 9.16 and answer the following questions:

(a) What do you think the author means when he says that 'Corporate social responsibility is a subject starting to be discussed in the boardrooms. It is too soon to be definitive, but it is possible that this represents the beginnings of a step beyond what has become known as economic rationalism'?

(b) It is noted that 'Business has traditionally ignored social issues, such as the provision of health, education and welfare. These have been matters for the government and the community. Business has been more comfortable tackling issues such as monetary policy, market access and the provision of infrastructure'. Do you agree with this perspective, and if this is no longer the case, what might have caused such a change in business focus?

(c) Linked to part (b), why will 'companies have to spend a lot more time and energy developing investments in the social infrastructure in a form that can be justified to their shareholders?' Is it appropriate to worry about justifying actions to shareholders, and if so, to shareholders alone?

(d) Why do you think the Business Council of Australia recently made the alleviation of unemployment the focus for its 'New Directions' task force?

EXHIBIT 9.16 A view that sound macro-economics is not enough to secure prosperity

Social concern and economic rationalism

David Uren

In a speech last month, Malaysia's Prime Minister, Mahathir Mohamad, pondered on why it was that no Muslim nation was a force of consequence in the international arena.

He said Muslim nations had been incapable of making progress to match that of advanced nations. 'While we are in the 15th century, the rest of the world seems to be in the 20th century.'

Mahathir noted that the inability to manage democracy had left Muslim countries without adequate governance and stability to meet the challenges of globalisation. 'The concepts of democratic governments have been largely mishandled by us,' he said.

Although Mahathir shows continuing difficulty with the concept of democracy, his acknowledgment of the role of government is an important component of an emerging global consensus.

The Asian crisis has contributed to a profound shift in thinking about the underpinning of growth and prosperity. Many of the Asian countries affected by the crisis had sound public finances and good savings rates. Some had respectable international trade accounts.

(continued)

EXHIBIT 9.16 *(continued)*

It is now accepted that it is not enough to get the macroeconomic settings right. The social and institutional framework is even more important. This fundamental point is gaining acceptance in developing and developed worlds. The president of the World Bank, Jim Wolfensohn, has been forceful in pressing the issue. In a speech to a conference in Tokyo last month, he set out what he saw as the conditions for economic development. He started with strong public institutions: 'If you do not have good governance and you have corruption, your financial architecture will not save you.'

He underlined the importance of a strong legal and justice system to allow a business sector to flourish and to protect a nation's citizens. And he spoke of the importance of a well-regulated financial superstructure, with supervision of banks and capital markets, and strong corporate governance and accounting systems. 'No country is going to have a sound financial system without company accounts that make sense, rules of company behaviour and disclosure that are applied, legal systems and bankruptcy procedures that work.'

Then he turned to the need for good health and education systems, a strategy to protect the environment, strategies for managing urban pressures and for ensuring cultural continuity. 'If our goal is equitable development and peace, what we must have learned recently is that stability also requires action to protect the most vulnerable.' This involves safety nets for the disadvantaged.

'I name all these elements not to beat a path away from our engaging debate on the financial architecture which we surely must attend to. I name them because I believe they should be an integral part of our debate as we seek solutions.' Many of the pre-conditions named by Wolfensohn are taken for granted in developed economies. Business executives do not mop their brow and thank the heavens for the Australian Securities and Investments Commission. Nor have they given great attention to the problems of single mothers.

Business has traditionally ignored social issues, such as the provision of health, education and welfare. These have been matters for the government and the community. Business has been more comfortable tackling issues such as monetary policy, market access and the provision of infrastructure.

There are signs that this is changing. The Business Council of Australia, for example, has made the alleviation of unemployment the focus for its 'New Directions' task force. Prime Minister John Howard has made increasing the level and awareness of corporate philanthropy a goal for his current term of office.

Corporate social responsibility is a subject starting to be discussed in the boardrooms. It is too soon to be definitive, but it is possible that this represents the beginnings of a step beyond what has become known as economic rationalism. It is not that the discipline of economics is wrong about the importance of balanced budgets, saving and monetary stability. They are all necessary components of a sound business environment.

However, they are not sufficient. Companies have to spend a lot more time and energy developing investments in the social infrastructure in a form that can be justified to their shareholders.

The Weekend Australian, **17 April 1999, p. 52.**

9.14 Collison (1998, p. 7) states that: 'Attention to the interests of shareholders above all other groups is implicit in much of what is taught to accounting and finance students. The very construction of a profit and loss account is a continual, and usually unstated, reminder that the interests of only one group of stakeholders should be maximised. Indeed it may be very difficult for accounting and finance students to even conceive of another way in which affairs could be ordered—even at the algebraic level, let alone the moral.'

(a) Do you agree or disagree with Collison, and why?

(b) If 'profit' maximisation is biased towards maximising the interests of only one stakeholder group, would you expect that over time there will be less emphasis on profits, and more emphasis on other performance indicators? Why? What might be some of the alternative measures of performance?

(c) Would Collison's comments provide a justification for moves towards profit measures that incorporate 'full costs' (that is, that consider the externalities of business)?

9.15 How would the following theories explain corporate social responsibility reporting:

(a) Positive Accounting Theory?

(b) Legitimacy Theory?

(c) Stakeholder Theory?

9.16 In publicly released reports a number of organisations are referring to their 'public licence to operate'. What do you think they mean by this, and is there a theoretical perspective that can explain what this term means?

9.17 Consider how the concept of sustainable development, as it applies to business entities, compares to the accountant's notion of a 'going concern'. Do you believe that they are similar, or are they quite different?

9.18 Read Exhibit 9.17 and answer the following questions:

After considering the implications (externalities) associated with the use of asbestos manufactured by James Hardie, what would be the implications for James Hardie's reported results if:

(a) conventional financial accounting practices were employed?

(b) triple bottom line reporting was employed?

(c) full cost accounting was employed?

9.19 In 1995, the Institute of Chartered Accountants in Australia (ICAA) established an Environmental Accounting Task Force (later renamed the Triple Bottom Line Issues Group). The Task Force has released a number of documents, one being *The Impact of Environmental Matters on the Accountancy Profession* (released in January 1998). Within this document the ICAA Environmental Accounting Task Force raised a number of environmental reporting issues that they believed require consideration. These included:

EXHIBIT 9.17 **A view on safety versus profit**

Hardie put profit before safety, asbestos hearing told

Claire Harvey

Asbestos paid Peter Russell's wages when he was safety officer at cement manufacturer James Hardie during the 1960s.

But he could not shake off his terrible fears about the health risks posed by the potentially fatal fibre, telling senior company officials they had a moral duty to do something about it.

His warnings were brushed off by executives whose only concern was 'covering their backside', a tearful Mr Russell yesterday told the Dust Diseases Tribunal, which is hearing an $800,000-plus negligence action against James Hardie & Company.

Mr Russell, 70, is giving evidence for the first time on how he resigned in frustration after unsuccessfully urging James Hardie to alert the carpenters and builders who used its products.

Canberra carpenter Peter Thurbon, who is not expected to live to his next birthday, claims he contracted the lung cancer mesothelioma from asbestos dust in cement sheeting manufactured by James Hardie.

Mr Thurbon, 51, wore no protective gear when he used power saws to cut the sheets, and would be white with asbestos dust from head to toe, his lawyer, Jack Rush QC, told the tribunal.

'James Hardie knew of the dangers of exposure to asbestos,' Mr Rush said, adding that Mr Thurbon never saw any warnings on the products.

'The prime concern of James Hardie throughout this period of time was the bottom line and, as far as it was concerned, its trading performance and its profits were more important than a warning.'

Mr Russell, who was James Hardie Industries' senior safety officer from 1961 to 1964, said yesterday he told company doctor Terry McCullough that asbestos was too dangerous to use. 'Don't forget, asbestos pays yours and my salary,' Dr McCullough allegedly responded.

'For dusty jobs, James Hardie should employ older men, because the older men will not live long enough for cancer to develop,' Dr McCullough said in a 1966 memorandum quoted to the tribunal by Mr Rush.

Mr Russell said yesterday that in 1966 he told another executive he wanted to discuss his fears with experts at Sydney University's Department of Tropical Medicine.

'He told me that it was not a problem to talk to the people at the Department of Tropical Medicine as they valued the annual grant James Hardie gave the department each year,' he told the tribunal.

'They covered their backsides and intended to tough it out in spite of what I was endeavouring to warn them of.'
The Australian, 18 June 1999, p. 3.

(a) Are standards or guidelines needed to assist companies to meet the information needs of stakeholders in respect of the disclosure of environmental information?

(b) Do environmental impacts, whether quantifiable in monetary terms or not, warrant some form of disclosure to the extent that the environmental implications are deemed 'significant', rather than material within the meaning of accounting standards?

(c) Does the provision of environmental performance information and advising on control aspects of environmental management systems fall within the core skills of accountants?

(d) Are the definitions of 'assets' and 'liabilities' in SAC 4 appropriate to environmental accounting? If not, how should they be expanded? Specifically: should SAC 4's definition of an asset based on 'control' apply?; should SAC 4 be amended to specifically recognise the environment as an entity, thereby allowing liabilities to be recognised without the intervention of a third party?

(e) Is the concept of materiality relevant to environmental reports?

(f) Should reporting of environmental issues according to traditional accounting concepts be progressed while the difficulties of monetary measurement are researched further?

(g) Should general or industry specific approaches be adopted to advance issues associated with environmental performance evaluation, reporting and auditing?

Required: Attempt to provide your own views on the above issues.

Chapter 10

Reactions of capital markets to financial reporting

Learning objectives

Upon completing this chapter readers should:

- understand the role of capital market research in assessing the information content of accounting disclosures;

- understand the assumptions of market efficiency adopted in capital market research;

- understand the difference between capital market research that looks at the *information content* of accounting disclosures, and capital market research that uses share price data as a *benchmark* for evaluating accounting disclosures;

- be able to explain why unexpected accounting earnings and abnormal share price returns are expected to be related;

- be able to outline the major results of capital market research into financial accounting and disclosure.

Opening issues

Assume that there are five companies from the same industry with the same balance date, 31 December. All five companies are to make earnings announcements for the financial year (the announcements being made in February), but the earnings announcements are spread over two weeks, with no two companies announcing their earnings on the same date.

(a) Would you expect the earnings announcements made by each company to impact on their share prices, and if so, why?

(b) If it is found that the share prices of some entities change more around the date of the earnings announcement than others, what might have caused this price–effect differential?

(c) Would you expect the share prices of larger companies, or smaller companies, to be relatively more impacted by an earnings announcement?

(d) Once the first company in the sample of five makes its earnings announcement, would you expect this announcement to impact on the prices of shares in the other four companies? Why?

Introduction

In some of the previous chapters we have considered various normative prescriptions pertaining to how accounting *should* be undertaken. For example, Chapter 4 discussed theories that had been developed to prescribe how accounting *should* be undertaken in times of rising prices (for example, General Price Level Accounting, Current Cost Accounting, and Continuously Contemporary Accounting). Chapter 5 considered the role of Conceptual Frameworks in providing prescription (such frameworks can tell us what the objective of accounting is; what qualitative characteristics accounting information *should* possess; how elements of accounting *should* be defined and recognised; and how assets and liabilities *should* be measured). Chapter 9 provided an insight into various approaches adopted to disclose information about an organisation's social and environmental performance (which has indeed become an area of accounting research that has grown rapidly in recent years).

While the abovementioned chapters provided a great deal of prescription, they tended not to provide any theoretical arguments as to the *motivations* for managers to make the disclosures. This void was filled by Chapters 7 and 8 which provided different theoretical perspectives about what drove management to make the disclosures. Chapter 7 discussed Positive Accounting Theory and it indicated that where management had a choice in selecting a particular approach to accounting, both *efficiency* arguments and *opportunistic* arguments could be advanced to explain and predict management's accounting choices. Chapter 8 provided alternative explanations of management's behaviour. It showed that the choice of a particular accounting method might be made to restore the *legitimacy* of an organisation (from Legitimacy Theory), or because such disclosure was necessary to retain the support of powerful stakeholders (from Stakeholder Theory).

While the above material provided a perspective of what motivates managers to provide particular accounting information, the material did not consider the further issue of how individuals, or groups of individuals in aggregate, react to accounting disclosures. This chapter and Chapter 11 provide material that addresses this issue.

This chapter and Chapter 11 examine the impact of financial accounting and disclosure decisions on the users of financial reports. Specifically, we look at research that focuses on the impact of alternative accounting and disclosure choices on the investment decisions of financial statement users such as sharemarket investors, financial analysts, bank lending officers, and auditors.

Reported profit depends on many financial accounting decisions. Managers have much scope in selecting between alternative accounting methods and accounting assumptions. For example, they will choose between expensing or capitalising particular costs; they will choose between alternative accounting methods such as straight-line or reducing balance depreciation; they will exercise discretion in relation to accounting estimates such as the useful life of assets to be depreciated; and so on. Further, decisions must be made in relation to how much information to disclose, the medium for disclosure, and, in some circumstances, whether to recognise particular items in the financial statements, or merely disclose them in the footnotes to the statements.

Financial reporting decisions impact on the information provided to users of financial reports. This in turn may have implications for the decisions that users make. There are two ways to assess the impacts of financial reporting decisions: (a) determine the impact of the information on the decisions of individual information users (behavioural research), and (b) determine what impact the release of information has on share price (capital market research). In this chapter we consider capital market research (which considers reactions at an *aggregate* or *market* level). In Chapter 11 we review behavioural research undertaken at the *individual* level.

An overview of capital market research

Capital market research explores the role of accounting and other financial information in equity markets. This type of research involves examining statistical relations between financial information, and share prices or returns. Reactions of investors are evidenced by their capital market transactions. Favourable reactions to information are presumed to be evidenced by a price increase in the particular security, whereas unfavourable reactions to information are evidenced by a price decrease. No price change around the time of the release of information implies no reaction to the information (the release does not provide anything that is *new*).

Conclusions about the market's reaction to particular information releases or events are generally based on evidence from a large number of companies, with data spanning several years. This type of research is often used to examine equity market reactions to announcements of company information, and to assess the relevance of alternative accounting and disclosure choices for investors. If security prices change around the time of the release of particular information, and assuming that the information and not some other event caused the price change, then it is considered that the information was relevant and useful for investment decision making.

In contrast to behavioural research (considered in Chapter 11) which analyses *individual* responses to financial reporting, capital market research assesses the *aggregate* effect of financial reporting, particularly the reporting of accounting earnings, on investors. By analysing share price reactions to financial information releases, the sum of individual investor decisions is captured in aggregate. But when considering such research, a possible question that comes to mind is why have so many research studies been undertaken that focus on the market's response to accounting earnings announcements? Brown (1994, p. 24) provides one answer to this issue. He argues:

> *Four reasons are that, according to the Financial Accounting Standards Board, information about earnings and its components is the primary purpose of financial reporting; earnings are oriented towards the interests of shareholders who are an important group of financial statement users; earnings is the number most analysed and forecast by security analysts; and reliable data on earnings were readily available.*

Another important difference between capital market and behavioural research is that capital market research considers only investors, while behavioural research is often used to examine decision making by other types of financial statement users such as bank managers, loan officers, or auditors.

Capital market research relies on the underlying assumption that equity markets are efficient. Market efficiency is defined in accordance with the Efficient Market Hypothesis (EMH) as a market that adjusts rapidly to fully impound information into share prices when the information is released (Fama et al., 1969). Capital market research in accounting assumes that equity markets are *semi-strong form efficient*. That is, that all publicly available information, including that available in financial statements and other financial disclosures, is rapidly and fully impounded into share prices in an unbiased manner as it is released. Relevant information is not ignored by the market.

Semi-strong-form efficiency is the most relevant for capital market research in accounting, since it relates to the use of *publicly available* information. Other hypotheses about market efficiency are the *weak-form efficiency* perspective, and the *strong-form efficiency* perspective. The *weak form* of market efficiency assumes that existing security prices simply reflect information about past prices and trading volumes. The *strong form* of market efficiency assumes that security prices, on average, reflect all information known to anyone at that point in time (including information not publicly available). According to Watts and Zimmerman (1986, p. 19) the available evidence is generally consistent with the semi-strong form of the EMH.[1]

The view that markets are efficient does not imply that share prices will always provide an accurate prediction of the value of future cash flows. Market predictions are sometimes proved in hindsight to be wrong, thus necessitating subsequent adjustments. As Hendriksen and Van Breda (1992, p. 177) state:

> It needs to be stressed that market efficiency does not imply clairvoyance on the part of the market. All it implies is that the market reflects the best guesses of all its participants, based on the knowledge available at the time. New information appears all the time that proves the market was incorrect. In fact, by definition, the market will not react until it learns something that it did not know the day before. One cannot prove the market inefficient, therefore, by looking back, using the benefits of hindsight and pointing to places where the market was incorrect. Market efficiency simply asserts that prices are appropriately set based on current knowledge; practical evidence shows that with hindsight the market is always incorrect.

The assumption of market efficiency is central to capital market research. But why is the assumption of information efficiency so important for capital market research in accounting? Simply put, unless such an assumption of efficiency is accepted, it is hard to justify efforts to link security price movements to information releases. A great deal of capital market research considers the relationship between share prices and information releases. The reason for looking at this relationship is that share prices in an efficient market are deemed to be based on expectations about future earnings. If particular information leads to a price change, then the assumption is that the information was *useful* and caused investors to revise their expectations about the future earnings of the organisation in question. That is, share prices and returns are used as benchmarks against which the usefulness of financial information is assessed. If we do not assume market efficiency, then there is an inability to explain how or why share prices change around the date of information releases. If share markets are not semi-strong-form efficient, they do not provide accurate benchmarks against which to assess alternative financial reporting choices. Overall, market inefficiency would render capital market research results to be at best less convincing, and at worst extremely unreliable, depending on the extent of inefficiency present.

Assumptions about market efficiency in turn have implications for accounting. If markets are efficient, they will use information from various sources when predicting future earnings, and hence when determining current share prices. If accounting information does not impact on share prices then, assuming semi-strong-form efficiency, it would be deemed not

---

1. Brown (1994, p. 14) notes that 'few if any investors would seriously accept the *strong form*, although many would accept the *semi-strong form* as their working hypothesis'.

to provide any information over and above that currently available. At the extreme, accounting's survival would be threatened.[2]

A share price reaction to the release of financial information is taken to indicate that the announcement has 'information content', while a high association between financial information and share prices or returns over an extended period of time indicates that the information provided by the accounting system reflects information that is being used by the capital market (and this information will come from a multitude of sources). Each of these roles for accounting information in equity markets is explored in the following sections. While the 'information content' of many types of financial information can be assessed using capital market research, the bulk of this work has focused on earnings as the primary measure of the financial accounting system. For example, one issue that has been the subject of many research papers is whether earnings announcements cause a movement in share price. This focus is reflected in the following discussion.

The information content of earnings

Many research papers have investigated capital market reactions to earnings announcements. That is, when a company announces its earnings for the year (or half-year), what is the impact, if any, on its share price? Assuming that capital markets are semi-strong-form efficient (they react swiftly and in an unbiased manner to *publicly available* information), a movement in share price is considered to indicate that the new information in the public earnings announcement has been incorporated into the security's price through the activities of investors in the market. It was *useful* in reassessing the future cash flows of the entity.

A number of studies have shown information about earnings to be linked to changes in the price of securities. But, why would we expect accounting earnings and share prices to be related? Modern finance theory proposes that share price can be determined as the sum of expected future cash flows from dividends, discounted to their present value using a rate of return commensurate with the company's level of risk. Further, dividends are a function of accounting earnings, since they can generally only be paid out of past and current earnings. It follows therefore that if cash flows are related to (a function of) accounting earnings, then the price of a share in company i, which we can denote as (P_i), can be viewed as the sum of expected future earnings per share ($\overline{E}$), discounted to their present value using a risk-adjusted discount rate (k_i).[3] That is, for company i today:

---

2. Once we relax notions of efficiency, and once we consider broader issues about corporate accountability to stakeholders other than investors, threats to accounting's survival tend to dissipate.

3. The risk-adjusted discount rate chosen should be commensurate with the level of uncertainty associated with the expected earnings stream.

$$P_i = \sum_{t=1}^{\infty} \overline{E}_t / (1 + k_i)^t \qquad \text{(Equation 1)}$$

Equation 1 shows that a relation exists between share price and expected future earnings. In general, companies with higher expected future earnings will have higher share prices. These expectations are formed, at least in part, on the basis of historical earnings for the company. However, all currently available information (for example, media releases, analysts' reports, production statistics, market surveys, etc.) are considered when predicting future earnings. Any revisions to expectations about future earnings per share, including those resulting from new information contained in announcements of current earnings, will be reflected in a change in share price.

Revisions to expectations about future earnings per share will result only from *new* information, since under the maintained assumption of a semi-strong-form-efficient market, price is assumed to already reflect all *publicly known* information, including expectations about current earnings. Therefore, only the unexpected component of current earnings announcements constitutes new information. That is, unexpected earnings, rather than total earnings, are expected to be associated with a change in share price. For example, if CMR Company announces annual earnings of $11 million when only $10.5 million was expected, unexpected earnings are equal to $0.5 million. Any share price reaction will be to these unexpected earnings rather than to total annual earnings of $11 million, since investors already anticipated most of this.

Such a change in share price results in a return to investors (R_{it}), since returns are a function of capital gains or losses, in addition to dividends received (D_{it}). Thus, for an investment in firm i for one holding period $(t - 1 \text{ to } t)$ the return would be:[4]

$$R_{it} = \frac{(P_{it} - P_{it-1}) + D_{it}}{P_{it-1}} \qquad \text{(Equation 2)}$$

The length of time over which returns are calculated (the return period) depends on the particular research focus, but is generally not less than one day, or longer than one year. In return periods where no dividend is paid, returns can simply be calculated as a percentage change in share price. This is generally the case when returns are calculated on a daily basis. For example, if CMR Company's share price moved from $5.42 to $5.56 during the day when earnings were announced, the daily return (R_{CMR}) is equal to ($5.56 − $5.42)/$5.42 or 2.6%.

Given that returns are a function of changes in share prices (from Equation 2), and share price can be expressed as a function of expected future earnings (from Equation 1), returns are related to changes in expected future

---

4. Where price at the end of the holding period (P_{it}) is adjusted for any capitalisation changes such as rights issues, or bonus issues.

earnings. This relation is often referred to as the earnings/return relation. For CMR Company, the unexpected announcement of an additional $0.5 million of earnings has resulted in a return to investors of approximately 2.6%, as indicated in the above calculation. This positive return indicates that investors expect future earnings to be higher than originally expected.

Of course, not all share returns are due to investors trading on information about individual companies. Share prices tend to change on a daily basis due to things that affect the whole market, or sectors of it. We can call these 'systematic changes'. For example, the Australian capital market tends to follow the US market, and daily returns for individual companies largely reflect this.

The market model (see Fama, 1976, for details about its early development), which is derived from the Capital Asset Pricing Model (CAPM), is used to separate out firm-specific share price movements from market-wide movements.[5] The CAPM explains how a market should decide the appropriate return on a share, given its riskiness. It predicts a linear relationship between expected returns and systematic risk, where systematic risk is the riskiness of an asset when it is held as part of a thoroughly diversified portfolio. Systematic risk is the non-diversifiable or unavoidable risk that investors are compensated for through increased returns. The market model is expressed as:

$$R_{it} = \alpha_{it} + \beta_{it}R_{mt} + \mu_{it} \qquad \text{(Equation 3)}$$

where R_{it} is the return for company i during period t, calculated in accordance with Equation 2; R_{mt} is the return for the entire market during period t (as would be approximated by the average return generated from a very large diversified portfolio of securities); and β_{it} is company i's level of systematic risk, which indicates how sensitive the returns of firm i's securities are, relative to market-wide (systematic) movements.[6] α_{it} is a constant specific to firm i, while μ_{it} is an error term that provides an indication of how the return on a security relates or moves with respect to specific events.

For the market model it is assumed that the variations in returns on individual securities are largely due to market-wide factors. As a portfolio of investments increases in diversity, the non-systematic risk of the diversified portfolio (measured by $\alpha_{it} + \mu_{it}$) tends to disappear, thereby leaving only returns that are due to market-wide movements (that is, $\beta_{it}R_{mt}$). The market model makes a number of assumptions, including that investors are risk averse and that investors have homogeneous expectations (they think alike).

---

5. For further information on the development of the CAPM, reference can be made to Sharpe (1964) or Lintner (1965).

6. For example, if the returns of firm i's securities are expected to fluctuate in period t at the same rate as a very large diversified portfolio of securities, then beta (β_{it}) would be approximately 1. If the returns of the individual are twice as sensitive or volatile as general market movements (indicating that the returns on the undiversified security are more risky than the returns on a very large diversified portfolio) then beta would be approximately 2, and so on.

Equation 3 shows that total or actual returns can be divided into normal (or expected) returns, given market-wide price movements ($\alpha_{it} + \beta_{it}R_{mt}$), and abnormal (or unexpected) returns due to firm-specific share price movements (μ_{it}).[7] Normal returns are expected to vary from company to company, depending on their level of systematic risk in relation to the market, while abnormal returns are expected to vary from company to company, depending on whether there is new information about the company that causes investors to revise expectations about future earnings.

The market model is used to control for share price movements due to market-wide events, allowing the researcher to focus on share price movements due to firm-specific news. For example, part of the 2.6% return earned by CMR Company upon announcing its annual earnings may be due to an overall rise in the market on the announcement day. A researcher analysing the impact of the earnings announcement would control for the impact of this rise in the market by deducting it from CMR Company's return. Assuming $\alpha_{CMR} = 0$, $\beta_{CMR} = 1$, and $R_m = 1\%$, this calculation would leave an abnormal return (μ_{CMR}) of 1.6%.[8] It is abnormal returns, or firm-specific share price movements, that are analysed by researchers to determine the information effects of company announcements.

Capital market research into the earnings/return relation analyses firm-specific price movements (abnormal returns) at the time of earnings announcements. These abnormal returns are used as an indicator of the information content of the announcement. That is, how much, if any, *new* information has been released to the capital markets. If there is no price reaction, it is assumed that the announcement contained no new information. That is, the information was already known or anticipated by market participants.

Results of capital market research into financial reporting

Capital market research has been a major focus of financial accounting research over the past thirty years. The research has investigated the information content of earnings as well as many other accounting and disclosure items. Results of this research are useful for both practising accountants and finance professionals such as security analysts. Knowledge of these results is considered to be particularly useful in relation to making financial reporting decisions. More informed choices between accounting and disclosure alternatives can be made

---

7. Normal returns can also be thought of as the level of return to investors that is expected simply as a reward for investing and bearing risk. Abnormal returns are the realised rate of return, less the expected normal rate of return (calculated by reference to the market model).

8. When returns are calculated on a daily basis, the assumption that $\alpha = 0$, $\beta_{it} = 1$ is not unrealistic.

if the expected impacts on share prices are anticipated when making financial reporting decisions. A summary comprising some of the more important capital market research results follows.

Historical cost income is used by investors

Ball and Brown (1968), in the first major capital market research publication in accounting, investigated the usefulness of accounting earnings under a historical cost model. Prior to their research, there was a widely held view that historical cost accounting methods resulted in 'meaningless' information that was not useful for investors and other users of financial statements.[9] Ball and Brown saw the need for empirical evidence about whether accounting earnings, calculated using historical cost accounting principles, provide useful information to investors. They state (p. 159):

> If, as the evidence indicates, security prices do in fact adjust rapidly to new information as it becomes available, then changes in security prices will reflect the flow of information to the market. An observed revision of stock prices associated with the release of the income report would thus provide evidence that the information reflected in income numbers is useful.

Using data for 261 US companies, they tested whether firms with unexpected increases in accounting earnings had positive abnormal returns, and firms with unexpected decreases in accounting earnings had negative abnormal returns (on average). Unexpected earnings were calculated (quite simplistically) as the difference between current earnings and previous year earnings. That is, they assumed that this year's earnings were expected to be the same as last year's earnings. Monthly share price data were used, with the market model being used to calculate abnormal returns for each company. Cumulative abnormal returns (CARs) were then calculated for each of (a) the full sample of companies, (b) firms with unexpected increases in earnings (favourable announcements), and (c) firms with unexpected decreases in earnings (unfavourable announcements), by summing the average abnormal returns for each of these groups over time.

They found evidence to suggest that the information contained in the annual report is used in investment decision making, despite the limitations of the historical cost accounting system. This result is evidenced by the CARs during the month of the earnings announcements (month 0). As can be seen from Figure 10.1, firms with unexpected increases in earnings (favourable announcements), represented by the top line in the chart, had positive abnormal returns, while firms with unexpected decreases in earnings (unfavourable announcements), represented by the bottom line in the chart, had negative abnormal returns during the announcement month (on average). Since Ball and Brown's early study, this research has been replicated many times using more sophisticated data and research methods. The results appear

---

9. For example, see Chambers (1965) and Sterling (1975).

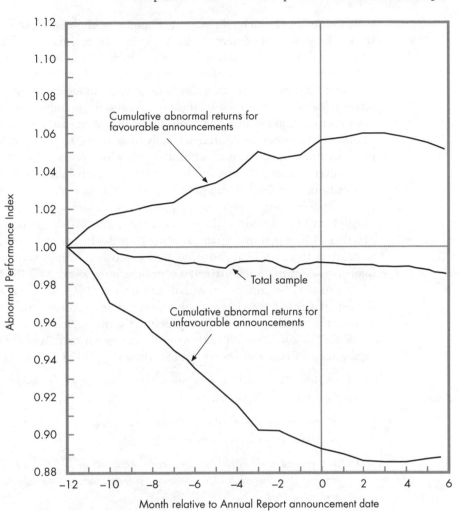

FIGURE 10.1 Movements in cumulative abnormal returns before and after the announcement of earnings

Source: Ball and Brown (1968)

to confirm the usefulness of historical cost income to investors. This is not to say that the historical cost accounting system is the 'most useful', since a present value or current cost accounting system may be more useful, but it gives some credence to the continued use of historical costs.

Prior to an earnings release, investors obtain much of the information they need from other sources

In addition to confirming the usefulness of the historical cost accounting model, Ball and Brown found that most of the information contained in earnings announcements (85–90%) is anticipated by investors. The gradual slope in the lines (which represent the cumulative abnormal returns) prior to the earnings announcements (which were made at time 0) in Figure 10.1 provide evidence of this. Anticipation of earnings changes by investors indicates that investors obtain much of the information useful for investment decision making from sources other than annual earnings announcements (perhaps from media releases, analysts' releases, information about the industry's production and sales trends, and so on). This is not surprising given that alternative sources of information such as conference calls to analysts, and press releases, are generally more timely than the annual report, which tends to be issued several weeks after balance date and less frequently than many alternative sources of information. Therefore, we can never expect to produce accounting statements that will tell investors everything they may want to know. That is, provision of *all* relevant information to investors is not a good basis for regulation or practice. When making financial reporting decisions, it is important to remember that, while accounting appears to be an important source of information for the stock market, it is not the only source of information.

In finishing our discussion of Ball and Brown (1968) it is perhaps worth noting that this paper is generally accepted as the most cited academic accounting article. It certainly represented quite a change from previous accounting research, which was predominantly normative. Reflecting on the significance of Ball and Brown (1968), Brown (1994, p. 24) states:

> *A number of reasons have been given to explain the paper's major impact on the accounting literature since 1968:*
>
> * *It was cast in the mould of a traditional experiment: hypothesis, data collection, data analysis, conclusion.*
>
> * *It expressed a view that ran counter to the critics of GAAP (these critics arguing that historical cost accounting information was meaningless and useless).*
>
> * *It was an early plea for 'empirical research'.*
>
> * *It emphasised the use of data to test a belief.*
>
> * *It adopted an information perspective.*
>
> * *It contained the basic elements of a research design that became a model for future research: the semi-strong form of the EMH was a maintained hypothesis, so the focus was on market behaviour around an announcement date; earnings predictions were modelled to identify the news in, or what was new about, the earnings report; GAAP earnings were compared with a primary version of operating cash flows; and abnormal returns were measured by the Market Model and the CAPM.*
>
> * *It was a particularly robust experiment, in the sense that it has been replicated for firms with different fiscal years, in different countries, and at different times.*
>
> * *It gave rise to many papers in related areas.*

As Chapter 7 indicates, Watts and Zimmerman (1986) credit the development of Positive Accounting Theory, at least in part, to the early experimental approach adopted by Ball and Brown (1968).

The information content of earnings announcements depends on the extent of alternative sources of information

Research indicates that the information content of earnings varies between countries and between companies within a country. For example, Brown (1970) found that when compared to US markets, the Australian market has slower adjustments during the year, with larger adjustments at the earnings announcement date. This result implies that annual reports were a more important source of information for the Australian capital markets than they were for US capital markets because there were fewer alternative sources of information for Australian companies. This difference in the extent of alternative sources of information is partly due to Australian regulations that required only semi-annual rather than quarterly reporting, and is also a function of differences in average firm sizes between the two countries. Smaller firms tend to have fewer alternative sources of information than larger firms, and are less likely to be followed by security analysts. This difference in the extent of alternative sources of information between smaller and larger firms causes differences in the usefulness of earnings announcements, with these being more useful for smaller than larger Australian firms. Therefore, the extent of alternative sources of information should be considered when making financial reporting decisions. (We return to the issue of size later in this chapter.)

The capital market impact of unexpected changes in earnings depends on whether the change is expected to be permanent or temporary

Following Ball and Brown's finding that the *direction* of unexpected earnings changes is positively related to the *direction* of abnormal returns, further research was conducted into the relation between the *magnitude* of the unexpected change in earnings, or earnings per share, and the *magnitude* of the abnormal returns. This relationship is often referred to as the *earnings response coefficient*. The results show that this is not a one-to-one relationship. Indeed, some research has shown that the average abnormal return associated with a 1% unexpected change in earnings is only 0.1 to 0.15% (Beaver, Lambert and Morse, 1980). This relationship varies, depending on whether the change in earnings is expected to be permanent or temporary. Permanent increases are expected to result in increased dividends, and therefore future cash flows, and this implies a change in the value of the company. On the other hand, temporary increases are discounted or ignored, since they are not expected to have the same impact on expected future dividends (Easton and Zmijewski, 1989). While some earnings changes such as those due to one-off restructuring charges are obviously temporary, it is more difficult to determine whether other earnings changes are likely to persist.

Earnings persistence depends on the relative magnitudes of cash and accruals components of current earnings

The accrual system of accounting differs from the cash basis of accounting owing to differences in when cash flows are recognised in the financial statements. Under the accrual system, some items are recognised before the cash flows are received or paid (for example, credit sales and purchases), while others are recognised on a periodic basis (for example, the cost of a fixed asset is recognised over its useful life through periodic depreciation charges). Therefore, the accrual process involves adjusting the timing of when the cash inflows and outflows of a firm are recognised to achieve a matching of revenues and expenses. Earnings, the summary performance measure of the accrual system, has fewer timing and mismatching problems than performance measures based on unadjusted cash flows (for example, cash flows from operations). However, application of the accrual system can be a subjective rather than an objective process, and depending upon the choices made, many different earnings figures can be achieved. For example, if the reducing balance method of depreciation is chosen over the straight-line method, reported profits will initially be lower, owing to a greater depreciation expense. However, reported earnings will be higher in the later years of the asset's life due to lower depreciation expense. Sloan (1996) undertook a study to see if share prices behave as if investors simply 'fixate' on reported earnings without considering how those numbers have actually been determined (that is, what methods of accounting have been employed). According to Sloan (1996, p. 291):

> *A meaningful test of whether stock prices fully reflect available information requires the specification of an alternative 'naïve' expectation model, against which to test the null of market efficiency. The naïve model employed in this study is that investors 'fixate' on earnings and fail to distinguish between the accrual and cash flow component of current earnings. This naïve earnings expectation model is consistent with the functional fixation hypothesis, which has received empirical support in capital market, behavioral and experimental research.*[10]

Sloan provides evidence that firms with large accruals relative to their actual cash flows are unlikely to have persistently high earnings, since the accruals reverse over time, reducing future earnings. However, share prices are found to act as if investors simply 'fixate' on reported earnings, thereby failing to take account of the relative magnitudes of the cash and accrual components of current earnings (fixation implying a degree of market inefficiency). In concluding his paper, Sloan (p. 314) states:

---

10. According to Watts and Zimmerman (1986, p. 160), 'the hypothesis of functional fixation maintains that individual investors interpret earnings numbers in the same way, regardless of the accounting procedures used to calculate them. If all investors acted in this way, there would be a mechanical relation between earnings and stock prices, and the stock market would not discriminate between efficient and less efficient firms'.

This paper investigates whether stock prices reflect information about future earnings contained in the accrual and cash flow components of current earnings. The persistence of earnings performance is shown to depend on the relative magnitudes of the cash and accrual components of earnings. However, stock prices act as if investors fail to identify correctly the different properties of these two components of earnings.

Hence, while earnings can be managed up through various discretionary accruals, this cannot be done indefinitely, and earnings will eventually be lower as the accruals subsequently reverse. Likewise, while it may be possible to increase share price through reporting higher earnings, this effect will be reversed when lower earnings are reported in the future. Although the lower earnings are due to the reversal of accruals, evidence indicates that the market *fixates* on the lower reported earnings, and share prices therefore fall as the accruals subsequently reverse. Notions of market efficiency, such as the functional fixation perspective, have been hotly contested in the accounting literature.

The earnings announcements of other firms in the same industry have information content

When a company announces its annual earnings, this generally results in abnormal returns for not only the company concerned, but also for other companies in the same industry (Foster, 1981). That is, there is information content for similar firms as well as for the announcing firm. This phenomenon, known as 'information transfer', reduces the surprise (unknown) element in earnings announcements of other firms in the industry who choose to announce their earnings later. The direction of the capital market reaction is related to whether the news contained in the announcement reflects a change in conditions for the entire industry, or changes in relative market share within the industry. Because information is gained from the announcements of similar firms, information releases about sales and earnings changes result in price reactions for other firms in an industry, as well as the firm making the announcement (Freeman and Tse, 1992). Therefore, in forming expectations about how information releases, such as earnings announcements, might affect share prices, it is important to consider the timing of information releases relative to those of similar firms, since information about a company can be gained from the information releases of similar companies.

Firth (1976) investigated the 'information transfer' issue. He sought to 'investigate the impact of a company's results being publicly announced on the share price behaviour of competing firms' (p. 298). His results indicated that when 'good news' was released about accounting earnings, the share prices of the non-announcing firms in the same industry reacted quickly (the same day) by showing a statistically significant increase. Interestingly there seemed to be no abnormal returns in the days before the announcement (limited anticipation) or the days after the announcement. That is, most of the adjustment appeared to occur fairly immediately. Similar results were found with respect to 'bad news' earnings announcements. The share prices of non-disclosing firms in the industry tended to fall on the day of the 'bad news' earnings announcement.

If the announcement of earnings by one company impacts on the share prices of other companies in the same industry, there would be an expectation that if a number of companies are about to release earnings information, then all other things being equal, the largest share price reactions might be generated by the entity that makes the first release. By the time the last entity releases its earnings announcements for a particular year end, it could be expected that a great deal of this information would already have been impounded in share prices and hence the last announcement would have relatively little impact on share prices. This expectation was confirmed by Clinch and Sinclair (1987). In summarising their findings they state (p. 105):

> *The directional association between daily price changes for announcing and non-announcing firms and the magnitude of the price change diminishes for subsequent announcing firms in the same industry over the reporting period.*

We can relate the view that announcements by one company can impact on share prices of another company to a recent newspaper article relating to banks. Exhibit 10.1 shows that when one bank released its profit figures, this seemed to cause share price reactions in the shares of other banks. This is consistent with the results reported above.

Earnings forecasts have information content

Announcements of earnings forecasts by both management and security analysts are associated with share returns. That is, not only do announcements of actual earnings appear to cause share prices to change, but announcements of expected earnings also appear to cause price changes. Similar to earnings announcements, earnings forecasts are associated with market returns in terms of both direction and magnitude (Penman, 1980; Imhoff and Lobo, 1984). These results are not surprising since earnings forecasts are expected to contain *new* information that can be used in the prediction of future earnings. Forecasts of expected future earnings appear to be an effective way of communicating information to the share market. Also, bad news forecasts about lower than anticipated future earnings may be useful for avoiding potential shareholder lawsuits (Skinner, 1997).

Earnings forecasts have also been explored in terms of the 'information transfer' phenomenon discussed above. Baginski (1987) generated results that showed that the share prices of firms within the same industry that did not provide an earnings forecast were positively correlated with the change in earnings expectation indicated by earnings forecasts released by managers of other firms within the same industry.

Exhibit 10.2 provides an example of where it appears that a profit forecast led to an increase in share price, consistent with some of the research results reported above. However, what must be remembered in research that looks at market reactions around particular events is that it is possible that share

EXHIBIT 10.1 An illustration of the 'information transfer' effect

Firm ANZ final sparks bank shares

Louise Brannelly and wire services

ANZ Banking Group Ltd's robust full-year net profit and unexpected plan for a $500 million share buy-back lit a spark under oversold banking stocks yesterday, buoying earnings expectations for others in the sector.

The Banking index kicked 129.8 points, or almost 2 per cent higher, to 6752.8 with ANZ the star performer, rallying 38.1c, or 3.61 per cent, to $10.94.

ANZ booked a $1.48 billion net profit for the September 30, 1999 year, up from $1.06 billion previously, representing an 18 per cent surge when adjusted for a $1.1 billion preference share issue and an accounting charge for software. The result came in at the top end of analysts' expectations for a $1.399 billion to $1.484 billion net profit.

'It's a good result—they set down their objectives and achieved them,' Hartley Poynton analyst Jamie Nicol said.

He noted that the planned $500 million ordinary share buy-back was a surprise.

For the sector overall, a strong performance in offshore bond markets and relief that an expected rise in official interest rates was restricted to 25 basis points also enhanced sentiment.

National Australia Bank, which the market expects to post a strong result today, jumped 58c to $25.44, while Westpac, reporting tomorrow, lifted 18c to $10.38 and CBA rebounded 40c to $26.70.

'The sector got oversold last month and suddenly with the outlook for inflation improving and the bond market stabilising, you are seeing investors refocus on the bank sector as a whole,' Wilson HTM analyst Mark Arnold said. He said the sector was expected to deliver a 13 per cent boost in earnings for the 1998–99 reporting season, slowing to 10 per cent in 2000.

ANZ chief executive officer John McFarlane flagged an improved result for the group in the year ahead, although he declined to comment on whether the first or second half would be strongest.

Mr McFarlane said the 1999 result demonstrated that ANZ was delivering on its promise to generate strong earnings growth, reduce costs, lower risk and improve the return on equity.

'At the same time, we have re-balanced our business mix towards higher return, lower risk businesses,' he said.

Net interest income rose 3 per cent to $3.645 billion and non-interest income 11 per cent to $2.32 billion, while the bad and doubtful debt charge climbed to $510 million ($487 million). The cost income ratio fell to 55 from 60.9 per cent and return on equity rose to 17.2 from 14.6 per cent in 1998.

Mr McFarlane said the buy-back of up to 48 million ordinary shares was the first step in addressing group surplus capital.

'The high level of internal capital generated from strong earnings growth, the implementation of risk reduction programmes and the preference share issue have all created a capital surplus for the group,' he said.

ANZ has a group tier one capital ratio of 7.9 per cent, up from 7.2 per cent previously and Mr McFarlane said a 6 per cent level was considered 'prudent'.

He said ANZ had examined a number of acquisition opportunities in South-East Asia and, with the exception of Panin Bank, these had not met the group's hurdle criteria.

One analyst said the market had been wary that ANZ could use its strong capital position to make an acquisition. 'Buying back ordinary stock is positive for earnings per share and also return on equity,' he said.

The final dividend will be 30c, bringing the full-year dividend to 56c, up 8 per cent from 1998.

The Courier Mail, **Thursday 4 November 1999.**

EXHIBIT 10.2 Profit forecasts and their potential influence on share price

Macquarie up 30c on promise of big profit

Andrew White
Financial Services

Macquarie Bank shares surged to a record close yesterday as investors swamped a high-yielding debt issue and awaited an expected bumper profit today. The shares reached $24.10, up 30c for the day and nearly 13 per cent in the past month as investors warmed to forecasts of a record profit for the full service investment bank. Analysts said comments by deputy managing director Richard Sheppard at a New York investment conference on October 15 had underpinned expectations for a record result.

Mr Sheppard said all divisions had performed well in the six months to September 30 and continued to be 'very busy'.

The shares have run up from $21 since then, but analysts said the result would have to exceed market forecasts to maintain momentum on the share price.

'It has had a tremendous run in the past month and it would be very hard to sustain that trajectory without surpassing everyone's forecasts,' one analyst said.

Profits are forecast between $83 million and $96 million, from $80.5 million in the previous corresponding half year.

Built in to expectations are a full contribution from the new retail broking network and two months of operations from the Bankers Trust investment bank, bought from Deutsche Bank for $100 million in July.

The bank's position was further strengthened yesterday with closure of a $400 income securities issue.

The issue was twice the original estimate and will be used to strengthen the bank's balance sheet.

Macquarie treasurer Paul Robertson said the issue was divided equally between retail investors through the bank's own retail broking network and fund managers, who asked for several times the available stock.

The notes pay 1.7 per cent above the bank bill rate and are guaranteed at least 7.25 per cent for the first three years. They list on November 25.

The Australian, **16 November 1999, p. 24.**

prices might actually be reacting to other unknown (by the researcher) contemporaneous events.

There are benefits associated with the voluntary disclosure of information

The disclosure of additional information, over and above that required by accounting regulations, has benefits in the capital markets. Voluntary disclosures include those contained within the annual report, as well as those made via other media such as press releases and conference calls to security analysts. For example, Lang and Lundholm (1996) show that firms with more informative disclosure policies have a larger analyst following and more accurate analyst earnings forecasts. They suggest that potential benefits to disclosure include increased investor following and reduced information asymmetry. Further, Botosan (1997) shows that increased voluntary disclosure within the annual report is associated with reduced costs of equity capital, particularly for firms with low analyst following. For these low-analyst firms, disclosure of forecast information and key non-financial statistics is particularly important, while for firms with a high analyst following, disclosure of historical summary information is beneficial. Therefore, these potential benefits of increased disclosure should perhaps not be ignored when deciding the extent of voluntary disclosure.

Recognition is perceived differently to mere footnote disclosure

Recognising an item by recording it in the financial statements and including its numerical amount in the financial statement's totals is perceived differently to merely disclosing the amount in footnotes to the statements. For example, Aboody (1996) finds that where firms in the US oil and gas industry recognise a write-down in their financial statements, the negative pricing effect is significant, whereas when firms in the same industry merely disclose such a write-down in footnotes, the pricing effect is not significant. In other words, the market perceives recognised write-downs to be more indicative of a value decrement than disclosed write-downs. Further, Cotter and Zimmer (1999) show that mere disclosure of current values of land and buildings indicates that the amount is less certain when compared to current values that are recognised in the statement of financial position (balance sheet) via an asset revaluation. These results indicate that investors place greater reliance on recognised amounts than on disclosed amounts. Therefore, while it is not necessary to recognise information in the balance sheet for it to be useful, since merely disclosing the information in the footnotes conveys the information to investors, disclosed information is perceived to be less reliable than recognised information.

Size

There is evidence that the relationship between earnings announcements and share price movements is inversely related to the size of an entity. That is, earnings announcements have been found generally to have a greater impact on the share prices of smaller firms relative to larger firms. This is explained on the basis that with larger firms there is generally more information available in the marketplace and therefore greater likelihood that projections about earnings have already been impounded in the share price. The earnings announcement for larger firms would have a relatively limited unexpected component. For example, research has shown that the relationship between the information content in earnings announcements and changes in share prices tends to be more significant for smaller firms. That is, in general, larger firms' earnings announcements have relatively less information content (for example, Freeman, 1987; Collins, Kothari and Rayburn, 1987). This is consistent with the EMH and is explained by the fact that larger firms tend to have more information being circulated about them as well as attracting more attention from such parties as security analysts. Hence, on average, earnings announcements for larger firms tend to be more anticipated and hence already impounded in the share price prior to the earnings announcement.

Grant (1980) also explored this issue. He investigated the information content of earnings announcements of securities traded on the New York Stock Exchange, as well as securities traded on what is known as the Over The Counter Market (OTC). Firms traded on the OTC are typically smaller than firms traded on the New York Stock Exchange. Consistent with the perceived size effect, the prices of securities traded on the OTC were more responsive to earnings announcements than were the prices of securities traded on the New York Stock Exchange.

Do current share prices anticipate future accounting earnings announcements?

The previous discussion in this chapter has provided evidence that accounting earnings announcements, because of their potential information content, can have some impact on share prices. That is, prices change in relation to information as it becomes available. However, this impact seems to be more significant for smaller firms. As we saw, this is explained on the basis that there tends to be more information available for larger firms (for example, through analysts paying particular attention to the larger firms). Hence, as firm size increases, the general perspective taken is that share prices incorporate information from a wider number of sources (including, perhaps, numerous forecasts of the larger entity's earnings) and therefore there is relatively less unexpected information when earnings are ultimately announced. Therefore, for larger firms, we might actually be able to argue that share prices *anticipate* future earnings announcements with some degree of accuracy. As Brown (1994, p. 105) states, if we take the perspective that share prices anticipate earnings announcements, then we are effectively 'looking back the other way' from traditional perspectives that assume that earnings announcements actually drive share price changes.

A more recent focus in capital market research investigates how well accounting information, such as annual earnings, captures information that is relevant to investors. This is a different focus from research considered previously in this chapter. Rather than determining whether earnings announcements *provide* information to investors, this alternative form of research seeks to determine whether earnings announcements *reflect* information that has already been used by investors in decision making. That is, this research views market prices, and hence returns, as leading accounting earnings, while 'information content' research (the previous focus of this chapter) views earnings as leading (or driving) market returns. Both perspectives have merit, since the earnings announcement is likely to contain some information about a firm's activities that was not previously known to investors, as well as information that investors have already determined (or anticipated) from alternative sources.

In considering why share prices convey information about future accounting earnings, Brown (1994, p. 106) argues:

> In a world of rational expectations, events that affect future distributions to shareholders will be reflected in today's share price, whereas accounting standards often require that the recognition of those events be deferred until some future accounting period.

Share prices and returns (changes in prices plus dividends) are considered by some researchers to provide useful benchmarks for determining whether accounting information is relevant for investor decision making. Share prices are deemed to represent a benchmark measure of *firm value* (per share), while share returns represent a benchmark measure of *firm performance* (per share). These benchmarks are in turn used to compare the usefulness of alternative accounting and disclosure methods. For example, this methodology is used to answer questions such as: are cash flows from operations a better measure of a firm's performance than earnings calculated using the accruals system? Each of these accounting measures of performance is compared to the market benchmark measure of performance (returns) to determine which accounting measure best *reflects* the market's assessment of company performance. This type of capital market research also assumes that the market is efficient, and acknowledges that financial statements are not the only source of information available to the markets, such that security prices reflect information that is generally available from a multitude of sources. In particular, it assumes that investors and financial analysts actively seek out relevant information when making investment decisions or recommendations, rather than awaiting the release of the annual report. Further, this area of the research allows researchers to consider questions about statement of financial position measures. For example, are disclosures about current values of assets value-relevant? That is, are they associated with, or linked to, the current market value of the company? Again, there is an assumption that market values reflect all publicly available information, including, but not limited to, information contained in financial statements.

This area of the research is based on a theoretical framework that is derived from the premise that market values and book values are both measures of a firm's value (stock of wealth), even though book value measures wealth with some error. That is, at any point in time, the market value of a company's equity (MV_{it}) is equal to the book value of shareholders' equity (BV_{it}) plus some error (ε_{it}):

$$MV_{it} = BV_{it} + \varepsilon_{it} \qquad \text{(Equation 4)}$$

This error is due to the conservative nature of the accounting system. Book value is generally expected to be lower than market value for a number of reasons. First, not all assets and liabilities are recognised in the financial statements. For example, human resources, customer satisfaction levels, and internally generated goodwill are not included in the statement of financial position, nor are their values amortised to the statement of financial performance (income statement).[11] Second, some assets are recognised at less

---

11. As another example, the appointment of a very reputable managing director would be value-relevant because it is an action that could be expected to lead to improved company performance, cash flows, and hence share value. However, such an appointment would not generally be reflected in the financial statements themselves.

than their full value. For example, fixed assets, that have not been revalued, and inventory are generally recorded at less than their expected sale prices.

If markets are assumed to be efficient, market value provides a benchmark measure against which alternative measures of book value can be assessed. As we see shortly, there is a deal of research that evaluates the output of the accounting system on the basis of how the accounting information relates or compares to current market prices of the firm's securities.[12]

If market value and book value of a company are considered as 'stocks' of wealth, then changes in each of these measures of wealth between two points in time can be considered as 'flows' of wealth. Just as market and book measures of stocks of wealth equate with error, market and book measures of flows of wealth (changes in value) can be equated, albeit with some degree of error:

$$\Delta MV_{it} = \Delta BV_{it} + \varepsilon'_{it} \qquad \text{(Equation 5)}$$

Change in market value (ΔMV_{it}) is simply the difference in the market capitalisation of a company between two points in time ($t - 1$ to t). On a 'per share' basis, it can be expressed as the change in the price of one share.

$$\Delta MV_{it} \text{ / no. of shares} = P_{it} - P_{it-1} \qquad \text{(Equation 6)}$$

Change in book value (ΔBV_{it}) is the difference between opening and closing total shareholders' equity. However, if we assume that there have been no additional capital contributions during the period, ΔBV_{it} can also be measured by considering the change in retained earnings for the period. On a per share basis, this is measured as earnings per share (E_{it}) less dividends paid per share (D_{it}):

$$\Delta BV_{it} \text{ / no. of shares} = E_{it} - D_{it} \qquad \text{(Equation 7)}$$

This formula is based on the concept of 'clean surplus' earnings, which assumes that all increases in book value pass through the statement of financial performance. Clean surplus earnings does not always hold in practice, since items such as asset revaluation increments are credited directly to owners' equity. However, the assumption of clean surplus is useful for simplifying our analysis. Substituting Equations (6) and (7) into Equation (5) gives:

$$P_{it} - P_{it-1} = E_{it} - D_{it} + \varepsilon'_{it} \qquad \text{(Equation 8)}$$

---

12. This research assumes, perhaps somewhat simplistically, that the market has it 'right' in its determination of the firm's value. Thereafter, accounting figures are compared with the market's 'benchmark'. Clearly, the benchmark figure of valuation might over- or under-value the entity relative to the value that would be placed on it if all private and public information was known and 'appropriately' used. As noted earlier in this chapter, market predictions are sometimes, in hindsight, proved to be wrong, thus necessitating subsequent adjustments.

That is, there is a theoretical relationship between change in price and change in retained earnings for the period. With a small amount of manipulation, this equation can be expressed to relate returns to earnings (the return/earnings relation). First, adding dividends to both sides of the equation, and dividing through by beginning of period price, gives:

$$\frac{(P_{it} - P_{it-1}) + D_{it}}{P_{it-1}} = E_{it}/P_{it-1} + \varepsilon''_{it} \qquad \text{(Equation 9)}$$

Since the left-hand side of the equation, $((P_{it} - P_{it-1}) + D_{it}) / P_{it-1}$, is equal to returns (equation 2), we are left with an equation relating returns to earnings:

$$R_{it} = E_{it} / P_{it-1} + \varepsilon''_{it} \qquad \text{(Equation 10)}$$

Equation 10 shows that we should expect returns (R_{it}) and earnings per share divided by beginning of period price (E_{it} / P_{it-1}) to be related.

In short, this perspective says that if market value is related to book value, returns should be related to accounting earnings per share, divided by price at the beginning of the accounting period. This analysis provides an underlying reason why we should expect returns to be related to earnings over time. However, it is interesting to note that it is *total earnings per share* rather than *unexpected earnings per share* that this theoretical framework proposes should be associated with returns. This is in contrast to research that assesses the 'information content' of earnings announcements by analysing the association between unexpected earnings per share and abnormal returns at the time of the announcement. We will see that there has been a number of studies that evaluate reported earnings on the basis of how closely the movements in reported earnings (or EPS) relate to changes in share prices.[13]

Beaver, Lambert and Morse (1980) was an early paper that sought to investigate how efficiently data about share prices enable a researcher to estimate future accounting earnings. Accepting that share price is the capitalised value of future earnings, they regressed the annual percentage change in share price on the percentage change in annual EPS. Consistent with Equation 10, they found that share prices and related returns were related to accounting earnings, but they also found that share prices in year *t* were positively associated with accounting earnings in year *t* + 1 (share prices led accounting earnings). It was accepted that share price movements provided an indication of future movements in accounting earnings. Because of various information sources, prices appeared to anticipate future accounting earnings. These findings were also supported in a later study by Beaver, Lambert and Ryan (1987) who regressed changes in security prices on the percentage changes in earnings.

---

13. Again, this research assumes, perhaps somewhat simplistically, that the market has determined the 'right' valuation of the organisation.

In previous discussion we showed that research indicates that share prices of larger firms do not adjust as much to earnings announcements as do the share prices of smaller firms. This was explained on the basis that there is more information available and analysed in relation to larger firms, and hence information about earnings is already impounded in the share price. That is, 'for larger firms, there is a broader and richer information set, and there are more market traders and more analysts seeking information' (Brown, 1994, p. 110).

Now if we adopt the position taken in this section of the chapter that share prices can actually anticipate earnings announcements ('looking back the other way'), as indicated in Beaver, Lambert and Morse (1980) and Beaver, Lambert and Ryan (1987), then perhaps share prices anticipate accounting earnings more efficiently in the case of larger firms. Collins, Kothari and Rayburn (1987) found evidence to support this view—*size does matter*, with the share prices being a better indicator of future earnings in larger companies.

As noted above, there have been a number of studies using stock market valuations as a basis for evaluating accounting information. In Equation 10 we indicated that, theoretically, market returns should be related to earnings. Dechow (1994) investigates how well accounting earnings reflect market returns. She also considers whether another measure of performance, based on cash flows, relates better to returns than earnings based on the accrual accounting system. According to Dechow (p. 12):

> *This paper assumes that stock markets are efficient in the sense that stock prices unbiasedly reflect all publicly available information concerning firms' expected future cash flows. Therefore, stock price performance is used as a benchmark to assess whether earnings or realised cash flows better summarise this information.*

According to Dechow, earnings are predicted to be a more useful measure of firm performance than cash flows because they are predicted to have fewer timing and matching problems. In her conclusions, she states (p. 35):

> *This paper hypothesizes that one role of accounting accruals is to provide a measure of short-term performance that more closely reflects expected cash flows than do realized cash flows. The results are consistent with this prediction. First, over short measurement intervals earnings are more strongly associated with stock returns than realized cash flows. In addition, the ability of realized cash flows to measure firm performance improves relative to earnings as the measurement interval is lengthened. Second, earnings have a higher association with stock returns than do realized cash flows in firms experiencing large changes in their working capital requirements and their investment and financing activities. Under these conditions, realized cash flows have more severe timing and matching problems and are less able to reflect firm performance.*

Using the market value of a firm's securities as a benchmark, a number of studies have also attempted to determine which asset valuation approaches provide accounting figures that best reflect the valuation the market places on the firm. The perspective taken is that book values that relate more closely to market values (determined through a review of share prices) provide more relevant information than other accounting valuation approaches. Barth, Beaver and Landsman (1996) undertook a study that investigated whether fair value estimates of a bank's financial instruments (as required in the US by SFAS No. 107) seem to provide a better explanation of bank share prices relative to values determined on the basis of historical cost accounting. Their findings indicate that SFAS No. 107 disclosures 'provide significant explanatory power for bank share prices beyond that provided by book values' (p. 535), thereby providing evidence that such values are the values that are relevant to investors.

Easton, Eddey and Harris (1993) investigate whether revaluations of assets result in an alignment between information reflected in annual reports and information implicit in share prices and returns. Again, share price data are used as the 'benchmark' against which accounting data is assessed. According to Easton et al. (p. 16):

> *Prices are used to assess the extent to which the financial statements, including asset revaluations, reflect the state of the firm at a point in time, while returns are used to assess the summary of change in financial state that is provided in the financial statements.*

They found that the revaluation of assets generally resulted in better alignment of market and book values. In concluding their paper, they state (p. 36):

> *Our analyses support the conclusion that book values including asset revaluation reserves are more aligned with the market value of the firm than book values excluding asset revaluation. That is, asset revaluation reserves as reported under Australian GAAP help to provide a better summary of the current state of the firm. Thus, allowing or requiring firms to revalue assets upward should be carefully considered by organizations such as the UK Accounting Standards Board, the Japanese Ministry of Finance, and the International Accounting Standards Committee as they debate the merits of various proposed changes in asset revaluation practice.*

Consistent with a view that market prices already seem to reflect the current values of an entity's assets, as indicated in the research discussed above, it is interesting to note that asset revaluations do not appear to provide information to investors over and above historical cost accounting information. That is, some studies have indicated that the provision of current cost data in financial statements does not have information content (Brown and Finn, 1980). These results suggest that investors are able to estimate current value information prior to it being disclosed in the financial statements. Therefore, while the provision of current value information does not provide new information to investors, it appears to reflect the information used by investors in making their investment decisions.

Chapter summary

In concluding our discussion on capital market research we can see that this research has investigated a number of issues. Central to the research are assumptions about the efficiency of the capital market. In the 'information content' studies considered in the earlier part of this chapter we saw that researchers investigated share market reactions to the releases of information, often specifically the release of accounting information. The view taken was that the accounting disclosures often revealed new information and in a market that was deemed to be informationally efficient with regard to acting upon new information, share prices react to this information.

In the latter part of this chapter we considered studies that investigated whether accounting disclosures reflected, or perhaps confirmed, information already impounded in share prices. The perspective taken was that in an informationally efficient capital market, market prices of shares will reflect information from a multitude of sources. If the accounting information did not reflect the information already impounded in share prices, then some researchers would argue that accounting data that do not relate to share prices, and changes therein, are somewhat deficient. The idea is that market prices reflect information from many sources and if the accumulated data provide a particular signal, the accounting disclosures should also provide similar signals. As we noted, this approach implies that the market has it 'right' when determining share prices, and hence returns. In practice, the market cannot be expected always to get it 'right'.

Because much knowledge about the performance of an entity will be gained from sources other than accounting, it is perhaps reasonable to expect that accounting information should relate (not perfectly) to expectations held by capital market participants, as reflected in share prices. However, because there will arguably always be some unexpected information released when accounting results are made public, we might expect that not all accounting disclosures will be of a confirmatory nature. Some information in the accounting releases will be new, and in a market that is assumed to be information efficient, some price revisions are to be expected.

Many share price studies have investigated the market's reaction to particular disclosures. Often, if no reaction is found, it is deemed that the information is not useful and therefore entities should not go to the trouble and expense involved in making such disclosures. This form of argument has been used to criticise accounting regulators for mandating particular disclosure requirements. What must be recognised, however, is that capital market research investigates the aggregate reaction of one group of stakeholders, the investors. While the share market is an important user of accounting information, provision of information to the share market is not the only function of the accounting system. Accounting information is also used for monitoring purposes (Jensen and Meckling, 1976; Watts and Zimmerman, 1990), and hence, financial statements play an important role in relation to the contracting process (see Chapter 7). Financial statements provide a relatively low cost way of measuring managers' performance and monitoring compliance with contract terms, thereby helping to reduce agency costs. Further, financial statement information can be used to satisfy people's 'rights to know', that is, to fulfil the duty of accountability (see Chapter 8 for an overview of the notion of accountability). Therefore, while investors are important users of financial statements, it would be foolish to focus solely on the investor-information role of financial reporting, to the exclusion of considerations about the monitoring/accountability role.

References

Aboody, D., 'Recognition Versus Disclosure in the Oil and Gas Industry', *Journal of Accounting Research*, Supplement, pp. 21–32, 1996.

Baginski, S.P. 'Intra-industry Information Transfers Associated with Management Forecasts of Earnings', *Journal of Accounting Research*, Vol. 25, No. 2, pp. 196–216, 1987.

Ball, R., Brown, P., 'An Empirical Evaluation of Accounting Income Numbers', *Journal of Accounting Research*, Vol. 6, No. 2, pp. 159–78, 1968.

Barth, M., Beaver, W., Landsman, W., 'Value-Relevance of Banks' Fair Value Disclosures Under SFAS No. 107', *The Accounting Review*, Vol. 71, No. 4, pp. 513–37, October 1996.

Beaver, W.H., Lambert, R.A., Ryan, S.G., 'The Information Content of Security Prices: A Second Look', *Journal of Accounting and Economics*, Vol. 9, No. 2, pp. 139–57, 1987.

Beaver, W.H., Lambert, R., Morse, D., 'The Information Content of Security Prices', *Journal of Accounting and Economics*, Vol. 2, No. 1, pp. 3–38, 1980.

Botosan, C.A., 'Disclosure Level and the Cost of Equity Capital', *The Accounting Review*, Vol. 72, No. 3, pp. 323–50, July 1997.

Brown, P., 'The Impact of the Annual Net Profit Report on the Stock Market', *Australian Accountant*, pp. 273–83, July 1970.

Brown, P., *Capital Markets-Based Research in Accounting: An Introduction*, Coopers and Lybrand Research Methodology Monograph No. 2, Coopers and Lybrand, Melbourne, 1994.

Brown, P., Finn, F., 'Asset Revaluations and Stock Prices: Alternative Explanations of a Study by Sharpe and Walker', in *Share Markets and Portfolio Theory*, R. Ball (Ed.), pp. 349–54, University of Queensland Press, St Lucia, 1980.

Chambers, R., 'Why Bother With Postulates?', *Journal of Accounting Research*, Vol. 1, No. 1, 1965.

Clinch, G.J., Sinclair, N.A., 'Intra-industry Information Releases: A Recursive Systems Approach', *Journal of Accounting and Economics*, Vol. 9, No. 1, pp. 89–106, 1987.

Collins, D., Kothari, S., Rayburn, J., 'Firm Size and Information Content of Prices with Respect to Earnings', *Journal of Accounting and Economics*, Vol. 9, No. 2, pp. 111–38, 1987.

Cotter, J., Zimmer, I., 'Why Do Some Firms Recognize Whereas Others Merely Disclose Asset Revaluations?', Unpublished working paper, Universities of Queensland and Southern Queensland, 1999.

Dechow, P., 'Accounting Earnings and Cash Flows as Measures of Firm Performance: The Role of Accounting Accruals', *Journal of Accounting and Economics*, Vol. 18, pp. 3–24, 1994.

Easton, P.D., Zmijewski, M.E., 'Cross-sectional Variation in the Stock Market Response to Accounting Earnings Announcements', *Journal of Accounting and Economics*, Vol. 11, No. 2, pp. 117–41, 1989.

Easton, P.D., Eddey, P., Harris, T.S., 'An Investigation of Revaluations of Tangible Long-Lived Assets', *Journal of Accounting Research*, Vol. 31, Supplement, pp. 1–38, 1993.

Fama, E.F., Fisher, L., Jensen, M.C., Roll, R., 'The Adjustment of Stock Prices to New Information', *International Economic Review*, Vol. 10, No. 1, pp. 1–21, 1969.

Fama, E.F., *Foundations of Finance*, Basic Books, New York, 1976.

Firth, M., 'The Impact of Earnings Announcements on the Share Price Behavior of Similar Type Firms', *Economic Journal*, Vol. 96, pp. 296–306, 1976.

Foster, G.J., 'Intra-industry Information Transfers Associated with Earnings Releases', *Journal of Accounting and Economics*, Vol. 3, No. 4, pp. 201–32, 1981.

Freeman, R.N., 'The Association Between Accounting Earnings and Security Returns for Large and Small Firms', *Journal of Accounting and Economics*, Vol. 9, No. 2, pp. 195–228, 1987.

Freeman, R., Tse, S., 'Intercompany Information Transfers', *Journal of Accounting and Economics*, pp. 509–23, June/September 1992.

Grant, E.B., 'Market Implications of Differential Amounts of Interim Information', *Journal of Accounting Research*, Vol. 18, No. 1, pp. 255–68, 1980.

Hendriksen, E.S., Van Breda, M.F., *Accounting Theory*, 5th edition, Irwin, Homewood, 1992.

Imhoff, E.A., Lobo, G.J., 'Information Content of Analysts' Forecast Revisions', *Journal of Accounting Research*, Vol. 22, No. 2, pp. 541–54, Autumn 1984.

Jensen, M.C., Meckling, W.H., 'Theory of the Firm: Managerial Behavior, Agency Costs and Ownership Structure', *Journal of Financial Economics*, Vol. 3, pp. 305–60, October 1976.

Lang, M.H., Lundholm, R.J., 'Corporate Disclosure Policy and Analyst Behavior', *The Accounting Review*, Vol. 71, No. 4, pp. 467–92, October 1996.

Lintner, J., 'The Valuation of Risk Assets and the Selection of Risky Investments in Stock Portfolios and Capital Budgets', *Review of Economics and Statistics*, Vol. 47, pp. 13–37, 1965.

Penman, S.H., 'An Empirical Investigation of the Voluntary Disclosure of Corporate Earnings Forecasts', *Journal of Accounting Research*, Vol. 18, No. 1, pp. 132–60, Spring 1980.

Sharpe, W.F., 'Capital Asset Prices: A Review of Market Equilibrium Under Conditions of Risk', *Journal of Finance*, Vol. 19, pp. 425–42, 1964.

Skinner, D.J., 'Earnings Disclosures and Stockholder Lawsuits', *Journal of Accounting and Economics*, Vol. 23, pp. 249–82, 1997.

Sloan, R.G., 'Do Stock Prices Fully Reflect Information in Accruals and Cash Flows About Future Earnings?', *The Accounting Review*, Vol. 71, No. 3, pp. 289–316, 1996.

Sterling, R., 'Towards a Science of Accounting', *Financial Analysts Journal*, 1975.

Watts, R.L., Zimmerman, J.L., 'Positive Accounting Theory: A Ten Year Perspective', *The Accounting Review*, Vol. 65, No. 1, pp. 259–85, 1990.

Watts, R.L., Zimmerman, J.L., *Positive Accounting Theory*, Prentice-Hall, Englewood Cliffs, New Jersey, 1986.

Questions

10.1 What is the role of capital market research?

10.2 What assumptions about market efficiency are typically adopted in capital market research? What do we mean by market efficiency?

10.3 What would be the implications for capital market research if it was generally accepted that capital markets were not efficient in assimilating information?

10.4 If an organisation releases its earnings figures for the year and there is no share price reaction, how would capital market researchers possibly explain this finding?

10.5 What, if any, effect would the size of an entity have on the likelihood that the capital market will react to the disclosure of accounting information?

10.6 Would you expect an earnings announcement by one firm within an industry to impact on the share prices of other firms in the industry? Why?

10.7 Researchers such as Chambers and Sterling have made numerous claims that historical cost information is *meaningless* and *useless*. Are the results of capital market research consistent with this perspective?

10.8 Some recent capital market research investigates whether accounting information reflects the valuations that have already been made by the market (as reflected in share prices). In a sense, it assumes that the market has it 'right' and that a 'good' accounting approach is one that provides accounting numbers that relate to, or confirm, the market prices/returns. If we assume that the market has it 'right', then what exactly is the role of financial accounting?

10.9 Review Exhibit 10.1 (newspaper article entitled 'Firm ANZ final sparks bank shares'). Explain the reason for the change in the price of ANZ shares. Also, what might have caused the price changes in the shares in the other banks?

10.10 In this chapter we have emphasised that the capital market appears to respond to information from many sources, including, but not limited to, accounting. As an illustration of how non-accounting information appears to impact on share prices we can consider an article by Stephen Romei that appeared in *The Australian* on 8 December 1999 (p. 1). The article entitled 'Aussies the real thing, Coke hopes' discusses how Douglas Daft will 'take the helm of the Atlanta-based global beverages empire in April following the resignation of chairman and chief, Douglas Ivester'. According to the article 'The news went down like a flat Coke with investors, with Coca-Cola shares falling 6 per cent to $US64, knocking about $US 10 billion off the company's market value. While Mr Daft is considered a star performer inside Coca-Cola, he is not well known on Wall Street'. Why do you think the market reacted the way it did to the announcement, and do you think that the announcement implies market efficiency or inefficiency?

10.11 Review Exhibit 10.2 (newspaper article entitled 'Macquarie up 30c on promise of big profit'). In an efficient capital market, why would a profit forecast lead to a revision in Macquarie Bank's share price?

10.12 Read Exhibit 10.3 and consider why we might expect, or not expect, the market to react to radio announcements made by Alan Jones. Would a market reaction imply anything about the efficiency of the capital market?

EXHIBIT 10.3 An example of an alternative source of information for the market

Jones helps himself to high-rise share of development deal

Amanda Meade

Broadcaster Alan Jones has been paid $250,000 a year since 1997 by major developer the Walker Corporation to promote its interests on Radio 2UE.

And if the company's share price rises, the breakfast show host receives a maximum bonus of $200,000.

But last year, Jones was so impressed by his own efforts on behalf of Walker, he wrote to his agent, Harry M. Miller, suggesting they ask for more money because the company was doing so well.

'I notice the press release from the Walker Corporation talking about the net profit before taxation of $18.6 million, an increase of 107%,' Jones wrote in February last year.

'They are boasting about all of that. Are we being paid enough!! Let's face it, they wouldn't be in the public place without moi! Tell me what you think?'

But yesterday, after being recalled to give evidence to the broadcasting inquiry for the second time, Jones claimed the memo was written in jest.

The Walker deal, which Jones has not yet terminated despite an order from 2UE chairman John Conde, includes an incentive fee.

The first time the share price hits $1.55 after the first anniversary of the July 1997 contract Walker had to pay him $100,000. The incentive rose to $200,000 by the second and third anniversaries, provided there was a further rise in the share price.

The Australian Broadcasting Authority inquiry heard it was significant because it provided almost exclusively for Jones to provide on-air support.

But Jones offered the same defence he has for all his seven personal endorsement contracts that are in breach of 2UE's rules—he has never actually given them any free plugs on air.

Counsel assisting the inquiry, Julian Burnside QC remarked: 'The curious thing is that what you have done, you weren't obliged to do, and what you were obliged to do, you haven't done.'

Jones was asked by reporters if he had any investment in the Walker Corporation's Finger Wharf apartments at Woolloomooloo.

'I have,' he said. 'I think it's a good development, but it's a bit slow. Yes I have, I have been impressed with the quality and finish of the product.'

A year after signing with Walker, Jones agreed a similar deal with another developer, Walsh Bay Finance, which was redeveloping the historic wharves in the Rocks.

David Mann, the Walsh Bay executive who arranged the deal, which runs until December 15, 2001, told the inquiry he approached Jones to 'minimise the negative publicity' the project was receiving.

Mr Burnside: 'Did he start broadcasting favourable comments about the Walsh Bay redevelopment?'

Mr Mann: 'Yes.'

These favourable comments appeared almost immediately after Jones signed the June 1, 1998 $200,000-a-year contract. On June 2, he broadcast the first of four

(continued)

EXHIBIT 10.3 *(continued)*

substantial editorials praising the 'magnificent' development.

Mr Burnside said he had recalled Jones in relation to the two development companies because the contracts 'stand in marked contrast' to evidence already given by the broadcaster.

'The Walker Corporation agreement seems to provide for nothing except on-air conduct apart from going to four functions a year,' Mr Burnside said.

He said if there was 'any doubt' the contract was concerned with on-air conduct, the panel should consider the four broadcasts that followed the signing of the deal.

The first of Jones' laudatory editorials came on the day The *Daily Telegraph's*

columnist, Piers Akerman, also praised the Walsh Bay project. The inquiry heard Akerman was also lobbied and provided with briefing notes by the developers.

Akerman said last night he had never been offered, nor taken, money for a story, although he had discussed the Walsh Bay project over lunch with an old friend, who was also a Transfield executive.

After the column was published, on June 2, Transfield had offered a case of Grange Hermitage wine, which Akerman said he declined.

The Australian, **Thursday 18 November 1999, p. 1.**

10.13 Read Exhibit 10.4 and, relying on results from capital market research, explain why the market price of Qantas shares would have fallen as a result of an announcement that Virgin might start operating airline services within Australia.

EXHIBIT 10.4 **An illustration of how an announcement by one company has apparent share implications for another company**

Virgin strips $872m off Qantas

Steve Creedy
Aviation

ANALYSTS predict a rough short-term ride for Qantas shares after investors yesterday wiped $872 million from the airline's value in the wake of plans by Richard Branson's Virgin Group to launch a third domestic carrier in Australia.

Qantas shares dropped 72c, or 15 per cent, as investors digested news that Mr Branson intends to start a low-cost airline that will offer half its seats on Sydney-Melbourne type runs for less than $100.

Prices dipped as low as $4.10 before recovering slightly to close at $4.15 on sales of 22 million shares.

Analysts said Qantas stock was particularly susceptible to changes in investor sentiment and the market was justifiably nervous about the potential effect of Virgin's entry on the established airlines.

The Virgin announcement also came on the back of rising fuel prices and a run of bad publicity for the airline, including reports about its involvement in the cash for radio comment affair and its September accident in Bangkok.

'We just think that in the short term, Qantas is a stock which is going to be afflicted by negative sentiment,' one analyst said.

Mr Branson plans to start the airline, which will be headed by Virgin Express

(continued)

EXHIBIT 10.4 *(continued)*

chief financial officer Brett Godley, using 143-seat Boeing 737-300s.

The Virgin boss has not yet revealed routes but Sydney and Melbourne airports said they saw no insurmountable obstacles to getting the start-up terminal space.

Analysts said it was too early to say exactly how the new airline would affect Qantas and Ansett. Uncertainty surrounding Virgin's plans included the sort of frequency it would be able to offer and the kind of slots it can secure in the crucial Sydney market.

And there were some doubts about Virgin's track record as an operator. Salomon Smith Barney analyst Jason Smith noted that Mr Branson had been forced to sell his main asset, his record business, to save Virgin Atlantic in 1992.

He said Virgin Express—a low-cost carrier similar to the one Virgin wanted to introduce in Australia—had had a patchy record and was likely to break even only this year. 'It's all over the place, so he doesn't have a great track record in that respect,' he said.

Mr Smith was also sceptical of Virgin's initial investment of $47 million. 'I would have thought they would have to spend in the range of $300 million to $500 million over the next three years and could potentially lose half of that in earnings over that time,' he said.

The shutters were firmly down at Ansett Australia and Qantas yesterday. The bigger airline responded to media inquiries with 'no comment'.

Mr Branson hosed down reports he was interested in buying News Ltd's 50 per cent stake in Ansett Australia.

The Australian, **Tuesday 30 November 1999.**

10.14 Read Exhibit 10.5 and, relying upon some of the capital market studies we have considered in this chapter, explain why BHP Ltd's share price might have reacted in the way it did.

EXHIBIT 10.5 Market reactions to particular operational strategies adopted by BHP Ltd

Market applauds BHP cuts

Richard Sproull
Resources

INVESTORS rushed into BHP yesterday after chief executive Paul Anderson unveiled radical financial surgery across the company and delivered an upbeat prediction for future earnings despite his gloomy outlook for commodities prices.

Swallowing a $1.8 billion writedown from mothballing BHP's Arizona and Nevada copper assets in two months time proved the key element in $3.3 billion of post-tax writedowns which produced a record $2.3 billion loss. Mr Anderson's decision to shut down the disastrous

North American copper business—eliminating 200,000 tonnes of copper supply—gave investors the opportunity to profit from an anticipated rally in the copper price.

The copper price spiked to a one-month high after the BHP announcement and the company's shares jumped nearly 4 per cent to $17.26. The stock slipped in afternoon trade to close 10c higher at $16.90.

Copper trading across Asian markets was electrified by the closure of the copper business, triggering high-volume sales for around 30,000 tonnes of copper

(continued)

EXHIBIT 10.5 *(continued)*

and pushing prices to around US69c a pound.

BHP analysts and resource fund managers were caught off-guard by the sheer size of the $3.3 billion writedowns which were partly offset by a $647 million abnormal gain from asset sales.

'They (the writedowns) were a lot higher than I thought they would be,' BT Alex Brown senior BHP analyst Keith Williams said. 'The extent of the writedowns and provisioning was significantly greater than our forecast of $1 billion.' The market had expected BHP to salvage some value from the US copper mines, though the company did provision heavily for the slump in hot briquetted iron prices ($531 million) and steel prices ($105 million).

Resources manager at National Australia Asset Management Richard Fish told Bloomberg investors were more comfortable about BHP after it put 'its house in order'.

'People are really thinking they have cleared the slate and the new regime has taken a hard line and some hard decisions in making these writedowns,' Mr Fish said.

Dramatically lower commodities prices shaved $1.08 billion off BHP's bottom line and 9 per cent off sales ($19.23 billion) over the last 12 months, though the company has managed to offset the impact by cutting overheads by $540 million.

The net result saw the company's operating earnings fall 72 per cent to $355 million with each of the four divisions reporting profit falls of 26 per cent or more. The major black spot was the North American copper business, which reported a $113 million loss. Iron ore profits held up well, though Mr Anderson said he was keen to extract greater efficiencies and flexibility out of the Pilbara business, and this had led to preliminary joint-venture discussions with competitor Hamersley Iron, a subsidiary of Rio Tinto.

While earnings from the Ok Tedi copper mine in Papua New Guinea looked stronger, Mr Anderson said the company had made no decision on its future, and was looking at all its options, including an exit.

Mr Anderson said he expected BHP to report higher earnings next year, albeit off a low base, but remained bearish on the future of copper prices.

'Looking forward, we see little relief in the marketplace—I haven't changed my view and become a raging bull on what's happening in the economy or commodities,' he said.

But analysts said closing the copper operations could ultimately benefit BHP's other copper operations, particularly the world's largest producer, the low-cost Escondida copper mine in Chile.

'He's painting a fairly tough year going forward and he's not expecting a substantial lift in prices,' Mr Williams said.

'That could be a bit harsh given the short-term impact from the closures (of the BHP copper operations).'

International ratings agencies Standard & Poor's and Moody's Investors Service yesterday affirmed their ratings on BHP after the results.

S&P said while 'profitability measures have been hurt by this abnormal charge . . . the cash flow to debt measure of about 30 per cent remains within Standard & Poor's expectations'.

Moody's said the restructure established 'a base for future improvement; the challenge remains to deliver results consistent with the company's potential'.

The Weekend Australian, **26–27 June 1999.**

Chapter 11

Reactions of individuals to financial reporting: An examination of behavioural research

Learning objectives

Upon completing this chapter readers should understand:

- how behavioural research differs from capital market research;

- how different accounting-related variables can be manipulated in behavioural research;

- how the results of behavioural research can be of relevance to corporations and the accounting profession for *anticipating* individual reactions to accounting disclosures;

- how the results of behavioural research can form the basis for developing ways to more efficiently use accounting-related data;

- the limitations of behavioural research.

Opening issues

The accounting profession often considers introducing new regulations relating to the disclosure of new items of information, or specifically requiring information to be disclosed in a particular format. A concern that often arises is how or whether various categories of financial statement users will react to the new disclosures which are potentially going to be mandated, particularly given that new disclosure requirements typically impose costs on those entities required to make the disclosures. How can behavioural research be used to assist the concerns of accounting regulators about financial statement users' reactions to the proposed requirements?

Introduction

In Chapter 10 we considered capital market research. Capital market research considers the *aggregate behaviour* of investors in the capital market. This aggregate behaviour is typically observed by looking at movements in share prices around the time of particular events, such as when earnings announcements are made.

In this chapter we consider decision making at the *individual level*. The research, which we refer to as behavioural research, involves performing studies to see how a variety of financial statement user groups (not just investors, as is the case in capital market research) react to a variety of accounting information, often presented in different forms, and in different contexts. By generating knowledge about how different categories of financial statement users (for example, investors, research analysts, auditors, bankers, loan officers, and so on) react to particular accounting disclosures, corporations and the accounting profession will be better placed to *anticipate* how different individuals will react to particular information.

Apart from the anticipatory implications associated with behavioural research, results of analysis of the decision making processes of individuals can also provide the basis for developing procedures to improve future decision making.

An overview of behavioural research

In Chapter 10 we considered research that investigated the aggregate reaction of the capital market to various accounting disclosures. In this chapter we turn to a different approach to research which considers how *individuals* react to various accounting disclosures. Research that considers how individuals react or behave when provided with particular items of information can be classified as *behavioural research*. According to Libby (1981, p. 2), research that attempts to describe individual behaviour is often grounded in a branch of psychology called *behavioural decision theory,* which has its roots in cognitive psychology, economics and statistics. According to Libby (1981, p. 2):

The goal of much of this work is to describe actual decision behavior, evaluate its quality, and develop and test theories of the underlying psychological processes which produce the behavior. In addition, these descriptions reveal flaws in the behavior and often suggest remedies for these deficiencies.

Behavioural research was first embraced by accounting researchers in the 1960s (Maines, 1995) but became particularly popular in the 1970s when embraced by researchers such as Ashton and Libby. It has been used to investigate a variety of decision making processes such as the valuation of market shares by individual analysts, the lending decisions of loan officers, the assessment of bankruptcy by bankers or auditors, and the assessment of risk by auditors.

Some of the various published behavioural research studies have been undertaken in a laboratory setting where a group of individuals are assigned a number of simple or complex tasks (which may or may not be reflective of 'real-life' decisions), while other research has been conducted in the individual's own workplace.[1] Behavioural research can have a number of aims. Some research has been undertaken to *understand* underlying decision making processes, while other research has been conducted to *improve* decision making. Some research manipulates the amount and types of information provided to particular subjects to assess how such differences impact on any final decisions, while other research provides all subjects with the same information and attempts to derive a model to explain how decisions by a particular category of decision maker appear to be made (for example, decisions by auditors, stockbrokers, bankers, or lending officers).

The Brunswik Lens Model

In explaining behavioural research, a number of researchers have found it useful to relate their work to a model developed by Brunswik, this being the Brunswik Lens Model (Brunswik, 1952). Libby (1981, p. 6) provides a simplistic representation of the Lens Model. See Figure 11.1.

Libby (1981, p. 5) illustrates the application of the Brunswik Lens Model to the decision by graduate schools to admit students. As indicated in Figure 11.1, the criterion event is the students' future success, denoted by $ (on the left-hand side of the model). Given that this event will take place in the future, the decisions made by admissions officers within particular schools must be based on a number of factors or environmental 'cues' (pieces of information), which can be probabilistically related to the particular event under consideration (in this case, student success). A number of cues can be used, for example GMAT scores, Grade point averages in prior studies, quality

---

1. A laboratory setting would constitute a setting different to where the subjects would normally undertake their work and where the researcher is relatively more able to control certain variables relating to the decision making task than would otherwise be possible.

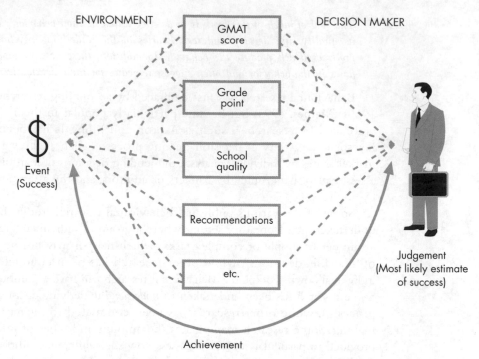

ENVIRONMENT

GMAT
score

Grade
point

School
quality

Recommendations

etc.

DECISION MAKER

$

Event
(Success)

Judgement
(Most likely estimate
of success)

Achievement

FIGURE 11.1 **A simple diagrammatic representation of the Brunswik Lens Model (after Libby, 1981, p. 5)**

of the undergraduate school attended, recommendations or references from various people, whether the individual participates in extracurricular activities, and answers to particular subjective questions.[2] As Libby indicates, none of these individual cues, or combinations of cues, can be expected to provide a perfect indication of the future success of the student, but some may be linked, with some degree of probability, to success. As Libby explains, in effect, perspectives about the environment (the issue in question in this case being student success) are generated (observed) through a 'lens' of imperfect cues. The relationships between these imperfect cues and the judgement about success are represented by broken lines.[3]

There would also be an expectation that some of the cues will be interrelated. For example the GMAT score might be expected to be correlated with grade point averages, as well as quality of school attended. Such interrelationships are represented by the broken lines linking the various cues, as indicated in Figure 11.1. To determine the weighting (or importance)

2. As we show later, in an accounting study such as the prediction of bankruptcy, the 'cues' might be information about various accounting ratios.

3. Libby (1981, p. 5) notes also that relative reliance on various cues is likely to change over time as a result of fatigue, special circumstances, learning, and so on.

of the various cues (independent variables) to the criterion event of success (the dependent variable which could simplistically be categorised as either success or failure in this case), as well as the correlations between the cues, various advanced statistical modelling approaches are applied. One model might be developed that provides a linear representation of the assessors' weightings of the various cues. This then provides a model of how the assessors actually went about their job of assessing applications. Knowledge of this model may be useful to a number of parties. For example, intending students would know what factors (cues) are particularly important to the assessors and hence the students may then know what factors to concentrate on. From the assessors' perspective it might be interesting for them to see how as a group they appear to be making their judgements. This might not be obvious until such a model is developed.

A model could also be developed that looks at the relationship between the actual outcome (student success or failure) and the various items of information available. That is, a model could also be developed by looking in the reverse direction from the event (the left-hand side) back to the cues (that is, not involving individuals making judgements). Obviously, such analysis could only be undertaken when a measure of actual success or failure can be obtained.

Libby (1981) provides an insight into the general applicability of the Lens Model to various decision making scenarios. As he states (p. 6):

> This structure is very general and can be applied to almost any decision-making scheme. Again, consider a simplified commercial lending decision in which the principal task of the loan officer is to predict loan default. Loan default–non default is mainly a function of the future cash flows which will be available to the customer to service the debt. The customer provides a number of cues, some of which are probabilistically related to future cash flows. These include indicators of liquidity, leverage, and profitability drawn from financial statements, management evaluations resulting from interviews, plant visits, discussions with other knowledgeable parties, and outside credit ratings. No individual cue or combinations of cues is a perfect predictor of future cash flows, and there is overlap in the information (e.g., credit ratings are closely associated with profitability and liquidity measures). In making this judgement, the loan officer combines these cues into a prediction of future cash flows. Even if the banker's judgemental policy is highly stable over time, some inconsistencies are likely to arise, which will result in a probabilistic relationship between the cues and the final judgement. At the end of the term of each loan, the officer's prediction of cash flows can be compared with the actual event, and any resulting losses can be computed to measure achievement. While this example is highly simplified, it illustrates the generality of the framework and its importance for accountants. The model's principal concern with information-processing achievements in an uncertain world coincides with accountants' interest in improving the decisions made by users of accounting information and their more recent attention to the quality of their own decisions.

In applying the Lens Model it is common for researchers to mathematically model both the left-hand and right-hand sides of the lens. For example, on the right-hand side of the model we are interested in providing a model (typically linear) of how the individual uses cues to make an ultimate decision about the issue under investigation. This is often the major goal of much behavioural research. This can be undertaken by considering how each particular cue individually relates to the ultimate decision (univariate analysis), or how the entire set of cues relates to the ultimate decision or judgement (multivariate analysis). If statistical regression is undertaken as part of the multivariate analysis, the decision maker's response might be summarised or modelled as follows:[4]

$$\hat{Y}_s = a_s + B_{1s}X_1 + B_{2s}X_2 + \ldots B_{ks}X_k \qquad \text{(Equation 1)}$$

where:

$\hat{Y}_s$ is the model's prediction of the judgement (for example, that the student succeeds or fails) based on the individual's judgements or predictions;

$X_1, X_2, \ldots X_k$ represent the set of cues (for example, the GMAT score, grade point average, etc.) for cue number 1 through to cue number k;

$B_1, B_2, \ldots B_k$ represent the weighting in the model given to each of the cues, based on the responses of the subjects.

If a cue contributes nothing to the prediction, it will be given a zero weighting. Because the model will need to be generated from many observations and because models such as the above assume that individual cues contribute to the decision in a linear manner, it is clear that the model will not explain or predict with total accuracy the actual judgements made by particular individuals—but as we would appreciate, it is not expected to— it is a model of individual behaviour. As Libby states (1981, p. 22):

> *It is important to note that the algebraic models resulting from these studies simply indicate the functional relationship between the* cues *and the* judgement. *These, like all models, are abstractions and do not purport to represent 'real' mental processes.*

Some researchers also model the left-hand side of the lens model (often referred to as the environmental side) which looks at the relationship between the *actual phenomenon* under consideration and the particular *cues* provided. Without relying on judgements provided by individuals, this equation can be used to predict a particular environmental event.[5] The model can be represented as follows:

---

4. We have elected to provide only a brief overview of this modelling. For further insight, interested readers are referred to Libby (1981, pp. 19–21) and Trotman (1996, pp. 33–6).

5. For example, Altman (1968) developed a bankruptcy prediction model by forming equations that related a particular environmental event (bankruptcy) with particular financial variables (derived from financial statements). Representative of modelling the left-hand side of the 'lens', no use was made of decisions of individual judges or experts.

$$\hat{Y}_e = a_e + B_{1e}X_1 + B_{2e}X_2 + \ldots B_{ke}X_k \qquad \text{(Equation 2)}$$

where:

$\hat{Y}_e$ is the model's prediction of the environmental event under consideration (for example, student succeeds or fails);

$X_1, X_2, \ldots X_k$ represent the set of cues (for example, the GMAT score, grade point average, etc.) for cue number 1 through to cue number k;

$B_1, B_2, \ldots, B_k$ represent the weighting in the model given to each of the cues, based on the modelling of the relationship between the actual event and the available cues.

Researchers often compare the results of the model derived from studying the decision making processes of individuals (Equation 1) with the results of the model provided by considering the relationship of the actual environmental event and the various cues (Equation 2). As we will see below, other issues focused on by researchers include how different individuals or groups weight particular cues, the consistency of the weighting, what issues associated with the presentation format of the cues might influence factor usage and weighting, and so on.

We can use the Lens Model to categorise a great deal of the behavioural research that has been undertaken over the last 20 to 30 years. The Lens Model explicitly considers *inputs* (uses of various cues), the *decision process*, and *outputs* (ultimate decisions). Libby (1981, p. 8) provides a summary of the type of issues that can be considered when undertaking research about how individuals process information when making a decision. These issues include:

At the *input* level (that is, issues pertaining to the cues):

- scaling characteristics of individual cues (for example, whether the presentation of the cues as nominal, ordinal, discrete, continuous, deterministic or probabilistic influences whether the cues are used in making a decision);

- method of presentation (for example, does the presentational format appear to impact on the use of the cue(s));

- context (for example, do perceived rewards, social setting, and so on, seem to impact on the use of the various cues).

At the level of *processing* the information:

- characteristics of the person making the judgement (for example, whether the demographics, attitudes of the judge, or the level of prior experience or interest impact on the decision that is made);

- characteristics of the decision rule (for example, how the individuals weight the cues; whether the judgements are stable over time; whether the judges use any simplifying heuristics when presented with potentially complex data).

At the *output* or decision level:

- qualities of the judgement (whether the response is accurate, quick, reliable; whether it incorporates particular biases; whether the judgements are consistent over time; whether there is consensus between the various judges);

- self-insight (whether the judge is aware of how they appear to weight various factors, etc.).

The use of particular information items and the implications of different forms of presentation

At the *input* level, the issue of how and whether particular cues (information items) are used in decision making is particularly relevant to the accounting profession. If it is shown that users of financial statements do not use particular information items (cues), it could be deemed that such information is not *material* and hence does not require disclosure, or associated disclosure regulation. The accounting profession would also be particularly interested in whether form of disclosure (for example, whether an item is provided in the statement of financial position, in a supplementary financial statement, or in a footnote) impacts on users' decisions. We now consider a limited number of papers that have considered such issues.[6]

In relation to the use of particular items of accounting information, Pankoff and Virgil (1970) investigated financial analysts' predictions of financial returns on particular shares. They found that the analysts acquired earnings and sales information (often through purchasing such information) more often than other types of information. In another study of financial analysts' information demands (cue usage) Mear and Firth (1987) also found that analysts believed that sales growth and profitability were particularly important for estimating returns on particular securities.

From time to time accounting professions throughout the world consider whether they should require reporting entities to provide additional information as a supplement to existing financial information. One particular instance of this was the accounting profession's move in the 1980s to require supplementary current cost financial information to be disclosed in corporate annual reports. Clearly, research can be useful in providing an insight into how and whether current cost information would actually be used by readers of

---

6. The overview of research provided in this chapter is certainly not comprehensive. Rather, the intention is to provide an insight into some of the different research that has been undertaken in this area. For those readers desiring a more comprehensive insight, reference could be made to Libby, 1981; Ashton, 1982; Ashton and Ashton, 1995; Trotman, 1996.

annual reports.[7] Such research includes that undertaken by Heintz (1973) and McIntyre (1973). These studies examined how three forms of disclosure impact on investment decisions. Subjects were provided with either historical cost information (only); current cost information (only); or both current cost and historical cost information. The results generally questioned the provision of current cost information, as the subjects did not appear to alter their decisions as a result of being provided with current cost information. Such results obviously challenged the accounting profession's move to require supplementary current cost information.[8]

Behavioural research has also been undertaken in human resource accounting, an area that has been typically neglected by the accounting profession. In related research, both Elias (1972) and Hendricks (1976) found that the disclosure of information on costs incurred in relation to recruiting, training and personnel development had an impact on subjects' decisions about acquiring shares in particular sample companies. We could imagine that such results, particularly if replicated across a number of studies, would potentially act as a stimulus for the accounting profession to put such issues on their agenda for consideration. In the absence of this type of research, the accounting profession might be ignorant of the fact that people would actually use such information if it were provided.

In relation to the *format of presentation* some studies have found that different presentation formats seem to impact on users' decisions. For example, some researchers have investigated how the presentation of particular graphics, such as the inclusion of bar charts, line graphs, pie charts and tables impact on the decisions of different user groups (DeSanctis and Jarvenpaa, 1989; Davis, 1989). In a famous piece of research, Moriarity (1979) examined whether the accuracy of subjects' (students and accounting practitioners) judgements pertaining to potential bankruptcy of merchandising firms was impacted by whether they were given a number of financial ratios, or whether they were provided with a series of schematic faces (referred to as

---

7. Also, behavioural research relating to reactions to particular disclosures can be done in advance of an accounting requirement being introduced. On the basis of the behavioural research findings, accounting regulators might determine that there is no point in progressing a particular issue past its initial stages of development. This can be contrasted with capital market research which relies on historical share price data; data which capture how the market actually reacted to the implementation or formal proposal of the particular requirement.

8. In Chapter 7 we discussed research that investigated the incentives for managers to lobby in support of, and/or to potentially adopt, a general price level accounting (which like current cost accounting, adjusts historical cost accounting information to take account of rising prices). Specifically we considered Watts and Zimmerman (1978). This research applied economic-based theory to explain lobbying positions of individuals. It did not directly involve any human subjects in the experimentation. Other research has considered how capital markets react to current cost information by investigating share price changes around the time of the information disclosure (for example, Lobo and Song, 1989). What is being emphasised here is that there is a variety of approaches that can be taken to investigate particular phenomena.

Chernoff faces, see Chernoff and Rizvi, 1975), where the faces themselves were constructed on the basis of the various ratios. Depending on the ratios, different facial features were provided (for example, mouth shape, angle of the eyebrow, nose length, represented changes in ratios). The findings of the research indicated that the students and accountants using the faces outperformed those using ratios in predicting bankruptcy. Further, the subjects using the faces were able to outperform models of bankruptcy that had been developed by other researchers (for example, Altman, 1968). The potential implications of this research are interesting. On the basis of the results, companies perhaps should provide numerous cartoon-like faces in their annual reports if they want to assist people in their decision making processes (perhaps the accounting profession might release an accounting standard on drawing faces?). However, to date, the disclosure of faces in annual reports is not an approach adopted by corporate management.

Another disclosure issue that has been addressed is whether subjects will make different decisions depending upon whether particular information is incorporated within the financial statements themselves, or included in footnotes only. One study that investigated this issue was Wilkins and Zimmer (1983). They studied the decisions of bank lending officers and how their decisions were influenced by whether information about leases was incorporated in the financial statements, or simply provided in the footnotes. They found that from the loan officers' perspective the format of disclosure did not impact on their assessment of the entity's ability to repay a debt. Again, such evidence should be of potential interest to the accounting profession when deciding whether to mandate adoption of particular accounting methods within the financial statements, or simply within the footnotes to those accounts.[9]

Research has also investigated whether the disclosure of segmental information will impact on the decisions of particular individuals. For example, Stallman (1969) found that providing information about industry segments reduced the subjects' reliance on past share prices when making choices to select particular securities. Doupnik and Rolfe (1989) found that subjects were more confident in making assessments about future prices of an entity's shares when they were also provided with information about geographical performance.

---

9. Consistent with a great deal of behavioural research, the results of Wilkins and Zimmer were contradicted by other research. For example, Sami and Schwartz (1992) provided evidence that loan officers' judgements about an entity's ability to repay a debt were influenced by whether information about pension liabilities was included in the financial statements or in the footnotes. However, because this research relates to pension liabilities, it is not clear whether the results contradict a general notion that users can equate information provided by way of footnote disclosure with information provided by financial statement disclosure, or whether the differences in the respective studies' results were due to the fact that one study considered pension liabilities, while the other study considered lease liabilities.

Decision making processes and the use of heuristics

In relation to research that considers the *processes* involved in making a judgement (the middle part of the Lens Model), a number of studies have considered issues associated with how the various cues (information items) are weighted. As an example of such research Schultz and Gustavson (1978) used actuaries as subjects (who were deemed to be experts) to develop a model to measure the litigation risk of accounting firms. They found that cues deemed to be important (relatively more weighted) were the number of accountants employed within the firm, the extent to which the work of the accountants was rotated among themselves, the size and financial condition of the clients, and the percentage of 'write-up' work performed.[10]

Another issue that has been considered is *consistency*. For example, do the individuals make the same judgements over time? Ashton (1974) investigated this issue. Ashton used 63 practising auditors in a study that required the auditors to assess the internal control system associated with an organisation's payroll. In undertaking the assessment the subjects were required to do the task twice, the second time being between 6 and 13 weeks after the first time. The findings indicated that the subjects were very consistent in their weightings over time and that the weightings between the various subjects were quite consistent. Further, the cue that was weighted the most was 'separation of duties'.

When considering how individuals make decisions, researchers have also found evidence that decision makers often appear to employ simplifying heuristics when making a decision.[11] Tversky and Kahneman (1974) identified three main heuristics often employed in decision making: representativeness, anchoring and adjustment, and availability. We can briefly consider them.

According to Maines (1995, p. 83), individuals who use the *representativeness heuristic* assess the likelihood of items belonging to a category by considering how similar the item is to the typical member of this category. For example, the probability that a certain person is an accountant would be assessed by how closely he or she resembles the image of a typical accountant. The fact that there may be few or many accountants is ignored. An implication of this bias is that individuals typically ignore the base rate of the population in question.

---

10. Another approach to gathering such information would simply be to send out questionnaires asking respondents to rank the importance of various items of information in terms of the various decisions they make. Of course this would be much simpler than a process involving the actual modelling of decision making which typically occurs in Lens Model-type research.

11. A heuristic can be defined as a simplifying 'rule of thumb'. That is, rather than fully considering all the potentially relevant factors, a simplifying rule may be employed which takes a lot less time but nevertheless generates a fairly acceptable (and cost effective) prediction or solution.

In some cases this bias has the effect of overstating the number of cases placed within a particular category. For example, in bankruptcy prediction studies, this bias may lead to an overstatement in the prediction of bankrupt firms as the base rate of real bankrupt firms is typically quite low.

The *anchoring and adjustment* heuristic indicates that individuals often make an initial judgement or estimate (perhaps based on past experience or through partial computation of the various factors involved) and then only partially adjust their view as a result of access to additional information. That is, they 'anchor' on a particular view and then will not move sufficiently in the light of additional information or changing circumstances. Joyce and Biddle (1981) undertook research that sought to provide evidence of this heuristic being used by auditors when they assess internal control systems. They found that new information (obtained through various substantive testing) was used by auditors to revise their assessments about the quality of internal controls, and that no evidence could be found of anchoring and adjustment. However, results of anchoring and adjustment were found when Kinney and Ueker (1982) investigated similar tasks. Other research to support the use of this heuristic is provided in Biggs and Wild (1985) and Butler (1986).

The *availability heuristic* relates to whether recollections of related occurrence and events can easily come to mind. That is, the probability judgements regarding the occurrence of an event are influenced by the ease with which the particular type of event can be recalled (Maines, 1995, p. 100). For example, in assessing the likelihood of a plane crash, a subject might overstate the probability as a result of remembering a number of highly publicised crashes. The actual base rates of such an occurrence are ignored. In a study of this heuristic, Moser (1989) found that when subjects were required to make an assessment about whether the earnings of a company would increase, their assessments were influenced by the order of the information provided to them.

We have briefly considered a number of heuristics, or rules of thumb, that might be employed in decision making. But, *so what*? Why would it be useful to know about such heuristics? First, if the heuristic results in inappropriate decisions being made (for example, lending funds to organisations that are not credit worthy, or accepting that internal controls are functioning soundly when they are not) then this behavioural tendency should be highlighted so that remedial action (perhaps training) can be undertaken.[12] Secondly, perhaps the heuristic employed by particular experts are efficient relative to costly data gathering and processing. If this is the case then perhaps novices should be encouraged to adopt the rule of thumb.

---

12. For example, Kida (1984) provides evidence that auditors when undertaking particular tasks often initially formulate a hypothesis to explain a certain event (for example, the reduction in bad debt write-offs) and then seek information to confirm this hypothesis (hypothesis-confirming strategies). Clearly, such information gathering is not objective and could expose the auditors to certain risks. Knowledge of this behavioural tendency would therefore be useful.

Issues of decision accuracy

When looking at the actual *output* of the decision making process (the decision or judgement) some research has considered how *accurate* the predictions are relative to the actual environmental outcomes. For example, Libby (1975) investigated the accuracy with which loan officers predict business failure. The results showed that loan officers were able to predict bankruptcies fairly regularly, with their various answers also being relatively consistent among them.

In a similar study, Zimmer (1980) investigated how accurate bankers and accounting students were in predicting bankruptcy when provided with a number of accounting related cues. The results showed that bankruptcies were typically correctly predicted. Also, a composite model of bankruptcy prediction generated from pooling all the bankers' responses typically outperformed the judgements of individuals.[13] A particularly interesting finding was that the students with limited experience performed nearly as well as the bankers.

Research has also considered the potential improvements to decision making that might result from combining the decisions of multiple decision makers. As noted above, Zimmer (1980) found that the composite model developed by combining the judgements of the different subjects was able to outperform judgements and models derived from individual subjects. Such findings are also presented in Libby (1976). Further, evidence indicates that decision makers working together in an interactive team can also outperform individuals working alone. Chalos (1985) found this result when reviewing the bankruptcy predictions of interacting loan officers, relative to predictions provided by loan officers working independently. Such results were subsequently explained by Chalos and Pickard (1985) as being due to the greater consistency in decision making that happens when groups, as opposed to individuals, are involved in making decisions. Again, these findings have implications for how organisations might make decisions in practice. Perhaps when major loans are being made, and assuming that these results are perceived as being reliable, banks should consider requiring approvals to be based on committee decisions.

Protocol analysis

Another approach to researching the decision making processes at the individual level that we can also briefly consider now is research undertaken using *verbal protocol analysis*. This form of analysis usually requires subjects to think aloud (that is, to verbalise their thought processes) while they are

---

13. As the composite model out-predicted the individuals, there could be a case to make the model available to the lending officers, particularly the inexperienced bankers. The model could provide a low-cost approach to screening loan applications at the initial stages of the application.

making decisions or judgements. The subjects' comments are taped and then transcribed for further coding and analysis.[14] This form of research has tended to be more popular in auditing than in other financial accounting areas. One of the first studies using this method was Biggs and Mock (1983) who reviewed judgements being made by auditors when assessing internal controls. Other auditing based studies to use verbal protocol analysis include Biggs, Mock and Watkins (1989) and Bedard and Biggs (1991).

According to Trotman (1996) there are a number of advantages and disadvantages in the use of protocol analysis. In relation to some possible advantages he states (p. 56):

One of the main advantages of verbal protocol analysis is the ability to examine the process by which judgements are made. Understanding how judgements are made is an important start in improving those judgements. Second, verbal protocols are particularly useful in examining information search. The sequence in which information is obtained can be traced and the amount of time a subject devotes to particular cues can be determined. Third, verbal protocol can be useful in theory development. For example, Biggs, Mock and Watkins (1989) suggest the need to 'begin gathering data about how auditors make analytical review judgements in realistic settings and attempt to build a new theory from the results'. (p. 16)

In relation to some of the potential disadvantages or limitations that arise from using verbal protocol analysis Trotman states (p. 56):

Consistent with all other methods of studying auditor judgements, verbal protocol studies have a number of limitations. First, it has been noted that the process of verbalising can have an effect on the auditors' decision process (Boritz, 1986). Second there is an incompleteness argument (Klersy and Mock, 1989) which suggests that a considerable portion of the information utilised by the subjects may not be verbalised. Third, some have described the process as epiphenomenal, that is, subjects provide verbalisations which parallel but are independent of the actual thought process. Fourth, there has been some criticism of the coding methods. For example, Libby (1981) notes that the choice of coding categories, the choice of phrases that serve as the unit of analysis, and the assignment of each phrase to categories are highly subjective. Libby suggests the need for comparisons using competing coding schemes. Finally, there are significant difficulties in communicating the results to the reader, given the large quantity of data and possibly large individual variations in decision processes.

---

14. This form of data collection can sometimes lead to many hundreds of pages of typed quotes which can tend to become quite unmanageable. There are a number of computer packages available to organise transcribed data into a more manageable form. One such package is NUDIST which stands for non-numerical, unstructured, data indexing, searching and theorising.

Trotman has provided a number of limitations in relation to protocol analysis which, as he indicates, can also be applied to behavioural research in general. In concluding our discussion on behavioural research, we further consider some of these limitations.

Limitations of behavioural research

First, as we have already seen in some of the material presented in this chapter, many of the studies that review similar issues generate conflicting results. This clearly has implications for whether the research can confidently provide guidance in particular areas. Unfortunately it is often difficult or impossible to determine what causes the inconsistencies in the various results because typically a number of variables differ between the studies (for example, the issue of concern, the realism of the setting, the experience and background of the subjects, the incentives provided, and so on). Further, within studies, differences in judgements between the subjects are frequently not explored to any extent, meaning that some unknown but potentially important decision making factor remains unknown.

Another perceived limitation relates to the settings in which the research is undertaken. These settings are quite often very different from real-world settings, with obvious implications for the generalisability of the findings. In the 'real world' there would typically be real incentives and ongoing implications from making particular decisions—this usually cannot be replicated in a laboratory setting.[15] Further, there will be no real accountability for the decisions being made.

Related to the above point is the realism of the cues provided to the subjects. It is very difficult to replicate the various cues that would typically be available in the workplace. Also knowing that the results on a particular judgement are being carefully scrutinised could clearly be expected to have an effect on the decision making processes being employed.

A number of studies also use students as surrogates for auditors, lending officers, and so on. This has also been seen as a limitation because such people perhaps have limited training in the area and have not had the same background experiences as the parties for whom they are acting as proxies

---

15. Interestingly, at one meeting of professional accountants held in Sydney some time ago (attended by the author) some researchers made use of the assembled attendees to undertake an experiment related to interactive judgements and their impact on bankruptcy prediction tasks. In an attempt to provide an 'incentive' (perhaps in an effort to increase the 'realism' of the task) at the commencement of the task the subjects were told that each member of the 'winning team' was to be provided with a bottle of whisky. Clearly this is an imperfect incentive and might actually introduce other unwanted factors into the analysis. For example, people with a 'drinking problem' might find this a tremendous incentive and really try hard to win. Others might be fairly indifferent, whereas others, perhaps with a religious objection to alcohol, might actually make judgements that guarantee that they and their team-mates will not 'win'.

(there has been some research that shows that students do make judgements comparable to those of particular experts. However, such findings are not universal).

A final criticism that we can raise is the typically small number of subjects used in experiments and again, whether results based on relatively small samples can be expected to apply to the larger population.

What still appears to be lacking in this area of research is a theory as to why people rely upon particular items of information, adopt simplifying heuristics in some situations, and so on. For example, much of the research tells us that some decision makers were consistent in their judgements, while others were not, or that particular groups seemed to adopt a particular heuristic. But we are still not sure *why* they did this. Perhaps theory will develop in this area.

Chapter summary

In this chapter we consider how individuals use information to make decisions. More specifically we consider how individuals use accounting information to make a variety of judgements. Research pertaining to individual decision making (behavioural research) has shed a deal of light on how various groups of individuals such as auditors, lending officers, bankers, and so on, make decisions. We found that financial statement users often employ simplifying heuristics when making particular judgements. The perspective taken is that if we know how individuals appear to make decisions, we can *anticipate* how they will react to particular accounting disclosures and forms of disclosures. This could be particularly relevant to the accounting profession when contemplating the introduction of a new accounting requirement. Knowledge of how financial statement users make decisions could also provide the basis for making suggestions about how decision making can be improved (for example, it might be found that a certain category of financial statement users are inappropriately adopting particular heuristics, possibly unknowingly, that could lead to potentially costly implications).

References

Altman, E.I., 'Financial Ratios, Discriminant Analysis and the Prediction of Corporate Bankruptcy', *Journal of Finance*, Vol. 23, No. 4, pp. 589–609, 1968.

Ashton, R.H., 'An Experimental Study of Internal Control Judgements', *Journal of Accounting Research*, Vol. 12, pp. 143–57, 1974.

Ashton, R.H., *Human Information Processing in Accounting*, American Accounting Association Studies in Accounting Research No. 17, American Accounting Association, Florida, 1982.

Ashton, A.H., Ashton, R.H. (Editors), *Judgement and Decision Making Research in Accounting and Auditing*, Cambridge University Press, 1995.

Bedard, J.C., Biggs, S.F., 'Pattern Recognition, Hypothesis Generation, and Auditor Performance in an Analytical Review Task', *The Accounting Review*, Vol. 66, No. 3, pp. 622–42, 1991.

Biggs, S.F., Mock, T.J., 'An Investigation of Auditor Decision Processes in the Evaluation of Internal Controls and Audit Scope Decisions', *Journal of Accounting Research*, Vol. 21, No. 1, pp. 234–55, 1983.

Biggs, S.F., Mock, T.J., Watkins, P.R., *Analytical Review Procedures and Processes in Auditing*, Audit Research Monograph No. 14, The Canadian Certified Accountants' Research Foundation, 1989.

Biggs, S.F., Wild, J.J., 'An Investigation of Auditor Judgement in Analytical Review', *The Accounting Review*, Vol. 60, No. 4, pp. 607–33, 1985.

Boritz, J.E., 'The Effect of Research on Audit Planning and Review Judgements', *Journal of Accounting Research*, Vol. 24, No. 2, pp. 335–48, 1986.

Brunswik, E., *The Conceptual Framework of Psychology*, University of Chicago Press, Chicago, 1952.

Butler, S., 'Anchoring in the Judgmental Evaluation of Audit Samples', *The Accounting Review*, Vol. 61, No. 1, pp. 101–11, 1986.

Chalos, P., 'Financial Distress: A Comparative Study of Individual, Model and Committee Assessments', *Journal of Accounting Research*, Vol. 23, pp. 527–43, 1985.

Chalos, P., Pickard, S., 'Information Choice and Cue Use: An Experiment in Group Information Processing', *Journal of Applied Psychology*, Vol. 70, pp. 634–41, 1985.

Chernoff, H., Rizvi, M., 'Effect of Classification Error on Random Permutations of Features in Representing Multivariate Data by Faces', *Journal of the American Statistical Association*, Vol. 70, pp. 548–54, 1975.

Davis, L., 'Report Format and the Decision Makers' Task: An Experimental Investigation', *Accounting, Organizations and Society*, Vol. 14, pp. 495–508, 1989.

DeSanctis, G., Jarvenpaa, S., 'Graphical Presentation of Accounting Data for Financial Forecasting: An Experimental Investigation', *Accounting, Organizations and Society*, Vol. 14, pp. 509–25, 1989.

Doupnik, T., Rolfe, R., 'The Relevance of Aggregation of Geographic Area Data in the Assessment of Foreign Investment Risk', in *Advances in Accounting*, Vol. 7, JAI Press, Greenwich CT, pp. 51–65, 1989.

Elias, N., 'The Effects of Human Asset Statements on the Investment Decision: An Experiment', *Journal of Accounting Research*, Vol. 10, pp. 215–33, 1972.

Heintz, J.A., 'Price-Level Restated Financial Statements and Investment Decision Making', *The Accounting Review*, Vol. 48, pp. 679–89, 1973.

Hendricks, J., 'The Impact of Human Resource Accounting Information on Stock Investment Decisions: An Empirical Study', *The Accounting Review*, Vol. 51, pp. 292–305, 1976.

Joyce, E.J., Biddle, G.C., 'Anchoring and Adjustment in Probabilistic Inference in Auditing', *Journal of Accounting Research*, Vol. 19, pp. 120–45, 1981.

Kida, T., 'The Impact of Hypothesis Testing Strategies on Auditor's Use of Judgement Data', *Journal of Accounting Research*, Vol. 22, pp. 332–40, 1984.

Kinney, W.R., Ueker, W.C., 'Mitigating the Consequences of Anchoring in Auditor Judgements', *The Accounting Review*, Vol. 57, pp. 55–69, 1982.

Klersy, G. F., Mock, T. J., 'Verbal Protocol Research in Auditing', *Accounting Organizations and Society*, Vol. 14, No. 2, pp. 133–51, 1989.

Libby, R., 'Accounting Ratios and the Prediction of Failure: Some Behavioral Evidence', *Journal of Accounting Research*, Vol. 13, No. 1, pp. 150–61, 1975.

Libby, R., 'Man Versus Model of Man: The Need for a Non-Linear Model', *Organizational Behavior and Human Performance*, Vol. 16, pp. 13–26, 1976.

Libby, R., *Accounting and Human Information Processing: Theory and Applications*, Prentice-Hall, Englewood Cliffs, 1981.

Lobo, G.J., Song, I.M., 'The Incremental Information in SFAS No. 33 Income Disclosures over Historical Cost Income and its Cash and Accrual Components', *The Accounting Review*, Vol. 64, No. 2, pp. 329–43, 1989.

Maines, L.A., 'Judgment and Decision-making Research in Financial Accounting: A Review and Analysis', in *Judgment and Decision-Making Research in Accounting and Auditing*, R.H. Ashton and A.H. Ashton (Editors), Cambridge Press, 1995.

McIntyre, E., 'Current Cost Financial Statements and Common Stock Investment Decisions', *The Accounting Review*, Vol. 48, pp. 575–85, 1973.

Mear, R., Firth, M., 'Assessing the Accuracy of Financial Analyst Security Return Predictions', *Accounting, Organizations and Society*, Vol. 12, pp. 331–40, 1987.

Moriarity, S., 'Communicating Financial Information Through Multidimensional Graphics', *Journal of Accounting Research*, Vol. 17, pp. 205–24, 1979.

Moser, D., 'The Effects of Output Interference, Availability, and Accounting Information on Investors' Predictive Judgements', *The Accounting Review*, Vol. 64, No. 3, pp. 433–44, July 1989.

Pankoff, L., Virgil, R., 'Some Preliminary Findings from a Laboratory Experiment on the Usefulness of Financial Accounting Information to Security Analysts', *Journal of Accounting Research*, Vol. 8, pp. 1–48, 1970.

Sami, H., Schwartz, B., 'Alternative Pension Liability Disclosure and the Effect on Credit Evaluation: An Experiment', *Behavioral Research in Accounting*, Vol. 4, pp. 49–62, 1992.

Schultz, J.J., Gustavson, S.G., 'Actuaries' Perceptions of Variables Affecting the Independent Auditor's Legal Liability', *The Accounting Review*, Vol. 53, pp. 626–41, 1978.

Stallman, J., 'Toward Experimental Criteria for Judging Disclosure Improvements', *Journal of Accounting Research*, Vol.7, pp. 29–43, 1969.

Trotman, K.T., *Research Methods for Judgement and Decision Making Studies in Auditing*, Coopers and Lybrand Research Methodology Monograph No. 3, Coopers and Lybrand, Melbourne, 1996.

Tversky, A., Kahneman, D., 'Judgment Under Uncertainty: Heuristics and Biases', *Science*, Vol. 185, pp. 1124–31, 1974.

Watts, R.L., Zimmerman, J.L., 'Towards a Positive Theory of the Determinants of Accounting Standards', *The Accounting Review*, Vol. LIII, No. 1, January 1978.

Wilkins, T., Zimmer, I., 'The Effect of Leasing and Different Methods of Accounting for Leases on Credit Evaluation', *The Accounting Review*, Vol. 63, pp. 747–64, 1983.

Zimmer, I., 'A Lens Study of the Prediction of Corporate Failure by Bank Loan Officers', *Journal of Accounting Research*, Vol. 18., No. 2, pp. 629–36, 1980.

Questions

11.1 Contrast behavioural research with capital market research.

11.2 How and why would the accounting profession use the results of behavioural research in accounting?

11.3 How and why would the management of individual reporting entities be interested in the results of behavioural research in accounting?

11.4 Briefly explain the Brunswik Lens Model and its relevance to explaining the various facets of the decision making process.

11.5 What is a 'heuristic' and why could it be beneficial for a group of financial statement users to be informed that they are applying a particular heuristic?

11.6 What is the point of modelling the decision making processes of different financial statement user groups (that is, for example, identifying how they appear to weight particular cues when making judgements)?

11.7 If the results of behavioural research indicate that a particular accounting-related information item (cue) is not used by individuals when making decisions, should this be grounds for the accounting profession to conclude that such information is not material and therefore does not warrant the related development of mandatory disclosure requirements? Explain your answer.

11.8 There have been a number of behavioural studies in financial accounting and auditing that have generated conflicting results. What are some possible reasons for the disparity in results?

11.9 What is 'protocol analysis' and what are some of its strengths and weaknesses?

11.10 What are some general strengths and limitations of behavioural research?

Chapter 12

Critical perspectives of accounting

Learning objectives

Upon completing this chapter readers should:

- have gained an insight into particular perspectives that challenge conventional opinions about the role of accounting within society;

- understand the basis of arguments that suggest that financial accounting tends to support the positions of individuals who hold wealth and social status, while undermining the positions of others;

- understand that the disclosure (or non-disclosure) of information can be construed to be an important strategy to promote and legitimise particular social orders.

Opening issues

Conceptual Framework Projects promote approaches to financial accounting that are built on qualitative characteristics such as *neutrality* and *representational faithfulness*. What are some arguments that challenge the *neutrality* and *objectivity* of financial reports?

Introduction

In previous chapters we explored numerous issues, including how accounting may be used to: assist in decision making (Chapters 4 and 5); reduce agency and political costs (Chapter 7); maintain or assist in bringing legitimacy to an organisation (Chapter 8); and to satisfy the information demands of particular stakeholders (Chapter 8). We also considered how the practice of accounting could be modified to take into account some social and environmental aspects of an organisation's operations (Chapter 9), as well as considering how accounting disclosures might impact on share prices (Chapter 10). In this chapter we provide an overview of an alternative perspective of the role of accounting. This perspective, which is often called the *critical perspective*, explicitly considers how the practice of accounting tends to support particular economic and social structures.

The view promoted by researchers operating from a *critical perspective* is that accounting, far from being a practice that provides a *neutral* or *unbiased* representation of underlying economic facts, actually provides the means of maintaining the powerful positions of some sectors of the community (those currently in *power*, and with wealth), while holding back the position and interests of those without wealth. These theorists challenge any perspectives that suggest that various *rights* and *privileges* are spread throughout society—instead, they argue that most rights, opportunities and associated power reside in a small (but perhaps well defined) *elite*.

This chapter considers various (critical) arguments about the role of the State (government); the role of accounting research; and the role of accounting practice in sustaining particular social orders that are already in place—social orders that some researchers argue function on the basis of inequities, where some individuals (with capital) prosper at the expense of those without capital. We will see that researchers adopting a critical perspective often do not provide direct solutions to particular inequities, but rather seek to highlight the inequities in society and the role of accounting in sustaining and legitimising those perceived inequities.

The critical perspective defined

The critical perspective itself is not easy to define. The term has been used to refer to an approach to accounting research that goes beyond questioning whether particular methods of accounting should be employed and instead focuses on the role of accounting in sustaining the privileged positions of those in control of particular resources (capital) while undermining or restraining the voice of those without capital. The researchers, who we call *critical accounting theorists*, seek to highlight, through critical analysis, the key role of accounting in society. The perspective they provide challenges the view that accounting can be construed as being objective or neutral, and these researchers often seek to provide evidence to support this view. Accounting is seen as a means of constructing or legitimising particular social structures. As Hopper at al. (1995, p. 528) state:

> . . . *in communicating reality accountants simultaneously construct it (Hines, 1988) and accounting is a social practice within political struggles and not merely a market practice guided by equilibrium in an efficient market.*

This view is supported by Baker and Bettner (1997, p. 305). They state:

> *Critical researchers have convincingly and repeatedly argued that accounting does not produce an objective representation of economic 'reality', but rather provides a highly contested and partisan representation of the economic and social world. As such, the underlying substance of accounting cannot be obtained through an ever more sophisticated elaboration of quantitative methods. Accounting's essence can be best captured through an understanding of its impacts on individuals, organisations and societies. Hence it is important for accounting research to adopt a critical perspective.*

Many of the critical researchers tend to be opponents of many aspects of the capitalist system and of accounting, which they see as a means of legitimising the capitalist order. They emphasise that systems of accounting are built around the prevailing social order. Reflecting on the role of accounting in a capitalistic society, Tinker, Merino and Neimark (1982, p. 178) explain:

> *Theoretical categories such as capital, rent, profit and wages are not universal to all wealth producing societies; they are (socially) specific to capitalism and therefore to its social relations because, in the final analysis, it is the social relations of capitalism that distinguish it from other social systems.*

As Gray, Owen and Adams (1996, p. 63) state, a major concern of the critical (or 'radical' theorists) is that:

> . . . *the very way in which society is ordered, the distribution of wealth, the power of corporations, the language of economics and business and so on, are so fundamentally flawed that nothing less than radical structural change has any hope of emancipating human and non-human life. The social, economic and political systems are seen as being fundamentally inimical.*

Given that the practice of accounting is in the hands of reporting entities, such as large corporations, and accounting regulation is in the hands of government and associated regulatory bodies (which are viewed as having a vested interest in maintaining the *status quo*), accounting information will, it is argued, never act to do anything but support our current social system, complete with all its perceived problems and inequities.

The critical perspective adopted by many researchers is grounded in Political Economy Theory, which we considered in Chapter 8. More specifically, critical accounting research tends to be grounded in 'Classical' Political Economy Theory. As Chapter 8 indicates, the 'political economy' has been defined by Gray, Owen and Adams (1996, p. 47) as the 'social, political and economic framework within which human life takes place'. The view is that *society*, *politics* and *economics* are inseparable, and economic issues cannot meaningfully be investigated in the absence of considerations about the political, social and institutional framework in which economic activity takes place. As Guthrie and Parker (1990, p. 166) state:

> *The political economy perspective perceives accounting reports as social, political, and economic documents. They serve as a tool for constructing, sustaining and legitimising economic and political arrangements, institutions and ideological themes which contribute to the organisation's private interests.*

As Chapter 8 also indicates, Political Economy Theory has been divided into two broad streams that Gray, Owen and Adams (1996, p. 47) and others have classified as 'classical' and 'bourgeois' political economy. The 'bourgeois' political economy perspective does not explore structural inequities, sectional interests, class struggles and the like.[1] It accepts the way society is currently structured as 'a given'. Many critical theorists consider that research that simply accepts the existing nature and structure of society without challenge effectively supports that (undesirable) society (Hopper and Powell, 1985). By concentrating on 'society' at a broader level it thereby tends to ignore struggles and inequities within society (Puxty, 1991). Prominent critical researchers such as Tinker, Puxty, Lehman, Hopper and Cooper have often considered it necessary to challenge the works of researchers such as Gray, Owen, Maunders, Mathews and Parker (these researchers, plus a number of others, have researched numerous issues associated with corporate social responsibility reporting); individuals who have for many years been promoting the need for organisations to be more accountable for their social and environmental performance (that is, to provide more information in relation to whether the corporations are meeting community expectations in their social and environmental performance).

While, to many of us, calls for greater disclosure of social responsibility information would seem to be a move in the right direction, the critical theorists argue that such efforts are wasted unless they are accompanied by fundamental changes in how society is structured. They would tend to argue that the disclosure of corporate social responsibility information only acts to legitimise, and not challenge, those providing the information. Cooper and Sherer (1984) argue that attempts to resolve technical issues (for example, how

---

1. Legitimacy Theory and Stakeholder Theory, which were both examined in Chapter 8, are embedded within a 'bourgeois' political economy perspective.

to account for environmental externalities) without consideration of the existing social and political environment may result in an imperfect and incomplete resolution, owing to the acceptance of current institutions and practices.

Reflecting on some of the views of critical theorists about the deficiencies of social and environmental accounting research, Owen, Gray and Bebbington (1997, p. 181) note:

> Early radical critique of the social accounting movement emanated from a socialist, largely Marxist, perspective. For writers such as Tinker et al. (1991) and Puxty (1986; 1991) society is characterised by social conflict. In Tinker et al.'s (1991) analysis, the social accounting movement, particularly as represented in the work of Gray et al. (1987; 1988), fails to examine the basic contradictions and antinomies of the social system under investigation and is therefore, at best, irrelevant, and, at worst, malign, in implicitly adopting a stance of 'political quietism' that simply benefits the already powerful (i.e. the capitalist class). Thus, for example, Puxty writing in 1986 suggested the irrelevance of social accounting, in noting that 'more radical critics of capitalist society have been more concerned with the broader issues of accountancy and accountants within that sociey than particular (almost parochial) issues such as social accounting which appears to be . . . rearranging the deck chairs on the Titanic'. (p. 107)
>
> However, by 1991, Puxty had taken his critique a stage further in arguing that by leaving basic social structures intact, social accounting can even lead to legitimation 'since the powerful can point to their existence as evidence of their openness in listening to criticism, it paves the way for . . . the extension of power'. (p. 37)

As accounting is deemed to sustain particular social structures, the introduction of new forms of accounting (for example, experimental methods relating to accounting for social costs) will only help sustain that social system. It is considered to be a wasted effort to use accounting (or additional accounting) to solve particular problems. Reflecting on the critical theorists' perception of the ongoing research being undertaken to explore how to account for the social and environmental implications of business, Gray, Owen and Adams (1996, p. 63) state that the critical theorists consider that by undertaking such research:

> . . . one is using the very process (current economics and accounting) that caused the problem (environmental crisis) to try to solve the problem. This is known as the process of 'juridification' and it is well established that one is unlikely to solve a problem by applying more of the thing which caused the problem.

As previously stated, the critical perspective tends to be grounded in a 'classical' political economy perspective. According to Gray, Owen and Adams (1996, p. 47), classical political economy is related to the works of philosophers such as Karl Marx and as such explicitly considers structural conflict, inequity, and the role of the State at the heart of the analysis.[2]

By adopting a research (and arguably, ideological) perspective that is grounded in 'classical' Political Economy Theory, such individuals can highlight particular issues that might not otherwise be addressed. According to Cooper and Sherer (1984, p. 208):

Social welfare is likely to be improved if accounting practices are recognised as being consistently partial; that the strategic outcomes of accounting practices consistently (if not invariably) favour specific interests in society and disadvantage others. Therefore, we are arguing that there already exists an established, if implicit, conceptual framework for accounting practice. A political economy of accounting emphasises the infrastructure, the fundamental relations between classes in society. It recognises the institutional environment which supports the existing system of corporate reporting and subjects to critical scrutiny those issues (such as assumed importance of shareholders and securities markets) that are frequently taken for granted in current accounting research.

When discussing the perspectives provided by critical researchers we should appreciate that the term 'the critical perspective' is a very broad term that captures a variety of different views about accounting. However, what these researchers have in common is that they seek to highlight the perceived role of accounting in supporting the positions of some people in society. As Hopper et al. (1995, p. 535) state:

Critical theory is an umbrella term for a wide variety of theoretical approaches perhaps more united in what they oppose than what they agree upon.

Critical theorists provide argument which is often driven by a desire to create a climate for change in social structures. By arguing for a change in the *status quo* it has been argued that 'critical researchers' are often marginalised to a greater extent than researchers adopting other theoretical or ideological perspectives (Baker and Bettner, 1997). The basis of some of this 'marginalisation' is that critical theorists often do not provide solutions to what they see as perceived problems. That is, they are often 'critical' without providing direct guidance on how the perceived problems can be

---

2. While a great deal of critical research is informed by the work of philosophers such as Karl Marx, Owen, Gray and Bebbington (1997) also refer to critical researchers who are identified as 'deep ecologists' and 'radical feminists'. The 'deep ecologists' question the trade-off between economic performance and ecological damage—they question the morality of systems that justify the extinction of species on the basis of associated economic benefits. The 'radical feminists' believe that accounting maintains and reinforces masculine traits such as the need for success and competition, and that accounting acts to reduce the relevance of issues such as cooperation, respect, compassion, etc.

solved.[3] For example, Owen, Gray and Bebbington (1997) argue that critical analysis alone is perhaps not enough. As they state (p. 183):

Restricting one's activities to critique, rather than actively seeking to reform practice, we would suggest, poses a minimal threat to current orthodoxy. Thus Neu and Cooper (1997) are led to observe that: 'while critical accounting scholars have illuminated the partisan functioning of accounting, we have been less successful in transforming accounting (and social) practices'. (p. 1)

As accountants, we are often trained to provide information to solve particular (predominantly economic) problems, hence 'culturally', many of us might be conditioned against criticism that does not provide *solution*. Reflecting on the 'attitudes and orientations' of accountants, Cooper and Sherer (1984, p. 222) state:

A critical approach to accounting, however, starts from the premise that problems in accounting are potentially reflections of problems in and of society and accordingly that the latter should be critically analysed. Thus if a major problem in accounting is identified, say as its overwhelming orientation to investors, then a critical perspective would suggest that this problem is a reflection of society's orientation and to change accounting practice requires both social awareness (e.g. identification of alternative 'accounts' and the roles of accounting in society) and ultimately social change.

Whether critical theory can in practice be applied to accounting research depends on whether researchers can free themselves from the attitudes and orientations which result from their social and educational training and which are reinforced by the beliefs of the accounting profession and the business community. For this socialisation process has produced accounting researchers who may exhibit subconscious bias in the definition of the problem set of accounting and the choice of theories to analyse and solve these problems. The criterion of critical awareness involves recognising the contested nature of the problem set and theories and demystifying the ideological character of those theories.

Critical theorists are often strong in their condemnation of accountants, and this in itself could also provide a basis for a deal of the marginalisation that many believe they experience. Consider the statement of Tinker, Lehman and Neimark (1991, p. 37):

---

3. From a research perspective it has also been argued that critical theorists have been marginalised because they do not tend to use mathematical modelling and statistical analysis—both of which have become (to many researchers, as well as to a number of editors of accounting journals) part of accepted accounting research. As Hopper et al. (1995, p. 532) state: 'Critical researchers emphasise the social embeddedness of accounting practice, consequently, they tend to neglect mathematical modelling, preferring detailed historical and ethnological studies of structures and processes which help identify societal linkages to show that accounting is not merely a technically rational service activity but plays a vital role in effecting wealth transfers at micro-organisational and macro-societal levels (Chua, 1986).'

The enduring nature of this 'Radical Critique' is attributable to the persistence of the underlying social antagonisms, to which it attempts to speak, and the complicity of accountants, which it seeks to elucidate.

Being informed that we, as accountants, are *complicit* in relation to 'social antagonisms' is not something that is likely to be seen in a favourable light by many accountants and accounting researchers. It is confronting. However, although we might elect not to necessarily agree with what a number of the critical theorists are telling us (perhaps because of some profound ideological differences) it is nevertheless useful, perhaps, to put ourselves under scrutiny from a broader societal perspective. The critical theorists encourage such scrutiny.

A review of the literature will show that a number of critical theorists have been vocal critics of research that has adopted Positive Accounting Theory as its theoretical basis, as well as being critical of related capital market research (we look more closely at this issue later in this chapter). Positive Accounting Theory focuses on conflicts between what might be construed as 'powerful' groupings within society (for example, owners, managers, debtholders) and does not consider conflicts between parties that cannot impact on the wealth of such powerful parties. Many critical theorists have also been particularly critical of the anti-regulation stance often advocated by Positive Accounting theorists because such a stance further advances the interests of those with power or wealth (for example, owners of corporations) while undermining the interests of those who might need some form of regulatory protection. Critical theorists would also argue that in assessing the usefulness of accounting information we really need to look beyond capital market (share price) reactions. The capital market response is driven (obviously) by those with capital. Capital market studies ignore 'other voices'.

In the discussion that follows, we consider perspectives about the role of the State, accounting research, and ultimately, accounting practice in supporting current social structures. Again, as has been emphasised throughout this book, the views that are presented below are those of a subset of the research community. There will, as we would expect, be other 'subsets' of the research community that challenge such views.

The role of the State in supporting existing social structures

Researchers working within the critical perspective typically see the State (government) as being a vehicle of support for the holders of capital, as well as the capitalist system as a whole. Under this perspective the government will undertake various actions from time to time to enhance the legitimacy of the social system, even though it might appear (to less critical eyes) that the government was acting in the interests of particular disadvantaged groups. For instance, a government might impose mandatory disclosure requirements for corporations in terms of the disclosure of information about how the corporations attend to the needs of certain minorities, or the disabled. Arnold (1990) would argue, however, that such disclosures (which, on average, really do not cause excessive inconvenience for companies) are really implemented to pacify the challenges that may be made against the capitalist system in which corporations are given many rights and powers. Relating this perspective to the development of various securities acts throughout the world, Merino and Neimark (1982, p. 49) contend that 'the securities acts were designed to maintain the ideological, social and, economic status quo while restoring confidence in the existing system and its institutions'.

It is generally accepted that to make informed decisions, an individual or groups of individuals must have access to information. Restricting the flow of information, or the availability of specific types of information, can restrict the ability of other parties to make informed choices. Hence, restricting available information is one strategy that can be employed to assist in the maintenance of particular organisations and social structures. Puxty (1986, p. 87) promotes this view by arguing that:

> . . . financial information is legislated by the governing body of society (the state) which is closely linked to the interests of the dominant power group in society (Offe and Ronge, 1978; Miliband, 1969, 1983) and regulated either by agencies of that state or by institutions such as exist within societies like the United Kingdom, United States, and Australia that are linked to the needs of the dominant power group in partnership with the state apparatus (albeit a partnership that is potentially fraught with conflict).

Hence we are left with a view that government does not operate in the public interest, but in the interests of those groups that are already *well off*.

Apart from the State and the accounting profession, researchers and research institutions have also been implicated as assisting in the promotion of particular (inequitable) social structures. We now consider some of the arguments that have been advanced to support this view.

The role of accounting research in supporting existing social structures

Rather than thinking of accounting researchers as being relatively *inert* with respect to their impact on parties outside their discipline, numerous critical theorists see many accounting researchers as providing research results and perspectives that help to legitimise and maintain particular political ideologies. Again, this is a different perspective than most of us would be used to.

As an example, in the late 1970s and in the 1980s there were moves by particular governments around the world towards deregulation. This was particularly the case in the US and the UK. Around this time, researchers working within the Positive Accounting Framework, and researchers who embraced the Efficient Market Hypothesis, came to prominence.[4] The researchers typically took an anti-regulation stance, a stance that matched the views of the government of the time. Coincidentally perhaps, such research, which supported calls for deregulation, tended to attract considerable government-sourced research funding.[5] As Hopper et al. (1995, p. 518) state:

> *Academic debates do not exist in a vacuum. It is not enough for a paradigm to be intellectually convincing for its acceptance, it must also be congruent with prevailing powerful beliefs within society more generally. The history of ideas is littered with research that was mocked but which subsequently became the dominant paradigm when other social concerns, ideologies and beliefs became prevalent. The story of PAT can be told in such terms. Its rise was not just due to its addressal of academic threats and concerns at the time of its inception but it was also in tandem with and connected to the right wing political ideologies dominant in the 1980s.*

Mouck (1992) also adopts a position that argues that the rise of Positive Accounting Theory was made possible because it was consistent with the political views of those in power (that is, the State). He argues that:

> *. . . the credibility of Watts and Zimmerman's rhetoric of revolt against government regulation of corporate accountability was conditioned, to a large extent, by the widespread, ultra-conservative movement toward deregulation that was taking place in society at large . . . I would argue that accountants have been willing to accept the PAT story, which is built on Chicago's version of laissez faire economics, because the rhetoric of the story was very much attuned to the Reagan era revolt against government interference in economic affairs.*

Consistent with the development of PAT, in the late 1970s a great deal of accounting research sought to highlight the economic consequences of new accounting regulation. This perspective (which we considered in Chapters 2 and 3) argues that the implementation of new accounting regulations can have many unwanted economic implications, and hence, before a new requirement, such as an accounting standard, is mandated, careful consideration is warranted. Economic consequences analysis often provided a rationale for not implementing accounting regulation. Critical researchers have argued that it was the economic implications for shareholders (for example, through changes in share prices) and managers (for example, through reductions in salary or loss of employment) that were the focus of attention by those who researched the economic consequences of accounting regulation. As Cooper and Sherer (1984, pp. 215, 217) argue:

---

4. According to Tinker, Merino and Neimark (1982), researchers within the Positive Accounting and Efficient Markets paradigm adopted 'a neoconservative ideological bias that encourages us to take the "free" market and implicit institutional apparatus as given'.

5. Consistent with this perspective, in 1979, Milton Friedman, a leading advocate of deregulation, became a senior adviser to President Reagan.

It seems unfortunate, however, that the 'rise of economic consequences' (Zeff, 1978) seems to have been motivated, at least in the United States, by a desire of large corporations to counter attempts to change the existing reporting systems and levels of disclosure. To date, it would seem that accounting researchers have generally reiterated the complaints of investors and businessmen about the consequences of changes in required accounting practice. Studies using ECA (economic consequences analysis) have almost invariably evaluated the consequences of accounting reports solely in terms of the behaviors and interest of the shareholder and/or corporate manager class (Selto and Neumann, 1981).

More fundamentally, studies adopting the ECA approach have focused their attention on a very limited subset of the total economy, namely, the impact on the shareholder or manager class. The effects of accounting reports directly on other users, e.g., governments and unions, and indirectly on 'non-users', e.g. consumers, employees, and taxpayers, have been ignored. The basis of such a decision can, at best, be that any such effects are either secondary and/or lacking in economic significance. Thus, these studies have made an implicit value statement that the needs of the shareholder and manager class are of primary importance and the concentration on those needs is sufficient for an understanding of the role of accounting reports in society. Unless the insignificance of the effects on other users and 'non-users' is demonstrated rather than merely assumed, the conclusion from this research cannot be generalised for the economy as a whole and these studies are insufficient for making accounting prescriptions intended to improve overall social welfare.

Apart from indicating that economic consequences research focused predominantly on the economic implications for managers and shareholders, Cooper and Sherer (1984) also note that major studies that adopted this paradigm were funded by the Securities Exchange Commission and the Financial Accounting Standards Board. It was considered that the interests of these bodies were aligned with the 'shareholder and manager class', rather than society as a whole.

In a similar vein, Thompson (1978) and Burchell et al. (1980) suggest that the research efforts into inflation accounting in the 1960s and 1970s were not actually motivated by the rate of inflation *per se*. Instead, they argue that the research had been motivated by a desire to alleviate the shifts in real wealth away from owners (in the form of lower real profits and dividends) and towards higher wages.

If research gains prominence because it supports particular political beliefs of those in power, then we might assume that as the views of those in 'power' change, so will the focus of research. In recent years many governments around the world have tended to move away from deregulation. Reflecting on this, Hopper et al. (1995, p. 540) note:

The environment is continually being reconstituted within changing economic, political conditions. Accordingly, the ability of PAT to resonate with the prevailing discursive climate may be subject to challenge . . . Following the removal of the Republican government in the USA, this particular period and form of conservative reform may have ended. In the USA President Clinton is adopting a more interventionist strategy and in the UK, the Major regime claims to espouse an alternative 'caring society', albeit with market forces, in contrast to the harsher face of Thatcherism. In the 1990s a new set of values may be emerging which do not emphasise so greatly the efficiency and effectiveness of unregulated markets, for example, ecology, health care in the USA, gender issues. The ability of PAT to resonate with this changed environment may be brought into question, for example, the consecutive failure of some business enterprises and the stock market crash of 1987 augmented the call for more regulation.

Critical theorists have also implicated the editors of accounting journals, arguing that these editors will reject research that does not have 'complementarity with themes prevailing in the social milieu' (Mouck, 1992). In relation to the role of accounting journals, Tinker, Lehman and Neimark (1991, p. 44) state:

Accounting literature represents the world in a manner conducive to the changing needs of capital accumulation. Journals such as Accounting Review, *adjudicate in secondary conflicts by filtering research, scholarship (and untenured scholars) in a manner conducive to this primary purpose. The hostility of this journal to even the tamest 'deviants' is well known.[6]*

We now move our analysis to the critical theorists' perceptions of the role of accounting practice in supporting existing social structures.

The role of accounting practice in supporting existing social structures

As we know, the qualitative attributes of *objectivity*, *neutrality* and *representational faithfulness* are promoted in various conceptual framework projects throughout the world as being 'ideals' to which external financial accounts should aspire. There is a view promoted by the profession that accounting can

---

6. In recent years, however, it does appear that more research of a critical nature is being published within accounting journals. One journal that has been in existence for a number of years (edited by David Cooper and Tony Tinker) and which publishes various 'critical' papers is *Critical Perspectives on Accounting*. According to the journal (as per its Instructions to Authors), it 'aims to provide a forum for a growing number of accounting researchers and practitioners who realize that conventional theory and practice is ill-suited to the challenges of the modern environment, and that accounting practices and corporate behaviour are inextricably connected with many allocative, social and ecological problems of our era. From such concerns, a new literature is emerging that seeks to reformulate corporate, social and political activity, and the theoretical and practical means by which we apprehend and affect that activity'.

and should provide an objective representation of the underlying economic facts.[7]

However, a number of critical theorists see a different role for conceptual frameworks; a role that involves *legitimising* the accounting profession, as well as the financial reports produced by reporting entities. Hines (1991, p. 328) states:

CFs presume, legitimise and reproduce the assumptions of an objective world and as such they play a part in constituting the social world . . . CFs provide social legitimacy to the accounting profession. Since the objectivity assumption is the central premise of our society . . . a fundamental form of social power accrues to those who are able to trade on the objectivity assumption. Legitimacy is achieved by tapping into this central proposition because accounts generated around this proposition are perceived as 'normal'. It is perhaps not surprising or anomalous then that CF projects continue to be undertaken which rely on information qualities such as 'representational faithfulness', 'neutrality', 'reliability', etc., which presume a concrete, objective world, even though past CFs have not succeeded in generating Accounting Standards which achieve these qualities. The very talk, predicated on the assumption of an objective world to which accountants have privileged access via their 'measurement expertise', serves to construct a perceived legitimacy for the profession's power and autonomy.

Hines (1988) argues that accountants impose their own views about which performance characteristics are important and thereby require emphasis (for example, 'profits'). Accountants also decide which attributes of organisation performance are not important, and therefore are not worthy of measurement or disclosure. Through the practice of accounting, attention will be directed to the particular measures the (apparently objective) accountant has emphasised and in turn these measures will become a means of differentiating 'good' organisations from 'bad' organisations. Hines argues that in *communicating reality*, accountants simultaneously *construct reality*. Accounting provides a selective visibility for particular issues within an organisation that dictates which financial issues are 'significant' (Carpenter and Feroz, 1992). Cooper, Hayes and Wolf (1981, p. 182) also adopt this perspective in stating:

Accounting systems encourage imitation and coercion by defining the problematic (by choosing which variables are measured and reported) and they help to fashion solutions (by choosing which variables are to be treated as controllable). Of course, the way accounting systems are used is highly significant, but nevertheless the structure and elements of accounting systems help to create the appropriate and acceptable ways of acting, organising and talking about issues in organisations. Accounting systems are a significant component of the power system in an organisation.

---

7. This is consistent with the argument provided by Solomons (1978) that to increase the usefulness of accounting reports they should be as objective as cartography. That is, just as an area can be objectively 'mapped', so can the financial position and performance of an organisation.

For those people who have not previously considered accountants in the same light as do the critical theorists, there may be some form of bewilderment. How can accountants have so much power? In part, some arguments for this issue have been provided in the discussion above. The accounting profession is portrayed (through such vehicles as conceptual frameworks) as being objective, neutral, etc. Such characteristics (if true) are apparently beyond reproach. In fact, accountants are perceived as so *objective* and *neutral* that they have a reputation for being very *dull*. But if we are to believe the critical theorists, this 'dullness' is a façade that perhaps hides a great deal of social power.[8] As Carpenter and Feroz (1992, p. 618) state:

> . . . *accounting may be viewed as a means of legitimising the current social and political structure of the organisation. Hopwood (1983) further suggests that the legitimising force of accounting derives in part from the apparently dull, unobtrusive, and routine nature of accounting procedures, which generate an aura of objectivity and legitimacy in the eyes of financial statement users. Far from being dull and routine, accounting and accountants can and do take sides in social conflicts.*

Tinker, Merino and Niemark (1982, p. 184), argue:

> *This image of the accountant—often as a disinterested, innocuous 'historian'—stems from a desire to deny the responsibility that accountants bear for shaping subjective expectations which, in turn, affect decisions about resource allocation and the distribution of income between and within social classes. The attachment to historical facts provides a veneer of pseudo-objectivity that allows accountants to claim that they merely record—not partake in—social conflicts.*

Earlier in this chapter (as well as in Chapter 3) we considered research that investigated the economic consequences of accounting requirements. Once a profession starts considering the economic consequences of particular accounting standards, it is difficult to perceive that the accounting standards, and therefore accounting, can really be considered as truly objective and neutral.

In Chapter 8 we considered Legitimacy Theory. We explained how organisations often use documents, such as annual reports, to legitimise the ongoing existence of the entity. While these disclosures were explained in terms of a desire by the corporation to appear to be acting in terms of the 'social contract' (which may or may not be the case), some critical theorists see the legitimation motive as potentially quite harmful, particularly if it legitimises activities that are not in the interests of particular classes within society. As Puxty (1991, p. 39) states:

---

8. We are again back to the position that we introduced in Chapter 2—accountants are indeed very powerful individuals.

I do not accept that I see legitimation as innocuous. It seems to me that the legitimation can be very harmful indeed, insofar as it acts as a barrier to enlightenment and hence progress.

As Guthrie and Parker (1990, p. 166) state, the political economy perspective adopted by critical theorists does emphasise the role of accounting reports in maintaining particular social arrangements.

The political economy perspective perceives accounting reports as social, political, and economic documents. They serve as a tool for constructing, sustaining, and legitimising economic and political arrangements, institutions, and ideological themes which contribute to the corporation's private interests.

Thus social disclosures have the capacity to transmit social, political, and economic meanings for a pluralistic set of report recipients. Even formalised social disclosures may be employed by corporations in pursuit of self-interest at the expense of social interests themselves.

It has been argued by a number of researchers that social responsibility disclosures are made to legitimise the ongoing operations of particular organisations.[9] While there have been a number of researchers who have made calls for corporations to provide greater levels of social and environmental disclosure (see Gray, Owen and Adams, 1996), critical theorists would be critical of such a position. As Gray, Owen and Adams (1996, p. 63) state, critical theorists take this position on the basis that:

Corporate social reporting (CSR) will be controlled by the reporting corporations and a State which has a vested interest in keeping things more or less as they are, CSR has little radical content. Furthermore, CSR may do more harm than good because it gives the impression of concern and change but, in fact, will do no more than allow the system to 'capture' the radical elements of, for example, socialism, environmentalism or feminism and thus emasculate them.

Applying a critical perspective to the large US company, General Motors, Tinker, Lehman and Neimark (1991, p. 39) state:

The General Motors studies (Neimark, 1983; Niemark and Tinker, 1986; Tinker and Neimark, 1987, 1988) focus on the various ways the company uses its annual reports as an ideological weapon, and the social circumstances that govern one use rather than another. The studies are based on a content analysis of annual reports over some 60 years; it provides a 'between the lines' reading that uncovers the conflictual and antagonistic situations that embroiled GM over that period, and the way the firm's reports were used to modify and ameliorate these conflicts. In the long perspective of history we see the rationale behind the selection of specific topics, concerns and policies

---

9. See Chapter 9 for an overview of research related to social responsibility reporting.

emphasised in the annual reports. This is not to argue that annual reports have a dramatic impact on business and political decision making. Rather, like other ideological materials (party political statements, advertising, public relations 'fluff', religious dogma) it is the repetition of the mundane and particularly the censoring of other points of view that make these reports most effective.

Chapter summary

This chapter provides an overview of research that has been undertaken by people who have been classified as working within the critical perspective of accounting. These researchers are very critical of current accounting practices. They argue that existing financial accounting practices support the current economic and social structures—structures that unfairly benefit some people at the expense of others. The view that financial accounting practices are neutral and objective (as promoted in various conceptual framework projects) is challenged.

The critical perspective of accounting is predominantly grounded in Classical Political Economy Theory in which conflict, inequity and the role of the State are central to the analysis. Critical theorists make calls for fundamental changes in how society is structured and, without this restructuring, they believe that any changes or modifications to accounting practices will have no effect in making society more equitable for all. Critical theorists also argue that governments (the State) tend to put in place mechanisms and regulations to support existing social structures. Many accounting researchers are also believed to be supporters of particular political ideologies with the results of their research being influential in supporting those people with access to scarce capital.

Although this chapter is relatively brief, the aim has been to provide an insight into a point of view that traditionally has not received a great deal of attention in accounting education or in accounting journals. Perhaps, as the critical theorists would argue, this lack of attention is due to the fact that this branch of the accounting literature challenges so many of the views and values held not only by accountants, but by many others within society. The literature can indeed be quite confronting. It does, however, provide a different perspective of the role of accountants, and one that we should not immediately dismiss. If the literature causes us to be critical of our own position as accountants within society, well and good. As a concluding quote, we can reflect on the following statement by Baker and Bettner (1997, p. 293):

Accounting's capacity to create and control social reality translates into empowerment for those who use it. Such power resides in organisations and institutions, where it is used to instill values, sustain legitimizing myths, mask conflict and promote self-perpetuating social orders. Throughout society, the influence of accounting permeates fundamental issues concerning wealth distribution, social justice, political ideology and environmental degradation. Contrary to public opinion, accounting is not a static reflection of economic reality, but rather is a highly partisan activity.

References

Arnold, P., 'The State and Political Theory in Corporate Social Disclosure Research: A Response to Guthrie and Parker', *Advances in Public Interest Accounting*, Vol. 3, pp. 177–81, 1990.

Baker, C., Bettner, M., 'Interpretive and Critical Research in Accounting: A Commentary on its Absence from Mainstream Accounting Research', *Critical Perspectives on Accounting*, Vol. 8, pp. 293–310, 1997.

Burchell, S., Clubb, C., Hopwood, A., Hughes, J., Naphapiet, J., 'The Roles of Accounting in Organizations and Society', *Accounting, Organizations and Society*, Vol. 5, pp. 5–27, 1980.

Carpenter, V., Feroz, E., 'GAAP as a Symbol of Legitimacy: New York State's Decision to Adopt Generally Accepted Accounting Principles', *Accounting, Organizations and Society*, Vol. 17, No. 7, pp. 613–43, 1992.

Chua, W.F., 'Radical Developments in Accounting Thought', *The Accounting Review*, Vol, LXI, No. 4, 1986.

Cooper, D., Sherer, M., 'The Value of Corporate Accounting Reports—Arguments for a Political Economy of Accounting', *Accounting, Organizations and Society*, Vol. 9, No. 3/4, pp. 207–32, 1984.

Cooper, D., Hayes, D., Wolf, F., 'Accounting in Organized Anarchies', *Accounting, Organizations and Society*, pp. 175–91, 1981.

Gray, R., Owen, D., Adams, C., *Accounting and Accountability: Changes and Challenges in Corporate, Social and Environmental Reporting*, Prentice-Hall, London, 1996.

Guthrie, J., Parker, L., 'Corporate Social Disclosure Practice: A Comparative International Analysis', *Advances in Public Interest Accounting*, Vol. 3, pp. 159–75, 1990.

Hines, R., 'Financial Accounting: In Communicating Reality, We Construct Reality', *Accounting, Organizations and Society*, Vol. 13, No. 3, pp. 251–61, 1988.

Hines, R., 'The FASB's Conceptual Framework, Financial Accounting and the Maintenance of the Social World', *Accounting, Organizations and Society*, Vol. 16, No. 4, pp. 313–32, 1991.

Hopper, T., Powell, A., 'Making Sense of Research into the Organisational and Social Aspects of Management Accounting: A Review of its Underlying Assumptions', *Journal of Management Studies*, pp. 429–65, 1985.

Hopper, T., Annisette, M., Dastoor, N., Uddin, S., Wickramasinghe, D., 'Some Challenges and Alternatives to Positive Accounting Research', in *Accounting Theory: A Contemporary Review* (Eds Jones, S., Romano, C., Ratnatunga, J.), Harcourt Brace and Company, Australia, 1995.

Hopwood A.G., 'On Trying To Study Accounting in the Context in which it Operates', *Accounting, Organizations and Society*, Vol. 8, No. 2/3, pp. 287–305, 1983.

Merino, B., Neimark, M., 'Disclosure Regulation and Public Policy: A Sociohistorical Reappraisal', *Journal of Accounting and Public Policy*, pp. 33–57, 1982.

Miliband, E., *The State in Capitalist Society*, Weindenfeld & Nicholson, 1969.

Miliband, E., 'State Power and Class Interest', *New Left Review*, pp. 57–68, March 1983.

Mouck, T., 'The Rhetoric of Science and the Rhetoric of Revolt in the Story of Positive Accounting Theory', *Accounting, Auditing and Accountability Journal*, Vol. 5, No. 4, pp. 35–56, 1992.

Neimark, M., 'The Social Construction of Annual Reports: A Radical Approach to Corporate Control', Unpublished Doctoral Dissertation, New York University, 1983.

Neimark, M., Tinker, T., 'The Social Construction of Management Control Systems', *Accounting, Organizations and Society*, Vol. 11, No. 3, pp. 369–96, 1986.

Neu, D., Cooper, D.J., 'Accounting Interventions', Proceedings of the Fifth Interdiscipinary Perspectives on Accounting Conference, University of Manchester, 1997.

Offe, C., Ronge, V., 'Theses on the Theory of the State', in *Classes, Power and Conflict*, (Eds A. Giddens and D. Held), Edward Arnold, London, pp. 32–9, 1978.

Owen, D., Gray, R., Bebbington, J., 'Green Accounting: Cosmetic Irrelevance or Radical Agenda for Change?', *Asia–Pacific Journal of Accounting*, Vol. 4, No. 2, pp. 175–98, 1997.

Puxty, A., 'Social Accounting as Immanent Legitimation: A Critique of a Technist Ideology', *Advances in Public Interest Accounting*, Vol. 1, pp. 95–112, 1986.

Puxty, A., 'Social Accountability and Universal Pragmatics', *Advances in Public Interest Accounting*, Vol. 4, pp. 35–46, 1991.

Selto, F., Neumann, B., 'A Further Guide to Research on the Economic Consequences of Accounting Information', *Accounting and Business Research*, Vol. 11, No. 44, pp. 317–322, Autumn 1981.

Solomons, D., 'The Politicization of Accounting', *Journal of Accounting*, pp. 65–72, November 1978.

Thompson, G., 'Capitalist Profit Calculation and Inflation Accounting', *Economy and Society*, pp. 395–429, 1978.

Tinker, A., Lehman, C., Neimark, M., 'Corporate Social Reporting: Falling Down the Hole in the Middle of the Road', *Accounting, Auditing and Accountability Journal*, Vol. 4, No. 1, pp. 28–54, 1991.

Tinker, A., Merino, B., Neimark, M., 'The Normative Origins of Positive Theories: Ideology and Accounting Thought', *Accounting, Organizations and Society*, Vol. 7, No. 2, pp. 167–200, 1982.

Tinker, T. Neimark, M., 'The Role of Annual Reports in Gender and Class Contradictions at General Motors: 1917–1976', *Accounting Organizations and Society*, Vol. 12, No. 1, pp. 71–88, 1987.

Tinker, T., Neimark, M., 'The Struggle over Meaning in Accounting and Corporate Research: A Comparative Evaluation of Conservative and Critical Historiography', *Accounting, Auditing and Accountability Journal*, Vol. 1, No. 1, pp. 55–74, 1988.

Zeff, S.A., 'The Rise of Economic Consequences', *The Journal of Accounting*, Vol. 146, pp. 56–63, December 1978.

Questions

12.1 What is a *critical perspective* of accounting?

12.2 What are some of the fundamental differences between the research undertaken by *critical theorists,* relative to the work undertaken by other accounting researchers?

12.3 From a critical perspective, what is the role of a Conceptual Framework Project?

12.4 From a critical perspective, can financial reports ever be considered objective or neutral? Explain your answer.

12.5 If it is accepted that there are many inequities within society, would critical theorists argue that introducing more accounting, or *improved* methods of accounting, would or could help, or would they argue that such a strategy will only compound existing problems? Explain your answer. Do you agree with the position taken by the critical theorists? Why?

12.6 Critical theorists would challenge the work of authors whose work is grounded within Positive Accounting Theory. What is the basis of their opposition?

12.7 Critical theorists would challenge the work of authors whose work is grounded within Legitimacy Theory. What is the basis of their opposition?

12.8 If accounting is deemed to be complicit in sustaining social inequities, how would critical theorists argue that accounting can be 'fixed'?

12.9 Tinker, Merino and Neimark (1982) argue that 'the social allegiances and biases of accounting are rarely apparent; usually, they are "masked" pretensions of objectivity and independence'. Explain the basis of this argument.

12.10 Cooper and Sherer (1984) argue that 'accounting researchers should be explicit about the normative elements of any framework adopted by them. All research is normative in the sense that it contains the researcher's value judgements about how society should be organised. However, very few accounting researchers make their value judgements explicit'. Do you agree or disagree with this claim? Why?

Index

Please note that page references followed by n (e.g. 144n10) refer to footnotes.